THE SEWARDS OF NEW YORK

THE SEWARDS OF NEW YORK

A BIOGRAPHY OF A LEADING AMERICAN POLITICAL FAMILY

THOMAS P. SLAUGHTER

THREE HILLS
an imprint of
CORNELL UNIVERSITY PRESS
Ithaca and London

Frontispiece: Silhouette outline of the Seward and Miller families in 1833. Courtesy of Rare Books, Special Collections, and Preservation, River Campus Libraries, University of Rochester, original in Seward House Museum, Auburn, NY

First published 2025 by Cornell University Press
Printed in the United States of America

Librarians: A CIP catalog record for this book is available from the Library of Congress.

ISBN 9781501782657 (hardcover)
ISBN 9781501782664 (pdf)
ISBN 9781501782671 (epub)

GPSR EU contact: Sam Thornton, Mare Nostrum Group B.V., Mauritskade 21D, 1091 GC, Amsterdam, NL, gpsr@mare-nostrum.co.uk.

To the librarians and tech staff who made sewardproject.org possible and the students and volunteer transcribers who were the project's heart

Contents

Cast of Principal Characters

The three-letter abbreviations for each of the names listed here are used in the notes.

CCS	Caroline Cornelia Canfield Schoolcraft Beattie (July 25, 1834–February 28, 1922)
LCC	Louisa Cornelia Seward Canfield (1805–January 4, 1839)
MDC	Mahlon Dickerson Canfield (November 26, 1798–January 5, 1865)
FWC	Frances Worden Chesebro (December 12, 1826–August 24, 1909)
GMG	George M. Grier (September 27, 1802–December 20, 1878)
CMM	Clarinda Miller McClallen (May 1, 1793–September 5, 1862)
ExM	Elijah Miller (April 11, 1771–November 13, 1851)
PTM	Paulina Titus Miller (1751–October 3, 1835)
JLS	John Lawrence Schoolcraft (September 22, 1840–June 7, 1860)
AWS	Anna Wharton Seward (March 29, 1834–May 2, 1919)
AHS	Augustus Henry Seward (October 1, 1826–September 11, 1876)
BJS	Benjamin Jennings Seward (August 23, 1793–February 24, 1841)
CAS	Clarence Armstrong Seward (October 7, 1828–July 24, 1897)
EPS	Edwin Polydore Seward (1799–April 23, 1872)
FAS	Frances Adeline Seward (December 9, 1844–October 29, 1866)
FMS	Frances Miller Seward (September 24, 1805–June 21, 1865)
FWS	Frederick William Seward (July 8, 1830–April 25, 1915)
GWS	George Washington Seward (August 26, 1808–December 7, 1888)
JWS	Janet Watson Seward (November 18, 1839–November 9, 1913)
MJS	Mary Jane Jennings Seward (November 27, 1769–December 11, 1844)
ORS	Olive Risley Seward (July 15, 1844–November 27, 1908)

SSS	Samuel Sweezy Seward (December 5, 1768–August 24, 1849)
WHS	William Henry Seward (May 16, 1801–October 10, 1872)
WJS	William Henry Seward Jr. (June 18, 1839–April 29, 1920)
AHW	Alvah H. Worden (March 6, 1797–February 16, 1856)
LMW	Lazette Miller Worden (November 1, 1803–October 3, 1875)

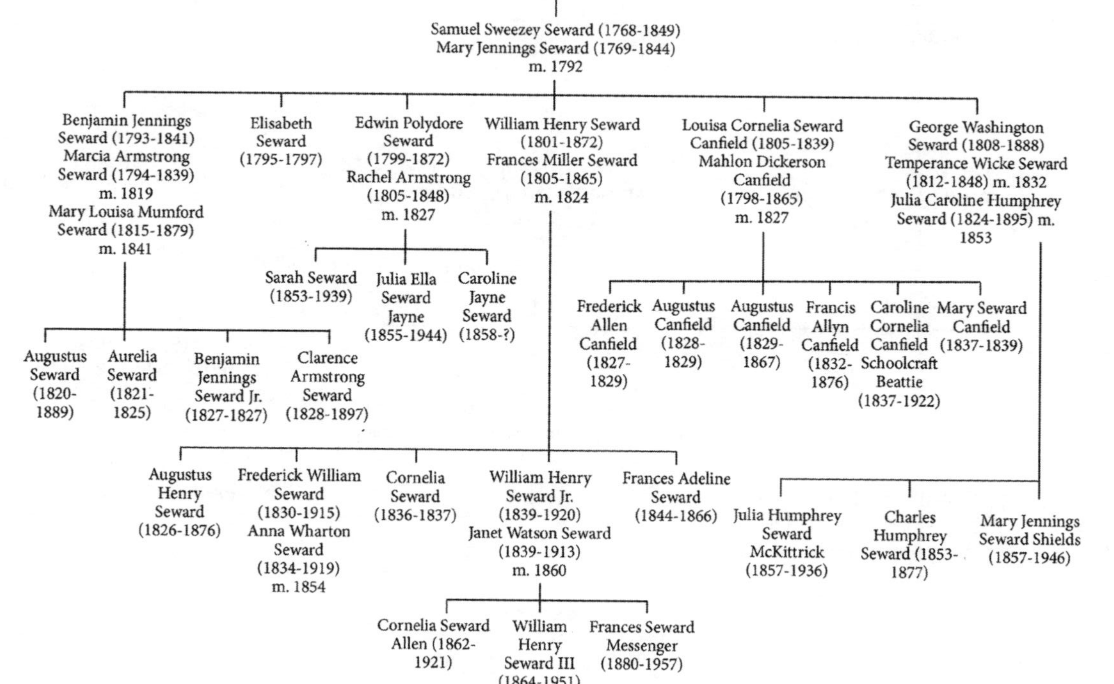

FIGURE 0.1. Seward family tree. Created by Maya Taylor-Bush.

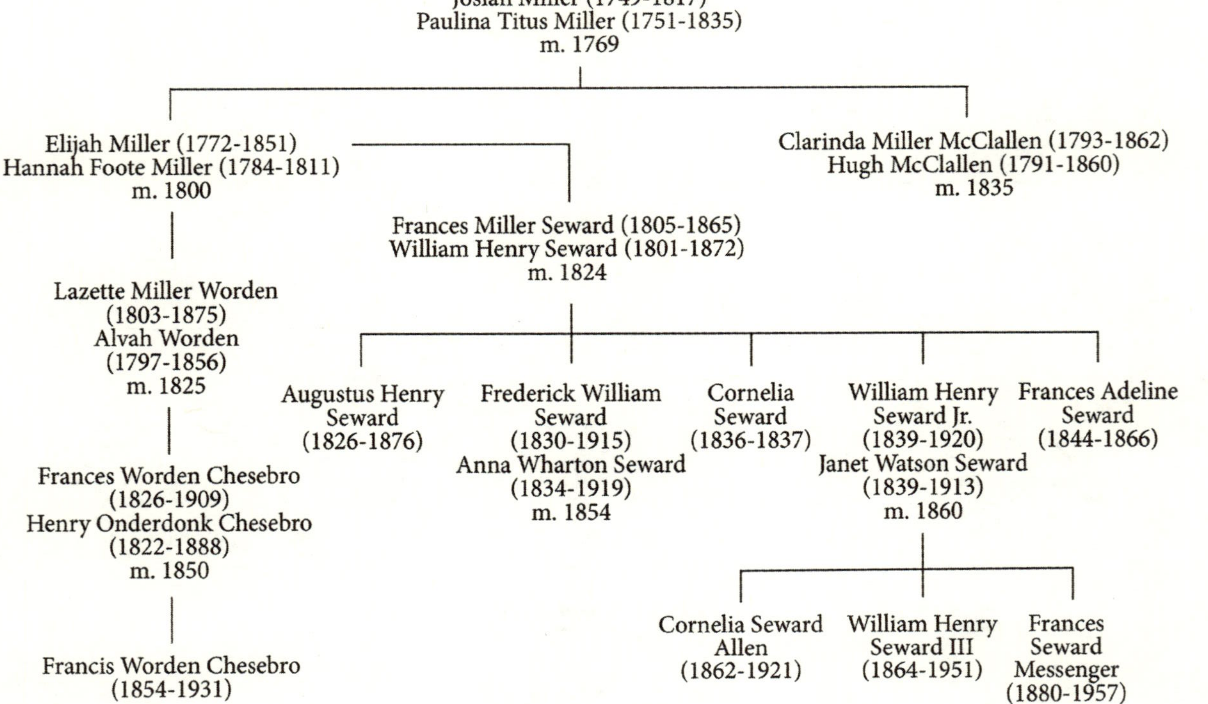

FIGURE 0.2. Miller family tree. Created by Maya Taylor-Bush.

Introduction

> When one has a story to tell, one is always puzzled which end of it to begin at. You have a whole corps of people to introduce that *you* know and your reader doesn't; and one thing so presupposes another, that, whichever way you turn your patchwork, the figures still seem ill-arranged.
>
> —Harriet Beecher Stowe, *The Minister's Wooing*

If you know anything about William Henry Seward, it is probably that he was responsible as Secretary of State for the purchase of Alaska from Russia in 1867, which his political opponents roundly ridiculed at the time as "Seward's Folly." Or you may know him for his survival of an assassination attempt in his Washington home on April 15, 1865, the same night that John Wilkes Booth shot Abraham Lincoln in Ford's Theatre. Or you may know of his "Irrepressible Conflict" speech in Rochester, New York, on October 25, 1858, in which he predicted escalating national strife because the two labor systems, one slave and one free, were "more than incongruous—they are incompatible. They never have permanently existed together in one country, and they never can. . . . It is an irrepressible conflict between opposing and enduring forces, and it means that the United States must and will, sooner or later, become either entirely a slaveholding nation, or entirely a free-labor nation."[1]

You may know that Seward came within a hair's breadth of being the Republican Party's nominee for president in 1860, which he lost as the presumptive candidate, partly because the nominating convention was in Illinois, Abraham Lincoln's home state, and partly because he was too polarizing a figure after a long career on the political stage, having served as governor of New York and in the US Senate. Republican strategists felt that Lincoln, as a blank slate on the national scene, was less controversial and thus a more promising nominee. Seward had the most votes in the convention on the first two ballots and then lost the nomination on the third after heavy overnight politicking.

This book is not a biography of Henry, although politics, and particularly the abolition of slavery, is crucial to the Sewards' collective biography. It is about the four generations of Millers and Sewards that dwelled at 33 South Street, Auburn, New York, between 1817 and 1860. The goal is to tell the family's story from surviving letters supplemented by published and unpublished sources, mainly journals, diaries, and memoirs. It approaches Henry more fully in his private roles than the biographies of him could do until now, so it shows him in a different light, not just as a politician and statesman but as a son, brother, husband, and father. The book ends with the election of Abraham Lincoln because that brought one chapter to a close and began another for the family.

The book's time span encompasses revolutions in commerce, education, transportation, and communication that affected the Seward family. Men worked away from home, although generally not as far away as Henry did; women ran the households, as his wife Frances and others from the rising professional classes did, on the backs of immigrants and people of color. Manufactured goods filled households in which Victorian clutter was not previously possible. More leisure lent itself to greater sociability; "calling" was a practice with formal etiquette. Private libraries, pianos, and sheet music became accessories to middle-class lives, as artifacts in the Seward House Museum display. Houses were redesigned to separate the functions of rooms and to provide members with their own designated sleeping quarters, which led to multiple renovations to their house over its first forty years. Play itself was new to most people. Literacy was no longer seen as the end but rather the beginning of education for both genders. The mass manufacturing of books, for children and adults, the proliferation of public libraries, and a taste for fiction as well as religious literature, advice manuals, the classics, and political and reform tracts were products of commerce and a flourishing publishing industry. The Sewards were far from the only family to accumulate a vast private library, although theirs is one of the few to survive today largely intact.

Nineteenth-century Americans were on the move from the countryside to towns and cities, and across the continent. Many more became tourists and travelers. Railroads, canals, steamships, and much improved roads moved more people farther, faster, but not more comfortably and safely as Henry experienced in journeys from Auburn to Albany, which took three days when he first entered public life and less than one by the time he was governor. The mail moved faster and sometimes more reliably, and the telegraph connected people in real time rather than over days between major East Coast cities and weeks across the continent. There were places to go, things to learn, money to make and lose, and more people to know and see than in the eighteenth century.

The impacts of the transportation and communication revolutions of the nineteenth century were as transformative as those of the late twentieth and early twenty-first centuries. The Sewards often received free rides, and railroad magnates who sought to influence politicians provided them free cars. The telegraph, railroads, steamships, and canals, as well as the proliferation of print in the mid-nineteenth century, impacted the circulation of ideas, news, and false information, much as commercial airlines, computers, the Internet, cell phones, and social media have over the past fifty years. More than once, erroneous newspaper reports led Frances to fear mistakenly that family members had died. She also learned where her husband was and accurate information about his health from such reports when he was too busy to write. Religious revivals, Spiritualism, phrenology, fad diets, water cures, homeopathy, and new religions such as Mormonism and others that have not survived were all products of dynamic change in the mid-nineteenth century. Some of the novelties intrigued the Sewards and some repelled them.

Illness also circulated more freely in closer quarters, in cities and on public transportation, and medical care failed to slow rising death rates from virulent diseases; as the Sewards experienced firsthand, doctors were as likely to kill as cure infants and children, women in childbirth, the poor, and the elderly, which is why women experimented and became their own physicians. Failure to recognize the role of bacteria and germs was a contributing factor in rising death rates. Anything from smallpox, tuberculosis, and cholera to measles, mumps, tonsillitis, the flu, a cold, or what started as a toothache or scratch could kill you, and the treatments, including bloodletting, purging, cupping, scarification, and the ingestion of mercury, opium, arsenic, belladonna, and ether could be even more lethal.

The Sewards are exemplary of such changes. They were privileged but reflected their times, which is also, besides their fame, what makes their story compelling. They left extraordinary materials behind for viewing families, which is what, in the end, enables the telling. We can know them as few others from two centuries ago and most families since. Separation of Henry from his wife and of his wife from her sister led to long journaling letters exchanged over decades. We know so much more about the family than we do about those that lived together and had no reason to bare their souls in correspondence. The opportunity to see life at the personal level rather than simply in aggregate statistics is part of what makes the Sewards' story engaging. With the Seward family's letters, we can look behind the curtain of the Victorian era's private sphere to see life as it was experienced by other Americans.

Until recently, Seward's public papers were the only accessible source on his family members' lives. Over a decade of excavation by students and librarians at the University of Rochester has now unearthed about 25,000 pages, over 4,000 letters, of family manuscripts that survive from the six decades that ended with Henry's death in 1872. The family papers were buried in his voluminous public correspondence, which librarians estimate at about 350,000 pages. Such unprecedented survivals enable a fresh approach to the Sewards from the multiple perspectives of its members, including women and children as well as the men.[2]

Although the rationale for this family biography is not Henry's importance as a public figure, it is possible only because one of the family's members was a notable man. If Henry's descendants did not believe the light of his stature reflected on them, they would not have preserved their correspondence in addition to his public papers. The rest of them were also famous in their lifetimes. They were a significant social presence in Washington in the 1850s and 1860s, when Henry was a senator and secretary of state, in Albany in the late 1830s and early 1840s, when he was a state senator and governor, and in their hometown dating back to the 1820s. Perhaps only the Adamses, diplomats, authors, and descendants of two presidents, were better known and revered in the North among America's nineteenth-century political families.

The very act of preserving their correspondence makes the Sewards of 33 South Street extraordinary for their times, which spanned an era of profound change in marriage, family, and childhood. Couples more often than in the eighteenth century married for love and in the expectation of companionate relationships, as Frances Adeline Miller and William Henry Seward did in 1824. Their children were objects of devotion rather than contributors to the household economy, and Gus, Fred, Willie, and Fanny were among the first generation of American children to hang their stockings with care for an annual visit from St. Nicholas, ride hobbyhorses, read children's books and magazines, and play with manufactured and paper dolls that performed on cardboard stages, toy soldiers, swords, guns, and tiny porcelain tea sets, many purchased in the first American toy stores.

Frances was sure she was not a leading character in her family's story as she is in this book. She would have found that a pretentious idea and unladylike; she was a timid homebody in her opinion, a nervous hypochondriac with weak eyes, bad teeth, afflicted with migraines and palpitations, depressive, habituated to opioids (which was common at the time), and obsessed with her family's health. In the medical diagnoses of the day, she was neurasthenic, the victim of an ill-defined medical condition that affected the nerves and her overall health. She was also a liberal Protestant, a member of the Episcopal Church in Auburn, an attender of services when up to it, if the preacher was thoughtful, had speaking skills, and it was not raining. She found Evangelicalism fraudulent and was increasingly attracted to Spiritualism, believing she was in communication with the dead. She knew that God is merciful and just. On balance, she favored the New Testament over the Old.

When Elizabeth Cady Stanton, the women's rights activist, abolitionist, and mother of seven, first met Frances in the late 1850s, Mrs. Seward surprised her. She wrote, "I did not know then the broad, liberal tendencies of her mind," which Stanton subsequently came to appreciate. "Mrs. Seward, approaching me most affectionately, said, 'Let me thank you for the brave words you uttered at the dinner table, and for your speech before the legislature, that thrilled my soul as I read it over and over.' I was filled with joy and astonishment," Stanton wrote of the meeting, because she had supposed that "all you ladies were hostile to every one of my ideas on this question," the question of woman suffrage. "'No, no,' said she, 'I am with you thoroughly, but I am a born coward; there is nothing I dread more than Mr. Seward's ridicule. I would rather walk up to the cannon's mouth than encounter it.'"[3]

Contrary to Stanton's story, Frances was quite capable of confronting Henry, had not always supported woman suffrage, prioritized abolition over women's rights, and continued to believe that her place was in the home and not in the public sphere, where she could undermine but not enhance her husband's political ambitions. Frances was more complicated than Stanton portrayed her. In private, she also mocked Stanton's bloomers.

Abolition was the major exception to Frances's domestic focus and deference to Henry on political questions. It was a source of contention between them over the course of their marriage, although she tried to keep her views private, sharing them openly only with Henry and her sister. While Henry saw himself as an abolitionist, he never was, and Frances challenged him often.

More accurately than her own self-deprecating views, Frances was a force of nature within her own home. She was admired in her town, respected in her church, adored in her family, a comfort to those in need, and the intellectual equal or better of those around her, whether she was in Auburn, Albany, or Washington, DC. If the Sewards' library was anyone's by dint of possession through reading, it was hers—and everyone knew it. Indeed, she personally purchased many of the books and left a record of inscriptions in those she gave to family members. It was Frances who oversaw the multiple newspaper and international magazine subscriptions that informed her family. She acquired many of the family's more than 3,500 pamphlets that they organized and had bound, and are preserved as an intact collection today. Frances also kept scrapbooks, mainly of Henry's career, which reflect her devotion and how closely she followed his life, often from afar and thirdhand.

Frances, more than her famous husband or accomplished father and sons, is the hub around which this family story revolves. She was more responsible for who they all were than she acknowledged, and she was minimized in her own eyes and in those of most others, as was the fate of women in her day. Her family knew just how essential she was. She was the general who commanded the home front; the quartermaster who supplied the family troops; the recruiter and drill sergeant who staffed the kitchen and laundry; the captain of the cavalry who oversaw care for their animals, of which there were dozens over the years; sometimes the skivvy when household staff fell short; and the master gardener of a landscape for which her absent husband is often credited. She was the family's moral and spiritual fountain, their doctor, nurse, and pharmacist of first and last resort. She was the seamstress who stitched their fabric into a family quilt.

Frances was the second of two daughters born to Elijah and Hannah Foote Miller, who married when Hannah was sixteen. She died at twenty-six, when her daughters were ages eight and six. Frances, known in her youth as "Fanny" before she had a Fanny of her own, had two heroes in her life: her father, Judge Elijah Miller, and her husband, the man who she thought would be president in 1860. She considered it entirely fortunate and proper that she should have two such worthy men as heroes, although the marriage, which she may have fancied at the outset to be right out of a Jane Austen novel, quite possibly *Emma*, was not what she had dreamed. Like the newlywed couple in the novel, the Sewards returned to the wife's childhood home to live with her aging father, but the outcome was not as romantic for Frances and Henry. As "you know," she later wrote to her husband, "I am opposed to marrying in general," which was a more extreme view of the institution than that of Austen's title character, who also had her doubts.[4]

Emma was reluctant to wed, an unconventional attitude that the unmarried Austen satirizes. Even after it dawns on Emma that her bête noir is truly her heart's desire, she cannot imagine leaving her hypochondriacal, widower father's home, Hartfield, drafts and all, to live in Mr. Knightley's Donwell Abbey. Knightley anticipates this problem and offers to move into Emma's home. The obvious solution was the heroic one, the one likely to melt the heart of a nineteenth-century heroine and never to have occurred to an eighteenth-century suitor. Henry was Frances's Knightley or, at least, so she had imagined him to be less than a decade after the publication of *Emma*: "She was sensible of all the affection it evinced. She felt that, in quitting Donwell, he must be sacrificing a great deal of independence of hours and habits; that in living constantly with her father, and in no house of his own, there would be much, very much, to be borne with."[5]

We could forgive Frances for interpreting Henry's decision in light of Knightley's. Family tradition recalls that Judge Miller, an eccentric widower set in his ways, insisted on Henry joining his household in return for permission to marry his daughter. Henry was no Knightley, but who is, and thus how many women have shared Frances's disappointment that their spouses had not actually stepped right out of a romance novel? As Henry explained to his father, he did very well for himself financially in negotiations for Frances's dowry and saved on household expenses by moving into his father-in-law's house.

After five years of marriage, Frances candidly shared with Henry her disappointment, not just with him. "I have been so foolish," she reflected, "as to form my ideas of beauty, I may say of human excellence from books. How many disappointments I might have spared myself had I never read a work of fiction, how many I might yet escape could I efface these romantic impressions." As Frances recognized rightly, she was a hopeless romantic; she kept reading and idealizing, and was disappointed by the failure of those around her, particularly her husband, to embody the ideals of nineteenth-century Anglo-American culture. "What a delightful life the numberless matter-of-fact people with which the world abounds, must enjoy. There is no bursting of bubbles with them all. All is tame reality." She, like others of her time and since who have escaped "tame reality" in the Gothic, which troubled her sleep, and the Romantic, both of which she preferred over the life that she found more harsh than tame for many of her days, the allure was too strong.[6]

Henry moved in after their marriage; Frances adored him for it, and was thus all the more disappointed when he did not stay long and failed to rescue her in her darkest hours. It was Judge Miller's house for the next quarter century. Her father refused even to reprimand, never mind fire, a member of the household staff who treated her like his servant and drank far more (sometimes with her father) than Frances could bear. Judge Miller decided which fireplaces and (later) stoves to stoke, in which room(s) he slept, and he even hammered nails into a wall of the front parlor, where the family received callers, to hang his wet socks. He frightened his daughters, both the one who lived with him and the one who escaped to a bad marriage. They also loved, admired, and mocked him privately. His sister Clarinda, the youngest of the ten siblings, who lived in the South Street house until the age of forty-two, said her brother was crazy and that she married in 1835 to escape him. By all accounts, Judge Miller's grandchildren, all four of the ones who lived in his house, simply adored him. They also adored Henry, but got to know their father better as young adults than they did in his absence during their childhoods.[7]

We would not know any of this if Frances was less diligent in preserving the family's correspondence, which she did as a sentimental record of domestic life and a commemoration of her husband's career. The letters that are missing were mostly lost by inadvertence, destroyed by Henry to secure his family's privacy in an age of inflamed politics, or discarded by their son Fred after he and his wife edited excerpts for Henry's autobiography, which he completed after his father's death. Most tragically for the historian, some of the letters written to Frances by her sister Lazette are gone from the collection, probably burned by Lazette after Frances died, which was consistent with the customs of the times. Frances wrote and received more personal letters than the rest of the family members combined. And hers were longer, more informative on family matters, and more thoughtful and candid on public events than those of the others.

The surviving correspondence between Frances and Lazette is a treasure; without it there could not be this book. Lazette was also the family member most active in the Underground Railroad, the most radical, reform-minded, and strong-willed. Lazette's activism, in both abolition and woman suffrage, was more engaged than her sister's, bolder, as was her nature, and without the anchor of a husband with the highest national political ambitions.

The women's letters in general are, not surprisingly, more informative about their families and more emotionally revealing than those of the men. The men's letters prioritized life differently, shared more about the business of the world and less about their feelings. It took a crisis to provoke the men to bare their souls and reorient their priorities. Henry was more guarded, rushed, and shallow in his correspondence, with the exception of his letters home when their marriage was on the ropes in the 1830s, after the death of their daughter, and during his second trip abroad in 1859, which provide more insight into his heart and mind than the rest of the manuscript collection combined.

All of the family's members made sacrifices in support of Henry's career and benefited from his influence, but Fred, the Sewards' second-born son, most closely followed his father's path. After a decade working for Thurlow Weed, Henry's political mentor, on his Albany newspaper, Fred served as his father's assistant in the Department of State. There was always a tug between the parents over Fred, whose skills were more useful to his father than those of their other two boys. Fred had attended his father's alma mater, Union College, and followed him into the practice of law, rather than following his older brother into the army, which was his preference. Everyone in the Seward family except Fred underestimated his wife, Anna M. Seward (née Wharton) of Albany, as a nineteen-year-old bride, a rather plain girl from a quite ordinary family; her father was a druggist. Anna, whom Frances had read on first meeting as "not pretty but . . . quiet & gentle," had become a formidable diplomatic hostess as this book ends.[8]

With Fred, Frances won the argument that she had lost with her husband over their eldest, Augustus H. Seward, Fred's senior by three and a half years, when Henry engineered Gus's admission to West Point. Gus teetered on the brink of expulsion for disciplinary infractions during his first two years, ultimately graduating thirty-fourth of thirty-eight. Gus served with the infantry in the Mexican-American War and in the Indian Territory—in Oklahoma, Utah, and Arizona—to his mother's moral outrage, among other assignments that included, most happily for all, the Coastal Survey mapping Key West, the Outer Banks, Chesapeake Bay, the Hudson River, and coastal Maine. His father intervened to keep Gus out of combat during the Civil War, with an assignment to the Paymaster Corps, in which he received a promotion to major in 1861, and lieutenant colonel and then colonel in 1865. He remained in the army until he died three weeks short of his fiftieth birthday, outliving his mother by a decade and his father by less than four years. Gus remained distant from the family emotionally and for long stretches physically throughout his mother's life; he was a loner, shy around women, and never married.

William Henry Seward Jr., born in 1839, was the youngest of the family's three sons. Known in the family as Willie when young, Will as he matured, he suffered from what today would be labeled learning disabilities. His parents only ever wrote about his educational challenges as "weak eyes," a congenital problem that he partly outgrew, although throughout his adult life he remained clumsy and often injured, which may have resulted in part from poor eyesight. His spelling and grammar were more primitive than those of his siblings, and the home education that ended without Latin or college enabled his mother to read aloud to him books that he would have had to read on his own at school. In his mother's eyes and despite her fears for him, Will was a civic stalwart in Auburn. He inherited the family's South Street mansion, where his three children grew up, and lived there with his wife, the former Janet (Jenny) MacNeil Watson of Auburn, whom he married in June 1861. The following year he volunteered for the New York Heavy Artillery, which he entered at the rank of lieutenant colonel and achieved the rank of colonel before breaking a leg in a fall of his horse during the Battle of Monocacy in 1864. He received a final promotion to brigadier general in September of the same year. For the rest of his life, the members of his family called him "the General," an identity he embraced with pride, to distinguish him from his more famous namesake.

Fanny, the youngest, was devoted to her father and predeceased him, outliving her beloved mother by only sixteen months. She was consumptive, fragile and spirited, immature, fascinated by the Washington social scene, an aspiring writer, and kept a series of diaries in the years prior to and during the Civil War. She was in many ways her mother's daughter. Given her fragile health and her mother's understandable fears for her life, Frances was Fanny's principal teacher, as she was Will's.

The final family member living in the house, the one easiest to overlook in retrospect, was Judge Miller's mother, Frances and Lazette's grandmother, Paulina Titus Miller, who was the household's matriarch and, more than her son and daughter, the family's closest link to the eighteenth century and the revolutionary generation. It was she who told the family's stories and defended traditional values, including those addressing wifely and motherly duties, home medical practice, household management, and relationships across lines of ethnicity, race, and class. She remembered (rightly and wrongly) the way things were and knew with a fierce certainty the way they ought to be. Paulina's devotion to Quakerism, including its pacifism, were no less staunch and no less influential in the South Street household than the bellicose patriotism of her late husband, son, and granddaughter's husband.

If the family members had all stayed contentedly at home together, we would not have the letters through which they communicated from across the state, nation, and eventually the globe, or the diaries, journals, and overflowing quantity of photos and artifacts that expand what we learn from their letters. Over the thirty-five years addressed in this book, Frances failed to convince Henry to become a family man. She drove him away by scolding and attempts to induce guilt. He never wanted children; he found his father-in-law's house confining and the cacophony of family life jarring.

The pulls of ambition were even stronger on Henry than those pushes. Whether his periodic claims to have spent his ambition were honest or self-delusional, they were simply untrue. His sights remained on the White House until the Republican Party rejected him and Frances bore the joys and burdens of family life in Auburn alone. Only the letters connected them for most of their days.

Chapter 1

Ancestors in the House, 1817–1851

Although the Sewards told their collective story in patriarchal terms with Henry's father Samuel and Frances's father Elijah passing the torch to Henry and then him passing it to Will Jr., "the General," there is another way to tell it that provides both gender balance and a fuller, more accurate picture. They agreed that while there were deeper roots to their family trees, the American Revolution provided the essential background to their collective history. There is also no denying that in the house at 33 South Street the font for accounts of their heroic past was not Elijah or Henry but Paulina, Elijah's mother. After all, she had memories of the War for Independence.

From December 1817 until her death in October 1835, Paulina Titus Miller was the eldest occupant of the Miller home. She moved into the new house with her second son Elijah, her tenth and youngest child Clarinda (Clary), and Elijah's two daughters, Frances and Lazette, after the death of her husband Josiah. She and Clary helped raise the two girls, who had lost their mother seven years earlier. There are no surviving letters written by Paulina, but there are numerous stories told about her by her granddaughters and letters that the girls wrote to her when they were away at school. She holds a prominent place in the manuscript biography of her son from the late 1870s, which the family commissioned. In it, the author cast her as a matriarchal heroine, "a daughter in Israel," of biblical proportions.[1]

The comparison of Paulina to Deborah in Judges 4 and 5 of the Old Testament was a grand flourish, as monumental a comparison as male Protestants could offer for a woman in her day. Indeed, it transcended the more common celebration of a woman for the accomplishments of her sons by linking Paulina to a woman who may not have had any. Depending on the translation, Deborah was a "fiery" or "spirited" woman, according to one biblical scholar, "one of the few examples of a strong, independent woman in the Bible." She was a judge, a prophet, and a military leader who accompanied her chosen general Barak into a celebrated battle from which the Israelites emerged victorious against their enemies.[2]

As the biography of Elijah Miller told her story, up until the war Paulina and her husband wore the Quakers' distinctive "plain dress"—nothing like the "red cloth cloak" she donned as an old woman—belonged to a Quaker meeting, and attended services religiously with the first three of their ten children, Robert (b. 1770), Elijah (b. 1772), and Anner (b. 1774). While family members never recorded the source of their estrangement from the sect, they owned four slaves and Paulina's husband served on the local Committee of Safety in Bedford, Westchester County, New York, before leaving the Westchester farm to fight at the rank of captain under General Lewis Morris in 1776. Either fighting in the Revolution or owning slaves could have caused their separation, but it was more likely in that time and place that taking up arms against the monarch was what alienated them from their meeting. Nonetheless, Paulina continued silent Quaker "meditation" throughout her life, and her granddaughters attended a Quaker school outside Auburn.[3]

When Josiah left to fight, Paulina ran the farm with the two male slaves working in the fields and two female house slaves who spun wool, made the family's clothing, and performed other household tasks. We know Josiah returned home periodically during the war, because Martha (b. 1777), Elisha (b. 1779), and Sarah (b. 1782) arrived during its course. Elizabeth (b. 1784), Lewis (b. 1787), Ezra (b. 1790), and Clarinda (b. 1793) arrived after the war ended. Not only had Paulina managed the farm, hiding its produce from combatants as best she could, taking refuge with her children when the battles got too close for their safety, but she actively supported her husband's decision to fight for the cause, according to the biography of Elijah.[4]

By calling Paulina a "daughter in Israel," the author put a patriotic spin on her stories about the Revolution. When the Sewards' second son, Fred, later recalled his great-grandmother's stories for his own memoir, he remembered her putting a greater emphasis on the danger, sacrifice, and horrors of war than on her own heroism. She recalled neighbors casting bullets in their kitchens from odd scraps of lead. She told of her home being in the "Neutral Ground," contested territory subject to the depredations of both sides. She said there were two gangs robbing their homes, one supporting each side in the war, "but one was about as bad as the other."[5]

The way Fred remembered Paulina telling the stories was closer to the experiences of other women in the Revolution than was the biography's depiction of her. Both sides plundered and killed, and civilians were caught in the middle. She was without her husband and just trying to survive, to keep her family fed and safe. Her husband had chosen their family's side. She told of Colonel Banastre Tarleton's forces burning Bedford to the ground in retaliation for the town's support of the Patriot forces when they controlled the area. She also recounted how Tarleton spared Paulina's house when her mother entreated him personally to leave it standing. "What was said," Fred explained, "can only be conjectured, but it was presumed that she told him that she was a loyal subject of King George. Probably she did not mention that her son-in-law, Captain Miller, was just then engaged in harassing Tarleton's flanks and rear. When night fell, all that was left of Bedford was one dwelling, and a dozen or two heaps of smoking ashes." Indeed, as told by a Quaker woman in New York, such a story of personal Loyalism rings true.[6]

In one story, which was apparently oft told by Paulina and then retold in the biography of Elijah and later by Fred, Paulina took refuge at a relative's home in Peekskill overnight, where she was introduced to a Major John André, who was also a houseguest. As both sources told it, she was suspicious of André, doubts she shared with her host. By the next morning, the major had fled. Shortly thereafter, they learned that forces under General Washington had captured André, who was the head of the British secret service in America, and hanged him as a spy for assisting Benedict Arnold's attempted surrender of West Point to the British.[7]

In the biographer's account, Paulina's patriotism overcame her pacifism when she reported her suspicions about André; her sense of justice overwhelmed her mercy and left her family with both a high standard

FIGURE 1.1. Elijah Miller, c. 1840, by artist Chester Harding. Courtesy of Rare Books, Special Collections, and Preservation, River Campus Libraries, University of Rochester; original painting in Seward House Museum, Auburn, New York.

and a moral tension to live with as her legacy. As Fred recalled, Paulina and Elijah argued over her story about André, Judge Miller taking the position that General Washington had no choice but to hang him and Paulina contending that Washington committed an unforgivable crime by hanging a prisoner of war who was simply captured doing his duty as a soldier. According to Fred, the argument recurred and Paulina never yielded in her judgment of Washington and her condemnation of the behavior of both sides in the war.[8]

The family members surviving in 1877, when the wife of the Sewards' third son, Will, commissioned Judge Miller's biography, expected the story of their legacy from the Revolution to be centered on the public accomplishments of the three successive patriarchs of the household, and for us to see the rest of them as a supporting cast for the great men who lived at 33 South Street. The role they imagined for the tiny old woman who lived in Elijah's house was as their link to heroic origins. Their story, as they told it and imagined it instructive to others, really began with Judge Miller, continued through the greatest among them, William Henry Seward, and finished with Will Jr. in the third generation, the one who inherited the house and was the only one of the children to have heirs, which included William H. Seward III, who bequeathed the house to become a museum commemorating the lives of his father and grandfather.

A decade after the war, Josiah and Paulina moved their ten children from Westchester to Rensselaer County, New York, and began to purchase additional lands for their offspring on the Military Tract in Cayuga and Seneca Counties, land set aside by the state government to compensate soldiers for their military service on the winning side. In this process, Josiah took advantage of his officer's rights to several 640-acre plots and moved himself and his wife to one of them in Romulus, southwest of Auburn.[9]

Josiah and Paulina's son Elijah moved to the area in 1795, before Auburn had a name, arriving in Cayuga County from Utica on foot. He worked in an Aurora law office as a clerk and law student for three years before beginning to practice in Romulus in 1798. On January 1, 1800, Elijah married Hannah Foote (1784–1811) of Williamstown, Massachusetts, who was a student at the Williamstown Academy. In that same year, they moved into a house south of Auburn on Cayuga Lake.

According to Elijah's biographer, he was known "as a safe and wise adviser, and especially in complicated real estate cases his standing was equal to the best in this part of the state." He was successful in land speculation and made much of the wealth he passed down in that way. Miller was "a Hercules in law from the start," one educated classically in Blackstone, Pufendorf, Locke, Paley, Burlamaqui, Montesquieu, Beccaria, Littleton, Coke, Grotius, and Vattel, volumes of which became the foundation of his family's unusually large library. Miller was not, by repute inside and outside the family, a patient man. One reflection of this personality trait was that "his writings were remarkable for their brevity. He was in the habit of saying that 'brevity was the soul of wisdom as well as wit.' He detested long papers of every kind, but particularly deeds."[10]

We know much less about Miller's wife Hannah, mother of Frances and Lazette. Her parents had reputedly moved to Williamstown just so their children could attend the academy. This puts the Footes on the precocious edge of revolutionary attitudes toward education, especially female education, which became the mark of nineteenth-century America's rising middle class and was reflected in the education of the Miller and Seward girls. Williamstown Academy was "the best school in New England for girls as well as boys." Hannah attended the school for several years. According to a fellow student, Hannah "was as large and mature at fourteen as most of the school girls were at twenty. From all that can be learned of her from anyone who knew her at and after she left that school, she graduated from the Ladies' Department of that Institution at the age of fifteen, a tall, bright, handsome, stately and highly accomplished lady."[11]

Hannah's move to Auburn was a step down socially, to a frontier town and the rougher, less-educated pioneers among whom she lived. Nonetheless, "she succeeded in receiving them when they called and dining them when they came to dinner in a way and manner which charmed them greatly and elicited general praise. The result was precisely that which the Judge anticipated." Henry Ammerman, a neighbor, remembered the striking couple from their attendance at church services. They were "tall, trimly built persons nearly of the same height. . . . He usually wore a blue coat with bright buttons and a black napped hat, and she a lustrous silk dress and a white napped hat with plumes. Ammerman described Elijah and Hannah as being the most conspicuous and royal looking persons he saw at those meetings and those who paid the most to the minister." Lazette arrived in 1803 and Frances in 1805. The way the family told the story, their house was in "a bleak situation, exposed to raking winds from the lake, and in winter seasons unpropitious as a residence to delicate constitutions. The Judge was strong enough to endure those winds without serious detriment to his health, but his wife was not."[12]

Hannah stuck it out through the winter of 1808, but the Judge escorted her and their daughters back to Williamstown the following summer to save her from the winter of 1809–10. Having been instrumental in Auburn's selection as the county seat, which secured the courthouse there, and having determined that the winter climate around the lake was unhealthy for his family, Miller decided that the town of Auburn was the ideal location for both his home and law office. On his return to Auburn, Miller proceeded to board at the Center House, where he lived for the next three years. His landladies found him a difficult tenant, demanding, particular, and extremely fussy about his laundry, but they suffered his long stay because Miller was willing to pay handsomely for their services. For his first year, Miller's room served also as his law office.[13]

According to Hall's biography, "Mrs. Miller never recovered her health, but died at her father's in Williamstown in the winter of 1810." The diagnosed cause of death was "pulmonary consumption." The daughters wrote a letter to Elijah informing him, which he did not receive in time to attend the funeral. That letter does not survive. Hannah is buried in the old Williamstown (now Westlawn) cemetery in the family plot, under a marker commissioned by Henry in 1842 at the request of Frances. Elijah brought his daughters home, and his sister Martha (b. 1777), called "Patty," moved in and took responsibility for the girls' care. The sisters returned to school in the autumn and the four of them boarded in what must have been tight quarters in Center House.[14]

The shock of Hannah's death almost killed Miller, according to the family's oral history, but Elijah rallied to the appearance of stoic calm. As Elijah's good friend Judge Gary Sackett recalled, although Elijah was "not by nature or habit very demonstrative generally . . . for several weeks he was nearly distracted." Although his intense emotions were not on display to the public, in private he was bereft. According to his daughter Frances, as her children recalled, Miller had a similar reaction to the death of his mother in 1835, whose passing was anticipated by a long period of decline; "when her death occurred in his mansion on South Street and was announced to him by his daughter, Mrs. Seward, he immediately swooned and fell from his chair."[15]

Judge Miller returned to his practice of real estate law, representing one of the parties in over 25 percent of the county's property cases. Miller also served a two-year term as county clerk, was one of the commissioners who chose the site and contracted for the construction of Auburn prison in 1816, and in 1817 he became the first judge of the Cayuga County Court of Common Pleas, the highest public office he attained. He held that position for six years but remained "Judge Miller" for the rest of his life. Enos Throop, who served as Miller's clerk and went on to serve as a judge himself and then governor of New York, said that Judge Miller, "although naturally diffident and modest, was from the first the most at ease on the bench with heavy lawyers before him, of any judge, inclusive of himself, he ever knew." Perhaps his greatest gift as a judge, however, was Miller's ability to summarize a case, whether it was for a jury or in a decision.[16]

In the summer of 1816, Miller purchased for $4,000 a plot of land on South Street. Over the rest of that year and the next, he had the two-story brick house built, and in 1817 he hired two men to plant trees and lay out a garden and two others to paint the woodwork before the family moved into the dwelling by the year's end. At that time, Miller's daughters attended a day school in Auburn. Later, the girls attended the

Quaker school at Aurora, then a private boarding school in Windsor, Vermont. Finally, they enrolled in the renowned Troy Female Seminary, founded by Emma Willard, one of the most progressive and intellectually demanding of the new schools that provided young women with educations that were the equivalent of what young men received in college.[17]

In the fall of 1817, while the South Street house was in its last stages of construction, Elijah's father died in Romulus. He attended the funeral with his sister Martha, who was still living with him. Martha remained in Romulus, and Elijah's mother and sister Clary moved to Auburn to run Judge Miller's household and help raise his daughters. It was the family's understanding in the 1870s that the arrival of Paulina and her sociable youngest daughter brightened the home's mood and connected them socially in ways befitting Judge Miller's standing in the community.[18]

There was household staff right from the start at 33 South Street, one of whom was Peter Crosby, an Irishman; there was also a former slave named Harry and "a young black boy" named Jack, but they were at the margins of the story that the Millers told about themselves and the only servants we know by name until the arrival of Nicholas and Harriet Bogart, who were also African Americans, and their family. The staff remains in the shadows of the sources that survive, so we have to imagine their perspectives in essential roles. Unless we romanticize their lives, the servants were not really family, although the Sewards included the children among them in holiday celebrations and Frances tutored them along with her own children; some of the staff became friends, like the Bogarts, but they all knew that they were both essential and peripheral, valued and dismissible by the Millers and Sewards.

Miller resigned from his position on the Court of Common Pleas and entered into a law partnership with the young attorney William H. Seward in February 1823. One month later, Judge Miller was elected town supervisor, in which position he supervised elections for town and county offices. While he was promoted as a candidate for Congress, nothing ever came of that, and his service remained distinctly local and mainly private for the rest of his career. In the same year that Miller took Seward as a law partner, Henry became engaged to Elijah's daughter Frances. As Seward reported the betrothal to his father, "I am anxious to see you here and introduce [you] to your daughter Frances. Judge Miller has adopted [me] as a son, yours sincerely." What Henry meant was that he and Elijah had reached an agreement on the dowry and Elijah blessed the match. Indeed, the two fathers got on famously, and both favored the marriage, which neither of them did for those of their other children.[19]

The family's letters complicate the stories about Elijah and Paulina that we get from the manuscript biography of Elijah, his own brief account of his arrival in Auburn, and the family's oral history. The family correspondence also extends our knowledge of the two of them through the rest of their lives. The letters portray Elijah as difficult and beloved, a man and not simply an institution. Frances saw Paulina as superstitious, a pessimist, and often a scold. The correspondence also shows that the family had a different center, a female hub to its wheel, than the one the commissioned biography of Elijah gave it. Paulina was both more of an independent presence than an appendage of her son and less patriotic, more of a Quaker matriarch than the "daughter in Israel" that she is in the biography. The stories family members told each other in letters recount the challenges of living with Elijah and Paulina, more fully describing privately the ancestors in the South Street house and the family's dynamics.

According to her granddaughter Frances, Paulina was healthier in her old age than her son, or she suffered rheumatism and the loss of hearing more quietly than he did. She was both loved by and annoying to Frances, who found her grandmother naive, uneducated, superstitious, bigoted, and harshly judgmental of her mothering skills. Only after her grandmother's death did Frances reflect on Paulina's gifts, which she came to miss. In an 1839 letter to her sister, who was most often the sounding board for Frances's complaints about Grandma during her life, she now regretted "kindness slighted, counsel neglected of affection like that of a mother deep and strong, thought of then as a commonplace feeling which was very natural and consequently unimportant. Dear, dear grandma; how differently now I should appreciate all those qualities which then called forth no enthusiasm."[20]

Paulina had an abiding prejudice against the Irish, which led her to predict only malicious incompetence from the immigrant girls who worked in the house. Frances had her own problems with the Irish girls (and they were girls, often barely teenagers) and her own hierarchy of staffing preferences that mirrored those of her grandmother, but she claimed inaccurately that "I have not Grandma's prejudices against the Irish and shall be glad to hear from that country of warm hearts and generous impulses." Paulina referred to Maria, one of the Irish maids, only as "that girl" and predicted that she "will set the house on fire." At one point the family had two Irish servants by the same name. "Maria 'le grand' does not improve in neatness or civilization," Frances complained to her husband, "and the 'petit' Maria keeps our well-beloved Grandmother in a very unpleasant state of excitement."[21]

Sometimes Frances felt that she and her grandmother disagreed about everything, but despite Frances's attempt to contrast her grandmother's anti-Irish prejudices with her own more progressive views, she shared her grandmother's assessment of the comparative worth of German, African American, and Irish servants, in that order; there was a labor shortage and she had to take what she could get, which meant Irish "girls" only if she could not get the others. The two women were actually very similar in a number of ways that Frances denied. She complained about her grandmother's failure to see either the bright side or the necessity for hiring the Irish girls, but she shared the same complaints in general while disagreeing on specific cases. "Maria is much better than no help at all and Grandma is an old woman who does not always feel a Christian spirit but is a good grandmother notwithstanding." Maria "continues to find no favour in the eyes of Grandma," Frances vented to Henry, "and is blamed for all the evil doings of the children." When Clary planned to move out after her marriage, she declared that she was taking the younger Maria with her. "Grandma is so prejudiced against the child," Frances explained to Henry, "that she is determined to see nothing but evil in her disposition. She makes me very uncomfortable with constant complaints." When Paulina saw an advertisement in the newspaper offering German immigrants as servants, she insisted that Frances write to Henry "to make enquiries and get a girl of 13 or 14 years for us if possible."[22]

Frances also saw her grandmother as "dark" and "gloomy," which is interesting in part because that is the way Frances herself is generally described by others. More than once to her husband, Frances referred to Grandma's "usual gloomy prescience." When Henry left on a business trip in 1829, Grandma, having meditated "a great deal about your going away this time, of course, from that circumstance presages some misfortune, all of which is very consoling." The sarcasm is typical of Frances. Paulina had what her granddaughter described as a "passion for the marvelous," seeing signs and portents in the weather or celestial events, or simply drawing on what came to her in meditative states. Grandma "always views everything on the dark side," Frances explained on another occasion. Indeed, Paulina's diagnoses of illnesses seemed always to end with predictions of death. "She . . . felt pretty much convinced that the Dr. would never get well again" after he too was struck down by the flu.[23]

Most annoying to Frances was Paulina's harsh judgment of her parenting. This reflected the changes in lifestyle from the eighteenth to the nineteenth centuries. Now that the rising middle-class wife and mother had more leisure time and more social commitments outside the home, she also left her children in the care of others, who often were not even family members. This practice struck Paulina as irresponsible. "Grandma considers it a crime of the first magnitude," Frances wrote to Henry, whom she believed did not share Paulina's views, "if I ever go out of the house, [she] says people ought not to have children if they cannot stay at home and take care of them." Only a week later, Frances wrote again, "I have been out three days in succession and Grandma does not look at me very kindly, so I came upstairs to write to one who always does look kind." Again, only a couple months later, she wrote that "Grandma by this time thought Frederick shamefully misused—three times in one day" because Frances went to church, stopped at her sister's for tea on the way home, and attended church services again the same evening. Another time, Frances returned only to be greeted by her grandmother "with a lengthened visage and [was] withal not very cordial in her reception of myself." The cause was that Gus had vomited in her absence, which Frances minimized by diagnosing that her son "had eaten something to occasion his sickness," to which Paulina replied, in what Frances took to be a foreboding and judgmental tone, that "she hoped this was all, but doubted exceedingly the probability of my explanation." In sum, "Grandma forebodes all manner of evil and thinks that I neglect the children unmercifully."[24]

Worst of all, though, was the time that Frances left home for a reception in the company of a man who was not her husband. As Frances wrote to Henry about the incident, "Grandma does not look very complacently at me this morning. She considers it a crime of the first magnitude for me to leave the children in pursuit of amusement, and then going with a young man is a heinous sin in her estimation."[25]

All such complaints from Paulina could be lumped in Frances's mind under the diagnosis of her grandmother as old and stuck in the past, but it is unlikely Paulina was just an eccentric. More likely, she was representative of her generation of women. Paulina simply did not accept that new ways could be better or, at least, not necessarily a failure just because they were deviations from the way things once were done. Whether she was talking politics, marriage, motherhood, or household management, Paulina judged the 1820s and even worse the 1830s as representing a decline from eighteenth-century norms as she knew them. In politics, according to Frances, "she cannot see into the propriety of anything that was not done by the members of the legislature . . . some 20 or 30 years ago." Such universal denunciation of change led Paulina, in Frances's opinion, to complain about everything, which wore on her granddaughter's nerves.[26]

There was a generation between Frances and her grandmother, so the amount of change that Paulina had lived through was vast. Late in her life, Paulina witnessed the transition to companionate marriage, which meant that love now mattered to women as much as the financial competence of their suitors; the rise of a new middle class, which meant that women had more responsibilities outside the home; and the invention of modern childhood, which led parents to indulge ("spoil") their offspring, consider them blank slates to be molded by love and education rather than creatures born into original sin who needed redemption and strict (physical) discipline. That was a lot for a woman of Paulina's generation to accept, even though Quakers were at the forefront of all three changes in the United States. Frances and Henry were among the innovators in each of those realms, and even Elijah saw the benefits of female education and indulged his grandchildren, although he too was impossibly slow to catch up, in his daughters' opinion.

More than a decade after Paulina's death, Frances recalled with greater sympathy her grandmother's plight. "How frequently do these words of our dear Grandmother recur to my memory," she wrote to Lazette, quoting Paulina, "'since my sister died I have been alone in the world.'" Although Frances still had Lazette, distance separated the sisters and letters were their more frequent recourse for support than time spent together, so Frances often felt that she was alone, without her husband or sister. She also tried to take comfort in her grandmother's other refrain about time, which had a more positive spin. "Well, as Grandma says," Frances wrote to Lazette, "seven weeks cannot last always and the time will come for us to go home if we all live." This was grandmotherly wisdom that Frances took to heart and repeated often. "Well, six months, as Grandma used to say," Frances wrote to Lazette when Henry was away in Albany without her, "cannot last forever." "Well, as dear Grandma used to say," Frances wrote at the beginning of Henry's second two-year term as governor, "two years cannot last always. I feel sometimes as though it would last long enough to deprive me of the little intelligence I possess."[27]

Frances consistently failed to recognize how much she had in common with Paulina. She was shocked to find, when sitting for a bust by the artist John Frankenstein, that she saw a physical likeness she had never previously noticed. "The bust in its present state looks just like dear Grandma Miller," she wrote to her sister. "I wish you could see it. It is unaccountable to me that it does, for I know that Grandma's features were unlike mine and altogether better. What a crowd of recollections throng upon my mind whenever I cast my eyes that way."[28]

While Frances was more inclined to see her grandmother as superstitious and naive while she was alive, later in life she was more likely to recall her as a source of folk wisdom, which compensated for a lack of education. In the 1830s, when she was still in her twenties, Frances ridiculed what she saw as Paulina's ignorant belief that "it must all be true because it was in the paper," but in the 1850s and 1860s Frances began to see her grandmother's prophecies fulfilled. "There are so many accounts, which remind me of events told us by Grandma," she wrote to her sister in 1859. By then, Frances's portents and diagnoses were as dark as her grandmother's, and she came to see in the 1860s fulfillment of all their worst fears.[29]

Frances eventually recalled that her grandmother was not always critical of her parenting, but rather recognized with pride the fine characteristics of her great-grandsons and suspected that her granddaughter was at least partly responsible for their good behavior. To be sure, Paulina's compliments could be left-handed, as when she admired Fred at the age of six months by saying that "Fred has <u>grown</u> to be very nice since he came here to live, but he will never equal Augustus," his older brother, which was likely intended to compare only their physical size, and in that sense only was true. Two years later, Fred had obviously grown on his great-grandmother in ways that pleased his mother. "Grandma says he is undoubtedly the best child in the world," Frances wrote to Henry. Paulina's compliments about the two boys even led to praise that Frances took personally. "There is something so peculiar in the disposition of our children," Paulina thought. "She could never make hers take any medicine or make them obey her in any way without a great noise."[30]

The family correspondence complicates more than conflicts with accounts of Paulina's son as well. Elijah Miller was public-spirited and generous to his community. He was a formidable presence in Auburn and dedicated to the community's growth, demonstrating a civic and national pride that transcended his pecuniary interests and personal affiliations. He promoted local causes such as a new bank, the business interests of friends, and the building of new schools and churches, even ones where he never attended services, but his generosity stopped short of toleration for evangelical revivals, which he dismissed as charlatanry.[31]

Judge Miller was a loyal friend and sociable, attending, dancing, and eating joyfully at more weddings, balls, and private parties than the other members of the household combined, except for Clary. At one such large party, Frances reported to her husband, the Judge "danced four or five times with Miss Conkling," which was almost enough to create a scandal. When Gus wrote home about a ball he had attended, Frances replied, "I was much amused with your account of the Christmas ball. Grandpa was reminded of the time when he first came to this part of the country when it was no uncommon occurrence to go forty miles to a ball." Throughout his life, the Judge had numerous social callers, traveled far and wide with his friends, and could be counted on as a companion to attend an afternoon tea.[32]

At home, though, he could be stingy and controlling, even mean and bullying, in his dictates on the interpersonal contacts and decisions of his daughters into their adulthood, home renovations, and the use of shared space in the house. In July 1833 a cousin Frances had never met called, the daughter of her mother's only sister, who lived only thirteen miles away in Marcellus. "She told me that Grandma Foot[e] was dead, has been dead two whole years. Oh Henry, how bitterly I feel now the effect of Pa's policy in keeping us in such utter ignorance of all my mother's relatives." There was a mix of guilt and blame in Frances's regrets, but the blame is consistent with Frances's resentment of her father's control over the women in his household.[33]

As a grandfather, though, especially as one who had no sons of his own, Judge Miller was unquestionably generous and beloved. Indeed, when Frances attempted to make her husband feel guilty about his time away from home, she held up her father as the epitome of familial commitment. Three-year-old Gus "went to sleep in remarkably good humor reflecting on the beautiful stories his Grandpa had been amusing him with about the dogs and foxes." "Augustus [age six] and his Grandpa have just departed for an evening ride. I wish you could arrange your affairs," she wrote to Henry in 1832, early in what became a multidecade and fruitless plea, "as to have a little more leisure. Your good

Frances scarce knows she has a husband and the little boys cannot realize that you are nearer to them than Grandpa." Gus and his grandfather attended the circus, went fishing, and had countless expeditions together.[34]

Late in his life, Judge Miller craved the company of his grandchildren, especially his grandsons. "Augustus and Willie have been driving about with Grandpa all the morning," Frances reported to Lazette in 1845. "Fred continues to entertain Grandpa without intermitting," Frances wrote to Henry in 1848. "Grandpa said he missed Willie more than any one of the family," Lazette wrote to Willie in 1850 when the family was in Washington. "I do not know what Grandpa will do without Fred," Frances informed Henry the year before Elijah's death. "He is uneasy now if he leaves him an hour." In a pinch, though, the sound of four-year-old Fanny "reading" to him before she could actually read also comforted her grandfather, who found her stories told with an open book before her comforting. As Frances wrote to Henry in January 1849, "Fanny continues to read Grandpa to sleep with a very demure face. It will not be possible to keep her from learning to read." "I have a good little book that I read Grandpa to sleep with," Fanny "wrote" to her Aunt Lazette at age five. "I like it very much."[35]

Judge Miller bonded with his grandchildren very early in their lives and indulged them in ways that were not even possible in previous generations. He transitioned to modern grandparenting seamlessly in a broad cultural context. When Gus was five, his grandfather purchased him a hobbyhorse, which was the most treasured of gifts. "Augustus and Grandpa are down stairs discussing the merits of the Hobby horse," Frances wrote to Henry in January 1831. It had arrived three days earlier and was stabled in a small and very cold room off the "little kitchen." "Augustus and his Grandpa make it periodical visits. . . . He asks my permission twenty times a day to go a 'little while and see hobby.'" Two weeks later, Gus and his cousin Frances "have rode poor hobby almost to death." Two months after Hobby's arrival, "Augustus still continues his military career. He has been general all day with a new paper cap and wooden sword." Had his mother known that Gus's fascination with a military life would outlast the hobbyhorse into adulthood, she would not have found his playful warfare so charming.[36]

Hobby was the first, but far from the last, of the ponies and horses, outfitted with saddles, wagons, and carriages, that Elijah purchased for his grandsons. The first live pony came a year after the hobbyhorse. "Tell Augustus that his colt will be well broken by spring," Judge Miller wrote to Henry when the family was in Albany, "so that he can drive or ride him as soon [as] he gets home." "I am about buying a horse," he wrote to Fred in Albany when his father was governor, "so that you can ride when you come here next summer." Frances wrote to Gus when Willie had just turned four that "Grandpa has purchased an old horse which he and Fred drive every day. Fred rides occasionally on horseback and Willie thinks he is old enough to be allowed the same privilege."[37]

Elijah's indulgences of his grandchildren included excursions, pets, and candy, cakes, and other sweets, as well as books and magazines for children, which did not even exist for his daughters. The invention of the modern child in the early nineteenth century built on a belief that active encouragement of children's development was more important than discipline, which gifted such children as those of the Sewards with the first generation of indulgent grandparents. The books and magazines aimed at them were an important part of the change, as was the prolongation of childhood into and ultimately through their teens, when education took the place that labor once had in the lives of middle-class teenagers.

The sharp decline in birth rates was one foundation of the changes in relationships across generations; birth control by abstinence, *coitus interruptus*, and the rhythm method all played a role. Induced abortion was also an increasingly common method of limiting births. As children to such families as the Millers and Sewards were no longer sources of income, fewer births enabled the rising middle class to invest the time, energy, and money in education necessary to prepare children for the new industrial and commercial world they were born into. Women now had their last child three to four years earlier than they had in the previous century, which suggests they and/or their partners practiced birth control after they had the desired number of offspring. The Sewards' generation was among the first in the United States to have a separate nursery in their home: actually Elijah's house, which speaks to both the elevated value of adult privacy and the passing down of such values to the next generation. It also reflected that Frances was among the modern mothers who relied heavily on the new wave of advice literature on housekeeping and child-rearing.[38]

There was a hardening of gendered assumptions about children, but not the same ones that informed previous centuries. Boys and girls of the rising middle class now often attended the same schools or, at least, had curricula that did not assume the inferiority of the female intellect. Elijah and Paulina apparently treated the Miller sisters and their children accordingly. Women were, however, viewed as physically fragile and conformed to the expectation. Femininity was the goal for girls, and lessons elevated self-sacrifice and service over the aggressiveness, daring, and independence that defined masculinity. Girls were confined, dependent, and restrained in the domestic realm, while boys roamed, rode, ran, fought, and competed. Middle-class children had many more toys than previous generations, but girls had dolls, tea sets, stages on which their paper dolls performed theatrically, music boxes, and books; they took piano and art lessons, and learned French. Boys had swords, hobbyhorses, guns, bugles, drums, toy cannons, tin soldiers, and firecrackers, and they studied Latin.[39]

Sometimes, looking back on her own childhood, Frances was grateful for her father's heavier hand with her than she and Henry imposed on their children. In retrospect, she understood his close supervision during her motherless childhood, but she still viewed him as unpleasantly controlling compared to her husband and their generation of paternal, rather than patriarchal, figures. This more modern view did not lead her to rebel often against Elijah's or all male authority in society. She was not one of the women of her generation who resented confinement to the domestic sphere; she did not seek the vote or aspire to a more public role than that defined by her duties within her father's house. Rather, she was of the more representative group of women who celebrated their roles as wives, mothers, and household managers in an elevation of housewifery and motherhood to higher regard even to the brink of seeing education in those roles as essential. These wives and mothers saw their authority in the home expand over that of the previous generation and estimated the value of themselves and their social contribution differently than their predecessors had. In the absence of Frances's late mother, the leap was from Paulina to Frances, which was undoubtedly jarring to Elijah as well.

The Judge retained a patriarchal presence in relation to the family's women. He could be loud when angry, and the women sometimes found his physical demeanor frightening. In one case, Elijah had a tantrum aimed at Frances, what she called "a frenzy at dinner over a piece of beef." As she was the one responsible for the meal, she bore the force of his rage. A dinner guest from outside the family tried to comfort her later by saying that "all men behaved so sometimes when they were disappointed about any particular dish." Loyally, Frances rose to her absent husband's defense, which reflected the generational change. "I told her I knew of one who did not," by which she meant Henry.

"Augustus, little rascal, was a witness of the scene. While reading his lesson in the afternoon, he came to the word meat, 'm e a t, meat, such meat ma, as Grandpa scolded so about,' said he. I tried to persuade him it was not scolding, but he appeared rather skeptical."[40]

Frances generally wrote on the subject of her father's patriarchal dominance when she resented rather than respected his commands. In an 1832 letter to her husband, for example, she was sarcastic in describing her father's supervision of "the putting up the fireboard in the north room which is beautified by nailing on three huge pieces of unpainted timber to prevent its coming to pieces." Her father's unaesthetic efforts to prevent fires caused by newly installed stoves, an innovation she did not embrace, continued throughout his life: "Saturday was employed by Pa and a very handsome man in nailing up sheet iron fireboards in the south chamber and front room. You will find the house considerably embellished when you come home if Pa continues as active as he has been." (The description of her father's assistant as "handsome" was another example of the Miller sisters' sarcasm, as was "embellished.") In Frances's view, her father's contributions of new technology (coal stoves and furnaces) generally made the house less attractive, uncomfortable, and more dangerous to the health of its occupants.[41]

Sometimes Frances attributed her father's dictates to eccentricity, sometimes to misguided frugality, but often to his lack of respect for women. The core problem from Frances's perspective was that her father declined to consult her or even consider her opinion about the house and grounds, whether the question was comfort, aesthetics, disrepair, or safety. She, in the true form of a modern homemaker, expected the residence to be her domain, which her husband but not her father welcomed. As she wrote to Henry, from whom she expected sympathy and support, "Pa has grieved me exceedingly by cutting down and mutilating our beautiful trees. It seems to be rather discouraging to attempt to ornament a place which does not belong to yourself. No one who has not experienced the same feeling can know how fondly I am attached to every tree and shrub about this place, which has been a loved home so many years." The Judge decided when they needed a new well and pump, when and how the trees should be pruned and the garden planted, when and what color the dining room and other parts of the house were painted, what repairs were called for and who should do them, which chimneys should be cleaned, and which rooms had fires. "Pa made himself wroth with the painters," Frances reported, "and a little vexed with me because the inside shutters were painted green first, determined that they should paint no more, and then concluded that he wanted the dining room shutters cupboards and all painted white. I remonstrated but without any effect. White, white was the thing. Pa does not appear to think I have anything to do but wash, paint or if I have it does not materially concern him."[42]

In other households, Frances would have been the final authority on the hiring and firing of staff, a role in which Henry had no interest. While this was true for female servants, Frances had no influence on the male staff, who reported directly to Judge Miller. "Peter [Crosby] will and must always make a part of our household until Pa dismisses him," she complained in a letter to Henry, "of which event there is not the shadow of a probability."[43]

The women were unable to confine Judge Miller to the use of a single bedroom in the private upstairs floor of the house. "You know his fancy for sleeping in public places," Frances wrote to her sister on one such occasion. "As for your father," Elijah's sister Clary wrote to Lazette, "he has his meals taken up in the North Room and then lies down on the settee and takes a sleep, has a fire built there for him." No one else ate or slept in that room on the ground floor. Frances was thoroughly exasperated with their father's habits when she wrote to Lazette in September 1834 that he "remained two days in the south chamber and then had a cot made and placed in the middle of the South Room, of course the front room is used for a hall. . . . I have said so many wrong things already about these movements that I will not trust myself to say any more now." Frances reported to Henry behaviors of her father that she came to accept in due course. "Pa grows since his illness more and more regardless of appearances," she complained. As an example, she reported that his "bed is to continue in the front room," the parlor where they received callers, "all summer, and he has been driving up nails in the wall in the sitting room to hang his clothes on. I hope people will not think we are all crazy."[44]

We might say that the Judge refused to respect boundaries, including very personal ones. Elijah invited a stranger, James Bowen, president of the New York and Erie Railroad, into Frances's dressing room before she was fully clothed, which was not something that a Victorian-era woman took lightly. In her opinion, it was her room, defined by her use even in his house. "What should Pa do but walk in and ask him into my dressing room," she wrote to Henry. "I had not one article of clothing that I could put on." The Judge grew increasingly exasperated with her slowness to join the men in the South Room, so he came again "to the head of the stairs . . . calling 'Frances.'" She sent a maid downstairs to inform her father that she intended to join the men shortly, but "she had hardly got upstairs before Pa came again and in an angry tone" tried to rush her. "I was vexed that I could not be allowed one of the two minutes to arrange my dress, but as they continued in the North Room until the last moment I was compelled to send up word that I desired to be excused." This was an act of defiance for which she expected to pay even as an adult. As she explained to her husband, "I was very, very sorry but these are grievances for which there seems to be no remedy." She was apparently sorry because Mr. Bowen might have thought her rude, but also because "the recollection of my former experience deterred me" from open defiance of her father. We do not know the previous event to which she referred, but it certainly discouraged further challenges to Judge Miller's authority in his house.[45]

As the household shrank from the losses of Paulina's death and Clary's marriage, the move of Lazette's family to Canandaigua, and the growth to adulthood of first Gus and then Fred, the Judge also became if not a less formidable figure in the eyes of his family members, certainly a more sympathetic one and even pathetic toward the end. During his last two years, Frances commented on Elijah's return to coherence. To Henry she wrote that her father "this afternoon . . . has talked considerably and rationally about the people in Auburn. The Dr. says I may safely say he is no worse. He does not think this improvement will be permanent." Grandpa Miller was always beloved by his grandchildren, and Frances began to see her father through other, more affectionate lenses. When he died, the Judge left an emotional chasm that turned to reverence and ultimately celebration.[46]

Never did Frances express greater loneliness than in the months immediately following her father's death in November 1851, a void she imagined filled by Henry replacing Elijah. Perhaps her husband would now be more comfortable at 33 South Street as the head of the household. The absence of caregiving for Elijah left a hole in Frances's life. "When I think of our home without Grandpa I feel as if my occupation were gone," she wrote to her sister four months after he died. Partly this was because he had always been there, but mostly she genuinely loved him and missed him despite, or even because of, his quirks and demands. "It was very sad to feel that there was no possibility of meeting Grandpa on the side walk," she explained to Henry on returning to the house after time away. "I hardly knew how to employ the first half hour which had always been given to him." "Grandpa's going away leaves a great void," she wrote shortly after her husband had returned to Washington from Elijah's funeral.[47]

Immediately after Elijah passed there was much to arrange, and with Henry's assistance as executor of the estate, Frances moved forward with plans for the funeral and burial. She met with resistance from the pastor of the Episcopal church, which had the capacity for the large attendance anticipated, who "would not venture to have the remains of our honored father taken into the Church until he had consulted the bishop." After all, Judge Miller was not baptized or a frequent attender late in his life; he generally preferred the Unitarians. As Frances rose in rage to her father's defense, she argued that "our father had done more than any man in the community towards making the church what it is. He never failed to contribute liberally to its support when all others have vacillated. He was an honest, upright man, irreproachable in morals. If the church which he has fostered could hesitate about rendering to him this poor tribute of respect I can no longer have any sympathy in his communion. This I feel constrained to tell Mr. Ayrault," who resigned as pastor the following year.[48]

Six months after Judge Miller's death, his absence in the house still left a void for his daughter. "I am again at the home of my Father," Frances wrote to her husband, "the home which your love has beautified and which I hope will in time become a haven of rest to you also. Everything is green and beautiful beyond my anticipation, and though much remains undone the garden is in tolerable order." The house and grounds seemed oddly empty, and she felt alone in Elijah's absence. The house was now hers, which is what she had long craved, but possession was more than a legal condition; it was also psychological and could be a burden, a responsibility that she feared was beyond her skills. "I find many things about which I want your advice," she continued to Henry, "but with the knowledge I have of the continual draft upon your time and patience I feel unwilling to ask you to share my cares."[49]

Frances rallied to the task, gained confidence, and eventually asserted her authority over her home with less consultation and more firmly fixed views. The death of Grandpa left a pall over the house from which she never fully recovered, and Lazette eventually preferred her own home down the street, where she lived after her husband's death, to a room in what she may now have seen as her sister's house rather than as mutually theirs. Their father had, after all, left the house to Frances, the younger of the two sisters, but the one whose marriage he approved and who cared for him.[50]

With the last two of the Seward children growing to adulthood in the 1850s and the family split between Washington, DC, and Auburn right through the Civil War, Frances's hope to have the entire family united in the South Street house, now finally her house, was never realized. Lazette preferred to live alone, while visiting often and helping whenever asked. Henry's retirement was Frances's dream and not his; Gus's return home from the army and Fred's from his careers in journalism and government never occurred, as Fred and Anna bought a house on the Hudson River and Gus never resigned as his mother long urged. Frances welcomed the return home of Will's wife and children for stretches during the war; Will also resided there for a time before he enlisted and then again when injured and ill. Even after Frances's death, Henry's eventual "retirement" was peripatetic, with trips across the continent and around the globe more attractive to him than the garden and the house were. As early as the mid-1840s, with Gus off to the army, Fred leaving for college, and Henry still always away, Frances lamented that the house was no longer filled. "I would it were," she wrote to Lazette, "still filled with the descendants of Paulina Titus."[51]

Frances does not refer in this letter to the family members as descendants of Elijah Miller or William Henry Seward, but of Paulina. Frances was entitled to such a matriarchal view of her home and family, but such a dream of a house full of Paulina's descendants would not be realized in Frances's lifetime. She was right that her family was as much descended from the women of 33 South Street as it was from famous men about whom biographies were written, but the family scattered to Albany, Washington, even Utah over the course of the decade, and Frances was unable to bring her children and husband home.

In 1851 Frances could still hope, though. In the immediate aftermath of her father's death, she joined Henry in Washington to escape the ghosts of Paulina and Elijah, but they never left her, nor did she really want them to go. From Washington she wrote to Lazette, who occupied the house in her absence. "I have your two letters from our dear, old, home," Frances wrote in January 1852. "How much it is like you and how unlike anybody else to go there and stay alone, and to like to be there. I think my heart has felt lighter since I have known that you were in the house." And yet, Frances's heart was never truly light, and was even heavier now. "Somehow or another," she continued to Lazette after the brief interlude of brightness, "since Pa died I have felt that everybody's life was much nearer a termination than it was before." With such a dark perspective Frances sounded much like her grandmother.[52]

Chapter 2

Henry's Backstory, 1801–1824

Henry was the only resident of 33 South Street who did not either live there from birth or from the house's completion in 1817, taking up residence on his marriage to Frances in 1824. When he heard the door slam behind him on his way into Elijah Miller's house, he felt imprisoned—perhaps not on first entry, but shortly after, and incarcerated by domesticity rather than the house's owner. Soon after arrival Henry plotted an escape, but the core problem was family, which rattled his nerves even before the arrival of children. The jangle of any household might have done that, but it was this one that did. In retrospect, it was a formula for conflict, and flight was the obvious choice for a man such as him.

The backstory that Henry shared publicly to explain the man he became did not include a physical description, but he was five foot six, slightly built, with blue eyes and red hair. Instead he wrote about his character formation and assertion of independence from his father, Samuel S. Seward, who would have attended university if "Columbia College, the only one in the colony of New York," had not been "disorganized during the war." Samuel was a practicing physician during Henry's childhood and youth, "to which occupation he added those of the farmer, the merchant, and county politician, magistrate, and judge, discharging the functions of all with eminent ability, integrity, and success, and gradually building up what at that day, and in that rural neighborhood, seemed a considerable fortune." Samuel Seward represented Orange County in the state legislature for one term when Henry was a toddler "and showed much vigor and ability in debate," according to his son. Henry's mother, Mary Jane Jennings Seward, attended country schools, and her son remembered her as "a person of excellent sense, gentleness, truthfulness, and candor." That is all he has to say about her. About himself, Henry wrote, "I was the fourth of six children, and the third son, born in 1801, May 16th. A daughter, older than myself, died in infancy; a second daughter and a son came after me. I have been told that the tenderness of my health caused me to be early set apart for a collegiate education, then regarded, by every family, as a privilege so high and so costly that not more than one son could expect it."[1]

Henry thought he most effectively prepared for college at a school close to home. "My daily studies began at five in the morning, and closed at nine at night," he recalled. "The tasks were just the utmost that I could execute, and every day a little more," which included driving the cows to distant pastures, running the family's errands, carrying grain to the mill and the flour back home, and fetching lime from the kiln. The stories that Henry told about his father presented Samuel as a hard taskmaster who drove his son to accomplishment by high expectations and threats to withdraw favor.[2]

Samuel Seward delivered his son a clear message, which Henry recalled as hard but inspiring. His father encouraged him to think that he could "ultimately become a great lawyer, like Theodore Frelinghuysen and Joseph C. Hornblower, of the neighboring State of New Jersey." Henry told this story as humorous, knowing that he had far exceeded his father's ambitions for him. His father chided him as a child for hubris, for not grasping the essential truth that an aspiration to public office must come from a place of humility, that it would be his neighbors who decided whether he was worthy of their trust. "My father took me severely to task," Henry recalled, "for not knowing that the office of magistrate was to be obtained through the favor of others, and not to be ambitiously usurped." From his father's correction, Henry learned never to appear above but always at the side of his fellow citizens. It was in such a spirit that Henry joined the local militia and proudly accepted the rank of colonel bestowed on him.[3]

The conflict imbedded in Henry's relationship with his father reflected fundamental change between Samuel's generation and that of his son. Samuel's generation was patriarchal: the man alone ruled the family and projected authority derived from his social standing. In the first two decades of the nineteenth century, new cultural values of self-made manhood emerged from republican government and democratic impulses that became highly valued, the expansion of the market economy, and the growth of the middle class. A man's public role rather than his standing by birth became the critical factor in his family relations. While Samuel felt obliged to prepare his son for the world he had grown up in, Henry chafed at restrictions that bound him to the old ways.[4]

Men in the new century sought to break free from the fetters of the past. The sources of their authority would be independence, competition, and ambition rather than the social class into which they were born. Although Henry's ambition initially focused unsuccessfully on a judicial appointment, his education sparked an early and deep interest in politics. Both the method and the subject of his schooling led him in that direction. Latin translations were often from political discourses, and public declamation and debate were key parts of both college and preparation for it. Henry thought that he did not have a natural talent for public speaking, but application to the skill both in college and the study of law prepared him for the courtroom, political campaigns, and legislative debates. He credited moot courts and his college debate society as the core of his practical education for public life. "If I were required now to say from what part of my college education I derived the greatest advantage," Henry reflected, "I should say the exercises of the Adelphic Society."[5]

Henry meant that he learned more from his fellow students in their self-made literary and debate society than he did from the adults who taught his college classes. In this belief he was far from alone, and the emergence of male clubs was one mark of not only nineteenth-century colleges but the larger American society in which they existed. The Adelphic Society was Henry's constructed family away from home, where he learned, competed, honed his skills, and made the closest friendships of his youth. In this, too, his experience was exemplary of change. Here young males bonded in relationships that were social and intellectual, where they asserted their independence in a masculine world that was more self-possessed than that of the generation that preceded them as boys made themselves into men fit for the changing times.[6]

It was in the Adelphic Society that Henry first debated the great public issues of the day, but his opposition to slavery began earlier, he thought, in his childhood home, which harbored "a social anomaly, which I long found a perplexing enigma." While he, his parents, and siblings occupied bedrooms and parlors in their house, there were also "in the family two black women, and one black boy, who remained exclusive tenants of the kitchen and the garret over it." The social distinction between the two groups was never a subject of conversation in his home that Henry could recall. "If my parents never uttered before me a word of disapproval of slavery, it is but just to them to say that they never uttered an expression that could tend to make me think that the negro was inferior to the white person." What was more, his parents displayed by their actions, if not by their words, that they rose above the white community's prejudices against Black people. "While the two younger of my father's slaves attended school," Henry recalled, "and sat at my side if they chose, I noticed that no other black children went there." Those were Chloe, two years Henry's senior, and an unnamed "black boy," perhaps her brother, who later ran away to escape his enslavement by the Sewards.[7]

Henry thought his early sympathy for African Americans began with those he knew as a child, his recognition of the injustice of slavery, and his family's progressivism on race for their time and place. New York had more slaves than any other state north of Maryland and was one of the last of the northern states to adopt a gradual abolition law, which it did in 1799, two years before Henry's birth. The discourse on slavery remained contentious in his youth; Quakers were a leading edge of abolition in the white community, but they were much less influential in New York than in Pennsylvania. Abolition had its advocates and the New York Manumission Society dating back to 1785, but the movement was not as vibrant as in Massachusetts and Pennsylvania. New York also had its share of southern sympathizers and the full range of opinions about race, slavery, and citizenship. In Henry's youth, people were arguing in public about personal independence, suffrage, and citizenship, all of which absorbed him as a teenager. "I early came to the conclusion that something was wrong," he wrote, "and the 'gradual emancipation laws' of the State, soon after coming into debate, enabled me to solve the mystery, and determined me, at that early age, to be an abolitionist." The mystery to Henry was why some people were free while others were not.[8]

Henry accepted a gradual approach to the abolition of slavery, which radical abolitionists, including his wife, found morally compromised if not bankrupt. Henry, though, still saw his approach as more practical and deeply moral. "Shall I not stop now to say that," Henry wrote, "while the family of which I was a member has increased, until it numbers more than eighty persons, all of whom hold respectable positions in society, and some one or more of whom are to be found in every quarter of the globe—the descendants of that slave family in my father's kitchen now number but seven, and these have their only shelter under a roof which I provide for them?" In other words, Henry recognized fully the injustice done to former slaves as he wrote in 1871, and he took personal responsibility for the role of his family in perpetuating racism.[9]

Although they go unnamed in the autobiography, the enslaved family to which Henry referred is that of Chloe, who married a man named William Coe. At the time Chloe was born, her status fell under New York's gradual emancipation law of 1799. This law dictated that females born into slavery after July 4, 1799, as Chloe was, would be free on reaching their twenty-fifth birthday. For Chloe that was on November 9, 1824, the same year as Henry's marriage to Frances. Chloe gave birth to a daughter, Mary, in 1819. She bore at least five other children, whose death dates are elusive, which makes it entirely possible that Chloe, who lived until 1877 and remained sometimes employed by the Sewards, had six other family members living with her under the roof that Henry mentioned.[10]

Henry also noted that "both of my father's female servants were seduced and disgraced," although he does not say by whom. Given what we know about the moral turpitude of enslavers, we ought to consider the possibility that it was one or more of his family members, and that the guilt that led Henry to feel responsible for his family's former slaves could have had biological roots. This would explain why Chloe pressed Henry and Frances to take her daughter Mary into their home from about the time she reached age fourteen. Perhaps Chloe felt her daughter would be safer with Henry and Frances, that she trusted Henry, whom she knew as "Harry" from his youth, more than she did other men in the family.

When Frances visited Henry's parents in 1832, Chloe regaled her with stories praising Henry's youthful generosity with the spending money that his frugal father dispensed grudgingly. "He would give it away to the first poor man he met," Frances quoted Chloe as saying. "There is many a negro man in Goshen who remembers Harry yet." Chloe also told Frances, "Well, I can say one thing of Harry; we lived together so many years and he never said a crass word to me." It took a decade of lobbying by Chloe to Henry and his parents before Mary came into the Sewards' household first as a maid and later as their cook.[11]

Henry tested out of his first two years of college, but its rules barred a student under the age of sixteen from joining the junior class, so he entered as a sophomore. He was young, immature, and emboldened by his newfound freedom. "I felt a conscious self-satisfaction," he recalled, "in being trusted to pursue my studies and govern my conduct without the surveillance of parent or teacher," and he, at the age of seventy, still knew "of no institution where a manlier spirit prevailed among the under-graduates."[12]

The language of manliness was very nineteenth-century and part of the cultural change that led men to value self-made independence. Henry's impulse to conform to the adolescent culture that he found so liberating was one aspect of the new values. This youth culture framed its members as in conflict with adults and independent of their governance. Adolescents challenged the very foundations of adult authority in pranks that disrespected the individuals and institutions that substituted for their fathers. They reveled in both bonding and exclusion: one belonged to his society or fraternity or class against others in a competitive environment where the members made the rules.[13]

A letter Henry wrote to a friend back in Florida (the village near Goshen, New York, where Henry grew up) in March 1817 reflects the immaturity of the not-yet-sixteen-year-old college sophomore and his playful approach to college. He was writing to Daniel Jessup because "Firstly, hem. I have got nothing else to do. Secondly, hem. To speak the truth, you are the laziest fellow about writing I ever knew and therefore can afford that time in reading which others spend in writing. Thirdly, hem. Nobody else will answer my letters, ergo—you must of course." In the letter, Henry reported that two nights previously the students had singled out the residence of one Professor Burt, whose crime against them was an "unsavoury savour." Burt smelled badly, so the students "attempted to wreak their vengeance" by burning his residence to the ground. Although they failed in that ambition, "no furniture was saved. Since that fatal night attempts have been made and successfully prevented to burn the other castles." In these assaults on the tutors' rooms, the students saw themselves through the lenses of the history they read, as descendants of Guy Fawkes, one of a group of English provincial Catholics sympathetic to Spain who failed in their attempt to blow up Parliament in 1605, masterminding "conspiracies dark mysterious and dangerous," not against "Kings Presidents Emperors Popes," but gunpowder plots against the faculty. Such details of vicious pranks, not surprisingly, go unreported in Seward's autobiography.[14]

Despite the pranks and a prideful run-in with one of the tutors, Henry was successful in his studies. "The college reports of my study and demeanor gratified my parents and encouraged me," he wrote. "There was only one drawback, and that was my entire failure to bring my expenses to an equation with the parental allowance." This, Henry explained, seemed to him at the time entirely his father's fault for being unrealistic about the real costs of living at college in a manly way. His father disagreed, unreasonably from the perspective of his teenage son, that Henry required financial supplements to cover his contribution to the "expenses of recreations, not to speak of the sums which I could not refuse to give away in charity, or to lend to juvenile borrowers, by whom I am not yet reimbursed. Moreover, the more I retrenched these expenditures, the more the quarterly appropriation was reduced."[15]

What Henry called his "financial misunderstanding with my father" was compounded by debts he incurred to tailors in Schenectady. "I would by no means imply a present conviction that the fault in the case was altogether with my father," Henry wrote, which is a grudging acknowledgment of his own complicity. "On the other hand, I think now that the fault was not altogether mine. However this may have been, he declined to pay for my bills that he thought unreasonable; and I could not submit to the shame of credit impaired. I resolved thenceforth upon independence and self-maintenance."[16]

According to Henry, Samuel simply did not understand the social pressures that led Henry to conform or be mocked and excluded, and his father failed to comprehend how essential being included was to his generation. There were standards of dress, informal financial relationships as both creditor and debtor, and responsibilities for taking one's turn to treat others. The youth culture had rules in utter conflict with those of Samuel, and Henry felt honor-bound to abide by the standards established by other boys in an assertion of independence from his father, which seemed to Samuel dishonorable.[17]

The solution hit upon by the youthful Henry was to hop on a stagecoach on January 1, 1819, head for New York with a classmate, and sail for Georgia on a schooner from that city. He and his friend hid on the ship from Samuel, who had pursued him to the docks in the hope of saving his son from what he feared could be a life-altering or fatal mistake. On landing in Savannah, Henry headed to a rural outpost that had advertised for a teacher to run a new school, in the hope that the board of trustees would hire him for the job. The five trustees who interviewed him for the position were headed by Major William

Alexander, "a genial planter," who agreed both to hire and board him despite his young age, which he and Henry agreed to keep from the other trustees. Henry contracted for a salary of $800 in the first year plus room and board, and recalled that he "accepted the position with an expression of profound thanks, and an assurance of determination to merit the approval of my generous patrons."[18]

The surviving letters from Henry in Georgia to his parents back in Florida, New York, suggest his flight may have been all along, or evolved along the way into, a ploy to extract the necessary funds for college from his father. While the story is generally told as one in which his father and especially his mother put pressure on him to return, what is missing from that version is the pressure Henry, his mother, and likely his sister and grandmother put on his father to bail Henry out of his financial struggles and pay for his return home. The first letter of Henry's is from Savannah, before he secured the teaching position he sought in Macon. It is addressed to his "Respected and beloved Parents," a salutation that perhaps overplayed his hand. He proceeded to insist, appearances to the contrary, that his parents held the "supremist situation in my heart" and appealed "to my former life and (if my life be spared) I appeal to my future conduct to confirm my assertions."[19]

Henry returned again to this theme of the risk to his life represented by his current path, knowing as he did that he "might be reduced to sickness and Poverty in a foreign land." And, he insisted, it was only "through necessity" that he was an "undutiful son." The blame rested on his father, and Henry had no choice under the circumstances but to risk his future, his good name—indeed, his life—to extricate himself as a "vagabond and prodigal" from the penury Samuel had imposed on him. He had a plan one month after his departure for an independent path, having "forfeited my right to expect assistance and support from my parents."[20]

Henry did not explain fully why he left the school and Alexander's plantation long before fulfillment of his contract with the school's board of trustees. He referred only to pulls from home, pleading letters from his parents, which may have induced guilt and homesickness, but his resentment of his father's overseeing hand and his need to assert independence had not, at least in his recollections from more than a half century later, diminished. His father authorized an agent to advance Henry the funds necessary to finance his return trip. Instead of invoking gratitude and remorse, though, and "by no means disposed to give up an independence which had been so dearly gained, I drew on

Mr. Richardson, as he had advised me I might, for one hundred dollars. With this sum I brought my person into more presentable condition, and returned to my patrons." In sum, Henry stole the money offered in peace by his father, who had hoped to smooth his son's path home for reconciliation.[21]

What, then, accounts for Henry's early departure for home? We know there was a second letter from his father addressed to Major Alexander in which he denounced Henry as "a much-indulged son, who, without any just provocation or cause, had absconded from Union College, thereby disgracing a well-acquired position, and plunging his parents into profound shame and grief." Samuel Seward then threatened Alexander and his fellow trustees with prosecution to the "utmost rigor of the law" for harboring the "delinquent." In Henry's telling, Alexander rose to the occasion as his friend, agreed to keep the letter to himself, and told Henry if he decided to remain in Georgia despite Samuel Seward's wishes, "your father may prosecute me as soon as he pleases. Had this been the whole of the case," the story continued, "it would have been easily settled." Henry wanted readers to know that he did not return because his father threatened him. That would have been unmanly by the standards of his generation.[22]

The clinching blow to Henry's plans, as he told the story, was a letter from his mother that "indicated a broken heart" and another from his younger sister confirming that "our mother was on the verge of distraction." What compounded his mother's pain, as she shared with Henry in her letter, was the fact that his "eldest brother had, two or three years earlier, come into a misunderstanding with my father, no less unhappy than my own; had left the paternal home, and was seeking, with uncertain success, to establish a fortune for himself in the then new State of Illinois." This would have been Benjamin Jennings Seward (1793–1841). His other older brother, Edwin Polydore Seward (1799–1872), had enlisted in the army and "was then writing to his mother mysterious accounts of his new occupation." All three of Mary and Samuel's adult sons had run off.[23]

The older brothers returned to Orange County but did not fully reconcile with their father. Samuel never forgave them for their transgressions, which included future financial crises as well as the past ones. To his dying day and through his immensely complicated will that took over twenty years to settle in probate, Samuel Seward held a grudge, a harsh judgment against the surviving older son, Polydore, whom he considered an irredeemable drunk. In our terms, Polydore was afflicted with alcoholism and depression, and struggled mightily against them throughout his long life. Jennings was, by all accounts, a loving and beloved man, whom his father considered a failure, incompetent and lazy despite ample evidence to the contrary.

Samuel S. Seward's patriarchal hand extended from Florida, New York, to Schenectady, Macon, and Auburn. His wealth influenced a web of family relationships. His reputation as a harsh man haunts Henry's backstory as it did his life and those of his siblings. Henry measured himself against his father, as sons do, and wanted people to know what he struggled against and what made him. The story was complicated, as it often is, and he was in many ways his father's son, both in reflection of and in opposition to the model provided.

There is another possible explanation, though, for why Henry left Georgia so shortly after committing to stay. While Henry could not have fathered Chloe's child, who would have been conceived around February 1819, when he was in Georgia, there was a claim by Rossetta Alexander in an 1866 letter to him that he fathered her by an enslaved woman named Milly at about that same time in Macon. Fred was perhaps the only family member who knew about the letter, because it came to the Department of State when he served as his father's assistant. Someone saved it in Henry's State Department correspondence, where a biographer recently found it. We do not know whether Henry provided Rossetta the financial assistance she sought from him upon her family being freed from slavery in Georgia after the Civil War. "This communication may excite much surprise & possibly indignation," she wrote to Henry in 1866. "For nearly forty-five years I have been a slave," Rossetta's letter continued, "& therefore I had no chance to assert my rights, & claim my real paternity."[24]

The letter went on to explain that she was born into slavery on the plantation of Major William Alexander of Putnam County, Georgia, and that she now lived in Macon. "My mother & my old Master who is now dead always said you was my Father. . . . I have been taught to claim you as my Father from my childhood now since my race have been freed and emancipated by the result of the war, I feel that I have a right to call on you for aid." She was the mother of eleven children, still had six to support, "& we are all very poor both black & white." What she wanted from Henry, what she felt entitled to as reparations, was "money to buy me a little house." It sounds as if Rossetta's mother was still living, but that is uncertain. "I will if you require it give you all the evidence of the truth of what I have said. My Mother knows more of the case than any other person." In another attempt to establish credibility, Rossetta Alexander added in a postscript, "I write myself my good mistress taught me to read & write. I forgot to say I am nearly white. My Mother's Name was Milly."[25]

Henry's failure to mention Rossetta is not surprising, and we cannot know whether what she believed was actually true. The evidence is circumstantial, but plausible. There are no holes in her story, which was an oral history before she wrote it down. The timing and location make it possible, and she claims two credible sources, Major William Alexander and Rossetta's mother, Milly. There is also Henry's decision to leave Georgia so soon after his arrival, but there is no evidence that the departure reflected tension with Major Alexander, with whom Henry claimed to have left on good terms. On balance, Rossetta's story rings truer than Henry's does. She believed the story, and he would not have admitted it if it was true.[26]

It may have been guilt and his mother's grief that led Henry to break his contract with the Union Academy in what he maintained was a responsible manner, only after securing a replacement whom the trustees found acceptable. Or it may have been Milly's pregnancy. "I felt well satisfied on arriving at home," Henry wrote, "on the ground, not that I had decided wisely for myself in returning there, but that I had relieved my fond mother and sister from anxiety and sorrow on my account, and I promised myself never thereafter to abandon them, however difficult my own situation might become." He said he returned for the sake of the women and pledged to take responsibility that he felt his older brothers had abdicated in their flight. Henry's father remained the crux of the problem. "I soon ascertained that I had no change to expect on the part of my other parent," who remained fixed in his opinions about Henry's behavior. "On the other hand," Henry explained in retrospect, "his former opinions of my great disobedience were confirmed by the discovery that, unlike the prodigal son in the parable, in coming home again I had come impenitent." Henry concluded to bide the short time he had remaining until he "arrived at my majority and acquired my profession," when he could "resume, lawfully, the independence I had seized upon prematurely, and given up with reluctance." He agreed to return to Union College in January 1820, one year after his departure, and to spend the intervening six months reading law in the office of a local attorney and paying off his accumulated debt "by earning fees as an advocate in the justice's court," which he could do without being admitted to the bar.[27]

In the interim, Henry again disappointed his father. Samuel sent Henry to collect debts. At the first stop, Henry collected $150, about a year's pay for an army private and double what a common laborer made in that time. At the second, he lost the cash, and he was unable to find it after returning for a thorough search of the grounds and road. Two years later, the woman who lived at the second address confessed to having found it on the ground, where Henry had dropped it in dismounting his horse. "My father submitted to the loss," as Henry told the story, "perhaps all the more cheerfully because he had mentally appropriated the lost money to the discharge of my indebtedness at Schenectady." In other words, Henry covered his debts to the tailors himself, debts he thought his father should have paid in the first place, and did not believe he owed his father anything for losing the money entrusted to him. There was no hint of apology in Henry's telling; it was simply the clinching anecdote in the larger story of his father's parsimony and his own quest for independence.[28]

"The resumption of my collegiate course was embarrassing," Henry wrote, although graduating at the age of nineteen, in the class behind him, should hardly have been a humiliation, especially after testing out of his freshman class. In his opinion it was a necessary price he paid for precociously asserting his independence. In a letter to his friend Daniel Jessup back in Florida, he reported a few weeks into the semester that "as yet matters prosper in my favor and I have so far been inferior to none in my own opinion. College is the same as formerly and the drama remains the same, some of the actors only have changed. There is still the same ambition and the same meanness, the same integrity, and the same dishonor."[29]

On graduation in July 1820, Henry returned home to the law office of John Duer in Goshen, where he read in preparation for his bar examination two years later. In the fall of 1821 he left Duer's office for that of John Anthon in New York City, for reasons he did not explain. He noted that Anthon had written a book on the subject of "Practice" and "this department received my more special attention." About six months later, Henry had an opportunity to replace Duer, who was retiring from his practice, in partnership with Ogden Hoffman. While Henry saw the benefits of training in New York City, where there was an active literary society in which he further honed his speaking skills, he accepted the partnership offer and returned home.[30]

Henry explained that the move and sacrifice of his preference for the life he had in New York City was purely financial. "My collegiate debts," Henry explained, "unavoidably increased on my return to Schenectady, had again become embarrassing, and I eagerly accepted the offer. The partnership continued six months," during which time he completed his study for admission to the bar, leaving the firm immediately upon admission. He did not say why he terminated the partnership at the point he was to become a full partner, although it is likely he was already drawn to Auburn. "Between two offers of legal partnership which I received at Auburn, I declined the one which promised the largest business, but involved debt for a law library, and accepted the less hopeful one which I might assume without new embarrassment." He returned home to announce his success and, "receiving fifty dollars from my father . . . I took leave of my native home and arrived at Auburn by stage-coach through the southern tier of counties on Christmas morning" in 1822.[31]

According to Henry's younger brother George, the decision about where Henry practiced law was a battle of wills with Samuel. "My father," George wrote to Will Jr. after Henry's death, "in the education of his children acted upon the assumption that they were given him for his own benefit and not their own, and that he was entitled to their services." While George was only eleven at the time of Henry's escape to Georgia and a teenager living at home when Henry embarked on his career, he remembered well Samuel's wrath at his son. "My father told me," George continued, "that he educated Henry as a lawyer for his counsel, which meant that he expected him to do all his business without compensation. My father bought a lawyer's office . . . in the village of Florida, expecting your father [Henry] to occupy it." Henry, whom George "commended" for the decision, acted in defiance of Samuel in moving to Auburn and charting an independent path.[32]

On January 1, 1823, Seward's partnership with Elijah Miller began and was a financial success for both men from the start. As Seward explained, although he enjoyed the study of law, he never enjoyed the practice. It was a necessary means of supporting himself, but never anything more. "Nevertheless," he confessed, "I resigned myself to the practice with so much cheerfulness that my disinclination was never suspected. Scarcely anyone would have believed me if I had told him that when I came to the responsibilities of a trial or an argument I would have paid a larger sum to be relieved from them than the fees which I had before received or stipulated."[33]

Henry boarded in the house of a widow, who had other young male tenants, "and I lodged in the back room, which, in the daytime, served as the counsel-chamber of my office. My senior partner gradually relinquished the business to me, only coming in to my aid in cases of difficulty." With an eye toward politics and away from the practice of law, Henry "took my pew and paid my assessments in the church, attended the municipal, political, and social meetings and caucuses, acting generally as secretary," and joined the militia. "And so, I rendered to my neighbors and acquaintances such good offices as my training and position made convenient." To him, right from the start, "politics was the important and engrossing business of the country." While the rest of the nation was "irreconcilably divided on the subject of politics and religion," he cared little for theological disputes, favored doctrines unanimously agreed upon by the various Protestant sects, and "decided to adhere to the Episcopal Church, into attendance upon which I had casually fallen."[34]

Unlike his church affiliation, Henry's choice of political parties was deeply deliberate, and it was a complicated one in such troubled times. He saw the Democratic-Republican Party of Thomas Jefferson and James Madison as his political roots but rejected its principles that led to nullification, which was a threat to the Union, and its support for the southern interest and thus slavery. The Democrats of Andrew Jackson, which was founded in 1828, "was unequivocally hostile to foreign immigration," so was less appealing to Henry as he told his political story. In voting for John Quincy Adams in the presidential election of 1824 and Dewitt Clinton for governor, Henry made a statement of principles that steered a course he felt he strictly adhered to through the turmoil of political controversy and changing parties over the next half century. "Though I thus chose my religious denomination and political party" at the same time, Henry explained, "I did so with a reservation of a right to dissent and protest, or even separate, if ever a conscientious sense of duty, or a paramount regard to the general safety or welfare, should require." His first affiliation was with the Anti-Masonic Party, which emerged in 1826 after Masons abducted Henry Morgan, who had threatened to reveal secrets of the first three degrees of Masonry, from Canandaigua. Morgan's disappearance led to a political reaction against Masonry as antidemocratic. Henry then became a Whig after the party was established in 1833 in opposition to Andrew Jackson and the Democrats, and then a Republican when the new party split from the Whigs over opposition to slavery in 1854.[35]

At about the same time Henry chose his church and political allegiance, he also proposed marriage to Frances Miller, who was a friend of his sister at the Troy Female Seminary. Henry explained it was his attraction to her that had led him to focus on Auburn as a possible place to live and work. Henry did not explain the relationship between Judge Miller's offer of employment and the romance he had with Miller's daughter, although he did discuss his attraction to Frances and their marriage in 1824. "On the 20th of October in that year, my marriage took place with Frances A. Miller. She was then nineteen years of age, daughter of my partner and friend, Elijah Miller. Of fine natural parts, with modesty almost approaching to timidity." She was, according to Henry, "thoughtful but cheerful," perhaps belying the expectation that thoughtful women were dour, and well educated at three female academies, where, "while accomplishments were not neglected, a course of study was prescribed corresponding in extent and fullness with the curriculum of our colleges."[36]

While these were the qualities that recommended Frances to Henry, he also recalled what became the family story about the condition that Judge Miller set for his consent to the marriage, a story that family members accepted as gospel. "Her father had been, from her infancy, a widower, and his consent to the union was given on the condition that she should not leave her home while he should survive. I thus became an inmate of his family." It is, of course, the choice of the word "inmate" that is critical here, a half-joking synonym for "prisoner," and possibly an unconscious excuse for his escape from the house that for him could be a prison.[37]

As a letter to his father of August 1823 revealed, Henry was just as deliberate in choosing a wife as in selecting a political party. "The first subject which claims my attention in your letter," Henry replied, "is that of my matrimonial expectations. These are at length settled in a manner which will I hope receive your approbation. If I have ever acted deliberately or thought seriously it has been upon this subject." Samuel had expressed doubts in his letter, quite possibly based on what he saw as previous impulsivity in his son. "My first principle," Henry further explained, "was that I would never unite my fortune with another's unless there was a strong and devoted attachment mutually existing between us. My next principle was that I would not unite myself to one who did not possess a strong mind together with a proper respect for me. And lastly, I was resolved that I would not unite myself to any person where poverty would be the result of my union."[38]

Samuel had previously heard from Henry that Mary Ann Kellogg, daughter of Auburn attorney Daniel Kellogg, was the focus of his courtship. The change in course did not inspire Samuel's confidence in his son's good judgment. "I grant you," Henry replied, "in view of all these circumstances that Mr. K is rich and if he lives long will die very rich. But he has seven children and may have a family increasing in the same proportion with his wealth, that his business is good and a connection in business with him might be most advantageous to me. But his property was obtained by extortion and oppression. And he has no friend who will attempt to defend him." Furthermore, Henry continued in his own defense, an association with the Kellogg family exposed his sister Cornelia to the same connection, making her vulnerable to the charms of Mary Ann's brother Augustus, which would only compound the problem, "and the result of that would so long remain in uncertainty and could so illy be calculated upon" that Henry was acting in the best interest of his sister as well as himself. Now, that was a stretch, but Henry was an enthusiastic young litigator making every conceivable point in defense of his client, himself.[39]

In sum, "the dowry of Miss M. cannot be much inferior if any to that of Miss K. He [Judge Miller] has no host of children to pamper all the rest at the expense of one. His honesty and his magnanimity are unsuspected. And if I should become his Son in Law he could not have any inducements to persecute me. These are arguments to the head. There are others of the heart," in which Henry expected his father to be less interested, but nonetheless "Frances M. is a girl of strong mind and of an undissembling heart. She says she returns my affection and I know she does. She respects me as the Man to whom above all others she would commit her destinies for life." Case closed, while "Miss K. has pretended to love me when I know she did not, not to love me when I know she did, and then again after wounding my pride appeals again to a passion which long since expired upon the altar of my own self-respect."[40]

When Samuel met her, Henry was confident his father would see for himself Frances's virtues if he had not already during her visit with his sister Cornelia to their home. As an independent son, Henry was now solicitous of his father's approval. "I therefore think that if there be any one person to whom on acquaintance you would be willing to join your errant son it is she to whom I have pledged my troth and she who in return has declared to me what she will one day say before the world, that she takes me to be her lawful wedded husband to love honor and obey for better, for worse, for richer, for poorer till death us do part." Then he tacked back to more practical matters, of the sort that

Henry knew his father cared more about. He had escorted Frances to her cousins' house in Ludlowville for a visit so that she was away when he proposed the marriage to Judge Miller and negotiated his terms, "of whose assent I have the vanity to think there can be little doubt. . . . I shall write to you the result next week."[41]

Three days later, Henry wrote to inform his father of his success. Henry had not waited for his father's blessing, but had again pursued his own independent path. "I have to claim your congratulations. The question is proposed and answered in the affirmative. This ends the negotiation." His father had no say in the matter. The two lawyers came to terms for Frances's hand in shorter order than Henry had anticipated. Although there was no written contract, the details were both financial and residential; the Sewards would live in Miller's house, and the Judge provided a substantial, although unspecified dowry.[42]

There is not another surviving letter from Henry to his father for over four months, at which time, shortly before Christmas, Henry apologized in a letter to Samuel that three letters from his father had gone unanswered by the son who claimed to be dutiful, but whose actions continued to belie the words. Most of the letter addressed state and national politics, about which Samuel and his son were in agreement. Perhaps the father and son had settled on the warmer path of politics to thaw their otherwise frigid relationship. Henry suggested as much by concluding, "May I hope the continuance of your correspondence, which has lately become so interesting."[43]

Nonetheless, another six months passed before Henry wrote again, this time to both his parents in apology for not responding to their letters. "I will grant to you that I am very undutiful in my long neglect of writing to you," he confessed in, for him, rare contrition that he offered more easily to his mother. "But I beg you to understand that it has been owing to no want of interest in your happiness with that of the rest of the family that I have written nothing." He was glad to learn from others about his father's return to health, something that was a recurring theme in their correspondence for the next quarter century of Samuel's life. Henry mentioned his coming marriage in October and his plans to visit the family in early July, after he delivered a July 4 oration, in the company of Frances's sister Lazette, who had recently "been unfortunate in her attachment and has become mellowed in a temper which bears sometimes too much of independence. Her intrinsic worth you know and appreciate. I commend her to your hospitality." In Henry's estimation, a woman could be too independent, unlike a man.[44]

We do not know who this was or who exactly broke it off, Lazette, the beau, or Judge Miller, but Henry implied that Lazette's temperament was the cause and that she was chastened, perhaps even reformed, in her attitudes toward men. What he did not say was that Lazette may have been increasingly desperate to find an escape from her father's household, especially with her younger sister's marriage on the horizon and the Sewards taking up residence in Judge Miller's home. During his visit to Florida of three or four days (Lazette would stay longer; he had business to attend to), Henry hoped to discuss arrangements for his marriage with his parents.

To Henry's shock and humiliation, Samuel refused his presumption of a visit accompanied by Lazette. Things were still not right, trust was low, wounds unhealed between father and son. This time Henry replied to his father's letter within twenty-four hours, expressing humiliation and feelings wounded by the snub, which he believed was based on Samuel's misunderstanding of Henry's "benevolent" intentions.[45]

Whatever the details, Samuel understood that there was tension in the Miller household, and Lazette and her father were at odds. Henry acknowledged the tension but asserted that all parties favored some time apart. In response to what Henry interpreted as his father's inhospitable refusal to harbor Lazette, Henry washed his hands of both households. "However, as matters seem to be more favourable with the parties concerned," which included the Millers as well as the Sewards, "I wish them a happy issue out of all their domestic difficulties and intend to leave them to the labour of extricating themselves." So much for Henry's efforts to bring peace. Instead, he figuratively walked away from the tension. Walking away already was, and continued to be, Henry's preferred response to domestic strife.[46]

Henry hoped that none of this conflict interfered with the celebration of his marriage. "On that score, I trust there will be no disappointment and that important business settled we shall appear in duty to receive your benediction." On October 20, 1824, Frances married Henry in Saint Peter's Episcopal Church. Although several hundred people witnessed the wedding, the reception was a small, private affair composed mostly of relatives of the bride and groom, and a select few local friends of the couple. After a honeymoon of one night at Rust's Hotel in Onondaga Hill, the couple returned via Syracuse to Judge Miller's home, where they resided for the next four years.[47]

According to Henry, the honeymoon did not last much longer than the young couple's overnight trip. "The joyousness of this event, after a short season, was broken by a serious illness of my own, from which, however, I entirely recovered. Subsequently her health gave way, and it was never fully and permanently restored." In the first month of their marriage, Henry and Frances were stricken with quinsy, an abscess in the area of the tonsils, which, in an age before antibiotics, could be deadly. Fifteen years later, Henry's sister Cornelia died of it at the age of thirty-four. On December 9 Henry wrote to his father, "I have continued to grow better. This is the first day of my coming to the office. The physicians bled, cupped, blistered, physicked & scarified me so severely that I cannot yet get strength enough to enable me to attend to business." Frances experienced much worse.[48]

This is the backstory that Henry provided to his family life. It is one perspective and likely true to his memory. Henry took up residence at 33 South Street with an enthusiasm—"joyousness" was his word—that diminished quickly and permanently. He also joined the family from what was perhaps a position of dishonesty that left the others disappointed too. Judge Miller believed he was welcoming a law partner into his home, when Henry already planned a political career. Frances believed she was embracing a husband and partner in a settled home, but Henry was unhappy there and she would come to feel betrayed.

Frances interpreted Henry's political career in Albany, as a state senator beginning in 1831, as a flight from South Street and their marriage. It is likely that his law partners, both in Auburn and Goshen, saw his withdrawal from their practices as breaches of understandings if not of contracts. He left his apprenticeship with John Duer in Goshen and also broke his apprenticeship contract with John Anthon in New York City. And, of course, Henry wanted others to know that he breached his teaching contract with William Alexander and the school's board honorably, although there is a case to be made that he entered into it without the intention to keep it, but rather to use it as leverage against his father. The pattern does not do Henry credit and is a weak defense against those who saw him throughout his adult life as propelled more by ambition than by principles, more of a nineteenth-century man than was honorable. He admitted that his dealings with the tailors of Schenectady and with his father showed him in a bad light, and that he stole and lost money that was his father's, apparently with little or no compunction. The backstory, as Henry told it himself, is more supportive of the portrayal of his political opponents than he realized in the telling.

Family letters complicate Henry's narration of his own life. While Henry's narrative could be self-deprecatory, his regrets fell short of apologies and he was more likely to share blame than to take it. Henry's account, focusing as it does on his public life, did not sweep up the backstories of other members of the household. There is more about his father and their relationship, less about his mother, and nothing about siblings and grandparents. He had precious little to say about his wife and children, and what he wrote for public consumption about Frances reflected regret more than gratitude. He also had nothing to say about friends, another set of private relationships that he did not discuss in public.

One omission from the way that Henry told his own backstory does him more credit. David Berdan was a fellow member of the Adelphic Society at Union College, who was two years Henry's junior. They rekindled an even closer relationship when they served as apprentices in the New York City law firm of John Anthon. Berdan's death of consumption (tuberculosis) in 1827 at the age of twenty-four was a loss Henry found emotionally wrenching. He spearheaded fundraising for a monument to Berdan's memory constructed on the campus of their alma mater, and he delivered the eulogy at graduation in 1828.

Berdan's was the first of Henry's close friendships with men. Historians have sometimes taken such closeness for physical relationships without evidence that they were. They paralleled similar relationships among women that cooled upon the marriage of one of the friends. They were youthful friendships and not to be confused with modern gender identities and preferences. These were ardent relationships that included unbridled expressions of affection that can confuse us in a post-Freudian, more self-conscious world. The rules of manliness still applied in an age when the term "homosexuality" had yet to be coined. Men loved their closest friends, male and female, with emotional abandon. Romantic friendships did not necessarily dissolve upon the marriage of one of the friends, but they generally lost the passionate intensity of youth. If it were not for the death of David Berdan, we can see the same happening upon Henry's marriage to Frances.[49]

In his eulogy, Henry said Berdan lacked worldly ambition. "He had a downcast air," Henry told the assembled graduates, "unassuming deportment, and retiring manners. His temper was cheerful, his conversation animated and enthusiastic, and his disposition gentle and confiding. . . . All distinctions . . . were worthless in his esteem. Collegiate honors never excited his emulation." In other words, David was a contrast to Henry in his introversion. "He early manifested a reluctance to engage in active pursuits, and to be concerned with the ordinary interests of society." Berdan's goal was a contemplative life, steeped in literature and the pursuit of life's meaning. He was sensitive to a fault, unfit for the rough and tumble of public life. Berdan was "inoffensive and retiring." Like Henry, he had a "repugnance" to the practice of law, although he saw it as a vehicle for the financial independence he sought. Upon admission to the bar, Berdan toured America east of the Mississippi River on foot, stopping at Auburn to say his last farewell to Henry before departing for Europe, a trip from which he rightly did not expect to return. Berdan was, in sum, young, gifted, and unfit for the kind of life to which Henry aspired.[50]

Henry's letters to Berdan do not survive, having been burned by the recipient to prevent possible embarrassment to their author in a Victorian-era gesture that reflected standards of privacy and the license letter-writing gave for such intimate communication between two people. Burning also circumvented the practice of circulating letters and reading them aloud; for some forms of epistolary communication sharing was appropriate, and for others it was not. Henry had bared his soul to his friend, revealed emotions, attachments, hopes, and fears, leaving himself open and thus vulnerable. "By my former letter you know of course that I have your letters with me," Berdan wrote from Seville. "I shall be compelled to burn them all when I reach Madrid so you will be put at ease about their contents. I am sorry to part with them but their memory will remain to cheer me hereafter." Two years earlier, Berdan had thanked Henry for writing letters that contained "a full and free and undisguised history of your joys and your sorrows. It is this frankness and this freedom which has won upon me and which will forever make me lay open my own heart to your survey. I feel there is nothing there that I would be unwilling to communicate and I should not to your eyes be ashamed of exhibiting it in its nakedness."[51]

In several letters Berdan apologized for his inability to match the frequency or eloquence of Henry's. From an 1823 letter of Berdan's, we know that Henry's recent letters had included discussion of his feelings for Frances and his happiness in love. "Do not believe that I am indifferent to your present happiness because I do not hasten to congratulate you," Berdan wrote in September. "I have found an excuse for my remissness in reflecting that you were so happy that there was not the same necessity for regularity and that love engrossed you so completely as perhaps to render you less anxious respecting letters." Here Berdan envied Henry, but he stepped back from such very human feelings in the name of friendship. "This shallow pretense could not however satisfy my conscience. Your two last letters are convincing proofs that in the midst of love you have remembered friendship. I assure you that I have been more pleased with the perusal of those letters than any you have ever written and from the certainty that your present attachment has not abated your friendship I have derived a permanent satisfaction." In a gesture that reflected his personality, and possibly the depths of his feelings for Henry, Berdan refused to see Frances when the two men met in Auburn to say their last goodbyes. Henry never again had a friend as close or as different from him as David.[52]

Chapter 3

Inmates All, 1825–1831

The courtship of Henry and Frances reflected their changing times. As the Miller sisters reached their late teens they had launched on a new phase of life. Lazette finished school before her younger sister and returned to their home, where she felt alone with Paulina, Elijah, and Clary. The script for girls of their class was for Lazette now to find a husband, preferably before she reached twenty, but she was miscast in a role that better suited Frances.

"Yours Theodora," the eighteen-year-old Lazette signed herself in a May 1822 letter to her sixteen-year-old sister, who was at school in Troy. It was a joke, an obscure one from a distance of over two hundred years, but one shared easily between two such literate sisters, steeped as they were in Gothic and Romantic fiction. "Theodora" was Theodore Wieland, the title character from Charles Brockden Brown's novel. Wieland hears voices calling him to murder his wife and children. Lazette implied she was feeling murderous and/or suicidal living with her father, grandmother, and aunt. Ultimately, Theodore kills himself after threatening his sister, who reflects years later on the limits of human reason and moral constraints.[1]

Lazette's letter continued in the same jesting, despairing, self-deprecating tone. "If you wish for any articles of clothing from home do write and I will make and send them," she wrote, making another joke on herself, because she lacked such domestic skills, which an eighteenth-century woman was more likely to have. The sisters were educated, but not in that way. "Now don't fail. Laugh. I will leave you in the comfortable enjoyment of your mirth to ask a few simple questions." Her queries were about men, first of all Frances's Henry. The others were suitors she had herself rejected. Lazette was trailing her younger sister socially and was reluctant to compromise her standards for the fools who had thus far courted her. First, though, a little jab at Henry, who had not offered to escort Frances back to school: "Are we to infer from this that he was so unaccustomed to using any politeness and so much fatigued with what he extended to you at Florida," when Frances visited Henry's family with his younger sister Louisa Cornelia, "and therefore was determined to give it up as a hard task?" Ouch, but she was just teasing because she continued, "No, I cannot believe this for to tell the truth after all I am a little prepossessed in his favour." Ah, Lazette's blessing was undoubtedly important to the motherless teenager.[2]

Frances said that beaux of other friends were still introducing her to potential suitors, but Lazette had no idea who the "Mr. F" was to whom she referred. "You say it was a Mr. F . . . but whether he was Dr. Fowler of whom you had before spoken or Sir J. Fallstaff or Mr. Frisk, a Fish or Fight or Fidget or Frump, or Flummery or Fool I cannot with certainty determine. Perhaps these names will all apply to him at different times." She went on and on in the same jocular vein, which could not conceal what a momentous decision lay before the sisters and their female friends. Beyond the obvious attractions and charms, did the young man in question project gentleness, generosity, ambition, financial competence, and which of the characters from a Jane Austen or Mary Shelley novel could they expect to emerge from the suit on their wedding night, when it was too late to turn back? It was a deadly serious game for the women, who lost their leverage upon marriage, when they surrendered themselves in law and social custom to their husbands, for better and for worse.[3]

Lazette had rejected that same Myron C. Reed, whom she mentioned as one of her sister's discarded suitors, proclaiming from the rooftop of 33 South Street that "'Myron C. Reed <u>sold poor civility</u> by the half ounce,' but our good grandma protested against it with all her might, saying 'he is a good Christian man who is honest and upright in his dealings.' Notwithstanding I thought myself 'as much a Christian man as he is such.' I concluded to hush up the matter for fear he might throw

FIGURE 3.1. Lazette Miller Worden, sister of Frances Seward, 1830. Courtesy of Rare Books, Special Collections, and Preservation, River Campus Libraries, University of Rochester, painting in Seward House Museum, Auburn, New York.

me into the N. River, for spite if ever we should meet there." These were not decisions the sisters could expect to make independently of their grandmother and, above all, their father, but they did have the power to dismiss suitors, which was hard-earned by those who came before them. While she was on the subject, "without turning Edinburgh Reviewer," Lazette found Frances's last letter annoying in the way she characterized a visit from Parliament Bronson, a local lawyer, to their home the previous Sunday. Frances owed her an explanation "for after disposing of the rest of the family in a manner at once agreeable and rational," she left Lazette alone with Bronson. "What is meant by such an insult. I have hardly spoken to the man since our 'unhappy difference' last winter and I have abundant reason to be thankful it took place. I suppose you thought it was a time for reflection and not conversation, but methinks meditations on the deformities of nature are rather unsuitable, unpleasant subjects for the Sabbath." Ouch again; Lazette could be pointed and spoke her mind, although describing the young man, whom she had already rejected as a suitor, as a deformity of nature, a monster right out of Mary Shelley's *Frankenstein*, is a bit harsh even for her.[4]

Frances was thrusting suitors, even recycling them, on her sharp-tongued older sister in an attempt to give her a nudge. Lazette pointed to the problem in this same letter by concluding, "I understand there were a great many Troy gentlemen at Florida to see you. Won't you tell us who they were. Do write soon." Not to exaggerate the case, it does look as though Frances had her choice from the top of the barrel and Lazette was left to choose from the middle or bottom, and they both knew it. Romance novels told them and real-life anecdotes confirmed, there was no guarantee that either of them would make a good choice—the right choice—among the candidates who presented themselves.[5]

Two months later, Lazette's next surviving letter to her sister confirmed the same story. She had attended a ball, accompanied by the mayor, an older gentleman who was a tolerable chaperone, perhaps arranged by her father, and thus preferable to any of the young men who might have volunteered for the job. Sadly, her description of the ball listed the men who asked about her sister. " 'I really wish your sister was here,' " said George Rathbun insensitively in greeting Lazette, who continued in her letter, "I can assure you my dear sister he was not the only one who regretted your absence." In the same vein, she wrote, "All your friends were there, particularly Fleming, who often reminded me of you, not that he spoke to me but as he was always one of your hangers-on."[6]

Lazette returned home with her father, having experienced no conquests of her own worth mentioning to her sister, and in a sour mood caused by her failure. To her chagrin, Judge Miller invited an unattached man and woman, who were both far from home, to spend the night at the Miller residence. The man declined and the woman accepted. "And here let me observe that Caroline is a fool and Wilkenson is as stupid as many others with whom I have the misfortune to be acquainted," she dished on them by name. When Henry M. Nichols, another unattached man, called on her, she reported to her sister that she fell asleep and remained that way throughout his call. "I did get my eyes opened before he went away." Not that Lazette looked down on everyone; she mentioned Dr. Ira H. Smith, another older gentleman, who relieved her from the "vexing dilemma" of spending more time with several "dumb" people and "the pretty Miss [Serene] Fosgate. I was really much pleased with her. She is agreeable, artless and unaffected." Serene was Frances's best friend. Lazette also spent an enjoyable evening playing whist with mutual acquaintances.[7]

Lazette continued to document her displeasure with the men who presented themselves to her and with herself for being less attractive than her sister. There was another caller, however, who intrigued the hard-to-please Lazette; with her younger sister romantically entangled with Henry, the pressure increased on Lazette to tolerate one of her suitors. "Garry Sackett has also been here," she wrote. That was not unusual, since he was one of her father's closest friends, a fellow judge, and a loyal companion of his ever since the death of their mother Hannah. But he was not there to see Judge Miller, "and made an engagement to come again next Sunday. Who knows what his business may be?!!" Now, that was enthusiasm coming from her. Judge Sackett was single, and most of the kind things she had to say about men were about older ones like him. A romance was not inconceivable with a man thirteen years her senior, and she seemed hopeful and enthusiastic in this letter.[8]

"It really makes me provoked with you," Lazette half-teased her sister, "to think how much interest you excite in Auburn. If I should stay [away] four years there would not [be] half as many enquiries made about me as there has [been] respecting [you] in two weeks." Lazette apparently took her sister's popularity, with both women and men, in stride. Frances was attractive, smart, charming, and friendlier than her sister, which Lazette fully recognized. The younger sister was the social butterfly of the family, albeit a shy one.[9]

Frances and Henry married; then came the quinsy, Henry's illness and recovery, and Frances's failure to bounce back to full health. Somewhere in this flurry of life's joys and sorrows, others occurred. Frances got pregnant and miscarried. Marcia Armstrong Seward, wife of Henry's brother Jennings, offered condolences, of a sort, in a letter of January 29, 1825, and referred to letters from Henry of January 12, 21, and 25, one of which revealed the sad news. Most miscarriages happen within the first twenty weeks of a pregnancy, which likely means the loss occurred shortly preceding one of Henry's three letters. Marcia believed Henry was exaggerating his disappointment and minimized the sympathy she offered him. "I should regret your loss very much," she wrote to her brother-in-law, "were it not that I trust your happiness will be prolonged by what I should term a misfortune did you not tell me Henry, when we were on our way to Goshen, that you sincerely believed that children would make you miserable."[10]

Henry's behavior as a husband and father, his frequent and prolonged absences from the household, especially around holidays, and the absence of family stories about his warmth as a parent would be nothing more than clues to his feelings if Marcia's testimony had not addressed his attitude toward family life. "You are now safe," Marcia continued, "and remember that it depends entirely upon your own dear self whether you shall be happy or wretched." Her lack of sympathy for him now ambled closer to an indictment. "Take heed to your ways; and lay no charge to your wife." Now, directly to Frances, whom she assumed would read the letter as well, "My Dear Frances, I am sorry to hear of your illness," which could be a reference her miscarriage, the quinsy, or both, in an age when pregnancy was often referred to vaguely as an illness, "but rejoice that you are so comfortable. Keep good courage my dear, this is but a faint emblem of what a married life will produce." This was not intended to cheer her sister-in-law. "I fear for your constitution," if Frances got pregnant again, which she did a year later. "You are but delicate and such hopes are exceedingly destructive. Henry certainly ought to have taken better care of you."[11]

Frances wanted and assumed children in marriage; she now knew, perhaps for the first time, that her husband did not. She also knew, if she did not before, that her constitution put her life in danger with each pregnancy. How seriously she took her sister-in-law's testimony on Henry's distaste for family life and whether Henry denied it is lost to us, but the implications for the family's happiness are not. Family size in the United States plummeted from the previous century, and contraception practiced by a thoughtful male partner was obviously effective, which is what their sister-in-law charged by blaming Henry. In 1800 the average was about 7.5 children per family in the United States. By 1850 the average was under 5.5; by the end of the century it was under four.[12]

A month later, Henry reported that Frances's health remained "so delicate I cannot often with propriety keep my light burning at the office so late at night as should be." She was "still convalescent," she remained weak, "and the tone of her system is not nor soon will be restored." In the middle of March, Henry told his siblings that Frances had "recovered." A month later, though, in a reply to a letter of Henry's, Jennings described what sounds like symptoms of depression that continued to afflict Frances for the rest of her life. He recommended to Henry a change of scenery, "a little jaunt with your love," and perhaps some time visiting friends, by which he meant family. On May 19 Jennings wrote again, saying, "I long to congratulate you that she is yet spared to you, and her that health has resumed his wanted seat in roses on her cheeks." Nine months after Jennings's letter, Frances was pregnant again. Augustus H. Seward arrived on October 1, 1826, without much fanfare or even notice in the family's correspondence.[13]

Back in Orange County, Henry's sister Cornelia and their father were at war over Mahlon Canfield, her choice of suitors. The showdown came on November 11, 1824, less than three weeks after Henry and Frances's wedding, while Cornelia's brother and sister-in-law were stricken with quinsy. Samuel had lied to his daughter, invoking the authority of her esteemed brother in judging Mahlon harshly. "Know then my dear Henry that I believed you the immediate cause of a furious & cruel overhauling on the morning of the 11th Nov (never to be forgotten day)." It sounds as though Samuel forcefully intervened in an attempted elopement. "This idea it was [in] the interest of more than one person to nourish and confirm." Cornelia saw a family conspiracy against her, which she thought also enlisted another brother, but more likely their mother, prevent Cornelia from realizing her heart's desire. Jennings, in advance of the arrival of Henry's letter, had alerted her to their father's lie about Henry.[14]

Two months later, when she became convinced that Samuel had lied to her, Cornelia apologized to Henry. "I thank you with all my heart for your respect for him [Mahlon] whom you can never cease to regard if you are at all acquainted with his excellency. Papa in his blow up declared that I was a child incapable of judging or acting for myself." She was the same age as Frances.

Canfield, seven years Cornelia's senior, was an apprentice to Samuel in his medical practice. He left in February 1825 for another position in New Jersey, having been dismissed by Samuel at the time of the blowup to which Cornelia referred in her letter. His crime against Samuel, according to Canfield's account of the conversation, was acting "dishonourably 'in stealing away the affections of his daughter,' [who] was a child, meaning that she had not arrived at years of discretion!!"[15]

At age nineteen, Cornelia plotted her escape. "Whatever my feelings were then," in 1824 when she accepted Mahlon's proposal, "I glory in saying and derive my greatest happiness in the fact that they are unalterable. I would as soon cease to exist as to deprive myself of my chief comfort. This it is necessary to smother [hide] (of shame to my father) until by a 'legal age' I may convince the world that I am not ashamed or afraid." She was trusting Henry with a big secret to keep from their father. Only Frances, Jennings, and his wife Marcia were also to know. Samuel did not relent two years later, when Cornelia had reached twenty-one, so the couple married against his will.[16]

The intervening two years were a family drama in multiple acts, in which no one came out a hero and the villains were a matter of perspective. Samuel did not trust his daughter and commanded her to sever the engagement and all contact with Mahlon Canfield. Cornelia swore that the relationship was over, apparently with her fingers crossed behind her back. Mahlon felt betrayed by his mentor and did not know whether he could trust anyone else in the family; eventually, he felt insulted and deceived by them all. Samuel remained suspicious and enlisted his wife and Cornelia's brothers as spies.

By March 1826 Cornelia lived with Jennings and Marcia in New York City and played the dutiful daughter in letters to her father. In these letters she was pleasant and downright chatty: my health is fully recovered, will you write to assure me that everyone is well, please send money for a new hat, "your affectionate daughter Louisa." Nothing amiss here, but her father remained suspicious that Canfield was lurking, and given what had already passed between Mahlon and his daughter, letters such as this one did not reassure Samuel. Four months later, he was even more certain that he had not misjudged either Mahlon or Cornelia. Jennings, now acting as Samuel's informant, reported that Canfield had visited New York City, "in high spirits, saying he had corresponded with Cornelia and all was well."[17]

To Cornelia, her father was a tyrant and her brothers were cowards. Samuel agreed that he had cowardly sons, who could have brought the whole episode to a close if they only supported him both to his face and behind his back. Cornelia bided her time, as she had told Henry and Jennings she intended, and pretended to accede to her father's demands until she reached her twenty-first birthday. Then, in April 1827, Mahlon and Cornelia eloped, and the Seward family of Florida, New York, and its branches in New York City and Auburn exploded. Samuel, Cornelia, and Mahlon were enraged and disgusted with the brothers. Henry, Jennings, and George (no Polydore to be found in the conflagration) were saddened and simply hoped to patch things up with the rest.

In an undated letter posted shortly after her marriage to Mahlon, Cornelia wrote to her "dear and respected parents," who were feeling neither by then. Cornelia testified to her love for Mary and Samuel, but she did not apologize nor regret that she pursued her heart over her father's will. "I have not for one moment," Mrs. Canfield continued, "doubted your affection for my interest and do sincerely believe whatever has been done was with a view to my happiness." But, she might have concluded, this was the second quarter of the nineteenth century, not the fourth quarter of the eighteenth; "'tis natural that each one of us should endeavor to seek our own happiness," and women had become more assertive in making decisions about their own lives. "I beg that my parents will not consider this a final separation. This idea is painful in the extreme. I hope and trust we shall yet add in no small degree to the comfort and happiness of each other."[18]

It was a matter of honor, not just of romance and pride; she had made a commitment to Mahlon and adhered "to those solemn engagements which I have made." She hoped "that you will forgive me all the trouble I have caused you," which was the "sincere prayer of your own Louisa." Her father never forgave her during her lifetime, and he was right that Mahlon would never secure a competence in support of his family. Nonetheless, Cornelia was also correct that in the new century women were freer to make their own mistakes. Were they happier in their marriages? Apparently not, if the Seward and Miller marriages are representative, and they were perhaps even less content for having higher expectations for spouses than their mothers had for theirs. Nonetheless, the daughters seized their households as realms of their own.[19]

When Cornelia gave birth to Frederick, her first child, less than nine months after their wedding, the suspicion that she was pregnant when she married created another grievance for Samuel and confirmed his low opinion of Mahlon. When the Canfields' second child, Augustus, was born in August 1828, Mahlon skirted the brothers and informed Jennings's wife, Marcia. The surviving record of reconciliation between Cornelia and Henry began with her loss. On February 23, 1829, she acknowledged the breach between them in news of six-month-old Augustus's death.[20]

Cornelia's letter reached Auburn on March 3. Henry was away from home, so Frances broke the black seal, which revealed what sort of news the missive contained. She transcribed the letter to save space and wanted to reply directly but had no mailing address for her sister-in-law. "Do go and see Cornelia," Frances prodded her husband. "As much as I wish to see you I will part with you another week gladly if it will be the means of her receiving any consolation. Why do I say consolation? She can receive that but from one source. He who gives us ills to bear can alone impart the courage to support them. Still, she wishes to see you and if it will be any gratification you should go. . . . Write immediately. I am anxious to write to Cornelia."[21]

Cornelia tried in the letter to be cheerful in the face of her loss, but she did not mention her first child, Frederick, who was not yet two. He died in 1829, a year before the birth of the Sewards' second child, whom the Sewards also named Frederick. The Canfields lost another child, Mary, named for their mothers, under the age of two as well. At the time, 45 percent of babies born in the United States died before reaching the age of five. The Canfields' other three children, two sons and a daughter, lived to adulthood.

The extended Seward family's crises were piling up. While Samuel was the central, indeed causal, figure in many of them, he could not be blamed for them all. There was the case of Polydore, now twenty-six, whom family members diagnosed as a hopeless drunk in a spiraling decline. It is possible that Polydore blamed his father for that too. The only hope for his survival that his siblings saw in spring 1825 was his professed love for a woman whose name they did not even know. "Polydore has at last made choice of a rib," Jennings joked to Henry in March. "Matrimony is looked upon by all his friends as the only salvation of his habits," Jennings continued, "and if he marries this must be the girl. He will no other." Nonetheless, their father stood against it, telling his son "if he does [marry] to separate from him and his farm." Samuel intended to cut him off financially, which was his usual threat that he delivered on with all but one of his children. "Poor fellow," wrote Jennings, "my heart bleeds when I tell you his indications of intemperance are increasing," and if "the doctor [Samuel] abandons him," his brother thought, it would surely be his end. The couple did not marry, but two years later Polydore wed Rachel Armstrong and fathered nine children with her.[22]

The sometimes loyal and generally sympathetic Jennings had his own tragedies. According to him, a dishonest business partner forged his signature on a series of notes (loans), and he was on the hook for thousands he did not have. His attempts to run a middle course between Samuel and Cornelia reflected his need to curry favor with his father, from whom he begged loans desperately. On April 8, 1825, he and Marcia lost their four-year-old daughter Aurelia when she succumbed within forty-eight hours of contracting an upper respiratory infection accompanied by a high fever. "Few have suffered more, none that I have ever known, either young or old, have borne their suffering with more patience," Jennings wrote to Henry on the day of Aurelia's death. "After successive convulsions for the last twelve hours, which agonized every beholder, how welcome the sound of the last respiration." Both parents, but especially Marcia in her husband's telling, were bereft, all the more so because Augustus, one year older than his sister, suffered the same symptoms. "Perhaps the next you hear of him," Jennings concluded his letter to Henry, it "may be from your doubly and now deeply affected brother." Ten days later, it became clear that Augustus would survive.[23]

Back in Auburn shortly after Frances's marriage to Henry, Lazette planned her escape from 33 South Street. Judge Miller had made his choice of Frances to stay to care for him and inherit the house. Lazette took that decision as an invitation to leave, which she did and quickly, marrying Alvah H. Worden against her father's will. Worden was in the picture by March 1825. The Judge's concerns were, as were Samuel Seward's for his daughter, both financial and a character judgment. The Judge was right on both counts, although Worden was marginally competent financially after a couple false starts.[24]

The family's oral history is, not surprisingly, more revealing on Judge Miller's approval of Frances's marriage than it is on his disapproval of Lazette's, so we have to imagine from subsequent events what Elijah saw in Alvah that warned him off. Worden had come to Auburn from Milton as a partner in a textile business that introduced weaving to the prison located there. When that venture failed, Worden read law, was admitted to the bar, and moved his wife and daughter to Canandaigua, where he practiced and pursued what became a rather modest political career, but they were always strapped for money.

Clary and Lazette had become the third and fourth women in the house now inhabited by two men. Lazette was on the verge of becoming an old maid as she approached her mid-twenties when she eloped, but Clary was already a spinster aunt, having crossed into her thirties the year before Frances's marriage. The situation of Elijah's sister in his house only worsened with the marriage of her beloved niece to Henry. Like Lazette, she felt herself an unwelcome dependent. Now she not only had her "crazy" brother and obstreperous mother with whom to contend. Her role as female head of cleaning and manager of staff fell to Frances, who became the woman of the house, the only married woman in it.

By 1828, if not sooner, the nieces were helping their thirty-five-year-old aunt shop for a husband. Henry's sister Cornelia promised to "procure the widower for a Sunday evening's beau for Aunt Clara," when she came to visit. After Margaret Nichols came to tea, Frances wrote Henry, "I am afraid Margaret is not going to marry all for love. . . . I do think no home at all would be preferable to a home with a man I did not love of all others." Aunt Clary disagreed and told Frances that if she were in Margaret's situation, she would do the same thing, consider financial competence over love as the highest priority. After all, Clary too was a member of Elijah's and Samuel's generation.[25]

Clary attended balls, and visited friends and relatives frequently for a number of reasons. Partly it was her sociability, loneliness, and the tension with her brother and mother at home, and partly she shopped for a beau. In February 1829 Clary went with a member of the household staff to a ball. Maria returned home after one dance, while "Clara did not come home until four o'clock as usual," Frances reported to Henry. "Thursday evening Clary went to the ball at the American [Hotel]," Frances reported on January 2, 1831, but was disappointed by how few single men attended. On September 25 Frances wrote to Henry, "Clary went to Compstons [Maryann and Samuel Cumpston] and I went to bed."[26]

On January 27, 1831, Frances told Clary that Hugh McClallen, a local man who ran a gun shop, planned to propose to her that day because he had rented a double sleigh and driver to take her out for a ride. Clary laughed off the rumor. In a letter to Henry, Frances told the story, which played out just as she had predicted. "Hugh, the two-horse sleigh and driver arrived at 2 o'clock precisely. . . . Clary is so queer I do not know what to make of her, ever. By what I can discover, Hugh has offered himself and she says she intends to marry him to get away from here. You know I am opposed to marrying in general, so I have been trying to persuade her that she will not better her condition. She says he is a fool and she does not care anything about him, but intends to have him notwithstanding."[27]

Hugh was two years older than Clary, so about forty at the time. Frances pumped Henry for more information about the man. "You are acquainted with him; does he know anything? Grandma did not like it because she went to ride with him, says he is a poor creature that cannot maintain himself and withal all the family are crazy but him." The women also held against Hugh that he was known to have once taken a local woman named Sarah Southerland on a sleigh ride too. "This he explains by saying she was very obliging while he was a boarder at the Exchange, rather a flimsy excuse," Frances thought. "There does not appear to be anything decided upon. I cannot ascertain that Clary did anything but laugh at him."[28]

Even after her argument with her mother over Hugh's prospects as a husband, "Clary says she still continues of the same opinion with regard to Hugh. Grandma does, too. I believe Clary does not appear to find much favour in her eyes." In his own defense, Hugh explained that he paid board for two of his sisters and had five workmen he was paying in his gunsmithing business. While he thought this information testified to his financial competence, Grandma and Frances feared he had financial albatrosses around his neck that he would never lose. Five days later, "Clary went to Compstons to tea, where she was rallied considerably about riding with Hugh," which Clary's mother still believed testified to moral failings of them both. Two days later, "Clary says I may tell you that Hugh is about jilting her. He invited himself to call last evening, did not meet with any opposition, but never came, after she had been to the trouble to have a fire made in the south room, being afraid Grandma would say something about his deranged relatives or something else equally improper."[29]

The only reason that Judge Miller was not a combatant in the household argument over Hugh is that the women told him nothing about the sleigh ride and proposal. On April 19, 1831, Frances wrote to Henry, "Hugh is here tonight to see Clary. She will not let Maria [household staff] go out of the room one minute. I conclude he will make little progress in his matrimonial calculations." On August 22 of the same year: "Last night I could not write because Lazette and Serene were here all the evening. Hugh came also and made Clary a visitation." In a letter of the same day Frances reported to her husband about the matter at hand. "I told Clary the other day after some conversation on the subject that she might tell Hugh that she understood he was somewhat embarrassed in his pecuniary affairs but must not tell who was her informant, supposing you did not wish to be implicated in the business." The informant was, indeed, Henry. Hugh took offense, "was much grieved" at the suggestion that "she should suppose he would make any proposals of marriage to her were he unable to make her comfortable." She replied that they should wait a year to see "what another year would bring," which left him "in a state of great despondency because she would not give him any satisfactory answer." On September 18, Frances wrote, "Hugh was here last night. Clary says this morning that he is a fool."[30]

That's how things stood at the end of 1831, depending on the day and Frances's accounts of the romance, if that is what it was. There were many obstacles to overcome. Hugh and Clary married four years later, by which time she was forty-two and he was forty-four. By any measure, that was a slow departure for Clary, who said often that she was desperate to get out of her crazy brother's house, but she had trouble making up her mind and feared from her nieces' experiences, as well as those of other women she knew and heard about. She could end up with an ogre like Lazette's husband, a drunk, like so many, or even, as was the case with Henry, whom she adored, a cold place in the bed where she expected her husband to sleep, although it is not at all clear that she sought a man to keep her bed warm. Her expectations appear to have been pretty low, and she married a man she often called a fool, as quoted by Frances, but she was expecting financial competence and was not at all sure Hugh could provide that for her. Perhaps the older she got the fewer suitors presented themselves, the better fools looked, and the lower her bar for competence became.

By the late 1820s, as Clary became more desperate to leave Elijah's house, she had three examples that gave her pause and contributed to her indecision as she aged and her pool of suitors dried up. The combined Seward and Miller families had three marriages from its first nineteenth-century generation that she saw as fraught to some degree. There were Cornelia's marriage to Mahlon and Lazette's to Alvah, in which the women chose their partners against the best judgment of their fathers, who turned out to have been right about both men. And there was Frances and Henry's marriage, which both families supported enthusiastically. Clary knew all three women were disappointed, but to different degrees and for different reasons.

The spread of the market economy, beginning in the eighteenth century, and the inability of eighteenth-century patriarchs to endow their married children with legacies that supported them were critical factors in the breaks from parental control in marriage choices. As we can see from the Seward and Miller examples, though, the change happened neither overnight nor without a struggle between the generations. The patriarchal fathers could still cause pain, if not prevent it.

The nineteenth-century husband, who was now more often a wage laborer, became the foundation of financial competence for the middle class, replacing the extended family and its landed or mercantile networks and legacy. His place in the world was more often determined by his job than by a fixed place in society, which was more fluid now, for good and for ill. Where the extended family had once been the primary unit of economic organization, the autonomous nuclear family now more often ran on its own. No longer did larger families mean more labor and thus greater productivity in the cities and towns; the child in the nineteenth-century family was an economic drain on resources, which contributed to shrinking family size and also to dramatic changes in the experience of childhood. The woman became the keeper of the home and the family's moral core. The husband and wife, who married for love with a keen eye on financial competence, now inhabited separate spheres, he the public and she the domestic one; he was more often away from home, at least during the day, earning a living, and she raised and in some cases educated their children. But this is all clearer in retrospect than it was to the people who lived through the changes without a blueprint for the future or any secure knowledge about how the new world they inhabited would work out for them. If people sometimes felt dizzy or had nervous attacks, we should not be surprised; it makes sense that they often felt at sea, even when they had both feet on shore. Despite their greater openness to sharing their feelings, it was not just the women who were overwhelmed and wanted to take to their beds.[31]

In February 1831 Frances wrote to Henry, "Next winter I intend to go to Albany with you. I do not think they treat me very well now you are gone." Frances too was unhappy at 33 South Street in 1831 with Henry off in Albany in his first year as a state senator and then pettifogging far from home after the legislative sessions ended. The Sewards had left 33 South Street in 1828 with their toddler, but they returned in December 1830 with Gus and baby Fred. Judge Miller's biographer gave the story a cheery twist, noting that although Elijah "willingly consented" to the Sewards moving into their own home, it "diminished the cheer of his household very perceptibly, and made him uncomfortably solitary for a year or two, and until he induced them to return."[32]

Henry's telling is more detailed, but even less candid. "While my residence in the family of Mr. Miller, my father-in-law, was in every way pleasant and desirable," he wrote, "the construction of his dwelling proved a severe trial to the health and comfort of my wife." It is unclear what he meant by that, and it leaves unanswered the question of why they then moved back if it was the house that he thought made Frances sick. "My return to the Senate involved a change in my domestic life," Henry explained. "My second son, Frederick W. Seward, was born on July 8, 1830, in the new house on South Street, which I had bought in the spring. I closed that dwelling for the winter, which I was to spend at the State capital, and in the last days of December, leaving my wife and two children with her father, proceeded to Albany by stage." It was a mere two months later that Frances wrote to Henry that she intended, with her sons in tow, to spend the next winter with him in Albany, because "they" did not treat her well in her father's house. It does not appear that the house's construction was her problem, so Henry's telling provided a fig leaf for domestic unrest.[33]

For Henry, the story of his family's moves was embedded in financial concerns. As he told it, "My professional pursuits had, by this time, become sufficiently profitable to assure me a competence for the country life which, on all grounds, I preferred. But that competence could not reach an abundance, by reason of the drafts to which I was subjected. Relatives unfortunate in business had, naturally enough, applied to me for indorsements and loans. I cheerfully gave the required aid, but, in so doing, depleted more than one-half the entire property which I possessed." The "relatives" definitely included Jennings and possibly Polydore. If indeed the relatives were plural, it was his brothers whose debts Henry absorbed. He was explaining that he bought the house for Frances's sake, but it strained his finances in light of the burden of his relatives and required him to take out a mortgage.

As Henry told it, he bought "the neat house and pretty grounds directly opposite to that of Mr. Miller. I paid one thousand dollars in hand, and secured the payment of the balance within five years . . . and removed to that dwelling with my wife and child (Augustus), then three years old. Impatient under renewed experience of debt, I laid aside all my gains with a miser's prudence and care, and extinguished the bond and mortgage in fifteen months." The moral of Henry's story was that he was no longer the spendthrift his father had labeled him when he was in college. He was a nose-to-the-grindstone family man and a responsible adult before he entered politics.[34]

Neither the biography of Elijah nor Henry's autobiography discusses Henry's two serious considerations of moves away from Auburn in the 1820s, which together suggest his lack of attachment to the town and his willingness, if not eagerness, to get out from under his father-in-law's roof. The two pursuits of moves contradict the family stories of attachment to the house and town and reveal that Henry's calculations weighed political ambitions and financial motives over personal ones. In neither case does the surviving record mention Frances's views on moving to Goshen or New York City, the two places considered by her husband. The pros and cons that Henry discussed in correspondence with his father and brother Jennings prioritized business concerns, but weighed political ones too.

After Henry's brief partnership in Goshen before he moved to Auburn, there was another business flirtation in 1825, also with Ogden Hoffman, so he had not burned all his bridges to home and pondered a return, although there is also the possibility that it was all part of a negotiation with his father-in-law, who was also his business partner. In a letter to his father on May 11, 1825, Henry wrote, "I have considered Mr. Hoffman's generous proposition in a pecuniary light and have endeavored to ascertain which residence will enable me to separate from the common mass of the root of evil the greatest proportion for myself." Ogden Hoffman, son of Josiah Hoffman, an eminent New York City attorney, had a firm in Goshen and was the Orange County district attorney. At this time, Ogden considered a move back to New York City, which he accomplished the following year. As Henry suggested to Samuel, he weighed both the money and the amount of time and energy he would have to devote to the practice of law, which he despised. The financial difference, as Henry calculated from the information Hoffman provided, was about $350 in favor of the Goshen offer—$1,740 versus half of the $2,750 that he and Judge Miller split, "which I regard as a fair estimate."[35]

Beyond that, the pecuniary calculations included comparative living expenses in Auburn and Goshen. "Now, as to the support of my family, Mr. Miller says that our living shall cost us nothing," Henry told his father. There was a negotiation or, at least, a conversation with his partner and landlord about the matter. "To this I object," Henry shared proudly, "that we shall not be supported by anybody and I insist on pay[ing] him $200 for our board, lodging, &c. This I cheerfully pay out of my pettifogging business, which is exclusively mine." In other words, it looked to Henry like a financial wash with the need for him to practice more law in Goshen than in Auburn. So the move to Goshen would not get Henry what he wanted, and Elijah's eagerness for the Sewards to stay also delivered counterbalancing financial benefits.[36]

"As to my feelings," Henry continued, recognizing that not only his feelings were in play, "I need not say how gratifying it would be to me to be once more a frequent visitor under my paternal roof." Henry laid it on pretty thickly: "dearer is it to me with its thousand little associations than are all my inbuilt speculations of wealth and honor," and he was not yet done: "Dear to me is my father for unnumbered acts of kindness and affection not least of all for his lively interest in my correct decision upon the present question nor shall this cease to be remembered by me. Dear to me is my mother for all the tenderness and all the affection which now ever and anew comes over my recollection like a drowning overwhelming flood."[37]

Henry went on to explain how dear his siblings were to him as well, but his father was too sharp not to see testimony to attachment as the preface to a decision against moving home. Samuel must have sensed the "but" coming: "But, I can no longer be the arbiter of my destiny," Henry laid the decision at the feet of his wife and his need to make the most conservative financial calculation, both of which argued against the move. "The time was when I would have hailed Mr. Hoffman's offer and accepted it, too. I can now only say that I thank him for it and decline it."[38]

On top of that, as a postscript to his explanation, Henry continued, "I have a loathing towards that same Goshen, a disgust which is too violent to be suppressed. A low, mean, and groveling race are most of its inhabitants, and it is questionable which is most to be desired, their love or hate. It is not so here, for here I have friends who wish me well, and I have no enemies who can injure me. I am removed above the scandal of the day and the peace of mind of my wife cannot be destroyed by the gossip of the village." That makes it hard to imagine Henry was even considering seriously such a move. The subtext was that the "groveling race" of his prospective neighbors in Goshen were not likely to support his ambitions for political office and indeed he never carried the town in his three campaigns for governor. Henry did not say in the letter to his father what scandal he anticipated the Goshen residents to gossip about. Everything—Elijah, Frances, legal practice, and political ambition—pointed in the same way, so it is unlikely that Henry considered this move for very long.[39]

A year later, shortly after the birth of Gus, Henry bragged to his father that "as to my business, it is confessedly second to none in the County. My reputation as lawyer or advocate is yet to be formed, of course. Whether or not it will be established at a high grade I am now less anxious than to secure a comfortable livelihood for myself and my little family. But I have no great misgivings upon that score." His father should not have believed the claim of declining ambition, but he may have shared Henry's concern that "Frances's health is precarious. She continues to be threatened with the puerperal fever, but I hope she will escape it. The boy grows finely."[40]

Another year passed, and we learn that Henry explored business opportunities in New York City with his brother Jennings, who lived there, as his agent. "I have felt some embarrassment in making the inquiries you desire," Jennings explained, "I could not judge for you who would make an agreeable partner, no more than I could choose a wife for you. Come down." A month later, Henry, who was just recovering from an unspecified illness, planned a visit to the city. "I am delighted with the idea of your visit to our city," Jennings wrote. "I will reconnoiter the ground thoroughly ere you arrive, and feel a strong conviction that we can do something handsome. But there is really a difficulty in asking a man to take a partner that is not present and that he has never seen."[41]

By mid-April, Jennings thought the move was a sure thing. Tell Frances, Jennings instructed his brother, "that Marcia is delighted with the idea of having her for a neighbor. Already she begins to count upon the solid comfort they are to have together." Jennings was in a giddy mood at the prospect of his brother's family joining his in New York. He believed, at least, that Frances had agreed and hoped she favored life in a more fashionable city over that in a country town. "I think if you have really made up your mind to remove to the city (doubtless it is so), you had better obtain from the ton, a license for your good lady to peramble Broad Way, without delay. You must know that the 'Navarinos' that are at present in vogue are larger by 9/11s than the Bolivars, and more delicate by far. Hence no more than between 9 and 10 ladies can be accommodated in front of one block at a time." The "ton" to which Jennings referred was short for "Breton," a type of ladies' hat with a turned-up brim all around, usually made of straw or felt, which became fashionable in the nineteenth century and again in the 1960s. It might do for Auburn, but not for fashionable New York women.[42]

Another month after that, in the third week of May, Jennings remained certain that the Auburn Sewards were moving to New York. The move was no longer a secret from their father, "who seems delighted with the idea of your coming to the City." Samuel believed the cost of living comparable but the income likely triple what Henry made in the country, at least according to Jennings. "Whether business can in every case be commanded, he [Samuel] is not exactly prepared to say. Many men of much cleverness do not obtain it, and although he seems to avoid the responsibility of advising your emigration hither, it seems evident to me that he does not consider the risk to be very great."[43]

The consideration of New York City disappeared from the family's correspondence without a resolution, except that Henry and Frances moved back into Judge Miller's house and there was no more written discussion. When Henry explained changes in his domestic relations between 1828 and 1830 he wrote that he preferred a "country life," which he apparently meant to contrast Auburn with New York City. Since he spent so little time in Auburn for the rest of his days and seized excuses to be away after short visits home, it is difficult to take his testimony on the subject of country life seriously. Indeed, his traveling patterns over the next thirty years reflect a preference for cities over his home. Henry's election to the state senate in 1830 likely led him to believe that his ambition was better linked to Auburn than to a new start. The affection he described for his neighbors compared to the scoundrels he believed populated Goshen was enhanced by Auburn's support for his campaigns.

How arrangements with Henry's business partner and father-in-law figured into the equation is also unclear, but it was not long after they moved back into Judge Miller's house that Frances described herself as badly treated in Henry's absence, and she used the plural "they" to refer vaguely to what could have included only three people—Paulina, Elijah, and Clary. Frances's health, the boys' attachment to their grandfather, and the family's clear affection for Gus and Fred all balanced the scales, and Frances really did love her crazy family and Auburn. The Sewards remained "inmates" of 33 South Street long after Lazette and Clary left home, and Henry spent increasingly more time over the years away pursuing his political career than in Auburn enjoying the country life.

Chapter 4

For Better, 1831

When the Miller sisters considered suitors in the early 1820s, the men were from one of a couple dozen local families that shared Judge Miller's success as land speculators and entrepreneurs. Auburn was young, having its origins in the mid-1790s, not long before Elijah's marriage to Hannah, so Frances and Lazette were among the first generation of marriageable offspring from the town's first families, first in time and first in influence and wealth. Some of these families came from New England, as Hannah did, and more hailed from downstate New York, as had the Millers. All saw Auburn as a potential boomtown, which had its value as a location on the Seneca Highway, through which east-west roads, canals, and railroads passed by the end of the 1830s, contributing to increased land value, commercial expansion, and the predicted prosperity and growth. The location also had industrial potential, given the power of the outlet from Cayuga Lake to the Seneca River, which brought the entrepreneurs more success than, for example, Seneca Falls to its west.

These factors contributed to a vibrant banking industry; an active staples market, particularly cornstarch, by mid-century; the financing of shipping and commercial corporations that became Wells Fargo and American Express; and the manufacturing of farm implements, shoes, and other commodities. Construction of the Auburn prison in 1816, which included commercial production by inmates, also contributed to the town's economic growth. First, though, came the land speculation, which grew the capital that was the foundation on which entrepreneurs built the rest. By the 1870s, when William Seward died and the South Street house passed to Will Jr.'s family, Auburn had breweries, starch companies, publishers, an opera house, four weekly and two daily newspapers, six banks including Will's, a business school, twenty-one churches, and trolley service to recreational sites throughout the Finger Lakes.[1]

The first families of Auburn included the Beaches, Beardsleys, Blatchfords, Bostwicks, Bronsons, Dills, Glovers, Hardenburghs, Hurlburts, Kelloggs, Millers, Morgans, Pomeroys, Throops, Vredenburghs, Watrouses, and Woodses, and from the mid-1820s, the Sewards. These were all families that had come to Auburn with money to invest or married into such families, and were thus at a competitive advantage in the first half of the nineteenth century, when they built the economy. They were better educated than their neighbors, they intermarried, and they partnered with each other in their investments and businesses. The form of capitalism they practiced was more organized and cooperative than it was competitive. Reputation and family were all; they were successful on the backs of their relatives and friends.

The origin of the community was its location on the Military Tract, land in central New York granted by the state, which was originally intended to compensate soldiers for their service in the American Revolution but actually brought wealth to officers and other speculators who bought the soldiers' bounties at huge discounts. The speculation resulted in a transfer of wealth from the poor, for whom a six-hundred-acre grant would have constituted a windfall had they been able to wait for the legislation, treaty rights, surveys, and actual distribution of the land that took more than a decade after the war, and if they had confidence those events would ever occur. Instead, the grants actually increased class differences and established communities of wealth in places like Auburn. Only 6 percent of the lots went to the families of soldiers who originally received the grants, while 38 percent of the officers' families actually settled on the land granted by the federal and state governments. The rest went to investors, mainly merchants from New York City, Albany, and New England, whose profits generally exceeded 100 percent over their investment.[2]

The town prospered and the population grew, from under 500 when the Millers arrived in 1808, to about 2,500 when Henry moved there in 1823, to over 20,000 by the time he died in 1872, and the leading families were the principal beneficiaries of the expansion of the market economy that accompanied transportation and communication revolutions in the nineteenth century. Changes in marriage and family accompanied movement of the population from farms to villages to burgeoning cities, and the economic growth and class differentiation that accompanied it. Although the changes in household management facilitated increased leisure for wives and mothers, the changes brought new responsibilities and required new skills, which resulted in a lifestyle that women did not experience as leisurely.[3]

The home became the domain of women, which was initially a liberating and ultimately a confining change. The wives and mothers now ruled the household more independently of their husbands than they had in the past, something that Elijah, Henry's father Samuel, and their generation never accepted. This role, which Frances only fully realized when she inherited the house from her father, elevated her life's work. She was responsible for her family's physical and spiritual health; their sustenance (shopping, growing, husbanding, and cooking) and clothing (manufacture or purchase, repair, and laundry); the upkeep and cleanliness of the home; the hiring, management, and care (feeding, clothing, health, hygiene, training, and supervision) of household staff, most of whom were children themselves; the education of her children; the maintenance of the kitchen and flower gardens; and the care and feeding of the family's animals. She also had social responsibilities, which included calls on neighbors to ensure their well-being and the maintenance of their community, charity through her church and social organizations, and the care of the ill and support of those in bereavement. She was also responsible for her husband, body and soul, and supported him in his work in the world.

Women experienced this all as a heavy load, which they described as hard on their nerves in an age when health was understood to derive from the nervous system. The best cure for illness was taking to one's bed, but that was not always possible for wives and mothers. Physicians, who were men, were often unsympathetic, prescribing opioids, which all who used them knew created dependency, led to symptoms of withdrawal that were often worse than the migraines, toothaches, cramps, and other ills they were intended to address, and could be permanently debilitating. Women could count on pregnancy with attendant postpartum complications five or six times, the tragic loss of at least one child, sometimes multiple miscarriages, and often undiagnosed and untreated gynecological disorders, which could not be discussed in the presence of children or men, or even in correspondence with other women, lest others might read about them. It is no wonder alternative medical treatments were widely entertained and homeopathy had its appeal among the educated classes, because, at least, it did no harm, which conventional methods (treatment by drugs, purging, bleeding, and surgery) often did. In the 1830s the physicians who practiced traditional medicine were under siege due in large part to their failure to address the plague of cholera that swept the nation.[4]

Women in Frances Seward's class were no longer personally feeding, killing, and plucking the chickens, collecting the eggs, planting and harvesting the vegetables, milking the cows twice daily, baking the bread and pies, and preparing meals for a dozen and more people, as rural women were, which did not mean they were women of leisure. She and her friends were more often than not exhausted, stressed, in pain, and burdened with the responsibilities of families and communities that depended on them in countless ways, and were expected on top of it all to serve as gracious hostesses to dinner and overnight guests, who might be relatives, friends, or business associates of their husbands. In the case of politicians' wives, the burden expanded to public as well as private duties in support of their husbands' careers, and a vast correspondence. Many, like Frances, were challenged and fulfilled in these roles.[5]

"'A happy New Year' to you dearest, if you have run away and left me alone with the two tiny ones." Frances began 1831 with what became the principal refrain of her marriage to Henry. And yet, she undercut her complaint with "they are dear creatures and I have no right to complain." No right, because Frances embraced heart and soul the prevailing norm that her place as wife and mother was in the home with her children, ages six months and four years at this point, and her husband's work was out in the world. But she had expected that, like her father, Henry's work would be in an Auburn office down the street, from which he returned nightly for supper, his family, and bed rather than spending months on end in Albany, where he was beginning in 1831, or even farther away in New York City, western New York, and ultimately Washington, DC, all places his work took him for extended periods of time.[6]

Frances had not anticipated Henry's political ambitions, because he denied them, claiming simply that he had responded to the call of his neighbors and friends, who had elected him to the state senate the previous November in his first bid for office. "I had neither expectation nor wish for office," he said. Despite the disclaimer, he calculated each political move with ambition and the support of his political mentor, the Albany newspaper editor Thurlow Weed. Over the previous three years, Henry had an opportunity to run for the House of Representatives and another for the state legislature, but he had withdrawn from both in the face of what he saw as certain defeat at the hands of the more popular Democrats, given his opposition to President Jackson and support for John Quincy Adams. This time, with the endorsement of Weed's *Albany Evening Journal*, Seward won the state senate seat handily, by a margin of two thousand votes. Frances hoped he would do his duty and return home after eight weeks away each year over the course of a two-year term. As she revealed in her letters, she was not going to make it any easier for Henry to be away; there was an outbreak of scarlet fever, there was nothing but rain and mud, she feared damage from ice and mice to their now-empty home, since she and the boys had moved back to her father's house in Henry's absence, and her "head aches so I hardly know what I write."[7]

Henry wrote to Frances from Albany on the same day, after an exhausting journey. On Wednesday morning, he left Auburn's American Hotel on the stage with eight other passengers, making it to Syracuse, where he spent the first night. At 2:00 p.m. the next day, Thursday, he got on another stage and continued overnight, making it as far as Utica by 6:00 a.m. Friday, the third day of his journey. There was "a tremendous storm" two hours after he arrived in Utica, so he made it only as far as Fonda, still forty-two miles short of his destination, which he reached on Saturday night at 7:00 p.m., January 1, "well and sufficiently fatigued." He had a room reserved at the Eagle but had to double up for a few days, and he had arrived too late for the New Year's open houses of dignitaries he had hoped to meet—governor, lieutenant governor, mayor, and former mayor, members of his Anti-Masonic Party, the nation's first third party, which disappeared before the end of the decade, after Henry and many others became Whigs, the next alternative to the Democrats. He attended services at Albany's Episcopal church Sunday morning. This was the launch of his political career, and he was not at all sure he would be successful in the new job.[8]

When Henry wrote to Frances on Sunday evening, he had "not yet been here long enough to know whether I shall be pleased or otherwise, though I was last night visited with more recollections about you and Fred and Augustus than you perhaps would give me credit for." Even before he received Frances's guilt-burdening letter that she wrote the same evening, Henry knew where she stood on his political aspirations. "All as yet seems pleasant," but the legislature did not convene until Tuesday, so it was too early for him to know what he thought of it all. Henry closed his first letter to Frances from Albany with the news that "Mr. Tracy called upon me this morning and went to church with me." Albert Haller Tracy (1793–1859), an attorney from Buffalo, was a three-term congressman as a Democratic-Republican and was now an Anti-Masonic state senator and became Henry's bosom friend.[9]

After being sworn in on Tuesday, Henry wrote to Frances again, a journaling letter that covered the previous two days, during which he had made calls on his colleagues in the company of Tracy. He presented himself to Frances as a man doing his duty, one of the "conscript fathers of the land," who would rather be home in Auburn with his wife and children were it not for his duty to the citizens of Cayuga County and his party. That evening, he attended the theater, which was "but a poor concern." In returning to his hotel, he and his companion, an outgoing senator with whom he was sharing a room, both had their hats knocked off by a wire strung across the road for the purpose of stealing them by "some thievish fellows. . . . My gloves, letters and papers were scattered over the walk. Fortunately, we recovered all our property and arrived safe at the Eagle."[10]

In Henry's absence, Frances was left to entertain overnight guests, the Jacobuses, "a couple of wonderful insipid beings," whom she hoped not to see again for another four years. She also received Deborah Dill Wood and her husband George, an attorney, as invited guests for tea. "George did not speak at all and Debby said very little to the purpose, but she can talk forever about nothing." Frances had some, but not much, sympathy for Debby, whom she was afraid was "not long for this world. She has a cancer, at least the Dr.'s so pronounced it, which is daily becoming more painful. She grows thin, but retains all her sprightliness. . . . It never appears to occur to Debby that cancers sometimes terminate fatally." Indeed, this one did not fell Debby, who survived for another fifty-four years. For the night of January 4, though, Frances was absorbed in nursing baby Fred and reading the second volume of the works of Lord Byron, "with which I am so much charmed that I found it almost impossible to lay it down this evening when my eyes refused any longer to distinguish the characters. Everyone in the house has gone to bed and Fred is getting quite uneasy about my long tarrying, so good night dear one."[11]

In that first week of his first session in the state senate, Henry continued to complain about one after another "tedious day of indolence," when the legislators met for only an hour or two and then ate, drank, and called on each other for the rest of the day and night. He was not alone in his room until almost midnight. Still, "I have nothing to do," Henry wrote to Frances mid-week, but he was assured that business would soon pick up and socializing decline. The next day he wrote again: "The senate was in session today including time occupied by the chaplain just forty-five minutes. No business as yet was matured and so we adjourned literally for want of anything to do."[12]

Henry bought a copy of James Fenimore Cooper's *The Water Witch*, which had just been published. He was bored and favored Cooper's novels. He intended to read the book and then mail it to Frances. Sharing the reading experience would enable him to bond with Frances through their correspondence, rather than the two of them just complaining to each other about how difficult life was when they were apart. His idea struck Henry as thoughtful but elicited no direct reply from Frances, who was not a fan of Cooper.[13]

The next day, which was January 8, the senate was in session for only twenty-five minutes. "There [in Auburn] are my friends, my home, my loved ones, my all. Here I am alone, a stranger." It was a man's world, no women in the legislature, only the old housekeeper in the Eagle, but some of the legislators had brought their wives. Henry socialized with Senator Trumbull Cary and his wife Margaret, who were from Batavia, and the Tracys, Albert and his wife Harriet, all of whom became "aunts" and "uncles" to the Sewards' children. About the Tracys, Henry wrote, "I very much like them. They are so free from all affectation. He is one of the most agreeable men in conversation I ever knew and she is a very independent little body, despising all the mock pretensions of our would-be great folks." In conclusion, Henry gave Frances reason to understand that his venture into politics would be short-lived: "I can hardly hope to make you understand how entirely the illusion under which I have labored in respect to the importance of my station has faded away. Seen through the vista of opposition, excitement, puffs, and abuse the post of senator of this great State seemed one of immense importance and dignity. One week has removed all the accumulating vanity of a year and I find the whole affair a dull everyday commonplace affair."[14]

Frances was not well and told Henry that she missed his moral support. For the previous five days, going back to the day she last wrote to him, she had been sick with a toothache, "which still continues to torment me." The morning after Frances wrote her last letter, Lazette sent her maid Nancy to get Fred, whom, against Paulina's protests, they took off his mother's hands so she could get some rest. "Notwithstanding some remonstrance from Grandma, I wrapped the little fellow up warm and sent him." She took to her bed that afternoon, but her teeth continued to ache through the night. "Of course, I did not sleep any, my taper went out, I had no Henry to call on to assist me in my tribulation, so I got up myself, went down stairs, lighted a candle, got some laudanum and brandy . . . but fire nor candle, laudanum nor brandy availed aught my teeth ached and ached until daybreak." The next day was even worse, because Frances awoke after two or three hours of sleep in the morning, "sick with the laudanum I had swallowed." The side effects, as she knew, could be worse than the symptoms they relieved for a time. She fed and changed Fred, "went to bed again, [and] with the assistance of a ginger poultice slept until dinner. . . . Well, toothache is the burden of my song. A hot poultice, which almost skinned my face, relieved my teeth so much that I slept very comfortably the next night."[15]

By mid-January Henry was beginning to get his footing in the legislature. Perhaps because he was young, enthusiastic, and naive, his colleagues assigned him to look into the salt monopoly that was a source of reliable graft to those in power. When he returned a report that recommended reforms, he got the unsavory attention of the so-called Regency, a powerful subgroup of the Democrats, and began to feel that he may have an important role to play after all. "I feel now," he wrote to Frances, "as if I had surmounted the diffidence which has oppressed me and unless all is dark before my eyes tomorrow I shall be able to assign my reasons for the measure I propose."[16]

Now Henry confessed to Lazette "that my ambitious hopes and desires sometimes, my feelings of attachment to others, sometimes, my feelings of indignation against wrong, sometimes have made me truant to the kindly affections of domestic life." And yet, he continued, Lazette could rest assured that she and other family members were never out of his mind. He knew she had seen the almost daily letters he was sending to Frances and thus understood that his illusions about politics as the profession of wise men had already dissolved. And yet, his views of politics continued to evolve from the early days of disdain with which he started the session. "Nevertheless, there is enough to interest me and

I begin to feel that I shall probably be no less happy in my new career than I have heretofore been." Yes, he was cynical about many, perhaps most, of the politicians, but there were good men such as Cary and Tracy, who were his natural allies and in wise pursuit of the public good. The senate was not entirely full of the likes of "Senator A, a Regency man who is always rather sullen when sober but the cleverest fellow imaginable when drunk, which does happen sometimes; Mr. Senator B., who is in the Senate about half the time and the rest of the time doing the bidding of the Regency. Mr. Senator C., who is stupid as an ass," and so on.[17]

For good reason, Frances was fearful with Henry away, as he was such an optimist that it countered her impulse to see darkness where he saw light. On January 16 she wrote to him that "I have the vapours most wretchedly," what we identify as psychological symptoms, but she saw as physical affliction of her nerves. The toothaches had passed their worst stage only to be replaced by dread that "the destroying angel still continues to visit the dwellings of our neighbours, and why shall we escape." Scarlet fever continued to plague the town. One family had lost two children, the younger of whom was only a few months older than Fred. Another baby was said to be dying, and Mrs. Gunn "was buried on Friday, the day after her disease. What a barbarous custom this is of hurrying people under ground the moment they have ceased to breathe," which reflected the panic that accompanied losses against which people had no defense.[18]

It was not that Henry, if he were home, could make it any less likely that one of their children succumbed, but Frances trusted his judgment more than that of Paulina, Elijah, or Dr. Pitney, whom she thought was a fool. Pitney believed, "like Augustus," their four-year-old son, that "one remedy may be effectively applied to all diseases." The doctor had increased the pain of a neighbor's "little sufferer by making an incision in its throat, because he chanced to be successful when he operated upon Mr. Mills' little girl, who had the croup. He did the same to Dr. Vaneps' child. It died and Vaneps now thinks had he followed his own judgment the child might have been living. I would give the world there was one physician in whom I might have half the confidence I had in poor Dr. Tuttle, but the best physician cannot always cure." Were Henry at home, he could reassure her that every little sneeze and sniffle was not the beginning of her baby's end.[19]

There was another solution, which was that she and the children join Henry in Albany. That is what he had proposed before he left and suggested again in response to her complaints, but she thought Fred too little and vulnerable to brave that trip. "It gratifies me to know that you think you would be more happy were I with you, but it cannot be. It would be almost cruel to take my little ones away from a home where they are so comfortable and happy this cold, cold winter. I am too foolish a mother to leave them, so it cannot be. I think you will feel less lonely when you become more accustomed to your new mode of spending your time." Given Fred's small size, the family had postponed his vaccination for smallpox until they thought he was strong enough to receive it, which was a gamble that traveling would undermine. He was vaccinated in April, at nine months of age, just as Gus had been.[20]

Henry's resolution on the salt mines went down to defeat on a party-line vote, but he felt encouraged nonetheless. "I said but little, very conscious of a considerable trembling of the knees," he wrote to Frances. "I feel much relieved by having surmounted the difficulty of making a debut. I can henceforth speak without fear, if occasion requires me to say anything." He felt launched and no longer out of his element; soon he owned the floor of the senate as if it were his true home. On the same night, after writing to Frances, Henry "finished reading 'the Water Witch.' I shall forward it to you at the first opportunity. It is a strange, improbable, absurd, and unnatural story, without the merit of one good character but yet one of the most bewitching books I ever read. . . . I will not again this winter be so much interested in a novel." He put it in the mail and hoped that she too found it "bewitching."[21]

When it arrived, Clary started reading aloud *The Water Witch* to Frances. On February 19 Frances finished reading the novel by herself late at night, perhaps because Clary dropped out of reading aloud a novel populated by bland heroines, while Frances stuck with it out of loyalty to her husband. "Except the two or three last chapters, I think the book very uninteresting," Frances wrote to Henry. "Many parts very improbable . . . Alida is as insipid as Cooper's heroines usually are." Henry had misread her gendered perspective on Cooper. In their time, the poet James Russell Lowell shared Frances's views, saying of Cooper, "The women he draws from one model don't vary, all sappy as maples and flat as a prairie."[22]

Henry did not see in Cooper's women what Frances did and modern critics do, that Cooper was a man out of step with social change, that he was deeply patriarchal, and that he did not accept women as full members of society. Henry was capable of buying into the romance of societies composed entirely of men, which enabled him to enjoy *The Pilot*, *Red*

Rover, and *The Water Witch*, all of which he mentioned in his letters to Frances as great literature. He might have anticipated his wife's taste but was apparently insensitive to her more modern views of gender relations, which she believed Henry shared at least more than her father.[23]

As she explained in a letter of January 19, Frances now read the daily proceedings of the senate in the *Albany Evening Journal*, so she had seen Henry's resolution on the salt mines. He need not have apologized to her for vanity in detailing his legislative actions in letters, even though some of the language and business was foreign to her. "I always read all the proceedings of the Senate in the evening journal, a thing I am sure I never thought of doing before. I read your resolution, hardly comprehended its import, and was very ignorant of the meaning of laying it on the table." She wanted Henry to continue to chronicle his daily activities in Albany; he should not assume her previous disinterest in politics extended to indifference to her husband's work. "I do not think you vain, dear one, I never did, that is I never have thought you vain since we were married; on the contrary, I shall scold you for your diffidence soon. If you could hear half the flattering speeches that are made to me about your talents and believe them half as religiously as I do you would not think you had any cause for embarrassment." Frances's affection for her husband remained strong six years into their marriage and her support for him unwavering. They corresponded multiple times a week in this, his first extended time away from home.[24]

By the third week of January 1831, Henry had settled into his new profession, neither so bored nor so cowed by the egos, pomp, and personalities that surrounded him. "You know I never did like my profession," he wrote to Frances, referring to his legal practice, "although the desire to have comfort and independence for you and Fred and Augustus and myself has made me its slave." He now liked politics better, found it more interesting and important, focused more broadly than the minutia that was the law. He waxed enthusiastically about those colleagues he admired, such as Thurlow Weed, the newspaper editor, and two of his Anti-Masonic Party friends, Assemblyman Francis Granger and Senator Albert Tracy, the last of whom he mentioned often.[25]

Henry feared his letters back home would make it sound like he was on vacation. He also knew that politics had a reputation for corruption that reached to the very roots of its participants' characters, but he thought he could avoid falling into that trap. And he realized that serving in the state senate kept him from earning more money by practicing law, so he needed to keep an eye on expenses. "Although I have heard so much and so long of the necessary dissipation of members of the legislature, I have thus far escaped it," he wrote to Frances. "I have been twice to the theatre. It must be some great novelty or a desire to oblige some particular friend which should induce me to go there again. At dinner, a glass of wine constitutes all the pleasures of that kind in which I indulge. I have eaten but one supper in a week. I spend one two or three hours in visits every day, and this is about the extent of my dissipation." He told Frances he worked hard, slept not more than six hours a night, and had a correspondence so vast that he could have used a personal secretary. And yet, he was much happier, much less stressed and harried in his work, and anticipated being pleasanter company for his family when he returned home. "Is it not passing strange that for four years past I have not had to my own use so much time which I might devote daily to domestic enjoyments as I now occupy in writing a page for your perusal. And, the time which I have had has been almost always swatched [splashed] with a feverish excitement from perplexities and cares which discolored most of the hours that might otherwise have been so happy."[26]

"Like a housewife's cares, my troubles are never ending," Henry concluded one of his letters to Frances that first month away. He did not mean that as a lack of sympathy for her plight, but rather as testimony to the fact that he understood how hard running the household and raising the boys was for her. He did not mean to diminish her loneliness, her suffering in his absence, and the trials she faced in a house where Paulina judged her, Elijah overruled her, and she witnessed the tribulations of Clary and Lazette. He knew she saw herself as a complainer, when her husband was out in the world doing important work that served the public, got reported in the newspapers, and supported his family with legal work that he despised.[27]

Frances thought her problems, which filled her letters, were really nothing compared to his. She was there to please, to serve, to defer, to wait, and to bear in silence or denial what came her way in return. Whatever he said or thought, she knew that was not Henry's fate. Frances's concerns continued to focus on scarlet fever, although she still suffered from toothaches. She promised to inform Henry if either of their boys showed any symptoms beyond those of the bad cold they, she, and Lazette all had in late January. "It makes me almost wild sometimes," Frances wrote to her husband, "when I think how far you are away and that four days would be the shortest time that you could attend any summons. Four days, how wretched four days might make me, but I will not think about it."[28]

Frances was also concerned about Henry's growing infatuation with politics, which kept him from home. "I do hope dearest that you will never be a 'political great man.' I believe they are all heartless and selfish, nay avaricious sometimes it appears, but I never suspected that. It is the ambition I so much dread, the ambition to be great that chills all the kindlier affections of the heart and throws its blighting influence on domestic happiness." Over the years, she repeated this fear or kept it to herself sometimes, but it never left her. She found laughable Henry's proposed solution to their separation that she, her father, and their sons join him in Albany. "You know how happy I should be to be with you, but it cannot be. I must content myself to remain a widow this winter." She refused to expose her children to the risks of travel in that most dangerous season.[29]

If longing plagued Frances's marriage in 1831, loathing marked Lazette's. "After finishing my letter to you yesterday," Frances wrote to Henry on February 1, "I went up and stayed a couple hours with Lazette, found her rather desponding. W[orden] had been very cross and struck her while she was attempting to punish Frances for some misdemeanor. I did not stay to tea and was so fortunate as not to meet him." Financial difficulties were a source of tensions in the Worden household, and there was a question about renting a house versus the wife and daughter boarding until Alvah could establish a reliable means of support. He hoped that Judge Miller would relent in his enduring opposition to the marriage and provide them one of his investment properties. Frances was against that. "I do hope Pa will never let it go into the hands of Alvah Worden. He would most assuredly mortgage or sell it before the expiration of one year. . . . If Worden cannot provide food for his family, I think he must be indeed past all hope."[30]

The Wordens lived in what Frances called "a miserable shell of a house," with a roof that leaked in every room. "No one knows half the privations my poor sister endures there." Tolerance for abusive husbands was declining in the nineteenth century; wife beating was now seen as lower class, a behavior beneath a "respectable" man. A good man was his wife's protector, the home a sanctuary from the world's violence. At every turn, Frances thought, Alvah was cruel. "Lazette says he is unwilling she show any fondness for little Fred, would not look at the little fellow the first day he came there. He says she likes Seward's children a great deal better than she does her own. He told her the other day that if he paid for her board it was as much as she must expect from him." That was a very eighteenth-century view of marriage.[31]

Frances was not alone among the women in the family in being torn between wifely and motherly duties. Such decisions were sources of friction between husbands and wives, but also among women who chose among wrenching alternatives. There was now a question about Marcia following her husband, Henry's brother Jennings, into new employment and leaving their children behind temporarily, another variation in marital relations. This was an intersection between marriage and parenting in the new, more mobile, wage-driven economy. The decision reflected on Frances's marriage, since she had declined to join her husband in Albany for the legislative session with her two small children as the explanation. "It is strange, indeed," Frances wrote to Henry, "that Marcia could leave her children to go among strangers, I think rather unnatural. But Marcia is strange about many things. She says I do not love my husband as well as she does. I know that he is satisfied with my love and that he loves me too well to ask such a sacrifice of my maternal feelings. There is not a particle of sympathy between Marcia and myself. We do not think or feel alike about anything, notwithstanding I think she is not destitute of goodness of heart."[32]

The disagreement between the two sisters-in-law was a relatively new one in the history of marriage. There was not the same tension between marriage and motherhood in eighteenth-century America, even when husbands went off to war for months or years. Of course, the women stayed home minding the family, and possibly the farm or store that supported it. The wives of politicians who had children still at home did not follow their husbands to Philadelphia for the Continental Congress or constitutional convention, but marriages were changing and the roles were more fraught in the nineteenth century. Frances struggled with the change, and her passionate denunciation of Marcia was as much a defense of her own decision as it was an indictment of Marcia's. The two women had words over their differences that are now lost to us. As Henry explained to Frances with anecdotes from Albany, her place and that of her children was with him when he was away serving the public interests of their neighbors. Frances was torn between hearth and husband, and she just wished that her husband remained home. On her one side, she had Henry and Marcia pulling her to Albany, while on the other, she had her father and grandmother, who knew where Frances belonged. Her heart was with her husband and home, which led to headaches, nerves, vapors, and the hypo, and she was far from the only wife and mother to endure the stress of separation and the desire to support her husband in his career.[33]

As April began, Frances hoped for an early adjournment of the legislature and was disappointed to learn that it remained in session until the end of the month. She was glad to read in the newspaper that Henry spoke on the floor of the senate, because the last she had heard from him he was ill and she did not know how sick he was. She was now sometimes learning more about her husband from the newspaper than from him, which blurred the line between public and private lives and left her profoundly uncomfortable, albeit in this particular case reassured.[34]

At about the same time, Frances regretted Henry's decision to sell "our beautiful house," although she knew "it were much better disposed of as the circumstances of the case are at present," by which she meant in light of Henry's new career in politics. From what she said in a letter to him, he looked to cut costs, labor, or both, suggesting that he might sell just the garden and she could keep the house, but Frances was not up to gardening alone as well as managing the household and parenting their children. "I am afraid I have troubled you too much about the garden. You write discouragingly, all your anticipations of a respite from your labours this summer appear to have vanished. They are all but a dream at best." This was apparently a negotiation; neither wanted responsibility for the garden. Henry had better things to do and did not want to be tied down to a home; Frances lacked the time and energy gardening or overseeing a hired gardener took; she was a manager and found managing the men a particular trial as they did not take her seriously. Henry was also concerned about the expense of another household staff member. "I would not sell the garden with[out] the house," she wrote. "You know I would <u>have</u> been and would <u>now</u> be satisfied with a smaller house and less ground."[35]

There were two strikes against remaining in her father's house from Frances's perspective, which led her to second-guess Henry's decision to sell theirs. One was the "retrograde situation" among those who lived there. Her father was difficult to be sure, but it was not her father alone. Her grandmother criticized her often. Judge Miller and his sister Clary were frequently at odds. Frances preferred either to keep their house (with garden) or find a new one, which was less expensive and demanding to maintain, rather than remain in the Miller house. The principal reason Frances gave her husband for wanting her own home was her sister's miserable marriage. "Lazette calculates so much upon our keeping house again in the summer when we can see each other every day or two that I could not find it in my heart to disappoint her." The previous summer, Lazette and her daughter had lived in the Sewards' house, where Lazette cared for her sister after Frances gave birth to Fred. "I would much rather be disappointed myself if but one of us was to be affected," Frances continued to explain to Henry. "I think I can say this without any affectation of generosity. I have so many more sources of happiness and comfort than have fallen to her portion." The sisters could not spend time together in her father's house, Lazette having fallen out with Elijah over her marriage. Alvah also forbade her to spend time there.[36]

Lazette had cared for her sister in the Sewards' own home not only over the summer of 1830 but right up until Henry left for Albany in January 1831. As Frances continued to explain to Henry when he considered selling their house, "she left me last winter after having nursed and cheered me so long that I [thought that I] could not live without seeing her oftener than I had done since before her marriage. But my poor health and my babe confine me much at home, and we do not meet oftener than once in two or three weeks." The decision about where the Sewards lived on a more permanent basis was obviously Henry's as the financial provider for his family, but Frances had made her needs and those of her sister clear. Both sisters wanted an end to the Sewards' residence in Elijah's house.[37]

Nonetheless, Henry sold their house and the Sewards remained at 33 South Street, unhappily for both Frances and Lazette. The reason was financial. Henry was still practicing law and soon took on another job managing mortgages, rents, and collections for the Holland Land Company in western New York to supplement the income from his legal practice and public office, but his political career still diminished his income. He was unable to increase his financial "competence" to an "abundance" because of the responsibility he took for the debts of his brothers after his father effectively disowned them. He was left "without an assurance of the pecuniary independence which I had already found indispensable to the social and political independence at which I aimed." Although he had paid off the mortgage on his house within fifteen months, before his first term in the state senate, by laying "aside all my gains with a miser's prudence and care," he was unwilling to put himself again in debt and thus make himself a slave to the practice of law by selling it and then purchasing another, smaller house and garden, and paying for staff in order to meet the emotional needs of his wife and sister-in-law. Although he insisted on paying his father-in-law rent, Henry was not paying anywhere near what it cost to run a household with staff. As he saw it, in order to do so and discharge his financial responsibilities for family members, he would have had to abandon his political career and recommit himself to the practice of law.[38]

Only four days after Frances wrote her pleading letter to Henry, she became herself a victim of Lazette's marital woes. "Such a scene as I have just passed through, I hope I shall never be placed in a similar situation," Frances wrote to Henry on April 17, 1831. "Worden has turned me out of the house and abused me in every possible way, and then says that my own Henry (who I know does love me) will and does approve of his conduct." She needed reassurance that she had her husband's support and his help to rescue Lazette, especially because she knew the sisters could not count on their father. "I did not weep then, but now I am home again and contrast my happy lot with the misery of my poor injured sister. I cannot dry my tears, can hardly compose my nerves sufficiently to tell you who are always so kind and considerate all my trouble." She needed Henry, really needed him, and he was in Albany. "I must try and make myself a little more intelligible or you will never understand me. I believe, Henry, that He has given me strength tonight whose assistance is never refused to those who ask it in sincerity. Am I wrong in thinking he listens to one so unworthy?"[39]

Frances tried to regain her composure by writing the letter, which was difficult and accounts for her long introduction to the story. She felt on the brink of incoherence—fear, anger, sadness, anxiety—and hoped that writing to Henry would be therapeutic, a substitute for throwing herself into his arms and sobbing out the story, but "the more I think the more cause I feel for sorrow. I am afraid you never will come home again. I know that I do not deserve so many blessings. How hard it is to write what it would be so easy to communicate to you were you here." All of Frances's worries, all of her arguments designed to bring Henry home and get her back into her own house now plagued her. Her failure to convince him to give up politics and settle with her in an Auburn house of their own now led to despair. If this story did not convince Henry to be the man of their house, she had no hope, no emotional resources left for the effort to persuade him. Yes, she was being dramatic, perhaps melodramatic before she even described the event, but that was the way people experienced and told stories in her lifetime, fiction and fact, as if they lived in a Gothic novel with the full range of tragic outcomes in play.[40]

It was Sunday morning, as Frances's story began. She had decided because the weather was unpleasant to skip church services and stay home with her boys. At that point, Lazette's lone household staff member, Harriet Bogart, brought a note from her sister. It said that Warren Worden, Alvah's younger brother and also an attorney in Auburn, had called in the absence of Alvah and "used the most insulting language to her." When Alvah returned home, Lazette reported to him in the presence of Warren and his wife Emily the abusive language, and Alvah replied that "Warren had done perfectly right and if she told him any more such stuff he would kick her out of the house." Frances sent a reply with Harriet, suggesting that Lazette come to her. "She came down as soon as Harriet returned and repeated the history of wrongs she had suffered, which would hardly be credited by anyone who did not know as we do the brute she lives with."[41]

After listening to her sister's recounting of events, which apparently included a ventilation of other incidents preceding the ones of that morning, Frances offered to return home with Lazette to serve as a buffer against Alvah's rage. "I went home with her as she desired it, [and] found them all gone to church. Nothing passed between us until after tea, after they came home. Then Warren came and came into the room where we were sitting, talked a while to Worden, came up where Lazette and I were, I know not for what purpose as I did not look at him, but I thought he was staring at us. He then withdrew." At that point, Frances's anger got the better of her. She "could not refrain from some observation on his impudence and added that I wished he had a man to deal with him." That was enough provocation to reignite Alvah's anger. In retrospect, Frances recognized that "I believe I was imprudent in saying this. Probably a moment's reflection would have prevented it, but my sister's wrongs were all present to my imagination and I hardly knew what I did say."[42]

In Frances's recounting of events, matters stood in a hostile silence until Alvah's brother and sister-in-law left. "As soon as Warren and Emily were out of the house Worden commenced abusing me. I cannot tell you half he said. I would not write the horrid oaths he utters. He concluded by saying if I did not go out of the house he would put me out 'neck and heels.'" Frances replied defiantly, challenging his authority as the man of the house. He, in turn, instructed Harriet to fetch Frances's hat and cloak. There was a question in Frances's mind whether Alvah would strike her, but she was confident, more or less, that he would not. "I took up a book and commenced reading. This only increased his rage," which she might have known that it would. "He came up to me and with a most dreadful oath snatched the book from my hands and threw it across the room." Having determined before she returned to the house with Lazette that she could "bear all manner of abuse in words," Frances endured the onslaught. "I can hardly account for it, but my composure increased with his violence. I said very little more notwithstanding he constantly showered upon me the most abusive epithets."[43]

Amid all the insults and anger, what most shook Frances's confidence in herself was Alvah's insistence that Henry was on his side, that "you approved of his measures," his efforts to rein in Lazette's independence, and that Henry and he "were on the most friendly terms and that you had often apologized to him for my conduct. He accused me of having said as outrageous things even as he does himself, and called me a liar if I contradicted them. This phrenzy continued I should think nearly half an hour."[44]

More troubling than the confrontation itself was the added detail that Alvah held their daughter while he vented his rage. "All the time he held Frances firmly in his arms while she was struggling and screaming to get to her mother, telling her all the time between his fits of raving at me that her mother did not care anything about her. Lazette was crying, but I did not shed a tear and indeed did not at all until I came home, which I did as soon as he released Frances and had stayed long enough to convince him that his threats did not intimidate me." The child was as much a victim as her mother of Alvah's abuse, but we can only imagine the wounds that he inflicted. She too was a hostage to her father's anger and not just this one time.[45]

The question concluding Frances's long story asked Henry what was to be done. Lazette feared losing custody of her daughter if she left Alvah and worried that she had no place to go. Elijah was unsympathetic, as he had warned her and she had made her own choice. She had no place to live and no means of support. She could not live with her sister in her father's house and could not expect Henry to support her. "You know my dear Henry with what an aching heart I then left my sister. She says it does seem impossible for her any longer to endure such treatment, that she would willingly cross the ocean, go into a strange land, and toil for subsistence if she could but take with her her child." That was a dramatic way to put it, but the core point was obviously true, which led to the sisters' conclusion.

> Of course, we have concluded to leave it all to you what must be done! I know it is a hard question. Men have framed laws I believe to uphold themselves in their wickedness. What right can a father have in case of a separation to take the children? Did they endure any of the agony of a mother in bringing them into existence? Can they feel that tenderness which is so intimately woven with every fiber of a Mother's heart? I believe he has made up his mind that he will no longer maintain Lazette, and he says repeatedly that he would turn her out of the house if she persisted staying there. But he said she never should have the care of Frances.

Frances Seward was right; the law was on Alvah's side.[46]

Worden blamed Frances for the fate of Lazette, who with her daughter lived with the Sewards before they vacated their house and Frances and her boys moved back in with the Millers. "In the next breath, he accused me of turning Lazette out [of] doors when we broke up housekeeping, said I was the most abandoned and depraved of mortals, and concluded all by saying that your opinion was the same as his with regard to his conduct. I am going to bed. My head aches so that I cannot write any more tonight. So, good night dearest," Frances broke off the letter she was writing to Henry, leaving it to finish the next day.[47]

Frances was clear that the Sewards' move back into Elijah's house had dispossessed Lazette, had thrown her back into an abusive relationship that had significant repercussions for Lazette's daughter Frances as well. She did not have to tell Henry that the decision had not been hers. The only explanation for returning to 33 South Street that emerges from the letters is economic; Henry said, "I closed up that dwelling for the winter, which I was to spend at the State capital, and in the last days of December, leaving my wife and two children with her father, proceeded to Albany by stage." The decision was his, which means that Lazette and her daughter also paid a high price for his ambition. If Frances expected her husband to defend her and right the wrongs that left the family in disarray she was disappointed, more likely distraught.[48]

By the next morning Frances had calmed, and by Monday evening she could pick up her pen and write to Henry that "I am in better spirits than I was last night, and I would not make you unhappy." Clary, whom she had told nothing about the trauma of the previous day, had stopped by the Wordens that afternoon. "She did not see Worden while there and heard nothing of the last night's storm, at least she told me nothing." In a postscript, Frances informed Henry that "Harriet has just been here with a note from Lazette. She says I must tell you that she attempted to write to you last night but failed."[49]

Henry arrived home on April 30 after a "wearisome" carriage ride from Albany. As the stagecoach entered Auburn, "the first glad countenance I saw was that of my dear sister, who was watching at her window as the stage passed her house." This was Lazette. After exiting the carriage at the American Hotel, he began the short walk home. As he approached Elijah's house, "the nurse was at the window presenting as the first object for my greeting little Fred, who was pleased with the chance of looking out at the window, but had no idea of the interest his sweet little face was to excite. My Aunt Clara opened the door and received me." His dog, "my affectionate and timid Frank, awaited me in the Hall. Grandmother in the sitting room and Augustus came soon after with a gratified but subdued look, which seemed to ask whether I recollected <u>him</u> in the joyous greeting which was taking place." Next to welcome Henry was Frances. "I found my dear girl comfortably well," he shared cheerily. "Augustus grown large and stout had under the assiduous tuition of his mother learned to read, though he has never been at school. Little Fred is fat but small. He was at first alarmed at my offers of attention to him, but has already become disarmed of all his fears and strives constantly to engross my attention. All the others of the household I found in perfect health and cheerfulness."[50]

In other words, all was domestic bliss, each family member well and situated in his or her place. No mention of Elijah, but all others eagerly anticipated Henry's return. "I am happy in the restoration to the family with all whose interests, affections, hopes, fears, joys, and sorrows I, though eight years ago a stranger to them," now found his comings and goings their "most important incidents." He shared his report with Albert because Henry knew that his friend cared about all that mattered to him, and "partly because of the deep interest you have manifested in their welfare." Henry knew that Tracy's wife Harriet was particularly interested in his domestic affairs, because "she is a woman, an unsophisticated one. The whole acquaintance has afforded no incidents upon which I shall dwell with more delight than the sympathies she has exhibited in my domestic griefs and pleasures, hopes and alarms." Henry had shared Frances's letters with Harriet, who served as a sounding board for his replies, none of which survive, which likely means the ones addressing the "domestic griefs" and "alarms" were destroyed, not something the family wanted to save.[51]

One piece was missing from Henry's ideal domestic scene, "being unaccompanied by you," he wrote to Albert. The family, from Judge Miller, whom Henry now mentioned for the first time, down to five-year-old Augustus, "who was dressed in his new pantaloons with the bright buttons to make a favorable impression upon his Aunty Tracy," and nine-month-old Fred, whose "new frock was brought out to show me how much the same Aunty had lost by going by us in the canal boat. Aunt Clara showed me how nicely your bed, room, etc., were prepared for your reception." The family's assumption was that Uncle Tracy, who was known by them to experience fragile health, must have been ill; indeed, "Judge Miller immediately came to the conclusion that you were left sick upon the road."[52]

Henry wanted Albert to have no doubt that their new friendship united the two families in a permanent bond. He had been a bit shy about sharing the depth of his feelings for Tracy when they were together. "I could not tell you," he now wrote, "because I am poor in speech, and on such matters I am dumb, and yet I always felt a strong desire for some opportunity to express to you the intense interest I have felt in relation to you, an interest whose intensity has continued to increase until it has become a passion, the disappointment of which would give me more pain than any event I can now anticipate, save the severing by death of some of the strongest cords bound around my heart." For two reasons, Henry had entered into their relationship with some trepidation. In the first place, Tracy was the Ajax Telamon of their party, the mythological hero of Homer's *Iliad*, the grandson of Zeus and cousin of Achilles, which left Henry awestruck from afar. There was also the rumor, which was bandied about in Albany's political circles, that Tracy was "dangerous," a man of "insatiable ambition and, of course, unmitigated selfishness," which led Henry to suspect Tracy of ulterior motives and "sinister designs," when Tracy first displayed an interest in him.[53]

Sometime after they had met, Tracy wrote Henry a letter from Norwich, Connecticut, which displayed an "up-bursting of a covered fountain of feeling such as has watered always every province of my womanish heart." That letter broke through Henry's reserve and penetrated "without resistance to the innermost home of my soul. God forbid that you should cease to desire to retain the place I yielded you in my affection." As far as his feelings for Harriet, Henry had easily fallen into what he termed an "uncle" relationship with her. "She hardly yet knows how foolishly I am devoted to her, how closely I have hoarded up in my remembrance the tears she gave me when I feared the death of my boy, the tender and unobtrusive sympathies she all winter long expressed for [the] health and contentment of my own dear Frances." These were her reactions to Frances's letters reporting illness. Finally, there was "the almost unbearable pain she caused me by involving me in the penance she inflicted upon you for some of your high crimes and misdemeanors," but Henry did not say what Albert's crimes against his wife were.[54]

At this early stage in the friendship between Henry and Tracy, Henry imagined a union of the two families in the ways that marriage brought him an additional sister, aunt, father, and grandmother among the Millers. He wanted the Tracys to embrace his sons as nephews and befriend his wife as a sister, to bond with the Sewards and Millers of Auburn, and to support Lazette without interfering in her marriage. In his reply to Henry from Buffalo, Tracy regretted only that he had not initial contact by mail after their separation; indeed, he was "mortified" that Henry's letter reached him before he had written his. "I do declare that I actually had my pen in hand for the sole purpose of addressing you the very moment that Edward [Albert's brother] returned from the Post Office with your letter. . . . You know I love you, but how much I dare not trust myself to enquire, far less to express."[55]

When Henry replied, four days after Tracy had mailed his letter, that "I am womanly apprehensive about your ill health," he was demeaning neither himself nor women. Likewise, the reference to his "womanish heart" in Henry's previous letter was intended to express the depths of his feelings, as nineteenth-century Americans believed that women had superior hearts, deeper feelings, greater warmth, and higher moral standing than did men. Henry meant that Tracy evoked his womanly side, his suppressed emotionality, which was inappropriate for a man to share in public, the true depth of his capacity to feel and to value another. He felt as much as he, as a man, was capable of feeling; indeed, it is possible, he wanted to say, that he felt even more. In return, he asked Tracy to assure him that Henry had done the right thing in selling his house, that "I have done wisely in taking this precautionary measure against the moth and rust which corrupt and the thieves which break through and steal the treasures of those who give themselves up to the service of the People."[56]

Henry caught grief from his wife, and possibly felt guilt for the plight of Lazette and her daughter, but he went ahead nonetheless with what he judged necessary financial measures to continue his political career. He wanted Tracy to know that he had sacrificed not only his wife's contentment but his own happiness in the name of public service.

> I am well satisfied of that and that the conviction is an abiding one, but just now I cannot avoid feeling rather blue when I think that my trees will yield their fruit and my honeysuckle, sweet briar, hyacinths, and polyanthus their sweets, and my hop vines and horehound beds their bitter to a stranger, especially when I reflect that the labor of my own hands was bestowed upon them to rear them for the gratification of a wife whose slumber was never disturbed by an ambitious dream and that she in meek and uncomplaining acquiescence resigns them all to the necessity caused by my indulgence of that sin for which angels fell.[57]

Henry was not without self-knowledge; ambition defined him. "I may as well say in plain English that I have sold out my domicile for $5,000 well secured, and am thrown back upon the enduring hospitality of our father Judge Miller, whose household I have always regretted on separation from it, and that this measure was adopted from consideration of prudence under the present circumstances as changed entirely from those in which I found myself a year ago with a flourishing practice and the hope of its continuance." The phrasing is cloudy, but the motivation is clear. The decision was financial and entirely Henry's with the acquiescence of his father-in-law. "That apprehension of all others most painful to me is the apprehension of being poor, and I know too well my want of prudence not to be fearful of being impoverished if I remain any length of time in political life." That consideration took precedence over all others. "It was therefore early determined after my election last fall to abridge private expense and I shall not grieve that in finding a purchaser for my establishment I have been able at once to bring down my expenses within the limits of my impaired income."[58]

Romantic theories about the Sewards' move back to 33 South Street notwithstanding, the reason for the return was not to please Frances nor to placate her father, although Elijah was undoubtedly glad to have his grandsons living with him and his daughter running the household. It is possible that Clary valued Frances's presence as a buffer between her, her brother, and mother until she could engineer her escape four years later. For all her complaints about Frances's mothering skills, Paulina was also grateful to have another woman in the house and to be relieved of homemaking responsibilities for the final four years of her life. Frances was ultimately grateful for the time she had with Paulina and Clary, but only in retrospect. The stress of the household wore her down.

The Sewards' return freed Henry from his law practice. He was less fond of living in his father-in-law's house with the tensions among the inmates and the complaints of his wife. Her infirmities also exhausted him. He was unwilling to take Lazette's side against her husband, so the move removed from him that responsibility too. Finally, and just as significantly, the return freed Henry, in body and mind, from living at home or being responsible for the house and grounds. Despite the paeans to gardening contained in his letter to Tracy, Henry abdicated direct responsibility for the gardens. Even after Clary moved out and Paulina and Elijah passed on, he had no desire to live at 33 South Street for more than a couple weeks at a time.

Whether Henry knew it in 1831, the return liberated him from much more than the expenses associated with owning a house. If we take his sister's and sister-in-law's testimony seriously, the move also freed Henry from family life. He loved his children, but more from afar when they were young and especially after they were grown and could serve his ambition rather than inhibit it. This was entirely consistent over his lifetime with views he had expressed prior to his marriage. His affection for family members did not stand in the way of his career. Frances did not get her way in 1831, a smaller house and garden that cost Henry less, one that she could better manage on her own, with fewer servants, a house that could be a refuge for Lazette and her daughter Frances. Instead, she was thrown back into her family with the burden of parenting and running a large household without the active presence and moral support of her husband. She did not know in 1831 what Henry wrote to Albert Tracy in May, when he confessed to "my indulgence of that sin for which angels fell." After only one session as a state senator, Henry was ready to launch a more ambitious political career than his wife ever suspected.

Chapter 5

And for Worse, 1832–1835

The friendship between Henry and Albert Tracy burned hotter through 1832, before threatening to engulf the Sewards' marriage. From then, the relationship between the two men chilled over the next two years, leaving Henry angry and Frances depressed. Frances was at first intrigued and suspicious, wondering whether, from what her husband and others said of him, Tracy could be trusted. Her instincts were on the mark, but she was seduced first by Henry's unbounded praise and then by Tracy, who revealed himself to be precisely the man against whom others had warned Frances's husband, one whose narcissism exceeded his ambition.

Henry was also wary at first, but he overcame his doubts about Tracy. In a letter to him of March 19, 1831, Henry testified to the "engrossing and absorbing affection for you which has swelled my heart since I unlearned the errors relating to you, disrupted my diffidence and found sympathy and congeniality in your feelings with all my disrupted and perhaps romantic joy-giving emotions. Besides yourselves I have found but two persons in a world who know or could understand me." During the break between legislative sessions, Henry wrote to Albert, "Perhaps you will smile at my conceit and say my very 'soul hath felt a fever of the mad' and my love for you would make me play 'some tricks of desperation,'" quoting Shakespeare's *Tempest.*[1]

"What more riches can a woman of feeling desire than the affections of such a man as you describe Tracy," Frances replied to Henry's enthusiasm during his first legislative session in Albany. She wrote to Lazette the following spring, "Henry told Tracy the other day that I was afraid of him [Tracy] and Tracy has been rallying [teasing] me about it ever since. I tell him it is actually the case, which he says is very silly. He is a singular being. I cannot tell you now what I do think of him. I believe at present that he could convince me that a chameleon was blue-green or black just as he should choose."[2]

Frances feared Tracy's power over her and Henry after a winter in Albany with them, Tracy's wife, and the Seward children. Thurlow Weed, the newspaper editor and Henry's political mentor, also distrusted Tracy, and Frances trusted Weed's instincts more than she did her own. "Weed has never come to see us," she wrote to Lazette from Albany in March 1832. "I am sorry for this, though I can hardly account for it." She eventually understood that Weed avoided Tracy's company while remaining discreet about his motives as long as Henry maintained his friendship with the man.[3]

To her sister, also in March 1832, Frances wrote, "Tracy has been in our room most of the day. He and Henry appear equally in love with each other." During the same month, Frances described Tracy to Lazette as "a singular being. I believe he has reasoned himself into a belief that he is not influenced by any of the impulses that actuate other people. Still, I do not think him vain. He certainly knows more than any man I ever was acquainted with, but I do not think I would have discovered this in a year of ordinary intercourse." It was only from living in Albany's Bement's Hotel during the legislative session that she got to know Tracy more intimately than she had any other man besides her husband and father. He felt free to stop by their rooms at any time of the day or night, sometimes after they were already asleep. Frances was surprised by how openly he talked to her and Henry about his wife when she was not in their company. On the one hand, Frances was intrigued; on the other, she saw his behavior as a breach of privacy and trust.[4]

Tracy also took liberties with Frances's children that she was powerless to resist. "The first thing he did after he came," she told her sister, "was to endeavor to persuade Augustus that St. Nicholas was an imaginary being. Little Gus don't exactly know what to think, as he can get no decided confirmation of his belief from his Pa; he has never applied to me." Less disturbing and more intriguing, "Tracy will talk to him

FIGURE 5.1. Painting of Augustus H. Seward as a child, by James Edward Freeman. Courtesy of Rare Books, Special Collections, and Preservation, River Campus Libraries, University of Rochester; original painting in Seward House Museum, Auburn, New York.

half an hour at a time with as much seriousness and very much in the same style he would to a man of 20." Gus was five at the time. Tracy was intense, focused, unlike any man she had ever known, even more charismatic than her husband. "Tracy's conversation reminds me of a book of synonyms," she told her sister in a letter that is more about him than about anything else. He hardly ever makes use of the same words to express ideas that have a shade of difference."[5]

Two weeks later, Frances shared with her sister again, "I am afraid of Tracy." She had gone shopping with Tracy and Henry, which made her nervous. "I put on my moccasins and Gus's great coat, warm as it was, because Uncle Tracy said I must." Later, "Tracy said I was a goose" for making a social engagement that she did not want to keep, "and I believe it to the letter." Frances was pleased when she awoke the next morning that "I found it raining 'vehemently,' to use Tracy's expression . . . so I shall have sufficient apology for staying at home. They [the two men] have teased me until I am quite nervous about it."[6]

In April 1832 Tracy "wrote me a short letter in one of Henry's. This you must wait until you can see. It is a kind of love letter." Henry apparently had no problem with that one, since Tracy wrote love letters to both of them. The Sewards continued to ride the wave that was Tracy, which Frances found thrilling and scary, an emotional tsunami for her. Henry was flattered, awed, in love, and Frances was frightened. She continued to extend "my love to the Tracys" in letters to her husband through 1832. "Please remember me to all our friends," she wrote to Henry, "to Weed particularly and above all to Tracy." In June she wrote to her husband's sister Cornelia that "his and Henry's friendship has not yet lost anything in fervor. To me, he realizes some of the imaginings I have often had of the love I should feel for a brother." "Tell Tracy," she wrote to Henry, "that he knows that I love him very much without my writing it down in a letter. Therefore, I shall do nothing of the kind."[7]

In November 1832 Frances was still resisting Tracy's insistence that she write him love letters in return, but what was his goal? He stopped by their rooms in Albany and their home in Auburn when Henry was not there. Frances, perhaps naively, thought that Tracy had inadvertently missed her husband.[8]

Tracy's best opening to meddle in the Sewards' marriage came when Henry left on short notice for an extended trip with his father. Shortly after the session ended in April 1833, Henry responded to the news that his parents were desperately ill, arriving in Orange County to find his father convalescing and his mother still in danger. "I rode out this morning," he reported to Frances, "and all along the road, at almost every house, some person came out to inquire concerning her. There is not one who does not love her; and in all this region there is none whose death can, in his caprice, select as a victim whose removal would excite so deep and general concern." According to Henry, as soon as she recovered, his father was eager to travel to Europe with his son.[9]

The two men sailed on the Liverpool packet, which took both Tracy and Frances by surprise when Henry had confirmed the plans one week earlier. As Henry later described the decision, "my father, at the age of sixty-five, although retaining all his intellectual vigor and much of his characteristic energy, had become a valetudinarian, and determined on a summer voyage to Europe. I cheerfully attended him, at his request. We sailed from New York on the 1st of June." Unlike Henry's subsequent journey to Europe and the Middle East, which is addressed in chapters 16 and 17, on this one Henry wrote letters that could have been cribbed from tourist guides and do not reflect on himself or his family.[10]

The correspondence that Frances considered "inappropriate" between her and Tracy began over the summer of 1833 while Henry was away, but the first surviving clue is in a letter from Frances to Lazette on September 9, when Frances wrote, "I found a long letter from Tracy on my table," but she did not have much to say about its contents, which was unusual for her. On September 27 she wrote again to tell Lazette that "yesterday while I was eating my dinner, Pa announced that there was a letter from 'Seward' upstairs." When she left the table to retrieve it, Frances also found one on the mantle from Tracy. "'Who is that letter from,' said Pa. 'From Tracy.' 'Let me see it.' I handed it to him and he very deliberately commenced breaking the seal for the purpose of reading it." Frances did not stand idly by while her father invaded her privacy. "My first impulse was to jump up and snatch the letter from his hand, which I did, and then apologized by saying I would prefer reading it myself first. He appeared very much astonished that I should be so unreasonable and said he did not suppose there was anything he ought not to see. I replied I presumed there was not but still insisted that I would rather have the first reading."[11]

How unlike Frances; no wonder Elijah was stunned. His suspicion was correct; she feared what he might see in that letter. Although Frances presented herself as the victim of her father's entitlement, his breach of etiquette while she was reading another letter simply reflected his usual impatience, as they either passed the letters around or read them out loud. Frances revealed guilt in her letter to Lazette, while trying to hide even from her sister the nature of a correspondence that she knew to be wrong.

On November 17 Frances wrote to Lazette that Henry was home from his trip and Tracy was also in Auburn to accompany him back to Albany for the start of the next legislative session. "Wednesday morning, we heard of Tracy's defeat in the election and the same day about noon I was called for and found Tracy himself seated upon the sofa in the front room. I was very glad to see him as I love him very much. He spent the remainder of the day with us. Henry will be on his way to Albany for the winter, having been at home nine days after an absence of nearly six months . . . and will [be] very much alone there when Tracy's time expires."[12]

After Frances and the boys settled into the Sewards' Bement's Hotel rooms in December, Tracy continued to take the liberties that were unusual for someone outside the immediate family circle. He sat with her as she combed her hair and dressed; he spent the evening with her when Henry went down to a tea to which they were also invited. She came home from church accompanied by Tracy, while Henry went calling. "I put on my hat and cloak the other day determined to go out" on a call to a sick friend, "but Tracy came in and opposed it so strongly that I could not." Again, Tracy accompanied Frances home from church, while Henry went his way and Harriet went hers.[13]

Over the winter 1833–34 in Albany, Frances confessed tearfully to Henry that she had exchanged scandalous love letters with Tracy while Henry was in Europe, which we know from a letter of Henry's to her later that year. She offered her husband the ones from Tracy, which he took from her hand and threw into the fire unread. In a December 1834 farewell letter to Tracy, Henry revealed that their friendship had foundered, not on the shoals of Henry's jealousy of Tracy's political skills, as Tracy had theorized, but on Tracy's betrayal. "But you will recollect," Henry wrote, "that this alienation on my part took place about a year ago," so in December 1833, shortly after he returned from the trip with his father. "And I shall now state its cause. It was that availing yourself of the relation existing between us, you did with or without premeditated purpose what as a man of honor you ought not to have done, pursue a course of conduct which but for the virtue and fineness of the being dearest to me would have destroyed if not her honor, her happiness and that of my children."[14]

Henry portrayed himself as too trusting of Tracy—"I refused to credit the evidences." "Can such a dishonorable [man] know that I burned without reading the letters which alarmed its [recipient?] and which she put [into my hands?] that I might determine whether you were not endeavoring to ruin complete peace." He had ignored the signs in the name of friendship. "I bore without [complaint?] that which I thought proceeded from weakness not criminal purpose and was content to see myself and my wife deprived of the friendship of yours lest I might bring into your family the evils you were bringing into mine."[15]

In true Victorian fashion, Henry decided to shield Harriet from the humiliation of public exposure, which, of course, could also injure Frances's reputation and Henry's political career. "I knew that you had failed to do me the injury you recklessly contemplated," Henry wrote to Tracy, but that was due to Frances's virtue rather than Tracy's intent. "How could I express my indignation without compromising the fair favor of one whose honor was, God be praised, unsullied and whose heart was pure. Thenceforth, Tracy, you lost that magic influence you once possessed over me." The knowledge of Tracy's "crime" came before Henry's run for governor, but while he pursued such a goal.[16]

Henry was jealous, hurt, and angry, and he blamed himself for abandoning his wife. He was inattentive in the best of times, and he left her alone with her dysfunctional family for weeks and months at a time. He also indulged his own lust for travel and his father's demands for a journey to Europe without consideration of her and his sons. He knew this was inappropriate behavior for a husband and father, but he took Frances for granted and believed her responsible for single-handedly raising the boys.

Over the summer of 1834, ignorant of the Sewards' marital trauma, Weed decided that Henry was the Anti-Masonic Party's best candidate for governor even though they did not stand a chance in the fall. He also reasoned that the nomination would advance rather than scuttle Henry's political career. The pressure on Henry from Weed and other party leaders increased during July and into August, when a combination of what Henry described to Frances as "vanity" and duty led him to agree to take one for the party in the middle of a cholera epidemic that engulfed Albany as well as New York City. The party convention, which nominated its candidates, met in Syracuse in late September, and Henry claimed to continue to hope that party leaders would change their minds before then about nominating him. In the meantime, he returned home, arriving on September 18, while Frances and the boys were in Aurora visiting Lazette in her new home. According to Henry, the *New York Times* reported that the party's nominee "is 26, has red hair, and a long nose." The last week of September, the Sewards were all in Auburn.[17]

After the convention nominated Henry, members descended on Judge Miller's home to congratulate the candidate. Frances reported to her sister that there must have been sixty carriages parked outside their house at one time and the next day she had six dozen wine glasses to wash. Eventually, after overflowing the parlors and hallways, the legion reconvened in the Episcopal church for speeches. "I told Henry that he had had glory enough if he did not get elected." The day after the delegates passed through Auburn on their way home, the party leaders arrived for consultations. "I do not think there was ever more enthusiasm manifested about a cause and a candidate," Frances reported to Lazette.[18]

In 1834 the relationship between Tracy and Henry fractured as Henry simply cooled to Tracy during the campaign and Tracy's enmity heated up. Finally, in November 1834, after the election had ended with Henry's defeat, with the two men in Albany for the end of the legislative session and Frances in Auburn with the boys, the tension came to a head. Weed finally exposed Tracy's political betrayal of Henry in a way that made it impossible for Henry to deny the public, if not the private, reality any longer. In the evening, following an afternoon of tension in Henry's room, in which "Weed ill-concealed a spirit of personal unkindness, which Tracy laboriously affected not to perceive," Tracy left in a huff about the rest of them becoming Whigs, which they were and Tracy was too. Their Anti-Masonic Party, the first of America's third parties, was dissolving. Its reform platform was too narrowly framed as an anti-elite, pro-Christian alternative to Andrew Jackson's Democrats and John Quincy Adams's National Republicans. In New York the Anti-Masons had replaced the National Republicans as an alternative to the Democrats in state politics, and their transition to Whigs was as yet incomplete. Henry asked Weed for "an explanation of Tracy's [political] course from last January to this time," which Weed gave and "in unmeasured language alleged that T. had been most anxious for my defeat" first for the nomination and then in the general election for governor.[19]

On October 29 Harriet gave birth to the Tracys' only child after nine years of marriage. It was a difficult delivery that left her invalided for a time. Why, Henry and Weed wondered, was Tracy himself not happier about this blessing? He struck them as "both exceedingly selfish and miserable." Perhaps it was jealousy over Henry's rise among the Anti-Masons and his promise now as a candidate for higher office. Possibly the unhappiness derived more from private than public affairs. Nonetheless, Henry persisted in his unexplained public coolness to Tracy, while Frances wallowed privately in her guilt.[20]

"Why," Frances asked, "was Tracy so depressed?" Henry had told her that Harriet was "overjoyed by the fortunate possession of a treasure, which, when she thought it could never be obtained, was despised." Frances wrote to Henry at the end of November that Tracy "has a new and bright tie to bind him to the world. It is strange that he should seem dissatisfied but you will say that this is a woman's reasoning and I admit that I am not very profoundly skilled in the science of metaphysics." Tracy served another two terms (four years) in the state senate. Frances asked Henry to "tell Tracy he must persuade Aunty to come home this way next spring that I may see that boy of theirs." Frances was downright chirpy, with Henry's long-hoped-for return home now imminent and what she assumed was his retirement from public life. She did not want to be selfish, knowing that Henry and his party were disappointed, "but I do find the quiet of home so comfortable, so necessary to me in my infirm states of health that I cannot feel otherwise than happy when I think of myself alone." This was the first time, but would not be the last, that Frances was ebullient at Henry's political defeat.[21]

In the wake of his election loss and the aftermath of Tracy's threat to his marriage, Henry claimed to have an epiphany about family life. On November 28 he wrote to Frances that he had seen the light. He had made calls in Albany, had gone to the theater with a friend and saw Fanny Kemble, the famed British actress, in one of her last performances before she married and retired from the stage for over a decade. Henry was also brushing up on the law, anticipating his return to a more robust and eclectic practice. He continued the letter daily over the weekend in much the same mood, before the breakthrough of insight that he reported to his wife on Monday, December 1. He delayed sending the letter because over the previous two days he slowly awoke "from a long, a feverish, and almost fatal dream, fatal to my love and mine, and your happiness. Even yet my mind is bewildered and my heart convulsed. It is now that I know the truth of what you have so often and with bitter tears doubted and I with cruel and unfeeling recklessness have censured you for doubting, that unworthy as I am I still love you."[22]

These are the testimonies of love for which Frances had waited for almost a decade, since she thought and then came to doubt that she had married her Mr. Knightley and still dreamed she would live in a Romantic comedy rather than a Gothic tragedy, which had, thus far, more closely approximated her life. Henry now knew that he had risked all in his selfish ambition. "How much suffering have I caused you, which can never be atoned for," he confessed dramatically. "What a demon is ambition," but he had now experienced "my deliverance from the idolatry of fame." Henry now glimpsed, after his loss in the election, what he thought should have been obvious if he had bothered to look.[23]

A lot of water had passed under the Sewards' marital bridge over the previous two months, but details are lost to us because the blowups occurred in person and went unreported in surviving correspondence until early December 1834. "I shudder now to retrace the past," Henry confessed in writing then. "Besides cruel neglect which has scarcely ever been omitted two consecutive days memory (conscience!) suggests so many prominent instances of unkindness. That night scarce two months ago," Henry recalled, so around October 1, "I upbraided you coarsely and with severe invective for unworthy deception followed as it was by the fearful illness which threatened to tear you from me forever. How has the memory of that night tormented me!"[24]

Among the charges Henry had laid against Frances, after her return from a visit to Lazette, was the one that had long divided them. "I have thought you the spoiled child of romance, for dreaming that love could be preserved amid the complicated employments and passions of life." He had "turned from you with pity for your feminine weakness, when you reminded me 'this is the anniversary of our marriage,' and 'do you remember loved one this is the birthday of our first born.'" Gus's birthday was October 1 and their wedding anniversary was October 20, so Henry's disregard for the dates elicited two reminders from Frances within three weeks, and triggered arguments during his campaign for governor.[25]

There was more that Henry now regretted. "I have looked with pity upon the struggles of your heart for an interest in the atonement made by our redeemer for the sins of all the human race." He "proudly despised and turned a deaf ear [to] solicitations of the spirit of Truth even when in his last effort to win my stubborn heart he appealed by your once-loved voice." He had bluntly charged her with being naive, for expecting him to bring higher Truth into the real world of politics. This argument was not over, and neither ever capitulated, but a round in their debate of the practical versus the True had ended with Henry expressing some humility on this score. In conclusion, "I have yielded to the belief that it was magnanimous in me to suffer you to cling to the fables which could afford you comfort and happiness far inferior as I thought to those which I sought in the glory of the world and your uncongenial spirit could not enjoy with me." He had rejected her principles and mocked her beliefs privately, even ridiculed them to her face.[26]

Henry called himself a fool, a man who should have known better than to waste "time, and heart, and happiness. And, I have now awaked from my delusion with fears that it is too late to win back to me the love I have despised." He did not deserve Frances, having "banished you from my heart." Henry said that he deserved what he had gotten, "when the wretched T. took advantage of my madness and offered sympathies, and feelings and love such as I had sworn, and your expelled heart was half won by his falsehoods. Still I did not know and see that

I was criminal." Tracy wrote Frances the love letters that Henry knew he should have written, sentiments that validated her feelings, showed her that which Henry claimed was impossible for a man who was not a character in an Austen or Scott novel. "The alienation which my feelings towards him have suffered was mainly wrought by his base conduct towards us last winter." Tracy was a cad, duplicitous to his bones, a traitor to friendship and requited love. Henry was taking half the blame and declaring Frances all but blameless, hoping that she would rally from the illness brought on by guilt and nerves, and give her husband another chance to redeem himself. "I have had time to reflect upon the values of that treasure I possess," Henry concluded his very long letter, and "repent of the wrongs and injustice I have done to you. Loved, injured and angel spirit, receive this homage of my first return to reason and truth, say to me that understanding my own feelings yours are not crushed."[27]

Frances believed that Henry was retiring from politics to become a lawyer and family man, because he told her he was and she hoped it was true. He was contrite; losing an election and the threat to the affections of his wife were blows to his confidence. But he hated practicing law, as he had explained in the past and repeated in the future, and he was little fonder of living in Judge Miller's house, with his wife's ill health and the household's tumult, which is not to say he was insincere in the moment. He thought he should have seen his comeuppance coming. His compatriots saw the election loss looming. Everyone predicted his defeat and thought the better of Henry for sacrificing himself to a losing cause. The epistolary romance between Tracy and Frances blindsided him, as did Frances's near-death illness. His public confidence was private arrogance, which he recognized. His mockery of fixed principles and the application of a higher law to politics were only privately shared, but he was second-guessing himself even there.

Henry's actions revealed his intentions; Frances's hopes are in her letters. If he planned to practice law in Auburn, the Sewards could move out of Judge Miller's house; if he intended to be away most of the time, they could stay to assure his wife's safety, what Henry perceived as a lesser burden on her for housekeeping and childcare, and lower expenses to him with a fixed rent that was a fraction of the actual cost of maintaining a household. In the short term, as 1834 ended with Clary packing up and 1835 began with Frances ill, the future was cloudy. Frances was hopeful, guilt-ridden, ill, and depressed. Henry apparently believed it when he wrote to Frances in December from Albany, "I mean to live for you and the boys." In the same month he wrote more fully on his enlightenment. "I am all solicitude my dearest to adopt some system of life which will enable me to be what I have never I fear been, a partner in your thoughts and cares and feelings; to have my place at the fireside in the evenings and devote the time to employments and thoughts and conversation congenial to your taste." This is exactly what Frances wanted to hear. "I would submit myself to the influence of your gentle and domestic spirit. I am grieved when I think that I am doomed to be a wanderer farther and farther from the source and foundation of what ought to be my truest happiness. I feel now determined to make the experiment."[28]

What a reversal of priorities, of lifestyle, of values, even of beliefs that "experiment" would be for Henry. He wrote that he was even praying before bed and contemplating whether to become a Christian, in fact rather than just in public form, aligning himself more closely to Frances's morals rather than mocking her desire to apply a higher law to politics. "Good night. I have learned not to retire without a select prayer to the great Being I have so long neglected." He attended church in Albany and listened to a "powerful sermon" that he did not feel compelled to argue against. "I felt happy, very happy, that for once my bias was with the preacher in this argument and I felt not the least desire to controvert a proposition so important to be believed." He was prepared to accept the Truth of biblical prophecies. "Heaven only knows whether I can become a Christian," he wrote on December 8. Only "your love can be my guide, my support, in producing the state of mind and feeling proper for asking that grace which is indispensable to the first step." He just prayed that all this was not too late for her, for him, and for the boys. "Does that love continue strong enough to undertake the task, and to preserve it. I feel the necessity for its aid. I feel at this moment, as I have all along, that if this important change is to be wrought in my heart, I shall, I must, in a humble and not irreverent sense owe it to you."[29]

Frances was overjoyed by Henry's incipient redemption, by his resolutions about family life and turning to God. She focused, as was her higher ambition, on the welcome news about Henry's soul, but she was ecstatic about the "experiment" she now hoped to undertake with her mate. "If you can give me the love for which my heart has so often yearned, if you will not resist or neglect the kindly influence of <u>this</u> spirit, if you will consent to make the praise and honour of erring mortals but a secondary object of ambition, I trust we may yet be more happy than in the earliest and brightest days of our union," she wrote to him on December 5. Contrary to Henry's previous charges, though, Frances was not naive; Henry's commitment to God and family might pass before he reached home. "I am impatient to hear from you again and hope with trembling that your feelings remain the same as when you last wrote." She waited, as always, hoped, prayed, but worried for another four weeks, as Henry completed the legislative session, argued his cases in court, visited his parents, attended to business in New York City, attended holiday celebrations, and *then* came home.[30]

Frances's illness was her second miscarriage, which the early Victorians only discussed indirectly. "That your health is convalescent is my hope," Henry wrote on December 1, "but you must not suppose [I am] at all chiding you for not being well. I trust never again to give you cause for sorrow as I have done heretofore in that way." The acceptance of blame and the swearing off of the behavior (sex) that caused her "illness" adopt the same pose that the letter from their sister-in-law Marcia did toward Frances's first miscarriage. Henry, knowing Frances's frailty, had failed to "take care of her . . . in that way," which would have safeguarded her health. There was also a "dreadful local inflammation," which persisted two months after the onset of the "illness." Even today, miscarriages sometimes result in vaginal infections, but there are antibiotics to address them and so they less often lead to life-threatening sepsis than they did in Frances's day. Henry apologized for being an unworthy husband who was to blame for his wife's "illness." He thought marital conflict triggered the loss, which came after he "upbraided you coarsely and with severe invective." Frances was sad and Henry regretted "the fearful illness which threatened to tear you from me forever."[31]

Through it all, Frances forgave him and did her best to deserve such a husband as Henry. "I will endeavor to make myself worthy [of] such love," she wrote to him on December 14. She intended to help him "become a Christian in such a world as this," knowing it would take more than his usual approach of "reflection and reason" to find the path to God. She also recommitted to making their home a place he wanted to live. "I have been devising a thousand plans to make home attractive to you and to make it more convenient for you to be with me. I have at length decided upon one which if it meets your approbation I think will be just right. We will talk it all over when you come home."[32]

Despite the best intentions of Frances and Henry, and notwithstanding Frances's efforts in support of the marriage, the experiment failed. Despite Henry's stated intentions, he did not make it home for the holidays. A week after Christmas with no Henry and no letter from him, Frances called the backsliding to his attention. "My Dear Henry, I am too much depressed by your unaccountable silence to write much." The world had again gotten in the way of Henry's connections to home and family. "You must have returned from New York no later than Wednesday," which was Christmas Day, "and might have written since that time (and your letter would have reached me) had you been well. You have always been so unvaryingly kind about writing that you see I am determined to believe you have been prevented by nothing but illness." Henry was just fine, simply preoccupied with business and other people's celebrations, ones that she would not have enjoyed as he did.[33]

Eventually, Henry replied. "You sent me wishes which belonged to Christmas," he wrote from Albany in a letter he started on Sunday but was still writing on Wednesday, the last day of 1834. "Accept my wishes that you may have commenced a happy new year, happy it may be if your health returns, and Providence be no less severe in its violations than it has been in the last year." Part of the reason for his serial absences from home over the holidays was professional—the courts and the legislature had kept him away—but he acknowledged that it was also avoidance behavior by him. "I have read and re-perceived many times your beautiful letter written to me on Christmas day," about church, the boys, their stockings, and their toys. "To me, it was not such a day as you described it, for I had not learned to regard it as a day in which I had a peculiar interest from its association with the origin of the Christian religion. But it did find me in some respects feeling very differently from what I did on preceding anniversaries. It found me as I trust willing and in some small degree desirous to be a Christian." "In some small degree?" Frances's fears were coming true; Henry's resolutions were slipping away.[34]

Henry no longer gave Frances a date for his expected arrival, having gotten her hopes up and then shattered them with his failures to meet the several dates he had already missed. This only increased her anxiety, since she always feared illness or accidents that might have waylaid him. She now thought he would arrive home sometime during the coming week, but she expected no certain answer or any further excuses. She still hoped, encouraged by his letter, that he was coming home and would stay once he got there. "I think you must feel relieved to be once more in Albany, which is quiet in comparison with New York. I feel more and more sensibly every day my incapacity for a life of dissipation and every day am better satisfied with the prospect of living in comparative retirement." In other words, if he declined to retire from politics for himself, she hoped he might still do it for her.[35]

Frances wrote to Henry again on January 2: "I will wish you a 'happy New Year,' although the 1st has passed by," and posted it to Albany the next morning. She had received the many New Year's Day calls, which began in the morning and lasted all day, mainly from men who had hoped to greet Henry, "and when night came I was very much fatigued." Lazette had arrived on New Year's Eve to be with her. Lazette and Clary enjoyed the day, before attending a ball that evening. "I was not quite well enough to enter into the spirit of the times," Frances wrote; nonetheless, she was expecting a number of women to tea.[36]

Henry's father, at least, expected a letter sent to Auburn on January 4 to reach him there. Samuel and Mary had been concerned for Frances's life, so they were heartened to learn that Henry, from Albany on December 28, believed she slowly recovered. Still, Samuel urged Henry "to be unremitting in your kind attentions and assiduity for her restoration to health. Remember us most kindly to her. Tell her we sympathize with her in her past affliction and earnestly wish for her speedy recovery." Henry still had to go home to do that. Samuel was proud of his son, who had received the votes of "an unquestionable majority of the un-collared," working-class voters, in the election for governor. "Duplicity" and "corruption" had won the day in "our misguided country." As usual, Samuel concluded a letter by reference to his own declining health and the short span of life left to him. He actually lived for another fourteen years.[37]

When Henry finally reached home in early January, Harriet Weed, Thurlow's sixteen-year-old daughter, accompanied him to help care for Frances and the boys through the end of the winter, freeing Henry to return to the practice of law. When Henry wrote to Harriet's father, to inform him of their safe arrival in Auburn, his resolutions appeared firm. "I am once more, thank God, and I hope for a long time, at home; really, I was so weary of the unprofitable life I was leading at Albany, that I was unable to regret, as I otherwise must have done, that the time had come when a termination must be set to our long, confidential, and intimate association." And yet, by January 18, Henry was already exhausted and frustrated by the practice of law. "An entire week has passed," he wrote Weed, "and I have found no leisure. All this would be comfortable enough if I were pleased with my employment. But I do not find that certainty in the results of long and painful investigation which compensates one for the trouble."[38]

Samuel wrote again to Henry on January 24, having still not heard of his son's safe arrival home or received a report on Frances's health. As a physician and family patriarch he expected to be informed, if not consulted. Rachel, Polydore's wife, wrote in early March that she was sorry to hear her sister-in-law's health remained "delicate." In March Samuel said he was distressed to learn that "after the marriage of A[unt] Clara the cares and business of the family devolved on her [Frances]. My dear children, this ought not to be. It will never do. Feeble and diseased as she is, the least exercise or stretch of mind is calculated to debilitate and throw her back. At whatever expense it may be, it is your duty to provide suitable persons to take charge of the house. You seem impressed with a belief that travelling will be beneficial. This, under any circumstances of your business, ought to be attended to."[39]

On March 11 Henry confided to Weed that given the distresses of home life, which he had now endured for about two months, "I am reckoning upon a visit of a week at Albany with as much pleasure as a child looks forward to the vacation." No longer could there be doubt in anyone's mind that Henry fled family life rather than surrendering to drafts from his party and constituents. He explained the situation at home more fully to Weed than he did to his other correspondents in and outside the family. "Mrs. S. has been until yesterday in very ill health, which continued ten days. She suffers under a complication of maladies, which waste her strength and resolution." Ever the optimist, Henry was hopeful. "I rejoice above measure that the spring is advancing, for I could have little hope that she would be able to go through another long, cold season like the last three months. If she can so far discipline her mind and feelings as to banish apprehension concerning her little boys, I have much confidence that she will derive great benefit from the proposed journey." And yet, he had neither hurried home nor kept his commitments to an "experiment" that involved him.[40]

Frances had fallen into a deep depression in her husband's absence over the holidays, what her sister-in-law Rachel called in herself "nothing but anxiety of the mind." Rachel also feared for her children's lives in the face of endemic scarlet fever. Henry meant to get Frances away from the children, which he diagnosed as the cause of her anxiety. He did not ascribe to himself any role in Frances's decline, but her elevated hopes for Henry's redemption and retirement from public life were dashed by his avoidance of home over the holidays. It is difficult to unravel the physical from the psychological symptoms, the role of postpartum hormonal causes from what they diagnosed as a "nervous" condition. Frances endured an intermittent fever, perhaps related to the vaginal infection she contracted in the autumn. It prostrated her again from mid-March through the first week of April. On April 7, eight-year-old Gus wrote to his cousin Frances that "Ma is still sick in bed. It rains so that she cannot go out to ride." On April 11, Jennings wrote to invite his brother to bring Frances to New York City, where his wife Marcia would "do all in her power to sooth her trials and relieve her pains."[41]

The Sewards were not a compatible couple, which became more apparent to them over time. Henry spoke of his "dissipation" and sometimes even guilt about his enjoyment of socializing without Frances. In a letter to Lazette, Frances referred to what was still an ongoing conversation between the sisters about their comparative sociability, which was relevant to tensions in the Sewards' marriage. Before they were married, Lazette had described Frances as a social butterfly, more popular than she could ever be. In 1834 the sisters still had not resolved their different perspectives. Frances was "very glad to hear you are alone and well pleased to be so. I have no fear of your becoming a misanthrope in as much as I make my own feelings a standard. I cannot remember the time when I did not feel more happy alone than with company that was indifferent to me and I always find it extremely irksome to make myself agreeable to people of that description more than half an hour at a time." On the other hand, in Frances's view, "the case is different with you. You <u>can</u> talk and love to talk much better than myself. With me, conversation is always an effort, when I am not talking to people who interest me, and, unfortunately, those who do not often come in my way. Now dearest, if you are not satisfied that I am the greater misanthrope of the two, I shall not try to convince you."[42]

When Henry was in Auburn, he was bored and beleaguered among family members. He sought out company; Frances avoided it, preferring family, neighbors, and friends over strangers. When Frances entertained guests, she got headaches. Lots of people were Henry's "friends." He was enthralled by the theater; she preferred her bedroom with a good book. The dinners and parties energized Henry, while they drained Frances of her last ounce of strength, the fate of classic extroverts versus introverts. He enjoyed what he called "dissipation." She understood the word in its heavily pejorative sense, as by definition a waste of time and energy. She continued to judge his social life and he judged hers. They were never on the same page.

The wonder is that Henry ever thought his "experiment" in family life could work for him. That impulse passed quickly and he did not endure a full season at home. He simply abhorred home, while loving his wife and children, and needed a "vacation" from them after several weeks in the South Street house. He found solace in flight. No wonder Henry suggested a trip to cure Frances's depression; in all good conscience, he knew that is what would help him if he were depressed. Henry had explained four years earlier in a letter to Tracy, who was ill at the time, that "travelling would cure me (if any remedy exists) of all the ills that flesh [is] heir to. . . . When I travel, I banish care and thought and reflection." Frances, on the other hand, preferred to stay home with her husband and boys, and she ruminated.[43]

Once Henry had time "to regulate my affairs," by which he meant practice law rather than attend another legislative session, he found his finances "somewhat more prosperous than I supposed." This meant that he could take his doctor-father's advice and travel with Frances "in a style somewhat more comfortable than I thought I would be able to command." He worked hard and found legal practice unpleasant, "floundering on from Monday's sunrise until Saturday's expiring hour," and "prostrate" on Sundays with exhaustion, so not spending much time with his family in any event, but Frances was grateful that he was living at home. Nonetheless, he still claimed in mid-March that he was done with politics. He wrote to Weed, "You talk about building more political cob houses with me. Pardon me. I have exhausted the entire interest of the game. No inducement would now prevail upon me to be at present reinstated in the Senate! I am happy in being out with the consciousness that I got honorably out!" But what about another, higher, office?[44]

In light of his eventual return to politics, a reader might find that Henry protested too much. He certainly was not burning any bridges, pleading with Weed in the absence of a letter in over two weeks, "Don't for heaven's sake cast me off. When I <u>see</u> you, you will be sorry for it." His correspondence with Weed was mostly extended dissections of state and national politics with some of the Sewards' most intimate domestic news included. For now, though, Henry "worked like the Devil. But I am cheerful and yet in health." At the end of March, "Mrs. S. has now been a fortnight confined to her chamber and principally to her room. I am at the office from 8 AM to 11 PM." Harriet Weed read to Frances, engaging her in "unaffected conversation" and filling "the important place at the table which Mrs. S. has left vacant."[45]

At the end of March, Henry was no longer fixed on taking Frances on a long carriage ride, as he had thought two weeks previously, but he was still determined to separate her from the boys. To Weed he wrote, "I am all uncertain yet where to go with Mrs. S. I have written to Dr. Williams, giving him a full account of her symptoms and the history of her long illness, and requested him to consult with Dr. McNaughton and give me their joint advice. If a voyage to Europe should be advised, I am determined to go. I cannot without remorse see her strength wasted by her protracted disease while a hope remains that health may be found on the globe." Charles Platt Williams and James McNaughton, a Scottish immigrant trained at the College of Physicians in Edinburgh, were prominent physicians practicing in Albany. Williams replied in a letter of April 12, 1835, and recommended a slow and careful increase in activity, first by walking and then by riding in a coach. If this "cautious" approach resulted in no pain to Frances's "hips and loins," she could safely embark on a trip, perhaps to the ocean where "sea bathing is generally a safe and good remedy for muscular debility and if the marine atmosphere should not disagree with her lungs it would impart strength to her whole system. The cutaneous absorbent vessels are soon invigorated by sea bathing."[46]

In mid-April Henry was still undecided about where, not whether, to take Frances on a long journey, but he was not considering a simple trip to the seashore as Dr. Williams advised, which Henry would find boring. Rather, Henry had in mind a more ambitious journey that interested him, promoted his renewed political ambitions, and supported his wife's fragile health. He had hoped that the physicians he consulted would support his argument for a much longer journey, possibly a yearlong European tour, but he was disappointed by Williams's medical advice. "Mrs. S. and I are yet undecided concerning our summer's journey. My mind inclines if she can endure the voyage to a trip up the Mediterranean and Levant. Her sister protests, and we are without medical advice. It would in my judgement be the surest means of recovering her health, provided she should spend the next winter in Italy, but to make a voyage to Europe requires the assent of all one's friends." Again, by "friends" he meant family, and the Millers were united against the couple spending a year abroad, likely because they saw Henry's idea as impractical, selfish, counterproductive to restoring Frances's health, and a huge burden on them to care for the Sewards' two sons.[47]

As usual, Lazette, who was the only one among the Millers named in Henry's letter, was outspoken about her views. Paulina protested when

Frances left her children for an afternoon. Clary had just made her escape from the household, and such an arrangement would scuttle her plans for independence. Judge Miller could hardly entertain Clary and Frances leaving 33 South Street at the same time, and he remained on the outs with Lazette. His mother was no longer of any use in caring for him but required someone to care for *her*. Who would care for Paulina in Frances's absence? Henry did not say, but what was Frances's view? Such a trip was more likely to exacerbate rather than relieve her anxiety about the boys at a time when scarlet fever and cholera stalked the state. No one suggested a long ride with both of the boys cooped up in a carriage as potentially restorative for anyone's health. Henry was mistaken if he thought there was a chance that the family would indulge his dream for another transatlantic journey with Frances's health as the excuse. "Frances and I are undecided," he wrote to Weed; no way. The Millers had ganged up against Henry; he had united the fractured family, and they told him that the idea of a yearlong cruise was a personal indulgence rather than an attempt to save Frances's life.

By April 12 Henry gained confidence that the winter of their discontents had passed. He wrote to Weed that he was enjoying gardening now that spring had arrived. "I watch the development of vegetation with a lover's interest. I have my hotbed in delightful success, my cucumbers are commencing their ramblings, the radishes begin to gather roughness upon the leaf, the sap starts from my grapes, and the polyanthus is in full blossom." Yet he had hoped to be abroad when the harvest came and most of the flowers bloomed. "To add to these pleasures, my dear F. begins to revive in health and cheerfulness." Frances was now reading Boswell's *Life of Samuel Johnson* and took a carriage ride daily. A week later, Henry thought she was still improving despite the "sour weather of the past week"; nonetheless, he estimated to Weed that Frances would not be fit for travel until at least the middle of May, after he argued cases in the Circuit Court and Court of Chancery.[48]

Without Frances writing letters from the depths of her despair, her voice is silent for more than four months after January 2, 1835, and we have precious few letters of hers for the rest of the year. Henry settled on a journey by carriage, with William Johnson as their driver, a twenty-nine-year-old African American man who made his living driving and caring for horses in Auburn. When he wrote about the trip as an adult, Fred made no mention of the reason for the journey, but he remembered the names of the horses, Lion and The Doctor, and that his parents packed lightly. "What little luggage was necessary was carefully stored in the boxes under the seats. A stout fishing-rod, and a few ropes and straps in case of accident, packed in front, and a tin cup and a pail hanging behind, for use at the roadside streams, completed the equipage for the journey, which commenced on the 23d of May," Fred wrote from memory.[49]

Henry explained that "when the time arrived, her heart was not set upon the journey, and I shrunk back from the confident anticipation I had indulged in relative to its effects upon her health." It began under the shadow of "melancholy forebodings and their sadness was increased by her solicitude about Augustus, whom she was leaving for the first time." This was a compromise, traveling with one child rather than two after the four of them rode for two days together—the best accommodation Frances would make to Henry's plans. After that, Frances still had Fred, who was a couple months shy of his fifth birthday, so Henry had lost two arguments: one about a voyage to Europe and the other about how essential it was to Frances's health that she (and he) get away from the children, whom he thought responsible for her anxiety of the mind. Henry insisted that Frances's family keep Gus because he "did not feel willing to carry back my dear wife to her friends [family] and say she was thenceforth to languish, no hope of relief but such as might be miraculously vouchsafed without exertion."[50]

When the Sewards departed, Frances began a journal of the trip in a book that Henry had used to keep track of his correspondence in the three weeks after the election, when he wrote on the order of one hundred letters, mainly to political supporters. "Left home May 23, 1835, sick and weary," she wrote, "lighter at heart than I should have been had I left my boys behind." It would be almost three months before they were back in Auburn, after a journey south as far as Virginia and then back north up the coast to the New Jersey beach before heading northwest toward home.[51]

The first night in Seneca Falls was a rough one for Frances: "no sleep until morning, nervous and restless, having talked for three hours before retiring." The journey was not, at least so far, recuperative; socializing did not restore her. "Boys slept on the floor by my side, which contributed much to my comfort. Augustus rolled from the bed to the floor 8 times according to his own account. Rose in the morning at 7 o'clock unrefreshed." Then they were off to Aurora, where they arrived at 2:00 p.m. and stayed "until 10 next morning, had a delightful visit, went away with a heavy heart. Left my dear A. crying, half repented undertaking the journey." The "delightful visit" was with Lazette, who accompanied eight-year-old Gus back to Auburn, where household staff and the Miller family cared for him until the Sewards returned.[52]

The three remaining Sewards and William, their driver, were then onto Ludlowville and Ithaca, where Frances reported herself "weary and dispirited, heart yearning for the company of my dear boy. Reproached myself for leaving him. Went to bed in no enviable frame of mind. Wept myself to sleep." She awoke the next morning, Tuesday, May 25, at half past six, "somewhat better in spirits but with bad headache." Fred was acting up, but that was likely more annoying to Henry than to her. "Fred full of all manner of tricks, which wonderfully discomposed my nerves. Glad I did not leave him at home, troublesome comforts better than none." She found Ithaca a "pretty place, superior to Auburn in the arrangement of the streets and buildings, churches inferior. Left there 9 o'clock, violent headache. After climbing an <u>insurmountable</u> hill over an <u>impassable</u> road, discovered we had lost our way." After retracing their journey from Ithaca, they made it only ten miles before stopping at Vickery's Tavern, where Frances spent an hour chatting with the landlady, a Swedenborgian whom Frances found fascinating and full of information about the religious sect, which believed in one universal church based on love and charity. She also found their spiritualism, a belief in the possibility of communication with the dead, intriguing.[53]

In Spencer, about twenty miles south of Ithaca, Frances wrote a letter to Gus, while Fred, Henry, and William went fishing. After a night in a cold room, she started the morning with rheumatism, but the landscape improved her mood. She found it "delightfully wild" with "bad roads," but "a profusion of wild flowers in the woods. Some places appeared like a variegated carpet. . . . Walked a few rods but soon exhausted my little stock of strength."[54]

Henry thought their stopover in Harrisburg on June 6, 7, and 8 was a turning point in the trip. "I should never forget how painful the journey thus far had been to the invalid under my charge. We remained there three days, hesitating whether the entire project was not conceived in error. But I did not feel willing to carry back my dear wife to her friends and say she was thenceforth to languish [with] no hope of relief, but such as might be miraculously vouchsafed without execution." Frances did not write in the journal during those three days.[55]

Henry wrote to Thurlow Weed on June 12, having now passed Harpers Ferry. At that point the Sewards and their driver had been on the road for about three weeks, and Henry was apologizing for being such a lax correspondent. "But the solicitude I continually feel concerning F's illness unmans me at all our stopping places," he wrote to his friend, "as she is always exhausted by the fatigue of the ride and requires all my attention." While he longed to see improvement, it was not easy to find. "She is not worse, and that (considering all circumstances) I am induced to regard as an evidence that she is better." That is the most hopeful view he could muster. She had been "very unwell" in Harrisburg and "was unable to see anybody during her stay. I found many friends." Frances appended a note to Weed's daughter Harriet in which she apologized for not writing, having been too unwell and exhausted during the trip. Nonetheless, she too mustered some optimism, saying that she had "enjoyed the journey more than I anticipated, with my indifferent health, am stronger than when I left home," which Henry was unable to discern, but "not materially improved otherwise."[56]

"The first impressions of Virginia by no means favourable," Frances wrote in her journal at about the same time as the letter; "never saw so execrable a road." Not only were they "enveloped in a cloud of dust, which prevented our seeing 3 yards," but she was "wearied to death, headache, toothache, &c, &c." On June 13 they drove twenty-seven miles from Charleston to Winchester on a "very bad road," had "poor accommodations," and she was "sick of slavery and the South." She found Winchester, an "unpleasant dirty town, built 150 years ago, I should judge, had remained stationary ever since from its present appearance." She had a "violent headache all day," which undoubtedly accounted, at least in part, for her mood.[57]

In a letter of June 15, Henry explained more fully than previously the principles that led him to plan their itinerary. The trip, he admitted, was not just for Frances's health; indeed, he knew that part of it made her more nervous. "It was necessary that I should travel in Virginia to have any idea of a slave state." Why, unless his interest in politics had not actually dimmed? Frances, as Henry well knew, preferred to avoid the horror rather than witness it firsthand. "I selected the Natural Bridge as our destination," Henry wrote, "because it is necessary in every journey, although it be taken for pleasure and health alone, to have some point before us, so that travelling may assume something of the character of employment, and for the further reason that curiosity to see that wonderful work of Nature serves partially to keep down that feeling of sadness which Frances and all persons like her must have in travelling through a slave state."[58]

In a letter to Lazette, which Frances wrote in Virginia, she noted skeptically that "we are told that we see slavery here in its mildest form. The plantations are cultivated much like our farms, and the slaves are principally domestics. But, 'disguise thyself as thou wilt, still, slavery, thou art a bitter draught.' I often think over the wrongs of this injured race." In this same letter, Frances wrote that she had always felt "a strong disinclination to travel in the Southern States, but I have so often been told that I might go from Maryland to Florida without meeting anything painful, that I began to believe my own impressions were incorrect, and my opinions prejudiced by education. So, I consented to try the experiment, with a faint hope that my fears were unfounded." She insisted, though, once she saw her worst fears realized, that the planned itinerary, which took them to Richmond, was altered and they headed north again once they reached Charlottesville and Jefferson's Natural Bridge. "I can only say," she wrote her sister, "that I envy not the apathy of those who can see every natural tie severed, their fellow-creatures transferred from one owner to another like brutes, without the least regard for their sufferings, and yet experience no painful feelings!"[59]

Henry kept those closest to him and Frances informed of their progress. Letters to the Millers in Auburn, Lazette in Aurora, and the Orange County Sewards do not survive, but replies summarize the general drift of his news, whether he was upbeat or despairing and how he portrayed Frances's health in general terms. When he wrote on June 24 from Charlottesville, Henry felt confident that Frances had taken a sustained turn for the better. "For the last ten days my dear F. had manifestly acquired strength, health and cheerfulness. She endures the fatigue of riding, walking, exploring caves and climbing mountains in a manner auspicious of great good." This exaggerated the case, as we know she did not explore the caves but stayed behind with Fred instead, and still reported exhaustion after her walks that were not up the sides of mountains, but the improvement that Henry reported as vindicating the trip was quite possibly real.[60]

On June 30 Henry was also sick, but Frances did not name his symptoms. She wrote that she walked alone through the woods about a mile to the ruins of the chapel where Washington was reputed to have attended church services, which was six miles from Mount Vernon. "Much difficulty in finding our way to Mt. Vernon, charming place on the bank of the Potomac. 1200 acres enclosed, but a part of the original estate. Fine collection of greenhouse plants in the garden. Vault new. Went through the lower part of the house, tasteful plan." Then they were off to Alexandria, Georgetown, and Washington, DC, where she was impressed to find Pennsylvania Avenue paved. She ascended the dome of the Capitol with Henry, which left her "completely exhausted," before they drove on to the White House and "saw the old general," Jackson, which tourists did in those days, just stopped in to see the president, who tried to receive them graciously. She found him "very polite" and left it at that. They departed the capital on July 4 and headed for Baltimore, where she heard they had ten letters waiting for them. On arrival, they found that the house they intended to stay in had burned down the night before, but the letters were safe, "all well at home."[61]

The final surviving letter from the batch that reached the Sewards in Baltimore was from Judge Miller to Henry. A letter that Henry had sent the family from Woodstock, Virginia, on June 15 had reached them. "From your account of Frances's health," Elijah wrote on June 23, "we think it has improved a little, but regret that it is so little." As for them, in Judge Miller's view, "we are all well. Augustus continues steady at school and is doing well." A hailstorm had destroyed much of the fruit on their trees and the vegetables from the garden that Henry had planted before they left. They had also lost some west-facing windows. "My best love to Frances & Frederick, & tell him that he shall have the toys he wished me to get (I have forgot what) as soon as he gets home."[62]

The Sewards crossed the Delaware River at Camden and, after a frustrating search for a boardinghouse in Philadelphia, stayed in a "very neat, quiet house" run by Edith Lloyd, "a Quakeress," on South Third Street. They remained in Philadelphia for nine days, during which time Frances got some dental work done and consulted Dr. Philip Syng Physick (1768–1837), who was one of the most renowned American doctors of the previous half century and had many famous patients. She found him a "good old man," which may have been dismissive or merely a sign that she was resigned to her fate. What she got from him was a diagnosis of neurasthenia, a term that was coined in 1829 from the Greek for "nerve" and "weak" to describe a mechanical weakness of the nerves. The diagnosis became extremely popular later in the century and has only recently been abandoned by the World Health Organization and the American Psychiatric Association. It denoted a condition with symptoms that include fatigue, anxiety, headaches, heart palpitations, high blood pressure, neuralgia, and depression. Frances's condition was a classic case.[63]

In the same book where Frances kept her journal of the trip, she wrote her notes from the consultation with Dr. Physick. It is no wonder

FIGURE 5.2. Painting of Frederick W. Seward as a child, by John Goodwin. Courtesy of Rare Books, Special Collections, and Preservation, River Campus Libraries, University of Rochester; original painting in Seward House Museum, Auburn, New York.

she found his diagnosis and prescription unhelpful: "Non-exercise of the brain and nervous system or inactivity of intellect & feeling a disposing cause to nervous disease—over tasking the brain produces irritability and disease. The intellect & feelings not provided with external interests—become weak & inactive or work upon themselves & become diseased." According to the best medical advice available, the "nervous disease" was all in her head. In the gendered diagnoses of the mid-nineteenth century, Frances was well advised to neither over- nor under-stimulate herself, and to stop dwelling on her symptoms. She should have gotten out more, found "external interests" apart from her children and home, and "exercised" without "over-taxing" her brain.[64]

The three Sewards and their driver left Philadelphia on July 27, a "cold, unpleasant morning," and crossed the Delaware River at Burlington. They had hoped to meet up with Thurlow and Harriet Weed at Long Branch on July 30 but missed them by two days. The "houses at the beach full, afford few comforts for an invalid. Too unwell to bathe today," Frances wrote on July 31. Henry bathed with Jennings and Marcia, who had joined them there. Henry's brother and his wife left for home on August 1, and Frances wrote that "I am too sick to write today."[65]

No other letters from Frances or Henry to friends and family members survive for the rest of 1835. Henry apparently wrote to his brother Jennings on September 6 that they had reached home safely after a stop in Aurora. They arrived home to "a scene of affliction upon which I may not dwell," Henry wrote to Weed. "Mrs. Miller, who has been the only mother Frances has ever known, is prostrated upon a sick and, as we fear, death bed. . . . My poor wife is in the most anxious state; I fear her strength is insufficient for the duties and solicitude so unexpectedly cast upon her."[66]

The morning after their arrival, Paulina spoke to Henry in words that he found eloquent. "'Henry,' said she to me this morning, 'this sickness has brought, in my view, the two worlds very near together. I feared you would not bring my daughter home to me before I died; but I felt assured that we should meet in a very short time, in a state where we could never be separated. Remember you have my treasure in your keeping. Take care of it while Providence leaves it in your charges.'" On October 4 Henry wrote again to Weed: "I have been three days confined to the house, in watching the dying bed of our deceased relative, in ministering to the comforts and wants of mourners, and attending the funeral. She was buried today in the Episcopal burying-ground by the side of the only one of her children who died before her."[67]

CHAPTER 6

Happy Christmas and a Sad New Year, 1835–1837

In 1831, when Albert Tracy tried to convince five-year-old Gus that Saint Nicholas was an imaginary being, the boy had appealed to his father, who recused himself. When Frances wrote Henry gushing letters in the 1830s about the joys of Christmas morning with small children, Henry replied that the holiday meant nothing to him as he did not consider himself a Christian. He declined even to reciprocate his wife's holiday wishes or to write to her on that day. Frances regretted Henry's absence from holidays with his family for decades to come; more often than not, he was away for legislative sessions, court cases, or other business, such as collecting rent and mortgage payments in Westfield for the Holland Land Company beginning in 1836, but he also avoided family celebrations of Christmas purposefully. Public celebration of New Year's Day was more appealing to him and avoided by Frances as best she could.

The Sewards' children were born into the first generation of Americans to turn Christmas into a celebration of family and childhood. It is difficult to find evidence of family gift exchanges of commercial goods in the United States before 1825, the year of Gus's birth. The traditions now associated with Christmas and New Year's Day were largely invented around then. Although the holiday has roots in European winter celebrations, Americans had previously resisted what they saw as anti-religious and socially disruptive festivities of the season. In New England, secular celebration of the holiday was illegal from 1659 to 1681, and children attended school on Christmas Day; in Pennsylvania, the Quakers simply did not tolerate what they saw as a celebration of excess. The New England Puritans observed that there is no biblical evidence supporting a celebration of Christ's birth in December; beyond that, they, like the Quakers, were not inclined to celebrate much, but by the 1770s Americans had begun to compose their own Christmas songs.[1]

The practice of "mumming" or costumed performing, accompanied by loud and persistent demands by lower-class folks for treats of liquor or food from those who were better off, rose up in the early nineteenth century despite attempts at suppression in cities. The practice led to outright rebellion against entrepreneurs and factory managers, who insisted that their employees work without respite or reward right through the holidays. By the 1820s, management and polite society saw misrule led by the working classes as a threat to the peace. In such an environment, a call from elites to return to the old ways, even when the "old ways" were new, made a stunning appearance. Washington Irving's *Sketchbook* (1819–20) drew on nostalgia for British rural customs. Irving had never witnessed such practices and romanticized them as unifying class relations in a paternalistic setting that had been largely abandoned in the competitive and class-fluid America in which he wrote. He tapped into the transatlantic upper-class guilt that had led to traditions of holiday charity long before children became its beneficiaries in family celebrations of the holiday.

New Yorkers Irving and Clement Clarke Moore, who were both part of the "Knickerbocker" set, are said to have "invented" the American holidays. The group, which was named for Irving's satirical *Knickerbocker's History of New York* (1809), was of English heritage, but often drew on fictitious Dutch roots in the state's culture. There were Dutch traditions associated with Saint Nicholas, but Moore, Irving, and other Knickerbockers embellished those stories and added the "miniature sleigh, and eight tiny reindeer" in Moore's poem, which we now call "The Night Before Christmas." There was actually no celebration of Saint Nicholas in seventeenth-century New York, when the colony was Dutch. The men who invented the child-centered Christmas and the social conventions of New Year's Day calling and reception were Episcopalian, culturally conservative, and fearful of the commercial growth and nascent class conflict they saw in the urban environment. The call for a "return" to "traditions" that they dredged up or created was in part an attempt to restore order and preserve class dominance in times of rapid and unsettling change for the patricians. The appeal was also generally embraced by members of the rising professional classes, who sought stability for their newly achieved status.[2]

Moore published his poem as "A Visit from St. Nicholas" anonymously in 1823 in the *Troy Sentinel*. Widespread publication of the poem began in 1824, the same year as the Sewards' marriage. Saint Nicholas was an authority figure in the Knickerbocker creations, rewarding *and* punishing children, but Moore cast him as a "right jolly old elf," whose appearance assured the narrator that he had "nothing to dread." This was a secular and plebian saint, who "looked like a peddler just opening his pack," and his pipe came directly from Irving. Frances quoted twice from the poem in a letter to Henry in December 1832. "Monday afternoon I went out to purchase the Christmas toys for the little boys' stockings. . . . When I came home I found the little boys' 'stockings hung by the chimney with care,' and 'the children were nestled all snug in their beds while visions of sugar plums danced in their heads.' Gus said he had dreamed all about his stocking being full of candy and Fred of course dreamed so too if brother did."[3]

Frances tried and failed to convince Henry that Christmas was a family holiday, that the father who narrated Moore's poem was the parental norm, and "mama in her kerchief, and I in my cap" should have "settled our brains for a long winter's nap" together in the same bed on Christmas Eve. From her recounting of the story about Tracy's intervention with Gus, Henry was clearly not the only man of his generation who did not embrace the new fatherhood and the indulgence of children. It is unlikely that Lazette's husband did either, but even Judge Miller played along and gifted the children with books, hobbyhorses, ponies, carts, and sweets in ways that he had never treated his daughters. "Augustus says I must tell you," Frances wrote to Henry, "his Christmas consisted of a Christmas cake, a little tin soldier, another on horseback, a tin basket, and a dancing man with the candies as usual and says I must tell he has kept them all nice." Gus and Fred, of course, bought deeply into Moore's story even though Gus no longer believed in the magical saint. The boys wanted to dream and they did.[4]

Frances's descriptions of Christmas morning in her letters to Henry made the case multiple times over the years for a family celebration with him as a participant. In that same 1832 letter she embraced the chaos that her husband sought to avoid. "Fred, of course, soon devoured all of his portion that was eatable and then proceeded to break the handle from his little basket, rub the paint from the strawberries, &c, &c. The work of demolition has continued until there is hardly the tip end of a tail left for a token. I think the organ of destructiveness must be pretty fully developed on his cranium. Gus is reserving his things to exhibit to Pa when he comes home, all but the candy and that he said did look so good to him that he could not keep it." Fred was two and Gus six.[5]

Two years later, after an intervening year that the family spent with Henry in an Albany boardinghouse over the holidays, Frances wrote to Henry, who was back in Albany without her and the boys, to describe Christmas in his absence again, and again she quoted Moore's poem. "I have been instrumental in making three glad hearts and smiling faces today. The children's stockings were all 'hung by the chimney with care' last night and this morning they found them 'overflowing' as Freddy says. The little boys are now arranging their toys and candies for a store and Maria is hurrying through her work that she may go home this afternoon and display her treasures."[6]

"There is so little of happiness in mirth," Frances wrote, "that I will not wish you a 'merry Christmas' dearest but I will wish you a 'happy Christmas' and a happy day it must surely be to all who think of it as the birth day of our blessed Saviour." "Happy Christmas" was from Moore's poem too, which accounts for Frances's quotation marks, and the choice of "happy" over "merry" emphasized her stand against raucous, inebriated celebration. Frances's gift-giving included household staff such as the younger Maria, who were often just children themselves; Maria was also a student in Frances's home school.[7]

This extension of charity at Christmas was part of an enduring tradition that was being adapted to the household and Saint Nick's stuffing of children's stockings. The feast was equally a part of the family celebration of Christmas, although the timing of the meal remained in dispute between Frances's father and grandmother during Paulina's lifetime. From the same letter: "Grandma wanted a Christmas dinner and Pa is to have a Christmas supper. Eating seems to be the end and aim of everything."[8]

The commercial classes co-opted Christmas from the patricians and monetized it right from the start. Toys, candy, fruit, and children's books were more widely available across geographical regions in the 1830s than they had been even a short time before. In 1832 Frances bought the children's presents from a "toy store" in Auburn. It is not surprising, then, that the children turned their "treasures," as Frances called them, into play "stores" that reflected the commercial culture.

"The children had a merry Christmas indeed," Frances wrote to Henry in 1832, and that was the idea. She had sent for Lazette and her daughter, thereby ensuring that her niece enjoyed a visitation from Saint Nick too, no matter Alvah Worden's views on the subject, which no one likely consulted.[9]

"Freddy kept Christmas all day Monday," Frances wrote in 1836. "He had a store on the sofa where he kept all his things for sale. Maria and Frances [cousin] came to buy." Fred, age six, also wrote to brother Gus, who was away from home with their father in Westfield, where Henry was just starting his new job collecting rents and mortgage payments for the Holland Land Company. As we will see over the years, Gus was the one of the children least attached to home and family throughout his life and most likely to be away over the holidays. Fred wrote to his brother about his gifts from Santa: "My dear Augustus, I got a man riding on a turkey in my stocking Christmas. He looks like a Irish workman. And a wineglass, a candlestick, a picture book, and some candy. Maria got a picture book, a little tin basket, a pair of gloves, and some candy. Give my love to Pa. We have made our New Year's cakes." In 1836 even five-month-old Cornelia, the Sewards' third child and first daughter, "sit[s] in her cradle and play[s] with her new rattlebox," which had appeared Christmas morning in "her little sock," a gift from "Aunt" Margaret, the wife of "Uncle" Trumbull Cary, from Batavia, who was a colleague of Henry's in the state senate.[10]

New Year's Day was a different matter, but connected to the "invention" of Christmas in the 1820s. The Squire in Irving's five Bracebridge Hall holiday stories, which are included in the *Sketchbook* that the Sewards owned in a first and several subsequent editions, orchestrated the reenactment of "ancient" practices that the author imagined. These commemorated "more honest days of yore," which were "more homebred, social, and joyous, than at present." The traditions threw "open every door" and "brought the peasant and the peer together, and blended all ranks in one warm generous flow of joy and kindness." Unfortunately, "the world has become more worldly. There is more of dissipation, and less of enjoyment." In seeking to revive the customs and recover the amity of society that Irving imagined lost, the Squire found that no longer could the entire peasantry be trusted to behave in his house. "The country people, however, did not understand how to play their parts in the scene of hospitality: many uncouth circumstances occurred; the manor was overrun by all the vagrants of the country, and more beggars drawn into the neighbourhood in one week than the parish officers could get rid of in a new year." So the Squire now invited only the "decent part of the neighboring peasantry to call at the hall." Irving's stories were about "the honest face of hospitality" rather than the child-centered holiday that Christmas became. When Henry wrote to Frances from Albany about his "dissipation" on New Year's Day, they both knew he quoted Irving.[11]

The reception of New Year's Day callers with food and drinks became an obligation for wealthy New Yorkers, especially for politicians who courted the goodwill of working-class voters. Those who were most generous provided savories, sweets, and alcoholic beverages, but the abstemious offered coffee for adults and special holiday cakes for children. Frances opposed serving hard liquor to guests but considered wine less of a threat to public tranquility. She shared Irving's fears of disorder. When Henry was away, callers received the minimum and were not greeted by the lady of the house but rather by substitutes from the family whom she recruited. Henry, however, was generous and made and received calls when he was in Albany, Washington, or Auburn.

Fred received callers on New Year's Day. To Lazette, Frances wrote the day after the holiday that "Freddy says we had 17 calls yesterday 'if we count Mrs Dean & Carlo' but I think he must have included Grandpa's visitors also." Carlo was their dog and Mrs. Elizabeth Dean was baby Cornelia's wet nurse, so neither counted in Frances's mind. Her point was that they had far fewer callers than usual. About the callers, she continued "I would gladly have dispensed with any for as usual I had a violent nervous headache. Tell Frances that Freddy had some wine in a little bottle and his little wine glass with some cake. I personated three or four different characters and made him as many different calls. When Mr. Cheadell called, Freddy produced his little decanter and glasses. He was much pleased that Mr. Cheadell drank some of his wine." John Hatch Chedell (1806–75) was a neighbor and silversmith in partnership with a jeweler in Auburn.[12]

Frances explained the reason for the small number of callers in the letter to her sister, which provides context for the family's coming tragedy in the midst of holiday celebration with Henry and Gus away. "There is a case of smallpox in our old office. I intend to have Cornelia vaccinated though she is so good-natured and playful I do not like to make her sick." She also mentioned in a letter to Henry that "there has been an alarm of smallpox in the village, the supposed case is one of the members of the family which occupies our old office. I have not heard much about it the last two days. I thought of sending for the Dr. to vaccinate Cornelia but Clara seemed to think it unnecessary and did not like to have the little creature made sick. I think both the little boys were vaccinated before they were nine months old."[13]

Harriet Weed wrote to Frances from her home in Albany on New Year's Day 1837 with wishes that are touching in light of what came soon after: "Dear little Nealy, I could not love her more if she was my own sister. I think of her every day, and can almost see her laugh and hear her say argoo." On January 3 Frances still had not heard directly from Lazette, so she despaired of her sister's health and still fretted over when to have Cornelia vaccinated.[14]

On January 7 Frances wrote to Henry, apologizing for adding to the "anxiety of a mind already so overburdened as yours," but explained that Cornelia displayed symptoms on January 4, when she was "slightly indisposed" and then vomited and was restless during the night. "Thursday, she continued to manifest symptoms of indisposition and I noticed a slight eruption about her throat without however thinking it of any importance." Cornelia was again restless through Thursday night, so Frances sent for Mrs. Dean "to see if she could tell me what was the matter. The eruption had by this time somewhat increased but still without exciting the least alarm." The nurse immediately diagnosed it as either chickenpox or smallpox but encouraged Frances to call a doctor as she could not stay and risk exposing another infant she was nursing to whichever it was. Dr. Humphreys confirmed the nurse's diagnosis. "He gave me little encouragement to hope it was not the smallpox." On Saturday, Humphreys was more certain but wanted another twenty-four hours to be sure. "The little sufferer is now covered with the eruption and seems very, very sick."[15]

By Saturday evening Frances learned that the doctor had come directly to her house for what we call a well-baby visit from the family with smallpox and had infected the Sewards' unvaccinated infant with the disease. "He has deceived me cruelly," Frances wrote to Henry, "and this is the man to whom I am obliged to entrust her precious life. Pa wishes me to dismiss him immediately. I am almost distracted not knowing what course to adopt." She wrote to Henry daily until he and Gus returned from Westfield.[16]

On January 8 Frances wrote to Henry that she had "nothing to communicate which will lessen your apprehension about our darling babe." Cornelia was by that point exhibiting symptoms of "an extremely violent case of smallpox. Pa has just been in to look at her and says it is very uncommon for a child to have so severe an attack. The Dr. even admits that it will be a fiery trial for one of such tender years." Frances tried to remain hopeful in the face of the symptoms, but witnessing her daughter's suffering was "wearing away my heart." She did not write again, anticipating Henry's arrival.[17]

The next letter is Henry's from Auburn to Lazette in Canandaigua dated Tuesday, January 17. Henry explained that he had arrived home at 4:00 p.m. on Friday, January 13, and that Cornelia breathed her last at 9:00 a.m. Saturday. During the intervening seventeen hours, he "was hourly expecting and impatiently hoping to see the beloved child expire under suffering that seemed to defy relief and for the last twelve hours [I] was plying with stimulants the exhausted and sinking frame that had survived the worst but had not strength to carry it through the searing convalescence." He had received a letter from Lazette that reprimanded him for not keeping her informed about Cornelia and Frances, which Henry thought harsh under the circumstances. He hoped that the letter Frances wrote to Lazette on Sunday "redeemed" him in her eyes. "Frances wisely preferred to write herself to you," he explained, "and did so at the earliest hour. We have buried our dead 'out of our sight.' We were compelled to do it almost alone, such is the excited state of apprehension around us. But this is indifferent to us and in no way aggravates our grief."[18]

In his letter Henry also thanked Alvah for his advice about keeping the rest of the immediate family safe in the aftermath of Cornelia's affliction. "Whatever precaution could be taken has been, and thus far (this being the thirteenth day) no indications exist that the horrible disease remains among us. Without a doubt we are all in danger." In addition to the bereaved parents, Elijah, Clary, and Fred had attended the infant, and thus "I feel that we are all yet in the shadow of the valley of death. But we think not of these things now—we wait the further development of the will of God in regard to us." Indeed, they all had been vaccinated and were still just fine.[19]

His real reason for writing, Henry explained, was not to vindicate his behavior in his sister-in-law's eyes or to report on events that he knew Frances had already described to her sister. He wanted to assure Lazette about Frances's condition in the aftermath of the greatest loss a mother can endure. "And now my dear sister I pray you rely with entire confidence upon the assurance that Frances is altogether as well and as cheerful as you could expect her to be after so severe a trial. She exhibits no indication of disease. Is able to be everywhere about the house, and to discharge all the duties proper for her to assume." Elijah was down with a bad cold, but the boys were just fine "and are playing at this moment with their miniature sleigh on the snow. Do not imagine any ill. Should we not rely on the assurance of god that he does not willingly afflict us?" Lazette should rest assured that Henry would notify her the minute any member of the family showed the slightest symptom of smallpox, but the passage of time suggested that the worst had passed. "Our child was enclosed in a double coffin. Upon the cover of the inner one is a plate with the inscription 'Cornelia Seward, died January 14th 1837' and her grave prepared under my own direction is at the side (leaving space for two others) of that of our sainted mother [Paulina], who I doubt not received the young adventurer with open arms in the world of the blessed spirits who have departed this life in peace."[20]

Knowing how much Frances suffered her miscarriages, as well as the absences and what she interpreted as neglect of her husband, we might wonder whether Henry understated her grief in that first letter to Lazette after the death of Cornelia. In the fall of 1834 and through the following winter and spring, she had seemed unable to rally, perhaps for reasons of physical as well as mental health, but her depression kept her from fulfilling her motherly and housewifely duties in the ways that Henry said she was in January 1837. Surely, he wanted to see a return to normal that would justify him heeding the call of business and returning to Westfield within three weeks of their infant's death. Apparently, though, Frances found solace in the religious beliefs that Henry echoed in his letter to Lazette. As we know from Frances's correspondence, especially after Cornelia's death, she knew many mothers who shared such a loss and found their beliefs consoling.

It would be the end of the century before rates of infant mortality began to decline significantly. As America grew more urban in the nineteenth century, infant death rates climbed. The greater concentration of population shifting from farms to villages, towns, and cities increased the communicability of disease that affected the very young, elderly, and poor disproportionately. Smallpox, measles, chickenpox, whooping cough, scarlet fever, cholera, and influenza all took their toll. Vaccination for smallpox was extremely effective but left unvaccinated infants vulnerable, as was the Sewards' baby. It was not the case that parents suffered the losses any less for the increased frequency of infant mortality; indeed, it is possible that in an age that celebrated childhood more than in the past, the losses were even more wrenching. Certainly, Frances's correspondents testified to their shared pain.[21]

Henry's sister wrote to their mother in late January that she had just heard about baby Cornelia's death. "I feel deeply for them," Louisa Cornelia wrote, "at the same time I very much fear for Frances that it will be prejudicial to her health." Less than two years after the carriage trip intended to help her recover from a miscarriage, infection, and depression, Frances faced an even greater mental health challenge that family members anticipated could again undermine her nervous system and thus her physical well-being. Marcia, Jennings's wife, wrote directly to Frances in early February, first apologizing for never having congratulated her sister-in-law on the baby's birth, which she blamed on Henry for having never informed her. Now, Jennings had learned of the death from the newspaper rather than from his brother.[22]

Cornelia had lost two sons, and Marcia wrote from personal experience about the loss of a daughter. "Yes, well do I know the sorrows of a bleeding heart mourning the loss of a beloved daughter. Had our dear little Aurelia lived, she would now be fifteen years old. I would not recall her back to this world of pain and sin and disappointments, if I could. I now look back to that affliction as one of the kindest acts of our Heavenly Father towards me, and yet I am humbled to the earth to think that the mercies of God were not sufficient to keep me in the path of duty." The newspaper account did not address the cause of death, about which Marcia now inquired. Whatever the cause and whatever the death was like, brutal or gentle, Marcia was sure "you have never passed through any scene that has caused your heart more to bleed like the sickness and death of your darling babe. None but a Mother ever can know those feelings and no pen, not even a parent's, can describe them." Marcia had just returned from visiting a friend whose thirteen-month-old daughter was at death's door, which brought home her own experience and heightened her feelings about what Frances was going through. On the positive side, though, in Marcia's Christian opinion, "Our natures are so deformed we never will grow in grace much while in prosperity. No situation seems so dangerous to the Christian as a cloudless sky of earthly enjoyments. I trust this affliction may be sanctified to yourself and Husband. God will be glorified in 'whatever comes to pass.'"[23]

This was particularly an opportunity for Henry, his sister-in-law thought, and a message from God intended specifically for him. She hoped the tragedy would occasion a rethinking of Henry's ambition and his relentless focus on work, and that he now considered his family and soul higher priorities than his career. "O, that this might be the means of teaching brother Henry the perishableness of all created things . . . How short, how very short at most is this life, and yet we live as if this were our everlasting home." Since Henry neglected to write directly to her or her husband, Marcia apparently thought Frances a necessary intermediary and likely a more welcoming recipient of her rather critical message in the aftermath of such a loss.[24]

Henry received a letter sharing a similar perspective from his brother George at about the same time. George had not learned the news directly from Henry either, but rather from Jennings after he read the newspaper report. "I may be permitted to sympathize with you at least in part," George wrote, "for some days we expected that our little one bearing the same sister's name would be taken from us, but she was spared. I would meet with you, mourn with you, but I would also console you with reflection, that we know not what is good for us but that we have a Heavenly Father who careth for us." Henry should, in his brother's opinion, take the loss with Christian fortitude and the knowledge that there was a message in it that Henry could work to discern and act on. "But this providence, however afflictive, may be an important lesson to you. Your heart may not have been sufficiently mindful of the one thing needful. You may have followed pursuits, however honorable they may be in the eyes of the world, and however worthy they may be of your effort in their proper sphere, yet have deprived Him."[25]

Henry eventually wrote to his mother and father about Cornelia's death. His father replied to him at Westfield the second week in February, looking at the bright side from a somewhat different perspective than Henry's siblings, from that of a physician who knew the uglier turn the infection might have taken. "We mourn with you at the great and solemn loss to your and ourselves," Samuel wrote sympathetically. "How uncertain are all things here below and still we are bound to be thankful that the hand of the destroyer was stayed here. Other valuable lives might have been taken. In the severe conflagration of Auburn, your property there must have been saved as it were by a miracle." The rest of the letter, about three-quarters of it, is about Samuel's business concerns and includes a plea for his son's help. "I find, my dear Henry, it is daily more necessary for you to be here often."[26]

Henry's mother wrote to the grieving parents, again with an injunction to accept God's will and to rededicate themselves to the living children rather than submitting to a self-indulgence in grief. "I hope a kind Providence will spare your other two children," Mary wrote, "and yourselves to be with them to guide them through their youthful life and guide them in the path of virtue that we may look to him that careth for us [and] our feeble endeavours." Mary believed that Frances's grandmother Paulina awaited Cornelia's arrival in heaven to comfort her and relieve any fears.[27]

Frances wrote to Henry in Westfield on February 11, in reply to a letter from him. It did indeed seem that she was able to stir from what could have been a debilitating grief by focusing on the needs of the boys. Two years earlier, Henry had thought it was essential to get her away from the children in order to recover her health, but then and now she believed that diving in, rather than Henry's preference for withdrawal, was the most curative path. "Dreading to be left to myself, I commenced my school the day after your departure. The little boys are very much pleased. I teach them four hours, two in the morning and two in the afternoon. . . . This arrangement occupies so much of my time that the days have passed off very well."[28]

This was the good news and rings true for Frances, who got great satisfaction from being her children's teacher. Her education had prepared Frances well, as it did other women of her generation, for such a role. Not all were gifted, as she was, at tailoring a curriculum to the personal needs of her students rather than trying to fit all with one size and what she saw as the wrong-headed discipline of many schoolteachers.

The news was not all good, though, which is a sign that Frances was sharing the full story with her husband, who had fled the sadness of home for the comparative peace of business halfway across the state. "The nights are more tedious," Frances continued. "My sleep is troubled with all manner of hideous dreams. I awake almost every hour during the night, watch the window for the first beam of light and rise from my bed unrefreshed. O, if I could only dream of my precious babe once as she was in health and beauty. That horrible disease does so haunt me. Do not allow this to distress you. Time will make it all smooth again, but it is such satisfaction to tell you just how I do feel." There was guilt, there was horror and the grief of the greatest loss a parent can know; she was facing down the nightmares alone in her bed. And yet, she did not want to "distress" Henry, simply to ventilate her feelings in correspondence because he was not at home.[29]

Frances continued to receive calls, which was difficult in the face of a raging headache that she had endured for four days before writing the letter to Henry. Clary stayed with her, so with her father, aunt, two boys, and household staff she was not really alone, but rather lonely for the support she needed from Henry, while he was in what she called his "other home." Gus was particularly solicitous of her because he perceived she was lonely, and Judge Miller was similarly attentive to the boys, often sleeping on the sofa in their room after listening to them read aloud before bed.[30]

Three days later, Frances wrote to Henry again. She had attended the boys' pretend church, where Gus and Fred alternately preached. She served as the congregation and they asked her to lead the choir, "but as I never sing when I am not happy, I found it very difficult to perform my part. My heart was too heavy. The last time we all played church, dear little Nealy was a member of the congregation. There is no time or place when such reflections do not crowd themselves upon me, endeavor as much as I will to occupy my mind with other things." Again, keeping busy, engaged with household duties, including teaching and playing with the boys, was keeping her emotionally afloat. "I feel the benefit of constant exertion and knowing as I do the sinfulness of yielding to despondence, I shall persevere in my present plan, 'hoping and believing, yea through faith knowing' that my endeavours will not be unassisted."[31]

Frances again raised with Henry the question of his relationship to God. He had once spoken "about receiving the sacrament of baptism. I always intended to talk more with you about it. I am afraid I assented to the reasons which you gave for delay without duly considering them. 'The world would think that your making a profession of religion was the result of a sudden affecting dispensation.' You know it to be the result of mature deliberation, that you designed making the profession before the recurrence of the calamity." She referred to another loss of a child, so to one of her miscarriages with which she was now equating Cornelia's death. "Think it over again dear one," she wrote on February 14.[32]

Frances had received letters now from Henry's sister, mother, brother George, and Jennings's wife Marcia. Frances felt obliged to respond to Marcia, who wanted to hear details about Cornelia's death. "I shrink from the task of recounting them, but I will try." There had been other losses since Henry left. "Poor Rathbone has lost his little boy." The infant born to Jared Lewis Rathbone, who was a business partner of Henry's, and Pauline Harris Rathbone of Albany was less than one month old when he died. Judge Gary Sackett, bosom pal of her father, and his wife Harriet had also lost an infant child to the croup. Understandably, Frances felt haunted by death, but far from alone.[33]

Frances wanted Henry to know that he worried too much about her, as she knew from his letters. She realized that her past depressions gave him cause for such fear, but for whatever reasons she now had more resources to cope with her grief. "You must not dearest give yourself so much trouble about me. I do not yield to the despondency you imagine I do. I believe I am most of the time as cheerful as you can desire. I do not forget our dear babe. This I know you would not ask. No, she is never absent from my thoughts, but I dare not repine while I have so many blessings still left me. I know it would be wrong." This was not to say that she was never down or fearful about the future; she was not in denial. "I am so much afraid of being the subject of still greater bereavements, of being left still more alone. This had always in some shape been a subject of disquietude to me and now that death had entered our dwelling my heart is often weighted down with a sickening apprehension." Frances was right about that too; her fears for the deaths of others close to her only worsened for the rest of her life in the aftermath of this crushing loss. Her anxiety about her husband, sister, and children endured, although all outlived her, albeit not all of them by much. We might imagine that Frances's gloominess came from the childhood loss of her mother.[34]

Finally, we see Gus's perspective on the family tragedy in a letter that the ten-year-old wrote to his aunt Lazette on February 19. While his mother had written about him, reading to his grandpa, in school, and playing church with his little brother Fred, this is the first glimpse of the effect of Cornelia's death on the Sewards' son. Gus was replying to a letter from Lazette, which is now lost. Gus had indeed contracted varioloid, a mild form of smallpox that was diminished by vaccination or previous infection. "I have had the varioloid, but I had it light. I did not lie in bed all the time." He caught it despite being kept away from the infected baby after he returned home with his father. "I did not see her after I came home because Ma said that I would think of her as I saw her last, but I do not now, because when I think of her I see her as I use[d] to, sitting in Ma's lap. She would laugh and say acoo, acoo, and make her little hands go. But she was too good to live in this world of trouble and if we are all good we shall see her again." Gus accepted his mother's narrative of the life and loss, which it was important for her to support with a reasonably cheery disposition in the presence of her sons. As Gus told it, Cornelia "is with Grandma singing to God, and with all good people," which was her reward for being so good.[35]

Frances now consulted a different physician. Dr. Joseph T. Pitney (1786–1853) was a traditional doctor with a long-established practice in Auburn. He encouraged her not to be overly concerned about Fred's symptoms, which were consistent with either a bad cold or influenza. Pitney administered an emetic, calomel, and a purgative, which had "so prostrated him that for an hour or two we were considerably alarmed. He lay with his eyes partly closed, seemingly unconscious of what was passing around him. After two or three ineffectual attempts to rouse him, I sent for Pa and the Dr. His pulse was very irregular and exceedingly rapid." By the time the doctor arrived, Fred had revived from the treatment and was sitting up. "He said it was not uncommon for children to be thus affected by the operation of an emetic," which led Frances's fear to subside, "but dear Clary (who could not love our children more were they her own) was too much frightened to come and look at him for a long time. . . . You can hardly imagine dear Henry how much at such times I feel the want of your advice and support, but perhaps it is better for me to [be] made to seek support elsewhere. Freddy rested tolerably last night, had less fever and coughed less than heretofore." Not surprisingly, he had a feverish thirst for cold water, undoubtedly caused by dehydration, "which the doctor says he must not be permitted to drink."[36]

Frances had gotten an inkling, perhaps from casual conversations and possibly from newspapers, that Henry was again a candidate for public office. His "retirement" after the loss in the election for governor the previous year had run its course, and the Whig Party owed him for running what all except Henry anticipated as a losing campaign. The party's prospects were brighter for 1838, and he was no more attracted to the practice of law in Auburn than he ever had been.[37]

On March 7, Dr. Pitney returned to bleed Fred, who still had a fever and cough. As Frances explained to Henry, "Dear Clary cried and said he should not be bled. I held him on my lap and Maria held the cup. His blood showed ardent marks of inflammation. Bleeding cooled his burning fever for a while. It returned partially in the course of the evening. I then bathed him with vinegar and water and gave him sufficient ipecac to vomit him. This diminished his fever. He slept quietly and breathed more freely through the night than he had done in some days." Ipecac syrup, which is mildly poisonous itself, was long used to induce the vomiting of other poisons but is now known to be ineffective even for that purpose. Frances reported that Fred was now, according to the doctor, "nearly free from fever. He breathes easily and coughs little." Dr. Pitney said that "unless he has a return of fever, he may be considered convalescent. Should that recur, he must be bled again.

I was very unhappy last night, but feel new courage this morning. I will write again tomorrow."[38]

In a letter that he wrote on March 8, Henry expressed concern about Fred. On the same day, Frances wrote to Henry that during the previous night Fred "was restless and wakeful. He seemed so much reduced by the medicines he has taken that I made up my mind in the night to write for you to come immediately home. This morning he appears much less languid, though weak." Dr. Pitney had just left, promising to return in the afternoon and bleed Fred again if the fever returned, which it did. The next day she wrote again. "He almost fainted in my arms. The Dr. took more blood than before. His fever is not subdued and yet he is very much reduced. I cannot but think the event doubtful. I am alone and sometimes disheartened. Can you come to me? I am so well assured that you will that I should not write again immediately."[39]

There are no more surviving letters for the next five days, and Henry did not return home. Frances referred to a letter she received from Henry in the interim, which he wrote the day after her last letter to him. "When I saw how much pain my communication of our little boy's illness has given you, I was half determined never again to apprise you of any sickness of the family until pronounced dangerous by the physician. I hope long before this that you have the assurance of our darling boy's safety." Dr. Pitney had written an assuring letter to Henry, in which he expressed confidence in his methods and their likely results. "I hope however the Dr.'s letter which accompanied mine may have operated as a sedative and prevented your setting out. In this view of the case, I regret that I have not written earlier. I know that an assurance from me would be more satisfactory. Freddy is now so well as to sit up half an hour at a time in the easy chair, free from fever, and but little cough. I think I may safely say there is no more danger to be apprehended from this attack."[40]

There remained lingering side effects to Fred's illness, both to the marriage and to Frances's nerves. She hoped Henry appreciated how crushing the death of Cornelia was to her and how well she was doing in the aftermath of the loss. She did not think an explanation should be required, but perhaps, now that Henry was anticipating a return home in the near future, she needed to explain again more fully. "No one can know without the same experience what I have felt while watching the progress of disease in my children, fearing that disease might have a fatal termination and yet knowing how perfectly useless would be all attempts to call you to their bedside." She knew it took about six days for even an exchange of letters if he responded immediately on receiving hers, which left her in "a sort of hopeless desperation" and feeling guilty at the same time. "I feel at least twenty years older than I did. My brow is wrinkled with care and my hair whitened with suffering. But, I am wrong to complain. God has been graciously pleased to spare the life of our precious boy and for many days I have felt renovated in strength and spirits."[41]

Henry likely gave his reply verbally when he reached home. Both partners were clearer now than they ever had been about the roles, the limits, and their disappointments in each other as spouses and parents. There were more apologies and more pledges of reinvigorated commitment ahead, but never again would there be the real hope by either of them that the other would change. Yes, they were "modern" parents, with different expectations for marriage and parenting than those held by their parents' generation, but such differences were no check on Henry's ambition, his intolerance of home life, and his expectation that Frances would take responsibility for the household and children. He carried the burdens of society on his back for most of the next three decades. Surely, he thought, Frances could bear the load of just one family.

By the time she wrote again to Henry on March 19, Frances was glad he had not come home, that he had taken Dr. Pitney's confidence more seriously than he had her fears. She also wrote, though, about the doctor that "I think the course he took with Frederick was an injudicious one and I feel it now a signal mercy that our precious child is restored to us," which she believed was despite Pitney's treatment. "We will talk it all over when you come home and until then I will not trouble you more about it. I am afraid I have already occasioned you more anxiety than I ought." She considered alternatives to Dr. Pitney, who was much too old-school, so eighteenth century; the purging and bloodletting struck her, as they do us, as extreme and counterproductive to a restoration of health. She was still exploring but had not yet settled on homeopathy as her choice.[42]

Frances also continued to suffer from debilitating headaches, which she described in a letter to Lazette of March 22. She had not read Lazette's most recent letter on the day that it arrived because "I was when it came suffering from an attack of sick headache rather more violent than I have ever before experienced. I was relieved by vomiting and bathing my head and feet, but was unable to sit up before the next morning." Since Frances was one of the many at the time who took laudanum to address pain, including gynecological symptoms, and nerves, the opioid was likely a contributing factor if not an outright cause of her recurring headaches. The opiate relieves pain immediately but causes intense headaches in withdrawal, which often led patients to take more rather than less in their addicted states. It was also unregulated at the time.[43]

Lazette had unsettling news about Frances's niece. "I hope Frances [Worden] has recovered from her cold by this time. I have thought of her many times. I find that the least appearance of illness in those I love alarms me much more than it did before the melancholy experience of this winter. Dear, dear Nealy, how glad I am you can dream of her and think of her as she was in the days of health and beauty." Clary was also now ill, having come down with what she thought was "a violent cold," but she had a "slight eruption on her face and neck, which increases" and caused concern. She also had a fever and a very sore throat, and her back and bones ached. Frances encouraged her to call Dr. Ira Smith, thereby avoiding the two local doctors whose practices she now questioned. The diagnosis was measles. "The Dr. thinks her symptoms favorable," Frances wrote to Henry. "The great danger is from inflammation of the lungs, which does not yet manifest itself. It is a severe ordeal for a person at her time of life. I hope Pa [can] escape, but he had already been more exposed than she was." Clary was a month shy of her forty-fourth birthday, and Judge Miller would turn sixty-five before that. At least it was not smallpox, which was a relief. Dr. Smith recommended bleeding.[44]

Judge Miller and Frances bickered again about whether she should send the boys to boarding school. It is unclear why this was an issue in the spring of 1837, unless Elijah felt the boys needed a male environment to thrive, especially with their father away, or perhaps he was of Henry's mind that Frances would be healthier if she dwelled less on her sons. Of course, she found in her teaching respite from grief, satisfaction that she was doing a good job, and distraction from her rumination, and she was certain that she would worry more rather than less if the boys were out of her sight for months on end. She recognized that she could not prepare Gus for college by teaching him Latin, but she believed that her comparative ability to teach him math and English compensated for that deficit. They could always hire tutors to address her limitations. Correspondence with a local schoolmaster convinced Frances that he was unable to spell. "This was pretty conclusive evidence that he could not teach others," Frances explained to her husband, "and

I believe it is the case with half the teachers we have in this age of rapid improvement."[45]

Frances noted that people in Auburn still avoided their family, no longer called or greeted them in public, in the aftermath of their household's infection with first smallpox and then measles. "We see no one," she reported to Henry; "I do not know but we shall lose cast[e] entirely by the fearful visitation of this winter. You will hardly credit that people can still fear contagion from coming to see us, but I was told a week or two ago that this was the case." In Frances's mind, what she saw as the irrational fears of her neighbors and the question of boarding school were connected, so perhaps she believed that the family was better off hunkering down in their home than trying to reengage the community with their unwelcome presence at that time. The moral of the story, to Frances, was that " 'the friendship of the world is but a shadow' in most instances. I cannot say that I have ever once felt this neglect painful to my pride, but I am afraid I have indulged too contemptuous a feeling for the weakness which occasions it. I am afraid I have little of that Charity which 'never faileth.' Why is it that generally we find more real magnanimity among the lower classes!"[46]

According to Frances, writing to Henry on March 29, 1837, Clary's eyes were still weak in the aftermath of her illness, and "she has a violent pain in her limbs much of the time. Her cough continues, but is not alarming. I hope Pa will escape. He has no symptoms yet and it is about time for them to manifest themselves if he had imbibed the disease." Thirty-three students at the Auburn Seminary had measles. "It is prevailing generally among children. The little boys send love and kisses." Frances expected Henry home in ten days, although it was actually another three months before Henry wrote to his brother Jennings that "it is with great satisfaction that I am at length hailing once more from my much loved home," where he had finally arrived on June 18 after almost five months away. Two weeks later, he was off again.[47]

Chapter 7

Panics, 1837–1838

A month after infant Cornelia's death, Henry offered his brother a business partnership, with Jennings as his on-site representative in Westfield for the Holland Land Company, which owned a large tract there and others in Pennsylvania. The company's American headquarters was in Philadelphia, which meant that Henry traveled there often and Jennings, who collected rents and mortgage payments, oversaw new contracts, made deposits, and kept his brother informed of problems. Henry made on-site visits, negotiated with banks, and liaised with partners in New York and Philadelphia. He also set local policy and devoted his considerable charm to assuaging investors on one side and tenants on the other, who had in the past been inclined to violence in protest over their payments. Henry saw this arrangement with his brother as a necessary compromise, an accommodation to Frances's needs and to his renewed quest for political office. Since he traveled for business and in pursuit of his political ambitions, spending more time away than in Auburn over the rest of 1837 and through the November election in 1838, Frances continued to live in the "hopeless desperation" that afflicted her.[1]

Frances wrote to Henry the last week in March, "you promise to come home in three weeks and I think I shall not allow you to leave me at home again alone." The next day, Jennings wrote to Henry accepting his offer, "part for Marcia's sake, and then for yours, and then for others as well as myself." He had regrets about leaving his work for a missionary society in Cincinnati, but "I hope God approves the motives by which I have been actuated," he wrote to his brother. "To Him and to you I am exceedingly thankful for what appears to be a great blessing in prospect for my poor affected wife, the opportunity of enjoying exercise and air. For most of the winter she has been unable to lift a chair." Perhaps Henry's offer enabled both brothers to do what they thought best for their families, but Henry's calculation was closely tied to his campaign for governor.[2]

Henry may have intended to spend more time at home when Jennings took over day-to-day management of rent and mortgage collection in Westfield, although the gap between his actions and his stated intentions only grew over time. To Gus he wrote on March 29, "I am happy to hear that you spend much of your time in reading with your Ma. Besides that it is a good thing to read much, it is very important to read for her when she is lonesome and thinks of your Pa that is far away and of her infant that was taken to Heaven." Henry was sympathetic to Frances's state of body and mind, but the two of them coped differently in the face of illness and death. Henry tried to avoid thinking about what he could not control and just pursued his career. He also had a sturdy immune system and enjoyed generally good health, while she decidedly did not. Home was for him a stressful place and Frances's worries were unsettling, so he found reasons to stay away. Lacking the same options or similar inclination to flight, Frances took comfort in her family and chose to ventilate in correspondence and surely in person as well, to her friends, but particularly to her sister and her aunt Clary now that her grandmother was gone.[3]

In 1837 and 1838 financial problems, both personal and global, compounded the domestic stress caused by Henry's ambition. By April 25 Henry was in Auburn and Jennings in Westfield, but Jennings's family remained in Cincinnati until the business could pay for their move. "Money is nowhere to be found," Henry wrote to his brother, "at any rate of interest. . . . We must abandon all idea of coercive measures for the present on bonds and mortgages. It would [not] be right or expedient to oppress [tenants] while this state of things continues." The Panic of 1837 had hit, and the financial crisis now affected everyone from rioters protesting the price of flour to tenants, landlords, banks, and politicians.[4]

The panic was a response to financial constrictions that had started the previous fall and reached crisis proportions by the spring. "In one word," a New York newspaper reported in April 1837, "excitement, anxiety, terror, panic, pervades all classes and ranks." The crisis endured over the next five years.[5]

The price paid for deeper integration of the United States into the international market economy was increased vulnerability to financial crises that had their origins abroad. The westward expansion not just in New York State but also across the continent was built on investments made possible by the canals and railroads, and financed by loans linked to the production of cotton in the slave-based economy of the South and textile manufacturing in Great Britain. Speculation such as that of the domestic purchasers of the Holland Land Company was a link in a very long and tenuously constructed chain across the Atlantic Ocean, one that floated on confidence rather than cash.

America's financial infrastructure was weak, with notes issued by upwards of seven hundred banks by 1836, circulating as paper currency. The only money issued by the federal government was gold and silver coins, so the bank currency was effectively a loan that greatly exceeded the amount of specie held in their vaults. The whole system depended on misplaced trust in the largely unregulated banks, a gamble that everyone eventually lost when the paper currency could no longer be redeemed for even a fraction of its face value. At every point of exchange, the bills were discounted, losing value that was subject to speculation. The whole system floated on the calculation of the worth of a note issued by an American bank by the time it was redeemed in London. With the expiration of the charter of the Bank of the United States in 1836, the whole system was even less regulated, with over one hundred new banks chartered by states in 1836 alone. Some people rejoiced that there was no central bank in a unified system, but the chaos that replaced it was riskier.[6]

On balance, the United States was Great Britain's debtor. While exports of cotton tripled in value between 1831 and 1836, the staple constituted over half of America's export economy, making it highly dependent on a volatile market for a single crop. Indeed, New Orleans, from which one-third of the cotton shipped to Europe, was the fastest-growing American city during the decade, exceeding the pace of New York and Philadelphia. When the price for American cotton realized in English auction houses plummeted in 1836, the ripple effects were catastrophic.

The political debate in America, often referred to as the "bank war," had undermined British confidence in the American banking system. In order to protect their investors against what they interpreted as volatility, British banks constricted credit, called in loans, discounted American notes more heavily, and triggered the very panic they attempted to prevent. The panic undermined the price of cotton and thus the amount realized back in New Orleans, which was most heavily dependent on the crop to finance banks and the construction of urban infrastructure to support the city's growth. The chain effect, from London to New Orleans to New York, by the end of 1836 spread on both sides of the Atlantic and brought the fragile structure down. By May 1837, when banks brought a halt to exchanging coins for banknotes, the economy was in a shambles from which it took six years to recover.[7]

For Frances, her own symptoms and concerns about family members' health took precedence over Henry's worries about money. She was glad to hear at the end of the first week of April that Lazette, while still weak, had recovered her health. As for herself, Frances reported on April 7, "I can do more about house and am really stronger than I have been in two years before, yet I felt very much fatigued with walking over to the Exchange buildings. So much depends upon the habit." Aunt Clary's eyes were still weak, but she was otherwise recovered from the measles. "Freddy runs out some, but it is not quite spring yet, the air is cold and generally damp." She had received a letter from Henry, but he did not mention returning home. "It will be nine weeks Tuesday since he went away, twelve weeks tomorrow since dear little Nealy died, and yet that seems but yesterday." A week later, still no Henry; the day he had predicted for his arrival in Auburn had passed.[8]

Henry arrived home on April 24. The next day, he wrote to Jennings that "you can have no idea of the consternation that overwhelms everybody," but he was talking about banks rather than family. The financial crisis loomed, and Frances's need for a stay-at-home husband fell before the demands of business that called him away. "Money is nowhere to be found, at any rate of interest. . . . What is to be the end of all this I cannot foresee. It is certain, however, that the crisis must come soon. There is but one step from the present to the general catastrophe." He was right: the crisis came in May, when banks stopped paying on other banks' notes and he needed loans to compensate for the shortfall until the economy righted itself. "I am settling my little affairs here with all the industry I can," by which he meant he was making arrangements with tenants on his Auburn properties and the bank; "my bank account [is] overdrawn and everything indicating that my tenants will not be able to pay their rent." He hoped to leave Auburn the following week. "We are all in usual health," which Jennings understood to mean that Frances and the boys were well enough for him to depart after checking in and addressing his local financial affairs. On April 28 Henry wrote to his brother again in the same vein: "the banks refuse to loan $50 to their best customers, and all stand trembling before the storm which threatens to sweep them all by the board." On April 30 Henry's sister Cornelia wrote to Frances that she hoped her brother was home. "I would never let him go away again," as if anyone could stop him. On May 2 Henry set off for Albany to consult with bankers and political friends.[9]

Jennings's replies to his brother's letters highlighted a difference between them. Jennings insisted that his duties to family took precedence over business demands; therefore, he refused to delegate the care of Marcia on her journey to Westfield either to Augustus, Jennings's seventeen-year-old son, or another man, as Henry suggested. She had not traveled with Jennings at the outset because an outbreak of mumps in their family prevented it. Her health was so frail that he was willing to fail Henry's "test of my devotedness to the interests of the company," however "fatal" to his own prospects and his brother's goodwill that might be. "But my dear brother you have asked of me a vast deal more than you think you have. Let me tell you. Your sister's [sister-in-law's] health and own life, is more deeply concerned than you have been aware of." It was only because of Henry's offer "of a house, and wagon, fresh air, and pure water" that Jennings leapt at the business proposition, "and it came like one of the dearest God sends that I ever noticed." He simply must return to Cincinnati to make arrangements and accompany Marcia, as "the poor woman is reduced to a shadow, with a most uncommon spirit. She is able most of the time to be up, but rarely has strength enough to set a chair to the table. Indeed, she is no more fit to go on a journey with a boy or a stranger than a little child would be to be a passenger among gentlemen in a stage without its mother or nurse. You would not ask it." Jennings meant that he begged Henry not to ask that of him. "If you do insist on my detention, I shall certainly think it the cruelest thing I ever knew of you."[10]

Jennings's letters reached Frances in Auburn in Henry's absence, so she read and summarized them in her letter of May 5 to Henry. About the family matters, she was succinct. "I think you will not hesitate to release Jennings. He certainly ought to go." By May 11 Jennings still had not heard back from his brother, having written by now six letters that had not caught up with Henry in his travels. From Albany, Henry went to Orange County in response to a summons from their father, who thought he was dying. Then he was off to New York City and Philadelphia in search of a bank that was willing to back the business enterprise in Westfield. Finally, he arrived in Bargaintown, New Jersey, to visit his sister before returning to Albany in the last week of May. "The unhappy and critical situation of my family requires my attention," Jennings wrote. "I leave in the morning to furnish them what relief I can. I hope this will be agreeable to you." On May 13 Frances wrote to Henry that in Auburn the banks were not even redeeming their own notes, never mind the notes of other banks. On May 17 she wrote again that she was glad he had taken the time to write to her while he was "wandering about." On May 19 Henry was in Philadelphia, where he secured from a bank the loan they needed for the Westfield operation. On May 22 he was in Orange County, where he found "father greatly improved; mother, blessed woman, making us most comfortable."[11]

By May 27 Henry learned that Jennings had left Westfield for Cincinnati two weeks previously, so the question of his permission was moot. "The panic and pressure having reached its crisis in New York seems to be carrying no less than its full measure of terror through the country," he wrote to his brother from Albany. "I find it of all places the most uncomfortable here and heartily wish myself again in Chautauqua." Henry did not wish himself in Auburn with his wife and children, but in Westfield, Chautauqua County, in his "other home." Nonetheless, on May 30 he was in Auburn, then back in New York City by June 3, and in Philadelphia again the following week.[12]

After a journey that was part business during the panic, part politics despite his denial, and part avoidance of his family, Henry was back in Auburn on June 18, but still only passing through. Henry was not keen on his father's proposed family trip to Westfield for a number of reasons, but he claimed travel exhaustion and his joy to be home. Both, it turned out, were flimsy excuses for avoiding travel with family members on a journey that he would be making anyway. "It is with greatest satisfaction," he wrote to Jennings the next day, "that I am at length hailing once more from my much-loved home." He had found "all my family well and Frances especially improved in health. I found also our parents here impatiently awaiting my return." Unfortunately, Samuel had come down with a cold a week earlier, which left him "feeble and sick ever since." Today, the doctor bled Samuel with good effect, Henry thought. Since he felt better, Samuel agitated for an immediate departure with the Auburn Sewards for Chautauqua County to visit Jennings's family. "I am very solicitous that they should go there," Henry wrote his brother, "much on my own account, but more on your and Marcia's. But after my long pilgrimage I am quite unwilling to leave home forthwith, and my little affairs can scarcely suffer it." Hence the dilemma: he did not want his parents to travel alone, but he needed a few days to address his finances. To summarize the fruits of his travels, Henry explained that he had secured the loan they needed, which would enable the brothers to issue new mortgages for the tract. "I rejoice so do all around me to hear that Marcia's health is improved and that she looks with satisfaction upon her new home," he concluded. Jennings replied that he was relieved to hear about the loan and understood entirely Henry's joyful return home, but he expected the extended family's imminent arrival in Westfield.[13]

Only three days after his last letter, Henry wrote to Jennings and explained that he was again off for New York City and Philadelphia "to close my affairs as early as possible." He did not explain what had changed, whether his attachment to home had diminished so quickly, and what had become of his father's demands and his wife's expectations. On July 1 the Sewards arrived with Henry at Jennings's Westfield home and stayed for about six weeks, apparently with Henry in residence much of the time. Gus and Fred exchanged letters with their grandfather Miller, who offered on July 24 to come and get them and Frances if it would expedite their return home. The boys explained a newfound fascination with silkworms, and Elijah reported on the progress of their vegetable garden, where the corn had grown tall in their absence. Frances and the boys were still with Henry in Westfield on August 19, and she was "very weary" of being so long from home.[14]

The financial panic and the family crises of Nealy's death, the serious illness of Fred, Gus's varioloid, and Clary's measles coincided with six months during which Henry was largely away. Unwelcome pressure on Henry from Frances, Samuel, and Jennings brought the Sewards together in Westfield, where they shared the same house for almost two months. That was longer than Henry had been at home in years. They were not together in Judge Miller's house, but Henry's business challenges were real and played a genuine role in his absence from Auburn for months immediately following Nealy's death. Their time together in Westfield broke the pattern of separation but left behind few details.

We do know from a letter of Frances's that Henry considered being baptized in February, once he was back in Westfield, but feared it would appear insincere if he received the sacrament so soon after Nealy's death. Frances encouraged him "to think it all over again" and not worry about the world's judgment of his motives. The two of them knew that he had been pondering the profession of faith for some time. Apparently, Henry received the sacrament of baptism from the Reverend Lucius Smith, who had presided over the Sewards' marriage, at some point soon after that, and he, among others, was confirmed by Bishop Benjamin Onderdonk while the family was in Westfield over the summer. As his family members had hoped, Nealy's death played a significant role in Henry's conversion. We cannot know whether the crisis deepened Henry's faith, or if he was placating the family or calculating the political gain in his next campaign. Possibly all three were true.[15]

The jobs that Henry and Jennings had in western New York working for the Holland Land Company were challenging and required Henry's travels and oversight even as he campaigned for governor. The summer of 1838, when the family lived in Westfield, was a sensitive one for relations with tenants, who had threatened vandalism if they were not released from their leases and mortgages. The brothers dealt with the financial crisis by refinancing loans and by assuring the tenants paid them in banknotes that were redeemable in Europe. The brothers' measured course on collections kept the peace and succeeded both politically for Henry and economically for the company. The Sewards accommodated reasonable requests for extensions and refinancing. They initiated some foreclosures, but they sought to keep those to a minimum and worked with the tenants as best they could.[16]

Henry and his family left Westfield the third week of August and arrived in Auburn on September 1 after a leisurely trip through Niagara, Buffalo, and then Queenston, Ontario, Lewiston, Lockport, and Batavia by rail, onward to Rochester and then Canandaigua to visit Lazette, who still had a bad cough. "There is universal despondency in this region about money," Henry wrote to Jennings when they arrived home. On their return, Frances sorted Nealy's clothes, a year and a half after her infant's death. It was sad and people still made thoughtless remarks that "grated horribly upon my feelings, but I must try and bear these things better, my dear baby . . . I must not complain." Clary did not look good and had been ill most of the summer. Frances ran her school mornings and received callers in the afternoons. Henry left for

Baltimore and Philadelphia four days after their arrival in Auburn, and Frances hoped for his return in two weeks.[17]

From Albany Henry wrote to Jennings on September 11, "An universal gloom pervades society here. The worst apprehensions are indulged." Henry was working on a speech about education in his campaign for governor. From Philadelphia he wrote to Jennings, "I am satisfied that it will not be necessary to make any more demonstrations of force either by . . . foreclosures or otherwise. We must take care not to excite . . . be mild and forbearing." Henry was off to Washington. As usual, Frances had a hard time keeping up with Henry's movements and often learned where he was and thus where to send her letters and forward his correspondence from others. From Washington Henry wrote to Jennings that he had secured what they needed, but he expected the contraction of currency to continue for several more months and that "the times are to grow more difficult." They must be very careful not to provoke the tenants to violence: "be cautious how we give occasion to complaints of harshness and severity. . . . I wish not <u>to be severe</u> and I wish moreover not to be esteemed more severe than I am. You will exercise therefore a discretion leaning towards forbearance, and especially being generous in the settlement of the mortgage foreclosures." Keeping his distance with Jennings as their point man was wise politically as long as Jennings showed discretion in his brother's name. "I have entire confidence in your discreet management of the affairs," Henry assured Jennings, "and therefore will not assume at this distance to suggest anything as to the business of the office."[18]

In September Henry's sister Cornelia weakly weathered another pregnancy and birth of a daughter Mary named for their mothers. In a letter to her mother, Cornelia described symptoms of puerperal fever, an infection commonly caused by birth attendants during delivery until more antiseptic practices were introduced later in the century. Frances had apparently contracted the bacterial infection in the past, and it was a common cause of maternal mortality. "I was confined on the 15th inst.," Cornelia wrote, "after a rather more tedious time than usual. I got along tho' for the first week very comfortably. The day my baby was a week old, I was taken very suddenly ill, and was worse than I had been at all, but am comfortable again so as to sit up a little, only suffering great debility consequent on a heavy loss of blood."[19]

During his travels, Henry took time to purchase marble slabs to mark the graves of Paulina and Nealy. "I do not know how much my feelings may be influenced by custom," Frances wrote to Henry in appreciation of his purchase, "but to me a grave wholly unadorned always appears neglected. Still, I do not measure the depth of grief or affection by the height or costliness of a monument. The more simple the memento the more congenial it would be to my feelings. A tree or shrub nursed by the hand of love is to me a more touching tribute of affection than the loftiest monument or 'proudest tale recorded on it.'" Here she quoted a poem by Bernard Barton, "Verses Supposed to Be Written in a Burial Ground Belonging to the Society of Friends," which had a perspective shared by her Quaker grandmother.[20]

Toward the end of October, Henry and Frances visited the graves of Nealy and Paulina in the cemetery of Saint Peter's Episcopal Church. "Someone has been recently buried close by her side," Frances wrote to Lazette, "so as to preclude the possibility of any other member of our family occupying that place. Henry thought it best to remove the coffin to some other place, but I cannot consent to this. I feel that she ought to be by Grandma, though the remainder of our family must find some other resting place." She hoped to have a railing installed around the two graves to prevent a burial between them, and to have the marble slabs carved and in place. "I hope to have all these things arranged before Henry leaves home again," she wrote to her sister on October 21.[21]

Jennings focused during the fall of 1837 on the financial challenges the brothers faced in Westfield. "A growing accumulation of remote paper has alarmed me," he wrote to Henry in early October. It now seemed wise to take only paper from local banks that he knew to be solvent, which was a change from practices in the past, when notes circulated freely nationally and even internationally. Henry worried about the impact of their business on his campaign for office. "The political season is approaching," Henry wrote to his brother on September 27, "and it is very important to us not to be compromitted in the angry feeling that may arise." On October 4 Jennings assured him that "the settlers are anxious about their business, but not distrustful of the justice or even leniency of the office." On October 5 Henry issued a policy statement limiting the paper they accepted in payment, exactly the sort of clear, fixed guidance that Jennings had sought.[22]

On October 6 Henry arrived home after another month on the road and the usual optimistic but mistaken estimates of his return; he hoped to remain in Auburn through the election in the first week of November. A few days after that estimate, he was off to Elmira for a railroad convention and then to Springport for a political meeting. Frances was left to receive visits from politicians and their wives who were overwhelming her hospitality. "I have lost, I fear," she wrote to her sister, "the little taste I once had for company. It was very irksome to me, but I suppose it will not answer to indulge this misanthropic disposition."[23]

Heavy politicking by Henry and his supporters kept him from another nomination for the state senate, which was not the office he had his sights on. There was nonetheless a political controversy that kept him home until he could cast his ballot in Auburn. "I am compelled in some sort to remain here until after the election," he explained to Jennings. "A conspiracy raised its head here in the Senatorial Convention taking encouragement from my absence, to eject me from the political concerns of this region on the ground of my change of residence and indifference to the local interests of the party. It has been well rebuked, but must not have the occasion for reviving which my absence from the polls would give. I shall leave here as soon as I shall have put in my vote on the first day." Henry spent so much time away from home that the question of his residency now caused him political problems.[24]

Samuel again predicted he was dying, having suffered from the "severest cold, asthma, and inflammation of the breast I ever had. I thought I must suffocate." Indeed, when his nephew George Grier and George's wife, Frances Tuthill Grier, lost a child the following spring, the second of two they lost to whooping cough, Samuel's letter of condolence described himself as a man who had lived "twenty years on the brink of the grave." At this point he still had another dozen years left. He hoped that Henry would visit him in January or February, "if I live 'til then." Fred sustained minor injuries when he fell from his brother's pony, which stumbled and kicked him in the head. He was frightened, bruised, and muddy, and his shoulder was sore for a few days, but nothing like the brain injury his family initially feared. Gus sprained his wrist trying to stop the runaway pony, but the hero of the day was Elijah's hired man Peter Crosby, who had grabbed the animal by the neck to slow him down. "An overruling Providence alone protected him in this season of peril," Frances attested.[25]

After the drama passed in the wake of the family's loss of a child earlier in the year, Frances wrote to Henry that the injury Fred received "was so slight that I never thought to mention it again. He did not even complain of any pain or soreness two days after the accident. He is unusually well this winter." Less than two weeks after the fall, she was back to worrying about Fred becoming too bookish, because he preferred to read rather than be outside riding the pony and playing with

Gus. "Do you think Fred will read too much?" she asked Henry. "He has a book in his hand continually." Here he was, at the age of seven, and "I can with difficulty persuade him to take the exercise which is necessary for his health," she continued; "he is sitting now at nine o'clock, like a Turk, on the sofa busily engaged with *The Lady of the Lake*," Walter Scott's poem.[26]

In early December Frances expected another Irish girl to replace the one who had left her with twenty-four hours' notice to keep house for her brother in Ohio. "Frederick [their son] would be far better calculated to perform a journey alone," she wrote to Henry. "I have, of course, been more than usually occupied with household duties or I should have written earlier." Frances's letter of December 6 also contains the sort of passive-aggressive passages that appeared more frequently around the holidays. "Monday, I received another letter from you, written the day before Thanksgiving. You are very kind to write to me so often. It is the principal thing that renders your absence endurable. It has been intimated to me a number of times that I am wonderfully neglected by my husband, but these speculations have ceased to move me, secure as I feel myself in your affection." Maybe, or maybe it was time for the Sewards to commence their holiday dance in which Henry predicted his imminent arrival and then disappointed his always hopeful wife.[27]

Frances moved from her testimony of faith in Henry's affection to reporting news of a local suicide. Unless we assume a random organization of the letter, this was a heavy burden of guilt to place on her husband one year after the last holiday season he missed, when their infant daughter took ill. There can be no mistaking Frances's identification with the woman, which she was direct about. "Sunday, a woman supposed to be deranged drowned herself in the Creek." This was the Owasco Creek, which ran not far south of their Auburn house. "On enquiring more particularly into the circumstances, I learned with surprise that it was Mrs. Crane," which was Mrs. Margaret Crane, age thirty-one, one year younger than Frances, "formerly Margaret Oliver, an old schoolmate of mine. What a host of melancholy recollections and somber reflections this tragic event has conjured up in my mind." As someone who had suffered from deep depression, Frances was better able than most to imagine the woman's despair. Some years ago, Frances had heard that Margaret attempted to take her own life, "occasioned by what she considered the injustice of her dying mother and the indifference of her husband." Frances left the story there, perhaps recognizing that Henry would see the connections without her providing any more clues.[28]

Their new Irish girl had arrived to do the family's laundry. She was soon gone. "We are again without a maid in the kitchen," Frances wrote to Henry. "The last girl or old maid was too fiery a temper to answer our purpose. After she had spent one week in wrangling, I dismissed her. . . . I shall try this time for a Yankee. The Irish have exhausted my patience." In the end, Frances was able to replace the Irish maid with Mary, "a coloured girl who is very smart and good-natured but not particularly neat," a step in the right direction in her opinion, but there could be a problem if a white girl to whom she had previously committed actually showed up for work.[29]

Frances inquired on December 12 indirectly about Henry's holiday plans, saying that the mother of a member of his law practice was wondering whether he would make it home from Westfield by January 1. Her eyes continued too weak to read. Mrs. Fosgate brought her daughter for a visit. "Perhaps she is more interesting to me being of the same age our dear Nealy would have been. The little boys were so pleased that they spent the whole afternoon playing with her and when she went home were so unwilling to part with her that I promised to borrow her, some fine day, for this amusement." The visit provoked the sharing of news about Nealy's grave. "The coffin of our precious one has been removed to the side of Grandma's. The stone is hewn and all is going on according to your direction."[30]

This year, there was not even the promise of Henry's return home for the holidays. In mid-December he predicted arrival at the end of the first week of January. Frances proposed that, weather permitting, she might plan a visit to Lazette and Mrs. Fosgate in Canandaigua, to coincide with Henry's return home. "My stay in Canandaigua will be a week, so if you can let me know about what time you will leave Westfield, and approve of my plan, I will arrange it so as to meet you there. If you write immediately, I shall receive your answer by Christmas. The little boys will both accompany me. Augustus is better than he has been, though his head is not entirely well." According to his brother, Gus took laudanum "three times a day."[31]

Henry wrote to share his grief over the death of Nealy and possibly even some guilt. He asked Frances to destroy the letter, which she apparently did. The feelings he expressed had embarrassed him. "The lines you sent me were very sweet and expressive," she replied. "No one but those who have had like trials can know how much I find every day to recall our precious babe to my memory. The bandbox containing her little wardrobe still stands at the foot of my bed." The approaching holiday season rekindled her grief. "I have looked forward with dread to the season of the year which is approaching. It brings all back so forcibly the time when the fatal disease was communicated." Again, Frances faced the nightmare alone. "The Happy New Year's Day when I received the congratulations of my friends and talked with pride of our new treasure, little imagining that even then that horrid disease was pervading her system, the ten dreadful days and nights when I watched its progress with agony not to be described, the closing scene, all, all are before me as if it were but yesterday." She tried to count her blessings and take solace in her sure knowledge that she would someday join in a better place those she had lost. "But, dearest, you must not think I am desponding. I am cheerful and content when I look on the numerous blessings which surround me. I should be ungrateful could I be otherwise."[32]

Frances's December 23 letter to Lazette showed how little had changed since the last holiday season. Two days before Christmas and she still hoped to visit her sister in Canandaigua, but she did not know when because Henry had not replied to her proposal to coordinate their travel plans. "If I do not hear again in two or three days, I shall think he is on his way home. I am concerned to hear that you have been sick again. Do you think you took cold? I hope you did not exert yourself to see the company that came to your house that evening . . . Now for St. Nicholas' duty so good bye." In the end Henry arrived in Auburn, apparently unannounced, on December 29, but he left for New York City on January 1, thereby managing to miss both holidays with his family and remaining home for less than seventy-two hours.[33]

As he recovered from his "last attack . . . two months ago, which I thought would be my last," Samuel Seward heard in Orange County that Henry was the leading candidate for the Whig Party's nomination for governor. He did not learn this from his son, as Henry studiously maintained the public fiction that he was not "running" but was open to a "draft." In truth, he had been running since he lost the 1834 election, which accounted for much of the travel that had kept him from home.[34]

The campaign started with a speech on internal improvements and education that Henry delivered on October 14, 1835, shortly after the family's carriage trip for Frances's health. The occasion was an Auburn ceremony laying a cornerstone for the waterworks at the mouth of the Owasco River. Two years later, on July 26, 1837, in a speech at Westfield, Chautauqua County, his "other home," he expanded on his education platform. Henry argued that those who advocated frugality, even in financially troubled times, underestimated the return in revenues, economic growth, and other benefits for taxes spent on schools, libraries, roads, canals, and railroads. Complacency, he thought, was likewise the enemy of progress. "Liberal confidence must be reposed," he explained in 1835, "in the abundant resources of the country." Resentment of spending for infrastructure in parts of the state far from a taxpayer's home disregarded the interconnectedness of the state's economy. "Now, in my humble opinion," he continued, "a state can no more wisely conduct its affairs than by contributing to the internal improvement of the territory within its limits a large proportion of its revenues and credits. Every such improvement develops new resources, adds to the capital and commerce of the country, and increases the mass of taxable property on which the government, in order to secure full accountability to the people, ought always to rely for its support."[35]

Likewise, the state's success in promoting literacy was important but insufficient in Henry's opinion. Teaching people to read and write was a first step. "But are the acquirements of reading and writing knowledge? No, fellow-citizens, they are only the means of acquiring it; and without some higher cultivation of the mind, the ability to read and write may be perverted to the perpetuation of error, as well as applied to the acquisition of truth. It prepares us to become the sport of demagogues, and the slaves of popular passion, caprice, and excitement. Something more is wanting." Hence, the need for public libraries, where citizens could continue their education in ways beneficial to a democracy.[36]

The 1837 speech, delivered six months after his daughter's death, expanded on the same themes from the one of 1835. "It is an interesting and important inquiry," he began, "how it has occurred that EDUCATION alone has been neglected in a country where the necessity for its improvement is so universally admitted; where all requisite facilities for that purpose exist; and where the necessaries and comforts of life are so cheap, and its cares so light, that those facilities are accessible to all its citizens?" Again, he thought complacency was the problem. Not even half of the citizenry read a newspaper, he observed, "of even the cheapest or most imperfect kind," and yet "we are accustomed to maintain that the people must and do in all cases, of necessity, decide wisely" in their public affairs. There endured a "miserable prejudice among us that we are wise enough already," which was a great threat to democracy unless addressed by the state.[37]

In this second speech on education, Seward went beyond an indictment of general ignorance and its threat to governance. For a New York politician in the mid-1830s, he boldly advocated public female education to address an error "scarcely less extensive or less pernicious than any I have mentioned." Although he believed there was no "degradation" of women in New York, there was also an unfulfilled duty "to make their education equal always to that of the other sex." Education was necessary for women to fulfill their roles in the home, as it was "the intention of the Creator to commit to them a higher and greater portion of responsibility in the education of the youth of both sexes. They are the natural guardians of the young." Education equal to that of men was necessary in order for women to succeed in "their proper sphere." Frances endorsed Henry's vision; indeed, she could have written the passages of his speech on female education and women's "proper sphere" herself.[38]

Henry had posted a letter to his father as the family left Auburn on the last day of 1837. His father replied to New York City, reporting that he was recovering from "a tremendous cold" while anticipating his son's imminent arrival for a "good long visit" to help with his business affairs. Henry's mother, whom Samuel described as well, would prepare a turkey she "had in waiting" for him. Samuel requested a bottle of Crème de Noyaux, an almond-flavored cream liqueur that contained trace elements of cyanide, which were known occasionally to float to the top of the bottle and poison the drinker of the first glass, or anisette, a safer aperitif, twelve dozen lemons, and the second volume of Matthew L. Davis's *Memoirs of Aaron Burr*, which was published in 1836. Mary apparently needed nothing more than a visit from Henry; she and Samuel did not know that Frances and her grandchildren now accompanied him.[39]

To Jennings, Henry wrote from New York City on January 10 that he was off to Philadelphia. His travels since the first of the year assured him that "Whig N.Y. seems to be unanimous for the Whig gubernatorial candidate of 1834," which he was. "There must, nevertheless, be much discussion of the question." Frances wrote to her sister the next day that she and the boys had joined Henry in Albany and were now staying at New York City's Astor House after a harrowing trip across a frozen Hudson River, "six hours before it [the ice] broke up, at the imminent hazard of our lives. I cannot think of it now without shuddering. I will never again expose my children in this way." Frances had a "sick headache" and had taken to her hotel bed, fully regretting the trip. "I need not say after relating so much of my experience how heartily sorry I am that I undertook a journey at this season of the year. I feel now that if we all get home alive and well we will have much cause for thankfulness." Henry admitted, in a letter to Weed, that the journey across the ice had been foolhardy. "Heaven forgive me for bringing into such peril those who ought not to be involved in the hazards of my irregular life!" Jennings wrote to Henry in the middle of the month that "we were delighted to hear that you had sister Fanny with you and mortified that we should be left to hear it from a stage passenger."[40]

At the Astor House in late January, Frances wrote to Lazette that she "took cold in Philadelphia, which was increased by my journey hither, and I am now laid up with a moderate intermitting fever, which I have so often had before." They had taken the train from Philly to Trenton, a stage from there to the Camden and Amboy Railroad, which they took to Amboy, and then a steamboat at midnight to Staten Island, after waiting two hours for the fog to clear. Travelers would soon be able to take trains from Auburn to Washington, DC, but not yet. "It was four o'clock when we arrived at New York. The boat rocked and creaked so dreadfully while we were crossing the bay that I was much alarmed." Henry laughed at her fears while the boys slept through it all. They did not reach the Astor House until 5:00 a.m., and three hours later she was ill with a fever and cough. That was Friday morning and it was now Monday. "I am still unable to leave the house," she wrote to Lazette, and she was living on "water gruel and slippery elm tea. Henry and my little boys are my nurses. We shall leave here as soon as I am able to leave the house."[41]

On Saturday, January 27, the Sewards left New York City for Orange County with a bottle of cordial for Henry's father, but the bottle broke and spilled its contents over several of their cloaks. In their hurry, they left behind a box of books, Frances's new hat, cloth she had bought for the use of her seamstress, and all of her handkerchiefs. It was raining when the steamboat started up the Hudson River, but the storm worsened and the rain changed to snow, which led the captain to stop at West Point. In a letter to her sister two days later, Frances recounted this harrowing leg of their journey. "The rain had changed to snow and the wind was blowing so violently that the pilot could not guide the boat." After a weather delay of several hours, the boat landed at Newburgh in the middle of the night and the family walked to the tavern through the wind and snow. "I was pretty much exhausted and quite disheartened when I discovered that I had left my pretty soft muff on board the steamboat. My anxiety was so great about the boys getting safe off from the boat that I thought of nothing else. I shall be exceedingly grateful if we all return from this wild adventure alive."[42]

The next day they continued overland through the snow and mud, eventually arriving in Florida by sleigh on Tuesday, after three days of travel from New York City. They visited with Henry's family for a few days before leaving for Albany, "I do not know what way as the river must have closed last night." Frances and Henry had both found the trip trying, Frances because of illness, the danger of wintertime travel, and the fact that "Henry is so busy all of the time." Henry complained that Frances's various illnesses were "vexatious" and the family simply slowed him down. Both agreed that Frances and the boys should have stayed home.[43]

The moral Frances drew from the misbegotten journey was that her grandmother was wise to tell the sisters that "experience is a hard teacher." She and the boys were down with colds, having had to travel in an open sleigh. Frances expected Henry to be detained two or three days in Albany, but she continued to hope for the quickest possible return home. "No one who has not had a similar experience can know how anxious I am to be once more at home with my children," she wrote to her sister on the last day of January.[44]

The Sewards arrived in Auburn on February 8, the journey from Florida to Albany having taken three days, during which they were undoubtedly slowed by the ice-covered Hudson River, remained in Albany for three days while Henry attended to political business, and then made the overnight trip to Auburn. Henry, contrary to Frances, believed that she and the boys "had some illness while absent, but no more probably than they would have suffered at home in the same season. They are all returned to their friends here in comfortable health and have no disposition to wander from home speedily," so he was not bringing them to Westfield as Jennings had suggested in his last letter. Neither Frances nor Henry wanted that.[45]

On their return home, Frances tried teaching Gus and Fred Latin, a necessary part of college preparatory education. She found her attempt to learn herself ahead of what she taught them unsatisfactory, so she hired a male tutor in 1838. "We have a teacher," she told her sister in April, "to assist me in instructing the boys. I will tell you more about him next time. He teaches them 3 hours each morning." To Henry, who was in New York City, she wrote that Benjamin Franklin Sanford, age nineteen, was "a very nice young man. He is so kind and gentle with the boys and withal so unwearied in his exertions to make them thoroughly understand their studies that I am much pleased with him." She described Sanford to her sister as Henry's protégé, since they had hired him based on a letter he wrote to Henry the previous summer seeking his patronage. A recommendation from the principal of the Cazenovia Academy represented him as "a young man of good moral character, a thorough Greek and Latin scholar, etc., etc., and entitled to confidence." Several months later, Henry brought Sanford home to tea and Frances agreed to give him a try. In the end, Frances found him "of more than ordinary intelligence, but extremely diffident." Gus insisted that his mother study Latin with him, so she too was Sanford's student and helped with the homework.[46]

Henry's neglect of correspondence with her triggered Frances's first complaint in a letter about her husband's rejuvenated political career. "And did you really think, dear Henry," she wrote to him in New York on April 20, "that it was a good and sufficient apology for not writing to me that you had been engaged in public business and could not find time?" Clearly not. "I had waited impatiently ten long days. Your letter came at last and caused some bitter tears, but I foresaw it all when you consented again to become a candidate for popular favour and ought to have been better prepared. These are hard lessons." She had learned where to send this letter from a passenger on the stagecoach from Albany, which in her mind compounded Henry's offense. He had not even taken the time to dash off a note informing her where she could reach him—this after so many sworn recommitments to her and their children. The path forward was fraught for the family, unless they could hope that he lost the election again, but she did not say that or likely even allow herself to entertain thoughts she considered disloyal. Instead, Frances wrote, "I hope you are not to be away from home all summer."[47]

Such frustrations led Frances to consider the state of Henry's soul. Nothing more provoked her to question her husband's moral fiber than his pursuit of elected office. Indeed, she found banking, for a local and upright institution, or the presidency of the New York and Erie Railroad, which had been rumored at the start of the year, less troubling. The practice of law in Auburn or an appointment as a judge was preferable both morally and personally to her. So when "old Mrs.

Hamilton" called and inquired about Henry's "spiritual condition," Frances did not need a second prompt to leap in. "What do you think I told her," Frances asked Henry rhetorically, "just what I thought, that you are a very good man, but too much engrossed with the world to devote much time to religious meditation. Was I wrong? But the time will come, dear Henry, 'when care and weariness and solitude will press heavily upon your heart and you will sigh for something better, greater, more permanent, more satisfying.'" Frances then proceeded to discuss the weather.[48]

In Henry's continued absence, Frances suffered from a "violent headache cold" as May began, which was exacerbated by her invitation to tea of what ended up being half a dozen of her friends, some with accompanying spouses and others with relatives. What she had originally planned as cake for a few friends left Frances "completely exhausted and firmly of opinion that I would never gather together 10 or 12 persons again to entertain. You people who talk and like to talk," she wrote to her sister, again disputing which of them was less sociable, "have no conception of the effort that it costs me with whom it always is an <u>effort</u> to talk to any person who does not interest me." Still, Frances thought socializing a moral obligation, as "a selfish seclusion is not right if it were practicable. I believe it is the duty of every member of the human family to keep up some sort of social intercourse." Still, she had her physical limitations to consider. "Four or five hours conversation when I feel any responsibility operates upon my nerves, produces headache and a prostration of all energy."[49]

On the evening in question, which lasted from about 5:00 until 10:00 p.m., when the last of her guests blessedly left her, Frances "came out of the room once . . . to rest a moment and then I could have sat down and cried like a child without being able to assign any adequate reasons. How do you like 'the confessions of a middle-aged lady,'" she asked without expecting a response. Perhaps Lazette could help her "devise some way for me to see in the course of a year the fifty or sixty families with which I am on visiting terms without permanently deranging my nervous system."[50]

Struggling as she had before giving up trying to teach Latin to Gus and Fred, Frances now had regrets about her own self-education. "Every new acquisition of knowledge opens another avenue of enjoyment," she lamented to her sister, as she understood only "enough of the Latin to make it interesting to me" and none of the Greek she heard recited when boys performed at a local school. She was pleased to see that the

Latin Gus had learned from his tutor was comparable to what the boys his age studied at the school, but her son got it from a gentler hand. "How often and how deeply I regret that so much of the early part of my life, for the want of proper direction, was wasted in reading novels, which were not even harmless as they fostered a morbid sensibility that will, I fear, always be the bane of my existence." Frances had expressed these same regrets about her own education in the past to Henry, one that she equated with what she now saw as unreasonable expectations for romance and love that she had acquired by reading fiction. The "morbid sensibility" that she now added to her regrets came from the untimely deaths of so many characters in romance novels, especially those of Sir Walter Scott.[51]

Both women thought themselves responsible for their children's education, so it was important that Lazette understood Frances's meaning; the distinction that needed clarification in this case was one about gender: "You ask me about Fan's studying Latin. I cannot say that I think it so essential for a girl as French. As [just] an accomplishment I would not urge a child to study anything." On the other hand, she now recognized that there were good reasons for children of both genders to study Latin, as "one obtains much knowledge of the construction of our own language." A child could just as easily learn the structure from the study of English grammar, but one or the other, grammar or Latin, were essential to education in her mind. Henry got his knowledge of grammar from the study of Latin, and "I believe there are few persons who write more grammatically," but Lazette's daughter could just as well get hers from English. Frances did have another firm opinion, though, on her niece's program of study. "In my judgement," she wrote to her sister, "Parley's Universal History is the only one suitable for children of her age. If you have not seen it, you cannot know its superiority. How clear it renders so much that was formerly so complicated." This too was part of Frances's job, evaluating texts used to teach her sons.[52]

Gus was on track for college preparatory Latin, although he had not yet started Greek at age eleven. He made adequate progress in reading, writing, and mathematics, even without the help of the tutor. His passion, though, indeed his obsession, according to Frances, was ducks. "Tell Frances," she wrote to her sister May 1838, "that Augustus, I think, in the course of the summer will turn into a duck. He talks of nothing else, sees and hears nothing else. I heard him telling his Grandpa this morning that he rather thought one of his ducks had commenced sitting," as in sitting on eggs that would hatch. "This has been an event of the last importance. If she should actually sit, I think Augustus will be obliged to have a bed in the barn to watch her and ascertain just the time when the little ducks escape from the shell." One week later, Frances reported to her niece and sister that Gus's duck "has been sitting just three days, eight hours, and some minutes. Gus spends all his leisure time in watching her movements and making an accurate calculation of the time when the young ducks will appear."[53]

At the end of May, Frances had a new "Irish woman in the kitchen, whose greatest failing is intemperance, though she has numberless of minor importance. She will give place to the next best we can obtain. So it goes. Seven in six months." The household was not running smoothly. Harriet Bogart, who was with her husband long an employee of the Millers and Sewards, could not help with the spring cleaning as she had made a previous commitment to a neighbor, who came to make her case to Frances. Although Frances surrendered Harriet reluctantly, she declined to give up her whitewasher to another neighbor, who also argued her greater need to Frances, "concluding that as the author of the laws of etiquette claims, 'it is one thing to be civil and [an]other to submit to imposition.'" Peter Crosby was uprooting and distributing plants from their gardens, including many dahlias, to his friends, "his countrymen" as Frances told it with her usual anti-Irish spin. "Peter has robbed the hot beds of the most thrifty plants. . . . If Peter could be kept out of the garden entirely, it would undoubtedly be more flourishing." She had no hope of change for the better as long as Peter worked for her father. After venting her frustration to Henry, Frances concluded rhetorically, "You have been gone seven weeks. How many more must be added?" She did not expect a reply that gave a reliable answer.[54]

CHAPTER 8

Ambition, 1838–1839

Never had the extended Seward family's branches in Albany, Auburn, Canandaigua, Florida, Bargaintown, and Westfield been in greater distress than they were in 1838 and 1839. Never before had Henry less time and patience for any of his family members, including his wife and children. Many eventually lost patience with him too, but not in the first flush of pride at his election as governor. They continued to excuse his domestic limitations as son, sibling, husband, and father for the better part of another decade as prices they all had to pay for his dedication to the public interest. For even the most loyal of them, though, their patience expired as his abdication of domestic roles large and small demonstrated that family was a burden from which he fled.

Whether it was campaign strategy or simply convention that led Henry to deny he sought his party's nomination, he wanted to be governor, and his ambition did not end there. When he arrived home on May 29, 1838, Frances had hoped he would stay two or three weeks before launching off again on his campaign for an office about which he claimed indifference. He wrote to Jennings that he was in Auburn until June 15. In the meantime he read Charles Dickens's latest, *Oliver Twist,* aloud to Frances. "Henry makes me cry every night over the wrongs of poor little Oliver," she wrote to her sister. "There is a deal of pathos mingled with the humour and satire." That was much different than *The Pickwick Papers*, which was simply funny. Again, though, Henry got too busy and stopped reading to her. "He hardly finds time to eat he is so hurried," according to Frances. Housekeeper troubles continued, but at least Harriet Bogart was now free to help with the spring cleaning. Their home school was coming to the end of a quarter and the boys were free for a two-week summer break from their studies. The open question was whether Sanford, their tutor, would return for another term.[1]

Gus's ducklings had not yet emerged from their shells, but it would not be long, Frances thought on June 8. By June 13 five of the ducklings had hatched and more were expected momentarily. There was now also a young hare, which needed a name; it came to Gus from Clara's husband Hugh, who got it from the man who had shot its mother. "They," which was the boys and their grandfather as their father was so busy, had constructed a pen to keep the cats and dog from killing the hare, and they fed the five-week-old pet clover and milk. "You are so happy in the selection of names, do send us one for the poor little hare," Frances wrote to Lazette. No matter; "the rascal ran away the first night Gussy put him in his new pen, which he had spent a week building. Was it not ungrateful?" Soon thereafter, they found the hare's skin and deduced that cats had killed it. Rats got the ducklings. Gus now tended pigeons, apparently in the house's rafters. "Poor Gussy has not had success with his pets. He is all the while engaged in building houses and pens, making yards and ponds, but his favourites make but a short stay." Fred was content with his kitten, Chitterbob.[2]

Sanford was unable to return, and Frances found Charles Anthon's *Caesar's Commentaries on the Gallic War* "altogether too difficult for my limited knowledge of Latin." This meant that Gus needed to leave his mother's school for the Auburn Academy, "very much against his inclination," according to Frances. In preparation for the start of the term, she devoted upwards of six hours a day with Gus to his math. As of late August, Fred was the lone student in her home school. Gus told his mother that at the academy "they spell once a week without study and write only when they choose, which is pretty generally equivalent to not writing at all." Frances planned to discuss the inattention to basics with the Reverend Josiah Hopkins, who was the principal.[3]

Frances experimented in August with a new (to her) treatment for headaches. She wrote asking Lazette's advice. "Now, I want to ask you what you know about the effect of ether. I have taken it three times when suffering with nervous headaches and found almost instantaneous relief." This was before she tried it while hosting a social event. As she explained to Henry afterward, "I believe the evening passed away agreeably to all. For my own part, I took some ether to allay a violent headache, which somewhat exhilarated my spirits besides curing my head." Then she passed out in company. "The little boys were very much afraid I had killed myself that night." Someone called a doctor. "I was felicitating myself upon having at last attained a very desirable object when Dr. Hamilton threw cold water upon all my glowing hopes by informing me that ether frequently produced apoplexy." The doctor told her that she really could have killed herself with the experiment. She also found the side effects brutal. "The effect of the ether lasted until about eleven o'clock. By that time the company had all dispersed and I retired to bed. Then came on my headache with renewed violence. I obtained but little sleep that night." Clara agreed with the doctor that ether was a bad idea, telling Frances that Marcia Hall, an acquaintance, regularly took it. "I reply that I should be very unwell to be in the state she is in now, whether produced by persecution or ether." Ether, also known as laughing gas, was first synthesized in the sixteenth century and was used successfully as a surgical anesthetic about eight years after Frances's experience. There were many deaths as patients, surgeons, and dentists experimented with dosages.[4]

With Gus off to school, Frances consulted Henry about taking French lessons. She proposed hiring a tutor for twice-weekly classes as her weak eyes permitted. "I have always been desirous of learning the language and would like to be able to assist the boys. Perhaps the leisure and inclination may not again occur. Tell me just what you think best." We can assume a positive reply because a few weeks later Frances wrote to her sister about invitations they had received to a wedding, addressed to "Mr. Seward & Lady," which she thought was in bad taste. "Don't the laws of etiquette say anything on this subject?" she asked her sister. "It is mauvais ton certainly. I put in those two French words to let you know that I am taking French lessons among a thousand other things. I intend to teach Fan [Lazette's daughter] and the boys."[5]

Henry called on his former friend and now nemesis Albert Tracy in Buffalo in early September. The issue between them was Tracy's opposition to Henry's pursuit of the Whig Party's nomination for governor and Tracy's support for Francis Granger, who had been the Whig candidate for vice president in 1836 and had lost campaigns for governor in 1830 and 1832. Henry liked Granger, considered him an honorable man and a friend, and also acknowledged in private, at least, that as the party's candidate in two previous elections, while Henry had been the candidate only in the last one, Granger had a prior claim to the nomination. To Weed, Henry insisted that he wanted to "withdraw if Granger was not inclined to do so." Luther Bradish, speaker of the assembly, was also a candidate. About him, Henry felt differently. "I am sorry to hear that Bradish has set his heart upon what warm friends of both say ought to be my point of ambition."[6]

Henry complained to Frances from Westfield about how busy he was and also claimed that he longed for rural tranquility such as others enjoyed in Chautauqua County, which was a beautiful place. "It is a bright and glorious morning," he wrote to her; "the scene is tranquil.... I suppose it is an idle dream, but it often seems to me that, if we were all here, I might enjoy tranquility and peace." She bought none of it, having succumbed to his claims of longing for family and home many times. "You must have had a pleasant excursion to Chautauqua, pleasant for you who enjoy hustle and much company and many strange faces. You do enjoy it, dearest, or you would not always be in the midst of it. It is distressing to me when I am ill, and wearisome when I am well." Henry knew she was right about him, and about herself, writing in response, "I know full well that it is the mind that makes peace or war; that it is my temperament and constitution that attract the thousand cares, and these would as certainly call them round me here as elsewhere."[7]

Someone in the Seward family spotted the famous author Washington Irving in church on Sunday morning, August 26. Henry was home, passing through on his political journey, and called on Irving in the American Hotel that evening, where he stayed overnight on his way to the wedding of a nephew in Geneva. Frances had missed meeting the author in New York earlier in the year, when she was too ill to attend a dinner with Henry. "He came home with Henry and spent part of the evening. . . . How different he appeared from the Washington Irving I had pictured in my fancy.... He is very plain, gentlemanly and affable but in no way remarkable in his appearance, not a particle of ostentation about him. He does not seem in the least sensible that he has written so many beautiful books."[8]

As September began, Henry was hopeful, but not confident, that the Whig nomination was his. On September 8 he wrote to Jennings that "there is nothing new politically. As we approach the sitting of the convention a thousand rumors gather about. . . . I discern no want of confidence among them upon whose information I rely for my own government, but my rule is to anticipate an unfavorable result. You will do well to prepare yourself for the same. We shall know soon." When the party convention met at Utica on September 12, the question was far from decided, and Henry had not withdrawn in favor of Granger. On the first ballot, Seward got fifty-two votes to thirty-nine for Granger and twenty-nine for Bradish. Politicking ensued. On the second ballot it was Seward sixty, Granger fifty-two, and Bradish ten. On the third ballot, Granger gained the lead, sixty to Seward's fifty-nine. On the fourth ballot Seward secured the majority with sixty-seven votes to Granger's forty-eight, and when the convention reconvened the following morning, it was unanimous for Seward with Bradish the nominee for lieutenant governor. "Well, Seward," Weed wrote to him from the convention, "we are again embarked upon a 'sea of difficulties,' and must go earnestly to work."[9]

Henry received congratulations from family members; letters from his father, his brother Jennings, and his brother-in-law Alvah Worden all expressed their pride. Other letters in August and September, from Henry's brother George, his sister Cornelia, and Cornelia's husband Mahlon, asked him for money. The same desperate plea came from Polydore's wife Rachel, but not until after the November election. Mahlon was $1,000 in debt for costs associated with exploring a move to the West. George had again failed in business with his store, and their father was refusing to help him out of yet another financial scrape. Apparently, Henry assisted George again, because there are no more pleading letters from him, and we learn later in the year that George had become a farmer. Samuel too was short of money and needed Henry to pay $140 that he owed. Jennings addressed Samuel's cash flow problem for his too-busy brother. Henry replied positively to Mahlon but said he could not help until after the election, which satisfied his grateful brother-in-law. Finally, that fall there was the letter from Rachel, which arrived in early December summarizing the situation with his brother dating back to early September. "Polydore has given up entirely to drink again. His father and mother told him the 1st of September he must go and look another place. They could not have him any longer." This led Polydore to work for wages with others, and he managed to keep sober until the election, when he "got intoxicated and has not been entirely sober since." Rachel was taking in wash, but it did not bring in enough to support the family through the winter, and she doubted whether Polydore's parents would relent and help her support the three children. Henry's mother had told Rachel the previous week that she "must leave Polydore and break up and trust to providence to take care of our children for father and her were too old to have the trouble of us on their minds." Rachel said she was writing to Henry for advice. She was willing to leave her husband if that is what his family thought she should do, but she was not prepared to abandon her children to an orphanage and the care of strangers. There was the question, though, of what to do with two-year-old Frances, who was named for Henry's wife. While she hesitated to ask, to put the burden of such a small child on her aunt Frances, she floated the idea with Henry. In the end, then, Rachel was asking for money to keep her family together.[10]

Samuel, who was still "tottering on the verge of the grave," as he did for another eleven years, was proud of his son. "I am immensely gratified," he wrote. He was offended, though, at newspaper accounts describing Henry as the offspring of Loyalists and concerned about the lie's impact on his son's political ambitions. "This is an absolute falsehood," he wrote. He believed that his father, John Seward, was among the first in Sussex County, New Jersey, to take up a gun in support of the Patriots. He fought in the battles of Long Island, White Plains, Stony Point, and Paramus and commanded a regiment in the battle of Princeton. "With his own rifle [he] brought many poor Hessian officers and soldiers to the ground." He was in "the hottest of engagements" at Trenton and Brandywine, and he also fought on the frontier "against the hostile Indians." With this proud heritage in support of liberty behind him, Samuel expected his son, as governor, to be a bulwark against corruption and to ensure against rampant election fraud. Henry should beware, as "political and personal friends, office hunters, speculators, and foundlings, each with his own selfish and interested views to gratify, will hang on to the skirts of your garment." Finally, a piece of fatherly advice that Samuel thought should be repeated often: "If elected, let this principle be riveted in your mind, that you are Governor of the state and not of a party."[11]

During the ensuing general campaign, Henry had to defend his role in the Holland Land Company's dealings, which he did, and he tried, as always, to steer a middle course on slavery, against the institution in principle, in favor of supporting fugitive slaves who passed through New York but refusing to endorse the path of immediate abolition, which was farther than his fellow Whigs were prepared to go. As he explained to his brother, "it will probably be unsatisfactory to the ultraists on both sides." As Fred explained the case looking back on his father's career, Henry had "the sagacity to foresee that to precipitate the issue prematurely in that canvass was simply to court defeat." Even though he, courageously as Fred told the story, avowed "more advanced sentiments than the bulk of the Whig party were yet prepared to sustain," that position was "only partially satisfactory to the antislavery leaders, who denounced them through the press." The abolitionists were not an effective political force in New York in 1838, and they split two years later between those who favored political engagement and formed the new Liberty Party, and the Garrisonians, who advocated nonresistance and opposed involvement in electoral politics. As for the approaching election, Henry wrote in late October, "on the whole it is my private opinion that there can be no safe calculation upon the result. My hopes exceed my apprehensions."[12]

Frances took ill in late October, which was her pregnancy with Will, who was born June 18, 1839. She reported her condition as nerves, which was a very Victorian way of not discussing such intimate details, and she was, as always, torn between her husband's ambitions and her own hopes for a settled family life in Auburn. Jennings's son Augustus stopped for what Henry described as "a cheerless visit" in light of his aunt's "illness." "Frances has been unable to sit up an hour since he came," Henry wrote to his brother. He described himself as "entirely absorbed in the perplexities and labors of the day." Two weeks later, after the election results were in, Henry again wrote to Jennings, "Frances has been unwell since I last wrote but not dangerously and is now able to sit up part of the day."[13]

Among the perplexities of the campaign that absorbed Henry was the concern among Henry's supporters that abolitionists would defeat him, but that turned out not to be true; Quakers in Ontario County did not vote in a bloc against him, while activists found more support for immediate abolition in Madison and Oneida Counties. The ticket even carried Chautauqua County, where Henry's role in foreclosures was thought to be a likely weakness of his candidacy. On November 12 Henry's father wrote to congratulate him "on the overwhelming majority" he won in the election, although it was no surprise that he had not carried Orange County, including Goshen. He received a majority in the town of Florida, where his cousin's husband George Grier worked tirelessly for him. The Whigs won both the governorship by over ten thousand votes and a majority in the assembly, while the Democrats retained control of the state senate. "For once," Henry's sister Cornelia wrote, "my good husband rejoices sincerely in the defeat of his party."[14]

On November 21 Henry wrote to Jennings that he was overwhelmed, and he was now less hopeful he could carve out two weeks to settle matters in Westfield and transfer responsibility for the business to his brother. Instead, he found himself unable to break free. "My dear Jennings," he pleaded, "here I am at last more in need of help and support than ever. With all the responsibilities of the most responsible office in the state to a jealous people. With private affairs confused and a family sick, yet all to be moved and transferred to the capital to maintain the dignity of a court and to perform its powers."[15]

Henry now hoped to be in Westfield for two or three days at the beginning of December rather than the better part of the month, when he had previously thought he would be free after the election. His inaugural message would take him four weeks to write, and he was buckling under the strain of rewriting the speech to suit various Whig Party factions. Shortly thereafter, Henry was off to Albany, and Jennings expressed gratitude for the confidence his brother showed by "promoting" him to head their business in Westfield. "I must say," Jennings wrote, "that I think the estate is suffering a little, because of my want of instructions and knowledge." Henry replied that he saw no way to come to Westfield at all and gave Jennings detailed instructions by mail of what he was to do before bringing the necessary paperwork to Albany for them both to sign after the first of the year. "Time is too precious," Henry wrote, "to expend even in grateful acknowledgements of love, affection, and gratitude to you and to my dear sister."[16]

Rather than basking in victory, Henry was deluged with cares. As Fred explained in retrospect, "while his supporters were thus giving themselves up to merriment, the newly-elected Governor had plenty of anxiety and work. . . . The house at Auburn was, of course, thronged with visitors at all hours, seasonable and unseasonable, and the mails brought him each day an increasing avalanche of letters." Henry must deliver the speech on January 1, which would steer his administration's course. He had a household to move and a sick wife who was a distraction rather than a help. He also had to find a place for them to live in Albany, as there was no state-owned governor's mansion. As a Whig, he could not live in a house that had been bought for the Democrats' governor, a mansion that his party had soundly ridiculed. "Several others were proposed, but the decision was finally in favor of the 'Kane Mansion,' at the corner of Westerlo and Broad Streets, the grounds around which were formerly those of a beautiful country seat of that family, but were now intersected by city streets. The house was a spacious yellow-brick edifice, with broad wings, surrounded by a grove of horse-chestnuts, hemlocks, and pines, and with about four acres of grounds. It was in all respects well adapted for an official residence."[17]

Rent on the Albany mansion cost about twice as much as Seward's annual salary as governor, and then there were the expenses of entertainment, housekeepers, and wait staff, so the office was a significant financial drain. Henry broke away from the chaos in Auburn, telling Jennings that "I leave Frances at home, sick all winter," so Henry traveled with Gus to their new home. Henry wrote to Frances on December 21, the day after their arrival, that "if I was oppressed with labor and cares at home, I have not found a bed of roses here." He was confident, though, that the house would meet with Frances's approval and not be a strain on her limited personal resources. "The carpets were laid in the nicest manner, the stove was heated, the lamps soon lighted, and some fine smoking-hot brook-trout were ready for our supper." While he was consumed by the people's business, he and Thurlow Weed "are of opinion that you will be tranquilly located when you come here, notwithstanding all the cares that may beset me; there is so much luxury in space, and so much comfort in the certainty that those you depend upon for the duties of servants understand and seek faithfully to perform them."[18]

Jennings felt rudderless in Westfield in the absence of guidance from his brother, and on top of it all, the landlord looked to cancel the lease on his house. "If you are so obliging as to buy me a house, it is due to you to determine when and where." Henry responded with what must have come as a bombshell. Jennings should reach an agreement with the landlord to vacate the house by June 1. The management of the business was not to be transferred to Jennings after all, but rather to William Duer, the son of one of the investors. "This deliverance you will appreciate," Henry wrote on Christmas Day, "and be more grateful than I can be. Preserve it for the present as a secret, known only to Weed, Bob Hunter, and my Secretary, who writes this. A merry Christmas to you." He assured Jennings, though, that "I will have a home for you."[19]

On Christmas Day Henry wrote again to Frances, acknowledging that "Christmas will be fully honored in your domicile. Its observance has been very different in mine." He continued to have "some friends to dinner daily, and we go on awkwardly, in some respects, for want of your presence and supervision." He continued to work on his inaugural message through the holidays, receiving callers, subjecting drafts to criticism from party elders, and attending to his correspondence as he had time; he had about 150 unanswered letters, a pile he had hoped to reduce after the inauguration. He now had a secretary, Samuel Blatchford, an eighteen-year-old who later became a partner in Seward's firm and, much later, an associate justice of the US Supreme Court. Henry dictated replies to Blatchford, and the secretary made fair copies of letters and documents from Henry's scrawl.[20]

Two days later, Henry wrote again to Frances and told her that when she saw the governor's message printed in the newspapers, she would not recognize it from the draft she had read before he left home. "It has been subjected to such criticism that I scarcely recognize a paragraph of the draft I read to you at Auburn." The message at least in part reflected the governor's personal ambitions and the demands of the various constituencies to which he answered. It might be viewed as a laundry list of agendas, but if so, it was a list befitting a queen's wardrobe. Critics saw it as "reckless" and "visionary." The opposition press called it a "curious piece of patchwork," the "labor of several hands," and "the effusion rather of the sophomore than of the statesman." There certainly had been many contributors, but Henry was consistent in his support for internal improvements, increased subsidies for libraries and schools, the improvement of education for females and African Americans, penal and court reform, a reduction in patronage offices, currency and banking reform, and new safeguards for "the purity of the ballot-box," particularly in the cities where party machines ruled.[21]

Henry's father had declined the invitation for himself and Henry's mother to attend the inauguration, "after much consultation and reflection on the delicate state of my health and the inclemency of the season." Frances too remained ill and unable to make the journey. "At midnight, the strains of a band of music from without announced to the governor the commencement of his official term. Henry invited the orchestra into the hall, and so began the first reception of the day." The inauguration itself was at the Capitol at 11:00 a.m. "While the clerks of the respective houses were reading the message, already in print, it was dispatched to the newspapers East, West, North, and South, forwarded by special engine over the Mohawk and Hudson Railroad, and sent by special messenger to New York." Back at the governor's mansion, "the old-time custom of undertaking to feed the multitude on an occasion of public rejoicing was still in vogue at Albany." The multitude was "orderly enough at first, though as the day wore on, . . . the graver visitors were succeeded by others less dignified, taking somewhat the air of a saturnalia, but not an unfriendly one. . . . With the slender police force then in existence, it is only remarkable that so few scenes of confusion, disorder, or riot, marked these tumultuous assemblages."[22]

The perspective of twelve-year-old Gus on the inauguration was different than his father's, as we might expect. The quantity of food was most remarkable to the boy. As he wrote to his aunt, "we had five tables set with turkey, ham, beef, corn beef, alamode beef, New Years cakes, crackers, cheese, champagne, [and] wine." He was on his own, which was the way boys his age lived back then. "I was up to the capitol and saw Pa sworn in his office. And, I went into the Assembly and saw some of the officers elected and heard the message read." His father returned home during the reading of the message and opened the doors of the house to the throng of about "two or three thousand people . . . and they crowded in so fast that they upset one of the tables." It was, then, a disorderly gathering right from the start. "When I came back from the Capitol, I tried to get in. I went up on the stoop and could not get in, nor could [I get] off the stoop again any way except to jump off the side." As he told the story, Gus then circled the house about three times looking for a way in and eventually climbed through the kitchen window. After some time inside, Gus exited by a sitting-room window and made his way down to Thurlow Weed's house, where he found a little peace. After staying at Weed's until he got bored, he made his way back home and climbed in a kitchen window again, but this time "with about a dozen boys at my heals. As quick as I got in another boy got halfway in, then we shut the window down. Then he began to squeal to get out. We kept him there about a minute, then we let him out."[23]

Frances read about what she termed in a letter to Henry "an assault upon your house by the mob," which had "caused much alarm." This was the same event that Henry described as "orderly enough at first" followed by "a saturnalia, but not an unfriendly one," and Gus navigated without harm in and out of a "crowded" house. Nonetheless, Frances was incensed in absentia, which did nothing to improve her attitude toward living in Albany. Her "friends," by which she meant her family, had kept the "rumors" of the mob assault on the governor's mansion from Frances for a couple days until they confirmed the safety of Henry and Gus. Her understanding on January 9 was that the Locofocos, an extreme wing of the Democratic Party that was responsible for the 1837 Flour Riot in New York City, had organized the mob action. She had also heard that Henry's "Whig friends behaved badly enough. They abused your house and stole your provisions upon the whole."[24]

Henry wrote a short note to Frances: "We are here. The ceremony is over. A joyous people throng the Capitol. This is the first message." Frances wrote to him the next day. "I intended to have wished you a 'happy New Year' yesterday, feeling unusually well in the morning, but a visit which Dr. Humphreys took occasion to make disturbed me so much that I was obliged to go to bed with the nervous headache." Humphreys was the physician who brought the smallpox contagion that killed Cornelia into their house three years previously. "I do not know why it is that he insists upon obtruding himself into a house when he is so unwelcome," she continued to Henry. "God knows I forgive him the misery and disappointment he has occasioned me. If I did not, I could not kneel with him at the same altar but his presence here distresses me exceedingly, bringing as it does so vividly to my remembrance all the painful circumstances relative to the sickness and death of our dear little girl in which he acted so unfeeling and unprincipled a part."[25]

Frances's dark perspective on her life and marriage was if anything gloomier as she entered the new year pregnant with their fourth child. "I suppose I may congratulate you," she reprimanded Henry, "upon having lived through the toil of New Year's Day as I see no account of your death in the papers." Lazette was still with her as comforter and nurse, but she would return to Canandaigua before accompanying Frances and Fred to Albany in mid-February. "I am getting better," Frances wrote three months into her pregnancy. "I still suffer so much with faintness and palpitations of the heart as to be unable to see any of my friends. I think I shall not only be invisible but silent also during my stay at Albany. I wonder you can really wish me to come." If she had an agenda, other than reporting, ventilating, and sarcastically congratulating her husband, this was it. Either she hoped to be relieved of the burden of being the governor's wife with an official role or was simply looking to lower Henry's expectations of her, which was probably unnecessary. She also offered Henry some advice on entertaining. "Avoid having a great variety of dishes. Your liberal spirit will be very likely to lead you into this error. . . . Too many indicates a want of taste and is now decidedly mauvais ton." This was exactly the sort of thing that Henry wanted Frances to address as the state's first lady. "I take it for granted that you have very little time for the consideration of these small matters. I have exhausted all my strength" in writing a letter, so they both realized how little she could contribute in Albany.[26]

On January 8 Frances left her room for what she estimated to be "the first time in three months," the first trimester of her pregnancy.

She continued to suffer from nausea, faintness, and "weakness of my breast," what she also described as "palpitations," and was still "able to sit up only a few hours at a time. Still, I am getting better slowly." She missed Gus terribly but had gotten used to life without Henry, as she explained to her husband. Gus had been "always ready when I was ill to read for me or perform any kind office within his power. You have been such a truant of late that I have become more accustomed to your absence. I hope it will not always be so." Fred was well and absorbed in his books. Elijah prepared to leave for Albany with a few of his friends.[27]

Henry's sister Cornelia died unexpectedly from quinsy, what we call tonsillitis, on January 4, three days after Henry's inauguration. Mahlon decided impulsively to return her remains to her parents in Florida, so he packed up their children and the coffin for the journey without informing anyone of his intentions. The Canfields arrived at the Sewards' home in Florida, from which Mahlon was long ago banished, on Thursday, January 10. The funeral and internment in a borrowed vault were on Saturday. As Jennings told the story, having heard about it after the fact, his father was out riding and found the party waiting for him on his return. "Their solemn countenances told him before they spoke that death had somehow fallen upon his household, but like all the rest of us he least expected it there. Poor dear old people, they were both overwhelmed. . . . Friends were invited, the funeral was held in the house and every room and every place was filled."[28]

Samuel began to dwell on the design and building of his own family's vault within two months of his daughter's death. They now had her coffin and that of Marcia and Jennings's daughter, also Cornelia, in a borrowed tomb. Obsessed as he was about his own death, Samuel found the Seward vault a matter of some urgency, the burden for which he put on Jennings, who received from him "a severe letter," the first among many, for not devoting sufficient time and energy to the task. Cornelia's parents did not attend the internment, as Samuel suffered from "an inflammatory fever, pains in my side, and [was] very feeble." Henry and his brothers were not there, which his father excused, because they were not notified in time for the January 12 funeral.[29]

Cornelia left Mahlon with four children, having previously lost Frederick and their first Augustus before they reached the age of two. Their sixteen-month-old Mary died of scarlet fever two months after Cornelia. Almost simultaneously, also in mid-March, their son Francis contracted measles and Caroline suffered a lung infection that "greatly alarmed" her father, who understandably considered himself "the most wretched of men," a physician who could not cure his own family. Fortunately, both of the children had recovered by the end of the month. It was Cornelia's dying wish that her parents take responsibility for her two daughters, soon to be one after Mary's death. According to Jennings, who heard the story from Mary and Samuel, Cornelia asked for a pen and paper the day before her death and scratched out a note. "Dear Parents, I am fast receding from the shores of time, pray remember my dear little girls." Others decided, given her parents' age and infirmity, that it was not possible for them to raise the children, although given the wording of the note, it sounds as if Cornelia may have had only financial responsibility in mind. In any event, the Sewards of Auburn accepted responsibility for the education of four-year-old Caroline Cornelia.[30]

After his inauguration, Henry was unable to escape the family and focus on his public duties. Frances's chronic illness, his parents' debility, his brothers' debts, Lazette's marriage, the loss of their own baby, and now his sister's death all distracted him. On top of the responsibilities of his office, the burden was heavy. About the loss of Cornelia, Frances believed that "probably none of her brothers feel it so acutely as Henry. They were very devotedly attached to each other."[31]

Henry's parents heard rumors reminiscent of his college days. Word had it that he was again living the life of an irresponsible bachelor in the absence of his wife and children. Perhaps their son was not so far removed from his youthful indiscretions as they had hoped. Samuel reminded his son that a widespread complaint about the previous administration was its "want of moral and religious feelings and profligacy." It was the expectation of the "thoughtful and sober" constituents who voted for Henry that they were electing a "sober, thoughtful, moral, reflecting man. To this course your message pointed," as did the "indisposition of a beloved wife, the loss of one of the finest and most accomplished sisters ever a brother had, [and] the painful decline and anguish of a father just stepping into the tomb." And yet, reports from Albany disclosed that Henry lived a dissolute life, surrounded by "a host of hangers on, that your dining hour is three [p.m.] and it usually is kept up until 5, 6, 7 & 8 o'clock at night, that these continued parties are enormous[ly] expensive and sometimes noisy." The published accounts of the raucous reception of the public at the governor's mansion on New Year's Day should have, according to Samuel, given Henry pause and reminded him "to reflect on the great responsibilities that rest upon you and cause you to determine that you would give no dining but those to the legislature and departments at proper seasons and in a temperate style." While Samuel recognized that both in his first month as governor and in his college days it was Henry's "noble spirit and generous soul" that got him into trouble, he needed to extrapolate the costs of such profligacy, which should make him realize that his debts would approach $50,000 at the end of his two-year term of office, "which is not required of you and for this nobody living will ever thank you."[32]

In mid-January Frances's head continued to ache "violently," and she was still hoping that Henry would relieve her of the unwanted responsibility of joining him in the governor's mansion. "I think if you still consider it advisable for me to come to Albany that I shall be able to go as soon as the 1st of Feb, about a fortnight hence." She counted on Lazette to accompany her. "I have felt so unwell for a few days past," she wrote to her sister on the same day she wrote to Henry, "that I have felt almost discouraged about undertaking the journey, but am in hopes to feel better." Three days later, Fred wrote to his aunt and cousin that "ma is a little better than she was when you went away." Frances now hoped that Henry would come to take her and Lazette to Albany. "Of course, I cannot think of going unless he does," she told her sister on January 24. "It seems to me like a journey across the Rocky Mountains to attempt to go at all in my present health." To Henry she wrote, "in the present state of my health, trifles appear formidable. I have no doubt that it will be inconvenient for you to leave, perhaps not possible." Again, perhaps this meant she could be relieved of the unwanted burdens of the journey and a formal role as first lady in Albany. By February 1 Henry had replied that he was coming for her.[33]

With the family in Albany, Judge Miller responded to a letter from Fred, who had inquired about his cat and Gus's pony, both of which were well; according to his grandfather, "there is nothing new in Auburn" as March came to an end. Henry spent one day in Florida in early April, during which he discussed without resolution the question of guardianship of Cornelia's children. "I found my parents about as I anticipated," he wrote to Mahlon. "I had some melancholy moments with my dear mother, who is grieved beyond even her power of resignation by the loss of her only daughter. They will soon be joined to part no more. The Spirit of my mother is broken." When Mahlon answered a letter from Frances on April 11, he said that "my children are all well and able to go out." He no longer feared for Caroline, whose lungs were now clear. Although Mahlon remained despondent over the loss of his wife and his younger daughter, he was grateful that Caroline had recovered. "The dear little creature seemed to be at the very gates of death, when I first wrote to Henry, and I felt as if I was not far off. I am sure I could not have sustained the loss of that child."[34]

Lazette returned to Canandaigua in early May, and Frances spent the next three weeks in confinement. With the legislative session ended, Henry accompanied Frances and their boys back to Auburn at the end of the month. It was Henry's opinion, communicated to Jennings on May 27, that "Frances, having been several weeks confined to her room, has obviously improved by the journey."[35]

"Frances gave birth last evening to a son," Henry wrote to his mother on June 19. The next day, he wrote to Jennings that "Frances has a son and is doing so well that I have ventured to leave her and go East." "Frances has a son," now two days old and as yet unnamed, so Henry headed back to Albany. When Jennings's son Augustus wrote to his uncle on June 24, he inquired about his aunt's health ("I hear she is quite unwell)" but did not know that she had been pregnant or that she had given birth. Jennings wrote on the same day to congratulate and express his surprise at the news. On June 27 Lazette wrote to Henry from Auburn that Frances "has passed the ninth day (a crisis is much demanded by physicians and nurses) and though extremely feeble is in good spirits and perfectly free from pain and other unfavorable symptoms. In good Doct. Mosher's language, 'she is doing remarkably well.' Today she has changed her meager diet of bread and water for more nutritious food and I hope to be able to say the next time I write that she has been much benefitted by it. The boy is quiet and increases in stature and favour with the whole family." Still no name for the baby, but Frances had now passed the postdelivery danger of puerperal fever. For the first time since the delivery, it could be said with some confidence that both mother and child would live. Gus wrote to his father on July 7 that Lazette headed home that week, a hired man weeded the garden, Peter Crosby was badly stung by bees, Gus and his grandfather had gone fishing, and "Ma is better than she was, the baby is well."[36]

The baby is first mentioned by name as Willie in a letter from Frances to Henry on July 13. The family had expected Henry to return by then, so she said they were all disappointed when she received a letter from him saying it would be another week until he arrived. She wrote from her bed as she was "able to sit up sometimes two hours at a time, but cannot walk without much pain. While in bed, I am very comfortable. Think I gain strength slowly." There were questions about household staff in Albany, and she suggested a Miss Simons, who was Black, if they wanted to replace the Irish Catherine in the governor's mansion. The Auburn gardens were beautiful, "Willie is not so pretty as Fred was but he is a nice little boy and very quiet," and it "grieves me to hear from you so seldom. I have at present little to amuse me but my own reflections."[37]

Then, that very evening, at 11:00 p.m., Henry appeared, having been "induced" at breakfast by a friend to travel from Albany spontaneously. Now it took only one very long day on the train, which was a big improvement over the three days it had taken by stagecoach at the beginning of the decade. "You may imagine," Frances wrote to her sister, "how much I was surprised when Henry walked into my bedroom at that late hour. I could sleep none in an hour or two and the latter part of the night Willie was so restless that he kept me awake. Of course, I awoke in the morning with the nervous headache." Henry and the other men with him attended church in the morning, which gave Frances some time to relax, and he made calls in the afternoon. "I did not see much of Henry. Mrs. Dean [the wet nurse] wondered that he could not see how much Willie had grown."[38]

Immediately, Frances and Henry were at odds about her return to Albany with him. He wanted her and the three boys to accompany him back to the capital after he made a brief trip to Chautauqua County. She flatly refused. "I shall not leave home with my babe before he is three months old," which was when she planned to have him vaccinated against smallpox. "Indeed, I do not think I will be able to do much myself before that time." On Monday morning, after a stay of about thirty-six hours, Henry was off on his westward journey.[39]

Jennings, who still lived and worked in Westfield trying to close the brothers' business affairs, was back in Florida in July trying to address his father's demands for a family burial vault. He found his father "suffering under one of his turns of coughing, cold sweat, and shortness of breathing . . . very feeble and without appetite or refreshing sleep it seems as if he could not last the day out. But he has stood it along much in the same way for years and I do not despair of seeing him about in a day or two and it is not improbable he will continue with us yet for several years." A week later, before the end of the month, Jennings wrote to his brother again with relief that "the arrangements for the construction of the vault are now nearly completed" and the work could commence in mid-August. The interment of their sister and

Jennings's daughter was now scheduled for the third week of October by Samuel's dictation.[40]

July was the time for making jelly, and Clary had made twenty-nine pounds from cherries and berries that Frances could not eat because it gave the baby indigestion. Willie was six weeks old when Frances wrote to Lazette and said she would be keeping the wet nurse to supplement her own production for several more weeks. The same day she dashed off an irate note to Henry, then thought better of it and toned down her temper before starting again. "On reflection, [I] concluded not to send it, fearing you might think I had said some things which were unkind. The truth is, your unwonted negligence about writing to me grieves and disturbs me more than you can well imagine. I have some difficulty in persuading myself at all times that you are not somewhat indifferent to one to whom you cannot afford to devote ten or fifteen minutes in as many days. I am not a believer in the entire supremacy of your official duties, which perhaps you may be."[41]

Frances gained strength slowly, which likely enabled her to vent her frustration with greater passion. Willie grew fat and was now aware of all that went on around him. She had "been out of my room a number of times, hope to be able to take my meals with the family next week." Henry Clay was in Auburn on the day that she wrote, and her father invited him to the house but "I would I were well enough to see him." Nonetheless, Frances did make the effort, as she wrote to Henry after the fact. "Henry Clay and his son both spent the night at our house. His son and some other gentlemen took tea with us. He did not come himself until after tea, when his time was occupied in receiving the calls of some of the ladies from the village. I saw him a few moments in the evening and the next morning at breakfast." As a result, she explained to her husband, "I was quite ill the day Henry Clay left, having made no small exertion to see him."[42]

Frances also reported to Lazette that Clay's visit had exhausted her, especially making it downstairs for breakfast, which Clary was unwilling to host on her own. "Upon the whole, I was not more than half satisfied. I suppose great men are always hurried through the world in this way, without much time to devote to forming acquaintances, with women especially." On matters of greater interest to her, Frances explained that the nursing was not going well. "I have much less nourishment for him and he is more hearty than any of my other children were." Mrs. Dean, baby Cornelia's wet nurse, "who from her own account always had pails of milk can make no allowance for me. I feel sometimes very much disheartened and fearful that I shall be obliged to wean my little boy, which I cannot think of with any composure." She appreciated any advice her sister could give. The baby refused a bottle; she had already tried that. She hoped Mrs. Benedict replaced Mrs. Dean in the coming week.[43]

Henry wanted Frances to bring the two boys to Albany in late August, while Gus remained home from school, disregarding her decision to have Willie vaccinated against smallpox in mid-September, before they made the journey. "There seems to be no particular necessity for my being there at present," Frances wrote to her sister, as Henry would be away from Albany much of the next month anyway. Such a plan, "of course, is out of the question." Henry was right, though, to report to Lazette that Frances was recovering her health. "Henry was so nearly correct about my health as a man whose mind is similarly engrossed could be expected to be. I probably looked better than he expected to see me and am much more cheerful than I could be last winter. . . . I feel faint and languid in the morning, am better in the middle of the day, and by 8 o'clock in the evening so completely exhausted that I am obliged to go to bed." Clary had a different opinion and was convinced that Frances would kill herself by nursing the baby. For now, though, Frances was supplementing her own milk with that from a cow to reduce the strain on her body. "We have succeeded in getting Willie to nurse a bottle by using a piece of fine sponge in place of a tube. It is a very pretty invention."[44]

Willie received his vaccinations "in both of his fat legs" on September 14. One week later, there were no physical signs that they had their intended effect, so he was revaccinated on September 21. The second time they had immediate results and he remained ill for over a week. At about the same time, Gus left in their wagon to pick up Lazette and his cousin Frances, who helped with the preparations for the move to Albany. Furniture and some luggage went by canal. Hugh McClallen drove Frances and her children from Auburn to the train in the first week of October. Lazette and her Frances followed a couple days later. Frances was in a sour mood as she packed and lamented that she did not have a house of her own in either Auburn or Albany. "Pa has grieved me exceedingly," she wrote to Henry, "by cutting down and mutilating beautiful trees. It seems to be rather discouraging to attempt to ornament a place which does not belong to yourself. No one who has not experienced the same feeling can know how fondly I am attached to every tree and shrub about this place which has been a loved home so many years."[45]

By October 1, Willie was recovering from the kind pox induced by his vaccinations, so Frances was ready to expose him to the world. She delayed their departure another few days as Fred "had a considerable fever last night, accompanied with nausea and pain in the head." The weather was cooperating, so she had hopes of setting out on October 3 if Fred had recovered, but she had to postpone for another day after that because "Frederick is better but not quite free of fever," which was a shame because "the day is so fine."[46]

When Henry was away from home in Albany, Auburn, or Westfield, he found time for distraction without always mentioning it to his wife. On October 1, as Frances dealt with their baby, sick son, and preparations to leave Auburn for Albany, Henry was in New York City, where Lorenzo N. Fowler, one of the leading popular phrenologists in the country, read Henry's skull. The practice had originated in Vienna as an experimental science situated somewhere between biology and psychology. It was an attempt to assess character from the contours of the skull, the bumps on your head. Its most sophisticated adherents were, indeed, scientists, who read tendencies in the development of thirty-seven different "organs" of the brain. The first adherent was a medical doctor, Franz Joseph Gall, who began his experiments in the 1790s. The second was a student of his, Johann Gaspar Spurzheim, who brought the practice to the British Isles in 1814. The path from student to collaborator to apostate took Spurzheim to Edinburgh where the brothers George and Andrew Combe became disciples. The brothers' books had greater influence in America than they did in the British Isles.[47]

The Philadelphia banker Nicholas Biddle, the educational reformer William Ellery Channing, and the Harvard physician Dr. John C. Warren, among others, welcomed the arrival of Spurzheim for an American tour in 1832, where he died during an exhausting schedule of lectures and events in the Boston area. The high watermark of the movement came during Henry's first term as governor, when George Combe, then the foremost international phrenologist, conducted his own American tour. Combe made the acquaintance of numerous influencers of popular opinion, including such politicians as John Quincy Adams, Martin Van Buren, and William Henry Harrison, who were all flattered to have their bumps read.[48]

The advocacy of Spurzheim and Combe spurred popularization, which the English writer Harriet Martineau attributed to America's provincial character. These "phrenologists of the studio" with no scientific credentials monetized the practice. Now anyone with the price of a reading received a practical application of the theory to explain his or her virtues, vices, aptitudes, and failures. Vocational and marital counseling were embedded in the readings, which in the hands of some charlatans became fortune-telling. Books and journals supported self-training in the art of skull reading, adding to the growing shelf of self-help literature that Americans read. It was, for a time, a popular form of entertainment, but it burned itself out in the 1840s.[49]

At its peak, the Fowlers' operation in New York City, where Henry had his reading, supported twenty-six lecturers in the field, all also selling the literature produced by the company. As Orson Fowler, one of the firm's owners and leading practitioners, bragged, "Let me plant a course of lectures in a little village, containing but a single tavern, two stores, and a blacksmith's shop, and a dozen houses, and they flock in from their mountains and their valleys for ten miles in all directions, and fill up any meeting-house that can be found." Among the hundreds of thousands of publications printed and sold was the booklet purchased by Henry for one dollar in which the phrenologist wrote his analysis of the subject directly in the printed explanatory text, on a line left blank for the entry. For an additional two dollars you also got a handwritten analysis that supplemented the printed commentaries.[50]

Henry's brain was large (5 on a scale of 7); his system was strong (also 5). He was very active (6) and excitable (6). Of the four "temperaments" identified by phrenologists, Henry registered as nervous (5), bilious (5), and sanguine (6), but his lymphatic system registered no number at all. This was the system "in which the various secreting glands are the most active portion of the system, [which] produces an ease-seeking disposition of mind and body, and aversion to effort." Henry exhibited no "love of ease" to the reader. Perhaps the governor was being flattered or was well enough known that the reading was not much of a challenge. In any event, the reading suited the customer.[51]

As far as the "classification of the faculties," Fowler read Henry as having strong "domestic propensities," loved and enjoyed his family, "yet not *passionately*." He was an "affectionate companion and parent; very happy with, and miserable without, or away from, his home and family." Finally, Henry was committed to home only to a "moderate or small" degree. He was "not well qualified to enjoy or perform family or social duties and relations; considers other interests as paramount."[52]

Henry had a high attraction to women (5), was attached to his children and pets (5), loved society and was fond of his friends (5). He had a high sense of honor (6) and self-respect (6), was firm and decisive (6), conscientious (6), and optimistic or hopeful (6). His faith or belief was more moderate (4), his command of language was high (6), and his capacity to be agreeable, to be likable and liked was also high (6). We might expect that Henry was flattered and recognized himself in such readings.[53]

The question of care for the children of Henry's late sister was still unanswered when Frances left for Albany. Frances was confused, perhaps because Jennings was her source of information about the family's deliberations, and he had confused everyone else. She also found Henry elusive when she wanted to talk about anything. Agreeing to raise one or more of Cornelia's children would be a major commitment by her. Jennings told her that Henry's parents returned the three children to Mahlon after several months. His father committed to paying for the children's education while declining to raise them. Jennings also told Frances that he and Marcia had likewise declined to adopt children they considered Mahlon's responsibility.

The good news was that the family vault would be completed that fall. The builder put the slate on the roof in mid-October. The workers carted the flagstone for the pillars and floor from the valley. "No pains or expense has been spared," Samuel wrote proudly to Henry, "in the creation of this structure, and I [am] confident it is one of the most permanent ever erected in the country. It will be ready for the reception of our departed relatives shortly after the first of November, when we should be pleased to see you and family."[54]

Five days later, on October 25, Jennings's wife Marcia died suddenly, so there was another body for the family crypt. She had collapsed in Chautauqua "in a fit of apoplexy," according to Frances, laid undiscovered for hours and never recovered, while Jennings was on the road home. She had never appeared healthier when Frances last saw her.[55]

Frances was back in Albany entertaining guests every night with only one servant, Ellen, to help her. She usually had three others, but the Sewards' manservant York, whom Frances described as "the very slowest mortal that I have ever seen in the capacity of waiter," was incapacitated by rheumatism. She also counted on their most dependable staff members, Harriet and Nicholas Bogart, but he was seriously ill with typhoid. "Poor Harriet is almost worn out with care and watching" her husband, who was delirious in his fevered state. "I believe you would be crazy to see the management of my kitchen," Frances wrote to her sister.[56]

The ease with which Frances moved from the news of her sister-in-law's death to a comparatively light discussion of the state of her household reveals better than anything said how little affection Frances actually had for Marcia, whose loss Jennings suffered alone. The rest of the family found her odd and annoying, a woman about whom Frances could only speak positively of Marcia's best intentions and other family members spoke hardly at all. On the last day of the month, Samuel and George had heard of Marcia's collapse but not yet of her passing. On the same day, when Marcia and Jennings's son Augustus stopped in Albany on his way home from New York City, it was Frances who broke the news of his mother's death to him. The next day, they received a letter from Jennings, confirming her passing, in which he showed himself "more composed, and resigned even, than I anticipated," Frances wrote to her sister. It was the servants who had found her paralyzed, perhaps from a seizure or stroke. She lingered for about twenty-four hours, eyes open and bulging, never regaining her faculties. They buried her near the house in Westfield, expecting to reinter her body in Samuel's vault at some point in the future.[57]

On November 13, Samuel wrote to Henry to inform him that "our family vault, 16 by 24 feet and 9 feet high of the best materials and I presume as well built as any in the state was completed this afternoon and the workman discharged." He had arranged to move the bodies of family members from different locations. It was a long list. "I have written to Jennings, but have as yet received no answer. Am very anxious to know whether he will be down or not." Samuel was impatient for Henry and Jennings to fix a date for the interments, including that of Marcia, in addition to Jennings and Marcia's deceased daughter. "Will you dispose of this suspense by conferring with your afflicted brother and letting us know as soon as possible the result." Jennings, in his grief, asked Henry to write and decline the summons for him. Henry replied, "I wrote to our Father that you would not be able to go to Florida. I go to New York tonight, stop at Florida on my return from there."[58]

Chapter 9

Governor's Family, 1839–1841

Christmas and New Year's Day passed with little notice in family letters from Albany as 1839 ended and 1840 began. Gus arrived with his grandfather on December 23 on a break from school that lasted until mid-January. "He has grown three inches since I came away," Frances wrote to her sister on December 26, "and, of course, has outgrown all his clothes. I could hardly realize that he was my boy." The next day, Christmas Eve, "we went to the tailor to order a suit of clothes for him, his present suit giving him somewhat the appearance of poor Smikes, who at sixteen appeared in the habiliments of six." Smike, a character in Charles Dickens's *Nicholas Nickleby*, which was serialized and then published as a book that year, first appears in chapter 7 of the novel, in "an extraordinary mixture of garments," a teenager tall for his age dressed in a suit "absurdly short in the arms and legs." Next, Frances continued, she "went to the toy shop for a Christmas present for Fred," then on to the bookstore for more presents before returning to their rented home. "Pa seems to enjoy himself exceedingly."[1]

Henry was so absorbed in preparing his annual message that he had no time for any of it or any of them. The rest of the letter was joyless and without the expectation of anything happy on the horizon. "Christmas has come and gone," she wrote, "the New Year is fast approaching before the advent of which I must write all that I intend to write for there will at that time be no peace or quietness anywhere, no withdrawing of one's self from the cares and vexations which that season will bring with it." January 1, 1840, began the second and final year of Henry's first term as governor, so there was another campaign ahead. For Frances, at least, life as a member of the governor's family was to be endured. The celebration of the new year brought less dissipation to the governor's house than the previous one, which Frances ensured.[2]

Fred shared his memories of New Year's Day 1840 almost a half century later. The celebration opened again, "like its predecessor of 1839, with a midnight serenade and a bountiful collation ready for all comers, spread in the hall of the executive mansion." Fred was nine at the time and thought they were conforming to the "old Dutch customs," which Washington Irving had imagined. "Immediately after sunrise, children began to perambulate the streets, to ring or knock at each door, wish the inmates a 'Happy New Year,' and receive in return a New-Year's cake stamped with 'pictures.'" The housewives kept a basket of cakes in the hallway to accommodate the children. By noon, the household was ready to receive gentlemen callers, who made the rounds of their acquaintances. These calls were short; the callers did not even sit down, but were welcomed and directed to a table where they could take a cake and a glass of wine before going to the next house on their list. At the governor's mansion, "the throng was great, though orderly, and less boisterous than the year before." There were barrels of cakes at the door for the children. "The great hall and all the parlors were thrown open to accommodate the crowd, whose movements were facilitated by an improvised place of egress, steps having been added to the large window that reached to the floor of the dining room." This was likely the same window through which Gus had entered the previous year. "The governor, surrounded by his staff, received his guests in the drawing-room. The refreshment-tables were resupplied as fast as cleared."[3]

The children embraced the family's new normal in their time away from Auburn. Fred needed his aunt Lazette to send him the Sewards' copies of Caesar's *Commentaries on the Gallic War*, so he could study his Latin, and Charles Davies's *Common School Arithmetic*, so thirteen-year-old Gus could study his math. Gus traveled alone on the train from Albany back to Auburn the last week of January for the new term of school. Aunt Clara was "very glad to have Augustus at home again." Frances had a cold but it did not keep her from attending a social event, where she "was looked at as a curiosity it being my first appearance in public." She hosted the governor's first dinner of the new year on January 31. There were two more in February and another in March. "How much I wish they were all over," she wrote to her sister. "It is decided that I am to see company two evenings, no particular invitation to be given. What shall I call them, 'At Homes,' 'Levees?' How I do wish you could come first. The ladies here seem to think it will be a dreadful affair for me to entertain company without any other lady." Frances was looking for ways to reduce her social responsibilities as the state's first lady; scheduled receptions by whatever name could reduce unscheduled visits that interrupted her days.[4]

"We are in the gall of bitterness and the bonds of affliction," Frances wrote to her sister before a social event scheduled for February 2. "How thankful I shall be when the next three days have gone by." Afterward, she wrote again, that "one week of toil has passed. Three dinners are disposed of. Upon the whole we get along." She was hoping that both Lazette and Jennings would be in Albany the following week. Judge Miller was there and out socializing most evenings. "Tuesday, Pa stayed at home to dine, saying he should do so but once." The roof leaked, "our dining room was afloat and we [were] expecting thirty men to dinner the next day."[5]

Among family members, eight-month-old Willie was least affected by their absence from Auburn. He played with a picture book that led him to moo like a cow. He could make himself understood with his versions of "cold," "hurrah," "cake," "Ma," "man," and "moo, grunt, and bark." On February 6 Fred wrote to his aunt Lazette that Willie "is very happy today" and deeply into mischief, trying to get his chair up onto the sofa, banging on the wall, and trying to tip over a basin full of water. Fred still missed a few of his paper animals—the lioness, monkeys, and their cages, which perhaps someone could find and send him from home. Gus and Henry were both ill, the former from eating buckwheat that inflamed his eyes, Frances thought, and the governor from exhaustion. Before the end of February, Willie could also stand on a chair and grunt like a pig, mew like a cat, and demand that his brother take some pretend snuff from an empty box.[6]

By June 5 Frances prepared to return home with Albany's legislative session and social season ended for the summer. Henry had Fred with him in New York City, and Frances wanted her son back before she left. "I must make my arrangements to return home next week," but she felt rushed, as she had three weeks of preparations to accomplish in one. "Should you be detained longer than next Tuesday," she wrote to

Henry, "will you send Fred on the day. . . . I am very lonely. You cannot imagine how much I miss Fred." Two days later, on Sunday, she wrote to Henry again to prod him to send Fred if Henry was not returning himself by Tuesday. "The day is gloomy; my spirits are oppressed with an unwanted weight. Perhaps I am only lonely." Fred arrived safely on the train Tuesday evening with a chaperone, just as Frances had asked. "He seems very much pleased with his visit." Willie had the whooping cough, which compounded Frances's anxiety, and she felt rushed by the nurse, who was eager to move on to her next job, when Frances and her boys left for home.[7]

Perhaps it was the stress of packing or the obligation of numerous calls before she departed Albany that led Frances to have words with Mary Boyce, one of the maids who was leaving her employ. "I endured Mary until I came away," Frances wrote to her sister, "after telling her just what I thought of her," before leaving the house in the able hands of Harriet Bogart, who would decide whether to allow Mary the favor of remaining in the house during a Baptist convention that was meeting in Albany. "I wondered at her impudence in asking the favour. . . . I left her to the tender mercies of Harriet and Eliza [another staff member] and fancy if they allow her to stay she will not find her home very agreeable."[8]

Frances, Fred, and Willie left for home on June 13, escorted by Sam Blatchford, who was still Henry's secretary, and Anna, a household staff member. To her sister, Frances wrote when she reached Auburn, "I hurried my preparations so much that I left many articles behind and many things undone. . . . It is unnecessary to tell you how glad I was when this irksome task was accomplished." As for the train ride home, "we had as comfortable and pleasant a journey as people can have in a rail road car where men spit all about you unceasingly." To Henry, whom Frances now assumed was back in Albany and soon would return home, she wrote that Fred was thrilled to be home with his swing and kitten, that Gus "has grown astonishingly. His voice has become harsh or hoarse and he is in many respects wonderfully like the young Millers who come from Romulus, but he is still a good, dutiful, affectionate boy. I must not quarrel about his entire deficiency in grace of manner and conversational powers, which though not unimportant are of much less moment than a good heart and good principles." She assumed that training would make up the deficits in social skills, so that he would not be as backward in such regards "as are some of his relatives on both sides of the house."[9]

This is the wonder of Gus to those who know him through his family's letters. As a boy, he was active, outgoing, socially engaged, and loving. As a teenager, he comes across as withdrawn and dull. He was far from the first or last moody teenager, but he maintained those traits for the rest of his life. The personality Frances described transcended their relationship but was influenced by tensions between them as he launched off on a career of which she strongly disapproved. He no longer shared his emotional life with anyone else in the family, as far as we know, and adopted a stoicism aspired to by many men. He also displayed, often by his absence, the awkwardness that his mother commented on here and elsewhere. He had changed, and Frances saw it as a reflection of her father's influence in her absence as the family split up between Albany and Auburn and Gus remained home for school.

Henry reappears in the family letters toward the end of June, when he arrived in Auburn for what he said was a few weeks. Almost a year after he had predicted an end to their business dealings in Westfield, Henry apologized to Jennings, who still lived and worked there, for being so long out of touch and so unresponsive to his brother's need for guidance on the closing of their business in Chautauqua County; it is unclear what became of the plan for Jennings to be replaced by one of the investor's sons. "I have been a long time silent and I doubt not much to your surprise," he wrote. By way of apology, he offered the pressure of the governorship as the explanation, which he did not doubt his brother understood; the legislative session had lasted more than four months. "The legislature adjourned, leaving me with several weeks labor but without the excitement which had sustained me during the winter. My health gave way while I was seeking to effect my escape from Albany to this place." We might say that his immune system succumbed in the absence of the adrenaline that had sustained him in the crush of work. "A brief visit to Orange County, which Frances felt that we were bound to make, and a stay of twelve days in New York, which the agitation of the Whig Party rendered necessary, delaying my return to Auburn until now." He was too weak to travel to Chautauqua County and hoped that resting at home would restore him in short order, likely within the week. Perhaps Jennings could come to him. He had seen Jennings's son Augustus in New York and he was fully recovered from the illness, including inflamed eyes, which he had experienced when he was with them in Albany.[10]

Frances had a different perspective on Henry's "rest." He had arrived with two other politicians, and the three of them had taken up residence for the last week of June. "Henry looks sick and careworn. He coughs more than I have ever known him to do before, but refuses to take any remedy," Frances wrote to her sister on June 28. "He has a constant succession of visitors of all descriptions, men, women, and children. He is more constantly occupied than when at Albany." She expected Jennings imminently, so the brothers could continue their work when Henry stole some time from the matters of state. Whether she was in Albany or Auburn, Frances felt like she was running "a tavern, let me be where I will. I think dear Clara will not be sorry to have my visit a short one." On top of the crowds to host, feed, and house, Frances had new staff members to train. She had parted company with the incorrigible Mary Boyce and now had a replacement who was "very raw material to attempt to make a chambermaid of." This put an additional burden on Maria, who had both to clean and wait on the guests.[11]

Frances also had her hands full with the two younger boys. Willie was fussy. Fred had a toothache that tormented him and kept her awake for two days before he walked over to the dentist by himself and had a molar extracted. "It hurt him badly, but he bore it like a man and has had many commendations for his courage." Gus and Fred prepared for the celebration of July 4 with many loud firecrackers and much gunpowder. "Tell cousin Frances that the boys would make her jump very frequently if she continues to be afraid of firecrackers." The previous day Gus had gone hunting with McClallen and Blatchford, and "brought home a number of pigeons. . . . He has a gun of his own and is said to be a very good marksman. Well, I would not have believed it once, but boys will grow into men, let their mothers be ever so timid." Henry was off two days later, on the last day of the month, after a "rest" of a day less than one week. He gave an Independence Day speech in Cherry Valley, Otsego County, between Syracuse and Albany, and planned to return after another week away from home.[12]

After a week on the road and another one at home, Henry was back in Albany the third week of July. Frances was still considering a visit to Lazette in Canandaigua, but she felt feverish, which delayed the decision for the rest of the month. Gus declined his father's invitation to join him for a visit to Schenectady, which was perhaps an attempt to inspire the boy's enthusiasm for college preparation with his father's alma mater in mind. Gus was still stymied by Latin, which was absolutely necessary for admission to any college. Neighbors whose relatives were disappointed office-seekers gave Frances the cold shoulder. A local attorney took personally a bill passed in the last session of the legislature and signed into law by the governor that limited his fees. According to Frances, he thought it was a "malicious attempt to 'ruin his family'" and considered "the Executive alone answerable for this enormity."[13]

Fred completed a note to his aunt and cousin after a delay of a few weeks, reporting that Uncle Jennings was visiting, and the kittens and his little brother were well. He anticipated visiting Canandaigua in two or three weeks, at which point he would regale his cousin with stories about the Independence Day celebration with his older brother. Willie was now thirteen months old and a terror. According to his mother, he "trudges all over the house and yard alone. He is so fearless that I am afraid some accident will befall him, was very wroth with Maria the other day because she would not let him put his finger in the old cow's eye." He persisted in grabbing the cat by the tail and the kitten by the ears, "regardless of the snaps and scratches with which his advances are met by the parties assailed."[14]

Frances was ill, but not sad and angry, the morning Henry left for Albany. "I do not distrust your affection. The gloomy fancies with which I have so often tormented both you and myself have been dispelled by the return of health, that great promoter of cheerfulness." She was upbeat despite the fact that she no longer had a nurse to care for Willie, so on "washing day" she tried to keep the toddler confined so she could assist with the laundry. She hoped it did not take long to find and train a new au pair, but there was none on the horizon during July. "Dear little boy," she wrote to Henry, "he is much less turbulent than he has been. I hope he will continue to improve." Fred was despondent and "cried bitterly" when he realized he had lost the penknife his father gave him. "I remonstrated with him on the impropriety of grieving so much about a trifle, but could obtain no answer other than 'Pa gave it to me.' His extreme sensitiveness causes me many sad forebodings about his journey through a thorny life." She also remained concerned about Henry's health and the lingering cough from his illness in mid-June. "Pray, smoke as little as possible," she advised. "I am afraid it injures you. Do get some sleep. Quiet, it is impossible for you to obtain. I hope you have sufficient strength of constitution to endure all the fatigue which you suffer, but have many fears." As Fred explained after his father's death at age seventy-one, Henry's smoking was a lifelong habit and increased during periods of intense work. "He usually lighted a cigar when he sat down to write, slowly consuming it as his pen ran rapidly over the page, and lighted a fresh one when that was exhausted." He seldom smoked fewer than six and sometimes as many as twelve a day.[15]

In early August Frances wrote to her sister yet again to postpone her long-pending visit. "I am at present in the hands of a dentist who will

FIGURE 9.1. Painting of Governor William H. Seward, by artist Henry Inman, 1843.

FIGURE 9.2. Painting of Frances M. Seward, by artist Henry Inman, 1843. Courtesy of Rare Books, Special Collections, and Preservation, River Campus Libraries, University of Rochester; original painting in Seward House Museum, Auburn, New York.

not complete his operations on my poor teeth until next Wednesday," she wrote on Sunday. Henry made no commitment on the timing of his trip to Chautauqua County, so she had no one to accompany her to Canandaigua, at least until Jennings again passed through on his way home from Albany. She also had heard from him that the workmen chopped down the pretty Siberian crabapple tree that shaded the dining room of the governor's mansion and replaced it with the new cistern that she had wanted. "It is the last place that any person of taste would have selected about the house. I am very thankful that I am not proprietor of the domicile. I should feel exceedingly indignant if I were." To Henry she wrote, "I would not have exchanged that tree for twenty cisterns."[16]

The sad story of the tree's destruction prompted Frances to ruminate on longer-term domestic arrangements. After all, the governor's mansion was not her house, so the destruction was not a permanent loss to the Sewards. "I believe you and I agree entirely in our taste about trees and shrubs," she continued to Henry, "and should we ever be blessed with a permanent home of our own we may escape the pain of seeing them mutilated or destroyed wantonly." The garden of her father's house had never been more lush. "I was wishing yesterday that you were here to see how beautifully our oleanders were blooming. . . . The frequent showers we have increase the verdure of the trees and shrubs so that the county never looked more beautiful." She could still dream of domestic bliss and try to convince her husband that it was a worthy ambition.[17]

The Auburn Academy that Gus and Fred now attended was in recess for most of August. Frances was pleased by the final exercises in which the students performed assigned public readings. Gus remained an unenthusiastic student and was agreeing "somewhat reluctantly" to study history for an hour each day with his mother during vacation. Fred, on the other hand, had "some ambition and does apply himself when he attends school," but his "feeble health" led her to keep him at home about half the time by her estimate. Gus preferred to be hunting, fishing, or swimming. He returned from Montezuma, which is now a nature preserve, with a number of dead ducks and a crane that he had shot on a weekend hunting trip with Clary's husband, this boy who had so recently fretted over the hatching of a brood of ducklings.[18]

Despite the dentist's weeklong labors in her aching mouth, Frances wrote to Henry on August 9 that "I am well, well for the first time in nearly sixteen years. I feel as if new life were given me and notwithstanding the increase of grey hairs at least ten years younger." She was thirty-five. One week later, she wrote to her sister that she suffered from palpitations. Snip bit Willie, who continued to torment the cat, which led Frances to fear tetanus. Maria Sibley, wife of Whig

Party congressman Mark Sibley, provoked Frances by stating in company that Henry's illness was caused by nerves, "that [his] disease was altogether imaginary. How silly it is to allow oneself to be provoked by such ignorant and unfeeling expressions of opinion but I was provoked and after Mrs. Sibley had gone expressed my opinion pretty freely to my guests." Elizabeth Conkling, wife of former congressman and now judge Alfred Conkling, insulted Frances at another social event by refusing to accept her extended hand. It was a gathering of about fifty people at Dr. Joseph Pitney's on a Friday evening in August, "no music or dancing, and too many people to admit of rational conversation. The truth is I do not enjoy such things and always think every time I go will be the last."[19]

Aunt Clary, who was Frances's most reliable help with the children and household, had left on a visit to Romulus. Willie was down with "summer complaint," digestive issues caused by food spoiling in hot weather. Frances had just one helper in the kitchen, so she had to be in there herself "most of the time, and the weather is so exceedingly warm that I have no strength for anything." She had failed to ween Willie, who "nurses almost the whole time. He rejects all that is offered him in the way of food except those things which he must not eat. Today I have the nervous headache in addition to the toothache, which I have had more or less every day since I was so foolish to employ a dentist." She received a note from a friend who said that Henry had asked him to tell her that he would write when he had time. "This is all I have heard from him in nearly a fortnight except by the report of others," she told her sister. "I suppose I shall feel better natured about it when my teeth cease aching."[20]

"Were I to do as you do," Frances wrote to Henry on the same day and in the same cranky mood, "put off writing until a convenient time, I might not send you a line for three weeks to come." Her teeth and head ached, their baby had diarrhea, Clary was away, and one of the kitchen girls had quit. She did not like learning where Henry was from the newspaper rather than from him, and she thought she should take up her father's hired man Peter Crosby's practice of making up stories when people asked. Instead, she continued "to express total ignorance" of Henry's movements.[21]

That letter provoked a response. "There is this difficulty in writing as often as I could wish: I cannot give you details of what happens to and around me." The reason he offered was because he was incapable of writing letters that were all about him. From Henry's perspective,

Frances was being harsh. The legislative session that ended on May 14 was the first in which the Whigs held the majority in both houses. As the governor and head of his party, Henry was simply buried in work. Fred gave us the context in reflection on his father's career; "except while receiving visitors, Seward usually sat in his writing-chair, pen in hand. Those two occupations consumed the whole of his waking hours; there were no idle moments, no recreations, no hours for reading. The amount of work accomplished by this persistence was simply prodigious, as the manuscript drafts, still preserved, attest." It had been a long and busy session, with controversial legislation to support the education of immigrants; infrastructure bills; prisons, law, and banking reform; and a firestorm over Henry's refusal to extradite to Virginia three African American men, who were charged with assisting in the escape of slaves.[22]

Frances then apologized for her "querulous epistle." In retrospect she thought herself "very unkind to trouble you when you have so many other sources of annoyance, but as I told you at the time I was suffering with neuralgia and ought not to have written in so impatient a frame of mind. I trust you will forgive me. I will try to behave better in future." Willie was so much better that she was considering leaving for Canandaigua the next morning, August 27, which she did with him, Maria, and Fred. Gus had "no inclination to accompany me." She was sick with a headache the day of their journey, but male passengers who were Whigs were very attentive to her.[23]

The press of business is visible in the changes to Henry's handwriting, which Fred noticed when he reviewed his father's correspondence after his death. "In the early years of his law practice, clients said his conveyances were 'plain as print.' It was not a hand, however, that could be written with great rapidity, and, when it became necessary to draft letters and paper hastily, his writing grew more and more illegible." During his governorship, "the first letter in each word and the first word in each paragraph would be clear and distinct, while the subsequent ones ran off in a hasty scrawl." It became worse when Henry was secretary of state, but both his health and handwriting were suffering under the stress of executive responsibilities, and writing letters to his wife was a lower priority as he suffered the indignities of what Fred called "the pouring out of all of these vials of wrath upon his head."[24]

Frances and two of her children stayed in Canandaigua for one week and then returned to Auburn with Lazette and her daughter Frances on the stagecoach. Several Democrat passengers "were anything but civil."

As Frances explained to Henry, "I am forced to be a politician whether I will or not." Willie was ill again with the same symptoms. He was awake and crying as she wrote and "my tooth aches so that I can hardly write intelligibly." She was now, at the end of the first week of September, planning to return to Albany with the two younger boys. Jennings was mysterious about an unexpected trip to Ohio in a letter to Frances on September 15. "You will query, perhaps, what it is that that takes me away, but I cannot spare the necessary room in this sheet to tell you. A moment's reflection of where I started from and the circumstances and the times will give you such a clue to it that with your knowledge of man and things, I do not doubt you will guess it but exactly."[25]

Judge Miller left home with two of his friends on September 14 for the Whig Party's convention in Syracuse that nominated Henry for a second term. Frances's two older boys agitated to attend and Frances was inclined to let Gus go. The doctor now attributed Willie's troubles to teething and so lanced his gums and administered calomel, which was mercury chloride. It had been used for centuries, but in the 1840s it was considered a miracle drug and prescribed in heroic doses, which could result in mercury poisoning, for everything from mumps to typhoid fever and teething. Administered orally, it could cause gangrene of the mouth and damage the gastrointestinal tract, often resulting in dysentery.[26]

On her return to Albany, Frances was again short one chambermaid. The new nurse, Mary Boyce, traveled with her, but "Maria refuses to come." Willie was shy of strangers and had not taken to the new nurse, so Frances had to carry him in her arms on the journey. Henry's parents were in Albany for a visit when Frances, the boys, and Mary arrived in the company of Sam Blatchford, whom Henry had dispatched to accompany the family. When she reached Albany, Frances wrote to Gus, who had again remained home to attend school. "Willie finds all strange faces here. Consequently, he is very uncomfortable. He cried about an hour while we were on the railroad." Within a few days, Willie only cried about half the time he was with Mary, by Frances's estimation. Frances was immediately challenged by the social schedule for which she was responsible, beginning with a breakfast for between thirty and forty men, which required her and her staff to be up all night.[27]

After a day out calling in Lansingburgh and Troy, Frances returned to find Willie violently ill, vomiting every ten minutes for two hours. She became so alarmed that she called the doctor, who ascribed the illness to "improper food" that he had eaten in her absence. Dr. Platt Williams left her with a quantity of calomel to administer to the patient, but she withheld the medication when Willie returned to normal without any. "O, the trials I have with Mary," Frances declaimed to her sister. "She is more thoughtless and heedless than Maria without loving Willie half so well. It appears a long time to November," when she would return to Auburn with her children. "I hope that Willie will not be permanently injured, but really think him in danger."[28]

Jennings wrote to Frances in October, two days after Clarence's twelfth birthday, to ask whether his "motherless son" could come to them for the winter. He was asking belatedly, because Clarence was already enrolled in an Albany school. "Will my kind sister look a little after Clarence if he calls, and restrain him from calling often, and tell me whatever you observe in him. The child is very dear to me: the Lord preserve him." Jennings hoped he was not tasking the good will of Henry and Frances, whom he knew bore the burden of "care and responsibility enough already," and he hoped they would "excuse it if it was any way wrong." Two days later, Henry wrote to Jennings that "Clarence is spending the day with me."[29]

Jennings wrote to his brother after the polls closed on November 4 that the entire Whig ticket had increased its majority over the election two years previously. Chautauqua County went for Henry as governor and William Henry Harrison as president by comfortable margins. Worden reported three days after the election that the Whigs did very well statewide, and the abolitionists, whom he considered the most threatening competitors with their new Liberty Party, had failed to diminish the Whig majorities. In the end, Henry ran behind the ticket, but by less than some had predicted. There was also now a Whig in the White House, as Harrison defeated the incumbent Democrat, Martin Van Buren.

The public-school controversy surrounding his support for state funding of Catholic schools was the most effective bludgeon against Henry. While he thought it advantageous to the state to have schools in which children were "instructed by teachers speaking the same language with themselves, and professing the same faith," his political opponents portrayed him as pandering to Irish Catholics, who overwhelmingly voted Democrat nonetheless. After Henry's reelection, he proposed using public money for immigrant schools, which the Catholic diocese of New York City embraced, but the plan was defeated by nativist, anti-immigrant politicians.[30]

Frances dismissed Willie's nurse Mary after the election. Mary Ann, the new chambermaid, watched over Willie in the mornings so his mother could get other things done. Willie's health was restored and his mood calmed as a result. Frances thought his imagination quite wonderful as he pretended to eat bread and milk from his father's shaving cup. In light of the gains and the relative postelection calm, Frances decided to try again to ween the now over seventeen-month-old. "As I apprehended," she wrote to her sister, "he cried almost the whole night. Dear little boy. His mother cried, too." The last month had been a frustration for both of them as she had all but dried up. "How often I have wished that you or Clara were with me during this trial." Not surprisingly, Frances's nerves were on edge and the usual bustle of her household was difficult to bear. Indeed, she and Willie were so indisposed that she was not up to the journey back to Auburn. As a result, she had "written for Gus to come down soon and stay two or three months. I am sorry to take him from Clara but am satisfied it is necessary. His father thinks he will be able to assist him in his studies." Frances had a new nurse for Willie, actually a previous nurse named Miss Brown, with whom she was only pleased in comparison to the previous one. "I am much better today. Willie was very dear and subdued last night."[31]

Five days before Christmas, in a letter to Frances, Jennings revealed his mystery. "I see in the workings of your face that you have guessed my malady. Yes, it is a disease of the heart!" Jennings asked Frances to break the news to his sons Clarence and Augustus. There were apparently two issues keeping Jennings discrete. The first was a lack of commitment as yet from the lady in question, although he expected a positive reply. The other was sensitivity about social convention, as his late wife Marcia was only one year in the grave. When she spoke to Clarence, Jennings asked that Frances "assure him for me that it is done with kind reference to the feelings of both Augustus and himself. Say, if you think so that it is all right, and will doubtless result in his improvement and comfort. None need doubt it. I would save the dear boy from falling into prejudice or unhappiness." He hoped that his sons, with Frances's assurance of their father's enduring love for them and for their late mother, would not resent their new, young stepmother as he anticipated an imminent marriage.[32]

According to Frances, Jennings, age forty-six, acted "like a boy of nineteen in love for the first time. He is to be married to Mary Mumford (I can write the name, though he is unable to do so) immediately." Frances was not thrilled that Jennings tasked her with breaking the news to Clarence, "who though he is very selfish retains some feeling for his mother, some respect for her memory, which I think will not make this communication very agreeable." Henry thought this was the last time she should expend any sympathy on a widower. Frances's letter to her sister dripped with sarcasm when the news was confirmed. "The young couple are to go to Washington or Philadelphia for a few days to 'cover our blushes,'" she wrote, quoting Jennings's letter. "Then, I suppose we may expect the minimum gratification of their company here."[33]

The governor's house was in disarray as the new year began and would get worse over the next week as family members and holiday guests filled the bedrooms. There were too few beds, so Nathaniel Jocelyn, the artist painting a portrait of Henry, had to move to the hotel until some of them left. Frances was better prepared than Henry had been for her first New Year's Day in Albany. The carpets were taken up and the furniture removed to limit the damage and provide more room for the throngs. A band would begin to play at midnight, by which time she had gone up to bed, "too sick to sleep." The boys, however, planned to take it all in. "Clarence and Fred stay up with the gentlemen. . . . We were awakened by day light with another band before the door, who were to be refreshed. I wish you could have seen the hall floor when I got up in the morning." By 2:30 p.m. she was "so ill that I was obliged to leave the room and go to bed." On the whole, she thought the celebration "rather more quiet than the year previous, but it was very fatiguing for us all."[34]

Frances's biggest social failure of her two terms as New York's first lady came on February 3. The dinner party was huge in an attempt to limit the number of social engagements she had to keep. She threw one big party and issued formal invitations for other "at home" events for women in which they were invited to call on her during set hours. This was intended to address her reputation for shirking her social duties and, as she frankly admitted, so she could say that she had invited people who publicly proclaimed that she had socially shunned them but had no intention of accepting her invitation. Six hundred attended the dinner, and it was a disaster by Frances's accounting. Seth Hawley, a lawyer from Buffalo, told her that he "attended a fete once when there were a great many thousand people beside Indians and Negroes, but among them all he did not see as much rudeness as was exhibited by the Albany Gentlemen last night."[35]

The problem was partly a result of the very idea that six hundred guests could be accommodated in such a house and by a staff of eleven, eight of whom were hired for the event. It was also a logistical disaster that resulted from Frances's decision to have the food set out on tables in a small room that she usually used as a spare bedroom. "As I knew it was impossible for all the ladies to [be] helped if the men were allowed to go in," she wrote to her sister in the wake of the fiasco, "I requested four or five gentlemen to stand at the door and invite them to wait until the ladies were served." When the gentlemen abandoned their post, the hoard of men rushed the room "before two-thirds of the ladies had entered and devoured everything before them." About one-third of the women, by Frances's estimate, were never served. "One man appropriated four or five plates of oysters, which were given him to pass to the ladies. Another took a decanter of choice wine to wash a plate for his own use. Two others took a bottle of champagne and each with a glass in his hand continued to drink until the bottle was empty." In the end, she thought "the third of February 1841 may be put down on the same list as the first of January 1839," the riot that accompanied Henry's first inauguration before her arrival in Albany.[36]

Jennings and Mary married on January 6 and began a tour that took them as far south as Richmond and through Washington, DC, before the couple returned to New York City. On February 1 the Seward family in Orange County awaited their arrival momentarily, and the governor's family expected them by the middle of the month. On February 15 Jennings wrote to Henry that he and Mary were in New York City and he was attending to the brothers' business affairs. On February 21 Frances wrote that the newlyweds were expected in Florida that day and in Albany "this week." On February 24 Frances wrote to her sister that "Jennings does not come yet. I regret that their visit is to be made just at this time. We expect them every stage. I shall not send this letter tonight but will write more in the morning." By the next morning, Henry had received a letter from his father announcing that the couple had reached Florida the previous Friday (February 19). Jennings was "a very sick man, has been growing worse ever since" they arrived, and "no possible hopes of recovery can be entertained. We all wish you home as soon as possible." In a postscript, Samuel added, "We shall retain the remains until your arrival." Frances wrote to Lazette that "our brother Jennings has probably breathed his last," which he had that very morning.[37]

On the same day that Jennings died, Frances despaired of his son Gus, whom their physicians in Albany had bled three times and administered additional doses of calomel for an upper respiratory infection. He had "diarrhea constantly, which is reducing his strength very fast," and was delirious. That afternoon, she had lost what little hope she still had and asked for Clary and Lazette to join her as she prepared for the worst. "I feel now that a day lost is everything. May God in his mercy grant that his gentle spirit may not have departed before you come." Henry had delayed a trip to Florida, where his father wanted him to deliver a eulogy for his brother before they interred Jennings's body in the new family crypt. By Sunday (February 26) Frances felt more hopeful about Jennings's Gus, and she had not yet mailed the summons to her sister.[38]

The death of Jennings led Samuel to "ask of myself under the controlling power of a wise providence, who is to be the next. The natural answer is it is I." Henry, still in Albany because of Gus's dire illness, missed his brother's funeral. "Your dear brother was committed to the family vault on Saturday (February 25) at one o'clock, attended by the mourning obsequies [funeral rites], of a whole surrounding country, three reverend clergymen officiating." Samuel, Mary, and their loyal servant Julia Van Brunt were all ill. Samuel was "looking almost daily for the great change. Too weak to dress myself, suffering with most afflicting pain and cough," he continued to predict his own death, which came eight years later.[39]

By Tuesday, Frances was getting more encouragement from the physicians, and Gus, who still complained of pain in his chest, had passed "a tolerably more comfortable day." Henry left for New York City to address the business matters left in chaos by Jennings's death. Samuel feared that he would resign the governorship to deal with the financial challenges, which he advised strongly against. Henry's next stop was Florida. Of his deceased older brother, Henry said that Jennings was "estimable and benevolent. I believe he has left more friends than any man of equal range of acquaintance; while I should be surprised to learn that [he] had an enemy."[40]

On March 6 Frances wrote to Henry with more confidence than she had for weeks that their nephew Gus "is so much better today that I cannot resist the inclination to give you the assurance myself. He has had no relapse since you left us and has today been sitting up twenty minutes." Jennings's son Clarence accompanied Henry when he arrived back in Albany, and "thenceforward became one of his family," according to his uncle.[41]

When the legislative session ended in May, Frances continued the countdown that lifted her spirits as she saw the light ahead. "You very well know," she wrote to her sister on the last day of May, "how thankful I am that I have but one more year of exile in prospect." She had a new nurse named Jane Lewis, who had arrived the previous day, but Willie was "still slow to make new acquaintances," so that was not going well. At the end of June, after Willie's second birthday, things were going better, so Frances was reasonably comfortable leaving Willie behind when she traveled with Henry to New England for some meetings and touring. "Henry was anxious to have me come with him," she wrote to her sister. "I think he will have cause to repent as my impatience to get back I know will prevent many excursions he would otherwise make. Dear little Willie. I suppose he thinks Ma has deserted him" by leaving him with Clary and the new nurse. A week later, she was back in Albany but could not leave for Auburn as Henry was ill. Willie had been just fine. On the other hand, she confided in her sister, Henry was sick with worry about the state of their finances. "His pecuniary affairs are in a condition infinitely worse than he has ever imagined. At present he sees no way through. This is entre nous."[42]

When Frances finally reached Auburn, on or about July 5, she was pleased to find that her "Augustus had not grown out of my remembrance, though he has out of all his clothes." She also found him "dispirited about his studies and desirous to give up Latin and study English, which he says he knows little about." To Henry she wrote, "We will talk of this when you come." Willie was happy to be back in Auburn and much amused by the cats and chickens, but he was "woefully afraid" of Snip, the cat he had tormented the previous year.[43]

At about the same time, in early July, Samuel wrote to Henry to complain about his neglect. While he knew perfectly well that the governor led a "distracted, hurried, confused, and irregular life," he also knew from the newspapers that Henry had passed up and down the Hudson to New York City several times without stopping in Florida. "Would it not have been possible, if not convenient, for you to have changed your course so far as to have called and spent one or two nights with us." Perhaps Henry did not know that Samuel had "for months past suffered every few days the most severe turns of sickness even to the borders of the grave." Possibly, had Henry known that "the blood was now settled under my nails, that there is but a hair's breadth between me and death, you would not have passed." If none of that was sufficient to elicit more frequent displays of filial affection, Henry's "pecuniary interest, which to say the least is as permanent as any other you may possess and which to do justice to yourself and family you ought to look at three or four times a year in my feeble and helpless state," should have inspired more concern. Samuel was threatening disinheritance as he did repeatedly with all his children.[44]

Henry explained to Frances, in a letter written in early July, why he had neither returned home to Auburn nor visited his parents in Florida. "My brother's death cast upon me all the business I have been accustomed to depend upon him to transact for me at Auburn, in Chautauqua, and in New York." There was still much business in Westfield. As for his days in Albany, "we are very quiet and staid here. I have brought the breakfast-hour back to seven, and I rise at six. My morning hours, until twelve, are devoted to business at home. I spend two hours in the departments. Weed comes after dinner and stays an hour, and then I return to business until the mail arrives at seven. The short, warm evenings I occupy with reading, writing to you, and in walks about town." As he described it, his was a lonely life of public service, nothing glamorous about it, and he would rather have been with his family, which, with the addition of Jennings's son Clarence, had grown yet again. At about the same time, Henry made clear to all who asked, first and foremost to Weed, but also to other political friends and newspaper editors, that he had no intention of running for a third term the following year.[45]

Frances was sympathetic to Henry's plight, but also buoyant upon her return to Auburn. "The boys Fred and Willie are the happiest creatures you ever saw," she wrote to Henry in mid-July. "Willie rides with his Grandpa, chases the cats, feeds the chickens, and amuses us all with his incessant prattle." She predicted that he would be much more sociable than her other two boys. As for her, "the boys' mother feels at least twenty years younger since her escape from the city. In truth, I am half alarmed at the buoyancy of my own spirits and fear that a shade is gathering in some unexpected quarter. Everything here is so green and beautiful, so natural, so quiet, and I am so relieved from care that existence does for once seem a blessing. My only regret is that you are shut up in the city and harassed by a thousand perplexing cares." She was also grateful that Henry had taken the time to write to her and found it predictable that Henry's father was complaining about his son's neglect without consideration of the other demands on the governor's time.[46]

Frances wanted Henry to give Clarence money for transportation and arrange for him to spend his monthlong holiday in Auburn. "The poor boy would like to feel as though he had a home somewhere, but it would be unsuitable for him to be at Albany even could he enjoy being there, which he would not while we were away. Clara and I think he had better come here." His stepmother Mary intervened and insisted he spend the time with her family in New York City, which Clarence did. Willie was almost always out of doors; Gus spent "a great portion of his in the water." Fred was constructing a camera obscura in the washroom, which despite the inconvenience his mother tolerated as an expression of his true nature and likely brilliance.[47]

After numerous predictions and several of what Frances considered promises, Henry arrived in Auburn on August 30 and was called away the very next day on state business. In the hubbub that required locating him and delivering important papers, Judge Miller was dispatched to the American Hotel, where he found General Winfield Scott and invited him back to his house. In the course of what Frances described as an agreeable social visit from a true gentleman, Scott's "soldier's eye" assessed Gus's fitness for the army and encouraged him to consider West Point as an alternative to college. Since applicants did not need Latin to enter the military academy, the recommendation struck Gus as a godsend, and he immediately began agitating to attend a preparatory school for aspiring cadets. "I do not like to think of having him away the next five years and in all probability become so weaned from home as never to desire to return," Frances wrote to Lazette, but she could see the attraction and the weakness of her capacity to resist. Gus immediately began to plan for school, and she prepared for a return of the rest of the family to Albany on about October 1, which was Gus's fifteenth birthday.[48]

With the help of her sister, Frances was on September 12 packing for a return to Albany and "preparing our Augustus to leave home, but not with any lightness of heart. A separation of this kind, though it may fail to benefit him as much as you seem to anticipate, will not fail to estrange him" from his family. At least, that was Frances's prediction to Henry, whom she blamed, along with her father and General Scott, for the plan. She had hired a tutor to give Gus a crash course in writing, hoping to improve his skills before he left for his new school.[49]

Frances was belatedly distraught that Henry had not provided her more information about the school they were sending Augustus to in what she considered a rush. With Henry, in a letter of September 19, she shared her second thoughts. "I would prefer to know something more of Mr. Kinsley's school before sending Augustus there, but the information which I would like to have I should not be likely to obtain from a man." As she knew from "bitter experience," many of the comforts of home were lost at any residential school, "but I consider it an act of positive injustice to keep a child at a school too much upon the

Squeers plan." She referred to Charles Dickens's fictional Wackford Squeers, the cruel headmaster of Dotheboys Hall in his novel *Nicholas Nickleby* and perhaps an explanation for why Frances and her sister held such strong grudges against Emma Willard, the head mistress of the Troy Female Academy that they both had attended. "I infer from what Augustus says, that he would consider it a disgrace to his manhood for me to visit the school and make some observations for myself, so I must e'en rest contented with what I can learn from others."[50]

On September 30 Frances sent Henry a short note announcing the delay of their departure because Willie's eye was inflamed. The doctor said it was unsafe for him to travel in such unfavorable weather and until the swelling went down. She hoped to leave only a day or two later than previously planned. At the same time, Samuel sent "a small colored boy named William Coe, belonging to my son William H. Seward" to Albany on a steamboat with a note to the captain. As the Coe family was no longer enslaved, and William was too young to have ever been a slave in New York, Samuel's language was inappropriate, but by arrangement with Henry, Mary Coe, age twenty, and "Bill" Coe, age twelve, would now live with Henry's family. The hiring of Mary had long been in the works at the request of their mother Chloe, the Sewards' slave when Henry was growing up. Chloe wanted them together working for the kind governor, whom she admired, rather than for his father in Florida.[51]

By early November Gus was in his new school, which was less than a mile from West Point and on the Hudson River. There were fourteen other students, who were also preparing for entry to the military academy. It was an intense and regimented curriculum, according to Frances: eight hours a day of study with Wednesdays and Saturdays off. "I believe it is as good a school as we could have found," she wrote to her sister. Henry received a letter from Zebina Kinsley, the Scotsman who ran the school, who wanted the governor to know about his son that "I am very much pleased with him, and my wife considers him the most amiable and gentle youth in the school." This, of course, warmed Frances's heart with pride about Gus and relief about the school. "He is permitted for the present to relinquish Latin and pursue mathematical studies, which pleases him much better. Very few of the scholars study the languages." Gus ultimately decided not to return home for the holidays. He said he did not want to interrupt his studies and that visiting home would only make him more homesick on his return to school. These were excuses that played well enough to his mother.[52]

For Frances, this was the "last winter I feel disposed to make all the required sacrifices without murmuring, which is as much as saying I should feel very rebellious were it otherwise." Her role as New York's first lady ended in just one more year, and she was counting the days. She was prostrated with illness the first two weeks of December, having contracted something at a wedding in Troy. "I was very sick two days before I would consent to have the Dr. and then I was sicker still. The quantities of medicine which I took produced such dreadful nausea that the next five days seem like a perfect blank. I have little recollection of anything except being dreadfully sick—physick, blisters, mustard poultices, etc.—finally produced the desired result. My cough became loosened and I breathed with more ease, then succeeded many days of nausea, languor, and debility, which have gradually departed." Henry was absorbed in his annual message, as usual over the holidays, and much "annoyed by pecuniary embarrassments."[53]

Frances had recited Moore's "Visit from St. Nick" to Willie countless times, which the two-year-old "understands perfectly." Clarence and Fred had "in a private manner purchased Christmas gifts for each other, as I could not go out, also for Willie and household staff." She still hoped for Gus's surprise arrival, even though he had told her not to expect him. Nicholas and Harriet Bogart's eight-year-old daughter Sarah was diagnosed with consumption in November and died two days after Christmas, so the new year would begin with a funeral. Frances cared for the Bogarts' younger daughter Harriet, age three, who played with Willie in the early days of her parents' grieving. Nonetheless, the household devoted the last two days of the old year to taking up carpets, moving furniture, and preparing food and drink for the governor's New Year's Day open house.[54]

Chapter 10

Lame Ducks, 1842–1844

Frances much appreciated that Gus's new school sent Henry periodic updates on his progress and health. One came the third week of January 1842, reporting that "your son Augustus is 'working his way' steadily onward. He is now nearly through equations of the second degree in algebra, and is doing very well in all his English branches. He possesses indomitable perseverance, and I doubt not will become a good mathematician in a few years. He is in very good health." Again, in February, Zebina Kinsley reported that Gus "performed his exercises excellently fifty-nine times, well thirteen times, tolerably three times, and badly zero times." He was absent but excused only once, when he did not hear the bell. Gus wrote to Lazette that he studied algebra, geography, grammar, and reading and spelling twice every day. He focused on admission to West Point but knew that admission to the academy was easier than remaining there. "You do not have to know as much as I thought to enter, but you have to accomplish a great many studies in a short time after you get there or get sent away."[1]

Samuel demanded from Henry a full accounting of the condition of his land office business. He wanted to ensure that the person he appointed executor of his estate was fiscally sound. "A person of force and determination, well qualified, clear of incumbrance with him sufficient to do justice to all interested in this distribution is a desirable object to me." He was now concerned that Henry's finances rendered him "a very unsuitable person to superintend the interest of other branches of the family as it may be years" of work to settle the estate. Indeed, it took decades, and he had good reasons for such concern.[2]

The last year of the governorship was wearing out Frances and Henry. He was ill with undescribed symptoms in mid-February, for which the doctor prescribed calomel and salts. According to Frances, that did not cure him but enabled him to return to work the next day. Through nursing her husband and children, Frances entertained a revolving door of houseguests and made her rounds of Albany calls. She did not think Henry had "any settled plan for the future, though he has many schemes. I shall go home as early as I can, but that probably will not be very early." Despite Henry's resolution to stop throwing dinner parties, Frances endured one for seventy people, mainly legislators, before the end of February. "The tables were swept so completely that I feared there had been a deficiency. . . . Hetty the cook is of opinion that they have been saving up their appetites by going without their dinners."[3]

The Sewards' time in Albany also burdened Clary back in Auburn, who was ill. Frances wished her father would come to stay with them so Clary could get some rest. Elijah had been confined all winter with rheumatism and was therefore not up to traveling, but he wrote to Fred in February to say that when the rail line from Auburn to Rochester was completed, he anticipated two trains leaving for Albany each day, "soon after which I intend to come down to see you all."[4]

According to Clary, Judge Miller was by early March "quite well" and had again taken up residence in the north sitting room, where he ate his dinner and slept on the settee. He arrived at the governor's mansion without warning on March 13. Elijah hoped to return to Auburn with Gus in two or three weeks, when Gus had a break from the military school. In the meantime, he slept in the parlor at the governor's mansion, even in company. "You know his fancy for sleeping in public places," Frances wrote to her sister. Clary used his absence as an opportunity to clean the house thoroughly.[5]

At about the same time that Elijah arrived in Albany, Henry took Fred and Will on the train with him and many others to celebrate a new line completed as far as Springfield and Worcester. At Springfield they met a delegation of Massachusetts politicians headed by Governor John Davis and stayed overnight with the governor and his wife, whom the men much admired. Frances reacted to their praise of Eliza Davis jealously by describing her to Lazette as unfeminine. "Mrs. Davis is a woman of a very strong, masculine mind, plain and unpretending, and I doubt not good hearted, but so unfeminine that I always felt as though I was talking to a man in petticoats." The men, including Sam Blatchford, were enthusiastic, downright "hyperbolic," she thought, in their praise of the Massachusetts governor's wife. They discussed "prominent political characters," Dickens (who had spent a night with the Davises), and animal magnetism, and Mrs. Davis did not withdraw so the men could continue their conversation without a woman present, thereby breaching a social convention that Frances endorsed.[6]

Henry's parties continued, without alcoholic beverages, despite his testimony that they had ended. Frances counted one a week through February and March, where somewhere between fifty and seventy guests each time feasted on oysters and pheasants, while she kept the fare simpler for her "at home" events, substituting coffee and chocolate. She threw a party for the young people as requested by Clarence. There was dancing, lemonade cake, and mottoes (place settings with inspirational words), and all the guests departed by 10:00 p.m. "Clarence devoted himself entirely to the fair sex, saying tender things to all individually and collectively." Fred was shy and more reserved. Frances continued the "at home" gatherings for women by formal invitation with another one the third week of March.[7]

Despite her support for the cause, Frances declined to sign the pledge of "The Temperance Benevolent Society," reformers who promoted total abstinence from alcoholic beverages. "A couple of damsels of a very uncertain age" presented her with a petition and displayed "an astonishing degree of horror" at her refusal. Her grounds were a personal policy against lending her name to any public pronouncements, but she was willing to make a financial contribution to their cause. "Now, I think," she wrote to her sister, "if women cannot make it consistent with their sense of duty to do good without publishing it in the newspaper, they may as well let it alone and especially, I believe that more than half of those who are most officious in public benevolence of this kind make the exhibition of their virtues at the expense of the comfort and proper management of their families at home." Perhaps she felt harshly judged, because she need not have explained her principles to Lazette. She closed this "very interesting lecture" with the observation that "if they must do good by associations instead of individually, let the societies be composed of women, if there are any such, whose domestic duties have not the strongest claims upon their time."[8]

Gus arrived in Albany about April 1, at the end of his session at school. The report from Zebina Kinsley was very encouraging. "Your son acquitted himself highly creditably in every exercise," he wrote to Henry. "He spoke very well in [the] presence of about thirty ladies and gentlemen without any apparent embarrassment. By unremitted industry he has won for himself, in my estimation, the first place of all my pupils in algebra, English grammar, and geography." There was still room for improvement, but his attitude was sterling. "As a most diligent student, and amiable, excellent youth, I set great store by him. His manner is still awkward, but the diamond is within and only wants polishing to make it shine with brilliancy." Nonetheless, Frances was "very uncomfortable" about Gus's school ever since Henry had visited and told her that "the boys are confined to the school room ten hours each day," as she wrote to Lazette. "I believe I have written this before. You will thus perceive how much it troubles me."[9]

On April 10 Frances awaited the adjournment of the legislature the following day to start her spring cleaning, which was hardly worth the effort before the politicians stopped tramping through. Gus was at loose ends in Albany with no focus for his energy, so he returned to Auburn with his grandfather. When he left for Auburn, Frances sent money with him for Lazette to pay for her transportation to Albany, so she could help her sister pack up for home.[10]

Mortality was still much on the Sewards' minds, and not only that of Frances. Harriet and Nicholas Bogart were about to lose another child that spring, seven-year-old Frances, whose liver failed. This led Frances Seward to focus on getting a stone to mark her mother's grave in Williamstown, Massachusetts. Toward the end of May, Henry informed his father that he had drawn up a new will that conformed to Samuel's instructions. He prefaced the long letter with compliments and gratitude for his father's generosity and confirmed that "it is your absolute right to dispense of your large estate, the fruits of a life of industry and frugality, according to your own pleasure." As a result of his father's rights and Henry's belief that "your views are sounder and wiser than my own, and it is an ungracious and unkind thing to intrude advice, suggestions, or wishes on such an occasion," Henry claimed to "refrain from making any suggestion of opinion concerning the will and its various provisions," before offering a long list of dissenting opinions that questioned his father's judgment, intensions, generosity, and good sense.[11]

While Samuel still favored the cudgel of an Old Testament patriarch, Henry advised a more equitable distribution that let the past rest. He wished, for example, that Samuel had not favored his deceased sister's daughter Caroline over her two brothers, and his own sons over those of his deceased brother Jennings and the children of George and Polydore. In making this recommendation of charity over his father's sense of justice, Henry assured Samuel that he was no fonder of Mahlon than Samuel was, but he wished affection for the late Cornelia took precedence over their mutual disregard for her husband. "Lest you may think I am moved by some too much kindness to Dr. Canfield, I deign to say that you hold him in hardly less esteem and respect than I do. . . . But his children are the children of my sister, who fondly loved us and whom I can never forget." Henry also offered to oversee the education of all the boys of Cornelia and Jennings if his father left a legacy to support it.[12]

As for his father's intentions to leave part of his estate to his three surviving sons, Henry was grateful for the preference Samuel showed him but thought it unjust. "They are both kind, confiding, and good men," he said of the two men. "I should not only prefer that the advantages you propose in my behalf should be omitted, but I would beg leave to ask that you would reconsider your views on that subject, and see whether more than a compensation for my future services is not given, allow me such a compensation <u>and</u> equalize the division with this <u>exception</u>."[13]

Henry flattered Samuel that he was appropriately generous to his mother and to his parents' loyal caregiver, Julia Ann Van Brunt, but he had one more reservation to add to the list, which was, perhaps, his most serious one. "I am oppressed with painful doubts concerning your proposition to establish a Seminary. I appreciate and honor the motive, and I speak under a liability to be pressed by motives of personal interest." But, Henry continued, "perfect your plan as much as we may, there is nevertheless a great hazard of a failure of the scheme, because very many, perhaps most, of such plans do fail. My death or removal from personal care of the trust would probably throw the whole into the hands of careless or sordid individuals, and strangers to you and to me and your family, perhaps ignorant, conceited, or bigoted men would combat your most munificent endorsement into means of self-engagement." He pointed to the examples of Girard College in Philadelphia, and Hamilton College and Hartwick Seminary closer to home, schools that had famously failed to realize the intentions of their founders. He might have added that his father was also leaving him a headache that he desperately sought to avoid.[14]

Not surprisingly, these entreaties fell on Samuel's long-deaf ears when it came to money. Julia Van Brunt took her employer's dictation, although his infirmity was related to his throat and not his hand. He acknowledged receipt of Henry's letter but postponed discussion of its contents until the two of them were together again. He expected to die in very short order from ulcers in his throat and a loss of appetite, which meant in his experience as a physician that "suffocation must soon take place." While Samuel appreciated "the importance of your business and weighty concerns, still I cannot help but think it is your duty to visit me every other Sabbath while I lie in the painful and critical situation." He lived for another seven years.[15]

Samuel wrote to Henry in mid-June that "I still exist," but barely, "through the mercy of a kind providence." He was sorry to hear that Henry had been ill, "especially as this deprived me of a visit." Samuel remained "literally too weak to live, with frequent faint turns that indicate speedy dissolution." He hoped that Henry was well enough to visit in the coming week, before it was too late.[16]

It was time for Henry and Frances to plan for a permanent return to Auburn. One problem was Jenny the fawn, whom the family had adopted in Albany without much previous notice in their correspondence. For her own safety, she needed to be confined, which was not easy at the governor's mansion. Moving her back to Auburn was risky and expensive, and Judge Miller thought there was no way to confine her on his property as she was quite capable of leaping fences that held horses and cows. She was tame and a target for neighbors who saw her only as fresh meat. "I am afraid we shall be unable to keep her if she leaps the fences . . . and it is a pity to confine the poor thing in a small space," Frances wrote to Henry from Auburn at the end of May. "Can you not give her to some person in the country?" she asked. "Fred is somewhat reluctant to part with her, but among the numerous pets he has here she will not be missed." Then, there was Bob, the family's pet bird and a virtuoso singer. "You can send Bob if you think best. Perhaps it is a more favourable time for moving him before he commences molting. The cats are so abundant here his life will be in some danger." She advised leaving the canaries in Albany for the same reason.[17]

One of the household staff, Harriet Bogart, had inadvertently poisoned Jenny the deer with arsenic that Frances had in the house to address rats. Frances thought Harriet had also endangered her own child by such carelessness, and she partly blamed herself for leaving the arsenic in the charge of others. "It is the last time so dangerous an instrument will be placed by me in the hands of another." If Jenny survived, which she did, Frances doubted that the deer could be taught to run with the cows, but even then she would remain in danger from the neighbors with guns, which accurately predicted her ultimate fate. Frances preferred to give up the canaries rather than Bob, but Henry had to sort that out before his return. "I have no doubt it is wise to dispose of the horses immediately," she wrote. Henry remained reluctant to leave behind Jenny the deer or Jenny the canary, who now sat on eggs, and he planned to bring Bob back to Auburn.[18]

The furniture could also wait to be moved until September, when Frances would be back to oversee the packing. "The truth is, I am so sick and probably shall continue to be so for two or three months to come, that I feel unequal to any existence." She was pregnant and miscarried, for at least the fourth time. She was also prepared to surrender the downstairs nursery in Auburn to accommodate Henry's need for an office. Having it near the north door facilitated the entry and exit of the expected stream of visitors Henry would continue to receive after his term ended. "I have said nothing to Pa about the office." The use of rooms was always a delicate negotiation, which she preferred to leave to Henry's superior diplomatic skills and greater influence.[19]

Frances wrote again to thank Henry for his sympathetic, and perhaps guilty, response to her news about the pregnancy. She apologized that her "expression [of] despondency should give you any pain. Had I not seen more energetic minds and more buoyant spirits than mine sink under the prostrating influence of a continuous nausea I should consider it an evidence of peculiar weakness. However, I hope soon to be better. My accustomed sickness after an interval of nearly nine weeks has returned and though I do not yet experience any great change, I trust a few days will restore my accustomed health," which was never good in any event.

Frances continued to have problems finding and retaining household staff. "I have engaged a fat Irish girl to come next week," she wrote to Lazette on June 16. "She says she can cook, but in that I have no faith. Maria is desperate lazy and so untidy about her person that I am ashamed to have her open the street door." Clary was still with her, but she and her husband were seeking to rent a house, an eventuality that

Frances hoped to postpone until fall. Frances and Clary continued to make calls, but the return of cholera frightened everyone. The kittens that lost their mother, which the staff fed with milk-soaked sponges, had all died, so Willie, who had his third birthday on June 18, sought a replacement. On June 26 Henry still was not home. "City servants are bad enough; country help quite intolerable," Frances had concluded by then. Mary had left her unexpectedly, apparently for higher wages. "The girl we have," she wrote to her sister, "is not deficient in head or body either, but the work of her hands is far from pleasing. I hardly think we shall form an acquaintance of six weeks standing."[20]

Fifteen-year-old Gus spent the July 4 holiday in New York City, escorted by his father, who then left him on his own when he returned to Albany. Fred planned and executed his own fireworks display in Auburn, where he would transfer to a new school from the one he had attended in Albany. He recounted the celebration in a letter to his aunt Lazette. "On Saturday evening, the fire companies came out with torches and marched about the village. They looked very handsome, each man having two torches. On Monday morning, the bells rang as if for fire and the engine companies ran about pretending that there was one, which however they very well knew there was not. . . . The procession formed at ten o'clock and marched on to Fort Hill. Willy has a box of wooden soldiers and after he had seen the procession he informed me that when they grew big they would march like those he had seen." Fred saved his own fireworks for the following evening to give them their due rather than compete with the larger public displays that he witnessed with his grandfather on the day of the celebration. He and Willie had a grand time.[21]

Frances had an unpleasant holiday in the absence of Henry. A drunken man had passed out in their yard, and she was alone with Willie for at least two hours as the man laid there. "Snip [dog], who is usually very courageous found his valour dampened by the noise of rockets and firecrackers, so I fastened all the doors and sat down with James's last novel, which so engrossed me that the time slipped away imperceptibly," she wrote to Henry, who was still in Albany on July 7. "I feel vexed with myself that I have been so absorbed with that book that I have allowed it to engross the whole of my leisure time for the last two days. Besides injuring my eyes and in truth being the chief cause why I have not written to you. The next novel I read, I shall commence with the last chapter first. . . . Everybody enquires when I expect you. I say I do not expect you at all."[22]

After an exchange of letters, the sisters learned that on the evening of July 4 they were both reading the same novel, George Payne Rainsford James's *Morley Ernstein*, which was recently published. "I am ashamed to say," Frances wrote, "that I found it impossible to employ my leisure time with anything else until it was completed," even though "I like the plot less than many of his previous works." She took this to mean that romance and fantasy overcame her critical powers. "I came to a conclusion that I was not yet quite old enough to read novels moderately and critically." Since she was thirty-six and did not consider herself young, Frances meant that she was incapable of maturing beyond the attachment to fiction that lured her away from the life that she lived.[23]

What James distracted her from on that day was the absence of Henry and Gus, her fears about Fred getting injured by fireworks, the drunk sleeping it off in her garden, the marching bands and crowds, the uselessness of their watch dog during the explosions of cannons and firecrackers, and the headache it all left with her. That same morning, a letter from Henry announced the imminent arrival of James and Eliza Bowen, president of the New York and Erie Railroad and his wife, people she did not know, who needed to be fed, entertained, and provided a place to sleep the following evening. Her kitchen helper had left for home the morning of July 4 with a sore hand shortly before Frances received news of the scheduled arrival of her guests. On Tuesday morning she sent out Maria, her slovenly maid, to find a substitute helper. Maria returned that afternoon with "another daughter of the Emerald Isle." The three of them, and probably Clary, who went unmentioned, "worked diligently and prepared everything for their reception." But the guests did not show on Tuesday, Wednesday, or ever. Through it all, Frances read *Morley Ernstein* to maintain her calm and escape the anxiety that accompanied her trials.[24]

A week after Gus left on his holiday excursion to New York City, Frances had not heard from him, so she was worried. She had received Gus's schoolmaster's report on his academic progress for the term just ended. "The report shows that he is studying with great diligence," she wrote to her sister. And then, she offered a curious observation. "I trust he does not still incline to enter the Academy." Why did a good report lead her to that conclusion? Possibly, it was just wishful thinking, but it ran against the grain of everything Gus had done since his father, grandfather, and General Scott endorsed his ambition. He showed an aptitude for the military academy's curriculum that he had never shown in his college preparation.[25]

Frances in her mid-summer "illness" found several things besides her household help annoying. One was her neighbor Sarah Hills, who was "much distressed that our grounds are not kept in as good condition as hers." Frances had also read in the newspaper that Henry attended a meeting of the "ladies association," an organization that she thought "calculated to foster love of display, which in most women requires no cultivation." In other words, this was one of those public organizations she thought distracted women from their domestic duties. "Vanity and envy are cherished under the specious name of emulation. Girls exert themselves for the sake of exhibition or with the hope of obtaining a reward. They are not taught to love knowledge for its own sake or for the good that its acquisition may enable them to do their fellow creatures." Apparently, the association and some of the schools for girls provided public exhibitions of female learning that Frances thought undermined the modesty that was more becoming to women. "Withal, these exhibitions are no test of scholarship. A bold girl with ordinary ability will often pass a better examination than a modest girl with higher order of intellect." She wished Henry did not patronize such organizations. And she really expected Henry to arrive back in Auburn the last week of July, with the birds and the deer, although no one thought the move was in Jenny's best interest; they simply had not come up with a humane alternative plan.[26]

On August 1 Frances was still ill, Henry was still not home, and she had heard from someone else that he was not coming. She "would much have preferred having heard it from yourself. I shall not expect you so confidently again." She hoped that Willie's eyes were slowly getting better, but she was discouraged by her homeopathic prescriptions so she stopped the treatment. In early September she took him for a consultation with a specialist in New York City, whom she discovered knew nothing other doctors had not already told her. The physician thought that Willie would outgrow the condition, which went undiagnosed with an array of causes theorized and treatments prescribed. Through it all, Willie continued "to suffer much from united effect of medicine and inflamed eyes."[27]

Over the summer Henry decided that he wanted Frances to return to Albany rather than him coming home with the animals. Fred, Willie, Aunt Clary, and Frances arrived in Albany on August 25. The company of Clary and the knowledge that it was not to be a long stay "prevented the depression I have heretofore experienced," Frances wrote to Lazette. Jenny the deer was still in residence. "I find her rather troublesome,"

Frances wrote to Gus, "as your Pa permits her to run about the house. I am not in favour of moving her to Auburn. Our other pets, the birds, are all well." She joined Henry at the end of the month for a trip to Long Island, New York City, Florida, and then back to Albany.[28]

Samuel made a few unspecified amendments to his will along the lines that Henry had suggested. He did this without materially altering its complexity or eliminating harsh judgments of his children and grandchildren, except for Henry's family. He required Henry to return to Florida in early August and again in September to formalize the changes, as he was "continually wasting away." Frances, who visited Florida with Henry, Clary, and Willie in mid-September, thought that her father-in-law exaggerated his own illness and minimized that of his wife Mary. When they arrived, Frances "found Mr. Seward much improved in health, mother quite ill." In what sounded to Frances like desperation, Mary asked to return to Albany with Henry's family to give her some rest from the demands of her husband and household, "as she could not live much longer there. Altogether, they are destroying this excellent woman very rapidly. She is wasted to a shadow, has a bad cough, and almost continual fever." Samuel was against the idea, for what Frances thought were entirely selfish reasons. "I cannot tell you now," Frances wrote to Lazette, "how difficult we found the task of persuading Mr. Seward to consent to her journey nor with how bad grace the consent was finally given. He is a bad man. She will not continue long a subject for his tyranny. This must not be mentioned to a third person."[29]

As Frances made her round of calls before she left Albany for the last time as the state's first lady, she was bewildered by the reaction she got from other political wives. "The people here wonder why I go home before Henry's term of office expires." While she plotted an escape, they thought she was being exiled rather than ending one. "Is it not strange," she wrote sarcastically to her sister, "that I am so insensible to the delights of Albany society that I prefer to pack up my things and make my arrangements for the winter in Oct. instead of waiting until the freezing month of Jan., thereby depriving myself of two whole months of intellectual intercourse with the citizens?" Even Henry, who surely must have known better, seemed surprised by her eagerness to leave Albany. "Well, there is no accounting for taste."[30]

By the end of October, Frances and Willie were back in Auburn. "I am home once more with all the furniture," she wrote to Lazette on October 30. "When I wrote last Monday, I was in the 'slough of

Despond' in consequence of a violent sick headache which continued all day, notwithstanding which I left 130 cards for the benefit of my acquaintances." The calling cards were sufficient evidence that she had tried and failed to return visits as etiquette required. She had more calls to make before she could leave the next day. Henry arrived back in Albany from New York City in the midst of it all. "I thought he seemed rather downcast that we had progressed so rapidly, as he thought when he left it would be time enough to see about the cars after he returned." The railroad had provided gratis on her request as many train cars as she required to move her family and possessions back home. "The directors very politely gave us a large car calculated for sixteen persons all to ourselves, a good fire and every attention possible. The birds came in the cars with us." The canaries made the trip fine, but Bob, their best singer, did not. "We have fed him spiders and worms. He seems [to be] surviving. So much for an unyielding disposition." Fred remained with his father through the end of his school term and then came home with Henry after the holidays. Gus accompanied his mother but returned to school after a few days of helping hang pictures. Lazette arrived to help unpack and stayed the rest of November and a few days into December.[31]

In early December Frances claimed she was now resigned to Gus attending West Point, although he had not yet been admitted. She was confident that Henry would get him in. In a letter to Henry the following week, she shared her reservations heavily. "I am afraid I shall never become reconciled to the path you have chosen for him. My continual anxiety is wearing away my heart." The day after Christmas, she wrote Gus a letter that has not survived, in which she tried to dissuade him from a military career. She had learned from Gus's schoolmaster that he was wavering. The news persuaded her that she should not have given up and therefore plunged back in once more. As she explained to Lazette on the last day of the year, the candid reply to her inquiry of Mr. Kinsley had led her to broach the subject with Gus one more time. "His father tells me I can have my own way about it," but she was convinced that her father, husband, and son remained united against her.[32]

On January 8, 1843, Frances wrote to Lazette from Auburn, "Fred is well and happy to be at home. I need not say that his mother is equally pleased." Henry had arrived home the previous evening after an exhausting round of farewell meals and calls in Albany. "Henry is very well, in fine spirits, more free from care apparently than he has been in four years," despite the financial trials he faced ahead. "Upon the whole," Frances concluded, "I think the termination of his official career is vastly more desirable than the commencement. Tomorrow the nursery is to be converted into a study or library." Henry also had an office in the Exchange Building, from which he intended to practice law. Frances had received a letter from Gus that he wrote on New Year's Day, in which he claimed never to have received the long letter she wrote before Christmas that laid out her argument against West Point. She wrote to him again, in the hope that he was wavering. As for Henry, she again misperceived his contentment and mistook what was far from the "end" of his political ambition.[33]

One week later, Frances had a clearer picture of what it meant for Henry to be home. "When he is here," she wrote again to Lazette, "the whole house is office, with the usual accompaniments of mud, spitting and smoking." She was hopeful that Harriet and Nicholas Bogart were the answer to her chronic housekeeping troubles, but they were as yet undecided about where they wanted to live. "I do not like to urge them to move back," Frances wrote; "they have no company here. The coloured people always sufficiently worthless have dwindled to but one or two who are decent." The Bogarts found, as other African Americans did, that density of the Black population made life in cities more tolerable than life in small towns. The Bogarts' daughter, also named Harriet, had scarlet fever. Nicholas was waiting for her to recover before heading to Albany, where he sought a job on a boat. Frances wanted them to stay with her, but Harriet (mother) "is discontented here. The truth is they are spoiled by a city life and will not be contented again out of it," which was a self-interested and unsympathetic view of the differences between their lives.[34]

As for Gus, "Henry continues to think me very unwise in objecting to his going to the Point." Once Henry was home, Frances renewed her lobbying against Gus's plans for the academy. She became convinced within a couple of weeks that Henry had not changed his mind after he declared her arguments against it "unreasonable and ruinous to my boy." Before the month ended, Gus also dashed her hopes that she would be able to dissuade him, when he wrote to her after three months of silence on the subject that he was "not willing at this late period to commence preparations for college" and that he hoped "when I reflected upon the unhappiness it would occasion him that I would change my mind." This led Frances to explain to Lazette, although apparently not to Gus, that "God knows I could make any sacrifice of my own feelings to promote the welfare of my noble boy, but I am called upon to make a sacrifice of principle, which I feel to be impossible. I never can approve of sending a boy like Augustus into the army." She blamed Henry more than she blamed Gus for the impasse. When Gus was on the ropes about returning to classical studies to prepare for college, his father and her father had failed to jump in on her side.[35]

Gus confirmed his commitment to Henry in a letter of January 18, which also described his mother as the one who had waffled rather than him. "When I left home last November, I thought that my mother was agreed on my entering the Military Academy next June, but recently she has changed her mind, of which I suppose you have been informed. She desires me to commence studies in preparation for college, thinking that it would be better for me. But of all things, I had rather do most any one instead of going to college at the age I will be when prepared." In Gus's opinion, he would graduate from the academy by the time he could possibly enter his second year in college. "I write for the purpose of soliciting you to procure my appointment if it is in your power as my education depends upon this step."[36]

When she learned of this letter, Frances wrote to her sister that she was now resigned to Gus's path. She had not changed her mind, as Gus believed, but had felt restrained from voicing more forceful objections back in November because she believed a father had more relevant personal experience out in the world. "My conscientious scruples with regard to a military education are in no manner changed. On this subject I have ever had but one opinion. It is in direct opposition to the precepts of the Gospel."[37]

Frances had not given up on Gus's career in February 1843, but she was now reduced to prayer, hoping for divine intervention or political failure on Henry's part. She wrote to Gus insincerely that she hoped he "will not be unprepared for a disappointment, as it is still possible that you may not succeed in getting a warrant, although I think the probabilities are in your favour." Within days of writing that letter, her hopes for Henry's failure were buoyed by John Canfield Spencer, a former cabinet official under Governor Seward, who was now President Tyler's secretary of war. Henry had gone right to the top on behalf of his son. Spencer replied to Henry that his hands were tied by new legislation that limited academy appointments to one in each congressional district, and the appointments went to residents of that district alone. Henry then wrote to his congressman, Christopher Morgan, explaining that he felt "a deep interest in this matter not because I wish to avoid the expense of educating him," but rather because "I ought to do for so just and pure a child whatever a parent can and my judgment approves his wishes." When he learned that Morgan had already committed his allotted appointment, Henry did not stop there but requested that Congressman Henry Bell Van Rensselaer "adopt him [Gus] as a constituent" in an attempt to circumvent the law. To Gus, Frances wrote at the end of the month that "you may be assured that your Father will leave no proper means untried to get your appointment. Still, you must not calculate too confidently upon it." Henry was back on the road to Albany and New York City.[38]

By March 7 Frances had her hopes up, as she shared in a letter to her sister. She had heard nothing from Gus in response to the news she had shared with him about the barriers to his appointment. "Poor boy; his disappointment will be very great if he loses his appointment, as is most probable, the bill I mentioned having passed both houses. I suppose Spencer has sufficient influence to get him appointed by the President, but doubt whether he will use it for that purpose." Several days later, Frances had heard that Spencer was no longer secretary of war, President Tyler having appointed him secretary of the treasury. She took this as additional good news. "The War department being left vacant, I suppose if he does not choose to use his influence to get a warrant this will afford him some sort of an agency, although it is none in truth. I feel perfectly willing to have it all in the hands of Him who 'seeth not as man seeth.'"[39]

Before the end of March, Frances learned that "the last of Mr. Spencer's official acts while Secretary of War was to transmit a warrant for Augustus, which he did very handsomely. Augustus will be very happy. I had a day or two previous written him a letter telling him there was very little chance of his succeeding after the passage of the new law. I must try to rejoice in that which makes my boy happy, though a mother's tenderness shrinks from the hardships to which her child will be exposed."[40]

At about the same time, Henry's parents arrived in Auburn and stayed for three months, during which time Frances almost daily expected one or both of them to expire. "Mr. and Mrs. Seward occupy the South Chamber and bed room, having a bed apiece, with one for Julia [their caretaker], coffee three times a day, &c. They propose remaining here all summer, a pleasing prospect," she reported sarcastically to her sister. One week later, she wrote again in much the same mood, as "Mr. and Mrs. Seward are, as usual, quite sick half the time." Henry, however, who remained away on business more often than not, saw it all differently, as he wrote to his cousin George Grier in mid-May. "My father and mother are about in the same infirm state of health as when they arrived here, but are cheerful and in good spirits. They seem confirmed in their purpose of remaining permanently here, though the change of residence at their advanced age would seem a matter of some surprise. Such a change, however, would be a welcome one to us." "Us" seems to have included Frances, which was far from true. At about the same time, Frances wrote to Lazette that "Mr. Seward was very ill two days last week and very sure that he would die, but as Mother and Julia were not alarmed, I was not."[41]

A month later the situation was just as dismal from Frances's perspective. "Mother has never been able to go out since she came." In early July, when Henry was again away, the family considered summoning him home as they doubted Samuel would last for long, but he rallied in response to a surprise visit to Auburn by John Quincy Adams in early August.[42]

On July 29 Henry heard that Adams was in Canandaigua, so he and twelve other local men escorted Henry's political icon to Auburn. Frances had no idea her husband was bringing Adams home until she saw the town's militia, a band, and firemen with torches marching down South Street. "We had barely time to light some candles for the parlour and hall before the procession entered the gate. I was sitting with a light gingham loose gown, . . . slippers and otherwise in dishabille owing to the exceeding heat. I put on a cap and the new cape only before my introduction to Mr. Adams and fifty others who followed him into the parlor." The delegation then adjourned to the front steps, where Henry and Adams addressed the assembled before retiring for the evening.[43]

As Frances wrote Gus, her attention was diverted from the procession "when I saw an immense multitude of men and boys climbing over the fence and crowding the court yard without showing any regard for our shrubbery or borders." As Frances told Lazette, she and Clary watched through the window. "'There goes a rose bush,' 'they have broken one of the Oleanders,' 'the gates are down,' 'the fence is falling' were the agreeable sounds which saluted my ears to the exclusion of Mr. Adams's speech. The old man seemed to be bewildered and fatigued. He declined eating anything, drank a glass of wine, and retired to his room as soon as it was prepared." The next morning Adams spoke at the Presbyterian church and expressed much gratitude for his reception before leaving. Shortly thereafter, with no explanation in the family's letters, Henry's parents with their caretaker returned to Florida, apparently no worse off than when they had arrived.[44]

By August Gus had been a cadet for two months, and Frances had distressing information from him. He had written to Clary with the details she sought about how he spent his days, as Frances explained in a letter to Lazette: "Awakened at 5 by the reveille, obliged to dress, fall into the ranks and answer rollcall within 5 minutes. From that time until ½ past 5 dress, wash and put tents in order. Infantry drill from ½ past 5 until ½ past 6, breakfast at 7, parade and guard mounting at 8, artillery drill at 9, cleaning fire arms from 10 to 11, dancing one hour, dinner, infantry drill again at 5 in the afternoon, parade at 7, supper ½ past 7, and all in bed at quarter before ten." It sounded to her exhausting and detrimental to his health. She planned a visit in coordination with Henry's September travels, so she could bring Gus more blankets and perhaps a comforter.[45]

Before August ended, Gus's parents had begun to receive reports of his demerits, which for his first month were a stunning sixteen and one-sixth. Two hundred would get him expelled; at the current rate he was right on the edge. Frances refrained from criticizing Gus in her first letter addressing the subject. Perhaps she was hopeful he now saw, as she did, that he was unfit for army life. Or, as she said, "I have your promise to do as well as you can, so I shall not remonstrate." It was the first week of October before she arrived at West Point, where she had ample time to grill Gus on various subjects, including his health, since she now heard from his physician what Gus had not shared with her, that he had been sick with a fever for over two weeks during the summer. "I think sometimes I should be quite reconciled," she wrote to her sister, "if Augustus could when ill be under the care of a homeopathic physician." She was during her stay "constantly hearing accounts of young men whose health has been injured or destroyed by a residence at the Point. The first five months is acknowledged by all graduates to be the most severe." Apparently there was a miasma, a swamp gas, that rose from the low ground on the other side of the Hudson River. Breathing it was known to be deleterious to one's health.[46]

Frances considered a second visit to West Point on her return upriver from New York City, where she had another dental appointment, but she understood that her son did not welcome further distraction from his studies. Instead, she sent him instructions on taking belladonna as a preventive against scarlet fever, "but do not take too much, a mistake which is often made with homeopathic medicine because the doses are so minute." To add authority to her recommendation, she shared the story of Colonel George Webb Morrell, who "never recovered from the effect of scarlet fever he had while there." Finally, she regretted that she was not directly informed by Gus's physician when he became ill but hoped that would be possible in the future, so she could assist in the diagnosis and treatment of whatever ailed her son.[47]

Five months into his residence, Gus still lived on the brink of expulsion for breaches of rules. His mother advised that he "not for the sake of getting the reputation of being a 'good fellow' do anything which you know to be wrong. You will always find the approbation of your own conscience of more value than that of your fellow students." It is unclear what he had done, but his roommate Henry Heth was also disciplined, and Frances suspected that Heth, who graduated last in their class, was the real culprit in her son's misdeeds. By the end of November, Gus's parents had only the reports through the end of September, by which time he had twenty demerits. The following week they learned that he got three more demerits during October, making his mother's tally twenty-three.[48]

Then came the deluge, in which the roommates were disciplined for cooking hash after taps. They were now well on the path to dismissal. Frances thought "sixteen hours additional guard duty a pretty severe punishment for such an offense," part of which he served over the Christmas holiday. "Today," she informed her sister on December 26, "his monthly report comes informing us that in addition to that he has thirty-three marks of demerit for this month, [from which] one would infer that they considered this cooking a breach of the decalogue." She and Henry had different concerns based on this news. "His father is, of course, much grieved by the apprehension that he may exceed his two hundred marks during the year. I suppose I shall never cease regretting that he ever went there, but these regrets are unavailing now." Frances's greater concern, though, was about the impact of the punishment on Gus's attitude toward authority. "This, I suppose is military discipline," she ruminated to Lazette. "It is unjust to my boy and like all unjust treatment will, I fear, make him reckless about his conduct in future." He had fifty-six marks for five months, as she told him unnecessarily in early January 1844. "You ought not to violate the prescribed regulations certainly, but I could not avoid thinking the punishment disproportioned to the offense." On January 21 Gus reported in a letter to his aunt Lazette that in his examination on January 2, "notwithstanding my fears, I was found proficient in my studies. Out of eighty who entered, fifty-two are only left in the class, some being sent away at this examination, some in June, and some have resigned."[49]

Gus's December report showed twenty-three additional demerits, which put him at seventy-nine for his first six months. "Now my dear child," his mother wrote to him at the beginning of February, "I wish you to write to me unreservedly on this subject. I cannot believe with principles formed as yours have been that you will persevere willingly in doing that which you believe to be wrong." She hoped that if his problems continued even after a "conscientious effort" to toe the academy's disciplinary line, "I think you will not doubt the expediency of resigning your warrant in preference to awaiting a dismissal. In the meantime, do not fail to write to me fully and freely explaining the difficulties of your situation. I shall then be better qualified to advise you what course to pursue."[50]

In a letter to Lazette of February 6, Frances quoted at length from a letter of Gus's that she had just received. She sympathized with his request that she stop sending him detailed reports, including up-to-date tallies on his demerits in reference to the two hundred that would get him expelled. He explained, "The punishment is so severe" that he was obviously doing his best to avoid the additional guard duty assigned for every minor offense. "I leave you to judge," Gus wrote to his mother, "whether I would be foolish enough not to try to keep from getting reports." Frances vented to her sister that "I have no sympathy from Henry," who reacted to the reports with "the cold assertion that boys must get accustomed to these things." Of course, "Augustus should not remain there another day were I to decide it for him. It is a wanton exposure of his health to say nothing of the other injurious effects of such injustice." Despite her better advice, she had no doubt that Gus "will do as his father advises, even were his life the forfeit. It is sinful so to task a noble, generous boy, and will someday bring fruit for repentance." Lazette wrote to Gus about Ira Cole, about whom Gus had asked, a young man from Canandaigua who had recently left the academy and spoke "of the discipline at the Point as very severe and tyrannical. His friends from the first were quite averse to his going there and undoubtedly encouraged his leaving."[51]

Gus insisted that he was doing his best and was the victim of overzealous discipline for acts that were often misunderstood. Frances wondered whether officers misinterpreted her son's "exceeding reserve," leading his superiors to think him "reckless and incorrigible." Perhaps he should try to explain himself to them. Henry advised Gus that he needed to conform to his superiors' expectations, while questioning Gus's vague accounts of the infractions. Frances continued to "disapprove of the severity of the punishment inflicted for trivial offenses," while being dismissed by her husband and father because "a woman was a poor judge of military discipline."[52]

To his cousin Frances, Gus wrote without mentioning the demerits and with little enthusiasm for the cadets' way of life. "The winter here would be rather dull for you, I presume; there are few or no parties, sleighs and 'sleigh riding' are very rare." Instead, most of his days were devoted to math. "Mathematics are here supposed to contain charms far superior to any of these amusements, and if I am not able to solve equations, find the area of surfaces and solids, and measure all lines straight, crooked, or curved by next June, it will not be because I have not been drilled enough at them, and the Professors I am sure can say that they have done their duty at least with good consciences." Only Saturday afternoons were open for some measure of fun. He hoped to see cousin Frances and her mother in June, after exams during the two months of break from the cadets' studies.[53]

The crisis surrounding Gus came to a head in the family toward the end of February 1844, when his January report arrived in Auburn. It showed, according to Henry, that "you remained during the month of January at thirteen in mathematics and at sixteen in French, that your demerit for the month was twenty-one and aggregate of your demerit for the academic year was one hundred, and the report distinctly says 'that you are not attentive to the regulations' as you should be, and your 'conduct not good.'" Henry had also received a private report from an anonymous source that Gus was "not doing well" and was "deficient in application . . . that there must be some evil influence operating upon you, some untoward circumstances in connection with your associates." His father took this to mean that Gus was overly influenced by his roommate, which led Henry to write a letter to the commandant requesting that they be split up.[54]

Frances had transcribed Henry's letter to Gus and imbedded it in one of hers, because her husband's handwriting had become almost illegible. "He writes so hastily from the extreme pressure of his business that I thought you might not be able to read the whole of his letter." His parents wanted Gus to know that they were now on the same page. "My duty is now too plain to be omitted," Henry wrote, in a manner he had never used to address one of his children before. "I say to you therefore with grief such as you have never before given me, that your conduct as exhibited in your monthly reports will lead to your disgrace and expulsion from the high and manly situation you occupy." As Gus well knew, he had accumulated in seven months more than half the demerits that would get him expelled at the end of the first year, and the number was escalating monthly. "Twenty-one marks per month," which is what he got for January, "from now until June would end in your disgrace, and there is no reason to hope you will have less, on the contrary there is every reason to fear you will have more." Gus had fallen to the very bottom of his class both in academics and discipline. "I cannot consent," Henry continued, "that you should be ignominiously discharged from your country's best academic institution. It would be a serious evil to you through all your future life. You must avoid it by a voluntary resignation. That resignation I insist upon your making; if you do not, I shall at once make it for you by writing to the Secretary of War."[55]

Henry's ultimatum, which he said that Frances fully supported, had an escape clause. Only if "you can resolve deeply, firmly, resolve to amend and restore yourself to your rightful standing in point of conduct and scholarship, and carry your resolution into effect" did his parents agree that Gus remain at the academy. "I allow you until the first of May for that purpose, provided you give me evidence in March and April that you are doing better. February is past. I expect no good account of you for that month, but it must not be so in March and April." Henry required that Gus write to his mother weekly, with a report of demerits and the cause. "Be independent of associates and adhere to these purposes and you cannot fail." His parents planned to tell none of the other members of the family—maternal grandfather, paternal grandparents, great-aunt, aunt, cousins, uncles, or siblings—about Gus's embarrassment. He must recall that his father had favored him attending college and his mother wanted him anywhere but in the military; it was his choice over their judgment that accounted for where he was.[56]

Henry remained willing to support Gus in the study of law or set him up in business or farming, if he decided to leave the academy of his own accord. Henry also told Gus in a postscript to his original letter, perhaps for the first time, about his own problems in college that had led to a hasty withdrawal before a recommitment after one year. "I know how to sympathize with you. I fell away from my collegiate studies and when I saw the end to which my heedlessness was carrying me, I made just such resolutions as I now recommend recourse to you, and I prevailed. I shall not cease to love and to respect you, whatever may be your academic misfortunes, but I shall not have a cheerful heart nor will your mother have peace until you write me all about these unhappy affairs and give us hope that you are doing well."[57]

One day later, Frances wrote to Gus again, withdrawing her endorsement of Henry's harsh judgment and demands on their son. "I cannot consent to have you consider the letter which I copied yesterday as an expression of my feeling or opinions." She supported Gus in what she interpreted as a principled opposition to the academy's rules. "That some adverse interest is operating against you is plain." Her "confidence in the uprightness of your intentions is undiminished." She "was not willing to trust the information of a third person," Henry's confidential informant, over that of "a child I have never had the least reason to doubt." Although others, such as his father, might lay blame at the feet of Gus's roommate, she was reluctant to do that unless Gus told her it was true. "Should you feel a resignation necessary I entreat you not to let it weigh down your spirits. You have health, strength, ability and perseverance. With industry and the blessing of your Heavenly Father you cannot fail to make your way through the world respectably. Withal you have loving hearts at home to receive you, a mother whose affection will remain the same through good and evil report."[58]

Despite Henry's assurance to Gus that his parents were not sharing the news of his troubles with the rest of the family, Frances continued to do so with Lazette, to whom she reported on Henry's letter and her own different take on the locus of blame. She only wished that Gus would share more of the details with her in letters or that she could secure a face-to-face meeting with him, during which she was sure that she could learn more, including whether Henry's anonymous informant was correct to blame Gus's roommate for most or all of his failings in academics and discipline. To her sister she wrote, "I know him well enough to be sensible that he will sooner be dismissed from the Academy than make any complaint of his roommate. It grieves Henry very much. I wish his ambition for his boys was like mine limited to their virtue and usefulness. It is better at present to say nothing on this subject, which can never be perfectly understood by anyone who does not appreciate Augustus."[59]

On March 11 Henry acknowledged a letter from Gus, which no longer survives. In it Gus resolved to improve in the hope of not being expelled. "Your letter addressed to me at Albany has made me very happy, for I have the utmost confidence in your fidelity to the resolution you have adopted." There could have been some embarrassment to Gus about changing roommates, but Henry thought the commandant had accomplished the switch with no need for an explanation or the implication that Gus had requested the change. Gus would lose face with his fellow cadets if it appeared that he had blamed his roommate for his problems or had received special treatment, which, of course, he had. Through the end of March, Frances had not heard directly from her son since the letter she transcribed from Henry to him. And, it seems, Henry had shared with her neither Gus's reply nor his correspondence with the commandant reassigning the roommates. This may have been inadvertence on Henry's part, his usual distraction from family affairs, or a function of tensions between husband and wife. She finally saw Gus's letter to Henry at the beginning of April, which neither explained the resolution of the roommate question to her satisfaction nor accounted for the specific behaviors that had led to the demerits.[60]

Frances was also concerned about Fred, who seemed depressed since a friend's death, and Willie, whose eyes were badly inflamed. Henry's mother declined precipitously and Frances doubted her survival through the summer; according to Jennings's son Gus, "she considers herself as rapidly drawing to the termination of her pilgrimage." Henry's father was "much complaining," as usual. Frances's father was incapacitated by gout. In mid-April Frances was extremely ill, according to Fred. We know now she was pregnant with Fanny. By the middle of May she felt a bit better and on May 28 Lazette wrote to Gus that his mother "desires me to say she is much better than she has been for a number of weeks past and hopes soon to be able to write to you herself. For a number of days past she has been able to sit up and enjoy the society of the family."[61]

At some point in July, Frances heard that Gus had passed his exams. He neither resigned nor was he expelled. She shared the news joylessly with her sister. "I have a letter from Augustus." she wrote. "He has passed his examination and is pronounced 'proficient,' so he remains." She hoped that she and Lazette could visit him early in August, but she had nothing else to say on the subject. On August 15 Frances wrote to inform Gus that they had safely returned home after a visit with him. Willie, Lazette, and his cousin Frances had accompanied her. "Aunty says all other young men appear rude and ill-bred in comparison with the cadets. Frances refers to her visit at the Point with much pleasure. It is a charming spot and will appear so to you one of these days when you escape from the tiresome routine of military duties. Willie imitates the regulations of the camp by summoning us frequently by the tap of the drum. He says we would not let him stay as long at the Point as he wished to."[62]

The family drama surrounding Gus's enlistment was apparently done, although his mother's worries did not end short of the grave. When she did not get a letter from him every two weeks during his time at West Point, she feared he was desperately ill. Until his reports came, she worried he had fallen back into the behaviors that almost got him expelled. He studied geography in addition to French and math in his second year, which his mother approved.[63]

Gus now prospered at West Point. Whether it was a change of roommates, an accommodation to the demands of military discipline, or a rededication to his studies, he successfully reversed course. He remained the shy, withdrawn, unsocial man that he had become, but he was now launched on a military career. An invitation to his cousin Frances to attend the academy's fall ball elicited a gentle, noncommittal reply. As far as we know, this was the last invitation and the only rejection he ever received from a woman over the rest of his life.[64]

Henry's mother declined through the summer and fall; he responded to one of his father's many summonses, which escalated in frequency in mid-November, culminating with one on November 13, in which he wrote "your beloved and always affectionate mother still lives and waiting with the most signal composure till her change comes, which we are hourly expecting." After staying with his parents for a few days, business called Henry away. He wrote Mary a parting note on November 24, in which he regretted that he had not bid his mother farewell when he left her for what was likely the last time, "but I could not say anything and we parted in silence. I hurried away lest my tears might excite you beyond your strength." When Samuel wrote again to Henry on December 5, it was to say, "Oh my child, this is truly a trying time. I am scarcely able to walk about the house without help and constantly lament that I cannot have you with us in those trying scenes." Two days later, his father wrote to him again in an effort "to mitigate my own agonies."[65]

Henry wrote to Gus on December 11 before he heard about the passing of his mother that day. "Your mother's illness renders it necessary that I be your correspondent for the present. We were all made happy on Monday the ninth by the advent of a little stranger, your sister. Your mother is quite comfortable and has no alarming symptoms. The babe seems healthy and we hope that before long the health of the mother will be quite restored. We have not yet bestowed a name on the child, but she will probably bear the name of her from whom she derives her being." Four days later, he wrote to Gus again, "I am just leaving home to follow the mortal remains of my dear Mother to their final resting place on the earth. She died on Wednesday last at the age of seventy-five. I am sorry that you have had so little opportunity to know her intellectual and moral worth. . . . Your mother is convalescent. Has sat up some time today. The infant is very well and all the family are in good health."[66]

Chapter 11

Domestic Perplexities, 1844–1848

The conflict between Frances's infirmity and domestic ideals, on the one side, and Henry's wanderlust and ambition, on the other, did not end with his term as governor. In the 1840s Frances realized that it was not just his political ambition that kept her husband from home but rather his disdain for family life. By the end of the decade she accepted that Henry longed to be elsewhere, that his mind and heart were not in Auburn even when he was physically present. There were no more domestic "experiments" for him, so from her perspective he might just as well be happy pursuing higher office rather than arguing cases in a local practice, which he just found boring. All this began to clarify in 1846, when Henry defended two inmates of the Auburn prison, motivated by both principle and ambition. Over the two years preceding the cases, it was still possible to imagine the Sewards living together at 33 South Street.

Henry had missed his mother's funeral in December 1844, when work delayed him. He arrived in time to sit with Mary Jane's remains before they were permanently secured in his father's vault. He stayed with Samuel for two weeks and left the day after Christmas. Four miles from Albany he was injured in a carriage accident. "The axletree of the stage broke," Frances informed Gus in a letter she wrote on New Year's Day, "and your father, who was sitting with the driver, was thrown the distance of fifteen feet upon the frozen ground, his shoulder dislocated and his body much bruised." She had received two letters from others saying that the former governor's injuries were not life-threatening as the newspaper reports had initially led her to believe. She had also heard from Henry, which she explained in a letter to Gus. He was barely able to write the letter with his lame arm. "At the same time the severe sprain of the muscles of my right leg has rendered it useless and more painful than the disabled arm. Of course, I have not been able to get in or out of bed, to sit up, turn over, or aid myself in any way. I suffer severely in my wounded limb when I cough, but I am getting better every day and hope soon to be able to return home."[1]

Frances did not expect Henry to reach Auburn anytime soon, but she underestimated his force of will, as he arrived home on crutches two days after she had written to Gus. "No one but himself would have thought of undertaking a similar journey in his situation," she wrote on January 13. "He was lifted to and from the cars in a chair by four men and then walked slowly with the aid of crutches. He is getting better, but very slowly, the pressing nature of his business renders him very desirous of recovery. The sprain of his leg is much more painful and will be much longer getting well than the dislocation of his shoulder. He has walked with his crutches once to the office but suffered much in consequence." In Frances's opinion, Henry was trying to do too much in frustration with the confinement and in the face of much pain, which she feared would undermine his overall health. On January 28 Frances wrote to Lazette in much the same way. "Henry is not materially better than when I wrote last. He allows himself no time to recover, is at work every day." He was in court daily and no longer using crutches in the house by February 1. By April Henry was back on the road after his most extended time in Auburn in at least fifteen years.[2]

Through the spring, Frances recovered comparatively well from giving birth to Fanny on December 9. "I am able to sit up much of the day, and [am] indeed more comfortable than I have been in many months," she wrote in her New Year's Day letter to Gus. "'Miss Frances A. Seward Jun' as Fred calls her is well and hopes to be tolerably well looking by the time her eldest brother comes home." Five-year-old Willie wanted his mother to write "Gusy that I had 9 presents at Christmas." "She grows fat and white," Frances reported to her sister about the baby two weeks later, but she was about to replace an older woman with a girl as her nurse, "and then I shall be chief nurse myself." Before Fanny reached two months, Frances wrote to Lazette that "Sister Fanny laughs often and talks a very little. Willie insists upon her being interested in all his toys. She seems more amused with Dick [pet bird] and his cage than anything else. Dick, for his part, never sings, only when she is crying very hard, which seems to animate him exceedingly." By February 1 Frances was on her fourth nurse, which was a major inconvenience and a strain on her nerves. At the end of April she wrote to her sister again to say, "I am, of course, left in sole charge of baby, which must be my apology for this scrawl." By May 14, in addition to nursing, Fanny took "three regular meals of bread and milk every day." Clary sat up with the baby until 10:00 p.m. or midnight, at which point Frances brought Fanny into her bed. Two weeks later, Frances thought that the baby was "getting very funny. She has taken a great fancy to the cats and when the bread and milk is unpalatable Mary brings in a young kitten, which never fails to restore her appetite. She is full of mirth all day. Monday, she never cried once, though she found it rather hard to go to sleep on my lap without nursing."[3]

"Within one week I had five different cooks," Frances wrote to Lazette in July. "Rachel remained but two days. She was engaged to another place when she came and they sent for her Thursday. I then had a white woman one day. Then Maria came two days, and finally John brought an Irish girl, who is no cook at all and I have had <u>that</u> to do myself." On top of the domestic chaos, Clary was ill and therefore no help. Homeopathic remedies were not helping their fifty-one-year-old aunt. "Dear Clara has been sick more than a week and every night after a toilsome day I have been down to see her. She has suffered greatly with pain having an inflammation of the kidney, some nights walking the floor nearly the whole night." As Frances wrote to Lazette during the same month, "I am looking for a coloured woman (drunk or sober) to hire as a cook for a season." The problem was much the same with nurses for the baby, and help with the cleaning and laundry was no more stable than it had been in other seasons. The whole domestic situation had reduced Frances to tears.[4]

The pregnancy, recovery from the delivery, and care of the baby through a revolving door of nurses, some of them not very much help, left Frances overwhelmed. Not surprisingly, her social calls continued to suffer. She explained to Lazette that "as the people made no allowance for my numberless visitors and indifferent health, I gave much offense by neglecting this law of etiquette." What she thought were "nervous" headaches returned. The steady stream of incompetent household staff, Willie's inflamed eyes, and the usual seasonal rounds of upper respiratory and lower gastrointestinal infections only added to her burden. She outlined for her sister a typical day: "rise at six, dust and shut up the parlour, overlook the breakfast and dining room generally, assisting in each department. After breakfast, spend one or more hours in the kitchen, wash and dress baby, the remaining part of the morning in the kitchen, after dinner nurse sister, lie down half an hour if not prevented," and then supervise the household staff and continue with nursing and baby care until "retiring wearily to bed" at about 9:00 p.m.[5]

During the months following Henry's carriage accident, Frances used her time as his amanuensis while he recovered the use of his right hand to communicate to Gus in her own words what she represented as her husband's ongoing concerns about their son. They were both pleased that he was no longer in conflict with military discipline, but she was torn between wanting Gus to succeed and hoping he would fail in his studies, so she attributed to Henry a lack of confidence in Gus when he had intended to convey encouragement. "Your father wishes you to determine whether there is a prospect of your being found deficient in any of your studies. If so, he prefers that you should resign previous to the June examination, as he thinks it may be a disadvantage to you in after life to be obliged to resign." She added, unnecessarily, that Gus was "already in possession of my wishes on the subject."[6]

Gus replied perhaps in anger, but certainly with hurt feelings, at what Frances had written and what he read as Henry's lack of confidence in him. She "was grieved to find that you had so misconstrued mine to which it was an answer. What your father said in relation to a resignation I think was said in all kindness and without an intention of conveying a reproach, as you seem to suppose. However, I will say no more about it. I hope and trust that in any event you will come home in the summer and not return again" to the academy for his final two years. By June 23, on Gus's arrival in Auburn on leave after passing his classes and exams, Frances was again in despair, which she shared with her sister. "He seems determined to return and with his father's influence on that side, mine will weigh but little. It is a bitter disappointment and will cause me many tears." If Gus ended up in the army, "it will be a sore trial for me, the grave of many fond hopes, but I must not anticipate. One suggestion from Henry, I think would change the whole matter; if he lives, I believe he will repent this immolation of a child of the high moral excellence and generous spirit of Augustus." Henry had a painful shoulder and leg, but Frances imagined him dead.[7]

Henry accompanied Fred to Union College for the start of his first term in August 1845, soon after Gus returned to West Point from his summer leave at home. To Fred's surprise and against his wishes, Henry boarded him with the college president's family, where he had less independence and got into less trouble than his father did at his age. Eliphalet Nott had been president of Union since 1804 and remained in the position until his death in 1866 at the age of ninety-three. Henry intervened to prevent a recurrence of the problems Gus had and recalled his own behavior at Fred's age more critically than he later shared in his autobiography.

During the same summer that Fred began college, six-year-old Willie accompanied his father to Rochester, where Henry had court cases to argue. When his cases delayed Henry, Willie returned with the carriage driver as his companion, a plan that Frances would have fretted about had she known before their youngest son arrived safely at home. Lazette joined Frances in Auburn, while Alvah and her daughter Frances were in Detroit. Nonetheless, Frances informed Gus that "I am more lonely than I can express now you are both gone," her two oldest boys. "How often the beautiful words of Irving occur to me—'our lives are made up of transient meetings and long separations.'" After two decades of lamenting the truth of this description of her marriage, Frances wrote to her son that "it is somewhat difficult to feel reconciled to this state of things, but as it appears unavoidable, I must endeavor to submit cheerfully."[8]

Jennings's son Clarence was still in Auburn until the commencement of his fall term at Hobart College in Geneva, New York, as was Mary Augusta Seward, age seventeen, a daughter of Polydore's, who was in Auburn for an extended stay and not happy about it. Henry declined her request to return to Florida on the grounds that he lacked the funds. Frances wrote to Gus that his father was owed legal fees but had no one to collect them. Clara Miller, a cousin from the other side of the family, who was about the same age as Mary, was also in residence.[9]

Frances lamented over the winter of 1845–46 that she had little milk to nurse Fanny, which made for a cranky baby. She contemplated weaning at about ten months, earlier than she thought ideal. Frances was still considering weaning when Fanny turned seventeen months in the spring. Frances always had trouble separating from her infants in this way. In letters Frances wrote for Willie to Gus and Lazette in the second week of May 1846, Willie reported that she "was going to wean Fanny tomorrow, but she is a little sick and I guess she can't wean her. She plays a good deal. As soon as she waked up she nursed. She don't like custard pie much, she has got tired of it." Frances finally thought she had weaned Fanny successfully a week later, having passed the first night without nursing, although the child continued to make demands. As she approached seventeen months, Fanny still did not walk, "owing to the weakness of one ankle. She talks incessantly to make up that deficiency," her mother told Gus at the end of April.[10]

Letters throughout the year emphasized Fanny's speaking skills and her love of books. "She is like Fred about books," Frances wrote in October. "It will be hard to keep her from learning to read. She already knows five or six letters," in contrast to Willie, who was much slower to read and was more interested in collecting nuts. "Dear little Fanny gets her book whenever she sees Willie read. She has already learned the names of half the letters," her mother declared proudly a month before she turned two. Frances wrote to Lazette shortly after a visit that "Fanny says 'Aunty gone home, baby sorry.' You can hardly conceive how much her vocabulary has increased in one week. She seems to talk about everything and tries to call the name of anything she hears."[11]

Fred returned home for Thanksgiving, the term and exams having ended earlier than his mother expected. He performed near the top of his class, which made his father proud and left Frances feeling jealous for Gus, whom she thought was in a much more difficult situation and thus had triumphed nearer the bottom than the top of his class. In the fall of 1845 and spring of 1846 his demerits were averaging in the single digits after being up to twenty a month the year before. He enjoyed chemistry, but he was not coming home for the holidays, which disappointed his mother.

Samuel had launched his school against Henry's advice, which he called an "institute," and he resented that Henry did not spare more time to admire it and assist him in its administration. He had found Elizabeth Parsons, a former tutor of Frances Worden's, to teach there and head it. While Frances predicted Miss Parsons to last all of ten days once she realized how difficult it was to work with Henry's father, she remained, despite, in Henry's opinion, being very unhappy for over a decade in different administrative roles. Henry wrote to her in November 1848 a long-delayed response to her urgent correspondence, trying to calm her down. Someone had poisoned her dog and she found his father impossible. "You have good right to be offended and grieved by the brutal treatment of your faithful dog," he wrote, but a lawsuit would accomplish nothing and could make matters worse. In the end, "it is a trivial loss," one that he had experienced himself, and "easily repaired" by getting a new dog. He had no advice to give on his father but would try to squeeze in a trip to Florida and reason with Samuel himself. Now that the November 1848 election was over, during which Henry had campaigned for Whig candidates, he said he hoped that "some unlooked-for change will return to something like domestic life for at least a part of the time," and he carved out three days from his schedule for a brief visit to Florida.[12]

The year 1846 began well enough for the family; their news was contained in letters written in Frances's hand but purported to be from six-year-old Willie to those family members who were away from Auburn. In those to his brothers, father, cousin Clarence, and Aunt Lazette, Willie reported that his now year-old sister was well, but she cried and screamed more than he liked. By mid-January his cousin Clarence and brother Fred had returned to college, and his father was in Washington, DC, arguing a patent case among others for about two months, but had sent him a book as a Christmas present. "It was a book of Cock Robin and the New Mother Hubbard," Frances wrote for Willie to Gus. Clarence and Fred had also given him books; perhaps this was a reprimand to Gus from his mother for not sending a present to his little brother. "I hope you will answer this letter very soon, as I shall expect an answer," Frances wrote for Willie. Willie wrote to his father to thank him for the book and to report that their dog's foot had gotten run over by a sleigh. "When are you coming home," Frances wrote for Willie. "I want to see you very much. Do come as soon as you can: won't you father?" He, she, or they hoped, "dear father, you will answer this letter soon, and remember your little boy in Auburn."[13]

There are surviving letters from all of them except Gus in response to Willie's letters in Frances's hand. Henry wrote to Willie that "your very nice letter, which came last night made my heart right glad. It contained almost the only information I have received since I left home about either yourself or your sweet little sister Fanny." He promised to return home "as soon as I can, certainly within two weeks." Fred wrote that he was glad to receive news from Willie about the family dogs. Lazette wrote that she was "glad to get a letter from you, written by yourself, and I hope I can write one so you can read it." She hoped he found that the two goats were better at pulling his wagon than the dogs had been. "Give my love to Grandpa and Fanny."[14]

Lazette's daughter Frances was in Auburn well into February. Frances Worden was of an age to be courted, and prospects were better in Auburn than in Canandaigua, where the Wordens lived. "Frances has attended numerous parties," Frances Seward explained to Gus, "Aunty, Aunt Clara & I a few. I have had two small parties at home, which were said to be pleasant." Henry remained home for only a week. "Write to Willie next time," she instructed Gus. "He is impatient for an answer to his letter."[15]

Henry arrived home in February 1846 not for family reasons but to argue a case. One year earlier, on March 16, 1845, Henry Wyatt, an inmate in the Auburn state prison, had stabbed to death a fellow prisoner. Wyatt believed that the man he killed with half a pair of scissors had implicated him in a murder committed in Ohio. Henry and his partner David Wright argued in February 1846 for a verdict of not guilty by reason of "moral insanity," that Wyatt had been so badly "flogged and tortured" in the prison that he was "unable to resist his passions." Shortly before Wyatt came to trial, a convict named Charles Plumb, age twenty-one, died after a guard whipped him. When prison officials attempted to cover up the brutality, the public became sympathetic to such arguments as Wright and Seward made in the Wyatt trial. Wyatt's jury deadlocked after thirty-six hours of deliberation, which led to retrial later that year. Frances was proud of Henry for taking the case without remuneration. "He will have the reward of a good conscience," she wrote to Gus, "which invariably attends such acts of kindness and mercy."[16]

Frances's interpretation of the Plumb and Wyatt cases was that they were each "a revolting instance of the depravity produced by placing one man completely in the power of another. As is too often the case in slavery, power makes man tyrannical and the abuse of power long persisted in assimilates a man to a fiend." She hoped the two cases inspired legislation restricting prison discipline. "I trust for the honor of humanity that such discipline may be ameliorated."[17]

In March, one month after Wyatt's first trial, a brutal mass murder led the local citizenry to their own inflamed passions. As Frances explained to Gus, "a murder so barbarous has never been committed in the United States except by Indians. Three of the family died instantly, one the next day, one wounded and still survives, and this immense sacrifice of human life the work of one poor degraded half-witted negro, but recently liberated from the state prison where he was confined five years for stealing a horse." People in the region now feared, in the wake of the deadlocked jury over Wyatt's sanity, that clever lawyers would defend successfully William Freeman, the African American charged with the inexplicable slaying of the Van Nest family. Freeman variously said that the Van Nests—husband, pregnant wife, son, and the boy's grandmother—were responsible for getting him falsely imprisoned, that he was owed compensation for his imprisonment, and that he did not know why he stabbed, and in one case gutted, family members in their home. He actually had no previous connection to any of the family members.[18]

People in Auburn and surrounding towns were now locking their doors. "The excited state of the community since the Fleming [New York] murders has produced a feeling of insecurity which I never experienced before," Frances wrote to Gus. "I wish I could persuade myself that the women in Auburn were more ferocious, more savage, more everything that is unwomanly than those of any other town, but I fear this is not the case," she wrote to her sister over the summer, "and as long as boys continue to be nourished and trained by she wolves, so long must men approximate towards barbarism."[19]

Elijah Miller and Thurlow Weed had warned Henry that in such an inflamed environment he would pay a high price for taking the Freeman case too. Henry had weathered the hung jury in Wyatt's first trial, but they thought the popular linkage of the two cases would ruin his reputation permanently. As he wrote to Weed, Henry knew that the defense of Freeman "will rain a storm of prejudice and passion, which will try the fortitude of my friends. But I shall do my duty. I care not whether I am to be ever forgiven for it or not." As he wrote in the fall to another political friend, "in that unavoidable and most righteous conflict, every friend I had here but my wife and sister, and every friend abroad abandoned me."[20]

While Henry had no record of opposition to capital punishment as governor, he believed that executing such a man as his client, who was clearly mentally unfit to comprehend the charges or his own motives, was unjust. He argued that Freeman was "a lunatic" who had "committed his crimes under the influence of an insane delusion." As governor, Henry had favored pardons for convicts who were clearly insane. The question of Freeman's race also played heavily in the case. Henry argued in his client's defense that if the roles had been reversed and a lunatic white man had murdered a Black family, the case would be handled with greater sympathy for the defendant. Henry thought that for once abolitionists would see him as on the right side, which not all of them did. As James McClune Smith, the African American physician and author, wrote to Gerrit Smith, the Liberty Party candidate for president in 1848, "My spiritual quarrel with Seward began in the very act for which you commend him." In Seward's defense of Freeman, he "used an expression about 'inferiority of race,' which I can forgive in no man. . . . I gave up all hope of him when I read that sentence, because no man can fight the true Anti-Slavery fight who does not believe all men are equal." According to Doctor Smith, Seward "advocated civil and political equality for blacks, while rejecting the idea of racial equality."[21]

Although Henry said that he did not care about popular opinion and felt a moral commitment to his client, he also made another calculation. "The argument in the Freeman case," he wrote to Weed in the fall, "is doing wonders for me professionally, and bids fair to secure me business of that better kind which is most profitable and least unpleasant." He had defended Wyatt once and also represented him in the second trial at least in part from the same motive.[22]

It is unclear whether the judges before whom Seward argued these two cases understood the precedents for insanity cases, and certainly the juries did not, based on deeply flawed judicial instructions. The legal interpretation in New York was more liberal than the British common law cases, but not by much. It was based on expert medical testimony that took seriously already discredited phrenology, the interpretations of bumps and skull shapes, which Henry found so flattering in his own case and had its origins in science before it was taken over by amateur performers. Wyatt was convicted in his second trial and executed in August 1846. Freeman died in prison in August 1847, after his conviction and before the scheduled execution.[23]

Through 1846 Frances continued to pressure Gus to quit West Point and the army. She remained fearful that he would end up fighting in the Mexican-American War, which she saw as a war of imperial aggression aimed at annexing vast swaths of the Southwest. Sometimes she was subtle, as in a letter of April 6, when she inquired about his preferences for a visit from Henry. "Shall he come now or would you prefer to have his visit delayed until after the June examination, when if you remain at the Point I intend coming myself?" The "if" reflected her hopes and opinion about his chosen career. In a letter to Lazette,

Frances dismissed her own chronic complaints about finding and retaining competent household staff as "petty vexations and constant labors to banish from my mind the corroding anxiety I feel about my boy. The war I apprehended has come. If Augustus passes his examinations one year more sends him into the army. As Frances [Worden] is a girl and not exposed to this danger, you will have difficulty in imagining what I feel on this subject. A constant foreboding of this result has embittered many, many hours of the time since he first entered the Academy and yet I have always been told my fears were absurd." A week later, she wrote to her sister in the same vein again. As always, Henry offered her no consolation on the subject of their eldest son's career. "Henry says nothing of Augustus in connection with the war. He is not ever in his thoughts as in mine, and then he could say nothing to allay my apprehensions. The shades will continue to deepen. God grant that they may not end in total darkness, that all my fearful foreboding may not be realized."[24]

On May 28 Frances even more frankly addressed the question with Gus for far from the first or last time.

> You may think it strange, but it is my earnest wish that you should not pass this examination. A dismissal or even being put back another year would be altogether preferable to the prospect of a successful graduation for the next year. Almost anything seems preferable to being engaged in the unrighteous war we are waging with Mexico. The prospect of any war has always appalled me. This has double terrors as it involves a dread of loss of life with a dereliction of principles. Will you think of this and be guided by the advice of one who would willingly resign her own life to preserve yours?[25]

When Frances learned that Gus had passed his exams, she softened her approach to him just a bit. "I received your letter communicating the result of the examination three or four days ago," she wrote on June 15. "As you seem gratified by the result I will endeavour to be pleased likewise." Clearly, though, she did not share Gus's elation or Henry's pride. "Your letter under the circumstances does you credit and was gratifying to your father. I can only pray that this wicked war may be terminated before the time comes when you may be called to take a part in it."[26]

In November Lazette mentioned in a letter to Willie that she expected Frances, Willie, Fanny, Fred, Clary, and Clarence for Christmas and very much looked forward to it. In the same month Frances wrote to her sister that Maria, a member of the household staff, was desperately ill, almost certainly dying, and Frances oversaw care for Maria and her two children. Frances also wrote that she was again entertaining for Henry, hosting a dinner for thirty, mainly local people with positions of public standing—town supervisors, overseers of the poor, "with a few others." Between the preparations for the supper and her care for Maria, she "had accomplished little the last two weeks." Maria, who was both ill and impoverished, "her husband having gone off last spring and left her with the care of two children," was "assisted now by the town, but has from us everything she needs to make her comfortable. An old colored woman has the children, who I presume expects to be paid for her services."[27]

By the end of November, Frances cautioned Lazette that the Christmas visit might not happen. "I should like very much to come out Christmas, but it is altogether uncertain. There are so many contingencies that I think it not best to expect us." She could only promise a visit from Fred, who had again made it home from college before Thanksgiving. The weather made the prospect of traveling with small children "uninviting." Then there were fears about illness, care for Maria, Clary's advancing age, their aged father, and the logistics of the trip to consider with no reason to count on Henry for help. Lazette apparently replied in frustration with Frances's usual pessimism, because Frances wrote back defensively, "I did not say I was not coming Christmas. I said I was very uncertain and you had better not expect me." Yet she continued in her negative posture and indeed eventually canceled the trip. "I very much doubt the propriety of taking a young child from home in the winter merely for a pleasure excursion. I know I felt reproached many times last winter for exposing Fanny so unnecessarily." Fanny had her second birthday two days after Frances wrote the letter, and Willie was seven. Indeed, by the time Christmas arrived, Frances was confined to her bed, sick with influenza and an attack of neuralgia that laid her low for more than two weeks beginning shortly after Fanny's birthday. "Most of our family have been or are now sick with it," Frances wrote to Gus on December 29.[28]

Fred too had become ill and so did not make the trip to Canandaigua. On the other end, Lazette's daughter Frances was also under the weather. "We had all intended spending Christmas there," Frances wrote to Gus, "but the illness in both families prevented." Willie no longer believed in St. Nick, but he hung stockings for himself and his little sister that his mother filled. "He was up before daylight Christmas morning," Frances reported to Gus, "took his lanthorn and went down to wish Aunt Clara 'Merry Christmas,' where he stayed to breakfast. He made molasses candy in the afternoon and in the evening had a show in the dining room. I believe so far as he was concerned Christmas was a very pleasant day." He had received a set of wooden soldiers. "Fanny says they are all 'Gusy.'" Henry was home for Christmas this year, but Frances only mentioned in letters that he attended church with the three boys, Willie, Clarence, and Fred. He left for New York on December 30, so he did not stay home for the entire holiday season.[29]

Frances was ill through much of January 1847, which she thought was from attending a wedding shortly after the first of the year. This was on the heels of her having been bedridden throughout the holidays. For much of January, Henry was away in Washington, DC, New York City, and Albany arguing cases and attending to business. In February, shortly after his return home for a brief visit, he was in a sleigh accident. One of the horses was seriously injured when the driver tipped the sleigh by inadvertently running off the road, but the inexperienced driver, Henry, and a Miss Darling were just fine. Frances also told Gus in February that she and Henry had received a letter from Dr. Nott, which reported that Fred "was attending a dancing school in the city 'in company with citizens of both sexes,' without the consent and contrary to the wishes of the faculty." Fred remained resentful throughout the spring that he had been singled out for enforcement of a rule generally ignored simply because his father had boarded him in President Nott's home. Nonetheless, he was doing very well in his classes and, according to his mother, "he appears to be quite an agreeable young man of twenty at least." He was sixteen at the time.[30]

Lazette and her Frances canceled a visit to Auburn, first due to illness, then because Judge Miller's house was undergoing renovations. "We are to have some alteration to the house, which will preclude visitors next month," Frances informed Gus in March. "The long staircase is to be taken down and the south room thereby enlarged. I am quite unable to decide whether the convenience of the house will be more increased or diminished by this arrangement, as what we gain in one way we lose in another, but we shall obtain a larger sitting room, which is a desirable consideration. I dread the pulling down of walls exceedingly." The Worden women deferred their visit until June, in order to arrive after the dust settled and the workmen were gone. On May 25

Frances hoped that the laborers would be done in another week or two. She also trusted that when Gus visited after his exams, "you will find the house much changed, but I hope it will not seem less like home. It will on many accounts be much more pleasant."[31]

Even Henry expressed concern that Gus might not pass final exams for the year, as his grades were plummeting and demerits ascending again through the spring. Gus attributed his scholastic failure in January to illness through the holidays, when he should have studied more. Henry addressed the problem in a letter of February 4, 1847. "I deeply regret the illness which you suffered in December, and sincerely hope that the fears your mother is inclined to indulge, of a permanent affection of your health, may prove groundless. We are both entirely satisfied that illness was the cause of you being unable to pass the semiannual examination. And thus the failure was a Providential misfortune." Henry also clarified that unlike Frances, he was "not at all concerned about your entrance into the army." On the other hand, if Gus found it "agreeable to yourself, you should adopt some occupation of a civic nature."[32]

His parents advised Gus that he needed an exit strategy that got him out of West Point and the army with as little embarrassment as possible if need be. Frances recommended resignation, either active or passive. "So long as there is a possibility of disappointment," she wrote to him in April, "it is wiser to have your mind in some measure prepared for it. I should, of course, consider it no calamity." Henry suggested the consideration of alternative careers that did not require a college education, but he emphasized in more than one letter that Gus had "a right to judge and determine for yourself." He thought it was a shame, though, if his son felt obliged to remain in the army only because the nation was at war. The April report from the academy showed seventy-eight demerits for the month, his highest monthly total by far. Despite all the hopes, fears, and concerns of his parents, Gus passed his exams and graduated from the academy without written comments from Henry and Frances, likely because they delivered their congratulations in person when he reached home in mid-June 1847. Gus stayed with his family for all of July and departed in August for what Frances assumed was the last time before he sailed for Veracruz, Mexico.[33]

During July, Julia Ann Van Brunt, the long-serving housekeeper for Henry's parents, died after a long illness and steady decline. George and Polydore reported the death in letters to Frances; neither imagined what their father would do without Julia to care for him, but they knew that the burden and their father's demands would fall even more heavily on them. George, anticipating Julia's demise, had written to Frances in June that "the old gentleman is evidently at his wits end. He is as close as ever and as severe in his exactions when he can make anyone yield, but those he has about him are breaking down and he finds it difficult to get along." Samuel was, as usual, threatening disinheritance to all around him, threats that he had already exacted in his most recent wills.[34]

In mid-September 1847 Gus boarded the ship *Ohio* with fifteen fellow officers and three hundred recruits for Mexico. Frances wrote to him at Veracruz on October 21, anticipating that "if no accident has occurred" he should have by then arrived after a journey of over one month. She followed news about troop movements and second-guessed General Scott's strategy. "It was a great disappointment," she wrote, that the treaty for peace failed so entirely, but "I am not at all surprised that the Mexicans thought the demands of our government unreasonable. They have little cause to acknowledge the justice of our claims to territory forced from them. I suppose all speculation about what will next be done is idle. I only know that my beloved child is in the country of enemies and that his life is continually subject to exposure. May God protect him. I have no hope from any other source."[35]

Three weeks later, Frances still had no confirmation that Gus had landed. "Before I can be assured that you have safely encountered the perils of the ocean," she wrote again, "you will be exposed to the equal dangers of the land." Finally, in the first week of November she received a letter from her son. He had landed in Veracruz; the newspapers simply had not announced the arrival of the *Ohio*. She continued to follow troop movements but did not know whether Gus was attached to the forces of Gen. Joseph Lane or Gen. Robert Patterson, and she was worried because she had learned of the death from disease of another lieutenant.[36]

Frances wrote to Gus on Christmas Day. Eight-year-old Willie had returned the night before alone. He had abandoned a trip to Albany with his father in order to be home for Christmas, a surprise the significance of which Frances did not miss. "He says he could not wait for his father as he <u>must</u> be at home Christmas. Fortunately, I had supplied myself with Christmas toys so that he and Fanny both putting up their stockings last night and today the table is covered with guns, swinging men, soldiers, horses, tea cups & saucers, chairs and sofas, dolls, &c, &c. They are very happy. Tonight, Abbey [household staff] is to make molasses candy, which is usually the conclusion of the Christmas sports." Frances had attended church that morning in the company of her niece Frances Worden, who had just turned twenty-one and spent the holiday with her aunt's family. Frances Seward wrote to Gus that she "was much affected by having Frances accompany me to the altar to take the Sacrament. It was unexpected to me and brought up so suddenly a thousand recollections, some pleasing, some painful, that I found it very difficult to restrain my tears. You and Frances are so nearly of an age and were so long playmates that every new era in her life seems intimately associated with yours." She hoped and prayed that her son, like her niece, made a testimony of faith and was baptized.[37]

As always, Frances hoped that Henry returned home, perhaps even that night from Albany, but she knew better after all these years than to count on it. She had gotten a first whiff over the summer of politics back in his life, although there were other clues that she had either missed or allowed to pass without comment. He spent much time in Albany now that the Whig Party had secured its largest majority ever in the state government, and there were Henry's speeches that she read about in the newspapers. Back in June, she had written to Henry that "the notice in the *Tribune* of your removal to Albany has excited much speculation. Was it authorized? I suppose so." He was running for office again with Weed's guidance, but this time the voters were members of the state legislature, which elected US senators on the governor's nomination.[38]

The rest of 1848 continued much as it started for the Sewards, with Frances fretting about her children's health—Willie's swollen eyes and toothaches; Fanny down with a mild case of scarlet fever, measles, and a bout of erysipelas. Clarence and Fred were again at their respective colleges. Clarence was in his last year at Hobart before studying law back in Auburn, and Fred was still doing well under the supervision of the college president's family. Judge Miller and Aunt Clary were both well enough for their ages, he at seventy-six and she at fifty-five, although his sight was going and he was periodically crippled with gout, she was prone to respiratory infections, and they both had lost a good bit of their hearing.

Lazette and her Frances, who was now engaged to Henry Chesebro (which they pronounced cheese-bro), both caught colds and succumbed to influenza in season as the rest of the family did. Over the summer and fall, Frances Worden also suffered a serious illness that was never named, although Frances wrote to Gus in December that "for the last six months, she has not been able to walk even in her immediate neighbourhood without much suffering." Lazette took her for a consultation with Dr. Adrian Vanderveer of Flatbush, Brooklyn, one of the first physicians to specialize. He was what became known as a gynecologist. According to Frances, the two women arrived in Flushing unaccompanied on November 3 and ended up staying into April for treatments that at first appeared to Lazette of no help. After several weeks in Vanderveer's care, however, she reported that Frances was able to walk two or three miles, and the doctor spoke confidently of an "entire recovery."[39]

Alvah was absorbed in state politics, which had Lazette concerned about their finances. He also remained as touchy and controlling as ever. Henry, who provided Lazette money and other assistance for her trip to Flushing with her daughter, had to be careful not to offend him. Lazette canceled a meeting with Henry in nearby New York City lest it rub her husband the wrong way. "I am obliged very reluctantly to forego the pleasure of my visit to N York, a pleasure to which Fan and I have been looking forward with high hopes." If Alvah got wind of it, there would be trouble. "I hope you will have time to come here," to Flushing, Lazette wrote to Henry by way of canceling the rendezvous, "and see us. That will not give the offense in meeting you in N.Y. will. Believe me, dear brother, that we fully appreciate and will gratefully remember this as well as every other evidence of your affection."[40]

Frances Seward apparently suffered no more or less from her chronic complaints throughout the year, principally headaches, toothaches, and a range of what she termed "nervous" ailments, along with the seasonal afflictions that many caught. Henry's absence remained a trial to Frances, and his time away was increasing in both frequency and duration as he returned to politics. He campaigned tirelessly for the Whig Party locally and the party's presidential candidate, Gen. Zachary Taylor, who won the November 1848 election. "Fanny says she will have a father one of these days," Frances wrote to Henry in January. In August she wrote to Gus that he should not expect any letters from his father, who "has little leisure to think of his family." At about the same time, Henry wrote to his cousin George Grier that he was "at home for one day" between political and business trips. At the end of September he made his way from Washington to New York, stopping to give speeches in support of the party's national ticket in Reading and Pottsville, Pennsylvania. In the last week before the election, he did the same in Ohio.[41]

The campaigning occurred in the context of the United States winning the war. The peace proposal offered to Mexico by the victorious Americans was harsh, initially rejected but eventually accepted in 1848 by a nation that had no choice in the face of a far superior occupying army. Frances was ever so grateful that her son escaped the war alive, healthy, and without killing anyone. "The news of the ratification of the treaty filled my heart with gratitude to Him who has preserved our boy in his dangerous career," she wrote to Henry in June. The Quaker values Paulina had raised her with made Gus's chosen profession even harder for Frances to stomach now that he was actually bearing arms. The fact that he served in a war of imperial aggression was more burdensome on her conscience. To Gus she wrote shortly after her letter to Henry that "you are once more at liberty to leave the army without having shed the blood of a fellow being."[42]

Having hoped so long and prayed so hard for Gus to leave the army with body and soul intact, Frances was ecstatic to learn he had reached first Pascagoula, Mississippi, and then New Orleans safely at the end of the war. Surely now that he had fulfilled his duty to the country in payment for the education he had received at its expense, he could return home and become an engineer or a farmer or whatever peacetime career attracted him. The new career would come, in his mother's dreams, after a long, leisurely visit in Auburn and a retirement in all good conscience, hers and his, from military life.

On October 1, 1848, Gus's twenty-second birthday, Frances wrote to him on the subject of his future yet again, having learned to her despair that he planned to travel straight to Indian Territory in Oklahoma with his regiment without coming home even for a short leave. Were it not for her health, Henry's distraction from family matters, her fears of travel in general, and her abhorrence of traveling through slave states in particular, she would show up at his barracks and make her plea to Gus in person. A week later, she considered a rendezvous with his troops as they marched from New Orleans to Fort Towson, on the Red River in Arkansas. "I cannot," she wrote to Henry, "so long as there is a possibility of seeing him feel reconciled to his leaving the boundaries of civilization without again seeing him." She waited for an answer from Gus on exactly where and when she could meet him. "My ignorance of the navigation of the rivers prevents my forming any conclusion."[43]

Although Frances's letter reached Henry in Washington, Gus had not received the last five letters she had sent him, or so he said. She also had learned that Henry's request to presidential candidate General

Taylor for a leave for their son contravened army regulations. In an addendum to a letter, which Frances dated October 19, she wrote that she had learned that "it is not customary to allow a furlough under two years. . . . I infer that the influence of friends in getting a furlough is esteemed rather unwarrantable interference by some of the officers." In doing her bidding and trying to help, Henry likely had only made things worse, at least for Gus.[44]

In this letter, the least restrained that she ever wrote to her son, Frances reflected on his young life and quoted at length from a novel that she had recommended to him, an army engineer who did not read much and no fiction. The title character in G. P. R. James's *Morley Ernstein: or, Tenants of the Heart* (1842) was the model man she had hoped that her son would become, the one that she saw inside him and knew that he still could be.

On October 20, Henry and Frances's twenty-fourth wedding anniversary, she wrote to her husband to remind him of that and to apologize for over the years "yielding to the despondency attendant upon continuous illness," which had led her to overlook "many blessings, and I fear been sadly wanting in gratitude to our Heavenly Father." She now hoped that Henry withdrew his request to the generals for Gus's leave. Gus would be embarrassed to learn that his father had made an "unwarrantable" request. "If this suggestion is made to Augustus," she wrote, "he will not avail himself of a leave so obtained should it be granted. Perhaps it is better that it should not be. His coming home would give me no pleasure while it occasioned him uneasiness or embarrassment. I have written to him at Ft. Smith, telling him to do what he thinks right without any reference to my feelings."[45]

On November 19 Frances wrote to Gus again to inform him that his father's request for a leave had been denied by General Taylor, the president-elect. She quoted from Taylor's explanation, which while disappointing at least reflected that his father had done Gus's career no harm. While he regretted that "the good of the service compels me at this time to deny your request," Taylor also agreed that when either of Gus's two superior officers returned from their respective leaves, and thus freed Gus from command responsibilities, Taylor would grant him a furlough to visit his family. Nonetheless, he suggested that Gus's parents advise their son "to proffer his application in the usual form, passing his request, at the proper time, through the channel pointed out in the regulations." In other words, please try to avoid any appearance of favoritism and a breach of the rules.[46]

Relationships, indeed roles, had changed at 33 South Street. Judge Miller appears nowhere in correspondence about the major house renovations in 1847 and 1848, including the failed installation and replacement of a coal-burning furnace. For decades he had made all decisions about the residence, but now Frances was acting independently of her father. The renovations took months, moved stairs, tore down walls, and added a new kitchen on the first floor to replace the one in the basement. Willie "wrote" to Gus over the summer that "we are building an addition to the house, in which I have a room. It is quite a large room." On September 20 Frances wrote to Henry, "Our house is making as rapid progress as we have reason to expect. The masons have today completed their work in the wooden parts. Next come the painters. The canopy over the front balcony is finished and is very pretty. There are so many closets etc. to be finished that it makes infinitely more work than was anticipated, so time is lost."[47]

While Frances had hoped the work would be completed in October, it dragged on through November. Eventually, the well got dug and the water was "tolerable." The walls were plastered and dried so the doors could be hung; the masons succeeded the carpenters, and she rushed the painters through their work. Finally, the kitchen was ready to use. "I wish you could see it while it is clean," Frances wrote to her sister, "which will not be for long." The kitchen was now on the main floor instead of in the basement, but "the girls are not as well pleased with it as the lower kitchen. I suppose it is too accessible to suit them."[48]

The best clue to Elijah's withdrawal from such matters, and Frances's lack of frustration with him as the renovations ensued, comes from his series of wills. The will of September 10, 1831, bequeathed $500 each to his mother and sister. The rest, including the house, went to Frances and her two sons with Henry as the executor. This first of his surviving wills cut Lazette, her daughter, and husband out cold, reflecting his opinion about the marriage and Alvah, from whom he wished to keep every penny of his estate. The second will of May 27, 1847, is more relevant in the context of Elijah's surrender of his house to the Sewards, when he had so doggedly defended his turf on every decision, large and small, in the past. In the new will he left Frances, "her heirs and assigns, my dwelling house, in which I now reside, and the lot, on which it is situate, in the village of Auburn, containing about three acres of land." The state law had changed so that he could leave the property directly to a woman without her husband becoming the owner. He left "the rest and residue of my real and personal estate, subject to the payment of my debts, unto the following named persons, to wit, L. M. Worden (wife of Alvah Worden), Frances her daughter, Augustus, Frederick, William, and Frances (the children of the said Frances A. Seward)." Again, Elijah named Henry the executor with authority to liquidate and disburse the estate according to these instructions.[49]

The final will, dated November 5, 1851, eight days before Judge Miller's death, put more of the estate into Frances's hands. The house and lot still went to Frances, as Elijah had always intended. Now, though, he left one-third of the estate remaining after the payment of his debts to Lazette and the other two-thirds to Frances. This left both of them to distribute funds to their children when and how they saw fit. None of these changes are explained in any of the family's correspondence, but it appears that Henry and Frances knew at least the general drift, if not the full details, of Miller's intentions.[50]

Henry was strapped for cash after his almost ruinously costly two terms as governor, but over the intervening six years his successful law practice had helped him recover fiscal competence. It was also true, though, that at the time of Miller's death in 1851, Henry's mercurial father still lived and threatened regularly to disinherit each of his children and all their offspring. Perhaps in the end Miller sought to give Frances more independence at the price of Henry's control. With the passage of the Married Women's Property Act in April 1848, New York became one of the early states to grant women the right to own property independent of their husbands. Judge Miller surely knew the different implications of leaving his house to his daughter in 1848 compared to that same bequest in 1831, when women could not own property. He also knew that Frances and Henry would look out for Lazette come what may in her turbulent marriage, including providing her a bedroom in Frances's house temporarily or permanently as Lazette wished. Elijah cut Clary out once she married, despite the fact that it was she who cared for him still whenever Frances was in Albany during Henry's governorship, confined to her bed, or traveling from the mid-1830s right through his death. Frances and Henry ensured that Clary was provided for too, through her death in 1862.[51]

On December 12, 1848, Frances reminded Henry that he had let their daughter's fourth birthday pass the previous week without notice. Frances also informed him that she was not traveling over the holidays, as her neuralgia confined her to the house. "No precautions are taken here against the cholera as in 1832, everyone taking it for granted that we shall escape as we did at that time." The recurrence of cholera, in Frances's opinion but not Henry's, made traveling problematic too. Of course, she hoped "to see you before Christmas, but cannot if your stay at Washington is much prolonged. Fanny dreams almost every night that her father is home."[52]

Chapter 12

Governor Seward Goes to Washington, 1849

The New York state legislature, with its large Whig majority, elected Henry to the US Senate in February 1849, which was the fruition of his campaign over the previous two years. He took the oath of office in March, on the same day that the new Whig President Zachary Taylor and Vice President Millard Fillmore, a New Yorker from Buffalo, took theirs. Henry and Frances sought a house in Washington, where the rental market was tight, eventually moving in with furniture, household staff, and extended family in early December at the start of the next full session of Congress.

Frances was more reconciled to Henry's election than recipients of her letters over the previous two decades might have expected. As she wrote to him in late January, when the question of his candidacy for the Senate was a matter of public discussion, on the one hand, she was proud of what she read about him in the newspapers. "People seem to be just awakening to the consciousness that you are a benevolent man and have many estimable qualities, a discovery which I made at least twenty-five years ago." On the other hand, she wrote further, "I am glad you are indifferent on the subject you mention. For the first time, I must say, I am not. I can tell you why some other time."[1]

Frances explained to her sister in more detail, "For once I am glad Henry was elected. The opposition papers represent him as a great bugbear [an imaginary creature used to frighten children] to the South. It surprises me how little he is understood even by his political friends. Disinterested benevolence must be very rare to be so hard to comprehend." As she explained further in a letter to Gus, "the next six years his winters, indeed two-thirds of the year, will be passed in Washington. He is so much away from home now that it will make very little difference with me. I shall probably spend some part of the time with him."[2]

Henry wrote often to Frances from Washington during March. The Senate floor intimidated him, even with his years of experience in Albany. He knew the names and reputations of many of the senators but few of them personally; he was new to the rules and protocols, and had yet to earn the respect of his peers. "For myself, I expect no influence until perhaps another year, but I am inclined to believe nobody will have any influence regularly." On March 7 Henry spoke on the floor of the Senate for the first of two times that month, rising to make a short response to South Carolina senator John C. Calhoun's opposition to the president's nominee for postmaster general on the grounds that he had spoken in favor of abolishing slavery in the District of Columbia. "I was short," Henry wrote to Frances the next day, "and I intended to show that I was uncompromising in my opposition to slavery, but at the same time calmly firm in my intention to abide by the Union and to accomplish whatever was attainable. My remarks were listened to with attention and curiosity, of course. I think they left a good impression upon candid and fair men, while they were regarded with favor by the very few bold and decided men of the North. . . . It is a great thing to have gotten over the panic which I always feel arriving to speak on a new stage."[3]

There was a real risk that Henry had no supporters for his views in the Senate, standing as he did for the Union over abolition and against the Democratic coalition that united pro-southern politicians in both regions. In a letter to his Auburn neighbor Judge Alfred Conkling, Henry responded to private criticism by saying, "I am alone, all alone in the Senate, in Congress, and almost in the United States. Alone, while adhering faithfully to the Whigs. I dare to build on the rights of disfranchised men. In this solitude I must stand or fall. The world is full of men who can avoid it dexterously and they do." Frances had never been prouder of Henry for taking such a principled and unpopular stand, one that led both abolitionists and southern advocates of slavery to revile him. "Is it not a pity," she wrote to Lazette, "that while there is one man in the Senate that dares to raise his voice against slavery that those who call themselves his friends must disapprove. For myself, whatever my timid nature might prompt me to do, I hope I shall never fail in the generosity which will enable me to encourage the actions of nobler spirits."[4]

Henry felt as isolated in the Senate as he had in Auburn when he defended William Freeman, the mad Black man who had murdered the Van Nest family three years earlier. He wrote to Frances of a dinner hosted by the vice president that he had attended. "Among the whole party was not one that sympathized or could sympathize with any sentiments in regard to the relief of the oppressed or could understand my principle of the political equality of Men." He saw himself as courageous in the company of cowards, "deserted by parasites . . . but with God's grace and blessing on his own truth, I shall win another triumph over the selfishness of the age." As Frances explained to her sister, in the Senate "not one voice was raised to support the only man who dared to disapprove the institution of Slavery. I only hope the time may come when they may appear as craven to themselves as they do to me. And come it will either in this world or the next." As she told Gus, "It requires a degree of moral courage which few men possess to take as your Father does a decided position on this subject and no small degree of Christian charity to maintain it with the moderation which can alone make it useful to the great cause he espouses." For now, at least, Henry had convinced his wife that he was on the right path on the question of slavery.[5]

With such feelings of isolation much on his mind, Seward's biography of John Quincy Adams was published in Auburn, including the eulogy Henry had delivered to the New York legislature the previous year. As biographies go, Seward's of Adams is more interesting for what it reveals about the author than what it says about the subject. There is also the caveat that a ghostwriter completed the book when Henry got distracted by his revived political career. In both venues Henry made the same case for Adams that he made for himself, as a lone man of integrity in conflicted times. His Adams was one of the great diplomats of the age, but it was his stand against slavery after he left the presidency where Henry found the "combination of virtue, courage, assiduity and modesty" that he so admired and made Adams distinct.[6]

In the halls of Congress, Adams "stood unmoved amid the storm" over slavery. He was not one of the radicals, who advocated immediate abolition, because "the work of emancipation abides the action, whether it be slow or fast, of the moral sense of the American People.

It depends not on the zeal and firmness only of the reformers, but on their wisdom and moderation also." In Henry's opinion, Adams's virtue lay in his resistance to the extremes of both sides. "If you ask," as Henry did in the 1848 eulogy for Adams, "what motive enabled him to rise above parties, sects, combinations, prejudices, passions, and seductions, I answer, that he served his country, not alone, or chiefly because that country was his own, but because he knew her duties, and her destiny, and knew her cause was the cause of Human Nature."[7]

A more radical stand was counterproductive, Henry thought. Adams and Seward approached the question of slavery with "wisdom and moderation. . . . If you ask," Henry asked, "why he seemed, sometimes, with apparent inconsistency, to lend his charities to the distant and the future rather than to his own kindred and times, I reply, it was because he held that the tenure of human power is on condition of it being beneficently exercised for the common welfare of the Human Race. Such men are of no country. They belong to mankind." Henry believed the charges against him and Adams took the short rather than the long view. Both Adams and Seward had to work in the world of the politically possible, which Henry did not see as a moral compromise. Indeed, he defended as high virtue the willingness to stand alone in the eye of the storm.[8]

An additional challenge to Henry in his early days in the Senate was his role in the distribution of New York's share of patronage by the new administration. This too tested his political skills. He had the goodwill of the new president, but that did not ensure the success of Henry's nominees for appointments. The onslaught of personal calls was overwhelming to him in the early days of his new office. "There is a world of care and strife around me," he wrote to his wife, "and I need your kind and cheering letters to console myself with. They would be only one out of a thousand full of selfishness . . . all but yours."[9]

The vice president was the greatest challenge, because Fillmore saw himself as representing New York Whigs in the nation's capital. "I am trying to get along with Mr. Fillmore," Henry wrote to Frances, "but he is selfish and cunning. He demands all for friends and associates, and gives nothing, leaves nothing for the great body of Whigs of the state." The next day, Henry shared his frustration again. "I have attempted to agree with him, but he agrees on nothing that does not proffer one of his small band to a place due to the Whigs of the state who have stood by me. I have about concluded to terminate this arrangement and to stand by my friends and the Whig Party and trust the conclusion to bold and independent conduct." Another day later, he complained to Frances that "the notable business of the week since I came here has been to recover my proper and just position as a Senator, the VP having modestly and quietly assured that he, too, was a Senator of New York." In other words, Henry thought Fillmore usurped his role as senator in the party that distributed patronage. "You can conceive how this has embarrassed me. . . . Of course, he differs from me in every appointment."[10]

For the fourth consecutive day, Henry stewed, "there has been a crowd of worshippers around the Vice President," whose influence with the administration was still in ascendance over that of Senator Seward. Finally, on March 14, Henry wrote in triumph that there was a breakthrough, when Fillmore made one appointment "a test question, and it was to decide whether I should be Senator or he. The Administration, wearied with the matter and disgusted with his pretenses, took it into their own hands and appointed the candidate most preferred by me, and this restored me at once to my rights and joint considerations." By the end of the third week of March, Henry reported that Fillmore "has sunk so low from his committed nepotism and selfishness that the Departments close their doors against him." New York's other senator through 1851 was Daniel S. Dickinson, a Democrat, who because of party affiliation had no standing in the patronage battles.[11]

By March 23 Henry had been in Washington for only three weeks but felt triumphant against significant odds on both policy influence and the distribution of patronage. He was "now the chief actor in the Senate for the Administration." He had made only one significant enemy in Vice President Fillmore, whom the administration marginalized in favor of Henry. On the matter of patronage, in Henry's opinion, the examples of Massachusetts senator Daniel Webster and Vice President Fillmore were instructive. Webster had inappropriately sought an appointment for his son, the result of which was that "this great man destroyed his mighty influence by being enslaved to selfish ends. He wanted an act of nepotism performed in his favor." As for Fillmore, he "had destroyed himself in the same way." Unfortunately for Henry's influence, he was wrong and neither man was destroyed; within six months Fillmore would be president and Webster his secretary of state. Henry was then on the outside.[12]

Henry wished Frances to join him in Washington for the president's inauguration and his own swearing in, but she declined. As always, there were challenges in the family that were her primary responsibility. "Your father wished me to accompany him this time," she wrote to Gus, "but my children as well as Grandpa require me here." She was homeschooling both of the children, because Fanny insisted at age four and at age ten Willie required it. "When she hears Willie recite his lessons, she wishes to join in them all." With Fred returning to college for his last semester, Frances also had a heavier burden of care for Elijah. "Grandpa misses Fred greatly," she explained to Gus. "Fred was so constantly in his room when he was at home, reading almost the whole time. Grandpa's eye sight is so much impaired that he can read very little for himself. Willie is just beginning to read, but his eyes are too weak for him to use them long at a time."[13]

Much of the family drama after Henry left for Washington surrounded Willie, who pleaded with Gus, in letters to Oklahoma, to send him an Indian pony. This fanciful plan lasted until Gus managed to convince everyone except possibly Willie that it was a bad idea. The Choctaw ponies were wild and therefore unsafe, in Gus's opinion, and in very poor physical condition. Gus did not know, in any event, how to get one to Auburn. "I do not think you would like them," Gus wrote to his little brother. "They are all similar to John's [John Richard, an Auburn man who groomed horses], worse looking if anything. The Indians do not take any care of them and use them to plough with, like large horses better to ride." The Comanche reputedly had good ponies, but they were over three hundred miles from where Gus was stationed. Even the Comanche ponies were undesirable, though, as they are nice looking, "but they generally teach them tricks, and I am afraid they would throw you off. They are taught to bite and kick when anyone comes near them that they do not know. I expect you had better try and get one at home."[14]

By mid-February, after months of agitation, Willie was disappointed but Frances thought that he finally understood. "He is reconciled, I believe," she shared with Gus, "by my arguments to giving up the pony. I have explained to him the impracticability of bringing one so far without much expense even were they less vicious than you represent them."[15]

In early March Willie was scalded when "he ran against Abbey [household staff] coming into the dining room and received a portion of the contents of a pitcher of hot chocolate in his face. With his usual perseverance he applied cold water without intermission for two hours, when the pain decreasing he went to sleep. His face is considerably disfigured but I think only temporarily. He was fortunate in not having his eyes injured."[16]

Lazette and Frances Worden remained in Brooklyn into April, so for more than five months. Although there was no doubt in their minds that Dr. Vanderveer's methods were working, the dates for leaving his care kept getting extended through December and the first three months of the new year. Lazette herself experienced significant health issues during 1849. Frances Seward wrote to Henry in late September that "Lazette is ill and much depressed in her spirits" because of her illness. Again, the discussions of women's health are vague, but Frances wrote to her sister from Philadelphia to say that she had consulted Dr. William S. Helmuth, her homeopathic physician in that city, about Lazette's case. "He says you ought to have an examination to ascertain whether this swelling is a hernia or a tumor, which cannot be determined in any other way, that it is unsafe to leave it unsettled, a hernia being at any time liable to strangulation should be kept in place by a truss. A tumor, which might be occasioned by a swelling of the glands, could if attended to in time, be dissipated by proper medicines, in no case to be removed by an operation."[17]

In June, after the return of Lazette and her daughter to Canandaigua, Henry had cases to argue there and decided, after "a visit of one day" in Auburn, to reside in the Wordens' home and borrow Alvah's office for several weeks. Shortly after his arrival, there was an argument between Alvah and Lazette about whether Henry should attend a party accompanied by their daughter Frances to which she had not been invited. Instead, Henry attended with Lazette against her husband's wishes, likely because Alvah had forbidden their daughter to join him and Lazette defied her husband. "I am so unfortunate as to be in the boat," Henry wrote to his wife Frances in the midst of the row. Henry had an attack of erysipelas while he was there and Lazette nursed him. In sum, he wore out his welcome and caused a rift between the married couple by being an intrusive guest at least to Alvah. As Henry explained to Frances in a letter of June 28, "When I came late to breakfast this morning, Lazette told me that Mr. Worden had quarreled violently with her because I disturbed his arrangement of the office, littered it, and threw the papers into confusion. . . . I therefore against her remonstrances and supplications removed my effects to the hotel, where I am now located. I am grieving for her sake, but I cannot consent to be an intruder or an unwelcome guest with my brother."[18]

Frances thought her homeschooling was going well in early summer. Willie had his tenth birthday in June and was now actually writing his own letters, which led his sister at age four to want to write too. His deficits in literacy contrast starkly with her precociousness, assuming that she actually dictated hers. Fanny "wrote" a letter to Willie on November 25, perhaps sharing the pen with her mother or their servant Abbey, which would explain the shaky handwriting. It reads in part, "Dear Willie, I have been to the Museum. I want to see you very much. But I don't know when I shall come to see you, unless you come to me first. . . . I think that you want to see mother Don't you? And I think you must be well, aren't you? How is Aunty? I guess that is enough. Your affectionate Sister Fanny." One from her to Aunt Lazette is even longer, more complex, and in her mother's clear hand: "My Dear Aunty, I have a nice red book named 'Fanny & her Mother' My Mother gave it to me on my birth day—Father bought me a nice book when I was sick in Philadelphia—it is Mother goose in hieroglyphics," and still it goes on. Willie's are much shorter. To Henry he wrote, "My der Father I should like to see you all I hope you will have a nice time I cannot rite much now it is late now. Yours affectionate." His others are much the same with shortfalls in spelling, grammar, and largely an absence of punctuation, but he was writing them himself.[19]

Fanny remained often ill. She had an "ulcerated throat" in mid-March, which was diagnosed as scarlet fever the next day. The severity and duration of the illness concerned Frances. "Great caution is necessary to prevent Fanny from taking cold," Frances explained to Henry, "and I do not feel willing to trust her to the care of any other person. Her relapse must have been occasioned by cold in some degree." Henry replied to the news on March 21, "Your letter answering to me that our very dear child was sick of that frightful disorder quite unnerved me, for a short time. But I felt sure that while there was a means of instantaneous communication you would not leave me in ignorance if she was at all in danger." With the advent of the telegraph, he thought there was less cause for any of them to worry. On March 24 Frances wrote to Gus that Fanny was now out of bed. By early April she was ill again, but with different symptoms. Henry wanted Frances to travel with him to Charleston, where he was to argue a case, but "I cannot leave Fanny at home, neither can I take her unless she is better than she is at present," Frances wrote to Lazette on April 3.[20]

Nonetheless, Frances and Fanny left Auburn with Henry the third week in April, and Fanny became ill before they reached Philadelphia, with a cold, "swollen face and some fever," Frances wrote to Gus from that city. "Fanny continued too ill to travel, so your Father was obliged to leave me here and go on to Charleston, where he is to argue a case this week. If Fanny is well enough, I shall meet him on his return at Washington."[21]

Harriet Bogart had joined Frances in Philadelphia to help care for Fanny, but Frances was nonetheless having premonitions of death from cholera, and she again took ill with an attack of neuralgia, "which has confined me to my room most of the week." Frances was well enough to see a dentist to be fit for dentures on April 25, which again induced symptoms that kept her from traveling. "My teeth disappoint me as I fear they will you," she wrote to Henry, who discouraged her from the whole process. On April 28 and 29 Henry was still hopeful that Frances and Fanny would join him in Charleston, but Frances had no such intention. Frances's party finally reached Washington on Monday, May 7, after a discouraging trip.[22]

Frances was too late, too exhausted, and too disinclined to travel again through the South, as she had in 1835, and by the time she reached Washington, Henry was on his way back. He had arrived in Charleston on April 28 and argued his case on May 5 after several delays. "Charleston is a city without a bourgeois," he wrote her. "The population is of two classes, white and black. The white people are gentry, the black are slaves. You see no crowds in the streets, no gatherings at the hotels, no curious or busy people. All is quiet and ease. This is fortunate for me, perhaps, for I come and go without being subjected to the curious stares that one coming with so obnoxious a character as mine would encounter in a crowd." Henry thought his reputation was undeserved. In his own eyes he was not the radical abolitionist that his refusals to support the return of fugitive slaves when he was governor had branded him in the South almost a decade ago. New York's abolitionists still agreed that he was not one of them.[23]

At a political meeting in Charleston that preceded Henry's arrival in South Carolina by about one week, his "election to the Senate was solemnly declared to be an aggression not to be forgiven and full of dire import. You may judge therefore," he wrote to Frances, "that my reception here is by no means warm, always excepting the people who stand behind the chairs at dinner. Nevertheless, there is courtesy and hospitality." The wonder is that having anticipated such a reception, Henry had wanted his wife and daughter with him. Perhaps he calculated that their presence would humanize him to people for whom he was more of a symbol of interregional conflict than an actual man. His perusal of the local newspapers suggested that the state of the Union was worse than he had thought. He was "grieved to find that Mr. Calhoun's nullification seed is maturing into a movement for dissolution of the Union or recipe for it. There is no mistaking this tendency."[24]

This firsthand experience was also the seed of two of Henry's most famous speeches, ones that cemented his reputation in the South. He now understood, as he apparently had not before, that the South was unalterably opposed to such efforts as the Wilmot Proviso, the unsuccessful proposal in 1846 to ban slavery in the territory acquired in the Mexican-American War. Henry, among others, had seen the proviso as a potential middle ground to preserve the Union without an extension of slavery. "I was quite surprised on taking up the newspapers," he wrote to Frances, "to find that the hospitable, intelligent, and generous men with whom I was dining every day oblivious of political differences constituted the Committee of Vigilance and Public Safety to see the South resist the encircling as they call it, even to blood." He now understood that among southern politicians the "abolition of slavery, the most atrocious of all creeds in their opinion, has no more inflammatory and dangerous advocate than I am. And, they have never stopped to inquire or consider whether I was anything more than this vile agitator."[25]

In light of the unalterable characterization of him, one that was reinforced on a regular basis by the *New York Herald*, Henry was inspired to take an uncompromising moral high ground in the Senate. He also now understood that a conflict over slavery that threatened the Union was imminent. "The good people of the state, alarmed by the progress of the cause of emancipation, are actually engaged in organizing a convention, which the leaders suppose will dissolve the Union or take the preliminary step for such a movement." No longer could he mistake southern hospitality for kindness or expect people there to listen to what he said unless it confirmed their preexisting opinions about his political views. After he appeared in court on May 5, he thought his argument in the case "satisfactory to my clients and to my friends. At least they say so," and he returned to New York a wiser man about the state of the nation if not about his own political career.[26]

They all, Harriet Bogart, Fanny, and Henry, returned to Auburn on May 28 after six fruitless weeks on the road for Fanny and Frances, who were with Henry for little of that time. "I am very glad to be at home again and wish I could remain here instead of going to Washington next Winter," she wrote to Gus, but "we made some arrangements for keeping house in a small way there."[27]

We cannot know the content of heartfelt conversations between the Miller sisters on the subjects of their marriages over the years, but we do know that Frances's views on women's rights were evolving. Lazette was ahead of her sister always in her more radical perspectives; Frances was more restrained, partly because it was her nature and partly in deference to her husband's career. Her sister knew that Frances felt deserted and lonely, and she had reservations about the institution of marriage that could have come right out of a Jane Austen novel. Lazette likely saw her sister as fortunate and at least somewhat naive, more Romantic than Gothic in her reading of fiction and take on life. Frances's library, which she shared with Lazette, contained numerous books on the subject. As was the case with fiction, science, and history, Frances awaited each of the volumes as they appeared.

In 1849 Frances loaned Lazette the first American edition of Mrs. Hugo [Marian Kirkland] Reid's *Woman, Her Education and Influence*, after she read it herself. "The book is written with much ability," she wrote by way of endorsement, "and did it not assert a claim to more rights than the lords of creation are generally willing to allow, I think it would have elicited some complimentary notices from the press." Frances's dissent is as revealing as her recommendation, because, as she continued, "although I cannot yet say that I think women ought to vote and become office holders, yet I will say that if there is no other way of elevating them I would rather see them more masculine than to see them what they are now." Her movement toward support for woman suffrage, a position she reached over the course of a few more years, was a significant change. "Mrs. Reid makes many sensible observations on the subject of education. Her book gives evidence of a strong mind combined with much modesty and delicacy." Here she contrasted Reid's style with that of the likes of Margaret Fuller and Harriet Martineau, two journalists with more radical views.[28]

Frances was a member of the target audience for Kirkland's book, the middle of the three classes into which the author grouped the women about whom she had something to say. The first she took to be a lost cause, "those who think that woman's sphere really and truly comprises only her domestic duties, and that her mind ought never to stir beyond these." This group also included most men. The second, into which Frances fell, were "those who think her mind ought to be enlarged, and her condition improved in some respects, but that she ought not to be equally privileged with man." Frances was not yet prepared to endorse a greater role for women in the public sphere, although after living for part of several years in Washington with Henry, she would reach a level of frustration with politics and eventually believe that only granting women the vote could possibly save the nation from destruction by its politicians. She too would eventually conclude, as Kirkland, Elizabeth Cady Stanton, and other reformers argued before her, that woman had "a just claim to equal rights with man."[29]

Kirkland and Frances already agreed about much, that "to improve and elevate woman, is but to elevate and improve man." They shared the belief "that our spheres are different, no one will deny. Woman is the natural educator of children" and thus needed to be educated herself. Women were uniquely responsible for "influencing the moral education of a family." For this role, society needed "a mother of a judicious, sensible, and cultivated mind." This was not the sole reason for educating women, but it was an important one. "The true reason for the culture of any human being is to be found in the benefit which that being derives from cultivation. The improved nature of the influence which the enlightened being exerts upon other minds, is quite a secondary consideration, although it is but too often urged as the only reason for the culture of the female mind."[30]

It was where Kirkland made the case for social equality that Frances was not quite in agreement. Kirkland was right about women such as Frances when she described the middle group of women as fearful that "the possession of equal civil rights . . . would take woman out of her sphere." For herself, Kirkland maintained over such objections "that woman has a right to social equality; and we also maintain, that the possession of this just right would not interfere in the slightest with her domestic duties, or 'woman's sphere,' as it is called. Nay, we go still farther, and assert, that the energy, self-reliance, and intelligence, which the possession of this right has such a tendency to foster and call into action, would be highly favourable to a more enlarged view of those duties and a more active discharge of them." Frances pondered such a position as she backed quietly into sharing such views, which she explained to Elizabeth Cady Stanton soon after. Kirkland and Stanton agreed that "civil rights are quite consistent with—nay, are almost necessary to—the proper performance of all her other duties," while Frances remained in 1849 one of those women who "start back from so atrocious a doctrine!" After reading the book, Frances wrote to Lazette, "I anticipate much pleasure in reviewing it with you."[31]

Frances failed to see that her unrelenting attempts to parent twenty-two-year-old Gus were driving him farther away. She continued to pester him in letters through 1849 about coming home, either on leave or permanently. Repeatedly, she pointed out that he had failed even to reply to her entreaties. She wanted to see his reluctance to come home as an overzealous commitment to duty, but she had good reason to believe that he preferred living in a fort in desolate Oklahoma to visiting his family. Both she and Henry provided Gus with guarantees of support if he left the army and launched a new career. His mother prodded him on his reading habits and reluctance to join an established church. "I hope and believe, my child, that you do not neglect reading your Bible," she wrote from Washington, DC. "It is there you will find the only correct rules for your guidance in all situations in life."[32]

When Gus enclosed a letter to his cousin Frances in a separate envelope with one to his mother, apparently not knowing Frances Worden's address in Flatbush, his mother opened and read it before forwarding. "It is much easier for young people to write to those of their own age, obviously," she shared with Henry. Gus had told his cousin more about himself than he ever shared with his mother. "I have gained sixteen pounds in the three months that I have sojourned here," he wrote to his cousin, "something of an indication that I may follow in the footsteps of my Maternal Grandfather." He never shared either such lightness or personal details with his mother, which wounded her now that she saw it. "Gus says nothing about a furlough," in letters to her. "I shall however hope to see him this summer," she complained to Henry. "I am much inclined to quarrel with you," she wrote to Gus in March, "because you do not tell me when you are coming home. It is a subject that engrosses a large share of my thoughts, sleeping and waking." Frances urged Gus yet again in April, "I will not, my dear child, urge you on this subject, for I can trust your judgment, but I want you to let me know when I may hope to see you." Frances informed Gus on August 12, "It is two years this day since you left us. It is a long, long time."[33]

The whole question of Gus returning home either for a visit or in retirement from the army came to a head shortly after the second anniversary of his departure for Mexico. "And now my dear child, about your letter," Frances wrote. "I was much grieved by the intimation that you might not come home until next Spring. Do reconsider this matter. I admit that it will be late in the season for you to go and return, but why need you return! You cannot seriously think of spending your life in the army and when will there be a better time for leaving it." She did not stop there, even after they both had yet again laid all their cards on the table. "Six years among such associations" had, in her opinion, warped his judgment, "but I know that a life of that kind is adverse to your real nature, is uncongenial to your taste and feelings, which are peculiarly domestic." His mother hoped that Gus did not prefer to live in a barracks with other men, in a remote wilderness outpost far away from the domestic tranquility that his father also fled. "Don't bring home an Indian Cousin for me," Lazette's daughter teased him. As we know in retrospect, women and returning home permanently were never part of his plan.[34]

Henry read Frances's letter before mailing it to Gus and shared her hopes for their eldest son. "I concur most earnestly in the advice and entreaties she addresses to you to return this summer in Auburn," he wrote earnestly, while deferring, as always, to Gus's right to plan his own life. "You will, of course, consult your own judgment and feelings about remaining in the army." Nonetheless, he wanted his son to know that "we shall be able to furnish a situation for you which will be comfortable and respectable if you choose to return to civil life, as I sincerely hope you will, but whether you conclude to remain here or to return to the army, it is quite time for you to return and renew your intercourse with the family and with its friends." Henry struck what was for him a melancholy tone. "Time is wearing on us all," he wrote to his son, "and we cannot consent that you remain a stranger to our trials, our sorrows, and the pleasures that through the kindness of heaven occasionally mingle with and relieve them." Henry tried to make Gus feel guilty. "Your mother is a mother to be cheered and sustained by the affection of her children." Fred, who had graduated from college and was training for the practice of law in Henry's office, was with the program, as were young Fanny and Willie. Henry failed to reel in Gus, who did not return for even a visit before the family left for Washington in early December. "So, my dear boy, come home if it is only for a few months and make us all happy."[35]

Henry's melancholy and Frances's assurance that they could finance a new career for Gus were reactions to the death of Samuel in late August 1849. After decades of prediction that he was on his deathbed, Samuel passed without the drama that readers of his previous letters might have expected. The family in Florida was exhausted by caring for him, and his wife and their caretaker predeceased him, so his sons George and Polydore carried the burden; nonetheless, he bequeathed them much less than their brother Henry and his family, and put their small portions under the control of Henry and his coexecutor. The drama would come from the two brothers' rage, particularly George's, which only grew over the years as the settlement dragged on and Henry doled out their small share in tiny portions spread over twenty years.

Henry's responsibilities as coexecutor of his father's estate defined his family relations for the rest of his life. Frances was the only wife to receive a bequest from Samuel, which was a sizable $10,000, about the same as George's and Polydore's, which she said was to balance out the distribution to the larger families of Henry's siblings. Each of the remaining heirs through the next generation eventually received something on the same order, but not soon. Questions and requests deluged Henry right from the start. Clarence asked, "How much is 1/20th" on September 2, less than a week after his grandfather was entombed. Clarence also wrote from Auburn several days later to offer his uncle help. Polydore wrote with the first of many requests for money, this time $200, on December 4. Henry often did not respond to such requests over the years, which made family relations worse.[36]

After a three-week stay in Florida, to attend Samuel's funeral, to mourn, to visit, and to help care for Fred and Henry as they combed through the patriarch's papers, Frances returned home without her husband. From Auburn she wrote to Gus, informing him that Henry estimated the estate was worth $300,000 after liquidation of property to be sold at auction. She also wanted Gus to know that his grandfather left the farms where his uncles Polydore and George now lived with their families in trust, with Gus's father in "constant guardianship." In Henry's opinion, Frances told Gus, "the land should not be disposed of in its present unfavorable condition. If he retains these farms, you might aid him essentially by superintending them or some of them. I think you would find it agreeable employment. . . . Should this fail to attract you, your father will gladly establish you in some other business; many places are open to those who have capital." To Henry, she inquired about the expected delay in the estate's settlement: "Cannot some ostensible employment be found for Augustus until something real shall offer?" The shares divided among Samuel's surviving children and grandchildren amounted to about $12,000 each. As executor, Henry oversaw distribution of the shares of his brothers, nephews, and nieces.[37]

Gus's parents agreed in 1849, if not sooner, that it was time for Gus to launch off on a second career. "Unless you have made up your mind always to remain in the army (which I pray may not be the case) now is the time to leave," his mother insisted. Frances was hopeful, if not confident, that this time she convinced Gus. "Your father thinks our united letters sent from Florida will not fail to bring you home. I trust it may be so. Your mother's heart yearns for a meeting after a separation of more than two years." As his cousin Frances explained to Gus, his paternal grandfather had attempted to determine his grandson's future. Samuel persisted from his deathbed in issuing patriarchal edicts, as he had done for decades, even though his wealth did not buy him the control over his descendants that he thought it should. "Grandpa Seward has despaired of you far less," Frances explained, "having settled you upon his farm." The rest of Samuel's plan was for Fred to share half of his uncle George's house, to assist Gus in managing the estate after his grandfather's death. The house went to Fred "upon condition he live there." As had been the case with his own sons, in whom, except for Henry, Samuel was sadly disappointed, his assumption was that his grandsons would live to serve him beyond his grave. Neither one did.[38]

Samuel's funeral was, according to Frances, "numerously attended, the church crowded . . . Grandpa's remains were deposited in the family vault. The mourners have resumed their usual avocations," she wrote to Gus. Henry felt badly, she said, that he was unable to respond to his father's final summons, which Samuel had repeated frequently over his last few days. "It was very painful to your father not to be present in the last hour with either of his parents. When I was here before [back in July] Grandpa Seward spoke affectionately of you, said he wished you would come to Florida and take a farm which he had recently purchased."[39]

With the death of Samuel, responsibility for the education of the family's children now fell on Henry as executor for the funds to pay for schools. Henry ceded much of his responsibility for the extended family's girls to Frances, as they made decisions that seemed best suited to each case. Willie and Fanny were still schooled at home, Willie because of his "eyes" and Fanny because of her age and eventually due to chronic ill health. Clarence was apprenticed to Henry's law firm; his uncle had denied him a year at Harvard Law School, which seemed an impractical indulgence and more of an unsupervised vacation, when hands-on practice was better training. On graduation from his father's alma mater in July, Fred dutifully joined the firm too, as Frances explained to Gus, "not precisely because he has any predilection of that kind, but because there seems to be nothing else for him to do."[40]

George's daughter Sarah was to attend the Troy Female Academy, as her aunt Frances and her sister Lazette did. "We are highly gratified to learn that your recollections of the seminary are so pleasant,"

John Hart Willard wrote to Frances for his mother, Emma Willard, who still ran the school. Another niece, also Frances, apparently wished to attend school in Rochester, but her aunt Frances opposed that because "Mary is not going with her." Frances (age thirteen) and her sister Mary were daughters of Henry's brother Polydore and his late wife Rachel. "I promised her mother many years ago," Frances explained in a letter to Gus, "that I would take Frances in the event of her death," but her niece favored staying close to her sister. Her aunt Frances thought the best options for Frances were Canandaigua, where Lazette could keep an eye on her, or Troy with Sarah, or back in Florida at her grandfather's school, which is where she ended up. "I love the child so well," Frances wrote to Henry, "that I shall not part with her without pain, but I do not think it would be well to take her to Washington." Mary, a third niece and the elder of Polydore's daughters, who was already twenty-one and engaged, declined the offer of school and remained in Florida, where she cared for her sister. "Mary has thrown off her mourning," Frances explained to Gus in early December, "and is to be married this month." "You will see my dear child," Frances wrote to Gus in November, "how many additional cares the guardianship of our four nieces brings."[41]

The greatest burden that had now fallen to Frances and Henry was for the fourth niece, the daughter of Henry's late sister Cornelia and her husband Mahlon Canfield. Caroline, age fifteen, was a handful in Florida, where she had lived under the care of her grandparents. After her grandfather's death, she wrote to her uncle, "I wish you were here. If ever I felt as if I was friendless it is now. I shall be very glad when I take up my residence in some other place than this." Henry and Frances decided over the fall to keep her close to them in Washington, where Frances could help tame her wild nature, which the Sewards attributed to the lack of a guiding maternal hand. They decided on a convent school in Georgetown, the "Academy of the Visitation," which Frances described to Lazette after she and Henry dropped Caroline there in mid-December. "We rang the bell, when a priestess opened an inside door separated from us by wooden grates and enquired our wishes. She was clad like the Sisters in black with a black hood. . . . The Lady Directress soon made her appearance and commenced a conversation on the other side of the grates. She was clad entirely in black with a white band around her head and a black hood."[42]

It was an alien environment to the Protestant Sewards and a scary one to Caroline, who was left there to live. "The regulations are strict,"

Frances wrote to Lazette. "Pupils are allowed to visit their friends one day every month, to see them at the seminary Wednesdays and Fridays. I think it altogether an excellent place for a child whose early education has been as sadly neglected as that of Caroline. If habits of neatness and order can be acquired anywhere, I think this is the place. Caroline is willing to go, but I think not very desirous."[43]

The enrollment of Caroline in the Catholic school was over the objections of her father, whose disinterest in the upbringing of his daughter was punctuated by periodic attempts to intervene from afar. Nobody in the family was fooled, though, by Mahlon's assertions of his parental rights, because when enforcement of them required any effort on his part, his concerns dissolved as quickly as they had appeared. "I have heard very recently, and much to my regret," Mahlon wrote to Henry in early October, "that the school at Georgetown is a Catholic institution. Had I known this, I would by no means have assented to the arrangement for placing Caroline there. . . . I wish Caroline to be placed at such a school as her mother would have preferred." He now had a list of alternatives, having offered none in previous discussions of his daughter's disposition. "I speak of the matter as a thing that I have a right to complain of, and one which you as the protector of my child expect to know. I trust you will impress upon Caroline the duty of respect to my wishes in regard to the choice of schools."[44]

In reply, Henry explained Frances's choice for Caroline but did not yield to Mahlon's anti-Catholic prejudice. "Caroline's moral culture has suffered the neglect consequent upon orphanage," he diagnosed, "and it has seemed to me that it was my especial duty to see that the misfortune should be corrected as early and as completely as possible, by giving her the discipline and society of Mrs. Seward, her aunt." Mahlon concurred in those observations, which put no blame on him. "We think that she can in no way be so well situated as to be home at Washington with us and receive her intellectual cultivation in the school at Georgetown, [with] which we are well acquainted and with its success in securing female virtue and cultivating moral principles without bringing the religious element into sectarianism, an evil which we do not fear when we consider the results of education there as well as the advantages of our own influence in contesting it if necessary." As for the school in New York that Mahlon had proposed as an alternative, Henry had no objection to Mahlon sending her there if he took responsibility for overseeing her care. "Of all our children and wards," which now numbered twelve by Henry's count, "we think however that Caroline is the one who would be most exposed to the unfavorable influences of a New York education."[45]

Henry and Frances conceded Mahlon's right to raise his daughter as he saw fit. "It only remains, therefore, for you to assume the entire responsibility and the control of the education of your child. You will please therefore come up and receive her into your own care and dispense of her as you shall think best." Henry agreed to pay for Caroline's education at the school of Mahlon's choice, but "it will be desirable that Caroline be removed as soon as conveniently may be, for her own improvement, as well as for our own convenience." That was enough to dissuade Mahlon from his path. "Although my opinion of the modern high fashion of placing Protestant children at Catholic schools is unchanged, yet, in view of the fact that Caroline has lived for so long a time without proper discipline and restraint, I am willing to believe that the quiet study and withal somewhat new and peculiar government of a Catholic institution may be best for her." In light of Henry's judgment and Caroline's express wish to conform with the Sewards' plan, "I therefore withdraw my objections to the proposed arrangement."[46]

The problem that gave Frances even more nervous headaches was finding a house to rent in Washington and getting her household—children, servants, wards, and furniture—settled in a second home. At the time of Henry's election, she had told her sister, "I suppose my Winters or a part of them will be spent there while he is in the Senate," which she thought meant at most six to eight months annually in Washington for six years. At first, Henry thought he preferred a house on Maryland Avenue; after looking at two he decided, "I shall take the house on Missouri Avenue." But they had not moved fast enough, and the landlord rented it to someone else the day before the Sewards' agent called on him to make their commitment. When the next lead materialized, Frances wrote to Thurlow Weed in the hope that he could find Henry in time. "The enclosed letter from Mr. Hall [their agent in Washington] related to a house in Washington, which will be reserved but one week from the 10th of this month, leaving only four days for an answer to reach that place. We have already lost one much more desirable by not replying in time and have now little choice left." She asked him to confirm her judgment that they had better leap sight unseen this time and, if he agreed with her, please forward the letters to Henry "if you know where he is to be found."[47]

On the same day, Frances also sent two copies of her plea to Henry, one to Albany and the other to Cooperstown, where she thought one of them might reach him immediately. The house in question was on F Street, which Hall considered "more desirable than any other to be found." According to Fred's recollections, "it was a respectable, unpretending, red brick structure on F Street, and was one of a block of three ordinary city houses, each twenty-five feet wide, and all just alike." It was between Sixth and Seventh Streets, just east of what became the city's commercial hub after the Civil War. At the time the Sewards moved into the house, the patent and post office buildings, both of which were constructed in the 1830s, were also on F Street, just west of there, as was the Herndon House Hotel and its restaurant on the corner of F and Ninth. At the far west end of the street was the Treasury Department. The house had three stories, a dining room in the basement, two parlors on the first floor, and ten rooms in all. "He represents the house as convenient, rent $400 a year to be paid quarterly, owned by an honest grocer in the city. . . . Mr. Hall seems to think he can do no better. You will answer by telegraph if you conclude to take the house." The next day Henry's father was dead, but he committed to the F Street house in time.[48]

After two weeks in Florida, Frances felt rushed at the end of September. "I have not had time to examine the plan of the house at Washington," she wrote to Henry on September 28, "or to do anything towards making preparation. I wish to consult you again before I purchase any furniture." By the middle of October it was decided that Fred would serve as his father's secretary, and Frances Worden was with them as well, hoping to enjoy the city's social scene before she got married. Fanny accompanied Frances and Willie joined them after they unpacked. They expected Elijah for a visit in late winter or early spring. In the meantime, Lazette and Clary cared for Elijah in his Auburn house while Frances was away; Clary had the duties most of the time.[49]

When Frances wrote to Gus in early November, she was stressed. "I am so hurried with preparation for Washington and when I reach there shall be so occupied with arranging the house that I shall have very little leisure. We leave here about the twentieth of this month, shall be more than a week on the way, as we are to stop in New York and Philadelphia." Her situation was even more desperate when she wrote on November 18. "The truth is," she wrote to Gus, "I am so hurried and bewildered by the multiplicity of my employments that I hardly know what I have done. We are now all ready to go to Washington. We leave the day after tomorrow." Caroline and their servant Abbey Vanwie also joined them eventually. Mary Coe came as their cook. Dennis Scollins, a Black man who had worked for the Sewards for some time, was with them temporarily in Washington and would return to Auburn when they got settled.[50]

The first trial of the journey came when Frances and Abbey were laid low in Philadelphia with "the sick headache," but Mary Coe nursed them and looked after Fanny until the two women recovered. When they arrived in Washington, they stayed in Willards Hotel overnight while awaiting their furniture. Since it was Thanksgiving, the shops were closed and there was not much they could do, but "the girls" were assigned to clean the floors of the house and "fill some straw beds, and with the carpets made beds upon the floor until our bed steads come. I went round again," Frances wrote to her sister, "and unpacked some sheets, comforters, and spreads, and left there feeling quite happy. The whole house requires cleaning. It is convenient for a city house, though there is not a closet on the first and second floor."[51]

In the warmer climate of Washington, they were back to open fireplaces and installed a wood stove in the hall, defying the opposition of their landlord, "who does not like to have holes made in the walls." They also added a "cooking stove or range. Mary prefers the latter." This was fueled by coal. Several days later, the bulk of their furniture had yet to arrive, and they were living, according to Frances, "with two chairs, a table, and half a dozen plates." She wrote to Gus, "I think you would laugh to see the incongruity of our housekeeping, with four servants and nothing to make them or ourselves comfortable. We have a coloured waiter or steward as they are called here, and tomorrow I expect the fifth in the form of a coloured chambermaid."[52]

The Senate convened on December 3. Furniture arrived on December 7. Frances expected more daily, a shipment from New York City, and hoped that what they had purchased in Philadelphia would be delivered before Christmas. On December 9 they celebrated Fanny's fifth birthday. "She is very happy with her presents," Frances wrote to Lazette, "a book from me and a silver cup from her father." They were all, including their tenant, Congressman John Lawrence Schoolcraft, a banker who represented the Albany district, still sleeping on makeshift straw beds in the parlor. Mary slept on a cot in the kitchen, and Dennis was in a room over the "outside or wash kitchen." The maid had already quit. "The ladies here say it is almost an impossibility to get good female help." As a result, and in light of the opinion of Mary and Abbey, Frances decided "to hire no chambermaid. I have a woman come to the house to wash and iron. Dennis is, of course, useful to us." If her sister and aunt could spare him from Auburn, perhaps he should stay with them in Washington for now. On December 21 Frances wrote to Lazette that "our furniture from Philadelphia has all come, except the crockery, of which we are much in need. Our parlor is furnished, curtains similar to those at home." They had not yet received callers, "today being the first that the parlor was ready, and today we were out from twelve to four leaving cards." Frances Worden, Fred, and Caroline were presented at the White House that evening at one of the president's Friday evening levees, which the ladies attended "in full dress."[53]

Christmas in Washington was much as it would have been for the children in Auburn. Willie and Fanny were nestled, all snug in their new beds. Fred had taken over as Willie's teacher, but Willie's mind was still more on ponies, and now Christmas, than on his studies. "Willie says I must wish you all Merry Christmas for him. I have been out this evening to buy toys," Frances wrote to Lazette. Fanny was "very well and contented. She is making great calculations about St. Nicholas." Frances and Fred went out again on December 22 to shop for more toys. The Episcopal churches were so crowded that Frances thought it best to leave the children home on Christmas, and anyway, it was a "cold, windy morning. . . . I am very sorry for this as the children will get out of the habit of going. It is not pleasant to take them when you feel that you incommode others." To Gus, Frances wrote, "St. Nicholas gave great satisfaction in the dispensation of presents. Their toys amused them a long time and when the day closed they wished Christmas would come again tomorrow."[54]

Holidays in Washington were, however, different for the adults, but preferable to Albany for Frances. "I like Washington very much," Frances wrote to Clary, who was likely surprised to hear it. Fred was invited to a "dejeuner a la fourchette," a sit-down lunch in Washington society. "I intend he should go," his mother wrote. On December 13 Frances reported to Lazette, "Henry and I dined at the President's with about forty guests, chiefly members of Congress and their wives. I being the only senator's wife present was honoured with the President's arm to dinner. . . . I enjoyed the evening very much. The President was very sociable. Henry says he looked at no one but me during dinner. I like him and his family. They are sensible, unpretending people. The President apologized for his slight knowledge of etiquette. I told him he had always been occupied with affairs which I considered infinitely more important." Frances and the president had that in common as she, too, struggled with protocol. "Washington, in this respect, approximates much more nearly to a court than any other society in the Union. I find it next to impossible to ascertain just what is required about visits. I told the Gen[eral] I thought they should have a book like the Army regulation and reduce such matters to a system that might be studied." Taylor also warmed her heart by mentioning Gus "two or three times . . . said you were entitled to a furlough," she wrote to her son. "I like the President and his family very much."[55]

The socializing wore Frances out before the calendar turned to 1850. "Visiting and receiving visits constantly is certainly not the kind of life adapted to my taste, feelings, or constitution, either physical or mental," she wrote to her sister on December 29. "When I dress at twelve to receive company and am thus occupied for four hours I am exhausted and unfit for any employment the remainder of the day and evening. The same effect is produced when I dress at twelve and go to make visits or leave cards. Yet, this is life in Washington." She fretted that she was again, as in Albany, not fitting in. "Other women differently constituted make these mornings only a prelude to a still gayer evening, while I am too much exhausted to do anything but go to bed, and if I am required to see company, which seems unavoidable almost every evening, I am stupid and listless, perfectly incompetent to entertain or be entertained, always hoping their visit will be short that I may seek rest." The problem was not simply Frances's chronically ill health. "I have fancied," she confided to her sister, "that with renovated health these duties might be less tiresome, but I am now compelled to admit that I am peculiarly, and considering my position, unfortunately constituted." She was again in a position where what was expected of her was more than she had to give.[56]

To Frances's surprise, on New Year's Day "the ladies visit as much as the gentlemen." This was different than both Albany and Auburn. "The President has a levee in the morning when everybody goes in full dress. I am excused from such gatherings this Winter as I wear mourning." Levees were adapted from English royal traditions in which the monarch received guests on New Year's morning. As far as Henry was concerned, Taylor was the best man to occupy the office of president since John Quincy Adams. Henry wrote to Frances on her return to Auburn, "General Taylor is a man to be loved."[57]

Chapter 13

Losses, 1850–1851

Frances Worden was still with the Sewards in Washington as 1850 began, happily socializing and supporting her aunt in that task. "Friday night [January 4] we went to the President's," she informed her mother, "had a pleasant evening and came away at ten." At age twenty-three, the social whirl could be exhausting even to her. "Our time is almost constantly comprised during the day paying or receiving visits and it is very unsatisfactory. We generally miss the very ones we care to see and see those we do not care to." Most of the people she had met thus far were either "frivolous and fashionable or stupid, and these it seems are divided into cliques. . . . Among the ladies of the Cabinet and some members wives I feel at home. We all being strangers makes us feel drawn together by our common bond of sympathy, and each one seems to feel not at home." Her aunt Frances shared such views, writing to Gus that "I find my time just now occupied much as it was at Albany, making and receiving unmeaning visits. I hope this will subside by and by," but with Henry serving as the administration's voice in the Senate, she supported one of its most important figures. She complained about the weather compared to Auburn. "I cannot say on the whole that I like it quite as well as our continuous cold weather for two or three months. Here, we never know upon what we may calculate."[1]

Nonetheless, Frances persisted. "Although our table can be made to accommodate only four guests, it is likely to be filled very frequently. I wish Henry were as well pleased to entertain his friends in some other way . . . but it is childish of me to complain of things which cannot be remedied." Mary Coe was "an excellent cook, but does not keep a tidy kitchen. . . . Our waiter, though very intelligent, is not neat and occasions me much trouble. Still, I have no encouragement for thinking I could improve by changing." When she established one day for receiving callers, as the wives of cabinet members did, Frances was more content with her social life. "I find that my time is much more at my own disposal and were it not that Henry wants to invite company to dinner very often we could live very quietly. One of these days I hope to have all the calls and cards returned." Her day to receive callers was Friday. "I am 'not at home' other days."[2]

Frances suffered less than she had in the past with the socializing required of her, especially in Albany, where she found her guests boring. Now, she wrote to her sister, "I must repeat it again that the society in Washington quite meets my expectations. I can count now among the acquaintances I have made half a dozen women of decided talents. This you will admit is quite a great deal." She continued in the same vein, "It is pleasant to be appreciated for the moderate share of ability one has. . . . People in Washington are not estimated by their dress or the furniture of their houses and, in this respect, it differs from any other city I have ever seen." She did not feel judged negatively, and "my 'reception' Friday was attended by the elite of the city," so she felt like a social success. "I will not complain while I have tolerable health."[3]

While Washington society was better in her home than Frances might have expected, out on the streets it was worse. One morning, when she was in the carriage making her calls, the horses spooked and knocked a man down. He was "a white man of the lower class," she wrote to her sister. "I saw him after getting up walk off apparently not much hurt." When William Johnson, the driver, got the horses back under control, he stopped the carriage in front of a boardinghouse to let out their passenger, at which point "a number of men rushed up and assailed William with the most abusive and threatening language." She tried to calm the crowd down by dropping the name of her husband, which did no good. There seemed to her a real danger that William, who was African American, would be arrested or worse, so she told him to drive to the Capitol, where they sent word for Henry to come out. His response was to instruct William that if he were arrested he should tell the authorities that Senator Seward would post bail. William's reply was that arrest was not his biggest fear. "Black men are punished without the form of a trial," Frances explained to her sister, "and the poor fellow was in bodily fear for two or three days." She later ascertained that the white man was not badly injured and that if he had not been intoxicated at the time, he probably would not have fallen down. "This little incident made me uncomfortable the whole day. Had William been severely beaten, there was no redress supposing the laws here to be such as they are in most of the slave states. Is it not disgraceful to a civilized community?"[4]

The Sewards hosted a dinner party for sixteen members of Congress in late February, so one of their servants "has been engaged in his capacity of carpenter in elongating our table. The china necessary is to be hired. I might just as well come prepared to entertain any amount of company as it is impossible for Henry to avoid having them." Frances was convinced "the dinner gave universal satisfaction to the guests." She was also flattered that spring by the attention given her by the British ambassador, Henry Lytton Lord Bulwer, and his wife, Georgiana Charlotte Mary Bulwer, who was the niece of the Duke of Wellington and sixteen years younger than her husband.[5]

Bulwer was the older brother of the famous author Edward Bulwer-Lytton, who wrote *The Last Days of Pompeii*, among other works that are less remembered today, and was one of Frances's favorite writers. Perhaps it was the family connection or that the diplomat was charming, as was his job, which flattered Frances. Maybe she was just awed by her first acquaintance with nobility, but she received warmly the attentions of a man the same age as her husband, and it contributed to her comparatively sunny disposition on the Washington social scene in 1850. She felt particularly "distinguished by considerable attention from him. He went with me to the supper room, talked with me some time after supper, and concluded by asking me if we would come and dine unceremoniously with them Saturday. I said yes."[6]

Shortly after she met Bulwer in early May, Frances returned to Auburn on short notice and devoted herself to the domestic sphere, where she felt more accomplished but with the confidence that she was, for once, handling society well. Dennis, the African American man who had come with her to Washington, was back in Auburn and had brought a cousin with him to work in what was still the Judge's house. Frances directed Clary to tell the new maid, before Frances arrived home, to start by cleaning the outhouses, the woodhouse, the carriage house chambers, where the groom and other hired men slept, and the soap house before she began the main house. At least one of the other girls could help her. "I wish you to have as little trouble as possible," she wrote Clary, "and would not suggest cleaning at all until I come home, but one month will not suffice to clean the whole of our house and the weather in June is generally too warm."[7]

When Frances arrived in Auburn with her entourage of children, Willie continued his obsession with ponies, traveling to Syracuse, perhaps with his grandfather, where he had heard of one that might suit him and his family, while Fanny was content to be home with her kittens. In early June the "housecleaning makes slow progress, as I have no cook housekeeping is rather more laborious than is agreeable." To Henry she wrote in early June that "our lilacs are just in flower and the red peonies are coming out." She had the hired men set out the verbenas. "Our place was never prettier. The grass in the courtyard is greatly improved. I suppose the old steps must last until you come home. They are unsightly enough and rather unsafe." Henry replied directly to Willie on the question of ponies. "I hear that you have been at Syracuse in pursuit of a pony. It is all very well for little boys to ride and amuse themselves, but I want you to know that in this world nobody has a right to live and act for himself alone. Each of us must find his own pleasure in helping others along as well as himself." Willie needed to make up the time lost in his studies to the chronic affliction of his eyes. And, his father wrote, "I hope especially that you try to find out every day what you can do to give comfort and help to your mother and to Grand Pa." Two days after his father wrote the letter, Willie had his eleventh birthday, which Henry neglected to mention when he asked his youngest son for a letter in return.[8]

On July 18, in a letter addressed to Fanny, Henry couched a suggestion for Frances in a joke. He now knew of a recipe that General David E. Twigs had discovered accidentally when trying to cure pimples on his forehead. The solution turned his beard from gray to the original hue from his youth. "How strange it would be now if Mother should put this solution for a few times on her head and all those white hairs that we all regret, though we they make us love her no less, should give place to the bright, glossy black such as she wore when she was of your own age. Will you propose to her to try the experiment?"[9]

On March 11, 1850, Henry rose to speak on the subject of extending slavery to the newly acquired territories in what has since been called his "Higher Law" speech, one of the most significant speeches ever delivered on the floor of the Senate. Inspired by his time in Charleston, where he learned two things—that there was no compromising with

FIGURE 13.1. Photo of William H. Seward and daughter Fanny, c. 1850. Courtesy of Rare Books, Special Collections, and Preservation, River Campus Libraries, University of Rochester.

FIGURE 13.2. William H. Seward Jr., William H. Seward, and Fanny Seward, 1850. Courtesy of Rare Books, Special Collections, and Preservation, River Campus Libraries, University of Rochester.

southerners on slavery and that the regional characterization of him as an antislavery radical was unalterable by anything he could do or say—he spoke his mind on the subject in support of the administration's policies. He read his remarks from a prepared text in what witnesses described as a quiet monotone, unconsciously twirling his reading glasses in his left hand while gesturing somewhat mechanically with his right. Reporters noted that Thomas Hart Benton read a book, other business distracted Daniel Webster, and Henry Clay appeared bored.[10]

Henry drew authority for his constitutional argument from such giants as Bacon, Burke, Machiavelli, Montesquieu, and Vattel in a day when educated men still read them. He denounced compromise, abandoning his previous accommodating tone, and no longer aimed for a moderate middle ground. The question was whether California would be admitted to the Union, the disposition of other territories acquired in the Mexican-American War, slavery and the slave trade in Washington, DC, and stronger legislation to secure the return of fugitive slaves. There were various arguments about precedents and details, but the real problem for some was California's state constitution, which banned slavery and thus constituted a threat to the institution nationally in the minds of southerners. Seward argued against southern opposition, saying that if California had sought admission as a slave state, he would have voted for it. "When the states are once formed," Seward responded to a question from Webster, "they have the right to come in as free or slave states, according to their own choice. But," he continued, and it was a significant but, "it is insisted that the admission of California shall be attended by a COMPROMISE of questions which have arisen out of SLAVERY! I AM OPPOSED TO ANY SUCH COMPROMISE, IN ANY AND ALL THE FORMS IN WHICH IT HAS BEEN PROPOSED, because, while admitting the purity and the patriotism of all from whom it is my misfortune to differ, I think all legislative compromises radically wrong and essentially vicious." Seward argued against accommodations to slavery on the grounds that the proposals of what came to be called the Compromise of 1850 were "radically wrong and essentially vicious," that such compromises were immoral.[11]

Senator Seward acknowledged a constitutional right for the states to choose their own paths on slavery. "I deem it established, then, that the Constitution does not recognize property in man, but leaves that question, as between the states, to the law of nature and of nations." It was in Seward's qualification to such states' rights that he made his most controversial claim, and it began with another significant conjunction.

"But there is a higher law than the Constitution, which regulates our authority over the domain and devotes it to the same noble purposes. The territory is a part—no inconsiderable part—of the common heritage of mankind, bestowed upon them by the Creator of the universe. We are his stewards, and must so discharge our trust as to secure in the highest attainable degree, their happiness." Here he quoted Francis Bacon on the power and responsibility of leaders, constitutions, and legislatures to "sow greatness to our posterity and successors." That brought Congress, then, to the question of whether to "establish human bondage, or permit it, by our sufferance, to be established." The Constitution left slavery in place where it was, as the founders saw no path for them to abolish it, but they left it to their descendants, in Seward's view, whether to create or establish it in new states. "Sir, there is no Christian nation, thus free to choose as we are, which would establish slavery." Indeed, Great Britain, France, and Mexico had already abolished it, and other nations were also on the path to abolition. And yet, others argued, compromise was essential to preservation of the Union. "I do not know what I would not do to preserve the Union," Seward averred. There was no question in his mind that a day of reckoning was at hand, that there was a threat to the Union posed by a civil war. The way to prevent that dissolution, though, was not for northerners to compromise on slavery but for southerners to accept that the institution was doomed. Southerners "could not roll back the tide of social progress," and no compromise by the North could help them do that.[12]

Radical or "immediate" abolitionists, those who argued for a full, immediate, and uncompensated abolition of slavery in the United States, were not satisfied with Seward's position, while he found them impractical and counterproductive to their cause. They also were disappointed, but not surprised, by what they saw as racism in his speech. California should be admitted to the Union, Seward argued, because it fundamentally conformed to the shared racial and cultural configuration of the United States: "The population of the United States consists of natives of Caucasian origin, and exotics of the same derivation. The native mass rapidly assimilates to itself, and absorbs the exotic, and thus these constitute one homogeneous people. The African race, bond and free, and the aborigines, savage and civilized, being incapable of such assimilation and absorption, remain distinct; and, owing to their peculiar condition, they constitute inferior masses, and may be regarded as accidental, if not disturbing political forces." In his mind, the Irish were examples of such white "exotics," but Indians and African Americans were permanently disqualified from being full Americans who could participate as equals. Even in this, his most progressive speech, Henry was no social radical, as were his wife, his sister-in-law, and their Quaker friends.[13]

Nonetheless, Frances was thrilled by how far Henry had come, how courageous he was in the face of Henry Clay's compromise, which proposed admission of California as a free state, allowing New Mexico to decide for itself, and retaining slavery in the District of Columbia while abolishing its slave trade. On the other side, such southerners as Senator Calhoun opposed the compromise because they thought the South would give up too much by agreeing to admit another free state. Even before the speech on March 11, Frances sat in the gallery on a number of days to watch Henry play his role in the unfolding drama that eventually ended with both compromise and the Civil War. "Much as I love Henry," she wrote to her sister after one of these occasions, "I feel that my love and respect are both augmented by his present position. When I looked upon his slight form, and thought that it embodied the only spirit sufficiently fearless to vindicate human rights, yet combined with a moderation and Christian charity, which can alone render such efforts' effect, I felt that it was good for me to be there, it was a sight calculated to make our 'Faith more strong in high humanity.' I have no misgiving about the final result; sooner or later the righteous cause must prevail."[14]

The speech was widely noticed, quoted, reprinted, and commented on in newspapers, which fixed popular opinion of Seward in the North as it already was in the South. He was now famous or infamous, depending on your political view. Horace Greeley, editor of the *New York Tribune*, argued that the "higher law" concept elevated the Constitution by imbuing the document with the authority of divine sanction. Others believed that Henry had diminished the significance of constitutional law.

With President Taylor on his side, in opposition to the compromise measures, Henry was not totally isolated in Washington. As the administration's spokesman in the Senate, there were conversations between the two men during Henry's many visits to the White House. From other quarters in Washington, though, the blowback was swift and forceful, which isolated the Sewards socially. "The first week after Henry's speech was made was a season of darkness" for both Frances and him, as he endured "unsparing abuse in the Senate, or coldness even from those who ought to have supported him." The reaction in the South was predictably vicious. A letter signed "Georgia Savannah" reflected the extreme: "I see you have commenced with your damnable abolition petitions again. Now, sir, allow me to say to you that if we ever find you in Georgia, you will forfeit your odious neck, you scamp. We have hemp and flax here for you, you scoundrel." Henry did not show such letters to Frances; Fred was the only other family member who saw them.[15]

In response to a letter from her sister after Lazette had read Henry's California speech in a newspaper, Frances wrote, "I knew you would like Henry's speech, but you can hardly conceive the moral courage it required to make such a speech in the Senate. You must not let it vex you that his course is not understood and appreciated by those who do not know him as well as you and I do." Although he started to receive supportive letters within days, Frances proudly believed that her husband was capable of standing alone. "He has many very highly complimentary letters from Northern men, but the only certain reward for such efforts is that which the world cannot give or take away, the reward of a quiet conscience."[16]

In less than two weeks, Frances gained hope that "now the light is bursting upon us. The Whig press at the North is making ample amends for the denunciation of the South. Letters innumerable from all quarters full of the highest commendation come daily . . . It is almost impossible to supply the demands for the speech." Henry was not as alone in the country as he sometimes believed. "I wish you could see the innumerable letters of congratulation Henry has about his speech, from all quarters. I am going to keep them for a book," she wrote to Lazette. "I never shall cease regretting, dear Sis, that you are not here to read with us the letters and papers about Henry's speech. They are coming now from Ohio and Michigan," she wrote on April 4. "I shall keep them for you. They amply atone for the abuse from other quarters." Frances beamed proudly, "Henry continues to receive very flattering testimony to the uprightness of his views. He has now some 1,600 letters unanswered. Among them are many of warm commendation from all parties. . . . I hope to bring a portion of them home for you to read." As she wrote to her sister, who was caring for their elderly father in Frances's absence from Auburn, "One of the clergymen who wrote to Henry about his speech prayed that God would give him grace to bear the persecutions which would inevitably follow the bold advocacy of a righteous cause."[17]

Union College president Eliphalet Nott wrote to Henry, his former student, "Amid that din of abuse in the midst of which you live and move, I cannot refrain from saying, that the wiser and better part of the community here sympathize with you. . . . Your speech has made and left an impression that no other speech has. It will be remembered and referred to when the outbreaks of passion it occasioned will be forgotten." Samuel B. Ruggles, a New York attorney, wrote to say, "I do most cordially and sincerely congratulate you on the result. . . . As far as I can now discern its outlines, they are grand, continental and majestic." Fred, working as Henry's secretary, sent out over 100,000 copies of the printed speech in response to requests.[18]

In the midst of the thunderous reaction and ongoing debate, Senator Calhoun died on March 31. He had served as vice president under both John Quincy Adams and Andrew Jackson, from whose administration he resigned for a seat in the Senate with only four months left in his term. He was an advocate of nullification, a constitutional interpretation that declared federal laws unsupportive of slavery null in his home state of South Carolina. He was an enslaver, endorsed slavery as a positive good, and supported the minority rights of states against what he saw as federal overreach. He was also a catalyst for the blossoming secession movement that Henry had underestimated before his visit to Charleston the previous spring.

On May 16 Henry wrote to Frances, "This is my birthday. From this time I enter my fiftieth year. It is a numeral very high in the progress of human life. The decline of life begins then if not already begun. The season for usefulness grows short, and for pleasure draws to a close. Give me your sympathies and your wishes that what remains hereafter may be spent more serenely and more wisely; commend me to all my dear children, and believe me more devotedly and ever yours." If that was truly his aim, he missed the mark, but the struggle at this point must have been exhausting for them all. Several days later, he wrote again of his devotion to home and family; as always, he wrote from afar: "How I should enjoy this Sunday in our home with our children, old and young, all about us, and our flowers and our birds." Within a week, though, Henry was planning to rise in defense of the president's plan after a ringing denunciation of Taylor by Senator Clay. The speech was "so bold, so arrogant, and so offensive that it will render it necessary that I shall at a proper time, if I can find it, and in a proper way, if I can do it, vindicate and defend the Administration and the noble old chief. This I feel a hope I can do in a good spirit." Still, he was discouraged about his ability to play a positive role. "The more I see of Washington," he wrote at the end of May, "the more I distrust my ability to work out the great ends I have cherished or to advance them." That is where the

Senate stood, in deadlock, as June began, unable to resolve the California question or to agree to adjourn. "The summer has come," Henry wrote, with no return home in sight. "It comes with chilly winds. But it has heat in reserve, I know." On June 11 he wrote again to Frances, "Your letters woo me home strongly by so many touching notices of my children, of the trees, and flowers, and of friends. But we are here in the beginning of the end; if, indeed, there is to be an end of this mighty strife." On June 16 he was more hopeful of an imminent adjournment.[19]

On July 7 the Senate was still in session. Henry wrote home that "General Taylor has been ill, but the newspapers have not got news of it." The next day, he wrote again, clearly more concerned about his ally and friend. "The President is sick, of a bilious att[ack]. The Vice-President is 'tempted to strange thoughts.'" On July 9 Henry was even more anxious and wrote home again. "Although the telegraph will anticipate by hours and days what I write, I cannot omit to speak my dreadful apprehensions about the President. He is in extreme danger. All that can be said of encouragement by his physicians is that 'there is hope.' My feelings are saddened by this event."[20]

Before the next morning, President Taylor was dead, which altered the path of the nation and the place of the Sewards in Washington society. "The President died like a brave, undaunted Christian," Henry wrote. Taylor was an enslaver himself, a Virginian by birth, a Kentuckian by upbringing, a Louisiana plantation owner at the time of his election, and a career military officer. He was a reluctant candidate and saw preservation of the Union as his highest priority. He did not advocate the extension of slavery into the territories that his troops had won in the Mexican-American War. Taylor sought intersectional harmony, which he did not believe the compromises provided. When he died suddenly of a stomach ailment at age sixty-five, he was succeeded by Henry's nemesis, the New York Whig Millard Fillmore, who endorsed the compromises that soon became law. "My own course of conduct will remain the same," Henry pondered, "but I do not see how it can help bringing me into opposition to the new Administration, if it takes the departure from the policy of General Taylor, which I apprehend."[21]

The news of the president's death reached Frances in Auburn on July 10; Henry was still in Washington. She lamented the loss in a number of ways. "I grieve for his family," she wrote to Henry, "for the loss of one I felt to be a personal friend, but above all for the irremediable loss which our Country has sustained. The nation has lost the guidance of a strong arm directed by an honest and upright conscience. How is this breach to be filled . . . I have wept till my eyes are dim. All about is gloom and sadness." Two days later, she wrote again in response to a letter from Henry, who was ill himself. "You write under evident depression of spirits such as you would not feel were you tolerably well yourself, even with this cause for sorrow. It is your nature when well to find hope everywhere." "Yesterday," Frances wrote on July 14, "the outward manifestations of mourning for our lamented President were made. The stores were closed, the bells tolled, cannon fired, and many of the buildings hung in black."[22]

Taylor's death changed much for Henry and everything for Frances, who no longer felt welcome or happy in Washington. She resented Henry's treatment even by his own party and felt judged and belittled for her unsociable ways. "I suppress in conversation with all others," Henry wrote to his wife, "what you may safely know, my apprehensions that his administration will be conducted in a spirit of war and proscription against me, and all with whom I act, and that this will occur simply because he does not at all know or understand his position or mine. All is dark for him and for the country, and there is not a ray of light to enable me to see through it."[23]

The cabinet resigned and Henry advised the new president to reappoint the same men, which he did not. Daniel Webster was the new secretary of state, and the administration's policy was now compromise. "The government is in the hands of Mr. Webster," Henry explained, "and Mr. Clay is its organ in Congress," replacing Seward. After Henry gave his advice to reinstate Taylor's cabinet, he was not invited back to the White House. "Henceforth, if I muzzle not my mouth on the subject of slavery, as I certainly shall not, I shall be set down as a disturber, seeking to disturb the Whig Administration and derange the Whig party. So we go, in this changing world!" While the omnibus bill that embodied the parts of the Compromise failed, its elements passed both houses serially in August. California was admitted as a free state, New Mexico and Utah were admitted with slavery; slavery was undisturbed in the District, although the slave trade there was restricted; the Texas–New Mexico border was settled to the advantage of Texas; and the fugitive slave law passed with many of the northern congressmen absent from the vote to avoid taking a stand. This led Thaddeus Stevens, the abolitionist congressman from Pennsylvania, to rise and facetiously move that "the Speaker send one of his pages to inform the members that they can return with safety, as the slavery question has been disposed of!" Many in both parties, but not Henry, exulted that the question of slavery was settled for good.[24]

To Weed, Henry wrote on August 2, "My responsibilities are much diminished." To Frances, on August 11, he said he had become resigned to his place in the new order. "There is now time on my hands. I employ it by reading some of the English classics–Swift and Beaumont and Fletcher. Half a dozen tragedies, really beautiful, make up all that is tolerable of the latter, but Swift is admirable throughout. I do not wonder at the 'inferior state' of your sex now, when I see how much lower it was less than one hundred and fifty years ago." Fletcher and Beaumont "had no idea of a woman, except that which degrades both sexes."[25]

On the domestic front, in 1850 Frances's principal concern remained Gus. It was taking about three weeks for his letters from Oklahoma to reach her in Washington, and he often did not reply to specific questions she had asked him about his plans. "He says nothing further about coming home in any of his last letters," she complained to her sister in mid-January. She wrote in frustration, having heard nothing from him. "You do not say anything about joining me here. If there is a shadow of a doubt [about] you coming home this spring, pray tell me and devise some way for me to come to you before I go North again. I cannot admit the thought that I may pass another six months without seeing you. I trust you will not decide to remain in the army before you see us again."[26]

Gus wrote to Henry, enclosing a copy of the request for leave he submitted on January 8. He hoped that his father could help secure an extension from two months to the six that he requested, "as this is so far out of the world that it would take nearly all the time to go and return." When Gus's letter arrived with the news in early January, Frances wrote, "Great joy pervaded the house. I suppose I shall not actually die, as poor Mrs. Bliss [Olive Hall Simons Bliss] did when her son came from Mexico, as I am not equally infirm, but I cannot think long on the subject with any composure." According to Frances, "Henry went immediately to the War Department and has since written to General Scott," who in a swift reply assured the Sewards that he granted the extension "with great pleasure," but he did not know when exactly Gus would receive the formal approval. Frances continued to fret about his arrival throughout the late winter and early spring.[27]

Finally, on May 4, Frances received a telegram from her niece's fiancé in Canandaigua: "Augustus arrived here last night. All well, goes to

Auburn today." Two days later, she was back in Auburn. The next day, Gus departed for Washington to see his father and already had other travel plans. "Augustus is going to Europe prematurely," she wrote to Henry. "He is impelled to this by the idea that he cannot honorably use a furlough granted upon such a suggestion for any other purpose. In this he may or may not be mistaken. The impression cannot be removed. All this may be obviated by resigning his commission at once. This I most earnestly desire. I know there are forcible reasons for a contrary course, but they are all swept away by the knowledge which I cannot disguise from myself and ought not to disguise from you that our child will be ruined if he returns to the army."[28]

Between the lines is news of a visit in which Gus and his mother were immediately at odds over his lack of communication with her, his surprise arrival where she was not, and his plans, both short term and long. He, much like his father, fled domestic conflict in very short order after a long trip. "We have caused him to pass through the fire and have no right to arraign the justice of God if he has not come out unscathed." By "we" she meant Henry, who facilitated Gus's path to West Point and the Mexican-American War. "While there is a doubt about his returning to the army, all my exertions are paralyzed. Relieved from this, I will go anywhere, do anything you think best." Having put all her cards on the table before Gus, who obviously had dismissed her hopes and fears, she again overplayed her hand with Henry, whose bottom line, as she should have known, was that Gus must plan his own life. "Do not allow any prospect of advancement [to] influence you." In other words, please support her in dismissing Gus's argument that he was on the path to a successful career. "I would not consent to Augustus's return to the army if he could tomorrow take the place of Gen. Scott."[29]

Interpreting Gus's silence as evidence of a stormy visit with his mother seems pretty safe. He, in the company of his aunt Lazette, left Auburn and his mother almost immediately. They rendezvoused with Henry in New York. One week later, after a leisurely visit with Gus and Lazette that was six days longer than Gus had stayed with his mother, Henry returned to Washington without a stop in Auburn and wrote to his son with advice on a European trip. His approach, no matter what he thought about Gus's army career, was advisory and supportive, an entirely different one than Frances took, which strengthened the relationship between father and son. "The object of travel, as you know," Henry advised, "is not to consume time or to find mere amusement in relaxation, but it is to acquire knowledge," so preparation and planning in advance of the trip was essential. He suggested a brief course of study: "a week or two, or three, will bring you accumulation of treasure." Henry thought books in their family library would "qualify" Gus for the journey. "The geography and the history of your own country" were a good place to start, "so that, when you are abroad, you can repay others by information of our country, for the knowledge they impart to you concerning theirs."[30]

Gus and Lazette returned to Auburn on May 14 after a cooling-off period for him and his mother and a day trip to the beach. They were, according to Frances, "much pleased with their jaunt." Gus remained restless, like his father, on his return home. "Augustus is impatient for action of some kind. He went to Canandaigua Tuesday for his cousin Frances," whom he accompanied back to Auburn at the end of May. The first week of June he was off to Washington, as was Fred. "I am anxious to learn what you advise Augustus," she wrote to Henry. "Let it be anything rather than a return to the army." Although Henry's reply does not survive, she summarized her disappointment in a letter to Lazette. "Henry thinks me unreasonable and in a fair way to prevent Augustus from succeeding in anything by my over anxiety. He is not willing that he should resign his commission at present. This is a subject on which we can never think or feel alike. My own course is clear. What influence I have will be exerted in every possible manner to induce Augustus to resign. If I had the shadow of a doubt before he came home, I have none now. Yet it makes our life uncomfortable to be in an attitude of opposition continually."[31]

Frances was wounded and Gus must have been too. He now planned his trip for September, which his mother learned from Henry, "but I have heard nothing in particular from Augustus himself on that subject. He undoubtedly has his own views." As far as she knew as June ended, Gus planned to travel with Fred, but the departure date was still unsettled and she heard nothing from Gus. She did not even know where he was on July 8, when she learned of a rail accident in which five people died, which led her to fear that he had been on his way home and was among the dead. And there were reports of cholera, both in Auburn and abroad. When she learned after an excruciating three days of no news that her fears were misplaced, it occurred to Frances that perhaps there was a silver lining in President Taylor's death. To Henry she wrote in mid-July, "It seems to be a very suitable time now for him to resign. His Commander-in-Chief, whom we all loved and honoured, is gone. I think your approval makes his resignation sure." On July 20

Henry replied but again ignored her futile obsession with Gus's career. "Augustus has gone to you. I shall return to see you and him before he leaves the country."[32]

At the end of July, Frances prodded their nephew Clarence to ask Henry if he could be Gus's companion on the European trip. She switched her advocacy from Fred to Clarence at the urging of Gus, and Clarence marshaled his arguments in a letter that reflected his training as a lawyer. "In compliance with the advice and request of Aunt Frances, I write . . . The concurring opinions of friends and my own reason both advise . . . Experience has demonstrated the wisdom of acting upon your advice. . . . Augustus wishes me to accompany him." The idea was Gus's, but we do not know why the preference over his brother or whether it was Henry or Fred who thought the trip inauspicious for Fred. Clarence's main concern was that if he took a leave of absence from the Auburn law office, he would lose the position, but, of course, his uncle could fix that. We learn in a letter from Frances to Henry three days later that it was all arranged. "I am glad to have him accompany Augustus. I was unwilling to have him go alone. They leave here Monday noon for Boston. The Asia, in which Augustus has engaged his passage, sails on the seventh." She was glad to know on August 3 that Henry approved the plan. They left Auburn the next day, as did Lazette, so Frances was alone again with the two children, her father, her household help, who were not much help, and her aunt Clary to pitch in. Fred was back in Washington, where his father needed him. Frances was now again free to return to Washington, which she did in late August. She and Henry rendezvoused in New York City and then proceeded on to the capital. Frances left behind Willie, whose aunt Lazette returned to Auburn to care for him and his grandfather, while Fanny traveled with her mother and now also with her father.[33]

Frances wrote to Lazette, who had sprained her ankle, on September 7 from Washington, where the "Thirty-First Congress has decided in favour of Slavery," as the Compromise measures were adopted. "Henry is content that he has done his duty." She hoped now that there was a prospect of adjournment and had heard from Gus, who wrote her a letter shortly before the ship sailed. "I have driven twice past the White House. It seems shorn of its glory," Frances wrote. "It is wonderful how much the occupants increase or diminish the attraction of a place."[34]

The last week of September, Frances wrote to Gus in London to wish him a happy birthday on October 1. "How long it has been since you have spent one with me." She wished Fred could go home to Auburn to read to Elijah, but "your father cannot spare him." On October 13 she received her first letter from Gus since he sailed. Several days later, the Sewards were at home for Frances Worden's wedding. On October 22 Henry wrote to Gus in Paris that he had authorized his bank to credit the cousins with $500 in additional funds as Clarence and Gus had requested. He also informed him that was all the cousins should expect, as the futures of both of them were as yet too insecure "to warrant great expense in seeing foreign countries. I have concluded therefore to advise that you so regulate your affairs as to return home without further remittance."[35]

By the end of November, the Sewards were all back in Washington, where Frances was again socializing, but much less. Fortunately, from Frances's perspective, the frequency and size of their dinner parties had plummeted now that Henry no longer worked in support of the administration. The only evidence of guests before the end of the year was the acceptance of an invitation to Christmas dinner from Mr. and Mrs. Hiram Mattison, who were friends from back home.[36]

The year 1851 started much as the previous one had ended for Frances, although this year she found the winters in Washington "decidedly preferable" to those of Auburn and thought that the weather perhaps played a role in her health being "much better than at home." Possibly that was because she was now forced by her social schedule "to spend two or three hours every morning in the open air." Nonetheless, there were "many, many days when I long for the quiet of my own home. Constant visiting wearies me, the excess renders it a business instead of a pleasure," and Henry had returned to hosting dinner parties at least once a week. The children were both well in January, but Fanny was ill with a fever by the end of the month; Willie's attentions were now focused on his pet squirrel, "who bites everybody but Willie and Abbey," the maid. Frances watched weather reports closely over the next month, when she expected Gus and Clarence to sail home. "I hope when Augustus comes to be able to persuade him to resign his commission and fix upon some mode of life which will not separate him entirely from his family." No one in the family was able to dissuade her from that course.[37]

Frances, the children, Abbey, the squirrel, and Dick their pet bird returned to Auburn in mid-March. Clary was glad to be relieved of her household duties, especially caring for her ungrateful and increasingly dependent brother. "He is as unwilling to be left alone as a child. He is nearly blind and lonely in his darkness." Frances found Fred, Gus, Clarence, and Lazette at home. "Augustus will leave here in two weeks more," she wrote to Henry, "unless he determines to resign his commission, which I confidently hoped when I came home. The uncertainty of his success in some other occupation makes him hesitate, and his hesitation fills me with indescribable pain and apprehension." She saw Gus's time in the army as "exile from his family" and believed that if he returned to his post the decision was likely "final. Independent of my dislike of the profession, this would cause me deep sorrow. Combined with that it occasions sorrow inexpressible." Her son's exile had now lasted eight years and her husband's over two decades. Both broke her heart.[38]

On March 19 Henry sent Frances a telegram announcing that General Scott had extended Gus's leave to July 1, likely at the senator's request, so a furlough of over fifteen months, when Gus was entitled to two months only. There is no mistaking the favoritism shown here. This was obviously no way to run an army, and the general did not run the rest of it this way. Frances understood that the extension of Gus's leave was connected to Scott's quiet campaign for president, to which Henry's support was critical. She noted that Gus had not himself received a letter authorizing the extension. "No letter comes from General Scott and none will come at present. He is too much engaged in being made President," she wrote to Henry cynically. On April 18 Frances wrote to Henry that "Augustus is uncomfortable under this inactivity. I do not wonder. He has spent five weeks almost wholly in the room or in the street with Grandpa. He does not complain, but his solicitude about a letter indicates the state of his mind."[39]

Again, Frances hoped that Henry would find his son a job that lured him safely from the army or kept him safely in it. "You have I know many things to perplex you, but there are no stronger claims than those of your own children. The jealousy of any interference in the army arrangements is such that I think your application for the Coast Survey will very likely fail." This is the first we learn that Senator Seward was trying to manipulate the system again, as he had to secure Gus's appointment to West Point, in an act of nepotism of the sort for which he had criticized the now president and secretary of state. The Office of Coast Survey was established during Jefferson's presidency and was the first scientific agency of the federal government. There was a struggle between civilian and military control, which resulted in two operations that divided up the work. Its funding was politically controversial at the time. In the 1850s the army and navy supplied manpower and vessels in support of the tasks of charting the coasts and the Gulf Stream.[40]

Henry was now reading Charles Dickens's *David Copperfield*, which had been published the previous year. Frances had already read the novel and wrote to Henry in early May, "I am glad you like David Copperfield. I think at our time of life it is well to keep the 'memory green' by reading occasionally a book of this kind independent of the pleasure which is afforded by the skill of the writer in drawing pictures so true to nature. Dickens has assuredly done much to make the world more loving and charitable." These same ambitions had led her to try to convince Gus to read Dickens or anything. "I have tried in vain to induce our Gus to read the book. He does not read far enough to get interested in the plot and works of imagination have few charms for one whose studies have been so entirely mathematical."[41]

As Frances predicted, the intercession of Henry through General Scott to secure a new assignment for Gus proved unavailing in the short term. General John Abercrombie, the commandant at Corpus Christi and Gus's commanding officer, had issued an order for the return of all the officers stationed there. "Gen. Scott regrets his inability to oblige you," she wrote to Henry in the middle of May. "Indeed, the disposition of both himself and the Superintendent to do so has been the cause of misleading us all." Under the circumstances, she thought that she and Henry were united in advising Gus to resign. On May 20 Frances informed Gus, who was on his way back to his unit, traveling through New York City and Louisville, that "tomorrow your father sets out in quest of employment for you, which I doubt not he will obtain. . . . I hope you will not give yourself more uneasiness than you can avoid as your father seldom undertakes anything that he does not accomplish. He has already written to some civil engineers." As she explained it to Gus, Alexander Bache, a great-grandson of Benjamin Franklin, a former army engineer, a professor of natural philosophy at the University of Pennsylvania, and now the head of the Coast Survey, had declined to have Gus assigned to him. He already had seven army officers, "when the usual number was four."[42]

"The hope which has lightened my heart for this last year has vanished," Frances wrote to Henry about Gus's refusal to leave the army. Fred was in New York City to study law with Judge William Kent, who was a Whig politician and circuit court judge appointed to the bench by Governor Seward. By early June Gus was back with his company, which had moved from Corpus Christi to Fort Gibson, Oklahoma. Henry left

Washington for Florida, New York, before the end of May, and then was in Detroit arguing a railroad case by the end of the first week of June, where he remained over the summer and into the fall. Clarence was now married and Caroline a student at the Troy Female Academy, Frances's and Lazette's alma mater, where she was reportedly much happier than she had been in Washington.[43]

It was not Caroline's discontent that had provoked the move from Washington to Troy. As we learn in a letter from Henry's brother George to Frances, the family feared her conversion to Catholicism. According to George, Caroline had shared in a letter to a Florida friend that "she had become a Catholic in sentiment and that she had been twice to the Confessional." That was enough. Her previous quarterly report reflected mixed success in her studies; her orthography was "sometimes incorrect," she had "imperfect lessons" in "profane history," but "good lessons" in mythology. She did well in arithmetic and botany, and was "very attentive" to "ornamental writing." In French she was "attentive and improved" and the same for piano; her conduct was "satisfactory." At the end of June we learn from Frances that "Caroline has become quite contented at Troy." The next we hear of Caroline is a short note from her to her uncle in late November, asking, "Will you please to send me some money?"[44]

Fred was admitted to the practice of law after an examination in Rochester for which he had prepared in what his mother thought was a dilatory way. As September began, it remained unclear what he would do next, but he did not want to return to New York City and work with Judge Kent. There was a discussion with his father about possibly moving to Michigan or Wisconsin to practice law, which his mother did not favor because that would take another of her sons away. Without discussion in the family letters, by October Fred had become the assistant editor of Thurlow Weed's Albany newspaper and was writing editorials that made his mother proud. As Frances informed Gus, "His immediate success seems wonderful. His taste inclines him towards literature as a profession and he is very happy in his new vocation." Apparently in reflection of his writerly turn, Fred abandoned the K in Frederick for a time.[45]

Over the summer, the Sewards also learned from General Scott that Gus would "have the preference in the next appointment on the Coast Survey. I shall see that he does not forget it," his mother wrote. Henry, following instructions from Professor Bache, had applied on Gus's behalf to General Scott and Adjutant General Roger Jones for the assignment that Bache now welcomed after some lobbying. It was, of course, Frances's hope, which she shared with Gus, that "we may get you nearer home by and by." There is no surviving evidence on what Gus thought about his family's maneuvering on his behalf.[46]

In late October Frances was not planning to accompany Henry back to Washington in December, "unless Grandpa's health improves. I cannot leave him as he is now." Instead, she was free to leave Auburn because Judge Miller died on November 13. The funeral at Saint Peter's and burial were three days later. As was the case with Henry's father, the family recorded few details about the death. "The house seems very, very lonely without him," Frances wrote to Gus. Elijah's internment was the first in the new Fort Hill Cemetery, where the remains of Paulina and the infant Cornelia were relocated near him in due course. There were now two estates to settle, Samuel's and Elijah's, and Henry was executor of both, but Elijah's was much simpler as almost everything passed through Frances, who saw to the interests of her sister, niece, and children.[47]

The other, and perhaps the most fraught, trial of Henry's year was his family's displeasure with the way he was handling Samuel's estate. The main problem was likely his distraction from the task, but his refusal to delegate or his coexecutor George Grier's unwillingness to take on the burden led his brothers and nephews to suspect bad will on Henry's part. In a letter to Frances in June, his brother George questioned Henry's motives, but he was willing to consider that Henry simply misunderstood his surviving two brothers' best interests. To be sure, the root of the problem lay at the door of their late father's vault. "Contrary to what I had good reason to expect," George wrote, which was not true, "my Father saw proper while to Henry he gave one-quarter of his estate unreservedly and while of the remaining fifteen shares he gave to thirteen of his heirs their individual share, also unreservedly and without condition, he gave to elder brother and myself each a share at the discretion of his executors." Samuel imposed controls over the spending of his money because he had so little trust in George's and Polydore's financial wisdom. While this was, in the minds of George and Polydore, obviously unfair, it was Henry's complicity in extending his father's control over them to which George objected angrily.[48]

There were only two interpretations that George could imagine for the executors' refusal to distribute the shares to which the brothers were entitled under the will. Henry's refusal to give them a straight answer to their faces or in writing was what frustrated them most.

Since Henry was always away from home and difficult even for his wife to find, their frustration was compounded by never being able to pin him down. Either the executors did not intend ever to give the brothers their shares "or they have created the impression that they did not as a course of policy to coerce me into their views and purposes." George, at least, had concluded that coercion was the executors' intent, which infuriated him. Henry apparently accepted the views of his father that George and Polydore were incompetent to handle their own financial affairs. This seemed to George hard usage in return for his care for his father in Henry's absence over the years. The injustice all but drove George mad. If his father had intended to disinherit him, why had he accepted "my services and care and attention to the exclusion of my own business to his person and his affairs for two years before his death, why did he permit me to do so even if I were willing, why was I allowed to stand at his bedside in his last illness, I who had forfeited his confidence when others upon whom he had much stronger claims than he had on me," and here he was talking about Henry, "and who were so much more interested, and whose obligations were so much deeper, sought their own"?[49]

Perhaps it was George's "supposed hostility to his favorite scheme," the establishment of Samuel's academy, that led their father, with Henry's complicity, to frustrate George from the grave. Or possibly it was George's "religious sentiments" that were "the spring of his action," which now denied George "this most sacred of rights, a right to which the humblest equally with the loftiest intellect is credible, too." The irony of this explanation was, George thought, that he had learned his religious devotion from his mother, whose deep beliefs he shared strongly. Samuel, like Henry, was more skeptical and less religious than Mary. George dismissed out of hand the alternative explanation that his father was right about the need for intervention to oversee his financial affairs.[50]

While George suspected that it was Henry's own debts that played a role in his decisions about how to control the estate, he only hinted at and then withdrew such an accusation to Henry's wife. He refused to give Henry a full accounting of his financial affairs, which George wished to hold "in my own hands." He also supposed that Henry held against him George's refusal in the fall of 1849 to relocate to Auburn, where Henry, who George might have pointed out was seldom in Auburn himself, could serve as guardian of his brother's affairs. He now questioned Henry's motives in his request that George sign a "Deed of Guardianship" for Henry over George's children, which he signed and then had second thoughts about; the request insulted him. George did not say it, but the act was not, in his opinion, merely to facilitate Henry's oversight of their education. It was also, which insulted George more, to ensure that he did not siphon money from their inheritance for his personal use. Finally, George suspected that Henry tried to control his love life, to keep him from marrying a woman to whom he had become devoted since his wife's death.[51]

George left Auburn in a huff on June 19, when he learned that Henry was away in Detroit. The next day Frances wrote to Henry, "Poor George. I should be in no way surprised if his infirm temper resulted in insanity. He evidently grows morose and irritable. We are quite uncertain whether he has gone back to Florida or to Detroit." Four days later, she wrote again to report, "I have a long letter from George, which, I think, indicates aberration of intellect. The subject of the letter is complaints of our injustice. It is incoherently written and has satisfied me that George is on the verge of insanity."[52]

Shortly before Christmas, George wrote to Henry a letter that was neither a retraction nor an apology, but rather grudgingly accepted that a letter from Henry, delivered by George Grier, explained to his satisfaction the motives that inspired the executors on their course. "I will not stop now to enquire who was in the wrong," George wrote, "and will only say that when your letter is carried out in its spirit and letter I shall be abundantly satisfied." While George acknowledged Henry's lack of bad will, he refused to allow Henry to help settle his debts, insisting that he had "the ability to adjust them myself. The question as to whether there should be a compromise or not I believe I should determine and I feel a just and honorable pride in doing it myself."[53]

In other words, George insisted that the executors immediately turn over to him his entitlement, one-twentieth of the estate, and he would handle his own finances. He was still angry that Henry inherited 25 percent of his father's vast wealth, while Samuel had bequeathed him a comparatively paltry 5 percent that remained under Henry's control. George still regretted signing a document that gave Henry the guardianship of his children. "I do not feel that I should relinquish control, right, and duty which I owe them as a father and in which I feel their interest as well as my own is involved." Those were his terms and he now hoped that the settlement concluded despite his refusal to surrender his rights as a man, the independence to control his own financial destiny. While Polydore took a much more accommodating tone with his brother, he also wrote in December in frustration with Henry's silence.[54]

As Frances left Auburn for Washington in mid-December, death was even more on her mind than usual. She was leaving twelve-year-old Willie behind, apparently at his request, to begin attending school. He, unlike his father and older brother, was very attached to their home. "I leave you very reluctantly," she wrote on December 14. "You are too young to be left to your own direction. With a very generous and affectionate heart, you combine some qualities which require watchfulness and restraint." Nonetheless, she had agreed to leave him. "The alarming illness which I had on Sunday has made me feel that I may be called suddenly away. Should this be the case, you must remember that you will be required to be more watchful of yourself when your Mother is gone." The illness was what she called "a spasmodic affection of the heart," which afflicted her on December 7, two days before Fanny's seventh birthday. Lazette had been called home by the illness of her Frances, but she was back in Auburn several days later, meaning Willie was alone with Clary and staff for a short time before his aunt returned and he started school. In the case of his mother's death, Willie should "strive to do what is right. Seek direction from your father and brothers, and ask strength from God."[55]

The year 1851 had been a rough one for Frances too, with the death of her father and her failure to dissuade Gus from a military career. It was also the first year that she suffered "palpitations" regularly, but this crisis was not the last of its kind. Heart palpitations now accompanied the headaches, toothaches, and colds that led her to take to her bed. During this trip to Washington, she consulted a homeopathic physician in New York City, Stephen Reynolds Kirby, who prescribed Veratrum or white hellebore, a flowering plant with highly poisonous black rhizomes, in very small doses, which was thought to diminish a variety of symptoms, including headaches, neuralgia, cramps, and gastric distress. Frances was now forty-six. Kirby also prescribed aconite to address her anxiety and headaches. In larger doses it is highly poisonous, and it can cause heart failure, hair loss, and diarrhea even in small doses.[56]

On Christmas Day Frances wrote to her sister for the first time since arriving in Washington. She had left Philadelphia on December 21 "in a violent snow storm, which continued nearly the whole day." The Susquehanna River was frozen, as was Chesapeake Bay and Baltimore harbor. "I should not have been here two days without writing had I been well, but I have not. I was sick every day I was on the railroad and have not been free from pain since I came." So it took her three days to write.[57]

Nonetheless, through it all, on Christmas Eve Frances caught a cold while Christmas shopping. She also met Senator Charles Sumner of Massachusetts, an antislavery radical new to the city, who eventually became her fast friend, her soulmate in politics who was bolder on the issue than her husband was. "I like him exceedingly," she wrote to her sister, "and so you would think. He is frank and fearless and sincere, very well looking in his deportment."[58]

Frances was in a melancholy mood as the year drew to an end. "How much I think of home and how sadly compared with former winters," she wrote to her sister, who was back in Canandaigua with Willie and his bird Bob, who was again ill. "When I write it seems as if my letters must be partly for Pa. Our old home standing alone and deserted in this cold, dreary winter time is continually before me."[59]

There was also good news. The War Department had notified Henry that "Augustus was detailed for the Coast Survey and required to report himself here." He would be in Washington with his family for at least part of the year. "I hope he will not come North until the weather is warmer, as I fear his health would suffer. It is quite uncertain how long he will be here or where he will be stationed. Professor Bache was in Maine the last I heard of him." There was reason for her to hope and less to fear for her eldest son in the coming year. It seemed reasonable to expect him in February and that he and his unit would remain in Washington until spring.[60]

Senator Sumner returned for dinner the day after Christmas, uninvited but welcome, which was unlike Frances, who generally found such social presumption rude. "He interests me very much," she wrote to her sister the following week. "I am reading a volume of his speeches on various occasions, chiefly in regard to slavery. He is evidently a disciple of Dr. Channing," the late Transcendentalist theologian, just as she was, "for whom he has great veneration. . . . I doubt whether he ever becomes a politician. His taste is evidently for a literary life and he is homesick enough here." This was not a romance or, at least, it was a platonic one, but it was apparently a mutual infatuation in which Frances and Charles were a principled match.[61]

Chapter 14

Bubble of Ambition, 1852–1856

The years 1852–56 might have been decisive for Henry's career, the culmination of his rise in the Whig ranks and then into a leadership role in the new Republican Party. While the Republicans positioned themselves as antislavery, they were divided nationally on tactics and goals. Again, Henry remained somewhere in the middle, between those such as John C. Frémont, their nominee for president in 1856, who opposed the extension of slavery into the new western territories, and the immediate abolitionists like Charles Sumner. Henry had moved too far and too quickly on slavery for those who supported Frémont and too little and too slowly for the abolitionists. This left Henry on the outside, with the late John Quincy Adams, and looking four years ahead to his decisive challenge for the party's presidential nomination. As for the family, there was also no resolution of the issues that had long challenged them.

George carried his grudge against Henry for his handling of their father's estate into the new year, starting off 1852 with a letter he prefaced angrily. "I wish to bring to your notice a subject deeply interesting to me, but which may not be sufficiently so to you as to lead you to give it any attention or bring from you any reply." That was George's experience with Henry and he expected no change; nonetheless, he wanted his older brother to know that he was courting Julia Humphrey of Tioga

County, and their mutual plans for the future were in abeyance until George's finances were settled; in other words, Henry was holding up their lives. "On other subjects," George continued, "you and I widely differ, and while I trust I have no wish and know it would be vain for so humble an individual as myself to question your perfect right to adopt such principles and views as you may believe to be just and safe for yourself, I claim as a man an equal right and liberty, but this subject and on all that concern me personally I shall claim and maintain it." George did not expect approval of his romance, knowing as he already did Henry's view "that I would be wise not to marry again," which George said was a quotation; Henry simply must, in all good conscience, give up his attempts to "control" his brother. "Has not the time arrived for you to come out and speak as a brother; may I not hope that kindly relations may be maintained?"[1]

In mid-January Willie arrived in Washington, having traveled by train from Auburn alone at age twelve. He began attending his mother's school and dancing classes the following week. "Willie came much sooner than I had calculated," Frances wrote to her sister. "He surprised us Tuesday morning by walking in while we were at breakfast. He seems quite happy here for the present." He had been disciplined for his behavior at his Auburn school, which explains why he left with no previous mention in the family's correspondence. "Poor Willie," Frances wrote to her sister, "will always be one of those who will suffer from misrepresentation. He is frank, fearless, confiding, and indiscreet without doing more wrong than other boys of his age would were the same latitude allowed them. He does it in so open a manner that he can never escape the observation, the malicious observation of those who delight in the shortcomings of others." His mother loyally blamed unnamed others for whatever trouble he had provoked. "That his heart is uncorrupted I have not the shadow of a doubt. He is generous, affectionate, humane, and manly." Finding her children blameless was a nineteenth-century mother's default, where in previous centuries it would have been more common to blame the devil or original sin. Frances was much happier having Willie with her, where she had resumed her role as teacher for both of her children. She now also taught them French.[2]

Henry's nephew Augustus was threatening legal action if he did not hear from his uncle about the estate settlement soon. His letters to both the executors were intended "to say, kindly, but most plainly, that unless some definite information is communicated within ten days from the date of this letter, I shall petition the Surrogate at once, to cite the Executors to show cause why distribution of the Estate should not be made immediately." The letter arrived in Henry's absence, and he had not seen it when the ten days expired. On February 3 Augustus wrote again to Henry, having now heard from his coexecutor, George Grier. "Why did you not send for me to meet out there [in Goshen]? Why have you never consulted me? Does the article of my Grandfather's will which bequeaths a legacy of ten thousand dollars create you a prefect Pope? Your treatment of me is ungenerous; it is more, supremely mean." According to Frances, "The heirs are about as amiable as usual."[3]

Frances's main complaints that winter were the usual ones, her poor health and the frequency of her hostess duties. Sometimes Frances felt that Henry invited men to dinner every night; at other times she thought it was more like once a week; she remained, however, always glad when Senator Sumner stopped by, which continued to be frequently. Ann Stephens, the dime novelist, arrived one afternoon with Francis Daines, the American vice consul to Turkey. The same day, James Shepherd Pike, the *Tribune*'s Washington correspondent, showed up for tea. "We had quite an agreeable evening," Frances wrote to her sister. Henry talked with Mrs. Stephens "while I was entertained by the gentlemen." Best of all, "Charles Sumner dined with us that day." The day after she wrote, their dinner guests were Daines, Senators Davis, Jones, and Sumner, an unnamed grandson of John Quincy Adams, whom she found "rather conceited," which does not help identify him, Mr. Pike of the *Tribune* again, and "five or six members of the House of Representatives." Frances dropped the names cheerily. She left the table at 9:30, when Sumner went home, to read the children to sleep, "after which I went to bed myself, very weary and coughed half the night." She thought the dinner came off well and felt good about that.[4]

Frances was not only entertaining at home, dinner parties that included Charles Sumner more often than anyone else, but also attended a performance by the Hutchinson brothers, singers "who being . . . abolitionists we felt obliged to patronize," and another by Jean Margaret Davenport, an English actress, "who was quite as attractive as when we saw her last winter." She also witnessed speeches in the Senate and House, for which she provided her sister capsule reviews. She was more content in Washington the first spring since her father died, because "when I think of our home without Grandpa, I feel as if my occupation were gone."[5]

At some point Gus arrived in Washington, but exactly when is unclear from the family's letters. He was assigned to the Coast Survey's unit charting the southern part of the Chesapeake Bay. He expected to work on the Hudson River in July, close enough to Auburn that family members could visit him. "Augustus seems pleased with his arrangements for the summer," Frances wrote to her sister. "He is a dear, good child" at age twenty-five.[6]

By May 18, 1852, Frances and the children reached Albany, and she sent Willie and Fanny onward to Auburn in the care of her maid. She lingered to visit Fred; Henry remained in Washington. Four days later, she wrote to Henry from Auburn, "I am again at the home of my father, the home which your love has beautified and which I hope will in time become a haven of rest to you also." Willie returned to Samuel Brown's school, which had an enrollment of twenty boys, including Willie's fast friend Charles Stowe. "Now, though Charlie is not a bad boy, he is exceedingly frivolous and being two years older than Willie, he exercises much influence over him." Frances blamed Charlie for the trouble Willie suffered the previous December, just as she blamed Henry Heth for Gus's disciplinary problems at West Point.[7]

George wrote to Henry in May that "there is an end of all human patience." George had exhausted his. "It appears as you can resist all appeal from the heirs of Samuel S. Seward deceased, that you feel you can treat them and their rights and feelings with impunity. I hope for your own sake that I may be wrong and that you are acting a part which will when explained remove all resentment and complaint." George again drew a line in the sand. "The object of this letter is to inform you of the necessity of our coming to an understanding, of saying kindly yet firmly that we are either to affirm the relation of Brothers in every sense of the word or to become enemies. The decision is in your own breast." Then came the threat: "A further delay until the first of May of a fair and amicable adjustment of my share and rights under and by the will of your father in accordance with what you have promised will result in the latter," and the brothers would become enemies. "From that day I shall take such steps as under the circumstances I may feel disposed to without any reference either to your wishes or any motive of forbearance towards the memory of your father."[8]

In other words, in the absence of receipt of his share of the estate forthwith, George would take undisclosed actions against Henry. There is a surviving note from Henry to George a month later that ignores his brother's threats. In it Henry says that he will ask George Grier to pay for work on the farm's fences that George Seward said was needed. Likely, this frustrated George even more, because it was so limited. On

August 2 he wrote to Frances, not Henry, to inform her of his marriage to Julia Humphrey; three weeks later he wrote again to accept Frances's invitation to visit her in Auburn on the newlyweds' journey home from Niagara Falls.[9]

Frances addressed her father's estate and consulted her two older sons and nephew Clarence, in his work for Henry's law firm, about its disposition. "There are many applications for the purchase of lots from the land left by Grandpa," she wrote to Henry. "We do not wish any more sold from the Burton farm," one of her father's investments. They ultimately split the farm into lots and had small houses built on each of them. The heirs of Elijah then sold the properties and held the mortgages on them. "All our friends advise us to keep it, as it is consistently rising in value. Will you direct that it all remain as it is until you come home." This was not a question but rather a request; she was not consulting her husband on the investments but asking him to act as the estate's executor in behalf of the heirs. "I believe I express the wish of all the heirs." She was concerned about how the unauthorized chopping down of four large trees affected the value of a pasture they intended to sell off in lots and advised her two adult sons on the investment of their inheritance.[10]

In Henry's absence, Frances engaged workmen to install a porch, but that was not going well. "The porch, as they were building it, would be suitable for a building about the size of the Court House, a very insurmountable appendage for a house the size of ours." She was confident of Fred's taste over hers, so if Fred returned home from Albany before Henry arrived, which was likely, she intended to consult him instead of her husband. The same for the walk, which she had already decided "should be covered with the same slate as the garden walks, uniformity in this particular being desirable," but there was still a question of design. Fred dutifully arrived home on July 31 and stayed just the one night, long enough to consult about the stone steps leading up to the street door. "It is not pleasant for me to superintend such work," Frances wrote to Gus, "and some superintendence is absolutely essential." Now that her father was dead, Frances wrote, "how much I miss Grandpa's judgment in such things." When the laborers finished what had turned out to be a monthlong project, she found the work shoddy. The mason had laid the bottom step without any foundation, which meant it was "exposed to the action of frost and would be ruined next winter." Rather than calling him back, she hired someone else to fix it. A week later, the steps still were not done, but men hung the large gate on their iron fence along the road. Frances felt that workmen responded more respectfully to her father, but she now had to handle such matters herself.[11]

Caroline Canfield, the daughter of Henry's late sister, graduated from the Troy Female Academy in July 1852. She planned to live with the Sewards, for now in Auburn with her aunt, but she and her cousin Sarah Seward, daughter of George, intended to spend the winter in Washington. Back in July, Frances had been "rather uncertain whether I shall go to Washington before the adjournment. If we keep the same house another season, I think I shall not go, but I shall go in September to Vermont" with her sister and aunt, accompanied also by Henry, who had a speech to give there. They returned from Windsor, Vermont, through Montreal, then down through Burlington and Lake George. After spending the time with Henry, Frances changed her mind and decided to return to Washington in December. While they were away on their trip, Willie's pony arrived, from where is not clear.[12]

Martha Coffin Wright, one of the regional leaders of the woman suffrage movement and a neighbor of Frances's, called "to lecture me," Frances wrote to her sister, "for want of boldness of which she certainly presents quite an example. She was disappointed not to have seen you and, I thought, received my apology with rather an incredulous air." They disagreed about bloomers, Wright for and Frances against; neither of them wore the loose pants under a shorter dress that fans of the fashion called the "Reform Costume" or the "American Dress," which was intended to make a political statement. The fashion embodied freedom and was more comfortable than long dresses with corsets.[13]

Wright also reported on an argument she had with other neighbors on "the absurdity of keeping the Sabbath." Frances said in the letter to Lazette about the short and testy visit, "I told her plainly that I could not disseminate opinions which I did not believe or such as I thought would not benefit others. She replied to this . . . that she thought the truth should be told at all times and in all places." Frances then "asked her what was her standard for truth if she disbelieved the Bible. She said any man's own conscientious conviction. I told her the Mormons and the Spirit Rappers held the same, but . . . she only added the more warmly that she thought the truth should be propagated. Not having any fancy for this circular argument, I did not prolong the conversation." This was easily the most full-throated argument that Frances ever reported with anyone to whom she was not related. The two women's differences were of style and substance, both of which mattered to them.[14]

By mid-December Frances regretted the decision she had made to spend the winter in Washington. "I cannot come again with such health as I have now." She had her second attack of neuralgia within a month. She was also having trouble with her false teeth at age forty-seven. "I am better today," she wrote to her sister on December 15, 1852. Fred and Caroline were now there and making calls in her place, leaving her calling card as evidence of a duty fulfilled. "Monday, I felt exceedingly depressed all day, not thinking it the precursor of another attack, I thought it was mere homesickness."[15]

Eight-year-old Fanny "had a Christmas party of little girls. They had a Christmas tree and were very happy," Frances wrote to Gus. This is the first time we learn of the family having a Christmas tree in their house. Fred considered a move to New York City to work for the *Tribune*, Horace Greeley's newspaper, and Henry argued "three or four cases" to the Supreme Court as the year ended. Gus was in Baltimore and did not join his family over the holidays. "We will not insist on your visiting any more than you choose," his mother wrote to him in disappointment at the end of the year, but she was also hopeful for Lazette's arrival soon, likely in the company of their boarder, Congressman Schoolcraft. Right before the new year, Henry sent a short message to Gus, who was in New York, which he favored visiting over his family. "Your mother has been very ill and continues so although she has passed the crisis. She needs constant care. I have written to Mrs. Worden to come and I wish you would watch for her at the Astor House, and either come on with her or furnish for her coming."[16]

As the new year began in 1853, there was still no Gus, and Lazette had canceled her visit to Washington in the company of Congressman Schoolcraft, who was at home in Albany and would be returning to Washington imminently. Caroline corresponded with Schoolcraft while he was away, which Frances saw as progress, a sign that she was maturing. Caroline was "very much more reserved since Mr. Schoolcraft has become her advisor," Frances thought. At age nineteen, Caroline was for once listening to an adult, a sensible man thirty years her senior. She traveled home with him in mid-March, but Frances never suspected a romance.[17]

Charles Sumner, who continued to join the Sewards in their home multiple nights of the week, called Frances's attention to "The Affectionate and Christian Address of Many Thousands of Women of Great Britain and Ireland to Their Sisters the Women of the United States of America," a petition signed by 562,848 women in support of immediate abolition. She was unsure how to participate in a reply and hoped that Lazette would advise her against her usual reluctance to take public stands. Sumner prodded her, but "I did not think those suggestions altogether practicable." She now hoped even more for a visit from her sister. "What do you think? I know if you were living here as I am, hearing every day accounts of inhumanity, which often keep me awake all night, that you would think there was little danger of doing too much." Still, Frances resisted any action that she considered "extravagant or unwomanly, because I think such action detrimental to any course." She thought she sent Sumner home "rather desponding" and now she felt on reflection "that I may have been wrong."[18]

Frances returned to Auburn with her children in mid-March. In mid-April Fanny rode the train to Canandaigua with her aunt for a visit of less than one week. "We had as comfortable a journey as could be expected," Lazette informed her sister after they had arrived, "on a train of cars in which we were the only persons who did not smoke, spit, and put our feet on the top of the seats. . . . I have never seen such a frightful set of passengers." When she noticed Fanny's eyes filled with tears and inquired why, her niece replied that she missed her mother, but she was reassured that she would have fun with Trippy, Lazette's dog, and return home on the weekend. "Her face was all smiles again." Lazette's daughter Frances and Trippy met them at the door. "The man of the mansion was, and is yet, in Geneva," Lazette wrote. "'There is at least comfort in <u>that</u>,' as Rip Van Winkle remarked, when informed his wife had died from rupturing a blood vessel." That was harsh even for Lazette. Fanny wrote to her mother too: "My dear mother, Are you better. When I started to come here I was a little home sick but now I am not. Dear little Trippy was so glad to see me." As the month ended, Frances still described herself as "quite ill many days."[19]

In June Frances learned from neighbors that Caroline had been baptized in Saint Peter's, the Sewards' Episcopal church, without informing her family. "It is my misfortune," she wrote to Henry, "to fail to win the confidence of our niece. For her own sake, I wish she would not so outrage propriety." Caroline wrote to her uncle at about the same time, requesting money but without sharing any news; when she did not hear back from Henry, she made the same request a week later. She said that she wanted to visit her family, which she did in July at about the same time Frances heard that Congressman Schoolcraft was about to leave for Europe.[20]

On August 1 Frances wrote to Gus sarcastically, "When you get married, please let me know and be sure to invite me to the wedding, though I will not come unless you wish it. If you look among the departures for Europe in the Atlantic on the sixth of August, you may find the names of Mr. and Mrs. John L. Schoolcraft. Mr. Schoolcraft came to see me on Saturday. He informed me that it was their intention to be married Saturday morning and leave immediately for Europe. . . . Caroline has not been home and has never said anything on this subject in her letters." Frances was angry and hurt. "I am sorry for her own sake that she subjects herself to the imputation of treating us with a want of consideration, which evinces either heartlessness or inexcusable thoughtlessness." Then, thinking better of ventilating her anger in ink, she wrote for one of at least six times in her life, "Please burn this letter," a request that Gus ignored. Frances finally heard from Caroline in mid-September. Frances summarized the letter to Gus as "singularly characteristic. She had a very disagreeable voyage, disagreeable company, no sunshine . . . Poor Caroline. She seems to have seen nothing in crossing the ocean, either new or pleasing." Caroline and her husband were in Paris when she wrote next to her aunt, "and [she] seems much happier than when she wrote before."[21]

Henry and George Grier made slow progress on settling Samuel's estate. Jennings's Gus, the Reverend Augustus Seward, and Jennings's younger son Clarence, received portions of their inheritance in the fall. Restrictions on funds released to George and Polydore still delayed theirs, to George's great frustration, as he wanted the entire amount so he could build a house, but the executors were releasing only much smaller amounts to him for specific construction items, not trusting him with even half of the $5,234.38 that he demanded for the full cost of the structure. Instead, Henry authorized a payout for sand and posts for early stages of construction. George replied that it was not enough. On September 21 Charles Humphrey Seward was born to Julia, George's wife of one year. On October 4 George wrote to Henry again. "I am much too excited to write discretely." His frustration was boiling over again. "At every application almost I make to Grier for money to carry on my building operations, he tells me there is none, and makes use of expressions at least wounding to my pride and as I firmly believe in derogation of my right." He was also angry that Augustus and Clarence had received some of their inheritance before he got his. Nonetheless, the construction continued into November.[22]

Henry was also handling his father-in-law's estate as executor and corresponding with Lazette about her affairs. This was a general oversight of her finances rather than just a solicitation of her approval for plans to sell off some of the property in lots. Interest-bearing mortgages went to the heirs. "I thank you," she wrote to Henry, "for your kind words you write in regard to my money affairs."[23]

The local militia camped out on a training exercise in early October, so fourteen-year-old Willie wanted to camp out too. Frances's initial condition was that his cousin Clarence join him "in playing soldier," but when Clarence took ill from sleeping outside in the rain, Willie persisted alone after changing his wet clothes for dry ones at his mother's insistence. She told the story in a letter to Gus, which she may have intended to make him feel guilty. "I was too much troubled about Willie to sleep and was troubled also with the conviction that I had done wrong to allow him to go, my conscientious convictions being against the cultivation of a warlike spirit. I fear that because you were in the army I have failed to impress these principles upon my younger children as I should have done."[24]

In the late fall Frances met Fred's fiancée, Anna Wharton, who visited over the weekend. She "is not pretty, but seems quiet and gentle," which Frances thought "esteemed desirable qualities for wives in general." She withheld an assessment of character until she had more firsthand evidence, but she trusted Fred, her most sensible son, to exercise his usual good judgment. She and Fred both regretted that Henry was unable to stop in Albany to meet Anna's family, which he did several months later. "I was pleased with her appearance," she wrote discreetly to Gus. "Of her character, of course, I can form no correct opinion. I was too ill when she was here to talk with her much, but if Fred is pleased I shall not be dissatisfied." Gossip had reached her from Albany "that Fred has not been sufficiently ambitious in this connection," but she tried to withhold such a harsh judgment based on Anna's father's profession as a druggist.[25]

On December 15, after a brief illness, Frances corresponded with Henry to show that she was well enough to write a short note. On Christmas Eve Lazette wrote again to assure Henry that Frances was recovering. "She has suffered much during the past week with excessive debility, owing to some little excitement she experienced Sunday and Monday. As she had no return of the pain in her side, I was not as much alarmed as on former occasions when that has been the exciting cause of her debility." Frances diagnosed the malady as neuralgia, nerve irritation, resulting from the "disturbed equilibrium of the nervous and vascular systems," from which she hoped she recovered once she was able "to drive in the open air next spring." For now, though, she was confined to a warm room. Lazette planned to stay in Auburn through Christmas to help with holiday preparations and to nurse her sister. "We are all planning to enjoy Christmas together. Fred is coming tonight and the children's baskets are ready for the gifts of Santa Claus. We are having Christmas weather, too. This morning the thermometer is at ten and the ground is covered with snow." On Christmas Day Lazette wrote to Henry again to wish him a happy Christmas and say that Frances was "not yet strong enough to write. Her nerves, from some excitement last week, are still very weak, though she has none of the alarming symptoms she experienced last winter. I shall continue here until she is better and will write to you immediately if I become alarmed."[26]

Fanny asked Lazette to tell her father that "she had beautiful gifts last night, which she intends to write about in a day or two." When she wrote, Fanny informed her father that they had a Christmas tree. She also listed the presents she and their child servant Matilda received. "I had so many things I can hardly tell you." Fred gave her a book by the author Fanny Fern and presented Matilda a fairy book. "Mother gave me the puzzle of Uncle Tom's Cabin" and Matilda a baby doll. Anna gave both the girls a scrapbook album and others sent them candy. "Willie gave me a little dog and Matilda a monkey." Aunt Lazette gave Fanny a book by Alice Neal titled *Contentment Is Better than Wealth* and Matilda a tea set. "Abby gave me a wax figure and Matilda a village. . . . Mother is not very well." Fred and Anna stayed through the holiday, which made Frances happy. On December 28 Lazette wrote again to inform Henry that her sister was "better than she has been in a week, says she will write for herself tomorrow." Frances wrote to Henry, but not until January 1.[27]

On New Year's Eve Willie came down with what his aunt described as "quite a severe attack of scarlet fever," so Lazette now had two patients and was concerned that Frances made herself sicker by insisting on nursing her son. The doctor consigned the active fourteen-year-old to his bed for two days and then insisted that Willie remain confined to his room for several more, although his "unfavorable symptoms have entirely disappeared."[28]

As 1854 began, Frances believed herself sicker than others did, but she refrained from calling Henry home to her bedside. Lazette returned to Canandaigua briefly, responding to a summons from her daughter, who was in the late stages of pregnancy. "I am confined to my room most of the time by the state of the weather," Frances explained to Gus, "but I am not materially worse than I was last spring. So say the doctors. My nerves are weaker and more unstable, so as to make both myself and those about me uncomfortable. I hope the return of milder weather will benefit me."[29]

Henry returned home for a visit in the middle of January and stayed for about a week. Frances wanted Gus to know that the newspaper reports were mistaken; his father had not returned home because his son was deathly ill, as Willie was fully recovered. On January 25 Frances wrote to Henry, who had returned to Washington, that she had gained strength, "and though I [am] seldom free from pain, when it is not in my head I feel better than I did a month ago." On his way back, Henry stopped in Albany at the home of Anna Wharton and her parents, and he declared "himself pleased with the young lady." Frances had failed to convince Fred that he should give up his journalism career and return to Auburn to practice law when he married. Fred, who was nonetheless concerned about his mother, returned for a visit at the end of the month. Frances was "gaining strength and cheerfulness every day," according to her sister, which was not the same story that Frances told about herself.[30]

By the third week of February, Lazette was back in Canandaigua and considered hiring a nurse to care for Frances; she was home for the birth of her only grandchild, Francis Worden Chesebro. "In the course of another week I can and will go back" to care for her sister, she informed Henry. Again, Lazette contradicted Frances by writing, "You must not leave Washington unless compelled by the most urgent circumstances to do so." Frances wrote to her husband on the same day, "I am just recovering from illness induced by reading your speech Sunday. It was a great and good speech and cannot have a bad effect upon anyone whose brain is in a less irritable state than mine." "The doctor says," Frances wrote, "I must not read any more long speeches, so don't make any." Reading the speeches was hard on her nerves. She also wanted Henry to thank Charles Sumner for his "kind letter commending highly your speech," and the next day she had Fred read Sumner's speech to her.[31]

Henry was again on what Frances considered the right, but losing, side with Charles Sumner in opposition to Stephen Douglas's Kansas-Nebraska Act, which repealed the thirty-four-year-old Missouri Compromise, opened the Midwest to slavery, and led to the violence called

"Bleeding Kansas." The Whigs then split over their approach to slavery; most of them in the North eventually joined the new antislavery Republican Party, and most southern Whigs joined the nativist American Party and then later the Constitutional Union Party. In national politics, it was the end of the Whigs and the beginning of the Republicans.

As Fred later told the story, "May 1854 was destined to be a memorable month in the history of slavery," and his father's speech was equally momentous in the creation of the Republican Party and the coming of the Civil War. Some saw an omen in the total eclipse of the sun on May 26, the same day as the Nebraska debate, which lasted all day. Senator Seward rose to speak in the evening, after the vote. "The sun has set," the senator began, "for the last time upon the guaranteed and certain liberties of all unsettled portions of the continent that lie within the United States. Tomorrow's sun will rise in dim eclipse over them. How long that obscuration shall last is known only to the Power that directs and controls all human events." As he had in his "Higher Law" speech, Seward cast the contest over slavery as inevitable and ultimately decisive. "Slavery and freedom are antagonistical elements in this country. . . . They have been at war with each other ever since the government was established, and that war is to continue forever." Despite the negative outcome of this particular vote, Seward boldly proclaimed, "Through all the darkness and gloom of the present hour, bright stars are breaking that inspire me with hope and excite me to perseverance. They show me that the day of compromises has passed away forever," which he saw as progress. The contest will not be settled, Seward concluded, until the opening of Kansas and Nebraska to slavery "shall be reversed" and likewise "to every other national territory, which will be a Constitution securing equal, universal, and perpetual freedom." Although the antislavery forces lost the vote on that day thirty-five to thirteen, Seward confidently predicted their ultimate victory.[32]

The Sewards learned in June, by happenstance, that Caroline and her husband were back in Albany. In the middle of the month, Frances heard a rumor that the Schoolcrafts were planning to visit them in Auburn, which they did without warning a couple days later, just for an afternoon, but Frances had little to say about it, except that she discussed politics with the congressman. In a letter to Gus, Frances wrote that the Schoolcrafts had "returned from abroad unexpectedly, being determined by the advice of friends and Caroline's health." Frances meant that Caroline was pregnant. She gave birth to a son on July 5.[33]

In October Fred asked Gus to be a groomsman at his wedding. Right up to November 9, no one in the family knew whether Gus would attend the event in Albany. He did not, but he sent a present. "Were it not that the beautiful case of jewels came," his mother wrote to him several days later, "and at the same time the certificate of the Express Office directed in your own hand, I should fear something unaccountable had befallen you." She also wrote to her eldest son that "the wedding passed off as such weddings do. There was certainly as much satisfaction given as is usual in these cases. The house was crowded with guests, more were invited than I supposed." Henry was there, but Willie was not, perhaps because of school. Henry's brother Polydore attended, but George did not. "We were all very sorry that you were not at the wedding," Frances wrote to Gus. She finally heard from him over a week after the wedding and, contrary to her fears, he was just fine.[34]

Chloe Coe, the former slave in Henry's childhood home, lost her daughter, who died a week before Christmas at age thirty-five. Fred shared the news with his father. "Mary was buried yesterday afternoon," Fred wrote on December 20. "They took her to what is called the Harmonia Cemetery. . . . There were two colored clergymen, and some thirty or forty neatly dressed colored people at the funeral. Lewis [Bogart], Robert [?], and William [Johnson] were among the pall bearers." Fred made the arrangements, and the undertaker "did everything with as much attention and propriety as I have ever seen." Henry paid for the funeral and Fred represented the family. Frances informed Gus that "Mary had an apoplectic fit, the result of previous disease. She lived until Monday at six o'clock, but without again speaking, though a few hours before her death she manifested a return of consciousness. . . . Her husband and his family were with her." It was a quiet and sad Christmas in Auburn, with the loss of Mary, Gus headed to Key West, where his team would map the islands and coast, and Henry in Washington. "I do not know what our people at Washington are to do without poor Mary. . . . Your father will miss her greatly. . . . I am much better than I was at this time last winter."[35]

Willie abandoned the study of Latin and the idea of college and looked for a new path in 1855. Six months short of his sixteenth birthday he considered work in a store. Later that spring he declined to attend school in Geneva, as his father proposed. "I do not know how he and his father will settle this matter," Frances wrote to Gus, but as long as Willie steered clear of a military career, she was willing to support him.

Henry headed from New York City, where he argued a case, to Washington, where the "gay season" was about to begin at the start of the new year.[36]

Henry was reelected to the Senate by the New York legislature in a joint session with eighty-seven votes, six more than he needed. "I have never known such a season of rejoicing among the Whigs since your father's first election as governor. They are firing one hundred cannons here, a salute of three hundred was given at Albany as soon as the vote was made known," Frances informed Gus. In Washington Henry received a serenade from a brass band. Lazette returned to Canandaigua to nurse her sick husband and then headed to Washington to supervise closing the house when the session ended. Alvah "had another ill turn" in late April. He remained very ill in July. "He is still confined to his room and most of the time to his bed," Frances informed Gus. "His physicians say that he will recover from this attack."[37]

When Lazette returned from Washington, Fanny went with her to Canandaigua for a visit. "Last night," her first there, "I felt, of course, a little homesick," she wrote to her mother the next day. "Morning has, however, dispelled it, although the sun does not shine." At age ten Fanny remained a precocious writer. She slept in her cousin Frances's "sitting room, where you say ladies receive their particular friends. [It] is Fanny's (mine) now, and I am writing in it; it is very light, has one window and large glass doors opening on the piazza. It has rained hard and a little bird but a moment ago sipped from one of the puddles left by it. There sits a little robin near my parlor window for me to see his beautiful red breast." Later that same day, having received a letter from her mother, Fanny wrote again. "I am sorry you have been sick. . . . I read my testament this morning and said my prayers morning and night." Again the next day, "I am glad to hear that Fred and Anna are coming to glad[den] home with their sunny smiles again." During the night that dawned on April 26, "Aunty and I both dreamed of Mr. Sumner last night. He kissed her, she said. . . . I don't know as I said my prayers last night, but I did this morning and read in my testament."[38]

Willie, now sixteen, wrote his mother a note of only a few lines from Canandaigua in August that his aunt corrected for grammar and spelling. His uncle remained unwell. "Frances and the baby war[e] going to nigh[t] they have shut up there their house."[39]

After about ten days in Canandaigua, Fanny returned home. Then she was off to Albany to visit Anna and Fred, where she made social calls and shopped; she returned with a pink dress, a white petticoat, and a drab skirt. Anna bought her a pair of kid gloves. She stayed with the Whartons. "Mr. Wharton dines or rather eats with a large cat on his lap, who refreshes herself by (after he has finished) switching her tail almost into his tea. We have a little wee, wee puppy here." Willie came from Auburn to accompany his sister home. She was invited to stay longer "but would rather come home, as I don't hardly know what to write."[40]

Frances, despite the effects that guests, dinner parties, and calls had on her nerves, and frequent recurrences of headaches, was planning to return to Washington for the winter on October 15. Within days of her planned departure, Frances received a commitment from Sarah Hance to serve as Fanny's tutor, a recognition that both Frances's and Fanny's health required an in-house tutor rather than Frances continuing as her daughter's teacher or sending Fanny to a boarding school. "I write a full acceptance of your offer without further delay. . . . I regret not staying longer with you and learning more of your views and wishes concerning your daughter." Sarah hoped that Fanny would reply "and tell me what she is reading and studying, whether canary learned to use his new swing and perches and now repays the care of his mistress with sweet songs?"[41]

On October 18 Frances was still nervously rushing around "in all the hurry of packing and shutting up the house." On October 22 she still had not left. On October 23 Willie, who had stayed behind, wrote to his mother that within an hour of her departure, the Irish woman "has brook but one peir of glass sence & cracket two more which cost me 37^{00} cent I hoope that she will not go on queit so fast or my meny will be all gone." He continued to have problems with the Irish housekeeper, who locked him out of the house when he returned after dark. "She is very mad at this time," he wrote to his mother, "because I will not have a carpenter come and make that door large enough for her to go through" and she refused to feed their dog Watch the same foods on the same schedule as the family normally did. "I shall git two or thr[ee] loves of b[r]ead for the dog so so that he can have sum thing but milk I have fed him all of the cake." At least, Aunt Clary was feeding Willie well.[42]

Henry returned briefly to help Willie pack up. He expected Lazette to join them in Auburn, but she wrote on November 17 that "Worden has another attack of hemorrhage," which delayed her departure. Henry left on November 28 and Willie followed him a week later. By November 20 Lazette had given up her traveling plans, as Worden "had frequent recurrence of the same. He is much reduced and appears to me very low." Several weeks later, when Worden's condition stabilized, she returned to Auburn to oversee the Irish house staff.[43]

Fred and Anna stayed in Washington over the holidays, and Anna remained when Fred returned to Albany on January 2, 1856. Anna, Henry, and Fred received callers on New Year's Day, serving "a great many gentlemen, giving them coffee and oysters with New Year's cakes, a box of which was sent us from New York. I was not quite as well as usual and saw no one," Frances wrote to Gus. "I am better again today," she wrote the day after. It was, so far in mid-January, "a winter of uncommon serenity" in Washington, for which Frances was grateful. Anna was "fairly initiated into the gay society, balls, parties, and receptions occupy days and nights." The Sewards had an evening party for one hundred guests. "Of course, I did not see them," Frances wrote to Gus, "though my name was included in the invitation. We had music and some dancing, refreshments, &c, &c." Frances looked forward to Lent, when the number of parties, what she called "the dissipation," slowed down. "There is an occasional party," she wrote disapprovingly in March. Henry planned to host one, which "I hope will be a small one. I wish I could do as Grandma used to, put on my bonnet and go to one of the neighbours until it is all over."[44]

In January Lazette was back in Canandaigua attending to Worden with her daughter Frances's help. Frances Seward did not expect him to survive the winter. In early February a letter arrived from Lazette, which no longer survives, saying that Worden "was failing very rapidly and he would not probably survive over a few days," so Henry took a train to Canandaigua to be at her side. Frances's thoughts "go back thirty-one years, when he was a young man just married, full of hope and health. The retrospect is painful," by which she meant the recollection of him in the intervening years brought no happy memories. Alvah died on February 16, one month short of his fifty-ninth birthday.[45]

A few days after Alvah's death, Frances received a letter from Lazette that described his end. "All day yesterday," she wrote, "I sat by his bedside with his hand clasped in mine. Often, when I put my face near his to know what he said, he made signs that I should kiss him, and I could not but think that the glimpses he had of a better world had removed the mists that hung over him while in this. Now his face has lost that unhappy troubled expression, and a beautiful serenity has taken the place of it." She reassured herself that in death her husband "now knows how much and how faithfully I <u>tried</u> to please him, though

I failed." Frances Seward never considered attending the funeral, but Henry, Fred, and Clary came. While Frances wrote to her sister that "I think of you constantly," she had no words of condolence to offer, except she was glad that Clary was with her. We might assume that Frances did not want to speak ill of the dead, so she said nothing about the deceased and thought her sister well rid of him. Lazette had turned over her Canandaigua house to her daughter, son-in-law, and grandson, and she moved her clothing and furniture to Auburn. Frances Chesebro, at least, missed her father, as she wrote to Gus. "It seems very lonely to me here now. I suppose that I shall become in time accustomed to his being gone, but as yet it all seems very strange. I probably feel it more here than if in any other house. . . . I wish he could have lived longer. Two years ago he seemed strong and well and apparently capable of long life."[46]

Now that Alvah had passed, others tried to plan Lazette's future, but, as always, she set her own course. Frances wanted Lazette to travel with Clary to Washington, where she anticipated remaining for much of the coming year. Judge Sackett, Elijah Miller's old friend, tried to dissuade Lazette from a plan to build her own house in Auburn rather than moving into 33 South Street with her sister's family, which resulted in an argument but not in changed plans. While she was sure that Gary Sackett was correct about the finances, Frances did not blame her sister for wanting a small house of her own. "It has always been one of my 'castles in the air,' which is not very likely to have a foundation on the earth."[47]

Frances prescribed aconite for Lazette's headaches in the aftermath of Alvah's death and funeral. As for her own symptoms, Frances had less hope of relief. "I begin to doubt whether there is any cure for neuralgia in my case, as I consider it only a manifestation of disease, either of the nerves or some other organ." She looked forward to returning home soon, and to Lazette and Clary sharing her house at least for a few months; as predicted, Clary's husband Hugh had chronic financial problems and he now suffered from ill health.[48]

There was a rumor, which Henry confirmed, that Gus's time in the Coast Survey was near an end. As Fred wrote to Gus at the end of March, their father looked for another prime posting for his lieutenant son. "There is a vacancy in the office of one of the captains in the Adjutant General's department," Fred wrote to his brother. "Our father went this morning to the Adjutant General and to the Secretary of War, and made application in your behalf for the place. He was informed that three weeks would probably pass away before the question will be decided." In the meantime, Henry asked Fred to inform Gus and suggested "that you transmit to him an application for the place, in due form signed by yourself."[49]

Fred and Anna agreed to stay a bit longer in Washington, at least through the end of March and the party to which Henry had invited 270 guests in anticipation of the upcoming Republican convention in June. Henry was rumored to be a candidate for the party's nomination for president or, at least, vice president. Frances thought that Henry would miss Anna very much, as she never tired of being his hostess. Before Anna left, Frances sent her to a house that Catherine Beecher was visiting with a note to invite Beecher for a short call. To her surprise, the famous author in her own right and sister of Harriet Beecher Stowe returned with Anna. Beecher had misread Frances's note, which invited her for the evening, when Henry was home, rather than in the afternoon. Frances knew Beecher only from her writings, but she knew those well. "I was prepared to find her very homely," Frances wrote to Lazette, "as that was about all that I could hear of her. I knew from her writings that she had strong, practical good sense, as she has, but I could not talk and she was afraid she might weary me." The strain of society exhausted Frances's vocal chords, so she was literally unable to speak to her famous guest.[50]

Beecher's "book on health has interested me greatly and suggested so many improvements that ought to be made in the education and social intercourse of women that I hoped I might be able to talk with her," Frances wrote to her sister. The book was *Physiology and Calisthenics*, published that year. In the same year her *Miss Beecher's Domestic Receipt-Book* appeared. "I shall have both of Miss Beacher's [*sic*] books by the time you come," she wrote to Lazette. Beecher promised to return before she left town, so she could meet Henry. Charles Sumner arrived with Henry for dinner, but Frances did not know he was there and missed him entirely. Beecher returned a few days later and spent an hour in close conversation with Henry. She said her sister was writing another book, nonfiction about slavery. It was published later that year as *Dred, a Tale of the Great Dismal Swamp*.[51]

There was much discussion in the newspapers and in the Seward house of the new Republican Party's 1856 candidate for president. "I could tell you many political speculations," Frances wrote to Gus, "which it is not altogether safe to write. Nothing positive will be done about the Presidential Candidate until the Philadelphia convention in June. In the meantime, many persons are talked of, a new one about every two weeks." Nothing was certain.[52]

Once Fred and Anna had returned to Albany, Frances felt obliged to remain downstairs with the family after supper. "Since Anna went away," she wrote to her sister the second week in April, "I pour the tea, which is brought into the parlour, and after that play a game or two of whist, the only recreation Henry allows himself." With the arrival of spring, she was again capable of short walks with Fanny, who "carried a portable bench for me to sit down upon occasionally." Fanny had drawing and dance classes. Frances still took her dinner alone, as there were usually guests, but then she joined her family after the politicians had gone. The exception was Sumner, with whom she always wanted to dine.[53]

After numerous additional letters and threats from George and more failed commitments from Henry over the fall and winter, Polydore wrote to Henry in mid-April 1856 to ask that he give George money to finish building his house; George had brought his family to live with Polydore's for what was supposed to be a few weeks and had now lasted four months. Sending the money would "save hard feelings on our part as we want the room." Frances dismissed the brothers as whiners, which likely reflected Henry's opinion. "They want another house," she wrote to Gus, "the new mansion not being large enough for the two parts of the family."[54]

Will, who was no longer Willie except when his mother forgot, returned to Auburn before the end of the month. Much to Henry's displeasure, he had now quit school at the age of sixteen; Frances accepted her son's decision without complaint. He was, at least, in Auburn to oversee the installation of gas lighting that connected their house to the street. There were other repairs to drains, the replacement of broken glass, masons, who were still there in June, and expenses for seeds, plants, and gardening that Will oversaw.[55]

Harriet Beecher Stowe "spent part of last evening with us" on April 16, but Frances had no details to share with her aunt, sister, or Gus. Eventually, she reported only that "Henry thinks her the most agreeable of the Beechers. She was too fashionably dressed for my taste, but that is a venial offence here." Frances had learned from the newspapers that John C. Frémont, the explorer, military officer, and former senator from California, would be the Republican Party's first nominee for president rather than Henry, although she was not sure it was true.[56]

Lazette was back in Auburn and looking for a small house to rent until she could have one built. When Will returned home, he found it mostly in good order, although Fanny the horse was in bad shape after being poorly cared for over the winter. He had overspent on clothes, for which he apologized to his mother. He had just received the bill and "had never expected it was such a large one. I am sure that I could have got along with much less if I had knowen how much I was spending. . . . You may be sure of one thing, that is that I shall never make another one if I have to go without clothes. I am ashames to send it any way." Someone unknown had poisoned the Sewards' dog Watch in Auburn. Lazette tried futilely to nurse him, and Will buried the dog in the yard; this came after someone in Washington had kidnapped their other dog and then returned it after a ransom. "Few human graves have had as many tears shed over them as has poor faithful Watch's," Lazette wrote to Henry. "I write to you instead of Mother, hoping you may open the letter before she sees it, so that you may tell her at a time you think most proper."[57]

Henry was not home and Frances opened the letter as soon as it arrived the next day. "I need not tell you how much Fanny and I are grieved by his loss," Frances informed Gus. "Fanny has cried herself sick." Frances now intended to return to Auburn no later than June 1. "I cannot sleep dear sister," Frances wrote after receiving the news. "I think I have never before truly realized how difficult it is to be a Christian, how hard it is to 'pray for those who despitefully use you.' . . . We both loved Watch too much and I doubt not our spirits needed the discipline this cruel act has given them. . . . I am so glad you and Willie were there. It is better that Fanny and I were not. . . . I choose to be sufficiently heathen to think so much of him still lives somewhere." Henry wrote too, and he saw a silver lining in the awful affair, a vicious act that none of them doubted had political motives. "In other times," he wrote to Lazette, "it would have been the master's life, not merely the dog's, that would have been demanded as a penalty for non-compliance with vicious and barbarous prejudices." According to Frances, Fanny had not learned to distinguish between humans and animals in her attachments.[58]

Frances also had mixed feelings about the ascendance of Frémont over Henry in discussions of the presidential nomination. On the one hand, she thought the plummet of Henry's candidacy unjust; on the other, higher office was the last thing she wanted for him and for them in their turbulent times. She felt restrained, however, from discussing the question in her correspondence, fearing that leakage of her views could damage them both. She thought Henry's brave stands against slavery, especially on admission of Kansas and Nebraska, worked against him, and there was nothing she was prouder of her husband for than his "Higher Law" speech and his consistent opposition to the compromise measures. "Although Henry is placed in an embarrassing position from which he would gladly relieve himself by declining to be a candidate under any circumstances," she finally wrote in a letter to her sister after declining to discuss politics in letters to Gus and Lazette over the late winter and spring, "this his friends or those who so call themselves will not allow." The poisoning of Watch confirmed how bad things already were.[59]

In early May, shortly before Frances returned home to Washington, Charles Sumner consulted her about the speech he intended to deliver advocating the admission of Kansas as a free state. Such readings were commonplace. As Will later recalled, "Charles Sumner was a frequent visitor at our house and a warm friend of my mother. He would occasionally bring one of his speeches for her criticism before their delivery." About this one she advised, according to Will, "Charles, I would leave that sentence out. It will do no good." In a subsequent note she clarified her meaning, which was about tone. "I objected only to the cutting personal sarcasm, which seldom amends, and is less frequently forgiven."[60]

Frances wrote on May 25 from Auburn to Gus, who had arrived in Washington after her departure to inform him of her arrival home. "Our garden never looked prettier. Perhaps it is that my health is better that the season appears unusually pleasant." Lazette was in Auburn with Frances. Henry was in New York. "I some expect Frederick today, if he can get away from the office. It is a long time since he has been home, for him." Gus would have understood his mother's implied criticism of her eldest son.[61]

On the same day that Frances wrote to Gus, Congressman Preston Brooks, a proslavery Democrat from South Carolina, caned Charles Sumner's head repeatedly on the floor of the Senate in retaliation for the speech the abolitionist Republican had delivered two days before without the changes in tone that Frances advised. It was in the heat of the "Bleeding Kansas" crisis, and Sumner's invective-filled "Crime against Kansas" speech indicted representatives of the "Slave Power" by name. "Not in any common lust for power did this uncommon tragedy have its origin. It is the rape of a virgin Territory, compelling it to the hateful embrace of slavery; and it may be clearly traced to a depraved desire for a new Slave State, hideous offspring of such a crime, in the hope of adding to the power of slavery in the National Government."[62]

One of the politicians Sumner attacked personally in the speech was Sen. Andrew Butler of South Carolina, a kinsman of Brooks. "The senator from South Carolina has read many books of chivalry, and believes himself a chivalrous knight with sentiments of honor and courage. Of course, he has chosen a mistress to whom he has made his vows, and who, though ugly to others, is always lovely to him; though polluted in the sight of the world, is chaste in his sight—I mean the harlot, Slavery."[63]

Frances returned to Washington immediately, out of concern for her friend. On May 30 she wrote to her sister that Sumner "continues dangerously ill." She had visited him, but only briefly, as he was considered near death from the injuries inflicted on his head. It was more than three years before he returned to the Senate, as he sought medical advice and treatment on both sides of the Atlantic.[64]

"It is sad enough to think of a man of such physical powers reduced to helplessness by violence which he had no power to resist. What shadows we all are," Frances wrote to her sister. Brooks had clubbed Sumner as he sat in his seat before he saw the attack coming. He then got pinned under his desk, which was bolted to the floor, and blinded by his own blood as the attack continued even after Brooks broke the cane. Someone asked Frances whether she thought that Brooks would be hanged if Sumner died. "I told her I thought he ought to be hung now, but that in the event of Mr. Sumner's death no law would be enforced endangering the life of Brooks. None are punished here but the poor slaves who rebel against their master and for these hanging is considered too mild a penalty." This all seemed to Frances part of the same breakdown of civility that had led to the poisoning of their dog. "I did not suppose anything could make slavery any more hateful to me than it was before, but the events of this winter have deepened that furrow in my soul, and the certainty that we are all becoming slaves ourselves is not calculated to make the grievance more tolerable." She and Henry waited to see whether Sumner's condition stabilized before deciding when to return to Auburn.[65]

In early June Henry was in New York, on his way to Philadelphia for the Republican convention June 17–19, but he changed his plans and continued on to Washington when his candidacy dissolved, maintaining the public posture of indifference. Frances was "very glad to see you view matters in so philosophical a manner. No person can be really independent who seeks political favour." As Henry explained to her his reasoning, "Buchanan's nomination at Cincinnati, by a unanimous convention, rendered the nomination of the preferred person at Philadelphia probably impossible, certainly undesirable." In the opinion of Henry and his advisers, the Republican nomination was not worth winning.[66]

Henry was withdrawing from the internal fight between the antislavery wing of the party and the Free Soilers such as Frémont. They endorsed the limited goal of preventing slavery from expanding into the western states without pursuing abolition, so they were considered more moderate than such Whigs as Seward and Sumner. Alexander Greene, a friend of Frances's from Washington, wrote to her with his analysis. "From present indications, Frémont, a South Carolinian by birth . . . thoughts, and associations will be nominated for the Presidency upon the heart sickening plea that the North must conciliate." On June 12 Frances wrote to Henry that "we are all dissatisfied with the admission of the *Tribune* that it is not yet time to nominate an Antislavery man for the Presidency."[67]

With such analysis of the political situation in mind, Henry wrote his wife a "truthful account of the explosion of the bubble of ambition, and the closing days of twenty years devoted, from the opening of to the ripening of manhood, to the advancement of the cause of justice and humanity. I trust that the record will not be a trivial one, or one destitute of the power to stimulate others." He wanted Frances to know that his quest was done: no more ambition pursued tirelessly. Frances wanted Henry to know that "the prospect of having you at home engaged in occupations more congenial to your true nature than those which now engross you is a very pleasant one for Lazette and I, who both know you well enough to feel assured that you will be much happier here," in Auburn, when he retired from politics at the end of his Senate term. The Democrat James Buchanan defeated Frémont and Millard Fillmore, the candidate of the Know Nothing Party, which was anti-immigrant, in the November election.[68]

Chapter 15

Sojourners, 1856–1859

Frances, among many others, blamed Horace Greeley and his *Tribune* for the nomination of Frémont and the betrayal of the antislavery cause. Greeley and Henry had a falling out over Greeley's desire to run for statewide office in 1854, and the two of them never reconciled. His newspaper opposed Henry's nomination for president in 1856 and again in 1860. "The Presidential nomination was the concluding dash of a cold rain which has pervaded here for some days," Frances wrote to Henry on June 20, after the news had finally arrived, slowed by downed telegraph lines. "The cup of disappointment overflowed when the nomination for the Vice Presidency was announced with the accompanying assurance from Greeley that [William Lewis] Dayton was a 'quasi American.' A tried and earnest anti-slavery man," like her husband, she meant, "would have helped Frémont here, but Greeley's subserviency to the K[now] N[othings] has produced a difficulty. Poor Dennis [the Sewards' Irish immigrant hired man] does not look as if he would smile again. Mr. McClallen [Clary's husband] declares with an oath that he won't vote for Frémont," and her friend Alexander Greene had assured her that he would not "vote for Frémont. . . . I don't think there is any difference between him and Buchanan."[1]

The Know Nothings were anti-Catholic nativists. They coalesced into the Native-American and then American Party in the 1850s. In

1856 they nominated former president Millard Fillmore, who received 21 percent of the popular vote and came in third behind Buchanan and Frémont.[2]

According to Frances, Lazette told Republicans in Auburn that "they need not console themselves with the expectation that you will be a candidate again, as you will do no such thing." Although Frances imagined Henry's pain at the outcome, not knowing he had withdrawn for tactical reasons, and believed it was the party's and the nation's loss, the joy leaked out of her pen. "I wait to hear your plans for the future, impatient for a good long talk." She hoped that he retired before the end of his Senate term, but, at worst, she was looking ahead to no more than four years of political life. "I feel like Grandma that though there is light somewhere, it will hardly get above the horizon in 'my day,'" so she hoped that Henry now rested content that he had fought the good fight and done his share on the national scene. She thought that nominating former New Jersey senator William L. Dayton as the Republican candidate for vice president, over Henry, would lose the party abolitionist votes in New York and elsewhere, so failing to balance the ticket with an antislavery man was both a moral failing and political suicide.[3]

In late June the Miller sisters were too ill to supervise the spring house cleaning of Frances's home. Lazette suffered an attack of neuralgia, and Frances had succumbed to her usual complaints. It was also eighty-eight degrees in the shade, which discouraged them from the annual task. "When our children are gone," Frances wrote to Henry, "I shall try boarding at Aunt Clara's for a season." Clary was now sixty-three, and yet still the family's workhorse even though the sisters were more than a decade younger.[4]

Frances persisted in her efforts to lure Henry home with reports of their garden's beauty, but she failed again. Lazette had selected a site for her new house and asked Frances to write Henry, as executor of their father's estate, to seek his permission "to build a small house for herself on the Little Farm. She has selected a lot on the West side, which she prefers if it will not interfere with others." On July 20 Frances wrote to Henry that "we have been twice to the Little Farm. The lot which you selected is a beautiful situation. I do not think there is a more desirable building lot in the town. The distance from our house and from any other house is the only objection there." The alternative was renovating an existing structure, which was closer to Frances, but if Lazette did that it would make Frances feel guilty, knowing as she did how much her sister wanted to design and have built for her a new house.

In the end, construction started before July ended. The masons had objected "so strenuously to stone and assign so many reasons that we have concluded upon brick." Heavy rain during August slowed digging the cellar.[5]

The sisters were incensed with the *Tribune*. "Does Greeley know what he is doing when he publishes that Charles Sumner is in danger of 'a softening of the brain?' True or untrue, it is cruel to publish it. Can't you persuade Sumner," she wrote to Henry in early July, "to stay away from Washington. I have always apprehended serious consequences from his wounds. Nothing can restore him but an entire freedom from irritation and excitement. . . . I wrote him a note last week congratulating him on his improved health, though I hear so many conflicting accounts that I hardly know what to think. I would write again and advise retirement if it would avail anything." On July 4 Frances wrote to Henry that bells rang and cannons fired in celebration of the anniversary of the nation's independence. "The telegraph from Washington announces intelligence which seems to make the Declaration of Independence a delusion. Where is our boasted freedom if Kansas is forced to become a slave state?" She had decided to be patient and await Christ's second coming, hoping for no redemption from Washington.[6]

Charles Sumner "wrote me a few lines before leaving Cape Island for 'mountain air,'" Frances informed Henry at the end of July. "He says, 'I am regaining my strength, but slowly very slowly,'" and he hoped to take his seat in the Senate during the current session. "Though his physician tells him he will be able to do so, I presume he will not." She informed Henry without comment that she had learned Henry and his friends conspired to lose him the party's nomination, which was a very different story than the one of disappointment that Henry had told her. It all now seemed like a political calculation that belied Henry's claim to have spent his ambition.[7]

Will pursued his future independently, but he did not anticipate the romance that changed his plans. He made his own investments and through Frances sought his father's permission to sell a house that he had built. He intended to use the proceeds to finance a move to the West to seek his fortune. By the end of July he had an offer of $800. Frances supported Will's plan to Henry, even though it would have moved another son away. "He is not satisfied with his present unprofitable life. He ought to have more occupation. Though he is still young, I am not sure but it may be best to allow him to make the experiment. He is old for his years and self-reliant. If he continues here two or three years longer, I do not see that he is to derive any benefit from it and I never had any faith in his remaining longer."[8]

Congress was scheduled to adjourn the third week of August, and Fanny wrote to her father, she said with her mother's support, to ask that he stop at a "fancy or toy store" in New York to buy her "'The Juvenile Theatre.' It comes in a box 10 or 11 inches square. The box and all is paper. Inside are about 20 small poppets with wire to move them by, and wooden stands to set them in. There are back and side scenes, a paper curtain, and small play book to speak from. Mother wishes me to have it. . . . Please give me an answer in your next letter to Mother. We both hope you will say 'yes.'" Fanny would be twelve on her next birthday. At the last minute, the president called a special session of Congress, which canceled Henry's travel plans. Again, the telegraph failed due to heavy rains along its East Coast route. Fanny eventually got her theater, as a Christmas present from her mother.[9]

Frances's preparations for a return to Washington remained hectic through the summer and early fall. The Auburn house was still "deranged" in mid-August from the workers installing fixtures for gas lights. The arrival of Sarah Hance as Fanny's tutor was postponed as a convenience to Sarah, who was ill and needed some rest, and Frances, who was unprepared for the move back to Washington. Lazette wrote to Sarah at the end of August endorsing the plan for her to take another six weeks. "The truth is, dear Sarah, you have confined yourself too strictly to your school duties and I am very glad to know you will have a month or two of rest before you again resume the task."[10]

Lazette also wrote to Sarah now that they no longer lived nearby her, and she looked back on her life in Canandaigua "as nineteen years of discipline, which though perhaps necessary, is not pleasant to remember." She wrote to Sarah that her house "will not be finished before next Spring, after your return from Washington and if we all live. What busy times it will be getting moved and visiting and all that." She would send Sarah her copy of Dickens's *Old Curiosity Shop* the next time she was in Canandaigua, where Sarah's family also lived. Lazette boarded with Clary and the two of them joined the Sewards for evenings of whist while Henry was home.[11]

Henry now planned to sail on September 17 by the *Persia* for a trip abroad, to recoup his health and avoid the presidential campaign. Three days before the scheduled departure, he wrote to his brother George, "I came home from Washington with health impaired so much that I was determined to seek a rejuvenation by a voyage up the Mediterranean.

But the condition of my affairs," which were financial, "prevents and I am here awaiting what time may bring forth of health or decline." Frances was worried, and she wrote to Gus about the canceled journey on September 15 that "I fear his health may be permanently injured by remaining here and working as he has for the last ten months. He is more than usually unwell." She also suspected that the change in plans reflected Henry's continuing ambition for the presidency. "I think Father's change of purpose is owing partly to the advance of the season and partly to the urgent remonstration of political friends." Despite his illness, Henry left for Detroit in early October to stump for the Republican nominees. About a week later, he was scheduled to speak in Cooperstown. He was also double-booked to speak in Buffalo and in Auburn on the same day. He spoke in Auburn and then in Buffalo before giving a speech in Lyons, Schuyler County, and Rochester before the end of the month. In any event, the Republican Party lost nationally and in New York, which Henry's political friends saw as a good sign for his candidacy four years hence.[12]

Fanny, Frances, and Clary arrived in Washington in mid-November. Will stayed behind and instead of moving west began to work in the hardware store of Lumen Barnes. Although he stayed in Barnes's employ for about two years, they had a rough start. Will showed up for work on Thanksgiving and told Barnes he refused to work that day, "to which he said I could not go. I told him that I did not ask him if I could or could not go, but that I was agoing and that was all that was said." When he returned to work the next day, there was no discussion of the disagreement, but Will told his mother, "I hardly think that I shall stay with Barnes three months, but I may do so." He ate Thanksgiving dinner with neighbors, Margaret and Robert Watson and their four children. One of the family members was seventeen-year-old Janet (Jenny), whom Will married four years later. It was likely the romance that scotched Will's plans to seek his fortune out west.[13]

The following week, Will wrote to his brother Fred inquiring about a position in the Albany newspaper office. "I have been thinking some of leaving my place here. I thought I would ask you something about it. Can you tell me any where near what I would get or what I would have to do if I could get the place." It is unlikely that Will's literacy made him a happy match for the printing and newspaper business. "I hardly think that I shall stay with Barnes this winter for several reasons. One of them is that he wants me to work until eleven or twelve every night and also all day Sunday. The latter of which I will not do any way. He is giving me $250 a year and offers to give me $300 if I will agree to stay with him two years."[14]

Instead of responding directly to his younger brother, Fred sensitively wrote to their father instead, enclosing Will's note. He wondered whether his father thought it wise to ask Caroline's husband, John Schoolcraft, to help arrange a position in a hardware store in Albany or whether he should advise his younger brother to stick it out where he was. "I would gladly have him here, but I think keeping or collecting accounts, collecting news items, or reporting would all prove more irksome to him than work about a store, and we have nothing else to offer him. I want to advise him to do whichever will be best for himself, and in order to do so, want you to advise me." When he did not receive an answer from Fred by the end of the first week of December, Will headed to Albany to ask him directly. As there is no further mention of the subject in the family's letters, and no response to Fred from Henry, the question was apparently settled without hard feelings between the brothers and with Will remaining in the Auburn hardware store for the time being. The fact that he continued unhappily there was several times mentioned. Fred also informed Henry that his brother was "employing his leisure evenings in reading Greek and Roman history. He came yesterday to get Gibbon and Goldsmith." His father sent Will an allowance.[15]

Lazette sent Henry bills for the construction of her house, which he paid in a timely fashion as executor of her father's will. This was, of course, an arrangement that he declined or ignored when his brother George pursued the same for himself from their father's estate. Had George known, he would have flown into another rage, but it is unlikely that he ever did.[16]

Clary was eager to return home before her first month in Washington ended, but she had to wait for Fred's arrival so he could accompany her on the return trip. Fred arrived on Christmas Day. Clary wrote to Gus, who was now in Charleston, that the family had all wished he would join them for Christmas dinner but were disappointed again in that expectation. They had all attended the theater on Christmas Eve. Clary and Fred left on December 30, and she expected to be back in her home with Lazette as soon as New Year's Eve. Frances Chesebro arrived in Washington with her son Frank soon after Clary left, so she could help the Sewards prepare to receive guests on New Year's Day. As 1856 ended, Frances reported to Gus, "I am much stronger than I have been in four years."[17]

Will was doing well in Auburn, not enjoying his job but prospering socially. He had not worked on Christmas Day and had dinner with others. “Oh, I nearly forgot to tell you,” he wrote his mother on January 5, 1857, “that I had a present of a beautiful watch seal on Christmas from Jenny,” which was a decorative charm to attach to the chain of a pocket watch such as his maternal grandfather carried. He went calling with other males his age on New Year’s Day. They started at about 11:00 a.m., “and did not get through untill 8 we made about 102 calls which was doing very well for one day I thought.” Will also wondered whether his father could use him in Washington that winter as a scribe, which others saw as another bad idea for him. According to Will, he was still not getting along well with his employer, who “has found out that there is not much use of trying to impose upon me, for he knows that I will not stand it.”[18]

Lazette wrote to Sarah Hance that in Auburn “we are having what the ancient people used to call an ‘old fashioned winter,’ not so intensely cold as it was last season, but steady and unchanging. . . . Years past, cold weather and snow and long evenings were only suggestive of fun and frolic and sleigh rides. Now I have much trouble in keeping myself warm while I sit by a hot stove knitting my grandson stockings.” She had just finished reading Elisha Kane’s book about Arctic exploration. “What a record it is of peril and privation and perseverance and courage.” She wrote from the kitchen, which she found the warmest room in the house. The dogs and cats were “disposed in a fanciful manner around me. Nep[tune] being an outdoor dog is obliged to be the circumference of the circle, the stove is so hot, and the cats with every variety of fur ‘shade off’ from him. The canary is hanging over my head, presenting a tempting lunch for our ‘wise cat’ Minz. . . . Trip and I are going out to look at the stars.”[19]

George made more demands on the executors of his father’s estate with few replies and much frustration. He wrote to Henry from Illinois, where he, his wife, and their child had spent the winter with relatives, demanding that the executors secure them a house for occupancy in Florida come spring, when they made their return journey. He also wrote that he was trying, as a favor to his brother, to convince the people of Illinois that Henry was not an abolitionist. Then, on March 21, whether out of pique or an unanticipated change of plans, George declined to take possession of the house that the executors had secured his family, the very one that he had requested in previous correspondence.[20]

Washington received ten inches of snow in mid-January, which drifted to five feet in some places, according to Frances. "I have seen but two men out and no wagon can pass through these drifts," she wrote to Clary. Henry was unable to reach the Capitol. "We are all shivering with the cold. The snow blows in at most of the windows. Eliza and I have taken up heaps of snow in many of the rooms." The cold brought on another attack of Frances's neuralgia. "I hope we shall all thaw out in a day or two. Invitations have been given for a dinner Thursday. . . . We shall have no mail today." Letters took over a week to get from Washington to Auburn. Henry again planned a trip to Europe, this time in the spring. "Please remind him," Will wrote to his mother, "that he has a son in Auburn that would not object to going with him." With Anna as hostess and despite the cold weather, in which the temperature reached as low as twelve degrees below zero, the Sewards had three dinners and one evening party during January. It was ten degrees colder in Albany. The ink on Lazette's table in Auburn froze overnight despite the fire she had going as late as 11:00 p.m. "Our climate now seems much like that of Canada," Frances wrote to Gus, who was still off the Florida Keys.[21]

When the thaw came, in early February, the flooding resulted in much damage along the Hudson River and elsewhere in the East. No one could cross the raging river at Albany. The Sewards' Washington home had two feet of water in the basement. Anna continued to host parties for Henry during February. There were 140 guests at one on February 10, which included music and dancing. "There are abundance of parties now that Ash Wednesday is so near," Frances wrote Gus. "The fashionable world are greatly pressed for time. Anna has morning receptions, which are largely attended." Back in Auburn, Lazette had invited Will's Jenny twice to tea and "seems pleased with her." Will had decided, since none of his other ideas had panned out, to remain in Barnes's hardware store for the present. Frances talked to Henry about returning home, but he wanted the family to stay in Washington until sometime in April.[22]

The Albany Burgess Corps and the Auburn Willard Guards headed to Washington for the inaugural and wanted to schedule a stop at Senator Seward's rented house to salute him if he was at home. Henry felt obliged to serve the 140 men light refreshments. He talked about a trip to either California or Key West rather than to Europe at the end of the session, "but nothing is fixed for present," Frances wrote at the beginning of March. If the extra session was short, Henry could travel and she could leave for home on April 1.[23]

Charles Sumner arrived in Washington for a few days at the beginning of March and Frances visited him twice in his rooms. "His face is very little changed," she wrote to Gus, "but he rises from a chair with great difficulty and cannot straighten himself for some time, is unable to sit up half the day. Next Friday, he sails for France in the steamer Fulton, hoping the voyage may improve his health. If he ever recovers, it will be a long time yet, though I feel more encouraged about him since talking with him. He seems cheerful and hopeful." He joined the Sewards for dinner. Frances wrote to Gus that "most persons think he is incurably disabled. He is sanguine in the expectation of great benefits or perfect restoration from his voyage and travels."[24]

In February Will had cut a gash above his knee, when an ax he weighed at work fell from the scales. "Dr. Briggs dressed the wound and attended him seven days. By that time Aunty discovered that the wound was not doing well and sent for Dr. Robinson. He made a different application and they think it is healing rapidly. Indeed, Will has been out of the house with crutches. I am anxious to see him," Frances wrote to Gus. Will had written to her to say he was just fine. Seventy years before the invention of a tetanus vaccine, such injuries could end in death.[25]

In early May Caroline's husband secured Will a job in an Albany hardware store owned by Alexander Davidson and Maurice Viele. Will liked Viele, but not Davidson so much, although he wrote to his mother that he had "no trouble in getting along with him." After two weeks, he was "beginning to get used to things here. We have to work pretty late nights at the store." It was a much bigger operation than the one in Auburn and was run very differently, which he thought all to the good, with thirteen employees who "all have all they can do." The spring rush was starting and he expected to work long hours at least into June. Will also looked for a new room with help from Fred and had outgrown his clothes yet again, so he hoped that his father would send money to buy new ones.[26]

"We are getting used to being alone," Frances wrote to Will shortly after he left Auburn and she had returned home accompanied by Henry after the session ended. "Father sleeps in your bed, but your room seems deserted during the day. Aunty consoles me by forming plans for your return and final settlement here. I hope they may be realized." Jenny had not yet called on Frances, but she hoped that happened soon. Lazette's stove was installed in her new house. She waited for the windows to be hung. Clary and her husband Hugh came to play whist while

Henry was home. "Fanny sends 'heaps' of love and says she is going to write tomorrow. We miss you morning, noon, and night." Frances also included some inspirational words from William Ellery Channing, the late Unitarian theologian: "the *greatest* man is he who chooses the *right* with invincible resolution, who resists the sorest temptations from within and without, who bears the heaviest burdens cheerfully, who is calmest in storms, and most fearless under menace and frowns, whose reliance on Truth, on Virtue, and God is most unfaltering" and another quotation in the same vein. Henry also sent Will a check for twenty-five dollars for clothes.[27]

Lazette was in her new house before the end of May, but she still did not sleep there in mid-July because the shutters had yet to be installed on her windows. "She has gone with the three dogs to Pisgah to protect the house from the incursion of boys," Frances wrote to Will, "it being one of the Sunday amusements to visit and mar a new house. Some person is needed there, especially on that day." Pisgah is the Hebrew word for "summit" and appears in Deuteronomy. Workmen finished Lazette's woodhouse and fence; she had a lovely garden and trees, according to Fanny, who wrote to Will that their aunt's "kitchen looked quite comfortable. She sits there all day." Gas lit the Sewards' front parlor for the first time in June.[28]

Henry was in New York City in mid-June, where he hoped to avoid being noticed, "although, of course, I meet everybody." High on his list of tasks was talking to Professor Bache about the approaching end of Gus's assignment to the Coast Survey team. "Of all the men I desired to consult about business for Augustus," he wrote to Frances, "I fail in finding any at home." He received a note from Bache the same day, informing him that "immediately on the receipt of your note of the 14th, I addressed the Department with a view to retain, if possible, the services of Lieut. Seward for another season." Bache would let Henry know when he heard back, but he hoped for a favorable response. Nonetheless, Henry planned to head next for Philadelphia to consult other businessmen about alternative careers for Gus. From New York City he wrote to Frances that "the political excitement here has subsided, and I am quite a harmless person." Nonetheless, he had difficulty convincing anyone that he was in the city on personal business rather than with a political agenda.[29]

Frances wrote Will a congratulatory note the day after his eighteenth birthday. "I thought of you much of the time," she wrote to him on June 19, and hoped to find time to write a line. Fanny was quite ill all day with her third attack of Quinsy. In the evening, Fred and Anna came. "Fred looks quite as well, even better, than I expected, but he is not well. His close application to business is hurting him." Gus had arrived in Auburn, so only Will and Henry were missing for a rare opportunity to have them all in the house, where the carpenters had finished installing new windows and blinds. "This is about the last of the improvements for this season, which is a comforting reflection. I have not seen Jenny since you were here." Still, it seemed to Frances that the work on their home was never done. "I have some doubts about our ever getting our house in order," she wrote to Will. "Neither the carpenters, masons, or painters are done yet." Fanny sent Will a pair of slippers for his birthday that she had made herself.[30]

Henry finally succeeded in meeting with one of the men he wished to consult about alternative careers for Gus. Asa Whitney, a manufacturer of railroad car wheels, was home in Philadelphia and glad to talk with Henry about his son. "After I had explained to him the matter in regard to Augustus, he quite approved of my idea of his going into the iron business and gave me an account of the three or four greatest iron manufactory establishments in N Jersey, Pennsylvania, and Maryland, and offered letters for Augustus or myself to the parties owning the establishment." The largest one was in Morris County, New Jersey, near the old patrimonial seat of the Seward family. As it turned out, several of the men associated with the company were "political and personal friends." Henry proceeded directly to the house of one of them in Jersey City. William Talcott was encouraging. He offered to give Henry a tour and to introduce him to members of their board, who were meeting the next day. After that, Henry proceeded to Goshen to address his father's will. Gus told his mother during a brief visit home that "he would soon be leaving his work" on the Coast Survey but did not know his next posting.[31]

Harriet Bogart, the daughter of Harriet and Nicholas who was a year older than Will, married Henry L. Simpson on June 17. "The wedding came off last Wednesday," Frances wrote to Will, "in a manner very satisfactory to all parties" in Auburn's Black Baptist church. "Every member of our family went. I stayed with the three dogs. . . . The church was filled, about one hundred guests, white and colored went to the house, where they had a supper which Father said seemed to him just like all others of the kind here and at Washington. Aunty made it her business to see that the white guests did not defraud the colored in the matter of eating. Being naturally less polite, some supervision was necessary."[32]

For Fred's twenty-eighth birthday on July 8, the family performed tableaux vivant, in which the guests cast themselves as characters from literature, art, or everyday life to perform for those in attendance. Fanny wrote to Will that the performances "came off in the evening. There were a good many: fortune telling, the rose-thistle and shamrock, Andromache weeping over the ashes of Hector, Red Riding Hood, the love letter, taking the veil, the bride and widow, Rebecca at the well, history, and painting and music."[33]

At the end of July, Henry was off on a trip across the state to Niagara, into Canada, and through Hamilton, Kingston, and on to Toronto, "a large and prosperous town at present the capital of Canada." He traveled with Anna and Fred, and his fellow senator from New York, Preston King, among others. The family thought that both senators needed a restorative journey to recoup their health. Henry sent long letters home addressed to Fanny, travelogues to read aloud to the family. "Tell mother that Frederick has gained five pounds in weight."[34]

In late August, before Henry's return, Frances was off on her own trip with Fanny to Gloucester, Massachusetts. "We reached this isolated place of rocks last evening at ½ six," she wrote to her sister on August 20. Fanny was thrilled that they were served six kinds of bread, "white, brown, graham, Johnny cake, rolls, whortleberry cake," all by a "real nice Irish woman." Frances wrote to Lazette on the same day. "I might throw a dash of umber on Fanny's pictures of couleur de rose, but it is better as it is. We are really very comfortable in our lodgings, having many more home comforts than are usually found at watering places," although they lacked an ocean view. Will and Jenny were with them; Will in the hotel and Jenny with Frances in a boardinghouse on the third floor. "Jenny's health is in a condition to make an anxious mother feel serious solicitude. She coughs much every night, has very little strength with a constant pain in her side and very little appetite." Fanny's face was swollen, but Frances hoped the bathing in her new red suit addressed her symptoms.[35]

Frances reached home on August 29, but Henry had still not returned. Despite Henry's chirping about the invigorating weather, a letter had reached Anna's mother in which she complained about chronic seasickness now lasting for weeks. Henry arrived home a couple days later, to everyone's surprise, bringing with him two puppies for Fanny.[36]

In mid-September Will looked to change his boardinghouse for the second time since May. "I have already been sick twice from the effects of eating spoiled food and the last time it has kept me away from the store nearly a week, although I am quite well now; and went to work again to day; I have concluded that I had better pay the money which I now pay the Doctor and get a little better board. I am now going to board with a Widow livg up in Broadway and if things are half as nice as they look to be (and boarders say they are) it must be a very nice place." He hoped his mother could spare him ten or fifteen dollars so he could buy some furniture. "If I ever have any money I will try and return it but I think it very doubtful. I should not have asked for this if it had not been that I have been away from the store so much this month that I have not hardly draw any pay while my expenses keep on here just the same. I would rather you would not say anything to Father about it and if is not convenient it will not make much matter, perhaps I can get along without it." Four days later he wrote to Fanny that he had moved and his new room "looks out on to the river and the Highlands on the other side. . . . Tell mother that I received her letter this evening and am much obliged." Frances had sent him five dollars and "will send you the remainder if this reaches you." She also wished he would "come home and let me take care of you when you are sick. . . . I shall insist upon your coming home; if your health continues as it now is you ought not to stay."[37]

There was a financial panic in the fall of 1857, which was exacerbated by the telegraph spreading bad news like wildfire. A collapse of Seamen's Bank in New York City lit the fire locally, and banks started to call in their loans. Frances hoped that the uncertainty in the commercial world did not lead Gus to dismiss his father's plan for him to enter the iron industry. "You know how gladly I would have you go into some business here which would keep you near us, but I have little influence in determining others." Fanny sent Gus slippers that she had knitted for him too. Henry was first in Westfield and then Cleveland on business as September ended. Sarah Hance returned and "Fanny commenced her studies rather reluctantly."[38]

On October 4 Will ruminated in a letter about the past year of his life. "It is just a year since I went into Barnes, fully intending at the time to remain there at least a year or more," but he did not get along with his employer and began to look for alternatives almost immediately. "I have been this morning thinking to my self and comparing the past five months which I have spent in business here," in Albany, "to those which I were with Barnes, and I must say this that the balance is greatly in favor of my present place as far a[s] business is concerned, but as for every thing else there is no place like home although that is a thing which I could hardly expect." His problem was no longer the place where he boarded in Albany, as he had no complaints about the new one. While he left it at that, both Jenny and his family drew him back to Auburn. How different Frances likely thought between Will, on the one hand, and his father and brother Gus on the other. Fred visited often but had married and moved close to Anna's family in Albany, where he had his job. Will came home for a short visit after sending this letter, so there is no direct reply.[39]

On a visit home in late October, Will, whom his mother again called Willie in a letter to Gus, helped fight a fire on Genesee Street, where "he came near losing his life by the falling of a wall. Monday night he was ill," Frances wrote, "with fever produced by the exposure, as he came home drenched to the skin." Two buildings burned to the ground; one was Elizabeth Graham's milliner's shop, the other Frank Goodrich's frame and gilding business, where a number of portraits and paintings were lost. In the back of the stores there were apartments rented by "numerous families of the poorer class. One man was burned to a cinder, supposed to have been asleep and intoxicated. The fire was so near us that we took Fanny from the house."[40]

Frances attended church services on the last Sunday in October, "the first time here in five years." Her health, the conflict over her father's funeral, and complaints about the pastor had kept her away, but she hoped that "none of my children will forget that the bible is the truest guide for lives pleasing to God in unison with that of His Son. I find no other which benefits my conscience," she wrote to Gus.[41]

The Sewards invited Henry and Elizabeth Cady Stanton to their house. "I have been long wishing to meet Mrs. Stanton," Frances wrote to Gus. "She is a woman of great abilities, and, now that she has laid aside the bloomer costume, is womanly and attractive, though she still has some rather ultra notions on the subject of the education of women. I should judge her own marriage not to be of the most fortunate kind. It was in opposition to the wishes of her Father, Judge Cady."[42]

For once, Frances had more applications for work than she had staff openings due to the bad economy that led many women to let household staff go. "So many girls have been dismissed from their places that we have constant applications to hire." Henry was again entertaining, a party of forty gentlemen in mid-November, before he left for Washington, which meant he was not abandoning politics anytime soon. "We have had snow here for the last month," Frances wrote on November 22, "except one day. The last week has been Winter in coldness, though we have no snow to continue on the ground. The ground is frozen hard. The last two days the thermometer has stood twenty above zero." When their twenty-year-old housekeeper and Fanny's fast friend, Catherine (Kate) Barrett, arrived in Washington to begin preparations for opening the house, she wrote Frances giving a sorry account of the situation in which she found the house at Washington.[43]

Henry headed for Washington at the end of November, with Lazette to open up the house. "I shall not go until February," Frances wrote to Gus. "I wish to attend to Fanny's studies here," and Sarah Hance was with her in Auburn. Gus went back to Key West for another season of charting. Will "has little work at this time. All business is dull. The poor of the large town are beginning to make themselves felt. I am thankful that with all the pecuniary troubles there is no scarcity of food in the country. It will, I trust, be distributed somehow," Frances wrote. She had several barrels of apples sent to Will, worried whether he had enough work and food. While he did not open one barrel until mid-December, he found the apples good.[44]

Henry stopped in Albany on his way to Washington, where he had Thanksgiving dinner with Will, Fred, Anna, and the Whartons. He attended a performance there by the famed actress Charlotte Cushman, who became a family friend, before leaving for Florida, meeting Lazette in New York, and returning to Washington. Will asked his mother to send him one of Henry's spare overcoats, which his father had suggested. Will found himself "without one and the weather being quite cold it would be very comfortable to have something besides a shell to ware." His mother found no such coat in Auburn. On November 28 Frances wrote to Will that "we are rejoicing in the second day of sunshine that we have had this month." Lazette passed Albany on Monday and met Henry in New York on Tuesday, December 1. Frances instructed Henry to see that her sister purchased "a cloth cloak, a black silk dress, and a new set of furs," charged to him, so she was dressed to fulfill her social role in Washington.[45]

Frances was relieved to hear from Lazette, by telegraph and letter on December 7, that she and Henry had arrived in Washington in time for the new session of Congress. She was also thrilled to learn that Lazette shared her high regard for Kate Barrett, a housekeeper with impressive skills. "Kate must feel very glad to see you," Frances replied. "I agree with you that few women would have remained there as she has done. It was her capacity for just such emergencies that made me anxious to have her at Washington. She has many noble traits of character." This was high praise indeed from Frances for one of her staff. Only Harriet Bogart and Mary Coe ever received anything close to this in her letters.[46]

Frances also now had a cook in Auburn, whom she lavishly praised. This was the silver lining for Frances to the economic panic that left so many household staff unemployed. “Mary does very well, indeed. I attempted the cooking but broke down after a few days, when I found that she could cook much better than I, so we changed work. She is not yet fifteen. Considering her want of an education, [she] is in many respects a remarkable child.” Mary had bought material for a dress with her first pay and was now making it in her spare time. Frances was also pleased with Eliza Freeman, an African American woman whom she had employed in a number of roles for more than a decade. She had “a sort of motherly care of me. She comes up every night to see that I am properly cared for and often stays all night, makes my fire in the morning. Indeed, we are getting along nicely,” except that Eliza was “afraid” of Willis Bogart, son of Harriet and Nicholas, age twenty-seven, who later served in the Civil War and then was convicted of larceny in Illinois, from which Henry secured him a pardon. Willis cared for the Sewards’ horses irresponsibly, but their Irish hired man Dennis Scollins was no better. They both drove the horses too hard, and one of the horses almost choked to death on an apple that Willis had failed to cut in half. “His heedless haste, his utter want of judgement to say nothing of entire irresponsibility frighten me,” she wrote. “I am constantly fearing some great calamity will come in consequence of his recklessness or wickedness, though I am by no means afraid of him personally.” She thought “his conceit prevents his learning.”[47]

In mid-December Will was deeply involved in the annual inventorying of the Albany hardware store’s stock. He stayed overnight with one of the bookkeepers, who was afraid to be left alone. “We are at this present time,” he wrote to his mother on December 16, “just in one of the most dirty and hard things in the hardware business ‘namely’ taking account of stock we have to weigh, count, and mark all the goods in the store even down to the smallest item although it may be nothing more than a paper of ‘tacks.’ ” He was proud that he had caught up on his bills, except for the one to a dentist. Since his mother could not find a spare overcoat at home, he hoped she would send him the money to purchase a new one before he took cold. He had in the past paid $25 or $26 for a winter coat, but he thought that one could be found for $20 that served just as well. Frances sent him $22, “which you may consider a Christmas present.”[48]

On December 23 Sarah and Fanny went to tea at Clary's. "I am alone in the office with the three dogs ranged around the stove for company," Frances wrote to her sister. "I should have gone, too, but could not leave Mary alone with Willis. Mary is making Christmas presents for her folks at home." Frances hoped to remain in Auburn until February, but if Lazette wanted to leave Washington sooner, Frances could change her plans. "It is impossible to leave this place in the care of Willis. He drinks so constantly that I am in continual expectation of some new explosion. He has had two affrays in the street, one with an Irishman, one with a Dutchman. For the latter he has been in the Justice's Court today. . . . It is impossible to control him. I shall try to endure him through the winter if he keeps out of jail."[49]

Gus had traveled to Cuba before reporting for duty in Key West. Neither Fred nor Will made it home for Christmas, but Clary and Hugh dined with Frances and Fanny that day. "Fanny and I will be quite alone after this week," she wrote to Gus. "Miss Hance is to leave us Monday. Her year expired a month ago, since which she has been visiting us." Sarah wrote Frances to say she had reached home safely on New Year's Eve. She took a new job as principal of a school in Palmyra. The weather over the holiday in Auburn had been "more than usually mild" with some snow, but not enough to sleigh. "We always wish you with us Christmas," Frances closed her letter to Gus wistfully. Lazette wrote to Will that she hoped he spent New Year's Day with his mother and that she planned to leave Washington immediately after helping with the preparations and entertainment for that celebration.[50]

Will arrived home on the last day of 1857, as his mother had requested. Fanny had a small gathering of girlfriends to welcome in 1858. The family postponed their New Year's Day dinner for twenty-four hours so those in Auburn could all be together. Lazette left Washington on January 11, having had all the socializing she could take. When she reached Auburn, the sisters had a four-day visit before Frances and Fanny left. Will accompanied his mother and sister from Albany to Washington, which they reached on January 22, at which point he returned so he did not miss too much work. Henry had sent for Anna to replace Lazette and then Frances as party planner and hostess; she arrived with her parents in early February, but Frances and Fanny stayed and Anna remained until the end of April, when she returned to Albany to oversee renovations to her and Fred's new house. In the meantime, Fanny attended a ball and commenced French and dancing lessons, but Frances did not find a suitable music teacher for a couple of months. The commitments she made to Fanny's teachers in Washington would end in late May.[51]

Charles Sumner again passed through Washington to vote on a bill. He stopped to visit Frances, who found him "less near entire recovery than he imagines himself to be. His face is unnaturally full and flushed." Gus expected to be transferred, but his father's intervention assured his stay in the Keys at least until spring. Frances hoped Gus would "come home and perhaps find something more agreeable to do than fighting with the Mormons." She continued through February and March to fear Gus would be sent to Utah, where his regiment now was. He came for a visit in Washington before she left for home in May; spring cleaning was completed at 33 South Street in mid-June. Frances expected Henry after the session ended in late June, but he had business along his route, including a stop in Florida, where his brothers continued to press him for settlement of their father's estate. George was "not pleased or satisfied with the course Mr. Grier pursues" at Henry's bidding. "Will you have the kindness enough," he solicited Henry, "to indicate to me your own wish or design." Polydore simply asked Henry to formally designate a burial place for his brothers in the family vault or nearby. Henry had promised him more than a year ago to attend to the matter but apparently forgot.[52]

Will had to change his boardinghouse again as his landlady was leaving Albany. He was not pleased that Mrs. Watson contemplated sending Jenny to school in Philadelphia. Frances wrote to Will when she heard what was up, taking Mrs. Watson's side in the dispute. "Jenny thinks you prefer that she should not go. I think if this is so, my child, that you are unwise. Jenny is not likely to be spoiled by a boarding school and if her health will admit of her giving her attention to one or two studies, it would be an advantage to her, which you will not regret later in life."[53]

By late September Frances had heard that Jenny was homesick at her new school. "I hope it is not to last," Frances wrote to Will, "for continued homesickness is very depressing and will prevent any benefits from change of air. I shall go and see Mrs. Watson and inquire about it." Will had heard from Lumen Barnes that he was considering selling his hardware store in Auburn, which Will thought would be a great opportunity for him. He expressed doubt to his mother whether Henry would back him financially in such an enterprise, and he was right that his father did not.[54]

At the end of October, Fanny had new puppies and Frances planned the family's return, puppies and all, to Washington. On November 1

Will announced in a letter to his mother that he had decided to quit his job and go to Washington to work for his father, if his father approved of the plan. "By being with him I shall at least acquire some knowledge of other business, which opportunity is not afforded me here. In taking this step I hope I am acting for the best and not in opposition to Fathers wishes." He realized that his decision might appear hasty, but if he was to accompany Frances on her journey, he should give his employers as much notice as possible.[55]

For some reason, now lost to us, the Sewards rented a different house in Washington, on F Street between Thirteenth and Fourteenth, very close to Willard's Hotel, which required some additional furniture and renovations. There was a bedroom for guests on the third floor in addition to the ones occupied by Kate Barrett and Anna, and the one shared by Nicholas and John. "We have just one room less than at the other house," Frances wrote to her sister, "much less pleasantly arranged but tolerably comfortable except those large halls, which are perfectly dark except that on the first floor, which is only lighted by three panes of glass over the side door. The house is pleasantly built and common in appearance on the outside." Fanny thought she had "a very nice little room." Fanny had kept Bell as her new dog and gave the other puppy, named Victoria, to her friend Mary Titus, "who has made a great pet of her." According to Frances, "Bell is a very boisterous little dog. Without room in the yard and without a playmate he reserves all his exercise for indoor employment and is always tearing some person or thing to pieces." In a postscript to her letter to Sarah Hance, Fanny included the news that on "Thursday I will be fourteen years old."[56]

Maria Freeman, a thirty-four-year-old Black woman who had worked for Frances since coming to her as a child, died suddenly back in Auburn, leaving behind her husband James and several children. "It is sad to look back thirty-five years," Frances wrote to her sister, "to the time when the helpless baby was left without a mother and it seemed to me then, thrown upon my care. That I have failed to do my duty by her in some way I doubt not, though the darkness in which we grope does not now enable me to mark the deficiency. May God take care of her now." Maria and James had long abused alcohol according to Frances, and Maria's death came so suddenly that there was a suspicion it might have been suicide. Mary, who was born before her mother's marriage to William and also worked for the Sewards, was twenty-two. "Mary has so long shared the care of the children that her duties will not materially increase. Still, she is but a child herself and I fear will not be able to manage them very well." Henry thought that Mary's younger siblings should go either to the orphan asylum or the alms house, but Frances disagreed. "The first will not be likely to take a family and the second is but one avenue to a life of crime. When is there to be a place provided for destitute children, where they may be made comparatively industrious. Until such a place is furnished, vice and crime must abound." To Lazette, Frances wrote, "I hope you drew money on Henry's account for the funeral expenses."[57]

Frances wrote letters to Lazette and Gus on Christmas Eve. Lazette celebrated the holiday in Canandaigua with her daughter and grandson. Gus was back in the Florida Keys. She finished the letter to Lazette the next day: "Christmas morning. I hope you may have a 'happy Christmas.' When will you ever spend this day with us again?" Fanny and Kate went to church. "Bell and I are at home enjoying the bright sunshine." Fanny and Will read Washington Irving's *Life of Washington* out loud together. "Maria's family get along pretty well so far."[58]

New Year's Day 1859 brought the usual onslaught of visitors, who may have been disappointed to find that with Mrs. Seward in Washington this year, there was no alcoholic punch. "I think the guests have been more quiet in consequence of this omission," Frances shared with her sister, "and some of the visits much less protracted." It all started about noon, and it was 3:00 p.m. when she wrote, "Still they come, a few ladies, not many." Fanny and Henry were out making calls, but not together, and Will, "who comes up occasionally to take breath," helped at home. "The box of New Year's cakes is reduced to half of the last layer. Kate superintends." Frances sent Lazette the first volume of Irving's *Life of Washington* when Fanny finished. Frances was upstairs reading one of the four remaining volumes, all of which she completed before the third week of January. "It is very interesting. I think Clara would like to hear it. It is by far the most clear and comprehensive account of the Revolution that I have ever seen. . . . There are so many accounts which remind of events told us by Grandma." At the end of the day, Henry thought they had received about four hundred callers.[59]

Henry and Will spontaneously invited some people over on January 3. "I did what I could to help entertain them," Frances wrote to her sister. "It was very little, but enough to exhaust such strength as I had and so discomposed my nerves that I sat up alone some time after all had retired for the night." Anna arrived with Fred on January 6 to serve as hostess. "It was a great relief to me to have Anna come," Frances wrote to Gus. "Father was in a hurry to commence a series of dinner parties, of which two have now passed [on January 22] besides the usual amount of company at other times." Will slipped and fell while running an errand for his father, "sprained his knee, partially dislocating the joint." Nonetheless, he limped around helping prepare a dinner for twenty. "Of course, it was much more swollen and painful that night. It is better now." Will walked without a cane and even went dancing before the end of the month. Frances had a bad cold that "keeps me much of the time a prisoner in my room," where she had now read "A House to Let," which was coauthored by Charles Dickens, Wilkie Collins, Elizabeth Gaskell, and Adelaide Proctor, and had appeared in the Christmas edition of Dickens's *Household Words* magazine. "Very good it is," Frances thought. "I wish Dickens had not quarreled with his wife and acted like so many other men." She, like others, thought he had left his wife of twenty-two years for the actress Ellen Ternan, who was twenty-one years his junior. Some modern biographers believe that Ellen was his illegitimate daughter. On Anna's reception day, when she received callers, Frances watched the carriages come and go from the third floor, where she and Fanny had "a quiet time of our own."[60]

Frances was concerned about a tumor on Clary's breast, so she consulted a homeopathic physician in Washington who had never seen the patient in question. He assured Frances that her aunt's tumor was not cancerous based on her description and prescribed small doses of several homeopathic remedies. "He says he has cured by homeopathic medicine two or three tumors in different stages of progress, which were pronounced incurable cancers by other physicians." Frances learned that Gus was promoted to captain, but she still hoped he would leave the army in the spring. She wrote to Clary with the prescription on February 26. In rotation she was to apply four globules of carbolic acid to the tumor. That was followed by a dose of conium (hemlock), then one of clematis and another of silica (horsetail); at least the last two would likely do no harm and the silica might even help. The first two are highly poisonous. Clary should continue this cycle for a month, "occasionally omitting one or two days." Frances assured her aunt that Dr. Jayne "insists that it is not a cancer" based on Frances's description. "The Dr. says about one in three thousand of the tumors which women have in their breasts are cancers. Does not think yours a cancer, says that all tumors may be dispersed by proper remedies, and that sometimes they are reabsorbed by an effort of nature alone. He considers it entirely unnecessary even to have them removed by a surgeon." Frances purchased and sent the remedies to Clary.[61]

On February 9 Henry had a dinner party for ten and two days later for twenty. "As the time of departure of the Congress draws nigh," Frances wrote to Lazette on February 9, "he thinks it necessary to have them more frequently. Anna is out today with cards for next week's dinner," the third in two weeks. "Poor Preston King," New York's other senator, "goes to so many dinners and parties, and grows so obese that he cannot keep awake, so he goes to sleep sometimes at the table, sometimes on a sofa with the women all about him. Anna always wakes him up, of course." Will managed preparations for a ball on February 17, which his father threw in honor of Lord and Lady Napier, who were departing for their next diplomatic assignment in Florence. "He continues to dance with his knee a little stiff yet, looks and seems well. He would like to have Jenny at the ball." To Lazette she wrote, "Will has had so much to do for a few days past that he looks quite care worn. I hope the ball will be a success but I think there is a chance of the reverse. However, that is entre nous." Three days after the event, she wrote to Lazette that "the ball went off successfully, everybody went and everybody seems pleased."[62]

Fanny was ill in mid-February: "her cough continues and she seems less strong than formerly"; she had missed many lessons over the winter due to illness. "Constant interruptions and the dissipation of time consequent upon our mode of living prevent any methodic course of study for Fanny, which is about all that I attempt with any degree of success." Frances hoped to engage a new tutor, but their uncertain departure date for Auburn made that difficult. Frances expected to return home in early April but could not be sure whether it would be sooner or later than that. She was also ill on the day her family hosted a dinner and the ball. "I was confined to my bed all day with fever accompanying this influenza, which I have had nearly two weeks."[63]

In the beginning of March the family still wondered where Gus would be sent next, but Henry thought not to Utah based on conversations he had with people in the War Department. Gus thought his promotion to captain was linked to the death of one in his regiment, so he was sure he was going to Utah. Gus was correct.[64]

Congress adjourned in early March, which relieved Anna of her hostess duties, so she left for Albany on March 6. There she reunited with her husband in their new home. Tragically, her sister Susy (age eight) died, "very suddenly," perhaps of a heart condition, five days after Anna arrived.[65]

Hugh McClallen was in deeper financial distress than usual, so Frances suggested that he sell their house and Clary move back into 33 South Street with her, but that did not happen. "Henry and all the children wish you to go there as well as myself. Everything is so uncertain about our movements that I do not pretend to look forward a year. I could make no calculation, even had I health, to be useful anywhere. As it is, I feel that I am only a sojourner for a season." This was apparently intended to make Clary feel needed rather than dependent, to assuage her pride, but was also true to Frances's beliefs about herself. "I enclose a check for $25," Frances signed off.[66]

The Sewards left Washington on March 29. Frances reached Auburn by April 2 with Fanny and Will. Henry traveled alone on a different route but arrived in Auburn on about the same day as the rest of the family. One month after they arrived home, Henry was again gone, this time to Europe again.[67]

Chapter 16

Launch, 1859

The *New York Times* reported Henry's send-off for Europe on May 7, 1859: "Among the passengers by the steamer *Ariel*, on Saturday, for Southampton, was the Hon. William H. Seward, who has gone on a visit to Europe to recruit his health, and, as he has publicly stated, in order to study the institutions and people of the Old World, that he may be the better prepared to labor for the benefit of his own native land." Fred and Anna were the only family members, but there were "friends," according to the senator, to bid him adieu.[1]

A committee of New York's Republican worthies greeted him at Manhattan's Astor House and proceeded to the *Josephine*, which they had chartered with his full knowledge for an orchestrated display of affection, despite, he claimed, his "resolute and persistent endeavors to avoid a show." As Henry wrote to Frances that morning, "I am to be met at the door of this hospitable house at ten o'clock by hundreds of citizens and escorted beyond the gates of the ocean by thousands of friends. There will be no lonely place, no leisure moment to take leave of you. I must do it now." In addition to the two hundred Republicans on board according to the newspapers, three hundred according to Seward, there was a band playing "a variety of lively airs" loudly, as well as "Auld Lang Syne" and "Sweet Home."[2]

'Mid pleasures and palaces
Though I may roam
Be it ever so humble
There's no place like home

Home! Home!
Sweet, sweet home!
There's no place like home
There's no place like home

"Home Sweet Home" was first performed in London, in American lyricist John Howard Payne's 1823 opera *Clari, or the Maid of Milan*. Englishman Sir Henry Bishop wrote the melody. In 1852 Bishop "relaunched" the song as a parlor ballad, at which time it became extremely popular in America, which explains the Seward family's copy of the sheet music for piano. The song was to be a favorite among both Union and Confederate troops during the Civil War. The song was actually banned in some Union camps for fear it would incite desertions.[3]

As we know from previous chapters, never were a song and a man more mismatched than "Home Sweet Home" and Henry Seward, who was always restless during his ever shorter and less frequent returns to the family homestead. He missed more Christmases than he made when his children were growing up; he acknowledged few birthdays and no anniversaries; and births, deaths, weddings, funerals, celebrations, and solemnities went on without him. Henry was always leaving.

Once in the harbor, a second steamer, the *Alida*, carrying hundreds of Brooklyn Republicans joined the party, "guns firing, bells ringing, handkerchiefs waving, flags flying, and people cheering." "I don't think I ever saw so grand a procession," Fred wrote to his mother the next day. "It was a scene and an event never, never to be forgotten," Henry wrote to Fanny. "The best possible good humor prevailed" as they sailed toward the Narrows at about 11:00 a.m. Refreshments were served; jaunty tales were told; it was a celebration of New York's favorite son and presumptive Republican nominee for the presidency. All were elated by the prospects for victory in the fall of 1860.[4]

At the Quarantine Landing, a mandatory stop for arrivals in an age plagued by cholera, in which smallpox had not yet been eradicated despite an effective vaccine invented in 1796, the health officer saluted Seward as the flotilla passed. "The Senator appeared in excellent spirits, and amused his friends greatly by his playful humor and anecdotes."

One was about a town in western New York, "where the people were all zealous Republicans except one man, and he was under conviction," meaning that from a sense of guilt and shame he had vowed to change. Not hilarious even then, perhaps, and the story translates badly to us, but a jab at the evangelical base of the Democrats, which resisted science and enlightened change such as abolition and vaccination on conservative, high moral, even biblical grounds.[5]

At the Southwest Spit, Seward's friends insisted on a speech, the first of two he modestly declined and then delivered from a settee, which helped raise the 5'6" politician to a height more befitting his stature. "It would, of course, be impossible," he began, "for me to convince you that I am insensible to the manifestation of such hospitality and friendship as I am receiving at your hands. I will, with your leave, however, undertake to interpret it, leaving out all its political bearings and relations, and will regard you, not as politicians, not as Republicans, but as fellow-citizens and as friends, who, against my will, followed me."[6]

If you leave out the sendoff's "political bearings and relations," though, you understand nothing about it; if you think it was against his will, you are wrong. The crowd cheered for "Governor William H. Seward, the next President of the United States." Preston King, New York's other US senator, introduced him as the Republicans' "next candidate," offering his opinion that Seward and "the principles he represents must and will prevail."[7]

It was a day of conventional modesty, a habit that survived from earlier times. Politicians served; they denied ambition; they sacrificed their own interests for the public good, or so they said. Men worthy of the position did not campaign for president. Seward sailed east to gather "the knowledge which I may derive from the sufferings of humanity in foreign countries, in order the better to labor for the elevation of my own countrymen. I will only say, gentlemen, in expressing my thanks to you, now that we are at the point of separation, that I trust it may be my good fortune to return amongst you and resume the duties now temporarily suspended in the great cause of freedom and humanity." He had no greater ambition than to continue to serve in the US Senate, in the office to which the New York state legislature had twice elected him in joint session. This was the political dance and Seward a *danseur noble*.

When Seward's steamboat approached the ocean liner, crew members lowered a ladder and he stepped on board, where the ship's officers and fellow passengers gathered to greet him. "The huge wheels of the *Ariel* slowly began to revolve, and she resumed her outward voyage. But the enthusiastic friends on the little steamboat were yet unwilling to part. Again and again they made the captain run up within hail of the *Ariel*, for one more parting cheer."[8]

From Sandy Hook, Henry wrote a last farewell to his wife, seizing an opportunity presented by a solicitous pilot who offered to post a letter for the senator on returning to shore. "The hordes of friends with Frederick and Anna dearest of all have left me after an ovation worthy of a Congress," he wrote to Frances, whom he knew was anxious about his safety and doubtful of the trip's necessity. She might also be angry, but she always had forgiven him for abandoning the family. He could be sure that Frances found his two explanations for the trip, his health and public duty, unconvincing. The band on board the *Josephine* continued to play "Yankee Doodle" until the departure scene ended at about 5:00 p.m., a full seven hours after it had begun at the Astor House, with the *Ariel* passing over the horizon and Seward's supporters returning to shore.[9]

Even the choice of the ship on which Seward sailed was a political calculation, but not *just* strategic. It was not one of the luxury liners but a more modest ship befitting a man of the people. Several days before the departure, Seward had written to Will that "she is considered a safer vessel than either of the Cunard steamers. She is as yet unknown in this trade and relatively to the Cunard ones a smaller vessel. I like her all the better, for she will not be crowded with frivolous people." He explained to Fanny that "the party onboard this ship consists largely of Germans and Frenchmen adopted by our country and returning to visit their relatives in their native lands." To Frances, Seward emphasized safety: "The sky is bright and the waters are calm. The ship is strong and swift. The season of storms is past. There is every reason to hope for a prosperous voyage." Still, there were risks and leave-taking was called for: "If I come back to you no more doubt not that whenever and wherever I taste of death my last thoughts will cling to the memories of yourself and my children. Adieu. Your own Henry."[10]

The *Ariel* was at best a second choice for the passage. In early April Henry and Thurlow Weed had not yet decided whether more speeches delivered in America or letters sent from abroad and edited for publication in Weed's newspaper were a better campaign strategy; other newspapers would pick up the stories after Fred and Weed published them. On April 7 Henry responded from Auburn to Fred's inquiry about summer speaking commitments, "It is quite out of the question. I cannot speak anywhere this summer. I would at Albany if anywhere."

The original plan was free passage on the *Vanderbilt*, gifted to Seward by the ship's owner and namesake Cornelius Vanderbilt. "The Commodore," as he was known, was the richest American ever and one of the wealthiest men in the world. He had long been generous to Seward and other politicians with free passage on his railroads. Weed thought there would be an April 30 departure, but the ship left New York on April 23, before Seward could get there, which required them to cancel or make other arrangements. According to Fanny's diary entry of April 26, "Father is decided to go in the 'Ariel,' his passage is taken. State room 59 on deck, next to the Captain's."[11]

Henry left Auburn on Saturday, April 30, for the departure one week later. First, though, Fanny crocheted her father "woolen shoes. They come to the ankle, button up the front, and have a scalloped maroon colored border, also crocheted maroon soles. I have not yet given them to him," she wrote in what was her first diary on April 27. "I think continually of his approaching departure. May God protect him, and restore him safe and well to us!" Frances had committed Fanny to a sleepover at her friend Ellen Perry's the night before Henry's departure, but Fanny canceled with her mother's permission, wanting to spend the last evening with her father. "I asked Father if he would play whist, his favorite amusement. He said 'yes' and I prepared the table. As usual, he played with me. Augustus and Mother were our opponents. They beat once, and we once. Dear, dear Father."[12]

Saturday morning, "I gave the sleeping shoes to father. He asked if I made them and said they were 'just the thing,' and amply repaid me with a kiss." Fanny "cut about 109 sheets of soft paper for his shaving book and then went out to buy him a brush and comb." She also made him lunch for the train—maple sugar, cheese, an orange, coconut pie, and raisins—and household staff prepared him more. At lunch, "old Neppy," the family's dog Neptune, "crawled under the table and stayed close to his feet. He seemed to know that he was going." At the table her father gave Fanny "a little gold dollar. How carefully shall I treasure it for the sake of the giver." Fanny, among others, rode the train to the first stop, which was Skaneateles, before bidding her father a tear-filled goodbye. Her brother Gus escorted Fanny off the train. "I was determined," Fanny wrote in her first diary when she got home, "that when he last saw my face I would smile, but every time I looked at him I burst into tears. At last, as he went, I was able to smile, but very tearfully. How kindly, sad, and compassionate was his dear face." Fanny was unable to eat dinner when she got home, "but gave unrestrained vent to my tears, after which I felt much better."[13]

By May 4 Henry was in New York City and on his way. To his son Will, he wrote, "I received your mother's letters last night, two of them, together with three from Lord Napier and Mr. Hamilton. The latter have determined me to stop in London for perhaps a week, long enough to organize my plan of travel on the continent." Napier was a diplomat and Hamilton a businessman. According to Fred, Seward "found himself free to accomplish a purpose he had long cherished, but hitherto had found no time for. This was to make another visit to Europe." Just a coincidence of unanticipated free time, which admits no political motive. "There would be now an interval until December, during which he could visit many of the European capitals," but to what end? "As his former trip, in 1833 had been chiefly devoted to the study of places, he desired now to study the people, to inform himself in regard to the condition of the masses, the character of rulers, and the working of governments, in the principal countries of Europe."[14]

As it turned out, there was little mixing with the masses and much hobnobbing with aristocrats, royalty, and political leaders, who were eager to meet the man they expected to be the next president. In retrospect, some said that Seward and Weed miscalculated, that the senator should have stayed home to campaign rather than leaving the field open to competitors in his absence, but he was too well known to alter fixed views about him and had already hit his ceiling of support within the Republican Party. As his family well knew, he had campaigned for decades. There was also nothing he could do about the convention being in Illinois, the home state of another candidate.

On the day of the ship's departure, Fanny and her mother heard by telegram from Fred that "at noon, my dear Father left his country. Heaven preserve him!" Onboard the *Ariel*, life quickly slid from celebratory to lethargic with twelve days of ennui, punctuated by seasickness, looming ahead, especially for the weak-stomached and inexperienced travelers who did not know to avoid alcoholic beverages and heavy foods consumed in quantity. Henry's last transatlantic journey, twenty-six years earlier with his elderly father, had been very fast for the days of sail, only eighteen days, and this one was faster by almost a week. He remembered and lived accordingly, while offering his voice of experience to those inclined to consider advice from the only famous man on board.[15]

In 1859 the weather cooperated for a smooth journey with no icebergs or other ships threatening the *Ariel* on dark nights and foggy days. "The sea is as calm as a river," Henry wrote on the second day out. "Our passengers are generally beginning to recover from their sea-sickness and to appear often on deck," he shared on May 12. They cleared the fishing banks off Newfoundland that day, so they saw fewer fishermen and more icebergs.[16]

"The chief difference between life on land and life on sea to the passengers," Seward wrote home, "is that the former is filled up with activity. The latter sinks into a monotony of indolence, and indolence gains power by habit and it produces lassitude." The ship averaged 10.5 mph through day three. "We are now about 700 miles from New York," he reported on May 10. "I have tried those beautiful socks which you made for me," he assured his daughter on May 11. "The ship's literature is not of high pretension," he wrote the next day. "Guidebooks, travels, and yellow covered pamphlets constitute our libraries and truth to say, life onboard ship generates an ennui that can endure nothing more severe." "At noon today we enter in the 7th day of our voyage, not quite half way across the Atlantic," Seward wrote on May 13. The days must have seemed endless to him, one of the most active of men onshore. He counted the miles: "Sixteen hundred and seventy-seven miles traversed, and a waste of fourteen hundred and seventy-three miles yet intervening between us and our destination," he wrote on May 14. The ship had a device that counted rotations of the steam-driven wheels, which could then be converted into nautical miles.[17]

There were problems with Henry sharing his thoughts by mail. The principal danger was publication of excerpted comments by hostile political forces within and without the Republican Party. Within the party, the concern was whether he was too liberal, too hated in the South, and possibly too much of a politician to suit the tastes of many voters; less moderate, inconsistent, and too much better known than candidates from Ohio and Illinois, Salmon P. Chase and Abraham Lincoln. Democrats would welcome ammunition to portray Seward as an immediate abolitionist, which he was not; an internationalist rather than a nativist, which he was; opposed to the fugitive slave laws and the extension of slavery to the West—true; soft on immigrants, Catholics, and people of color—yes, compared to the Democrats and Know Nothings, he was not a bigot; an opponent of states' rights and secession—to his dying breath; quite possibly an atheist or, at least, an agnostic—no, but he was not a devoted churchgoer and his views were unorthodox.

Seward had a keen eye for his legacy as well as his career. Writing letters helped him process experiences, filled his time alone, and tethered him to home. He fixed on a plan, a shorthand designed to address the problem of career versus legacy, public versus private, thoughtful ramblings or candid views versus calculated speechifying. As he explained in a letter addressed to Fanny from London on May 26, "The journal which I keep is intended for the perusal of your dear mother, who is entitled to the most complete account of all my experiences in this journey which she has so magnanimously consented that I shall make alone."[18]

Henry intended that the correspondence addressed to Frances was not private to her or the immediate family. He wrote such a letter "with the belief that she will very purposely show it to such of my friends as have a right to be informed of my travels and so that it may obtain some publicity." If the letter was addressed to Frances, it was intended for discreet circulation and edited publication by his political friends.[19]

On the other hand, "there must be personal experiences which delicacy would forbid me from revealing to any but persons of my dear family." These, he addressed to his daughter, and were not to be shared outside the closest circle of family and friends: "In preparing an account of them and dedicating it to my only daughter I feel sure that your mother will regard it as equally or even more designed for her perusal, and will even approve of this small contribution towards your education, now the chief object of her own care as well as of mine." The code was in the salutation: "My dearest Frances" was for public consumption; "My dear Fanny" was strictly private. It was even the case that parts of the same letter were internally addressed to one or the other of them, so Frances had to be careful. It was complicated but provided Seward cover, gave him space for candor, and left us a key to what he preferred to keep from public view.[20]

The instructions trusted Frances to know which of Henry's "friends"—and a successful politician had many, many friends—had "a right to be informed of my travels"; these were men he could trust. Apparently, she knew whom to include on the other list of friends, the "public" friends who published what he wanted published, but she was not sure with whom she could share the letters and parts of letters addressed to Fanny and reserved for "family." Almost two months later, in a July 12 letter to Fanny, Seward clarified in response to a letter from Frances, now lost. "Your mother asks," he wrote privately to his daughter, "whether she shall send my letters to Dr. Henry, or show them to Col. Carpenter"; Frances did not trust her judgment about where she should draw the line on "family" and thus her husband's privacy. She was right that she drew the line in the wrong place, as Dr. Caleb Sprague Henry, an Episcopal clergyman, was left off Henry's list. The letters "are written under a belief that Frederick, Anna, Mr. and Mrs. Wharton [Anna's parents], George Grier, and other relatives may like to read them," including, for example, Caroline Schoolcraft (niece and ward) and Mrs. Schoolcraft, a relative of hers and thus his by marriage.

Henry explained that there were seven friends he considered "family," all of whom were neighbors in Auburn and thus likely to call at the Sewards' South Street home and ask about him. These included several local politicians whom Seward had known for ages—Christopher Morgan, a former law partner of Seward's who would be elected Auburn's mayor the next year; Edwin Barber Morgan, Christopher's brother, a Republican congressman; William H. Carpenter, owner of a livery stable in Auburn, for whom Seward secured an appointment as US consul to Foochow (Fuzhou), China, when he became secretary of state; Ethan Warden, also a neighbor; and two local ministers, George Peck (Methodist Episcopal) and John Mather Austin (Universalist), all of whom had supported him personally and politically throughout his career. He trusted them, although none was a principal in his national campaign. There was a different group, headed by Thurlow Weed and Fred, that handled the publicity he hoped to generate with the public letters.[21]

With his experience as a trial lawyer, Seward was curious about the operations of the British judicial system, which he indulged with the intervention of friends in London. "It is certainly a very pleasing thing to see partisan contention within moderate bounds and yet be free from implication in the strife," he wrote to Frances in late May. He also gained admission to the Athenaeum and Conservative clubs, which enlightened him on the range of influential men's political views. In the same letter for public consumption, he informed Frances that "both of them have allowed me the privileges of their societies respectively, and I hear with much interest their discordant speculations."[22]

Seward was pleased by his access to the powerful in and outside the aristocracy. He learned that whatever his own hopes and dreams for his political future, the English had already decided he would be the next president of the United States and treated him accordingly. "The hospitalities of this capital so completely engross my time that I have scarcely leisure to record them," he wrote to Fanny.[23]

The extravagant socializing often reduced his descriptions to lists: breakfast with Lord and Lady Haverton; dinner with George Mifflin Dallas, former vice president of the United States and mayor of Philadelphia, and his wife Sophia; a most enjoyable afternoon in a grove of ancient cedars of Lebanon discussing "the political affairs of the world" with Lady Granville; "a long and agreeable tête à tête" with the Duchess of Sutherland, "the most accomplished and elegant lady in England," whose husband was "old, infirm, and almost absolutely deaf but honest benevolent and amiable," after a "lunch" held in his honor at Stafford House, "the finest and most magnificent private dwelling in England." The aristocrats he dined with on another occasion were the "nobles and statesmen of the liberal class. It would be tedious to recount their names"—then he recounted them. The Lords included St. Germans, Stanley, Granville, John Russell (former prime minister), Derby (current prime minister Edward Smith-Stanley), and his wife the Countess of Derby. It was challenging for an American to keep their titles straight—Sir James and Lady Tennent, the Earls of Shaftsbury and Carlisle, the Duke and Duchess of Sutherland, the Marquises of Westminster and Landsdowne. He also met the archbishop of Canterbury and Cardinal Wiseman, Roman Catholic archbishop of London.[24]

There were, of course, famous people without titles, such as Madame Erminia Frezzolini, an Italian operatic soprano who did not speak English but was off to America and esteemed by the English "the finest artist of the age"; John Blackwood, the English editor of *Blackwood's* magazine, who groused in reply to Seward's compliment that despite the magazine's popularity in America he was not receiving royalties for the copies sold there; Louis Kossuth, the Hungarian freedom fighter whom Seward had met in America and found "the most serene dignified and graceful person in address and convention whom I have ever met"; and the people whose names escaped him in the crush of meetings, a grandson of Major General Lafayette, among others, all within his first two weeks on land and before the month of May ended: "I must not try to recall the names of the manly persons of all classes to whom I was presented. Suffice it to say," in private, "that two or three of the most spirited attended me to my lodgings at half past twelve." He need not tell his family, he told them, "that all of our party were Republicans of the American school," partisans who were extremely pleased to make his acquaintance and those he already knew. Sometimes, as on May 30, "our party at dinner . . . was nearly [all] American." Seward was having a grand time "in the midst of excitements and pleasures" in London society. He found it amusing that the treatment he received in his hotel on arrival as an apparently obscure American tourist was improving "as the great and titled visitors successively appear to call on me." "The world seems to grow small," he explained to Fanny on May 30, "as I find myself introduced every day to some personage or monument that has heretofore been regarded as forever inaccessible to me."[25]

The greatest monument was Queen Victoria, the very apex of the British social pyramid that Seward scaled. There was initially a glitch. Protocol dictated that Seward could not "be invited to any Court entertainment until he has first been presented, and no person can be presented except at a levee," a formal royal reception. Given his travel schedule, that was inconvenient. There was no levee until June 20, but an invitation to a concert at the palace at 9:30 p.m. on June 8 arrived at Seward's room on June 2. This event served in lieu of a levee with the intervention of the Lord Chamberlain, who presented Seward to the queen. Lord Napier, the former British ambassador to the United States, had apparently arranged it and then "put tailors, shoemakers and hatters in requisition" that very afternoon to make Seward presentable—sword, scabbard, top hat, tails, shoes, shirt, cummerbund, and tie.[26]

During the intervening days, Seward attended a luncheon at Kensington Palace hosted by the Duchess of Inverness, where he met the Duke of Bedford, "one of the first statesmen of Great Britain but now retired from public life." That same evening, he dined at Pembroke Lodge in Richmond with Lord John Russell, "one of the most eminent and active of the statesmen of England, and lately Prime Minister." Mrs. Pulszky, one of the Hungarian exiles, hosted a party in his honor on June 6. "It brought around me many of the reformers and strong-minded women as well as men in London," he wrote to Fanny, "and the reception was a most hearty one by them all." The next day, June 7, he attended the opening of Parliament, "appareled in the free dress of the American Legation, black coat, white vest, breeches, silk stockings, buckles, black sword and chapeau. . . . I stood by the side of three Indian Princes in the small gallery by the side of the throne. The scene was a very brilliant one."[27]

Promptly at 9:30 p.m. on June 8, Seward presented himself at the gates of Buckingham Palace; the doors of the ballroom opened a half hour later. He entered the reception line and passed before the queen and royal family. Each member of the diplomatic corps "bowed to her majesty and the Princesses and Prince consort," he reported to Fanny, "and each received a gracious salutation." He continued, "The Prince Consort said How do you do Mr. Seward and gave me his hand. . . . Everyone who entered the room, and there was 1000 or 1500 saluted the Queen in the same manner at some stage of the evening. . . . The ball was like all balls. The queen danced gaily and joyously many hours. At 12 there was supper . . . after which I repassed through the Drawing rooms, and was surprised to find that I already had a very large acquaintance with the great and fashionable ones of this grand metropolis."[28]

The next day, Seward "dined with a large party composed of Whig and Tory statesmen and ladies at Lord Lyndhurst's, who has been earnestly courteous to me," and so it went for his next two weeks in London. On June 14 he received his second batch of letters from home, dated May 27, in which he learned that Fanny was ill yet again. Since Henry did not save the letters he received during the trip, we only learn of their contents from his replies, which means that we lose the voices of family members in the correspondence with him. Trying perhaps to assuage his guilt for being away during a time of family crisis or simply reflecting his generally sunny disposition in contrast to his wife's pessimistic nature, Seward replied that he regretted Fanny's illness, but "I should be much alarmed about your health if I did not remember that for a long time Frederick and William's feebleness gave me what proved afterwards an unnecessary degree of solicitude." He also concluded that "England is beautiful in June, but so is our own country."[29]

Seward booked his days in London through June 26, when he anticipated a wider tour of the island. "I have declined all invitations beyond the 26th," he told Fanny, "and on the 27th I shall bid final farewell to this great capital, make a hurried excursion to Manchester, Birmingham and Sheffield," then possibly a brief jaunt to Scotland before proceeding "to Paris, where I shall stay probably ten days or two weeks." Before leaving London, he spent more time in the British Museum viewing the relics of Greece, Rome, Egypt, Nineveh, and Babylon, but he brought Fanny catalogs rather than cataloging in his letters what he saw. He referred her to a book on the subject by a British author.[30]

Henry also made day trips to Oxford, which left him "fagged and wearied to the verge of death" but elated by a "devotional performance" of Handel's *Te Deum* by a combined choir and orchestra of 3,500 and an organ that required seventeen men to pump the bellows. "It was the first time I ever felt the full power of that Divine Art," he wrote Fanny. "Henceforth I shall never again be a sceptic. Their devotional performances rose above the earth and earthly things and showed that our religion does reach the spiritual sphere." Another day he went to Cambridge, where he found that "the town indeed is nothing, the University is everything." He also enjoyed a weekend respite at Rowfant, a grand six-hundred-year-old country house purchased by the American fur merchant Curtis Lampson. There he strolled down the avenues of linden trees, "a grove from which I heard last night the song of the nightingale," walked at leisure through the "apparently limitless fields," 180 acres of which were maintained as a wild habitat for thousands of rabbits, and five hundred acres devoted to the raising of pheasants for the fall hunting of gentlemen. Sunday morning he attended church and then returned to his gambols before riding out to view the ruins of Brantridge House, a castle demolished by Cromwell's army during the English Civil War.[31]

When Seward returned to political networking, he was "unable to find time to continue the desultory notes addressed to your dear mother. She must therefore take this letter for all," he wrote to Fanny. Now that he had been formally presented to the queen with a bending of protocol, he was required by the rules of court etiquette to attend other events, including Victoria's Saturday morning drawing room, in which the great officers of state and the diplomatic corps paid their respects. In this ceremony, "the ministry and the diplomatic corps advance from the antechamber, enter the salon, and pass in review before her Majesty in long single files. One bows and receives a royal salutation." Madame Delepierre, wife of the Belgian consul, threw what was by comparison a small party for Seward. "The company was chiefly literary persons and artists" whose names did not bear reporting to his daughter, although she, as an aspiring writer herself, was more interested in authors, actors, and performers than in politicians, except for Senator Sumner.[32]

Lest his family think his travels were smooth sailing, Seward shared some of the frustrations, such as being denied reentrance to the debates of Parliament after he ducked out for supper, by a doorkeeper "who did not know me." His reservation had failed to secure his rooms at Fenton's Hotel on arrival, which necessitated him moving twice. And the one he most regretted was when he mistook the date of a dinner engagement for the address and returned from Cambridge to find "that I blunderingly not only lost a dinner which I anticipated with so much pleasure . . . but had disorganized the whole party." Nonetheless, on returning from Oxford, "the day closed with a very intellectual dinner party at the Vice Chancellor's, Dr. Jeunes, in which as the representative of the Republican Party of the United States on which the hopes of freedom rest I had much attention." He enjoyed it, but "do not on any account let this letter get into any hand that will suffer its reflections to become known." He had his doubts about the endurance of the British monarchy and nobility, the British subjects' comparative deference to rank, their elevation of rank over achievement, and yet "I am under a thousand obligations here to all kinds of persons and I would on no account violate them." Again, "London does not seem as weary of me as it ought, but I am beginning to feel that my time might be better spent elsewhere."[33]

It was difficult to walk away from what felt to Seward like vindication after two decades in the trenches of America's political wars over slavery, when both anti- and proslavery forces had vilified him. "Nor can I admit [omit] to say to yourself," he wrote his wife, breaking with his plan to write privately only in letters to his daughter, "and yourself alone that there is a recompense, a most consolatory one for long years of endurance of contumely at home in the universal respect and sympathy which my poor efforts for freedom and humanity there have won for me here in this enlightened and more impartial land." His London calls for goodbyes took him past the planned departure date; everyone wanted to talk. He described the good wishes of noble people, but in particular the Duchess of Sutherland, as "a trophy worth carrying away." They all seemed to admire and respect him, and to wish him well in his next public role. On his last visit to the Metropolitan Club, "what a gathering was there—all on equality—authors, poets, painters, historians, princes, and diplomats."[34]

"At last I am out of London. But by how great an effort," Seward wrote to his wife on June 29. From Warwickshire, he gushed, "How delightful it was to wake up to a bright sunshine and the music of birds at five o'clock in the Country, and to feel once more that I was free." What he meant was free to explore, to be a tourist, and to move at his own pace and by his own lights. He toured Warwick Castle and the ruins of Kenilworth, and he paused in Stratford-upon-Avon, where he shared with his family scenes and scents that Shakespeare once had experienced. "Here are some leaves from the well of Ann Hathaway's cottage," he explained to his daughter, "perhaps derived from the bushes planted by herself," he encouraged Fanny to imagine, however unlikely. He continued on to Leamington for a view of the Lucy estate "described by Washington Irving in Bracebridge Hall."[35]

What Seward had come north for was a glimpse of Birmingham, "to study the manufacturers." He started at sunrise the next day, touring a cut-glass factory and one that manufactured chemicals and glass. The first employed eighteen hundred workers, the second six hundred. "I have learned I think two things already," Seward wrote to his wife for publication, "first that manufacturers in the United States have a hard competition with those numerous establishments here which have secured a large trade throughout the world and second that the manufacturing population of England are its only real republicans." This was the class that gave Seward the most hope for a socially transformed Great Britain, one that would be an ideological and commercial ally of America's farmers and industrialists in their competition with the capitalist alternative built on slavery and exploitation of American slaves and the developing world. "Here," Seward shared with Frances for public consumption, "is the seat of that firm antagonist to the landed aristocracy which is working steadily and right on but only imperceptibly at political change in Great Britain." He saw the linkage between the British landed aristocracy and southern plantation owners as at the heart of the problem. Likewise, the political consequences of a new system built on the foundation of free labor was obvious to him and his fellow Republicans. "So true it is," he wrote, "that if men are trained only to mechanical arts they become soon self-governing, or in other words republican." Again, on visiting Glasgow and Leeds, Seward had similar ruminations. To Fred he wrote, "Artisans and manufacturers are republicans." It was their employers who were Tories: "how like the United States!"[36]

Seward found the South of England and the Midlands "painfully monotonous," and he carped that only a "permuted American mind," by which he meant "confused" or "addled," traveled to the Lake District for a view of lakes and mountains rather than staying home to see Greenwood in Orange County, his birthplace, or Lake George and the Thousand Islands, also in his home state, which he thought "far surpassing anything on this island in native richness and beauty." The Finger Lakes "at home are infinitely more varied and attractive." Fifty years hence, he predicted, the "worship of fashion" for the English lakes would pass, and the superiority of the American ones would be celebrated by an influx of European tourists.[37]

Henry had not come to the Lake District for the scenery but rather to intrude on the solitude of Harriet Martineau, the English writer so revered by his wife, and one whose blessing as an abolitionist he craved personally, perhaps even politically, more than his audience with Queen Victoria. Martineau was a contemporary of Frances and Henry, having been born in 1802 in Norwich, the sixth of eight children in a Unitarian family descended from French Huguenots and members of the same rising professional class as the Sewards. She received the sort of broad education at home that Frances and her sister acquired at the Troy Female Seminary, and that Frances provided at home to her sons and daughter. This was highly unusual for a girl in that time and place—the classics, modern languages, mathematics, and English composition. Martineau's education continued at two excellent Unitarian schools, which belied her claim to parental neglect, although her emotional needs clearly exceeded the capacity of her parents to meet them. Reflecting back on her childhood education at the age of twenty-one, she had observed that "we find as long as the studies of children of both sexes continue the same, the progress they make is equal." It was obvious to her that the so-called inferiority of women was a product of inferior education, a view that Frances Seward shared without the same critical edge. Harriet was a sickly child, like Fanny, and inclined to depression and perhaps unwarranted (according to her brother James) blaming of her parents for her unhappiness. Her misery was clearly compounded by deafness, which left her to communicate with others from the age of eleven through an ear trumpet.[38]

After achieving greater emotional stability as an adult, Harriet's world was rocked by the death from consumption of her eldest brother in 1824, her father's death in 1826, the mental breakdown and death of her fiancé in 1827, and the failure of her father's cotton-cloth factory in 1829, which left her family destitute. The family's poverty compelled Martineau to depend financially on her budding literary career, which she did brilliantly. Her first and most enduringly successful effort was a twenty-four-part series in the *Monthly Repository* on political economy, which began in 1832 and secured her both financial independence and celebrity in London literary circles. Her popularization of the arguments of free-market economists, including Adam Smith and Thomas Malthus, brought her a large and sympathetic audience among the more progressive elements in British and American politics. While her opposition to tariffs, restrictive taxes, monopolies, striking workers, and counterproductive charity and her support of the immutable laws of science and the free market were controversial enough, the fact that she entered into such discussions as a woman ensured resistance. Dating back to the 1830s, then, Martineau was the most influential woman writer in the United Kingdom and had a large audience in the United States, where she was perhaps an even more controversial figure.

In 1834, after a journey that took six weeks compared to the two weeks it took Seward in 1859 with the change from sail to steam,

Martineau arrived in America for a two-year tour that led her to write two books. Her views on slavery, which she freely shared in the North (in public) and the South (in private), avidly supported the work of the more radical immediate abolitionists and led to death threats. Her timing and celebrity amplified her impact; William Lloyd Garrison's abolitionist *Liberator* began publication the year before her arrival, and the American Anti-Slavery Society formed during her tour. Her embrace of women's rights and advocacy of woman suffrage were likewise controversial but less incendiary. She did, however, charm Americans with her admiration for their spirit and belief in the promise of their new nation.

The Sewards owned Martineau's *Retrospect of Western Travel*, which was published in London and New York in 1838, and aimed at a popular audience. They also owned her novel *Deerbrook*, which appeared a year later, garnered her high literary praise at the time and is generally seen as a direct literary descendant of Jane Austen's novels, particularly *Persuasion* (1817), and as a precursor of George Eliot's *Middlemarch* (1871) and the fiction of her good friend Charlotte Brontë. At the time, she was compared favorably to Madame Germaine de Staël, the woman of letters, political theorist, and exile from the French Revolution, which was very high praise indeed for the early Victorians.

In her *Autobiography*, which was published a year after her death at the age of seventy-four, Martineau reflected on her failure to marry in terms that Frances and Fanny Seward, had either of them still been alive, would have found to reaffirm their own views. "I am, in truth," Martineau wrote, "very thankful for not having married at all. I have never since been tempted, nor have suffered anything at all in relation to that matter which is held to be all important to women, love and marriage." She credited mesmerism (hypnosis) for curing her debilitating illness, which also impressed Frances, who was on the lookout for modern alternatives to traditional medicine. From the Seward family's library, we know that Frances saw Martineau as a trusted source on a range of topics from medicine to literature, politics, and especially abolition.[39]

A meeting with the deaf and chronically ill Martineau was even harder for Seward to secure than a place in the queen's reception line, so he did not take silence in response to his written request for an audience as an English gentleman would have. He simply knocked on her door like the brash American he was. A woman answered. "Does Miss Martineau live here. She does, is she at home, She is. I have called to inquire whether she would see me—You are aware that Miss Martineau is an invalid and obliged to deny herself to society. Yes, and I did not expect that she would receive me now—but I had a hope that at some time during my stay here she might not be unable or unwilling to see me. Please give her this letter with my card and I will wait to know her pleasure." After some time, Martineau's niece, Maria Martineau, returned: "My Aunt will be delighted to see you—and she has been looking for you—but just now she is more than unusually unwell—Perhaps tomorrow? Said I. Oh no—an hour or two hence—say eight o'clock—At that hour I was there again."[40]

Martineau was influential on both sides of the Atlantic, and Seward campaigned for her support that evening in her parlor. She was, after all, the "leader," head editorial writer, for the influential *Daily News* dating back to 1852, as she would be through 1866; her influence crossed the Atlantic to northern liberals who had their own doubts about Seward's moral spine. The fact that she agreed to see him, however reluctantly, as she had other Americans more attuned to her views on women's rights and slavery, such as Transcendentalists Ralph Waldo Emerson and Margaret Fuller, may have reflected curiosity, the fact-gathering for which she was famous, or possibly even the hope that she could influence him; the last seems unlikely given her low opinion of politicians such as Henry.

With his foot, and the rest of him, in the door, Seward approached Martineau, who sat in her drawing room. He found her "florid and really handsome, something past sixty, a benevolent countenance with matronly ways and manner. She applied her ear trumpet and we talked right on an hour and a half, chiefly of course about the great American question." Clearly, Seward hoped to change Martineau's mind about him and where he stood on slavery. He felt that she wrote her columns in London's *Daily News* without the full perspective on what was possible in the American political environment. "Her intercourse has been chiefly with Garrisonian Abolitionists," he wrote to Frances (not Fanny), "and she spoke almost constantly from their stand point and of course she was very despondent. I gave her my own more practical views, and spoke of course hopefully if not confidently."[41]

Seward should not have been surprised by Martineau's directness, which "she betrayed or rather confessed [as] an opinion that I was a politician rather than an abolitionist of her school." He countered "that there was need of organizers of the anti-slavery movement as well as of disorganizers of the pro-slavery forces, and that I believed even Theodore Parker and Wendell Phillips," two of the most radical abolitionists, "were content that I should act in my own way." Seward told his wife that Martineau "readily understood and accepted all these explanations."[42]

If Seward truly believed that he had won either woman over to his views on the subject of immediate abolition, he was wrong. Both Frances and Martineau looked to Charles Sumner as their best hope for the cause and to William Lloyd Garrison as less extreme than Seward saw him. Martineau continued to think of Seward as a moral coward and compromiser, a trimmer in British political terms dating back to the late seventeenth century, and Frances tried hard not to see her husband that way. Two years after his visit, Martineau described Henry to a correspondent as inclined "to go over to the strongest party." A year after that, as the Civil War continued, Martineau believed only pressure from the likes of Sumner kept Lincoln and Seward on the path to "conquer the South," because "Seward will always succumb to sufficient pressure." Conquest in the war and the abolition of slavery were the only path she imagined, although had politicians such as Seward followed Garrison in the 1850s, she believed the moral blot of slavery would have been expunged and the republic saved sooner and without a war.[43]

Martineau probed Seward's status as a candidate for president. As he reported to Frances, Martineau asked "about our prospects of Republican success next year adding 'I know your interest in it.'" According to Henry, he "replied that I did not have any assurance of such an interest, as she alluded to, nor was I so sanguine as others were of success <u>next year</u> for the cause, but that I was sure of onward progress and of ultimate triumph." At that point, she dismissed him, but, again according to Seward, with an invitation to return the next day, which he declined in light of his travel schedule. Martineau then returned to her needlework, asserting that she had earned the equivalent of $350 for the abolition cause by selling it that season, "and that will go a good way you know in mustering papers and lectures. I bade her adieu at ten o'clock with sentiments of uncensored respect and affection, and with rather serious promises to go there again."[44]

What Seward apparently never understood was that Martineau saw him as the moral equivalent of Martin Van Buren, another New York politician, who was vice president during her tour of America and succeeded Jackson as president in 1836. What she wrote about Van Buren is so similar to what she implied to Seward on their meeting twenty-five years after she met the vice president and what she wrote to correspondents about Seward during the 1860s that it appears the two were, in her mind, a political type for which she had little respect. To her, Van Buren's career "exhibits no one exercise of that faith in men and preference of principle to petty expediency by which a statesman shows himself to be great." Consequently, in her mind, "with all his opportunities, no great deed has ever been put to his account, and his shrewdness has been at fault in some of the most trying crises of his career."[45]

The contrast here was to the likes of William Lloyd Garrison. "In any future historical review of the case," Martineau wrote of the abolitionist, "the most striking feature of his mind and his course will probably be his political sagacity. He has been so constantly right in his anticipations, and so successful in his counsels, that few will now question that if his countrymen had had courage and conscience enough to follow his lead at an earlier time, the inevitable revolution might have been wrought without warfare and without ruin to any section of the country."[46]

What Van Buren and Seward lacked in comparison was courage and conscience in Martineau's judgment. What she said about Seward, that he "will always succumb to sufficient pressure," she also wrote about Van Buren. Seward was, to Martineau, charming, weak, and if not unprincipled at least cowardly. She did not mistake charm for character, and she was quite capable of finding him likable without trusting him to do the right thing. There was no endorsement of his candidacy from her, and he was no more successful in getting the abolitionist wing of his own party to trust him. They had too much evidence of his vacillation over the years; they knew him too well and preferred someone they knew less about, who was possibly even more prone to vacillation and even less committed to the cause of antislavery, which they found in Abraham Lincoln. Seward may have been a "temporizer," as Martineau read him, and so was Lincoln, who grew in the job.[47]

From Martineau's home, the next day Seward was back on the road, mainly railroad, to Scotland, again combining the roles of statesman and tourist, touring factories, observing ports, walking public gardens, and visiting stately homes. He remained focused on the economic engine that drove British manufacturing and the political implications of the kingdom's global reach. In the same letter in which Seward described his tête-à-tête with Harriet Martineau, he leapt across miles and cities at a quickened pace. "I tarried in Glasgow only long enough to change from one train to another," Henry wrote to Frances, headed for Kier, outside Stirling, home of William Sterling, MP, whom he described as "a gentleman of leisure fortune and letters, with a distinguished taste for what is called vertu or curiosities in art. I cannot describe the place to you so that you can appreciate it," but he described it nonetheless, including galleries, a library, gardens, walks, fountains, waterfalls, terraces, gates, and statuary, a testament to wealth well spent, in Seward's opinion, and to current tastes in garden design that he admired.[48]

The next day, which he noted was Independence Day back home, Seward toured Roman ruins, Stirling Castle, and other sites significant in Scottish history, Shakespeare, Macbeth's reign, and Walter Scott novels. "The scenes of Scotland's heroism and chivalry lay nearly all beneath my feet and Walter Scott's remembered descriptions of them made them intelligible almost without a prompter. Today for Edinburgh," he closed the letter. He wrote next from Yorkshire four days later, where smokestacks replaced the settings for romance novels. He hoped to launch for the continent the following week.[49]

On July 10 Seward was in Manchester, reflecting back on his tour of Edinburgh, which he found much changed, more British, than when he last visited with his father twenty-six years earlier. Everywhere, though, he was struck by the clash of history and modernity, tradition and factory smoke. He made time, seeing only what passed his view through the train's window as he headed south along the island's east coast until he reached Leeds, where he toured a linen factory that employed three thousand hands, and then onto Bradford for a tour of Crossley's carpet works, which employed four thousand. Everywhere he was confronted by industrial workers in rags and the rags-to-riches stories of their masters, in whose fine homes he received hospitality. "It will not be long," he predicted, "it cannot be long before the struggle in this country between an ancient class struggling to keep up without labor, and a modern community seeking to rise by it will seriously change the political Constitution, which all affect at least to venerate alike." America, he thought, was in a far better place to embrace modernity without bloodshed and with a Constitution more suited to global economic competition. How hopeful, how wrong, but how understandable his mistake on the very brink of the Civil War.[50]

Seward was, he thought as he wrote from Manchester, "at last out of the regions of wonder and romance, and dragging in the swamps of reality and fact," which would, he was sure, make his letters less interesting to his wife and daughter but more relevant to his political audience. "I quite enjoy the idea of leaving England," he told his daughter, continuing his practice of praising his hosts in public and denouncing them in private. "All I have seen here," he continued in a retrospective mood, "confirms my conviction that our American trade is enriching England and not relatively enriching ourselves."[51]

British factories turned American cotton into cloth, which profited the factory owners to the loss of free northern laborers and manufacturers; "the system is made so prejudicial to us by the influence of the Slave states in their desire to abridge the importance of the free states." The competition for economic success pitted North against South with Great Britain the victor. About this Seward was right, we now know; the two forms of capitalism were already at war. The question was when it came to actual fighting, whether Great Britain would join the war on the side of the slaveholding South.[52]

On July 20 Henry was finally set to depart for the continent, and the letters from home written on July 4 reached him just in time. In his last days in London, he met up with Charles Sumner, who spent several weeks there before returning to France for more medical treatment. Henry noted in his parting letter to Fanny that Sumner "is the idol of society in London," which deflated the presumptive presidential nominee. Seward was unable to confirm rumors that Sumner planned to marry while in Europe, but he could not let the question pass without a jealous dig. If Sumner ever married, and Frances knew the gossip about him, "it will be in Europe," Seward explained discreetly, "where his principles and opinions find favor enough to lift up a proud man, as he is with all his virtues," comments intended for Henry's wife.[53]

If Seward's jealousy over Sumner's greater popularity in Europe was personal, that was one thing, simply the deflation of an inflated ego whose triumph in Great Britain was immediately one-upped by the stylish, flamboyant darling of the abolitionists on both sides of the Atlantic. The sniping also had a political root, because Sumner revealed by his very presence one of the weaknesses of Seward's candidacy. Despite the differences in their styles and Sumner's more ideologically pure antislavery stand over the past decade, the two men were, after all, on the same team. They were both founding Republicans and united in their opposition to the extension of slavery. And yet, meeting up with Sumner made Henry insecure.

Although Sumner's relationship with Henry was cordial and collaborative as senators from the same party, they were never friends. "I was happy several hours with your husband," Sumner claimed to Frances in a letter that summer, which she learned from Henry's letters had not been enjoyable for him. During their conversation, Sumner wrote guardedly to Frances, "He told me that our glorious cause is already won." What could Henry have possibly meant, as politics remained as fraught (if not more so) as it had been when Brooks whacked Sumner over the head? The nation was closer to, not farther away from, the Civil War, and the South had not bent on the question of extending slavery across the continent. Henry may have implied or asserted that the Republican nomination was his. That is the only thing that makes sense in such a context. Sumner, however, was buying none of it, as he shared obliquely with Frances. "Would to God this were true! If so, then would I retire contented to some congenial retreat. But no! There is much of work and contest before us all and I welcome it."[54]

What we now know in retrospect was that, when asked, Sumner said in public that he too assumed Seward would be the Republican nominee for president in 1860 and, more significantly, that he believed Seward was the right choice for the party and the nation. As Sumner explained to the Duchess of Argyll, he regretted the increasingly conservative, compromising tone of Seward's speeches with an eye on the Republican convention, but he understood that Seward meant to "plead the good cause, and at the same time to avoid disturbing the prejudices of those who differed from him" on the slavery question. Nonetheless, Sumner persisted in his public assertions that Seward was sound on the issue and would do the right thing as president.[55]

While Seward may have feared that Sumner would undo all the good Seward had done his own cause during his two months in Great Britain, he need not have worried. If, on the other hand, Seward recognized that England's antislavery progressives trusted Sumner, who was all but martyred for his courageous stand against slavery, and adored for his consistent claim to the moral high ground on the issue, he was right. Sumner was a hero in Europe among the very elites Seward most admired, and Seward was a mere cigar-smoking politician, comparatively short in both physical and moral stature to the six-foot-two Bostonian with more polished manners and a higher style, who was also more socially amiable to them; Sumner's friends back in Boston fondly called him "the Earl," in a teasing reference to the English affectations he brought back from previous trips abroad. Yes, the Duchess of Sutherland invited Seward to spend a few days at Trentham, when she was not in residence; she entreated Sumner to live at Stafford House, her London home, when she was there. Yes, Harriet Martineau granted Seward a two-hour audience when he forced himself on her, but she adored Sumner and all he stood for against the mere politicians in the US Senate. Martineau had even thrown Sumner a party.[56]

Seward met the famous people he listed in letters to his wife and daughter, but William Makepeace Thackeray and Thomas Babington Macaulay were Sumner's friends, as were others in Martineau's circle, including the free-trade reformer and Liberal MP Richard Cobden, and John Bright, the Liberal MP and one of the great orators of the age. The Duchess of Argyll, Lady Sutherland's daughter, took a personal interest in Sumner's recovery from the attack on him three years before; Lord Palmerston, Lord John Russell, and William E. Gladstone dined privately with Sumner, while they met Seward only at public events. Seward knew much or all of this and it stung, even though he and Sumner remained cordial.[57]

Seward squeezed in a performance of Shakespeare's *Henry VIII* on his last day in London, in which the famed actor Charles Kean starred in the title role. Henry's takeaway for his daughter, though, was how inferior the portrayal of the dying Queen Catherine was to that of their family friend Charlotte Cushman, one of the great Shakespearean actresses of the day. His other takeaway for his writerly daughter was a consideration of whether America's democratic society would handicap its authors from writing the sort of truly great literature of such geniuses as Walter Scott and Shakespeare. "Our republican system banishes Kings, Queens, nobles and even women from all public occasions. It sinks them all to the level of humanity!" This, he implied, perhaps by way of discouraging his daughter from her career aspirations, sapped drama from the American experience. "Take Paris and Helen and [A]eneas out of the Iliad," he continued in the same vein, "and what would be left?"[58]

In a connected observation, Seward shared how torn he remained about his views of British society now that he had witnessed its operation for two months. He found the classes to "harmonize better than might be supposed and England improves by their eternal conflict. I would not be an Aristocrat, God knows I could not be a Plebeian." There was no place for the likes of him, an American of the rising professional class, in this alien culture, despite its allures. Time to move on; a mere ninety-minute voyage on a calm summer sea was between him and Calais; an 11:00 p.m. departure from Dover on Wednesday, July 20, got him there in the middle of the night: "Good-bye to England. Good night to my loving little reader!"[59]

Chapter 17

Home Sweet Home, 1859–1860

Life went on at 33 South Street in Henry's absence, as it always had. There was illness; there were social calls; there were even local trips by the family's women. They got on just fine without him, while fearing for his health, looking forward to his letters, and reading them together aloud. They also experienced, for good and for ill, the attention that his career brought them and the privileges they enjoyed as a result. Niagara Falls was in range by train for even timid travelers like them.

The daredevil Frenchman Jean François Gravelet, also known as Charles Blondin, crossed Niagara Falls on a tightrope more than three hundred times between 1858 and 1896. He last performed the feat at the age of seventy-two, one year prior to his death from complications of diabetes. A number of those crossings were in the summer of 1859, while Henry was in Europe and the Seward women visited the falls. On June 30 Blondin had an audience estimated at twenty-five thousand. Men bet on the likelihood of his death, women fainted, children screamed. Hucksters hawked food and drinks, alcoholic and non. At 5:00 p.m. Blondin appeared on the American side in spangled pink tights. About one-third of the way across, he sat down on the inch-wide rope, hauled up a bottle of wine from the tourist boat *Maid of the Mist* anchored below him, drank from the bottle, and then broke into a run. As he reached the Canadian shore, a band played "Home Sweet Home." After a twenty-minute rest, he returned, this time with a camera strapped to his back. About two hundred feet into the walk, he attached his fifty-foot balancing pole to the rope, set up the camera, and photographed the crowd before packing up to complete the crossing. The *New York Times* reported the performance and condemned "such reckless and aimless exposure of life" and the "thoughtless people" who fancied "looking at a fellow creature in deadly peril."[1]

On July 4 Blondin, five-foot-five and 140 pounds, about Henry's size, crossed again, this time without his pole. About halfway across, he did a flip and walked backward the rest of the way to Canada. He returned with a sack over his head to walk the rope blind. Congressmen, senators, and other politicians were in the crowds on June 30 and July 4. Former president Millard Fillmore was there to see Blondin cross on July 15. This time, he walked backward to Canada and returned pushing a wheelbarrow. Two weeks later, he backflipped and somersaulted his way across. He would later make the crossing at night, in shackles, carrying a table and chair; he once hoisted a cooking stove and utensils on his back, set them up on the rope, cooked an omelet, and lowered the lot to passengers on the *Maid of the Mist*.[2]

The Sewards had started to receive Henry's letters from England shortly before Blondin made his first crossing of the summer. In mid-July, just after Blondin had completed his third performance of the season and was planning a fourth, Fanny reported to Sarah Hance, "my dearest teacher," that her father had smooth sailing and did not suffer at all from seasickness on his Atlantic crossing. By July 17 family, friends, and newspaper readers were up to date on Henry's travels through June 29, when he left Leamington for Birmingham, so they were only about two weeks behind in his news. "O Miss Hance! He has sent me a leaf of ivy from Kenilworth Castle! And some rose leaves from Ann Hathaway's cottage! Are they not treasures worth having?"[3]

At that time, according to Fanny, Frances, Great-Aunt Clary, and Aunty Lazette were "all quite well, that is mother is quite well for her, Aunt Clara uncommonly so, and Aunty much better than she has been for some little time." Cousin Frances Chesebro was also well and her five-year-old son Frank "very happy in the possession of some pet Guinea-pigs." It was Fanny's hope and her mother's, reinforced by a postscript in Frances's hand, that Sarah would come and stay with them in Auburn for two weeks in August, after Fanny's journey by train to Buffalo to visit friends and her short trip from there with her mother

Figure 17.1. Augustus H. Seward. Courtesy of Rare Books, Special Collections, and Preservation, River Campus Libraries, University of Rochester.

and aunts to Niagara Falls. In the meantime, Fanny studied grammar, geography, and music, and her brother Fred tutored her in Latin during a two-week visit.[4]

On July 20 Frances Chesebro wrote a letter to Gus and sent it to Auburn because his mother had expected him there for weeks. Frances invited her cousin Gus, just two years her senior, to join her, Frank, another child, and the children's nannies on what she called a camping trip to Walton Point, near the southern end of Lake Canandaigua, near Naples, about twelve miles from their home at the northern end of the lake. Her entourage sailed by steamboat to a house that would be "rough" on their arrival "but large and clean after we make it so." Gus could expect "a pretty beach for bathing and good fishing" that was "inaccessible except by water, and no person has a right to come while another party is there, unless invited by us. So that you will see no one but ourselves," an assurance Frances expected was necessary to entice her shy cousin. By July 28 still no Gus, who was spotted in Buffalo and New York City but remained elusive to his anxious mother, whose feelings were repeatedly hurt by his travels everywhere but home.[5]

FIGURE 17.2. William H. Seward Jr. Courtesy of Rare Books, Special Collections, and Preservation, River Campus Libraries, University of Rochester.

Fanny may have been right on July 17 that her mother was unusually well, but Frances's health did not endure for the rest of the month. "I was pretty sick yesterday," Frances wrote to Fanny in Buffalo on July 28, the day after Fanny, escorted by her brother Will, had departed Auburn by train. The next day, in a letter to Fanny, Frances explained, "I have not been well since you went away but am now about the house again, neuralgia consequent upon the exertion of going to the store Tuesday," three days previously. Aunt Clary planned to join her two nieces on their trip to Niagara Falls with Fanny, and Frances encouraged the women to expect Gus to join them.[6]

No Gus, so twenty-year-old Will accompanied the women as far as Lockport on August 2 and returned home by 9:00 p.m. that same evening. It was not a difficult or long trip, but the ladies were more comfortable with an escort on what was for them an exhausting ride. Will wrote to his mother the next morning to allay her concerns about him getting home safely. "I found everything as we had left it in the morning, and Eliza [household staff] reported that nothing of importance had happened during the day. She appeared quite relieved to see me, as she was commencing to be a 'little' afraid and had every door and window in the house barred and bolted. The dogs, all three of them, seem quite contented and were stretched out on the sofa and chair in a general manner when I came in last night." Will knew his mother expected his brother, who was still AWOL from the family. "As yet I have heard nor seen nothing of Gus. Perhaps he thinks it unsafe to return before you have got back for fear he may be impressed and made to visit at Rochester." Funny and right on the mark. His brother was quite possibly avoiding his mother's impressment. His elusiveness was intended rather than careless, but it is unclear whether Frances realized that or was simply in denial about her son's nature and her relationship with him. Gus much preferred to travel alone than on a train car full of the family's women or to reside in a lakeside house with his cousin and small children.[7]

On August 3 the three Seward women—Frances, Lazette, and Clary—met Fanny and her friend Ellen Perry at the Cataract Hotel. "Ellen went to see Blondin walk," Fanny wrote in her diary, "but mother did not wish me to see him so none of us went." Their rooms overlooked the rapids, "my first view long to be remembered," Fanny continued. "The roar of the waters lulled me to sleep after a day of pleasures." Fanny and Lazette walked to Goat Island and rode the *Maid of the Mist* under the falls. Words eluded Fanny to describe the sights and sounds, and she stretched to find something to say that captured her thrill. "It were vain to attempt to describe my impressions of the grandeur of the falls. It did not strike me all at once, but grew upon me at every look. . . . I liked the Canada Falls best. Aunty and I went without the usual oilskin dress under the 'sheet of water,'" which was Fanny's greatest thrill. "Thursday evening we went to Buffalo, Mother was sick." They reached Rochester on Saturday, where they found letters from Henry waiting for them, and then rode the rails onward, reaching home that evening.[8]

In mid-August Henry was in Rome, and Will, who was handling the family's finances in his absence, wrote to update him about the collection of mortgages and rent. They had developed some additional properties on land passed down through Judge Miller's estate, which was still not settled under Henry's executorship. Numerous stories have arisen over the years about one of their house sales to Harriet Tubman, a heroic figure in the history of abolition and the Underground Railroad. In fact, though, Tubman is mentioned in only four of the Seward family's letters through the start of the Civil War. Her name appears twice in 1859 letters written when Henry was in Europe, one from Fred to Will and one from Will to their father. These are the first two family letters mentioning her, and both presume Henry did not know who Tubman was, that he had never met her and Will thus needed to explain.

The first letter, from Fred to Will on May 27, mentioned in passing that if they built their "next house" on land from the Burton tract "and it adjoins Mrs. Tubman's it will save part of the cost of fencing," presumably because they could connect the new fence to one side of hers. The second letter that mentioned Tubman by name was a three-month account of family finances sent by Will to his father in Rome on August 15. At the time he wrote the letter, Will was proud to explain that "there are now no vacant houses, all are either sold or rented." One of the rentals was to "Mrs. Cromwell, a colored woman, for $4.50 a month. She pays promptly and so far has been a good tenant." The only other client identified by race in the August 15 letter was in connection to a sale with a mortgage the Sewards held. "On the 25th of May," Will informed his father, "I sold the house to Harriet Tubman (a colored woman from Rochester) with seven acres of land for $1200. The house you will remember cost $500, and you valued the land at $100 per a[cre]. She has already made a pay[men]t of $225 on her contract and promises another $100 by the first of Sept. This, I think, is a larger payment than has ever been made down on any of the lots heretofore sold." The Sewards did not make a gift or support Tubman's work on the Underground Railroad by giving her a sweetheart deal on a house. There is no evidence that she was a family friend or even an acquaintance of Frances's as the 1850s ended. It was an advantageous business transaction in which the Sewards realized a higher down payment than what they received for any of the other houses they sold.[9]

As he crossed the English Channel in late July, Henry knew that Martineau and Sumner exposed chinks in his political armor, the latter by his greater popularity in London, the former by her candor about the right side of history. There were other chinks too, exposed over the next year. The tide was turning on Seward's presidential prospects as he campaigned abroad. Although it was a very short trip across the channel, he was now on a different journey, where he was just another American tourist, a status he claimed to seek but was disappointed to find.

Nobody knew him in France and he did not speak the language. He was displeased by everything that was different about France. The court had retired to Saint-Cloud for the summer, and after a month of frustration he gave up on being received there. He was reduced to eating meals with Americans, including a phrenologist and the inventor of a smokeless stove. He toured the Louvre, Notre-Dame, the Elysian Fields, the catacombs, and a porcelain factory alone. Henry secured an audience with Alexandre Walewski, the French secretary of state, but neither man spoke the other's language and Walewski had no idea who Seward was. Henry called on Alphonse de Lamartine, hero of the progressive forces in the 1848 revolution, but Lamartine's English was "imperfect," according to Seward, communication was minimal, and they parted as strangers.[10]

On August 10 Seward reached Rome, where he was still a mere tourist and toured with other Americans the Colosseum, Saint Peter's Basilica, Roman aqueducts, the Circus Maximus, churches, art galleries, more catacombs, the tomb of Raphael, and the Temple of Vesta. Before he left the city, Henry secured an audience with Pope Pius IX, who did not speak English, but he had an excellent translator. In a letter addressed to Frances, Henry described the pope as "a venerable grey haired gentleman" who had been prepped on who he was and offered him "good wishes for my higher advancement."[11]

After more than two weeks in Rome, Henry sailed by steamboat on August 27 to Naples, where he toured Capri, Pompeii, Herculaneum, and museums, and climbed to the summit of Vesuvius with other tourists. He rode on the back of a donkey and was carried the last stretch in a chair by two men. On September 6 he was again at sea; on September 13 he first viewed the city of Alexandria, Egypt, and was unimpressed. He took a train to Cairo, toured pyramids and museums, and saw the Nile, which he thought not a very great river; "perhaps it may be compared to the Hudson at Catskill." He was no more impressed by Cairo, which was twice Alexandria's size. On September 26 he reached Jerusalem after a multiday sail in a fruit boat to Jaffa. He visited biblical sites, including the reputed birthplace of Jesus in Bethlehem, the tomb of Rachel (in Genesis the favored wife of Jacob and mother of Joseph and Benjamin), the "desert haunts" of John the Baptist, and Calvary before sailing again, this time for Constantinople.[12]

Henry was back on the continent in early October, where he lingered in Vienna before traveling by train to Venice and Milan, on to Paris, and eventually climbing on board a Liverpool steamer. In early November, as he left Italy, Henry thought more of home and the future than he did of Europe's past. He first remarked on John Brown's raid on the federal arsenal at Harpers Ferry in his November 15 letter to Frances. Since a detachment of Marines defeated Brown's attack with his company of twenty-two on October 18, the news had traveled fast to Europe. Henry already knew the story, the outcome, and the fact that Brown and survivors would be executed in short order. He also knew this was bad news for his candidacy. "I almost fear to write anything," he explained to his wife. Brown was a hero to the uncompromising abolitionists and became a martyr to the antislavery cause. To southerners and northern Democrats, Brown was a madman, a creature of reckless speeches delivered by abolitionists. Seward's private opinion was that the raid was a tragedy, a politically harmful loss of life that was, indeed, "mad," which "filled me with sadness."[13]

Henry foresaw no political middle path on the raid but rather a significant narrowing of options for moderate voices such as his. His views were too well known, his speeches going back decades already published; there was no way to convince conservatives that he was not part of the problem. His moral fiber, his consistent and devoted dedication to the cause of antislavery were already doubted by the Garrisonians and British progressives such as Harriet Martineau. Should he stand up for Brown or show himself yet again a mere politician, whose views blew in the political wind? This was not how Henry saw himself, but it was politics. As was his nature, Seward offered a positive spin to his wife. "I do not fear," he wrote, "that this affair will do political harm to our good cause, although the adversary so shamelessly answers their hopes for it." Seward knew that his political enemies would use Brown to denounce him and like-minded Republicans. His presidential candidacy, which Seward had believed likely but never thought certain, was clearly in trouble, not just because of John Brown's raid but rather because the event revealed his limitations as a candidate, to which he had found other clues in Europe. He was too well known and defined, had drifted too far in both directions on the slavery question, and presidential elections were not really about the candidates' qualifications in any event. The fact that he was easily the most qualified, even more qualified now given what he had learned and who he had met in Europe, did not matter in the end.[14]

Not for the first time, the hostile political environment even reached the Seward family's pets. Their dog Neptune took ill on November 9. The diagnosis was arsenic poisoning. Will found a man who had ministered to other family pets, but he could do nothing. Will advertised a reward of ten dollars for information leading to identification of the perpetrator. "Poor dear Neppy," Fanny wrote to Sarah Hance, "he must have been killed from spite to us for he [was] so gentle, never harmed anyone. Dear Neppy, we are very, very lonely without him. Bell seems quite changed and looks for him a great deal. My little graveyard under the apple tree grows. Neppy lies next to his old playfellow. About six weeks ago I had an ambrotype taken of Bell and Nep together. How glad I am to have it now!" In a postscript to the letter, Frances added that "our little girl was very sick for some days and confined to her room nearly two weeks. She is now regaining her strength." The most recent letter from Henry had him ascending the Adriatic on his way to Vienna. Fanny noted in her diary that her father had sailed from Le Havre on December 13.[15]

Henry was on board the *Arago*, captained by the man who was first mate on the ship on which he and his father returned from Europe in 1833. "The ship seems comfortable," he wrote to Fanny, "the passengers nearly all Americans and many of them personal friends are very agreeable." On Wednesday, December 21, Fred wrote Will, "They say the Arago will be due at New York about Tuesday. Can't you stop and spend Christmas with us, if you go down?" To Sarah Hance, Fanny wrote that she and Lazette were ill. "We look for father about the end of the month. . . . We shall probably go to Washington soon after his arrival."[16]

On his way to New York City to meet his father's ship, Will stopped in Albany to spend Christmas with his brother and sister-in-law. On December 27 he wrote from the city that there was still no sighting of the *Arago*, but all were hopeful it would land the next day. Will assured his mother, "I will not fail to telegraph you immediately on her arrival."[17]

Fanny reported on Christmas in her diary, this year from Auburn. Her mother gave her "a beautiful cologne bottle or vase of blue and white parian ware." Her aunt Lazette gave her "a very handsome album of rich colored engravings . . . as well as a very pretty yellow sugar rose with a face peeping out from the leaves." Friends gave her an Italian wax figure, a china Red Riding Hood, and a "very rich heavy chased gold ring." Will had left Fanny "a beautiful blue bound and tinted paper illustrated copy of 'The Merchant of Venice'" before departing on the train for New York to meet their father's ship. Fanny crocheted her mother a pair of slippers and gave her aunt Lazette an ambrotype of her and Lazette's dog. She sent a copy of the same photo to Sarah Hance.[18]

The last letter the family had received from Henry estimated his arrival "Christmas or soon after," which had gotten Fanny's hopes up and then crashed them as her mother's had been by such absences on past holidays. Since she heard from New York City that people were not anticipating the *Arago* until December 29, Fanny said to herself, "I will not expect him until then, so that I may not be impatient and disappointed. Days and weeks passed by, and many were the kind inquiries of friends as to when we expected him. 'Not till the 29th,' I replied," but she continued to hope and succeeded in not being seriously disappointed until Monday, December 26, "yet when night came and brought no tidings, disappointment would visit me. . . . Tuesday came with no news of the Arago." On Wednesday they heard that the ship had been sighted from shore.[19]

On Wednesday, December 28, Henry wrote again to Fanny as the *Arago* approached the harbor. "Land, Ho, we are running down the forest cover[ed] shore of Long Island, and already our leave takings have begun. For myself, I tremble between the hope of meeting and the fear of hearing ill news of those who have indulged me in erratic travel so long." He and his fellow passengers spent Christmas besieged by a gale: "no one could keep foot on the decks covered with ice and sleet. The ship rocked and plunged under the heavy weight of ice on the decks, masts, spars, rigging, pipes, boats, everything. The waves raged in response to the reckless shrieks of the wind." The passengers gathered in the cabin and prayed, but "a new gale more violent than the last met us fiercely as if to repel us from our nation's shore. For two days we heard that last storm, and this morning the sun had broken through the gloom, the sea is calmer, the land rises from its horizon covered with trees and Home with its cheerful fires and glad unions seems to lay past behind a thin mist spread out before us."[20]

According to Fred, "it was a bleak, cold, wintry night, near the close of December, when the *Arago* entered the harbor of New York," not conditions amenable to a public reception, so only a few people were there to greet the candidate. Nonetheless, Henry received a hundred-gun salute in City Hall Park, and "throngs of friends" met him at the Astor House, from which he had launched his journey. From Fanny's diary entry for Thursday, December 29: "We looked anxiously for a telegraph to tell us if the Arago did get safely in. Will telegraphed, we received it at about ten o'clock A.M. He said Father was at the Astor House and they would be home 'Friday.' How busy, how happy I felt. Mother seemed so much happier after the telegraph."[21]

A committee of the Common Council accompanied the senator to city hall Thursday morning, where Mayor Daniel Tiemann formally welcomed him on behalf of the city. Senator Seward told the assembled that Europe had changed greatly in the twenty-five years since his last visit. There was "decided progress" and "substantial improvement," but the continent balanced "between the desire for beneficial changes and the fear of innovation." Europe's governing institutions and the ancient principles that underlay them were holding it back, and the United States needed to support those who sought to reform their own countries. "But this we can always do: we can conduct our affairs, and our foreign relations, with truth, candor, justice, and moderation, and thus commend our better system to other nations. This republic may prove to them, that its system of government is founded upon public virtue; that as a people we are at unity among ourselves, and that we are seeking, only by lawful means, to promote the welfare of mankind."[22]

The chamber where Henry gave his remarks on the morning of December 29 was packed, as were the galleries, hallways, and streets outside city hall. After the speech-making finished, "two hours of handshaking followed, only terminated by the announcement that it was time to prepare for the train that was to take him to Albany." There Seward spent the night with Governor Morgan in the mansion now assigned to his office. On Friday Henry proceeded by the Central Railroad to Auburn. Fred described the trip. "Bleak and cheerless as was the wintry landscape, the whole journey was one of warmth and enthusiasm. Salutes and welcomes greeted him at every city. Crowds awaited him at the stations. Old friends and political followers boarded the train, to grasp him by the hand." When the train reached Auburn late in the day, Henry "was met by an outburst of popular pride and pleasure. The streets were decorated, banners waved 'Welcome Home,' the citizen-soldiers, the local authorities, societies, and even the children of the public schools were waiting to escort him in procession to his home." In his reply to the welcoming speech, Henry testified to his love of home. "Seward remarked that 'although in this journey I have traversed no small portions of four continents . . . it is not until now that I have found the place which, above all others, I admire the most and love the best. . . . I prefer this place, because it is *my* place.'"[23]

Not all the welcomes were so warm; others were heated. John Brown hung over Seward's head, as he had realized Brown would when he first heard the news in Europe. Now he was home to see he was right. As the presumptive Republican nominee for president, Henry had become in his absence the lightning rod for political attacks on the party. He was a polarizing figure and vulnerable to politically motivated charges that had no basis in fact. An advertisement in a Richmond newspaper offered $100,000 reward "*for the heads of the following traitors*": leading abolitionists such as Charles Sumner, Horace Greeley, Henry Ward

Beecher, and dozens more. At the end, in a separate paragraph, the ad singled out one national politician: "And I will also be one of one hundred to pay five hundred dollars each ($50,000) *for the head of William H. Seward*, and would add a similar reward for Fred Douglass, but regarding his head and shoulders above these Traitors, will permit him to remain where he now is. RICHMOND." When Seward returned to the Senate there was an investigation, hearings, and a report on "the Harper's Ferry" treason, which, again, was not good news for Seward. He was the only one among the major candidates for the Republican nomination to be singled out and so vulnerable to attacks based on his record on slavery.[24]

Fanny's new diary, the second of the ones she kept over the last nine years of her life, picked up the Sewards' story on Sunday, January 1, 1860. "This is Father's first Sunday at home since the 7th of May when he sailed for Europe in the Ariel," she wrote in her first entry. Henry attended church with Fred and Anna that morning and then again in the afternoon for Judge Charles Perry's funeral, this time with Will, Fred, and Fanny. "During morning service, a prayer of thanks for Father's return was offered." Auburn celebrated Monday as the secular New Year's Day, a day of calls and feasting. Henry was so much in demand that he simply stayed home to receive his many well-wishers. Tuesday, Judge Miller's old friend Gary Sackett called, among others duly recorded by Fanny, and Abby Hall threw a party in Henry's honor. Abby was the wife of Benjamin F. Hall, former clerk of Judge Miller and then partner in the law firm until its 1846 dissolution. Hall would become the first chief justice of the Colorado Territory in March 1861, an appointment he secured from President Lincoln with Henry's support. Hall would also be Judge Miller's biographer, commissioned by the family seventeen years later. "I am invited," noted the now fifteen-year-old Fanny, "but am too young. Aunty and Mother are too sick. Father looked very handsome."[25]

On Wednesday Henry was off to Washington at 9:00 a.m., after less than a week at home, traveling with Julia Warden, a friend of Fanny's five years her senior from an Auburn family. Fanny, Will, and Jenny were at the train station with many others to see her father off; Julia's parents, brothers, and their spouses were also there. Senator Preston King and the other Republican members of Congress "came in a body to welcome him" when the train arrived in Washington. The reception by Seward's well-wishers continued at his Washington home, where the Massachusetts, Ohio, and Wisconsin delegations each called in a

FIGURE 17.3. Frederick W. Seward and his wife Anna W. Seward playing chess in their garden, c. 1860. Courtesy of Rare Books, Special Collections, and Preservation, River Campus Libraries, University of Rochester.

body, and throngs of visitors passed through during the week before his family arrived.

The newspapers had covered Seward's movements, so the Senate galleries were populated by visitors eager to see how he was received by his colleagues in the aftermath of the Brown raid. Republicans greeted him warmly; southerners did not want to be seen talking to him. Many in the gallery believed the rumors promoted by some newspapers intent on thwarting his presidential nomination that Seward was somehow implicated in the raid on Harpers Ferry, at least as its inspiration with his "Irrepressible Conflict" speech. Some of the visitors, at least, expected him to be arrested on the floor of the Senate when he appeared. Never had American politics been more divided, and Seward was a lightning rod for division. Secession was openly discussed. "You may elect Seward to be President of the North," said one congressman in the course of debate, "but of the South, never!" It took forty-four ballots to elect a Speaker of the House, a Republican, former governor William Pennington of New Jersey, by one vote. The investigation and the bill to admit Kansas as a free state brought all other business in the Senate to a standstill.[26]

As 1860 began, the sun appeared to be on the horizon to family members other than Frances. In her diary Fanny recorded that she spent January 5 with Aunt Clary and cared for a stray dog. The next day another stray followed her home. On Saturday, January 7, there was a thaw and she "received first allowance, am to have $8.50 per month.

In case of more expense mother will furnish me with funds. [I] don't pay my travelling expenses or tuition." For comparison, laborers made about six dollars a week, firemen and carpenters about as much a week as Fanny received per month, and the Union army paid privates eleven dollars weekly. Over the next few months, Fanny spent money on treats and a ball for her dog Bell; cash and gifts for "Aunt Margaret," a poor African American woman she knew in Washington; two books, both romance novels set in Scotland; and some maple candy, but mainly on ribbons, hair accessories, and clothes. She duly noted in her diary that she had four cents left from December and that she spent $12.38 during the month of January, for which expenses her mother reimbursed her an additional five dollars for clothing. So she actually underspent her month's allowance by about a dollar.[27]

On Monday, January 16, Fanny and her mother packed. Fanny used one of her father's trunks, which had now arrived, so she had to unpack it first. Inside were the clothing and shoes he wore for his presentation to Queen Victoria, some candy for her, and mottoes from either the table of the queen or the Duchess of Inverness, he could not recall which. Fanny and Frances made calls in anticipation of their departure. On Tuesday Frances and Fanny "packed and packed." More calls and goodbyes were made to Aunt Clary and her husband, and Ellen Perry "brought me a very pretty pair of undersleeves made on the machine by her mother, white with fine tucks." Will's "pretty Jenny called in AM" and then came back to tea. At 9:00 a.m. on Wednesday, January 18, Fanny, Frances, Will, and Fanny's dog Bell left for the train depot with their two large trunks and sundry bags.[28]

"Cars came. We started. Bell's second journey to Washington. No dog could behave better. He lay in my lap quietly, all the way, getting out with Will at Utica. Arrived at Albany at four. Fred met us at Depot" and they stayed the night with him and Anna. After breakfast Thursday morning they got back on the train. They spent one night in New York City at the Astor House and another in Philadelphia at the Grand, where Will had his watch and thirty-five dollars stolen from his room when they were out walking the dog. Frances had an appointment with Dr. Helmuth, one of her homeopathic physicians. They left Philadelphia at 11:00 a.m. on Saturday, January 21, and arrived in Washington at 6:15 p.m. "Father met us at the depot. Bell knew him and was very glad. Anna, Julia met us at home."[29]

If Auburn sometimes seemed a social whirl to Fanny and her mother, one happily, one resentfully, Washington was exponentially better or

FIGURE 17.4. Frederick W. Seward by Matthew Brady, c. 1860. National Portrait Gallery, Smithsonian Institution; Frederick Hill Meserve Collection.

worse, depending on which of them you asked. Fanny tried to keep up with the names, titles, and capsule reviews of clothing and personalities, but it was hard to do much more than that in her diary, so it sometimes reads like lists of people and events that she name-dropped. Nevertheless it is priceless for its details on social life, individuals, the political campaign first for her father and then with her father for Lincoln. For Fanny, the whirl was thrilling.

On Monday Fanny began to unpack and then went for a walk with Julia to Lafayette Park, in between the Sewards' rented house and the White House, which they thought might be Fanny's new home the following year. Charles Sumner called while they ate dinner, one of many casual visits he made to the Sewards' Washington home now that they were all back. Fanny read aloud to Anna from Charles Dickens's *Bleak House,* which was a family favorite.[30]

Fanny and Julia read Ann Porter's *The Scottish Chiefs*, one of the nineteenth century's early and influential historical romances, aloud to each other. The novel focuses mainly on William Wallace, the Scottish knight who led the defeat of an English army at Stirling Bridge. "Bright was the summer of 1296," it begins, a year before the famous battle. "The war which had desolated Scotland was then at an end. Ambition seemed satiated; and the vanquished, after having passed under the yoke of their enemy, concluded they might wear their chains in peace. Such were the hopes of those Scottish noblemen who, early in the preceding spring, had signed the bond of submission to a ruthless conqueror, purchasing life at the price of all that makes life estimable—liberty and honor." Or, at least, that was the state of Scotland before William Wallace rose up from retirement, "too noble to bend his spirit to the usurper, too honest to affect submission," to lead his countrymen to victory.[31]

"Read in 'Scottish Chiefs,'" Fanny wrote on January 30. "What a splendid person is William Wallace." She found Wallace a "grand and faultless character. . . . How pleasant to think that these noble characters still exist, and that we may sometimes see them." She attended a dinner at the British ambassador's house on February 1 and entered on the arm of Senator Sumner. She and Julia still read aloud from *Scottish Chiefs* at the end of the first week of February. "I am perfectly infatuated," she wrote. On February 8 they finished the book, "over which I became so excited as to really feel sick and faint."[32]

The question was whether Fanny's father proved to be the Wallace of their times. Or, as was true for her mother, was Charles Sumner Fanny's knight in shining armor? Was Henry a noble knight to lead the United States against the slavocracy in politics or war? If it came to that, Henry would do everything in his power short of tolerating the splintering of the Union to avoid a conflagration. Despite his desire to be on the right side of history and his vision of himself as an abolitionist, Henry had no desire to be the president who sacrificed the lives of 620,000 men to free African Americans from the yoke of slavery; he was not that bold or brave or committed, but then again, neither was Lincoln when the war began. Or would Henry be the next president to preside over the political equivalent of Jarndyce and Jarndyce, the multigenerational court case imagined by Dickens in *Bleak House*, which pitted the heirs in a legal battle lasting for generations and drained a formidable estate dry in a struggle that could not be won? Or would Henry be the next president to succeed in leaving slavery for another generation of Americans to resolve at the price of the four million people then enslaved in the country and those who came after them? The last sounds more like the Henry who had been on the national

Figure 17.5. William H. Seward. Library of Congress Prints and Photographs Division, Washington, DC.

Figure 17.6. Frances M. Seward in her garden. Courtesy of Rare Books, Special Collections, and Preservation, River Campus Libraries, University of Rochester.

stage for the past decade. Each fate was possible for the next president, but victory was far from assured for whoever won the nomination and the election.

These were heady days for the Sewards in January 1860, which led Henry to attend church every Sunday for the first time in his life. Whether that was simply good optics for the campaign or a reflection of the hope and fear that inspired him to pray is uncertain, but Fanny documented the services and sermons that she and her father heard during her three months in Washington. She also recorded the names of dozens of people who streamed through their house before the Republican convention in Illinois. Senators, congressmen, journalists, New York politicians, and often their wives wanted to meet, greet, lobby, and advise Seward. And, of course, there was Charles Sumner, whom Fanny adored above all, "an excellent man, and one of deep religious feeling, even his servants bear testimony that like Daniel, he 'kneels three times a day before the Lord.'"[33]

Will headed back home, arriving in New York City on January 30, then Albany on New Year's Eve, and took an overnight train to Auburn, reaching home the morning of New Year's Day. He found "Aunty and Aunt Clary were both well and glad to see me. Everything seems to have gone on very smoothly since your departure and things are just as we left them," he wrote to his mother. He ate dinner at Clary's on Thursday and began hauling ice from the lake on Saturday, with the six laborers hired for the heavy lifting. Some would be stored for summer use, and he intended to sell the rest. Will remained busy collecting rents for his father. He found his fiancée Jenny "as well if not better than when we went away. Mrs. Watson is by no means willing to have her leave home but of course makes no objections. Now that the time is definitely settled, sewing operations, and preparations in general, will commence, and continue in full force for the next four or five months" until the wedding.[34]

Frances replied on February 6, reporting with annoyance that Ohio congressman Thomas Corwin, invited to dinner on Friday, had mistakenly showed up on Thursday and then neglected to return on Friday, "leaving a vacancy." Corwin was a former governor of Ohio, US senator, and secretary of the Treasury. President Lincoln appointed him minister to Mexico the following year, but more importantly in the short term he was a delegate to the forthcoming Republican Party convention. "Anna's reception was what is called 'brilliant,' which means I believe in fashionable parlance a well-lighted room filled with well-dressed ladies and gentlemen. Our new [gas] burners gave plenty of light without candles in kerosene."[35]

More importantly to Will, Frances reported that Henry approved Will's plan to enter into a banking partnership with Clinton MacDougall. "I mentioned the partnership with Mc . . . of which he spoke very approvingly. He says there can be no more lucrative or better business if it is well managed and understood than that you propose. I do not think there is any doubt but that he will give you all reasonable assistance. I left that part of the subject until I should hear from you again. I hope Mc. may continue constant in his intentions." Perhaps Will worked through his mother because his father was preoccupied with politics. It could have been because Frances, as the principal heir to her father's estate, now had some financial leverage in the family. In any event, her intercession was successful.[36]

Will replied on February 12, grateful for his father's promise of financial support of the William H. Seward and Company bank. "I need hardly say how much I was surprised and pleased to learn that Father thought favorably of a partnership with Mac. I had not the slightest idea that he would have time either to think or express any opinion in the matter." Will and his partner estimated that each of them needed between $2,000 and $2,500 to capitalize the venture by the coming spring.[37]

Lazette had moved out of 33 South Street a week previously, Will wrote, "and I am spending my second Sunday at home alone. The house looks quite deserted and cold and had I not been busy most of the time during the week I should have been very lonely." Clary was well in a rented house and handling her boarders successfully, with the exception of one, "who is under the continual temptation of eating more than is good for him." Also, "Dennis has been sick for the past few days, and I have another man in his place, who takes excellent care of the horses and cows." Will continued to supervise filling the icehouse. The men were hauling thirty loads per day, which was considerable. "Yesterday I worked with them myself from seven in the morning until six at night during which time we got in and packed away 78 loads. I hope that with one more such days work we shall have it finished."[38]

Those in Auburn were startled to read in the newspaper that "Mr. Seward was called home by a death in his family." After confirming that all were well enough, Fred determined that the death was Frances Grier, Henry's cousin and wife of George, in Orange County, New York, whose funeral the senator attended before making a brief visit home. All remained well in Auburn. "The sun has just come out brightly and bids fair to spoil my ice for tomorrow. Love to all. Jenny sends love also, affectionately your son Will." One week later, Frances reported that Henry agreed to pay Will's half of the investment if MacDougall raised his share. In the meantime, though, Frances hoped that her son "will not fill another ice house. Such labour breaks down constitutions much more hardy than yours, and a broken constitution is a great calamity to anyone, especially to a young person." Finally, "when you think of your mother on Sunday, I wish you would read at least one chapter in your Bible. It is the best moral guide given to mankind."[39]

Will was elated with the signs of a successful launch into adulthood, something about which he and especially his mother had worried, what with his home education and the challenges they considered a result of his weak eyes. His impending marriage was the other happy sign that Frances could worry less about her youngest son. On February 26 Will reported to his mother that all was well in Auburn. "Jenny continues to improve in health, and sends much love to you and Fanny. They are all very busy at Mrs. Watson's for some reason or another, and the amount of linen and cloth in general that has made its appearance lately is perfectly alarming. Mrs. Watson has promised to give Jenny a handsome piano next June. Aunty continues quite well and takes much interest in the building of the barn. Father's speech is looked for anxiously by the Republicans here. Love to all."[40]

On February 12 Fanny and Julia met Senator Sumner on the street. "He looked very handsome," Fanny recorded in her diary. Sumner called on February 20 and told the women "a great deal about the different kinds of jewelry" that Fanny's father had sent them from Europe, which had just arrived. Out of concern for his health, Fanny hoped that Sumner would not make a speech on the floor of the Senate, but he did, so she read it, "a clear argument, beautifully written." When she met Zylpha Clark, daughter of former New York governor Myron Clark, Fanny "quite liked her, and rather wished Mr. Sumner would take a fancy to her. She is very intelligent." When Fanny was in Matthew Brady's photo gallery, she "saw an excellent, a very handsome one of Mr. Sumner. Oh, how I long to possess it."[41]

On February 14 the Free Constitution of Kansas came before the Senate, and Senator Seward, taking the lead for his party, moved to refer it to the Committee on Territories and to have it printed. Resistance to such traditional pro forma measures came from those opposed to admission of Kansas as a free state. Debate ensued on February 29 in this leap year and Seward again took the lead. As reported in the *New York Daily Tribune* the next day, Seward spoke for two and a half hours, during which time his colleagues and spectators were riveted to their seats. "The audience assembled to hear Governor Seward's speech filled every available spot in the Senate galleries, and overflowed into all the adjacent lobbies and passages, crowding them with throngs eager to follow the argument of the Senator, or even to catch an occasional sentence or word. . . . Every Senator seemed to be in his seat. . . . The members of the House streamed over to the north wing of the Capitol, almost in a body."[42]

According to the *New York Daily Tribune*, "Governor Seward has so long been stigmatized by a reckless and ribald press as a Jacobin and a radical that those who now first study his inculcations carefully will be astonished to find him so eminently pacific and conservative." How many, though, were willing to listen to what Seward actually said? Most, perhaps too many, had already made up their minds about him. To southerners, as one congressman put it, "Seward is a perjured traitor, whom the Southerners could neither consistently support, or even obey, should the nation elect him President. Should the Republican party succeed in the next Presidential election, my advice to the South is to snap the cords of the Union at once, and forever." Small wonder, then, that Republicans considered nominating a less polarizing candidate for president.[43]

On the morning of February 29, Frances wrote to Will, enclosing an Etruscan scarf pin, a gift his father purchased in Italy, one of the items for family and friends that had recently arrived. She also sent a cameo for Father Michael Creedon, pastor of Holy Family Catholic Church in Auburn, which "has been blessed by the Pope. . . . This is the morning the speech is to be made. I wish it were over." She always wished the same, and undoubtedly did for the presidential campaign as well. "There are many people here from the North to hear it, and we are told the South too will be in attendance. All are going to the Capitol but Bell and I." She was not much help as a campaigner, which her son already knew. "I do not go to dinner but when I am able meet the guests at tea."[44]

On March 4 Will replied that "a full report of Father's speech reached us on Friday and was published in both the dailies. There is but one opinion in regard to it here, and judging from the papers from different parts of the state it seems to be universally concluded to be the greatest speech he ever made. . . . Nobody appears to find anything exceptionable in it." Three days later Frances wrote again to say that "commendations of the speech still come from all quarters" and the campaign continued apace. "We have an extra large dinner today, as Anna wishes to get through with the women before she goes home. She will probably go next week. She needs the rest." Frances was pleased that Jenny, who played so well, liked the new piano, and "must not neglect her music" after she married Will. On March 12 Henry and Anna left for New York, taking the campaign on the road. On March 13 Will received a telegram warning him to expect them and the throngs that gathered around Henry to arrive in Auburn the next day. It was such a crush that Henry stayed in the American Hotel rather than at home. Anna left for Albany alone the next day; Henry had "a constant succession of visitors," according to Will, "and was allowed just about as much time as he usually is when he remains in any place for a day or two." The local newspapers reported that Henry was home "'expressly to attend his son's wedding which was to take place during the present week' (and everyone was to be invited.)"[45]

When Senator Sumner came to dinner at the Sewards in Washington on March 16, he read aloud a book review, a performance that the infatuated Fanny gushed over in her diary: "beautifully written and assuredly beautifully read, slow and pathetically. Julia and I have determined to read slow." On March 17 Sumner called on her mother. On March 23 Fanny and Julia dined with Mary Martin, a twenty-two-year-old heiress, who lived on her family's estate on Lake Owasco, just south of Auburn. "I like Mary very much. I wish dear Mr. Sumner might only take a fancy to her. She would be such a good wife and he a kind husband." When introduced to President Buchanan, according to Fanny, "the President began to say something very flattering, when Mary said, 'Yes my father is a Democrat and I am the only Republican in the family.' Pretty bold and honest, I like that about Mary." Sumner called on March 26, 27, and 28, not always when her father was home, but the two men dined together on March 29 and again at the Sewards' house on March 31. "Mary Martin came in just before he left."[46]

Back in Auburn, Jenny was not at all well. Dr. Robinson had diagnosed her illness as "a cold in the face," but Will doubted him and his medicines. "I am inclined to think," he wrote to his mother on March 25, "that it is the same headache with which she used to suffer so much, brought on by continual excitement, and that one day's quiet would effect a much sooner cure than all the medicine Dr. Robinson can give, but between the Steam Engine across the road, Lucy's sewing machine downstairs, the baby in the same room, and her brother George (who like other boys takes much delight in making all the noise possible, merely because he is requested to keep quiet), she is kept so excited and nervous all the time." Nerves, Frances diagnosed from afar. She feared that Jenny suffered from neuralgia, which is pain along the course of a nerve. "I would advise that she take no medicine or as little as possible. Dr. Robinson's wife was an evidence of the mischievous effects of too much medicine for neuralgia. I wish Jenny would go and stay a week at the Lake . . . or somewhere else where she could be quiet. I think that would be the best medicine." Mary Ann Robinson, wife of the doctor, had died two years earlier.[47]

Will also asked his mother whether she had read that Wendell Phillips, a leading figure in American abolitionism, had denounced Senator Seward in a lecture he gave in Brooklyn on March 20. Phillips objected to Henry's "State of the Country" speech on the floor of the Senate and the logic that underpinned it. He thought Seward no more an abolitionist than Thomas Jefferson, George Washington, and John Jay, Founding Fathers who had owned slaves. In other words, Seward was no abolitionist and avoided the claim in public, at least while he was running for president. He, like the Founders, elevated the Union over liberty. By valuing preservation of the Union over the freeing of the enslaved, Seward showed himself to be no better or worse than other national politicians, in Phillips's opinion, and to have his priorities upside down. "No parchment however sacred, no machinery of government however venerable," by Phillips's lights, "is anything to me compared with the rights of the lowest individual that walks on the surface of our thirty-three States. I do not like Mr. Seward's motto." Phillips was not convinced that "Liberty and Union" could both be achieved, and he dismissed the idea that both could be preserved when "liberty" was denied to four million Americans. The reviews of the speech from other abolitionists were even more scathing.[48]

On April 18 a telegram brought bad news from home. According to Fanny's diary, an arsonist had set fire to the Sewards' "stable, carriage house, and shed, and worse than all Fanny and Dick, the horses, were burned last night. Only the cows saved, impossible to save horses. Poor dear Fanny, my own favorite horse. What a dreadful thing. Dick was Will's new horse, bought within two months. This is indeed sad news."[49]

Will also wrote a letter addressed to his father, which arrived a day or two after the telegram. "Our Barn together with the carriage House and sheds were entirely burned down this evening. The two horses were smothered before it was possible to get them out, although every effort was made." The fire apparently started in the cowsheds while Will was having his tea. He wanted his father to know that there was no chance the fire was an accident as the buildings were locked and dark before it started and none of the family or staff had been in there with lamps for more than a week. He wanted his mother to know that the horses were overcome by smoke before the fire reached them, so they suffered little. He wrote her that "Fanny and Dick are buried with Watch and Nep under the apple tree."[50]

Sumner called on Frances and Fanny on April 21, "asked a good deal about our going." Fanny wrote on April 22, "Last evening Mother rec[d] a beautiful letter from Aunty about the fire. Will behaved nobly, with great energy and perseverance, so much as remarkable presence of mind. I am so proud of him. The letter was sent to Mr. Sumner by mother to read. He returned it with a note saying 'This is a charming insight into your son's character. I am very grateful to you for sharing it with me.'" He closed the note, according to Fanny, with an observation addressing Will's heroism. "There is so much sham in the world, and so little true principle that I feel more and more alone, and sometimes very unhappy." Sumner contrasted Will's character with that of the common lot of men.[51]

Frances delayed their departure for home because a large dog had bitten Bell, which left Fanny's dog too ill to travel. She also hoped that Henry and Julia would accompany them. Frances and Fanny headed home on April 23, without Julia, who was extending her stay, and with Henry, who accompanied them part of the way. Two weeks prior to their departure, Frances had assured Will she did not expect him to have the house up and running on her return. She advised him to try to get Mrs. Adams or Katy, possibly Catharine Fanning, whose mother might be able to help her, to do the housekeeping. "Nothing need be done in the way of cooking," wrote Frances. "Fanny can go with you to Aunt Clara's and John to the hotel. I live on chocolates just now. You are doing so much I fear you will be sick, too."[52]

When they reached the station in Washington, there was a dispute with a "cross, rude official about getting Bell on the train," which required the intervention of Henry to get the dog onboard. Henry continued with the women and dog to Baltimore, where they had a layover of several hours, and Henry dined with Fanny and Frances before returning to Washington. "Reached Harrisburg without complaint about Bell by the officials," according to Fanny. They continued on the next morning. Will met them in Elmira at 4:00 a.m. on April 24. They "took boats at Jefferson, cars at Geneva, reached home at noon, snow all the way." Lazette and her dog Trip met them at the front door. Fanny's friend Mary Titus came to tea, as did Aunt Clara. Bell and Trip were well. Fanny's diary entry for April 25 ends "HOME, SWEET HOME."[53]

Conclusion

Homes Again, 1860

Frances was ecstatic to be home in Auburn. "The sun is bright today," she wrote Henry on April 29, 1860, "the weather much warmer, all traces of snow have disappeared. The birds are singing merrily." She was eager to housekeep. "There is much work to be done to put the place in order independent of repairing the ravages of the fire. Many inquiries are made about your coming home." She thought Henry hinted about retirement, when he wrote from Washington on May 5, "Next week this time I trust I shall be with you, mayhap to remain." At least, that is how she took such statements, although he did not actually say for how long, and he remained for only three weeks. Henry did not attend the convention because, as Fred later explained, it was his "habit during life to abstain from participating in any contest respecting his own candidacy. 'That work,' he used to say, he preferred to leave 'to those to whom it belonged,'" meaning Thurlow Weed and other supporters of his candidacy, his political friends.[1]

The Democrats met in Charleston from April 23 to May 3, where they were unable to nominate candidates for president and vice president, because southern delegates denied Senator Stephen Douglas of Illinois the two-thirds majority necessary for the nomination. They reconvened in Baltimore in June, splitting into two factions, one of which nominated Douglas and the other proslavery faction walked out of the convention and nominated Vice President John C. Breckinridge of Kentucky for president. Douglas and Breckenridge split about 48 percent of the popular vote in the November election.

The Republicans convened in Chicago May 16–18. Frances, who followed the newspapers closely, had her own hopes about the outcome. "When Mr. Greeley succeeds in nominating Judge McLean," she wrote to Henry, "we shall have you to help us beautify and enjoy our pleasant home." Horace Greeley, editor of the *New York Tribune*, was once a protégé of Henry and Thurlow Weed, as well as a member of Congress, but he split with Weed and Seward six years previously, a grievance he aired spitefully after the convention. Greeley's grudge against Seward translated into his newspaper's support for associate justice of the Supreme Court John McLean and, when that failed in the convention, former Missouri congressman Edward Bates. Greeley favored Abraham Lincoln for vice president but ultimately supported him as the party's presidential nominee with Hannibal Hamlin of Maine for VP.[2]

Southerners had their hopes too, which were not all equally inflammatory, but they agreed about Henry. "Gentlemen of the Republican party," said one of them, "I warn you. Present your sectional candidate in 1860; elect him as the representative of your system of labor; take possession of the Government as your instrument in this 'irrepressible conflict,'" quoting Seward's 1858 speech, "and we of the South will tear the Constitution to pieces, and look to our guns for justice." "We will never submit," said another, "to the inauguration of a Black Republican President." Republican moderates had good reason to hope for a less polarizing candidate, although there was no way for the Republican Party to appease the "Fire-Eaters," those proslavery southern Democrats who agitated for secession. A southern newspaper described Henry as "at once the greatest and most dangerous man in the government." Seward was to secessionists "the biographer of John Quincy Adams, and the follower in his footsteps." The mantle that William Lloyd Garrison, Harriet Martineau, and Charles Sumner denied him is the one that secessionists draped over Seward. He was damned for faintheartedness by one side and radicalism by the other. There was no escaping his many words during his previous three decades in public life. Over one million copies of his February speech in support of the admission of a free Kansas already circulated. More copies than that of his "Irrepressible Conflict" and "Higher Law" speeches were out there.[3]

In Auburn Frances prepared for a permanent full-family return home or movement into the White House; what she did not expect was a return to their Washington rental. Harriet and Nicholas Bogart had arrived to help return the 33 South Street house to its former state, before the Sewards had abandoned it for Washington. "I have 3 women cleaning house and 2 men whitewashing," Frances informed Henry on May 2. "I have some faint hope of seeing the house in order again, though it looks improbable at present." Will was overexerting himself as man of the household. He had a bad back and did not get enough sleep, according to his mother. "He went to bed at 11 and was up writing again at 6 this morning. He must not do this." She wrote to Henry about Will, "I think he will destroy himself while young by immoderate exertions"; starting his new bank, handling the tenants and real estate for his father, and filling the icehouse were simply too much for one person in her opinion. There was more than enough work at home for Will and his father if return to Auburn was their fate.[4]

Although Frances knew Henry was very busy in Washington in the weeks leading up to the convention, she expected him home as soon as Congress adjourned and knew he had decisions to make about closing up their Washington rental, which were probably not at the top of his mind. Although she wanted to keep Nicholas Bogart with her in Auburn to help bring the gardens up to their seasonal glory, she knew that Henry needed him more, so Nicholas headed back to DC. Frances was now reading the *Herald* instead of Greeley's *Tribune*, "as I prefer open enemies to secret friends, if friends at all." She thought the deadlocked Democratic convention "ludicrous" and hoped the Republicans did not quarrel in theirs. George Seward, who also wrote to Henry in May, knew his brother was busy but asked him to stop in Florida on his way home and approve, as he must as coexecutor of their father's estate, improvements George wanted to make to the family farm.[5]

Fanny followed the political news almost as closely as Frances did. On May 16 she wrote in her diary, "Today the Chicago convention begins. The New York delegates are all for Father. Many of his friends have gone." Henry stayed home, posing as a husband, father, patriarch, and country lawyer who preferred Auburn over Washington. The next day Fanny wrote, "No balloting of consequence. Prospects divided between Father and Bates. Horace Greeley, having gotten himself appointed as delegate from Oregon ~~is very bitter~~ is acting against Father and for Bates, and Blair of Silver Spring is bitter against the Seward party and strong for Bates." The next day Bates dropped out and "Lincoln taken up by Greeley & Co. Father votes highest on second ballot, 108. 3rd Ballot Abraham Lincoln of Illinois nominated . . . Father told Mother and I in three words, "A. broomstick Lincoln nominated.'" That is four words, but she inserted "broomstick" above the line. "His friends feel much distress. He alone has a smile. He takes it with philosophical and unselfish coolness." On Saturday, May 19, she wrote, "All father's friends disheartened, he alone cheerful. People act as if a great calamity had befallen the nation and 'Strong men weep like children.'"[6]

Gloom settled over Auburn. According to Fred, who quoted an anonymous traveler through the village, "Seward was the only cheerful man in town." In a letter to Fred on May 18, Henry wrote, "We are all well, and I think the least unhappy of all the families in our little city." To Weed, he said much the same in a letter written the same day. "You have my unbounded gratitude for this last, as for the whole life of efforts in my behalf. I wish that I was sure that your sense of the disappointment is as light as my own. It ought to be equally so, for we have been equally thoughtful and zealous, for friends, party, and country, and I know not what has been left undone that could have been done, or done that ought to be regretted."[7]

Henry spent the next week consoling those friends, many of them delegates returning from the convention. When asked how he maintained his good humor in the face of a devastating defeat, Fred quoted his father as saying, "Why should I not . . . I have been breasting a daily storm of censure. Now all the world seems disposed to speak kindly of me. Look at that pile of papers—Republican and Democratic—and you will find there is hardly one unkind word. When I went out to market this morning . . . I had the rare experience of a man walking about town after he is dead, and hearing what people would say of him. I confess I was unprepared for so much real grief, as I heard expressed at every corner."[8]

Fred and Anna had arrived in Auburn on the day the delegates chose Lincoln, summoned home by Henry to address domestic matters and await the convention news. The family focused over the ensuing six days on designs for the new barns and other renovations now that they believed they would be returning home. The barns were two stories, made of stone, and the construction had commenced under close supervision. The Sewards also planned a new library: "our old one will not accommodate the books now at Washington. We have a number of plans, the last is to make the 'little library' into a round tower with books on all sides and a spiral staircase all the way up to a little upper room. We are beginning to decide on this, I think."[9]

In another five days, Henry was back in Washington, where Frances sent her letter of May 30. "I fancy you in Washington this morning. I know it is not so pleasant as it is here among the trees, flowers and birds." She had failed to slow him down, keep him at home, dissuade him from pouring all of his energy into politics. And yet, "It surprises me that hardly one of the friends who have written to you recently seems to place the least value on a life closed in retirement from the wrangling, the envy, hatred and malice attendant upon political life." Was she really surprised or was this simply another approach to a subject that she had surely discussed with her husband before he left? "I believe Weed is the only one who has spoken of your withdrawal as a thing to be desired by yourself. It may be because he knows you better than others." Again, really? Did Frances really believe that she and Weed were the only ones who knew Henry well enough to expect him to retire in the aftermath of his failure to secure the nomination? If so, she was fooling herself; Henry had once promised an "experiment" in family life, but that was twenty-five years earlier and it failed in short order. Even wounded, as he was by the outcome of the convention, defeated by a broomstick of a man, Henry bounced up and returned to the fray.[10]

Yet Frances persisted in her hope that the family's time in Washington had come to an end and Henry would return soon to join them. She felt sorry for Greeley, not for Henry: "Poor Greeley has succeeded in outraging the feelings of his oldest friends. At the age of 50 he will not be likely to find new ones that will supply their places." Lucky Henry: "I am sure you will not be persuaded to return again to the Senate." She was confident her husband wanted no part of what lay ahead for the nation, because that is what he told her. "The more I consider the matter, the more obvious it appears that your determination is right and wise. 25 years of the best part of a man's life is all that his country can reasonably claim. Let those who are disposed to cavil go and do as well as you have done. You have earned the right to a peaceful old age." If Henry entertained thoughts of retirement, and in a fit of pique declared himself done with politics, that is understandable. It also makes sense that Frances wanted to believe him. But those who knew him well should not have understood such an utterance as any more than a gust rather than the gale that propelled him. Even if he was sick of the Senate, another opportunity might present itself. Another office, a new role, could entice him to remain in public service. For now, though, it was back to the Senate and on the road to campaign for the

Republican ticket, which did not include him. He was anything but retiring. Perhaps Frances was simply whistling into the wind of ambition that hurled her husband of thirty-six years.[11]

Family members thought they were gathering to comfort Henry, but he was off before they could even assemble. After Henry left, Frances continued to console Henry's friends, who called expecting to find him at home sulking. The latest was Colonel William Henry Carpenter, keeper of a livery stable, who had recently returned from the convention, where he had been one of Henry's loyal delegates. He was "much disappointed to find you gone," Frances wrote. "He looks as if he had buried all his friends. I tried in vain to make him smile when he was here. I hope your friends will some time or another regain their cheerfulness. It is melancholy to meet them now." What a role reversal for Frances, who was usually the one who needed cheering but was smiling now. "The weather is delightful. I wish you were here."[12]

Frances remained passionately committed to abolitionism even while wanting Henry home from the political battlefield. She expected Charles Sumner to carry the torch. "I am reading Mr. Sumner's 'terrible' speech," Frances wrote to Henry. "He chooses the example of 'John' rather than that of 'Jesus.' All well as usual." John the Baptist is portrayed as a strong but humble preacher who preceded the Messiah. Frances now hoped for a new leader to redeem the nation. She did not think Sumner's "The Barbarism of Slavery" was "terrible," but others did. He delivered the speech on June 4 to address the admission of Kansas to the Union, and it was his first speech on the floor of the Senate since the caning that had almost killed him four years previously. "Barbarous in origin; barbarous in its law; barbarous in all its pretensions; barbarous in the instruments it employs; barbarous in consequences; barbarous in spirit; barbarous wherever it shows itself, Slavery must breed Barbarians, while it develops everywhere alike in the individual and in the society to which he belongs, the essential elements of Barbarism. In this character it is now conspicuous before the world." Never one to mince words, Sumner's was a provocative and powerful return for a hero of the antislavery cause. He cited John Wesley, the founder of Methodism, John Locke, the political philosopher, and John Quincy Adams, another hero of the abolitionists, and he mentioned John Brown in passing, but not in praise. Sumner did not enlist Jesus in his cause, but he did elevate Adams as a founder of abolitionism.[13]

Senator James Chesnut, Democrat of South Carolina, replied. "Sir, in the heroic ages of the world, men were often deified, but they were deified for the possession and exercise of some virtue, wisdom, justice, magnanimity and courage. Yea, Sir, in Egypt they deified beasts and reptiles, but even that bestial people worshipped their idol on account of some supposed virtue. It has been left for this age, for this country, and for the Abolitionists of Massachusetts, to deify the incarnation of malice, mendacity and cowardice." This was the politics from which Frances expected Henry to retire contentedly, but she continued to cheer Sumner, and to fear for him, in his fight for the cause.[14]

On May 30 Henry wrote to Frances from Washington, a letter that again gave her hope that he would retire. "The journey and the reappearance at Washington in the character of a leader deposed by my own party," he explained, "in the hour of organization for decisive battle, thank God are past—and so the last of the humiliations has been endured." In what became an extremely long letter for Henry, he talked of kind people he met on the train, the awkwardness of some of the first meetings with Republicans, whom he knew or assumed to have abandoned him in Chicago, and dinners with true friends, including Charles Francis and Abigail Brooks Adams. "Good men came through the day to see me, and also this morning. Their eyes fill with tears, and they become speechless, as they speak of what they call 'ingratitude.' They console themselves with the vain hope of a day of 'vindication'; and my letters all talk of the same thing. But they awaken no response in my heart. I have not shrunk from any fiery trial prepared for me by the enemies of my cause. But I shall not hold myself bound to try, a second time, the magnanimity of its friends."[15]

Frances read such statements as plans for retirement; Henry only said, though, that he lacked the fire to run for president again. At least, that was how he felt as May 1860 ended, two weeks after his fifty-ninth birthday. If he ran again and won four years hence, he would be the third-oldest president inaugurated to that time. William Henry Harrison, who lived only a month into his term, and James Buchanan, the sitting president, were the only two who were older. On June 4 Henry wrote to Frances, "This morning I found your very beautiful and touching letter, which is very just as well as very natural." He did not reply directly to her "very natural" hope that he would retire.[16]

To Weed Henry wrote, "I am content to quit with the political world, when it proposes to quit with me," and not the other way around, as Frances had hoped. "But I am not insensible to the claims of a million of friends, nor indifferent to the opinion of mankind." This was by way of explaining to Weed that he was in no hurry to jump into the campaign in support of the Republican ticket, lest he appear "most falsely, to fear that I shall be forgotten. Later in the canvass, it may be seen that I am wanted for the public interest." Rest assured Henry was available as the party wanted him, but he hung back for now until he was called, in early August, a little more than a month later.[17]

On June 5 Henry learned by telegram that his old friend Congressman John L. Schoolcraft, husband of Henry's niece and ward Caroline, had taken desperately ill on his way home from the convention. He embarked immediately for Saint Catherine's, where Schoolcraft died on June 7, shortly after Henry's arrival at his bedside. On June 13 Henry was back in Washington. "I am at home; that is at this home, again." Frances would catch that reference to their Washington rental as home and fear it was true. "I came here last night," Henry continued; "at eleven I shall go to the Senate tread-mill, for day and night, cheerful, however, in the thought that responsibility has passed away from me, and that the shadow of it grows shorter every day." He claimed to look forward to returning to his Auburn home, but "an uncertainty hangs over the adjournment of Congress. The day fixed is next Monday," he wrote on Tuesday, June 19, the day after Will's birthday. "We are packing up here, and I mean, adjournment or no adjournment, to be at home with all my retinue, on Saturday night, Monday night, or Tuesday night, at all events, in time for Willie's wedding." Frances grew increasingly unsure, given Henry's long record, that he would prioritize family over politics this time. Despite her hopes and dreams, and the opening she saw in his rejection by the party, she feared that his heart remained in Washington. "It will be a grievous disappointment not to have you at the wedding," Frances informed him, having not yet received his letter of June 19, in which he promised to be there whether or not Congress adjourned.[18]

Henry chose family over politics by putting off a summons from Weed to attend Will and Jenny's wedding, but it was a postponement and not a cancellation. "I escaped on Friday," Henry wrote to Weed on Tuesday, June 26, "to give the needful attention to Willie's marriage, which comes off tomorrow. I had not been able, until this last moment, to inquire into the condition of his affairs, and to hear and counsel, as a child has a right to expect, in so important a transaction. So, of course, I cannot be in Albany tomorrow evening." "Will's wedding day," Fanny wrote in her diary on June 27. "At two o'clock today Will and Jenny started on their trip—to Canada and the St. Lawrence," Fanny wrote the next day. "How lonesome it seems without dear Will. . . . Aunty, Mollie, and I went to the depot to see the bridal folk off." From Niagara Falls on their honeymoon, Will wrote to Frances on June 29 that he and Jenny were well. By return mail, Frances hoped that Jenny's mother did not miss her more than Frances missed Will. "This day is so charming I almost wish myself at the Falls with you." Fanny too sent her regards and said that Will and Jenny would be missed at Auburn's July 4 fireworks display. Will sent his father, still at home in Auburn on the Fourth, a box of fish he caught in the St. Lawrence and asked him to forward some of them to his new mother-in-law.[19]

In early August Henry left home for New England, his first trip in support of the Republican ticket. He traveled from Windsor, Vermont, through New Hampshire, to Bangor and Portland, Maine, and then on to Boston, where Charles Francis Adams met him at the train depot. After his speeches, Seward spent the next day in Quincy with the Adamses before heading home. Some in the national party felt the ticket was in trouble, that they needed Seward to help revive confidence and enthusiasm for the cause. More invitations came and the party scheduled a trip through the Midwest for him.

On September 1 Henry again left Auburn, on the next leg of the campaign tour. The previous day Fanny entered in her diary that she was "sick this A.M. from crying last night. Concluded not to go." She accompanied her father reluctantly, having cried from anxiety about the trip, but "Father proposed to take some of my friends, proposed Ellen Perry [and] he seemed anxious to take me," so she went. "Mother and I went to ask her. She will go. Afternoon packed. Felt right, homesick about going . . . Mother not well." The first stop was Niagara Falls, which they reached at 8:00 p.m. "International Hotel, Splendid torch light procession brought Father. Roman candles. Speaking." On the morning of Monday, September 3, the party crossed over the Canadian border to Windsor and reached Milwaukee later the same day. "Ferry boat, rockets, evergreen trimmings. Introduction at Milwaukee depot, crowds. Frightened horses . . . Father brought up soon after by a long procession. . . . Speaking, large crowd, supper." Much the same on September 4: "Procession more than mile long . . . Father in midst, cheering of each company at house, went with Mrs. C. [Letitia Grace Chandler] to hear speaking, in Milwaukee depot."[20]

At Detroit there were cannons, speeches, and a meal for hundreds. There was an impressive torchlight procession of Wide Awakes, a new paramilitary organization formed across the northern states in support of the Republicans. It was the self-proclaimed voice of young voters eager to promote the antislavery cause. Seward spoke from a balcony to a large crowd.

> John Quincy Adams, the purest and wisest statesman I ever knew, died despairing of a peaceful solution of the problem. . . . Put this great cause into the keeping of your great, honest, worthy leader, Abraham Lincoln. Believe me sincere, when I say, that if it had devolved upon me to select from all the men in the United States a man to whom I should confide the standard of this cause, which is the object for which I have lived and labored, and for which I would be willing to die, that man would have been Abraham Lincoln.[21]

Truly, Henry believed himself the torchbearer of John Quincy Adams's cause, but his public support for Lincoln was Seward's contribution to the party's campaign. Then on to Dewitt, from which two hundred horsemen escorted his party to Lansing, "where a great crowd had gathered." There were more speeches and frequent stops to acknowledge crowds of well-wishers. At the State Agricultural College, the students addressed Senator Seward. "Procession formed. Took in our carriages. It was between two and three miles long. Girls dressed as states," according to Fanny. As her father began to speak, the stage gave way, but Henry escaped without injury. Another public dinner, another torchlight parade with roman candles that evening. In Kalamazoo on September 8, a band of fifty little boys, called "Little Giant Kittens," saluted the speakers with cheers, fifes, and drums. Again, her father spoke and Fanny estimated the crowd was twenty thousand, after which a delegation of forty mounted ladies presented him with a bouquet.[22]

On September 9 Fanny and Henry heard that the *Lady Elgin*, out of Milwaukee, went down in Lake Michigan, off of what is today the Chicago suburb of Highland Park. About three hundred lives were lost. Most of the passengers were headed to a speech of Stephen Douglas, one of Lincoln's opponents. The *Augusta* rammed the steamer below the waterline and sailed off, its captain believing the *Lady Elgin* remained seaworthy. Ninety-eight passengers survived. It remains the worst open-water ship disaster in the history of the Great Lakes. When Henry's campaign party reached Chicago that morning, they rode up Michigan Avenue, which Fanny found elegant, but in light of the accident the candidates canceled campaign events. They left by train at 9:00 p.m. and reached Milwaukee at 1:00 a.m., having "slept nicely," according to

Fanny's diary. There was likewise no public reception in Milwaukee, "as the whole city is in grief." On Tuesday, they left by train for Madison and stopped several times along the way for cheering crowds. "Once cannon shattered window glass in the railroad cars. Reached Madison at 4 o'clock, a very handsome procession." More speeches and another torchlight parade greeted them.[23]

On Friday, September 14, Fanny awoke on board a Mississippi River steamboat, which landed them in La Crosse, from which they traveled overland across the prairie. The next morning, they took another steamer from Prairie du Chien, which reminded her of the Hudson River steamboats. They were in Saint Paul, Minnesota, on Sunday, where Fanny attended church. They reached Dubuque, Iowa, on September 20 and road the rails to Fort Leavenworth, where they boarded another boat. They left Saint Louis on September 24, where her father addressed serenaders, and Fanny received "the most rare and exquisite bouquet of hot house flowers I ever saw," and "a German confectioner sent a box of exquisite French candies and bon bons to the ladies of Governor Seward's party."[24]

From Saint Louis they traveled by train to Springfield, Illinois, the home of the party's presidential candidate. Seward and Lincoln shook hands while the crowd cheered and cannons boomed. The stop was only twenty minutes, which included "a few moments devoted to a hasty private conference in regard to the political situation," according to Fred. "We are happy to report to you," Seward shouted through the cheers, that "although we have traveled over a large part of the country, we have found no doubtful States," and he guaranteed the vote of New York. "That is the way she did with John Quincy Adams; that is the way she sustained General Taylor, and that is the way she will sustain Abraham Lincoln."[25]

The whistle blew and the train was off to Chicago. Fanny stopped making diary entries on October 2, after remarking again that she liked Michigan Avenue and thought Chicago "a fine city." The train stopped for speeches at Cleveland and Erie, arriving back in Auburn on October 6. On October 8 Seward wrote to Lincoln, reiterating his belief that the candidate could count on the voters of New York. A week later Seward was back on the campaign trail in New York, speaking at Lyons, Binghamton, Fredonia, Seneca Falls, and elsewhere. On November 2 he spoke at the Palace Gardens in New York City. On November 6 every free state except for New Jersey voted for Lincoln; in New York the Republican ticket won by fifty thousand votes.[26]

In mid-December Henry met Weed in New York City to discuss their next political move. Without consulting Frances, Seward dispatched Weed to Illinois to lobby Lincoln for a cabinet appointment. On December 28 he wrote to inform Frances that he had accepted Lincoln's nomination as secretary of state. She advised him to decline, knowing that her advice came too late and, in any event, he would ignore it. His reply on New Year's Eve rejected her plea and included the line, "I could not be well or happy at home," which she had long known.[27]

Henry did not retire in Frances's lifetime. He followed the path of John Quincy Adams and continued in public service through some of the most trying times in the family's and American history. He did not share Frances's belief that he had done his share, was entitled to retirement, and would enjoy quiet time in her Auburn house and garden. To say that his seven years as secretary of state were fraught, personally and politically, understates the case and is another story.

While the Seward family had good reason to believe their public roles were over in November 1860, their lives would be anything but private in the decade ahead. The tension between hearth and home resolved, but not in favor of 33 South Street. All of them, including Frances, spent more time in Washington than ever before. When Frances and Jenny, with her small children, huddled in Auburn in fear of a Confederate assault on Washington, they nursed Fanny, who remained chronically consumptive, and Will through scarlet fever and a battlefield injury. The Seward men all rose to defend the nation, each in his own way, but only Will in battle, despite Gus's military career and his mother's fears.

Will remained his family's man of action, impulsive and possibly clumsy, due to his weak eyes, through illness and multiple leg injuries. Gus accepted, and sometimes sought, his father's intervention to keep him safe. Fred remained irreplaceable to Henry in the Department of State, and his wife Anna served the country as her father-in-law's diplomatic hostess par excellence. Lazette supported Frances in the domestic sphere, particularly after they lost Clary early in the decade. Fanny and Frances remained ill until Frances's palpitations and Fanny's consumption killed them after the 1865 assassination attempt on Henry, which also badly injured Gus and nearly killed Fred.

Henry, who was more often than not absent from home over the three and a half decades chronicled in this book, became a family man in the 1860s, but not in Auburn. He brought the family to him in their rented Washington house, and they supported him in his public role as they had never before. He replaced Frances as the family's hub even before her mid-decade death. He lived to mourn the loss of his two favorite women and persisted in public life after returning to Auburn to bury them.

Henry's greatest challenges and triumphs came as secretary of state through two administrations. His brief retirement of less than four years after that (1869–72) was also spent largely away from Auburn. Free to pursue his wanderlust without restraint despite physical infirmities, he circled the globe with new additions to the family: his adopted daughter Olive, who was Fanny's age, and her younger sister. The journey provided a model for diplomatic tours that long survived Seward. He collected artifacts from his travels that turned Elijah's and Frances's house into his home and eventually a museum that reflects his public career more than it does Frances's domestic sphere. Ray (Buzz) Messenger, a great-great-grandson, remembered that the house while still occupied by his great-uncle, William H. Seward III, was already a museum full of contents for which "Don't touch!" was the frequent warning.[28]

Since Henry outlived Frances by more than seven years, that is what we might expect to have happened, a house turned into a museum commemorating his illustrious career. There is also good reason, though, to expect that if Frances had been left to assimilate Henry's life and artifacts into 33 South Street, she would have done much the same thing. She was proud of Henry and aspired to make their home a place he was happy. After her death, the house went to Henry and then to Will, Jenny, and their three children, Cornelia Margaret Seward Allen, William Henry Seward III, and Frances Janet Seward Messenger. The third William inherited it from them and donated it as a museum under the care of the Fred L. Emerson Foundation.

As a museum, it reflects more of Henry's accomplished career than it does Frances's domestic scene—a room that was once a nursery now tells the story of the assassination attempt. Another in the basement adjacent to the old kitchen, where the family dined informally, now tells the story of the Underground Railroad. There is a diplomatic gallery of photos, rotating displays of china used to serve dinners in Washington, items brought back from Alaska and China, gifts made to Henry as governor, senator, and secretary of state, and busts and portraits of Henry and family members. Most of their books, including Fanny's library, remain in the house; perhaps those are the clearest legacy of Frances on display.

If the Sewards' story is less monumental and darker than you expected, and more complex, perhaps you should not be surprised. Think about the Lincolns, Roosevelts, Kennedys, and Bidens. We know that wealth, ambition, and power are not necessarily paths to personal happiness, and family life is complicated and full of losses. Authors often help us romanticize the past and underestimate the challenges for everyone, of however much success and of whatever class, ethnicity, and race, who lived between 150 and 200 years ago. In the case of the Sewards, that would be hagiography, romance, or fiction. If the Sewards had their share or more of sadness and failure, dashed hopes and crushed dreams, illness and losses, they also led lives of privilege and fulfillment, and they shared in each other's triumphs and joys.

The Sewards and Millers loved each other, perhaps more than the generations before them were capable of. If they were disappointed in that, it was because, as Frances thought, their reality was much less romantic than a Walter Scott novel, although equally tragic. Finally, we should recognize that others who lived through the Victorian era were more successful in keeping their flaws private, as the Sewards would have done too, if they only knew how much of themselves they left in the boxes, trunks, and baskets of letters stored in their attic for eighty years after Henry died before ending up in a university library where librarians, students, faculty members, and other researchers would find their story as instructive as those of their great men.

Postscript

Reflections on Genre

Family history is not experiencing a renaissance, mainly because it has not gone out of fashion, but it is evolving fashionably. Looking back half a century, it was the laboratory of the town-study historians in the 1960s and 1970s, who wrote about communities of families and the transfer of property across generations.[1] Some crunched data with computers, others embraced psychological theory in their analysis; all approached families as interactive units of vast social significance within specific historical contexts. For me, the inspiration was Lawrence Stone's *The Family, Sex, and Marriage*, which led me to graduate school at Princeton, where he became a life-inspiring mentor. At about the same time or shortly after, I found several other family historians and their scholarship also inspiring; in their own ways, Michael Zuckerman, Phillip Greven, John Demos, and Kenneth Lockridge became mentors. Historians of their generation saw families as both the engines and cabooses of change. The second modern wave was a product of women's history, as one wing of it evolved in the 1970s and 1980s to gender history and the family became a prominent setting for exploring marriage, reproduction, parenting, adoption, childhood, medical practice, gender roles and relations, and law in the eighteenth and nineteenth centuries.[2]

Another influence evolved in tandem with the others. There was and remains an intellectual/cultural slant to the collective biographies of prominent literary figures, including the James, Huxley, and Alcott families, and those of Emily Dickinson, Ralph Waldo Emerson, James Fenimore Cooper, and Lydia Maria Child, among others.[3] Biographies of the families of major political figures is its own subgenre, perhaps most persistently the families (slave and free) of Thomas Jefferson, but not of his alone, as the families of such first-line political figures as John Adams and John Quincy Adams have also had their share of biographers. So too have the wives of politicians from Washington, Adams, and Madison to Polk and Lincoln been the subjects of biographies.

The fact that they were presidents does not make their families more significant in the history of families, and they are certainly less representative of their time and place. The same can be said about the corporate (Carnegie, Ford, Rockefeller, etc.) and political (Roosevelt, Kennedy, Bush, etc.) dynasties in the generations to follow them.[4]

As the authors well knew, in the town studies of Greven, Lockridge, Zuckerman, and those who came after them, the analysis was skewed by the comparatively rich survivals of records for the wealthiest and most prominent families, but, nonetheless, those historians succeeded better than any before them in recovering the experiences of families in the middling and lower ranks of society. The same is true for social/cultural historians who have utilized the records of prominent planters to access the experiences, if not the perspectives, of those at the very bottom of American society. The gaps, of which there are many, include a much thinner understanding of the internal lives of people more typical of the middle than the top and bottom rungs of society. This would include, but not be confined to, our understanding of middle- and upper-middle-class consumers of culture rather than just its producers, of second- and third-line public figures and their families, of the rising professional classes, of women and men who did not leave an enduring legacy of radicalism or accomplishment, of writers whose work we no longer read, but who were more representative of their times than were the Emily Dickinsons, Abraham Lincolns, Walt Whitmans, Henry David Thoreaus, and Elizabeth Cady Stantons of the nineteenth century. We also have a solid transatlantic perspective on writers, including, for example, the families of Charles Dickens, Jane Austen, and the Brontës.

There is an argument to be made, then, for reaching out from the cultural centers to broaden the base of our understanding of Americans of both genders during the early American and antebellum eras in their family contexts, for exploring the links between public and private spheres, and for recognizing that the genders and spheres were never entirely separate but rather often entwined. Writing history from a family perspective outward decenters gender and public historical significance in ways that historicize the human condition.

Acknowledgments

There are always people to thank, but seldom so many. The project started with an idea fifteen years ago of the then director of the Department of Rare Books, Special Collections, and Preservation at the University of Rochester. Richard Peek thought that the 350,000-page William Henry Seward Collection, the department's largest and most prestigious, might be a good candidate for a documentary edition. Peter Lennie, then dean of the Faculty of Arts and Sciences and later provost, wondered in another context why the humanities did not adopt the sciences' laboratory model for research and teaching. Then came along an initiative in the digital humanities, supported by then dean of the River Campus Libraries, Mary Ann Mavrinac. Dean of the School of Arts and Sciences Gloria Culver was equally supportive. Somehow these unconnected ideas morphed into a digital humanities project focused on the Seward family's correspondence, a subset of the larger Seward Papers manuscript collection that intrigued students for their relatable intergenerational candor and their inclusion of the voices of women, children, and men.

Our collaboration with the Seward House Museum in Auburn gave the students introductions to the material artifacts, including the very house, that gave the Seward family's correspondence and lives recoverable meaning. Students, librarians, and the senior citizen volunteers who contributed so much to our transcription accompanied us on our annual visits, complete with box lunches and bus drivers who never seemed to know the way. My thanks to the museum's director, Billye Chabot, and its education director, Jeffrey Ludwig, for tolerating us by the busload and making those visits and picnics on the grounds so wonderful.

Nora Dimmock, then head of Digital Scholarship in the River Campus Libraries, was essential in the project's technological foundations and ultimate product. Nora helped us design a website, insisted that we document our processes, and taught students coding for several years before passing that on. Josh Romph and Jeff Suszczynski were the programmers who launched and sustained our website (seward-project.org), which the students designed with Nora's guidance. Emily Sherwood replaced Nora when Nora moved on to Brown; Lisa Wright helped us with photography and digital images, as did the late Jim Barbero, visual technologist, musician, long-distance runner, one of the noontime gym rats, and all-around great guy. Matt Mann, university photographer and videographer, helped train students in those skills; Blair Tinker taught us GIS, and Joe Easterly helped teach coding.

In the Department of Rare Books, Andrea Reithmayr, Rare Books and Special Collections librarian, provided essential support in the workflow over the life of the project. Alison Reynolds, Autumn Haag, and Melinda Wallington gave us hands-on support with manuscripts, not the least of which was physically locating letters in the vast collection. Melissa Mead, now university archivist, helped us launch and kept us on the path through alien technology, a labyrinthine electronic collection guide, and an antiquated but essential research tool called a "card catalog"—actually two.

There were too many student collaborators to try to name them all, but the student managers of the project started with my initial collaborator, Michael Read, whose idea it also was to enlist senior citizen transcribers as volunteers. When Mike had his fill after several years, Serenity Sutherland took his place and was eventually succeeded by Michelle Furlano and Lauren Davis as comanagers, and then Lauren saw the project through to its end. Camden Burd, Kate Hughes, Rhianna Gordon, Corinna Hill, Carrie Knight, Tallis Polashenski, and Demeara Torres were all part of the management team. The transcribers were legion, including many undergraduate and graduate students, and the senior citizens who worked with us at The Highlands and elsewhere; we certainly could not have done it without all of them, and we would not have wanted to.

The project was ultimately supported by about $1.2 million in grants. The National Historic Publications and Records Commission, Fred L. Emerson Foundation, and Robert D. L. Gardiner Foundation were our principal donors, the last two of which supported us through the pandemic, when we learned how to do it all remotely. Very early on we received a gift from an alumna, Pamela Lessing, which paid student salaries over the project's first couple of summers. Pam called it "seed money," and indeed from it our tree grew. Without the late Debra Haring, assistant dean for grants and contracts, our first grant applications would never have gotten off the ground, never mind been successful.

To say that Debra was the most overqualified person for her job I ever worked with at the university would be an understatement. The support of Dean Mavrinac was both creative and essential, as were the efforts of Ellen Speer, assistant vice president of foundation relations, and Mairead Hartman, director of foundation relations. I much appreciate their support, skills, and efforts on the project's behalf. I also enjoyed our brainstorming sessions.

Lou Masur, friend for over forty-five years, who writes shorter books so there are enough trees left for mine, read parts and helped me see the flaws. Mike Read was there at the beginning and read the whole thing at the end. I am always grateful for these two friends. Denise, as always, tolerated a sometimes hyperfocused and frequently cranky husband. Friends at Lake Geezerbegone, where we now live, were tolerant of a new and eccentric neighbor. My dogs, first Joe and now Rose, lifted me by example and love through the past decade of trials and trauma. They are both the best dog. Manny (cat) could not care less but was available when he felt like it for comic relief. It takes a village and I am grateful for mine. It has been a rough last decade in which the losses have piled up. The death of Moses at age twenty-seven left a hole that will never be filled. Peter Miller lived and laughed with me to a ripe old age, but I miss him daily no less. Allen Harrison, my first college friend and college roommate, and Val Martinez, my fellow alien in our first year of graduate school, both left way too early at age sixty-eight, making me feel older and less wise than ever. And yet, we go on.

At Three Hills/Cornell, I am extremely grateful to Meagan Piel Levinson, who saw the project's promise and was essential to whipping it into the shape it is now. India Miraglia, acquisitions assistant; Karen Laun, assistant managing editor; Lori Rider, copyeditor; Alex Vlahov, publicist; Martyn Beeny and Alfredo Guttierrez Rios, marketing; and Kimberly Glyder, cover design, were consummate professionals and did a great job. Enid Zafran did a great job with the index. It was a pleasure working with them all.

This book and the one I am now writing on the Seward family's Civil War are products of the many students, classes, and conversations about the letters and family members. Going back more than a dozen years now, I have taught both the history that provides the letters' context and the documentary editing that gave us all an intimate relationship with our historical subjects. I remember walking into the lab in the early days and coming upon one of the students crying. Romantic breakup? Illness of an elderly relative? No, "Aunt Clary died," the student sniffled. Well, yes, Clarinda Miller McClallen died in 1862, over 160 years ago now. Never in my experience had teaching history more effectively connected students to the past. Now I am crying too. Thanks everybody for the best experience of my professional life. This book is for all of you.

Notes

Introduction

1. William Henry Seward, "On the Irrepressible Conflict," speech delivered in Rochester, New York, October 25, 1858, available at New York History Net, http://www.nyhistory.com/central/conflict.htm.

2. On Seward, see Doris Kearns Goodwin, *Team of Rivals: The Political Genius of Abraham Lincoln* (New York: Simon & Schuster, 2005); Walter Stahr, *Seward: Lincoln's Indispensable Man* (New York: Simon & Schuster, 2012); Peter Charles Hoffer, *Seward's Law: Country Lawyering, Relational Rights, and Slavery* (Ithaca, NY: Cornell University Press, 2023); Ernest N. Paolino, *The Foundations of the American Empire: William Henry Seward and U.S. Foreign Policy* (New York: Cornell University Press, 1974); Joseph A. Fry, *Lincoln, Seward, and U.S. Foreign Relations in the Civil War* (Lexington: University Press of Kentucky, 2019).

3. Elizabeth Cady Stanton, *Eighty Years and More: Reminiscences, 1815–1897* (New York: European Publishing Company, 1898), 154.

4. FMS to WHS, October 27, 1831. Unless otherwise noted, manuscript correspondence is from the William H. Seward Papers, Department of Rare Books, Special Collections, and Preservation, Rush Rhees Library, University of Rochester.

5. Jane Austen, *Emma* (London: Mathew Carey, 1816; New York: Penguin Books, 2015), vol. 3, chap. 15, 363–64.

6. FMS to WHS, March 17, 1831.

7. FMS to WHS, January 27, 1831.

8. FMS to WHS, December 1, 1853.

1. Ancestors in the House, 1817–1851

1. Benjamin F. Hall, "Genealogical and Biographical Sketch of the Late Honorable Elijah Miller," Elijah Miller Papers, box 6, folder 7, p. 11, University of Rochester, River Campus Libraries, Department of Rare Books, Special Collections, and Preservation (hereafter Elijah Miller Papers).

2. J. Cheryl Exum, "'Mother in Israel': A Familiar Figure Reconsidered," in Letty M. Russell, ed., *Feminist Interpretation of the Bible* (Philadelphia: Westminster Press, 1985), 76, 83–85; Irene Thelle Rannfrid, "Matrices of Motherhood in Judges 5," *Journal for the Study of the Old Testament* (May 7, 2019).

3. FMS to LMW, January 31, 1841; Hall, "Genealogical and Biographical Sketch," 3.

4. Hall, "Genealogical and Biographical Sketch," 4; genealogical chart apparently prepared by Adeline Schooley Gurnee (b. 1809), cousin of Frances M. Seward, box 6, folder 10, Elijah Miller Papers, inserted in Hall, "Genealogical and Biographical Sketch," 2.

5. Frederick W. Seward, *Reminiscences of a War-Time Statesman and Diplomat, 1830–1915* (New York: G. P. Putnam's Sons, 1916), 5.

6. Seward, *Reminiscences*, 6.

7. Benjamin F. Hall to William H. Seward Jr., September 26, 1877, pinned on blank page between pp. 5 and 6 of Hall, "Genealogical and Biographical Sketch." The source for the story is Benson J. Lossing, *Pictorial Field Book of the Revolution*, 2 vols. (New York: Harper & Brothers, 1860). Hall apparently delivered the manuscript on or about November 7, 1877; notation on original copy.

8. Frederick W. Seward, *Reminiscences*, 8–9.

9. Hall, "Genealogical and Biographical Sketch," 5–13; typed nine-page manuscript in Seward House Museum, titled "The Early History of Cayuga County, by Hon. Elijah Miller, and Also His Personal Biography." It has very little biographical information.

10. Hall, "Genealogical and Biographical Sketch," 14–21.

11. Hall, "Genealogical and Biographical Sketch," 34.

12. Hall, "Genealogical and Biographical Sketch," 35–37.

13. Hall, "Genealogical and Biographical Sketch," 67–69.

14. Hall, "Genealogical and Biographical Sketch," 72–73.

15. Hall, "Genealogical and Biographical Sketch," 37–39.

16. Hall, "Genealogical and Biographical Sketch," 74–79.

17. Hall, "Genealogical and Biographical Sketch," 80 and two-page addenda on the Miller girls' education.

18. Hall, "Genealogical and Biographical Sketch," 81–82.

19. Hall, "Genealogical and Biographical Sketch," 83–84; WHS to SSS, July 15, 1823; SSS to WHS, September 26, 1828.

20. FMS to LMW, November 26, 1839.

21. FMS to WHS, June 13, August 5, November 25, 1833.

22. FMS to WHS, November 18, 1832.

23. FMS to WHS, August 5, 1833; FMS to WHS, February 17, July 26, 1829; FMS to WHS, February 1 and 7, 1831.

24. FMS to WHS, February 1 and 27, 1831; April 3, 1831; June 24, 1832; June 13, 1833.

25. FMS to WHS, July 22, 1833.

26. FMS to WHS, January 16, 1831; FMS to LMW, September 22, 1844.

27. FMS to LMW, October 3, 1846; August 31, 1833; December 23, 1840.

28. FMS to LMW, November 26, 1839.

29. FMS to WHS, March 28, 1831; FMS to LMW, January 1, 1859, March 28, 1860; LMW to FMS, May 19, 1822; FMS to WHS, January 16 and 27, 1831, January 23, 1851.

30. FMS to WHS, January 16, 1831.

31. FMS to WHS, February 25, March 11 and 28, 1831; ExM to WHS, February 23, 1833.

32. FMS to WHS, December 21, 1836; FMS to AHS, February 13, 1849.

33. FMS to WHS, July 22, 1833.

34. FMS to WHS, June 24, 1832, February 24, 1829; AHS to WHS, July 7, 1839.

35. FMS to LMW, June 23, 1845; FMS to WHS, December 12, 1848; FMS to LMW, December 7, 1848, January 7, 1849; LMW to WSJ, January 1, 1850; FMS to WHS, May 25 and June 9, 1850, January 19, 1849; FAS to LMW, 1850; FMS to WHS, November 20, 1844; FMS to LMW, September 22, 1844.

36. FMS to WHS, January 23, February 1, March 17, 1831.

37. ExM to WHS, January 31, 1832; AHS to WHS, December 11, 1838; ExM to FWS, February 24, 1842; FMS to AHS, June 25, 1843, February 13, 1849; FMS to LMW, June 9, 1844.

38. Steven Mintz, *Huck's Raft: A History of American Childhood* (Cambridge, MA: Harvard University Press, 2004), chap. 3.

39. Mintz, *Huck's Raft*, chap. 3.

40. FMS to WHS, January 23, 1831.

41. FMS to WHS, November 18, 1832.

42. FMS to WHS, September 20, 1839; WSJ to WHS, July [?], 1848; FMS to WHS, September 29, 1836.

43. FMS to WHS, May 24, 1838.

44. FMS to LMW, March 28, 1842; CMM to LMW, March 9, 1842; FMS to WHS, March 29, 1837, March 27, 1831.

45. FMS to WHS, December 11, 1842.

46. FMS to WHS, [?] 1851.

47. FMS to LMW, March 25, 1852; FMS to WHS, May 22, 1852, November [?], 1851.

48. FMS to WHS, May 22, 1852, November [?], 1851.

49. FMS to WHS, May 22, 1852.

50. FMS to LMW, March 25, 1852.

51. FMS to LMW, April 17, 1845.

52. FMS to LMW, January 25, 1852.

2. Henry's Backstory, 1801–1824

1. Frederick W. Seward, *William H. Seward: An Autobiography from 1801 to 1834* (New York: Derby & Miller, 1891), 19–20.

2. Seward, *Autobiography*, 21–22.

3. Seward, *Autobiography*, 21–22, 27.

4. E. Anthony Rotundo, *American Manhood* (New York: Basic Books, 1993), introduction.

5. Seward, *Autobiography*, 21, 25.

6. Rotundo, *American Manhood*, chap. 1.

7. Seward, *Autobiography*, 27, 28.

8. Seward, *Autobiography*, 27; David N. Gellman, *Emancipating New York: The Politics of Slavery and Freedom, 1777–1827* (Baton Rouge: Louisiana State University Press, 2006).

9. Seward, *Autobiography*, 28.

10. On the Samuel Seward estate and Chloe's house, see Clarence A. Seward to WHS, June 17, 1870; on Chloe's family, see biography of Chloe Coe, Seward Family Digital Archive, https://sewardproject.org/person-public-fields/4388; on New York's gradual emancipation laws, see Gellman, *Emancipating New York*.

11. FMS to WHS, April 22, 1832.

12. Seward, *Autobiography*, 31.

13. Rotundo, *American Manhood*, chap. 3; Jane Fiegen Green, "'An Opinion of Our Own': Education, Politics, and the Struggle for Adulthood at Dartmouth College, 1814–1819," *History of Education Quarterly* 52 (2012): 173–95.

14. WHS to Daniel Jessup Jr., March 10, 1817.

15. Seward, *Autobiography*, 34.

16. Seward, *Autobiography*, 36.

17. Rotundo, *American Manhood*, chap. 3.

18. Seward, *Autobiography*, 39, 40.

19. WHS to SSS, February 2, 1819.

20. WHS to SSS, February 2, 1819.

21. Seward, *Autobiography*, 42.

22. Seward, *Autobiography*, 43.

23. Seward, *Autobiography*, 43.

24. Walter Stahr, *Seward: Lincoln's Indispensable Man* (New York: Simon & Schuster, 2012), 14; Rossetta Alexander to WHS, April 11, 1866.

25. Rossetta Alexander to WHS, April 11, 1866.

26. George Washington Seward to Louisa Cornelia Canfield, April 21, 1827.

27. Seward, *Autobiography*, 44.

28. Seward, *Autobiography*, 45.

29. Seward, *Autobiography*, 46, 47; WHS to Daniel Jessup Jr., January 24, 1820.

30. Seward, *Autobiography*, 48.

31. Seward, *Autobiography*, 48, 51.

32. GWS to WSJ, August 4, 1873.

33. Seward, *Autobiography*, 52.

34. Seward, *Autobiography*, 53–54.

35. Seward, *Autobiography*, 54–55; Sean Wilentz, *Chants Democratic: New York City and the Rise of the American Working Class, 1788–1850* (New York: Oxford University Press, 1984); Eric Foner, *Free Soil, Free Labor, Free Men: The Ideology of the Republican Party before the Civil War* (New York: Oxford University Press, 1970); Michael F. Holt, *The Rise and Fall of the American Whig Party: Jacksonian Politics and the Onset of the Civil War* (New York: Oxford University Press, 1999); Glyndon G. Van Deusen, "The Life and Career of William Henry Seward, 1801–1872," *University of Rochester Library Bulletin* 31, no. 1 (Autumn 1978), https://rbscp.lib.rochester.edu/3452.

36. Seward, *Autobiography*, 62.

37. Seward, *Autobiography*, 62.

38. WHS to SSS, August 12, 1823.

39. WHS to SSS, August 12, 1823.

40. WHS to SSS, August 12, 1823. On the Kellogg family, see Stephen W. Phoenix, *The Whitney Family of Connecticut, and Its Affiliations* (Hartford, CT: Bradford Press, 1878), 760.

41. WHS to SSS, August 12, 1823.

42. WHS to SSS, August 15, 1823.

43. WHS to SSS, December 20, 1823.

44. WHS to SSS, June 21, 1824.

45. WHS to SSS, August 5, 1824.

46. WHS to SSS, August 5, 1824.

47. WHS to SSS, August 5, 1824.

48. Seward, *Autobiography*, 62; WHS to SSS, December 9, 1824.

49. Rotundo, *American Manhood*, chap. 4; Richard Godbeer, *The Overflowing of Friendship: Love between Men and the Creation of the American Republic* (Baltimore: Johns Hopkins University Press, 2009); Richard Godbeer, *Sexual Revolution in Early America* (Baltimore: Johns Hopkins University Press, 2004); Carroll Smith-Rosenberg, "The Female World of Love and Ritual: Relations between Women in Nineteenth-Century America," *Signs* 1 (1975): 1–29.

50. George E. Baker, ed., *The Works of William H. Seward*, vol. 3 (New York: Redfield, 1853), 117–27.

51. David Berdan to WHS, March 12, 1826, March 21, 1824.

52. David Berdan to WHS, September 16, 1823.

3. Inmates All, 1825–1831

1. LMW to FMS, May 19, 1822; Charles Brockden Brown, *Wieland; or, The Transformation, an American Tale* (New York: H. Caritat, 1798); FMS to WHS, February 24, 1829.

2. LMW to FMS, May 19, 1822.

3. LMW to FMS, May 19, 1822; Stephanie Coontz, *Marriage, a History: How Love Conquered Marriage* (New York: Viking Penguin, 2005); Karen Lystra, *Searching the Heart: Women, Men, and Romantic Love in Nineteenth-Century America* (New York: Oxford University Press, 1989).

4. LMW to FMS, May 19, 1822.

5. LMW to FMS, May 19, 1822.

6. LMW to FMS, July 7, 1822.

7. LMW to FMS, July 7, 1822.

8. LMW to FMS, July 7, 1822.

9. LMW to FMS, July 7, 1822.

10. Marcia Armstrong Seward to WHS, January 29, 1825; "Miscarriage," Mayo Clinic, September 8, 2023, https://www.mayoclinic.org/diseases-conditions/pregnancy-loss-miscarriage/symptoms-causes/syc-20354298.

11. Marcia Armstrong Seward to WHS, January 29, 1825.

12. Shannon Withycombe, *Lost: Miscarriage in Nineteenth-Century America* (New Brunswick, NJ: Rutgers University Press, 2019), 12, 13, 20.

13. WHS to SSS, February 21, May 11, 1825; LCC to WHS, March 19, 1825; BJS to WHS, April 19, May 19, 1825.

14. Louisa Cornelia Seward to WHS, January 31, 1825.

15. George Washington Seward to Louisa Cornelia Seward, April 21, 1827; Louisa Cornelia Seward to WHS, January 31, March 19, 1825.

16. George Washington Seward to Louisa Cornelia Seward, April 21, 1827; Louisa Cornelia Seward to WHS, January 31, March 19, 1825; Mahlon D. Canfield to WHS, April 2, 1825.

17. Louisa Cornelia Seward to SSS, March 20, 1826; SSS to WHS, July 26, 1826; MJS to WHS, October 15, 1826.

18. LCC to SSS and Mary Jennings Seward, 1827.

19. LCC to SSS and Mary Jennings Seward, 1827.

20. BJS to WHS, August 29, 1828; LCC to WHS, February 23, 1829.

21. FMS to WHS, March 3, 12, 16, 1829; LCC to FMS, March 16, 1829; Aaron O'Neill, "Child Mortality Rate (Under 5 Years Old) in the United States, from 1800 to 2020," Statista, August 9, 2024, https://www.statista.com/statistics/1041693/united-states-all-time-child-mortality-rate/#:~:text=The%20child%20mortality%20rate%20in,it%20to%20their%20fifth%20birthday.

22. BJS to WHS, March 14, 1825.

23. BJS to WHS, April 8 and 19, 1825.

24. BJS to WHS, March 14, 1825.

25. LCC to FMS, February 25, 1828; FMS to WHS, October 17, 1727.

26. FMS to WHS, February 24, 1829, January 2, September 25, 1831.

27. FMS to WHS, January 27, 1831.

28. FMS to WHS, January 27, 1831.

29. FMS to WHS, January 27, February 1, 7, 20, 1831.

30. FMS to WHS, April 19, August 22 (two letters), September 18, 1831.

31. Coontz, *Marriage*, chap. 9 and 10.

32. FMS to WHS, February 21 and 27, 1831; Hall, *Genealogical and Biographical Sketch*, 84–85.

33. Seward, *Autobiography*, 75–76, 80.

34. Seward, *Autobiography*, 75–76.

35. WHS to SSS, May 11, 1825.

36. WHS to SSS, May 11, 1825.

37. WHS to SSS, May 11, 1825.

38. WHS to SSS, May 11, 1825.

39. WHS to SSS, May 11, 1825.

40. WHS to SSS, October 12, 1826.

41. BJS to WHS, February 8 and 21, March 7, April 17, 1828.

42. BJS to WHS, February 8 and 21, March 7, April 17, 1828.

43. BJS to WHS, May 21, 1828.

4. For Better, 1831

1. Scott W. Anderson, *Auburn, New York: The Entrepreneurs' Frontier* (Syracuse, NY: Syracuse University Press, 2015), 6; Henry Hall, *History of Auburn* (Auburn, NY: Dennis Bros., 1869); Elliot G. Storke, *History of Cayuga County, New York* (Syracuse, NY: D. Mason, 1879).

2. Anderson, *Auburn*, chap. 1.

3. "Population of Auburn, NY," last updated 2016, https://population.us/ny/auburn/.

4. Charles E. Rosenberg, *The Cholera Years: The United States in 1832, 1849, and 1866* (Chicago: University of Chicago Press, 1968).

5. Nancy F. Cott, *The Bonds of Womanhood: "Woman's Sphere" in New England, 1780–1835* (New Haven, CT: Yale University Press, 1977).

6. FMS to WHS, January 2, 1831.

7. Seward, *Autobiography*, 80; FMS to WHS, January 2, 1831.

8. WHS to FMS, January 2, 1831.

9. WHS to FMS, January 2, 1831; Seward, *Autobiography*, 83.

10. WHS to FMS, January 5, 1831.

11. FMS to WHS, April 4, 1831; Lord George Byron, *Works of the Rt. Hon. Lord Byron*, 8 vols. (New York: William Borradaile, 1825).

12. WHS to FMS, January 6 and 7, 1831.

13. WHS to FMS, January 7, 1831.

14. WHS to FMS, January 8 and 9, 1831.

15. FMS to WHS, January 12, 1831.

16. WHS to FMS, January 16, 1831.

17. WHS to LMW, January 16, 1831.

18. FMS to WHS, January 16, 1831.

19. FMS to WHS, January 16, 1831.

20. FMS to WHS, January 16, 1831.

21. WHS to FMS, January 17 and 18, 1831.

22. FMS to WHS, January 18, February 15 and 20, 1831; James Russell Lowell, *A Fable for Critics* (New York: George P. Putnam, 1848), quoted in Nina Baym, "The Women of Cooper's Leatherstocking Tales," *American Quarterly* 23 (1971): 696.

23. Baym, "The Women of Coopers Leatherstocking Tales"; Chuck Zeitvogel, "Gender Power and Social Class" (MA thesis, SUNY Brockport, 2004), available at James Fenimore Cooper Society website, http://www.oneonta.edu/external/cooper/articles/other/2004other-zeitvogel.html.

24. FMS to WHS, January 19, 1831.

25. WHS to FMS, January 24, 1831.

26. WHS to FMS, January 24, 1831.

27. WHS to FMS, January 21, 1831.

28. FMS to WHS, January 23 and 27, 1831.

29. FMS to WHS, January 23 and 27, 1831.

30. FMS to WHS, February 1, 1831.

31. FMS to WHS, April 9, 1831; Coontz, *Marriage*, 148.

32. FMS to WHS, March 28, 1831.

33. FMS to WHS, April 3, 1831; Coontz, *Marriage*, chap. 9.

34. FMS to WHS, April 4 and 7, 1831.

35. FMS to WHS, April 9, 1831.

36. FMS to WHS, April 9 and 13, 1831.

37. FMS to WHS, April 13, 1831.

38. FMS to WHS, April 9, 1831; Seward, *Autobiography*, 75–76.

39. FMS to WHS, April 17, 1831.

40. FMS to WHS, April 17, 1831.
41. FMS to WHS, April 17, 1831.
42. FMS to WHS, April 17, 1831.
43. FMS to WHS, April 17, 1831.
44. FMS to WHS, April 17, 1831.
45. FMS to WHS, April 17, 1831.
46. FMS to WHS, April 17, 1831.
47. FMS to WHS, April 17, 1831.
48. Seward, *Autobiography*, 80.
49. FMS to WHS, April 17, 1831. Frances completed the letter on April 18.
50. WHS to AHT, May 1, 1831.
51. WHS to AHT, May 1, 1831.
52. WHS to AHT, May 1, 1831.
53. WHS to AHT, May 1, 1831.
54. WHS to AHT, May 1, 1831.
55. AHT to WHS, May 4, 1831.
56. WHS to AHT, May 12, 1831.
57. WHS to AHT, May 12, 1831.
58. WHS to AHT, May 12, 1831.

5. And for Worse, 1832–1835

1. WHS to AHT, March 19, 1831, sc15305_b2-f128; WHS to AHT, July 19, 1831, sc15305, both in the New York State Library, Albany (hereafter NYSL).
2. FMS to WHS, March 8, 1831; FMS to LMW, March?, 1832.
3. FMS to LMW, March [?], 1832.
4. FMS to LMW, March 12, 1832.
5. FMS to LMW, March 12 and 24, 1832.
6. FMS to LMW, March 24, 1832.
7. FMS to LMW, April 25, 1832; FMS to WHS, April 13, June 20 and 24, November 18, 1832; FMS to LCC, June 24, 1832.
8. FMS to WHS, June 20, 2832; FMS to LCC, June 24, 1832.
9. Quoted in Seward, *Autobiography*, 229.
10. Seward, *Autobiography*, 104; AHT to WHS, May 26, 1833; FMS to WHS, June 4, 1833.
11. FMS to LMW, September 27, 1833.
12. FMS to LMW, November 17, 1833.
13. FMS to WHS, November 25, 1833; FMS to LMW, December 20 and 23, 1833, January 23 and March 9, 1834.
14. WHS to FMS, December 29, 1834, which contains a paraphrased extract of the letter Henry sent to Tracy in response to a parting letter from him.
15. WHS to FMS, December 29, 1834.
16. WHS to FMS, December 29, 1834.
17. WHS to FMS, September 19, 1834; FMS to WHS, September 21, 1834; FMS to LMW, October 2, 1834.
18. FMS to LMW, October, 2, 1834.

19. WHS to FMS, November 23, 1834.
20. WHS to FMS, November 23, 1834.
21. WHS to FMS, November 23, 1834; FMS to WHS, November 27, 1834.
22. WHS to FMS, November 28–December 1, 1834.
23. WHS to FMS, November 28–December 1, 1834; WHS to FMS, December 1, 1834.
24. WHS to FMS, November 28–December 1, 1834.
25. WHS to FMS, November 28–December 1, 1834.
26. WHS to FMS, November 28–December 1, 1834.
27. WHS to FMS, November 28 and December 1, 1834.
28. WHS to FMS, December 1, 6, 8, and 29, 1834.
29. WHS to FMS, December 1, 6, 8, and 29, 1834.
30. FMS to WHS, December 5 and 14, 1834.
31. WHS to FMS, November 28, December 1 and 29, 1834; Karen Grewal et al., "Chromosomally Normal Miscarriage Is Associated with Vaginal Dysbiosis and Local Inflammation," BMC Medicine 20 (2022), https://bmcmedicine.biomedcentral.com/articles/10.1186/s12916-021-02227-7.
32. FMS to WHS, December 1, 14, 21, 1834.
33. FMS to WHS, December 28–31, 1834.
34. WHS to FMS, December 28–31, 1834.
35. FMS to WHS, January 2, 1835; Ann Saunders, "There Is Nothing True but Heaven" (Providence, RI, 1827), https://searchworks.stanford.edu/view/8140243.
36. FMS to WHS, January 2, 1835.
37. SSS to WHS, January 4, 1835.
38. Letters quoted in Seward, *Autobiography*, 249.
39. RAS to FMS, March 5, 1835.
40. WHS to TxW, March 11, 1835.
41. RAS to FMS, April 5, 1835; WHS to TxW, April 7, 1835; AHS to FAW, April 7, 1835; BJS to WHS, April 11, 1835.
42. FMS to LMW, January 23, 1834.
43. WHS to AHT, June 21, 1831.
44. WHS to TxW, March 11 and 15, 1835.
45. WHS to TxW, March 29, 1835.
46. WHS to TxW, March 29, 1835; Platt Williams to WHS, April 12, 1835.
47. WHS to TxW, April 12, 1835. In WHS to TxW, May 3, 1835, Henry refers to Harriet Weed's father as her "friend."
48. WHS to TxW, April 12 and 19, 1835.
49. Seward, *Autobiography*, 260.
50. FMS journal, Seward Collection, Department of Rare Books, Special Collections, and Preservation, River Campus Libraries, University of Rochester, 7–8; WHS to AHT, June 24, 1835, sc15305_b2-f142; WHS to AHT, June 24, 1835, sc15305_b2-f142, NYSL.
51. FMS journal 1835, d7.
52. FMS journal, 7–8.
53. FMS journal, 8–9.

54. FMS journal, 9–10.
55. WHS to AHT, June 24, 1835, sc15305_b2-f142, NYSL.
56. WHS to TxW, June 12, 1835.
57. FMS journal, 17–18.
58. Seward, *Autobiography*, 268.
59. Seward, *Autobiography*, 272.
60. WHS to AHT, June 24, 1835, sc15305_b2-f142, NYSL.
61. FMS journal, 25–26.
62. ExM to WHS, June 23, 1835.
63. John Mason Good, *The Study of Medicine* (New York: Harper & Brothers, 1823; 3rd ed., 1829), 4:370. The WHO (World Health Organization) ICD-11 formally adopted in 2019 is the first of the eleven revisions of the International Classification of Diseases to exclude the diagnosis. The most recent release is "ICD-11 2022 Release," February 11, 2022, https://www.who.int/news/item/11-02-2022-icd-11-2022-release.
64. FMS journal, 36.
65. FMS journal, 30–33.
66. Quoted in Seward, *Autobiography*, 290–91.
67. Quoted in Seward, *Autobiography*, 290–91. Robert Miller died in 1813.

6. Happy Christmas and a Sad New Year, 1835–1837

1. Stephen Nissenbaum, *The Battle for Christmas* (New York: Knopf, 1996), 3–33, 156, 161.
2. Nissenbaum, *Battle*, 62–65, 71.
3. FMS to WHS, December 27 and 30, 1832; Nissenbaum, *Battle*, 76–78.
4. Clement Clarke Moore, "A Visit from St. Nicholas," December 23, 1823, available at https://poets.org/poem/visit-st-nicholas?gclid=Cj0KCQiA4OybBhCzARIsAIcfn9k5TnNUU-0UT_Bw6gJU5SjKpuoL-I42IY7fNB6gXNHOg4aIkz5ek10aAlj_EALw_wcB.
5. FMS to WHS, December 27, 1832.
6. FMS to WHS, December 25, 1834; Nissenbaum, *Battle*, 84.
7. FMS to WHS, December 25, 1834.
8. FMS to WHS, December 25, 1834.
9. FMS to WHS, December 27, 1832; Nissenbaum, *Battle*, 132–34.
10. FMS to WHS, December 25 and 27, 1834; FMS to AHS, December 27 and 28, 1836.
11. Washington Irving, *The Sketchbook of Geoffrey Crayon, Gent* (New York: C. S. Van Winkle, 1819–20; Library of America, 1983), "Christmas" and "Christmas Day," 911–47.
12. FMS to WHS, December 28, 1836, January 1, 1837; FMS to LMW, January 3, 1837.
13. FMS to LMW, January 3, 1837.
14. Harriet Weed to FMS, January 1, 1837; FMS to LMW, January 3, 1837.
15. FMS to WHS, January 7, 1837.
16. FMS to WHS, January 7, 1837.
17. FMS to WHS, January 8, 1837.

18. WHS to LMW, January 17, 1837.
19. WHS to LMW, January 17, 1837.
20. WHS to LMW, January 17, 1837.
21. Michael R. Haines, "The Urban Mortality Transition in the United States, 1800–1940," *Annales de démographie historique* (2000/2001), 33–64, https://www.cairn.info/revue-annales-de-demographie-historique-2001-1-page-33.htm.
22. LCC to MJS, January 29, 1837; MAS to FMS, February 2, 1837.
23. MAS to FMS, February 2, 1837.
24. MAS to FMS, February 2, 1837.
25. GWS to WHS, February 6, 1837.
26. SSS to WHS, February 9, 1837.
27. MJS to WHS and FMS, February 11, 1837.
28. FMS to WHS, February 11, 1837.
29. FMS to WHS, February 11, 1837.
30. FMS to WHS, February 11, 1837.
31. FMS to WHS, February 14, 1837.
32. FMS to WHS, February 14, 1837.
33. FMS to WHS, February 14, 1837.
34. FMS to WHS, February 14, 1837.
35. AHS to LMW, February 19, 1837.
36. FMS to WHS, March 4, 1837.
37. FMS to WHS, March 4, 1837.
38. FMS to WHS, March 7, 1837.
39. FMS to WHS, March 8 and 9, 1837.
40. FMS to WHS, March 14, 1837.
41. FMS to WHS, March 14, 1837.
42. FMS to WHS, March 19, 1837.
43. FMS to WHS, March 23, 1837.
44. FMS to LMW, March 22, 1837; FMS to WHS, March 23, 1837.
45. FMS to WHS, March 29, 1837.
46. FMS to WHS, March 29, 1837.
47. FMS to WHS, March 29, 1837; WHS to BJS, June 19, 1837.

7. Panics, 1837–1838

1. BJS to WHS, March 17, 1837.
2. FMS to WHS, March 26, 1837; BJS to WHS, March 27, 1837.
3. WHS to AHS, March 29, 1837.
4. WHS to BJS, April 25, 1837.
5. Jessica M. Lepler, *The Many Panics of 1837: People, Politics, and the Creation of a Transatlantic Financial Crisis* (New York: Cambridge University Press, 2013), 2, 3, 4–7.
6. Lepler, *Panics*, 18–23.
7. Lepler, *Panics*, 50.
8. SSS to WHS, March 29, 1837; FMS to WHS, April 2, 1837; FMS to LMW, April 7 and 14, 1837.
9. WHS to BJS, April 25 and 28, May 1 1837; LCC to FMS, April 20, 1837.

10. BJS to WHS, April 29, 1837.

11. FMS to WHS, May 5, 13, 17, 1837; BJS to WHS, May 11, 1837; WHS to BJS, May 19 and 22, 1837.

12. WHS to BJS, May 27 and 30, June 3 and 9, 1837.

13. WHS to BJS, June 19, 1837; BJS to WHS, June 23, 1837.

14. WHS to BJS, June 22, 1837; AHS to ExM, July 8, 1837; FWS to ExM, July 19, 1937; ExM to FWS, July 20, 1837; ExM to WHS, July 24, 1837; SSS to BJS-WHS, August 13, 1837; FMS to LMW, August 19, 1837.

15. FMS to WHS, February 14, 1837; FMS to LMW, August 19, 1837.

16. BJS to WHS, August 31, 1837.

17. WHS to BJS, September 2, 3, 4, 1837; FMS to LMW, September 3, 1837; BJS to WHS, September 6 and 9, 1837.

18. WHS to BJS, September 11, 14, 15, 17, 20, 1837; FMS to WHS, September 15, 1837; AHW to WHS, September 20, 1837.

19. MDC to WHS, September 24, 1837; LCC to MJS, September 28, 1837; Judith Walzer Leavitt, "Under the Shadow of Maternity: American Women's Responses to Death and Debility Fears in Nineteenth-Century Childbirth," *Feminist Studies* 12 (1986): 129–54; Shellie Marie Clark, "Frances Seward: Nineteenth-Century Politics in the Private Sphere" (PhD diss., University of Rochester, 2023), 76.

20. FMS to WHS, September 25, 1837; Bernard Barton, *Poems* (London: Baldwin, Cradock & Joy, 1822).

21. FMS to LMW, October 21, 1837. The bodies were subsequently reinterred in the family plot in Fort Hill Cemetery at some point after it opened. The modern slab that replaced the nineteenth-century one mistakenly identifies Cornelia's age as five years rather than five months and gets her mother's middle initial incorrect ("A" and not "E").

22. BJS to WHS, September 25 and 26, October 2 and 4, 1837; WHS to BJS, September 27, October 5, 1837.

23. WHS to BJS, October 6 and 10, 1837; WHS to LMW, October 13, 1837; FMS to LMW, October 13 and 29, 1837; AHW to WHS, October 18, 1837.

24. WHS to BJS, October 23, 1837.

25. FMS to LMW, November 22, 1837; FMS to WHS, November 19, December 6, 1837; Seward, *Autobiography*, 362.

26. SSS to WHS, October 28, 1837; SSS to GMG, April 23, 1838; FMS to LMW, November 22, 1837, May 20, 1838; FMS to WHS, November 19, December 6, 1837.

27. FMS to WHS, December 6, 1837.

28. FMS to WHS, December 6, 1837.

29. AHS to WHS, December 11, 1837; FMS to WHS, December 16, 1837; FMS to LMW, December 23, 1837.

30. FMS to WHS, December 12, 1837.

31. FMS to WHS, December 16, 1837; FWS to WHS, December 16, 1837.

32. FMS to WHS, December 16, 1837.

33. FMS to LMW, December 23, 1837; WHS to BJS, December 30, 1837.

34. SSS to WHS, December 18, 1837.

35. WHS, "Internal Improvements and Education," speech delivered at Auburn on October 14, 1835, in *The Works of William H. Seward*, ed. George E. Baker, vol. 3 (New York: Redfield, 1853), 128, 129.

36. WHS, *Works*, 3:132, 133.

37. WHS, "Education," speech delivered at Westfield on July 26, 1837, in *Works*, 3:135, 136, 140, 143.

38. WHS, *Works*, 3:148, 149, 150.

39. SSS to WHS, January 8, 1838.

40. WHS to BJS, January 10 and 18, 1838; FMS to LMW, January 10, 1838; WHS to TxW, January 9, 1838; BJS to WHS, January 16, 1838.

41. FMS to LMW, January 22, 1838.

42. FMS to LMW, January 22 and 29, 1838; WHS to BJS, January 30, 1838.

43. FMS to LMW, January 22 and 29, 1838; WHS to BJS, January 30, 1838.

44. FMS to LMW, January 31, 1838.

45. BJS to WHS, February 7, 1838; WHS to BJS, February 9, 1838.

46. FMS to LMW, April 8 and 16, 1838; FMS to WHS, April 13, 20, 22, 1838.

47. FMS to WHS, April 13 and 20, 1838.

48. FMS to WHS, April 22, 1838; AHW-WHS, February 10, 1838. I am unable to locate the source of Frances's quotation. It is not quite biblical, although it rings of several of the Psalms; it is not quite from William Wordsworth, although it hearkens to "Tintern Abbey" (1798). Perhaps it is from a published sermon.

49. FMS to LMW, May 2, 1838.

50. FMS to LMW, May 2, 1838.

51. FMS to LMW, May 13, 1838.

52. FMS to LMW, May 20 and 24, 1838.

53. FMS to LMW, May 13 and 20, 1838.

54. FMS to LMW, May 20 and 24, 1838; FMS to WHS, May 24, 1838; WHS to TxW, June 2, 1838.

8. Ambition, 1838–1839

1. FMS to LMW, June 3, 8, 30, 1838; WHS to BJS, June 4, 1838; FMS to WHS, July 2, 1838.

2. FMS to LMW, June 3, 8, 30, August 10, 1838; FMS to WHS, July 2, 1838.

3. FMS to LMW, September 2, 1838; Charles Anthon, *Caesar's Commentaries on the Gallic Wars* (New York: Harper & Brothers, 1838); FMS to WHS, August 12, 1838.

4. FMS to LMW, August 2, 1838; FMS to WHS, August 3 and 12, 1838; Ravindra Chaturvedi and R. L. Gogna, "Ether Day: An Intriguing History," *Med J Armed Forces India* 67, no. 4 (October 2011), 306–8, https://www.ncbi.nlm.nih.gov/pmc/articles/PMC4920664/.

5. FMS to WHS, August 3, 1838; FMS to LMW, September 2, 1838.

6. Seward, *Autobiography*, 366; AHW to WHS, August 18, 1838.

7. WHS to FMS, August 7 or 8, 1838, quoted in Seward, *Autobiography*, 370; FMS to WHS, August 12, 1838.

8. FMS to LMW, September 2, 1838.

9. WHS to BJS, September 8, 1838; TxW to WHS, September 15, 1838, quoted in Seward, *Autobiography*, 374, 377–78.

10. GWS to WHS, August 16, 1838; MDC to WHS, September 10 and 24, 1838; RAS to WHS, December 5, 1838.

11. AHW to WHS, September 15, 1838; SSS to WHS, September 16, October 22, 1838; BJS to WHS, September 17, 1838.

12. TxW to WHS, September 15, 1838, quoted in Seward, *Autobiography*, 374, 377–78; WHS to BJS, October 26, 1838.

13. WHS to BJS, October 26, November 12, 1838; FWS to FAW, November 15, 1838.

14. AHW to WHS, November 4, 7, 8, 9, 1838; BJS to WHS, November 8, 1838; SSS to WHS, November 12, 1838; LCC to WHS, November 14, 1838.

15. WHS to BJS, November 21, 1838.

16. WHS to BJS, November 21, December 17, 1838; BJS to WHS, November 29, December 13, 1838.

17. WHS to BJS, December 17, 1838; Seward, *Autobiography*, 381–82.

18. WHS to BJS, December 17, 1838; WHS to FMS, December 21, 1838, quoted in Seward, *Autobiography*, 383.

19. Seward, *Autobiography*, 379; BJS to WHS, December 21, 1838; WHS to BJS, December 17, 1838.

20. WHS to FMS, December 23 and 25, 1838.

21. Seward, *Autobiography*, 384–87; WHS to FMS, December 27, 1838, quoted in Seward, *Autobiography*, 384.

22. SSS to WHS, December 27, 1838; Seward, *Autobiography*, 385.

23. AHS to LMW, January 7, 1839.

24. FMS to WHS, January 9, 1839.

25. WHS to FMS, January 1, 1839, quoted in Seward, *Autobiography*, 385; FMS to WHS, January 2, 1839.

26. FMS to WHS, January 2, 1839.

27. FMS to WHS, January 9, 1839.

28. SSS to WHS, January 12, March 20, 1839; FMS to WHS, January 17, 1839; BJS to FMS, February 13, 1839; SSS to BJS, March 21, 1839; BJS to WHS, April 1 and 4, 1839.

29. SSS to WHS, January 12, March 20, 1839; FMS to WHS, January 17, 1839; BJS to FMS, February 13, 1839; SSS to BJS, March 21, 1839; BJS to WHS, April 1 and 4, 1839.

30. BJS to FMS, February 13, 1839; SSS to WHS, March 20, 1839; MDC to WHS, March 24 and 26, 1839.

31. FMS to WHS, January 11, 1839.

32. SSS to WHS, February 6, 1839.

33. FMS to WHS, January 17 and 28, February 1, 1839; FMS to LMW, January 17, 20, 24, 1839.

34. ExM to FWS, March 30, 1839; WHS to MDC, April 9, 1839; MDC to FMS, April 11, 1839.

35. WHS to BJS, May 28, 1839.

36. WHS to MJS, June 19, 1839; WHS to BJS, June 20, 1839; AxS to WHS, June 24, 1839; BJS to WHS, June 24, 1839; LMW to WHS, June 27, 1839; AHS to WHS, July 7, 1839; Christine Hallett, "Attempts to Understand Puerperal Fever in the Eighteenth and Early Nineteenth Centuries: The Influence of Inflammation Theory," *Medical History* 49 (January 2005): 1–28.

37. FMS to WHS, July 13, 1839.

38. FMS to LMW, July 16, 1839.

39. FMS to LMW, July 16, 1839.

40. BJS to WHS, July 22 and 28, 1839.

41. FMS to LMW, July 24 and 25, 1839; FMS to WHS, August 1, 1839.

42. FMS to LMW, July 24 and 25, 1839.

43. FMS to LMW, July 31, 1839; FMS to WHS, August 1, 1839.

44. FMS to LMW, August 25, September 15, 1839; FMS to WHS, September 15, 1839.

45. FMS to WHS, September 20 and 29, 1839.

46. FMS to WHS, October 1 and 3, 1839.

47. John D. Davies, *Phrenology: Fad and Science, a Nineteenth-Century American Crusade* (New Haven, CT: Yale University Press, 1955), 3–11.

48. Davies, *Phrenology*, 12–29.

49. Davies, *Phrenology*, 28.

50. Davies, *Phrenology*, 30–64.

51. Reading of William H. Seward's skull by Lorenzo Niles Fowler in O. S. Fowler, *Synopsis of Phrenology*, 5th ed. (Philadelphia: Fowler & Brevoort, 1838).

52. Reading of William H. Seward's skull by L. N. Fowler.

53. Reading of William H. Seward's skull by L. N. Fowler.

54. SSS to WHS, October 20, 1839.

55. FMS to LMW, October 29, November 4, 1839; SSS to WHS, October 31, 1839; GWS to WHS, October 31, 1839.

56. FMS to LMW, October 29, November 4, 1839; SSS to WHS, October 31, 1839; GWS to WHS, October 31, 1839.

57. FMS to LMW, October 29, November 4, 1839; SSS to WHS, October 31, 1839; GWS to WHS, October 31, 1839.

58. SSS to WHS, November 13, 1839; WHS to BJS, November 18, 1839.

9. Governor's Family, 1839–1841

1. Charles Dickens, *The Life and Adventures of Nicholas Nickleby* (London: Chapman & Hall, 1839; New York: Penguin, 2003), 89–90; FMS to LMW, December 26, 1839.

2. FMS to LMW, December 26, 1839.

3. Seward, *Autobiography*, 458.

4. FWS to LMW, January 22 and 31, 1840; FMS to LMW, January 26, 1840.

5. FMS to LMW, February 2, 1840.

6. FWS to LMW, February 7 and 24, 1840; FMS to LMW, February 7, 1840.

7. FMS to WHS, June 5, 7, 10, 12, 1840.

8. FMS to LMW, June 19, 1840.

9. FMS to LMW, June 19, 1840; FMS to WHS, June [12–18?], 1840.

10. WHS to BJS, June 25 and 27, 1840.

11. FMS to LMW, June 28, 1840.

12. FMS to LMW, June 28, 1840; WHS to BJS, June 29, 1840.

13. FWS to LMW, July 20, 1840; FMS to LMW, July 20, 1840.

14. FWS to LMW, July 20, 1840; FMS to LMW, July 20, 1840.

15. FMS to WHS, July 25, 27, 29, 1840; FMS to LMW, July 29, 1840; Seward, *Autobiography*, 481.

16. FMS to LMW, August 2, 1840.

17. FMS to WHS, August 2, 1840.

18. FMS to WHS, August 9, 1840.

19. FMS to WHS, August 9, 1840; FMS to LMW, August 16, 1840.

20. FMS to LMW, August 23, 1840.

21. FMS to WHS, August 23, 1840.

22. FMS to WHS, August 26, 1840; Seward, *Autobiography*, 460–64.

23. Seward, *Autobiography*, 492; FMS to WHS, August 26, 1840.

24. Seward, *Autobiography*, 460–64.

25. FMS to WHS, September 6, 1840; BJS to FMS, September 15, 1840.

26. FMS to WHS, September 15, 1840; John S. Haller Jr., "Samson of the Materia: Medical Theory and the Use and Abuse of Calomel in Nineteenth-Century America, Part I and Part II," *Pharmacy in History* 13 (1971): 27–34, 67–76.

27. FMS to WHS, September 23, 1840; FMS to CMM, September 27, 1840.

28. FMS to LMW, October 4, 1840; FMS to CMM, October 4, 1840.

29. BJS to FMS, October 9, 1840; WHS to BJS, October 11, 1840.

30. BJS to WHS, November 4 and 5, 1840; AHW to WHS, November 7 and 12, 1840; SSS to WHS, November 13, 1840; Seward, *Autobiography*, 460; Ian C. Bartrum, "The Origins of Secular Public Education: The New York School Controversy, 1840–1842," *NYU Journal of Law & Liberty* 3 (2007), https://papers.ssrn.com/sol3/papers.cfm?abstract_id=1019159.

31. FMS to LMW, November 24, 1840.

32. BJS to FMS, December 20, 1840.

33. FMS to LMW, December 23, 1840.

34. FMS to LMW, December 30, 1840–January 3, 1841.

35. FMS to LMW, February 5, 1841.

36. FMS to LMW, February 5, 1841.

37. GWS to FMS, February 1, 1841; BJS to WHS, February 15, 1841; FMS to LMW, February 21, 1841; SSS to WHS, February 23, 1841; GMG to WHS, February 23, 1841; GWS to WHS, February 24, 1841.

38. FMS to LMW, February 24–26, 1841.

39. SSS to WHS, March 1, 1841.

40. FMS to LMW, February 28, 1841.

41. FMS to LMW, February 28, 1841; FMS to WHS, March 6, 1841; SSS to WHS, March 10, 1841; SSS to FMS, March 17, 1841; Seward, *Autobiography*, 525.

42. FMS to LMW, May 31, June 20 and 27, 1841.

43. FMS to WHS, July 6, 1841.

44. SSS to WHS, July 12, 1841.
45. Seward, *Autobiography*, 554–55.
46. FMS to WHS, July 14, 1841; FMS to LMW, July 19, 1841.
47. FMS to WHS, July 22 and 25, 1841; FMS to LMW, July 26, 1841.
48. FMS to LMW, August 31, 1841.
49. FMS to WHS, September 12 and 15, 1841.
50. FMS to WHS, September 19, 1841.
51. FMS to WHS, September 30, 1841; SSS to Captain Alexander Hamilton Schultz, October 3, 1841; FMS to LMW, October 3, 1841; SSS to WHS, October 4 and 7, 1841.
52. FMS to LMW, November 5, 14, 22, 1841.
53. FMS to LMW, November 29, December 15, 1841.
54. FMS to LMW, December 22 and 29, 1841.

10. Lame Ducks, 1842–1844

1. Zebina James Duncan Kinsley to WHS, January 22, February 4, 1842; AHS to LMW, January 29, 1842.
2. SSS to WHS, January 29, 1842.
3. FMS to LMW, February 20 and 25, 1842.
4. ExM to FWS, February 24, 1842.
5. CMM to LMW, March 9 and 16, 1842; FMS to LMW, March 20 and 28, 1842.
6. FMS to LMW, March 6, 1842.
7. FMS to LMW, March 13, 1842.
8. FMS to LMW, March 20, 1842.
9. FMS to LMW, March 28, 1842; Zebina James Duncan Kinsley to WHS, April 1, 1842.
10. FMS to LMW, April 10, 1842.
11. WHS to SSS, May 15, 1842.
12. WHS to SSS, May 15, 1842.
13. WHS to SSS, May 15, 1842.
14. WHS to SSS, May 15, 1842.
15. SSS to WHS, May 25, 1842.
16. SSS to WHS, June 16, 1842.
17. FMS to WHS, May 26, 1842.
18. FMS to WHS, May 29, 1842; FMS to LMW, June 1, 1842.
19. FMS to WHS, May 26, 1842.
20. FMS to LMW, June 16, 19, 26, July 3, 1842; FMS to WHS, June 23 and 26, 1842.
21. FWS to LMW, July 10, 1842.
22. FMS to WHS, July 7, 1842.
23. FMS to LMW, July 10, 1842. See also FMS to AHS, October 1, 1848.
24. FMS to LMW, July 10, 1842.
25. FMS to LMW, July 10, 1842.
26. FMS to WHS, July 18 and 24, 1842.

27. FMS to WHS, August 1, 1842; FMS to LMW, August 4, 6, 14, 17, 28, September 20, 1842; SSS to WHS, August 10, 1842; FMS to AHS, August 28, 1842.

28. FMS to WHS, August 1, 1842; FMS to LMW, August 4, 6, 14, 17, 28, September 20, 1842; SSS to WHS, August 10, 1842; FMS to AHS, August 28, 1842.

29. FMS to LMW, September 20, 1842.

30. FMS to LMW, October 23, 1842.

31. FMS to LMW, October 30, 1842; FMS to WHS, December 3, 1842.

32. FMS to WHS, December 11 and 27, 1842; FMS to LMW, December 31, 1842; CMM to LMW, October 19, 1842.

33. FMS to LMW, January 8, 1843.

34. FMS to LMW, January 15, 31, February 7, 1843.

35. FMS to LMW, January 22, 1843.

36. AHS to WHS, January 28, 1843.

37. FMS to LMW, January 31, February 7, 1843.

38. FMS to LMW, February 10 and 27, 1843; WHS to Christopher Morgan, February 13, 1843; FMS to AHS, February 27, 1843.

39. FMS to LMW, March 8 and 12, 1843.

40. FMS to LMW, March 22, 1843.

41. FMS to LMW, May 7 and 21, 1843; WHS to GMG, May 18, 1843.

42. FMS to WHS, July 5, 1843; FMS to AHS, July 9, August 3, 1843; FMS to LMW, August 10, 1843.

43. FMS to AHS, August 3, 1843; FMS to LMW, August 1, 1843.

44. FMS to AHS, August 3, 1843; FMS to LMW, August 1, 1843.

45. FMS to LMW, August 10, 1843; FMS to AHS, August 11, 1843.

46. FMS to AHS, August 30, 1843; FMS to LMW, October 6 and 10, 1843.

47. FMS to AHS, October 29, 1843.

48. FMS to AHS, November 26, December 10, 1843.

49. FMS to LMW, December 26, 1843; FMS to AHS, January 8, 1844; AHS to LMW, January 21, 1844.

50. FMS to AHS, January 8, 28, February 4, 1844; FMS to LMW, February 6, 1844.

51. FMS to LMW, February 6, 1844; LMW to AHS, February 9, 1844.

52. FMS to AHS, February 11, 1844.

53. AHS to FAW, February 16, 1844.

54. FMS to AHS, with her transcription of WHS letter, February 27, 1844.

55. FMS to AHS, with her transcription of WHS letter, February 27, 1844.

56. FMS to AHS, with her transcription of WHS letter, February 27, 1844.

57. FMS to AHS, with her transcription of WHS letter, February 27, 1844.

58. FMS to AHS, February 28, 1844.

59. FMS to LMW, March 3, 1844.

60. WHS to AHS, March 11, 1844; FMS to AHS, March 30, April 8, 1844; FMS to LMW, March 3, 31, 1844; AxS to FMS, March 2, April 5, 1844; Helen L. Webb to FMS, March 21, 1844.

61. WHS to AHS, March 11, 1844; FMS to AHS, March 30, 31, 1844; FMS to LMW, March 3, 31, 1844; AxS to FMS, March 2, April 5, 1844; Helen L. Webb

to FMS, March 21, 1844; FWS to AHS, April 21, May 19, 1844; FWS to LMW, May 12, 1844; LMW to AHS, May 28, 1844; Samuel Blatchford to FMS, May 29, 1844.

62. FMS to LMW, July [?], 1844; FMS to AHS, August 15, 1844.

63. FMS to AHS, September 16, 1844.

64. FAW to AHS, September 22, 1844; FMS to LMW, September 22, 1844.

65. SSS to WHS, November 10, 11, 13, 25, December 5, 7, 1844; FMS to LMW, November 20, 1844; FMS to AHS, November 24, 1844; WHS to MJS, November 24, 1844.

66. WHS to AHS, December 11 and 15, 1844.

11. Domestic Perplexities, 1844–1848

1. FMS to AHS, January 1, 1845.

2. FMS to AHS, January 13, February 1, 1845; FMS to LMW, January 10, 18, 28, 1845.

3. FMS to AHS, January 1, February 1, 1845; FMS to LMW, January 18, 28, April 28, May 14 and 21, 1845.

4. FMS to LMW, July [?], 1845; FMS to LMW, July 6, 1845.

5. FMS to LMW, January 10, 1845; FMS to LMW, July [?], 1845.

6. FMS to AHS, January 13, February 1, March 3 and 25, 1845; FMS to LMW, January 10, June 29, 1845.

7. FMS to AHS, February 14, 1845; FMS to LMW, June 23, 1845.

8. FMS to AHS, September 5 and 20, 1845.

9. FMS to AHS, September 5 and 20, 1845.

10. FMS to AHS, April 26, November 1, 1846; WSJ to AHS, May 10, 1946; WSJ to LMW, May 10, 1846; FMS to LMW, May 17, October 3 and 15, 1846.

11. FMS to LMW, October 1, 1845; FMS to AHS, September 5 and 20, 1845; FMS to AHS, April 26, 1846; WSJ to AHS, May 10, 1946; WSJ to LMW, May 10, 1846; FMS to LMW, May 17, October 3 and 15, November 1, 1846.

12. FMW to AHS, November 20, 1845; FMS to LMW, November 23, 29, 30, December 7, 1845; FMS to AHS, December 14 and 18, 1845; WHS to Elizabeth Parsons, November 9, 1848.

13. WSJ to AHS, January 18, 1846; WSJ to WHS, January 19, 1846.

14. WHS to WSJ, January 25, 1846; FWS to WSJ, January 27, 1846; LMW to WSJ, February 13, 1846.

15. FMS to AHS, February 8, 1846.

16. FMS to AHS, February 8, March 1, 1846.

17. Andrew W. Arpey, *The William Freeman Murder Trial: Insanity, Politics, and Race* (Syracuse, NY: Syracuse University Press, 2003), 15; FMS to AHS, February 8, 1846.

18. FMS to AHS, March 18, 1846.

19. FMS to LMW, July 1, 1846.

20. WHS to TxW, May 29, 1846; WHS to James Bowen, September 15, 1846.

21. Quotations from Arpey, *William Freeman Murder Trial*, 125, 137; see also 54–55.

22. WHS to TxW, September 8, 1846; Weed papers, quoted in Arpey, *William Freeman Murder Trial*, 124.

23. Arpey's is the only book on the Freeman trial and the best secondary source on the case, but see also Earl Conrad, *Mr. Seward for the Defense* (New York: Rinehart & Company, 1956) and the relevant portions of Stahr, *Seward*, 99–105, and Van Deusen, *William Henry Seward*. Van Deusen mistakenly believed that Wyatt was also Black. Primary sources include Benjamin F. Hall, *The Trial of William Freeman* (Auburn, NY: Derby, Miller, 1848); *Report of the Trial of Henry Wyatt* (Auburn, NY: J. C. Derby, 1846).

24. FMS to AHS, April 6, 1846; FMS to LMW, May 17 and 24, 1846; Amy S. Greenberg, *A Wicked War: Polk, Clay Lincoln and the 1846 Invasion of Mexico* (New York: Alfred A. Knopf, 2012).

25. FMS to AHS, May 28, 1846.

26. FMS to AHS, June 15, 1846.

27. LMW to WSJ, November [?], 1846; FMS to LMW, November [?], 1846; FMS to AHS, November 26, 1846.

28. FMS to LMW, November 30, December 7 and 29, 1846.

29. FMS to AHS, December 29, 1846.

30. FMS to AHS, February 15 and 28, 1847; FMS to WHS, April 7, 1847.

31. FMS to AHS, January 22, March 20, 1847; FMS to LMW, April 3, 1847.

32. WHS to AHS, February 4, April 11, 1847; FMS to AHS, April 19, 1847.

33. WHS to AHS, April 11, 1847; FMS to AHS, April 19, May 25, 1847.

34. EPS to FMS, July 26, 1847; GWS to FMS, June 3, July 26, 1847.

35. FMS to WHS, September 16, 1847; FMS to AHS, October 21, 1847; AHS to FMS, November 20, 1847.

36. FMS to AHS, November 6 and 14, 1847; AHS to FAW, November 20, 1847.

37. FMS to AHS, December 25, 1847.

38. FMS to WHS, June 14, 1847.

39. FMS to AHS, April 7, June 18, December 24, 1848; FMS to WHS, November 9 and 28, December 3, 1848; FMS to AHS, June 18, 1848; FMS to LMW, December 7 and 17, 1848; LMS to WHS, December 19, 1848.

40. LMW to WHS, December 19, 1848.

41. FMS to WHS, January 24, 1848; FMS to AHS, August 16, 1848; WHS to GMG, August 21, 1848; Burr W. Griswold to FMS, September 30, 1848.

42. FMS to WHS, June 6, 1848; FMS to AHS, June 18, 1848.

43. FMS to WHS, October 7, 1848; WHS to AHS, October 10, 1848.

44. FMS to AHS, October 18, 1848.

45. FMS to WHS, October 20, 1848.

46. General Zachary Taylor to WHS, October 24, 1848; FMS to AHS, November 19, 1848.

47. WSJ to AHS, July 2, 1848; FMS to WHS, September 20, 1848.

48. FMS to WHS, September 28, October 4, 11, 20, 29, November 28, 1848; FMS to LMW, November 7, 1848.

49. Elijah Miller Legal Papers, University of Rochester, Department of Rare Books, Special Collection, and Preservation (hereafter Miller Legal Papers), box 6, folder 6.

50. Miller Legal Papers, box 6, folder 6.

51. "Married Women's Property Acts in the United States," Wikipedia, last modified August 27, 2024, https://en.wikipedia.org/wiki/Married_Women%27s_Property_Acts_in_the_United_States; "An Act for the Effectual Protection of the Property of Married Women," passed April 7, 1848, https://www.womenshistory.org/resources/primary-source/act-effectual-protection-property-married-women.

52. FMS to WHS, December 12, 1848.

12. Governor Seward Goes to Washington, 1849

1. FMS to WHS, January 27, 1849.
2. FMS to LMW, February 12, 1849; FMS to AHS, February 13, 1849.
3. WHS to FMS, March 8, 1849.
4. Letter quoted by FMS to LMW, December 29, 1849.
5. FMS to LMW, December 29, 1849; FMS to AHS, December 30, 1849; WHS to FMS, March 18 and 29, April 1, 1849.
6. William H. Seward, *Oration on the Death of John Quincy Adams* (Albany: Charles Van Benthuysen, 1848), 5.
7. Seward, *Oration*, 14, 15, 24, 26–30, 33; William H. Seward, *Life and Public Services of John Quincy Adams* (Auburn, NY: Derby, Miller, 1849).
8. Seward, *Oration*.
9. WHS to FMS, March 6 and 7, 1849.
10. WHS to FMS, March 9, 10, 11, 1849.
11. WHS to FMS, March 12, 14, 20, 1849.
12. MDC to WHS, March 11, 1849; AHW to WHS, March 20, 1849; AxC to WHS, March 26, June 25, October 10, 1849; WHS to FMS, March 15, 16, 18, 23, 25, 26, 1849.
13. FMS to AHS, January 20, 1849; FMS to LMW, March 8, 1849; FMS to WHS, March 8, 1849.
14. AHS to WSJ, January 9, 1849.
15. FMS to LMW, March 8, 1849; FMS to WHS, March 8, 1849.
16. FMS to AHS, February 13, April 23, June 11, 1849; FMS to WSJ, September 15, 1849.
17. LMW to WHS, [undated, but December 1848]; FMS to WHS, September 28, 1848; FMS to LMW, November 26, 1849.
18. FMS to AHS, May 29, June 11, July 1, 1849; WHS to FMS, April 4, June 19 and 21, 1849; FMS to WHS, July [?], 1849; WHS to LMW, July 13, 1849.
19. WSJ to WHS, September 26, 1849; FAS to WSJ, November 25, 1849; WSJ to WHS, November [?], 1849; WSJ to FMS, November [?], 1849; WSJ to WHS, November [?], 1849; FAS to LMW, December 29, 1849; WHS to WSJ, March 16, 1849.
20. FMS to WHS, March 16, 17, 19, 20, 1849; FMS to LMW, March 16, 1849; WHS to FMS, March 21 and 24, 1849; FMS to AHS, March 24, April 18, 1849; FMS to LMW, April 3, 1849.
21. FMS to AHS, April 23, 1849; FMS to WHS, April 25, 1849; WHS to FMS, April 25, 1849.

22. FMS to WHS, April 26, May 2, 1849; WHS to FMS, April 28 and 29, 1849.

23. WHS to FMS, April 29, 1849.

24. WHS to FMS, April 29 and 30, May 1, 1849.

25. WHS to FMS, May 2, 3, 5, 1849.

26. WHS to FMS, May 3 and 5, 1849.

27. FMS to AHS, May 29, 1849.

28. FMS to LMW, January 15, 1849.

29. Mrs. C. M. Kirkland, *Woman, Her Education and Influence* (New York: Fowler & Wells, 1847), 48.

30. Kirkland, *Woman, Her Education and Influence*, v, 37, 39–40.

31. Kirkland, *Woman, Her Education and Influence*, 49, 51; FMS to LMW, January 15, 1849.

32. FMS to AHS, December 16, 1849.

33. AHS to FAW, February 15, 1849; FMS to WHS, March 23, 1849; FMS to AHS, April 23, August 12, 1849.

34. FMS to AHS, August 31, 1849; FAW to AHS, February 26, 1849.

35. WHS to AHS, September 3, 1849.

36. CAS to WHS, September 2 and 6, 1849; EPS to WHS, December 4, 1849.

37. FMS to WHS, October 17, 1849.

38. FMS to AHS, September 16 and 23, 1849; FAW to AHS, August 5, 1849.

39. FMS to AHS, August 31, 1849.

40. FMS to AHS, October 18, November 4, 1849.

41. John Hart Willard to FMS, October 2, 1849; FMS to AHS, March 24, June 11, October 18, November 4, December 2, 1849; FMS to WHS, September 28, 1849; MSJ to WHS, October 17, 1849; FMS to LMW, November 23, 1849.

42. CCS to WHS, September 26, 1849; FMS to LMW, December 14, 1849.

43. FMS to LMW, December 14, 1849.

44. MDC to WHS, October 4, 1849.

45. WHS to MDC, October 14, 1849.

46. MDC to WHS, October 19, 1849.

47. FMS to LMW, March 24, 1849; WHS to FMS, June 7 and 12, 1849; A. E. Hall to FMS, August 9, 1849; FMS to TxW, August 23, 1849.

48. A. F. Hall to FMS, May 12 and 14, June 4, 1849; FMS to WHS, August 23, 1849; Frederick W. Seward, *Seward at Washington, as Senator and Secretary of State: A Memoir of His Life, with Selections from His Letters, 1846–1861*, vol. 2 (New York: Derby & Miller, 1891), 111 (this three-volume work is also known as *The Autobiography of William H. Seward*, although it was completed by Fred); "A Closer Look: F Street, Heart of the Old Downtown, in the 19th Century," *Streets of Washington* (blog), October 18, 2017, http://www.streetsofwashington.com/2017/10/a-closer-look-f-street-heart-of-old.html.

49. FMS to WHS, September 28, 1849; FMS to AHS, October 18, November 4 and 28, December 2, 1849; FAW to LMW, November 29, 1849; FMS to LMW, November 30, 1849.

50. FMS to WHS, September 28, 1849; FMS to AHS, October 18, November 4 and 28, December 2, 1849; FAW to LMW, November 29, 1849; FMS to LMW, November 30, 1849.

51. FMS to LMW, November 30, 1849.

52. FMS to LMW, November 30, 1849.

53. FMS to LMW, December 9 and 21, 1849.

54. FMS to AHS, December 17 and 30, 1849; FMS to LMW, December 21, 1849; FMS to CMM, December 22, 1849.

55. FMS to LMW, March 8, December 14, 1849; FMS to AHS, December 16, 1849; FMS to CMM, December 22, 1849; WHS to FMS, March 8, April 26, 1849.

56. FMS to LMW, December 29, 1849.

57. FMS to LMW, March 8, December 14, 1849; FMS to AHS, December 16, 1849; WHS to FMS, March 8, April 26, 1849.

13. Losses, 1850–1851

1. FAW to LMW, January 6, 1850; FMS to AHS, January 13, 1850.

2. FMS to LMW, January 13 and 18, 1850.

3. FMS to LMW, February 3, 1850.

4. FMS to LMW, February 10, 1850.

5. FMS to LMW, February 24, March 3 and 10, May 2, 1850.

6. FMS to LMW, May 2, 1850.

7. FMS to CMM, April 7, 1850.

8. FMS to WHS, June 9, 1850; WHS to WSJ, June 16, 1850; FMS to LMW, June 30, 1850.

9. WHS to FAS, July 18, 1850.

10. William H. Seward, "Freedom in the New Territories," March 11, 1850, available at https://www.senate.gov/artandhistory/history/resources/pdf/SewardNewTerritories.pdf.

11. "Classic Senate Speeches: William H. Seward, 'Freedom in the New Territories,'" United States Senate, https://www.senate.gov/artandhistory/history/common/generic/Speeches_Seward_NewTerritories.htm.

12. "Classic Senate Speeches."

13. "Classic Senate Speeches."

14. Quoted in Frederick W. Seward, *Seward at Washington*, 2:120–21.

15. FMS to LMW, March 19 and 21, 1850; "Georgia Savannah" letter quoted in Frederick W. Seward, *Seward at Washington*, 2:130.

16. FMS to LMW, March 19, 1850.

17. FMS to LMW, March 21 and 26, April 4, 10, 27, 1850.

18. Quoted in Frederick W. Seward, *Seward at Washington*, 2:127, 128, 129.

19. Quoted in Frederick W. Seward, *Seward at Washington*, 2:132, 133, 134, 136, 137, 139, 140.

20. Quoted in Frederick W. Seward, *Seward at Washington*, 2:143–44.

21. Quoted in Frederick W. Seward, *Seward at Washington*, 2:144, 145.

22. FMS to WHS, July 10, 11, 12, 14, 1850.

23. Quoted in Frederick W. Seward, *Seward at Washington*, 2:145.

24. Quoted in Frederick W. Seward, *Seward at Washington*, 2:148, 155.

25. Quoted in Frederick W. Seward, *Seward at Washington*, 2:146, 147, 151, 154.

26. FMS to LMW, January 13 and 18, 1850; AHS to WHS, January [?], 1850; FMS to AHS, January 13, 1850.

27. FMS to LMW, February 3 and 24, 1850; Winfield Scott to WHS, February 5, 1850; FMS to LMW, February [?], 1850; FMS to LMW, March 10, 19, 21, 26, 1850; FMS to CMM, March 12, 1850.

28. HOC to FMS, May 4, 1850; FMS to WHS, May 7, 1850.

29. FMS to WHS, May 7, 1850.

30. LMW to WHS, May 13, 1850; WHS to AHS, May 24, 1850, quoted in Frederick W. Seward, *Seward at Washington*, 2:134–35.

31. FMS to WHS, May 19, June 1 and 9, 1850.

32. FMS to LMW, June 23 and 30, 1850; FMS to WHS, July 8, 14, 23, 1850; WHS to FMS, July 20, 1850.

33. CAS to WHS, July 28, 1850; FMS to WHS, July 31, August 3 and 13, 1850; FWS to WHS, August 15, 1850; LMW to WSJ, August 28, 1850.

34. FMS to LMW, September 7, 1850.

35. FMS to AHS, September 26, October 14, 1850; WHS to AHS, October 22, 1850; WHS to Richard Milton Blatchford, October 23, 1850.

36. Mrs. Mattison to FMS, December 24, 1850.

37. FMS to LMW, January 12, 1851; FMS to WHS, February 2, 1851.

38. FMS to WHS, March 14 and 15, 1851.

39. WHS to FMS, March 19, 1851; FMS to WHS, April 18, 1851.

40. FMS to WHS, April 18, 1851; Office of Coast Survey, "History of Coast Survey," https://nauticalcharts.noaa.gov/about/history-of-coast-survey.html.

41. FMS to WHS, May 8, 1851.

42. FMS to WHS, May 17, 1851; FMS to AHS, May 20, 1851.

43. FMS to WHS, May 16, June 8 and 19, 1851; FMS to AHS, June 9 and 25, 1851.

44. GWS to FMS, April 1, 1851; Academy of the Visitation B. V. Mary, Georgetown, DC, quarterly report, December 1, 1850; CCS to WHS, November 24, December 5 and 7, 1851.

45. FMS to AHS, September 1, October 20, 1851; FWS to WHS, December 2, 1851.

46. FMS to AHS, October 20, November 25, 1851.

47. FMS to AHS, October 20, November 25, 1851.

48. GWS to FMS, June 20, 1851.

49. GWS to FMS, June 20, 1851.

50. GWS to FMS, June 20, 1851.

51. GWS to FMS, June 20, 1851.

52. FMS to WHS, June 20 and 24, 1851.

53. GWS to WHS, December 16, 1851.

54. GWS to WHS, December 16, 1851; EPS to WHS, December 22, 1851.

55. FMS to WSJ, December 14, 1851; FMS to WHS, December 10, 1851; FMS to LMW, December 17, 1851; FMS to WHS, November [?], 1851.

56. S. R. Kirby to FMS, December 19, 1851.

57. FMS to LMW, December 25, 1851.

58. FMS to LMW, December 25 and 29, 1851.

59. FMS to LMW, December 25, 1851.

60. FMS to LMW, December 25 and 29, 1851.
61. FMS to LMW, December 29, 1851.

14. Bubble of Ambition, 1852–1856

1. GWS to WHS, January 2, 1852.
2. FMS to LMW, January 15 and 25, 1852; FMS to WHS, January 27, 1852.
3. AxS to WHS, January 24, February 3, 1852; FMS to LMW, January 31, February 6 and 12, 1852.
4. FMS to LMW, February 3, 6, 12, 16, 1852.
5. FMS to LMW, March 18 and 25, 1852.
6. CMM to FMS, April 11, 1852; FMS to LMW, April 12, 1852; FMS to CMM, May 13, 1852; AHS to WHS, July 18, 1852.
7. FMS to WHS, May 18 and 22, 1852.
8. GWS to WHS, April 14, 1852.
9. WHS to GWS, May 14, 1852; GWS to FMS, August 2 and 22, 1852.
10. FMS to WHS, May 23, 1852; FMS to LMW, July 17, 1852; FMS to AHS, August 9, 1852.
11. FMS to WHS, July 19 and 26, August 2, 7, 9, 1852; FMS to AHS, August 2, 1852.
12. FMS to AHS, July 19, September 22, 1852.
13. "Bloomers," Wikipedia, last updated September 9, 2024, https://en.wikipedia.org/wiki/Bloomers; FMS to LMW, October 21, 1852.
14. FMS to LMW, October 21, 1852.
15. FMS to LMW, December 15, 1852; FMS to AHS, December 29, 1852; WHS to AHS, December [?], 1852.
16. FMS to AHS, December 29, 1852; WHS to AHS, December [?], 1852.
17. FMS to LMW, January 1, 1853; FMS to AHS, January 3 and 14, 1853; CCS to WHS, March [?], 1853.
18. FMS to LMW, January 16, 1853.
19. WHS to WSJ, March 19, 1853; LMS to FMS, April 12, 1853; FAS to FMS, April 12, 1853; FMS to AHS, April 19 and 30, 1853.
20. CCS to WHS, June 9 and 15, 1853; FMS to WHS, June 13, 1853; FMS to AHS, July 19, 1853.
21. FMS to AHS, August 1, October 10, 1853.
22. GWS to WHS, June 6, July 19, 1853; CAS to WHS, June 22, 1853; WHS to GWS, August 9, 1853; GWS to WHS, August [?], 1853; GWS to WHS, September 8, November 14, 1853.
23. WHS to LMW, November 23, 1853; LMW to WHS, November 23, 1853.
24. FMS to AHS, October 10, 1853.
25. FMS to WHS, December 1 and 4, 1853; FMS to AHS, December 18, 1853.
26. FMS to LMW, April 24, 1853; LMW to WHS, December 24 and 25, 1853; FMS to WHS, January 1, 1854.
27. LMS to WHS, December 25, 1853; LMW to WHS, December 28, 1853; FAS to WHS, December [?], 1853; FMS to WHS, January 1, 1854.
28. LMW to WHS, January 4, 1854; CAS to WHS, January 4 and 31, 1854.

29. FMS to AHS, January 6 and 21, 1854; FMS to WHS, January 10, 1854.

30. FMS to WHS, January 25 and 31, February 2, 9, 14, 1854; FMS to AHS, February 7, 1854; LMW to WHS, February 8, 18544.

31. LMW to WHS, February 21, 1854; FMS to WHS, February 21, 23, 27, 1854; "The Kansas-Nebraska Act," May 30, 1854, United States Senate, https://www.senate.gov/artandhistory/history/minute/Kansas_Nebraska_Act.htm.

32. Frederick W. Seward, *Seward at Washington*, 2:239–44; *Speech of William H. Seward, on the Kansas and Nebraska Bill, Senate of the United States, May 26, 1854* (Washington, DC: Buell & Blanchard, [1854?]).

33. FMS to WHS, June 2, 20, 27, July 11, 1854; FMS to AHS, June 27, 1854.

34. FWS to AHS, October 10, November 12, 19, 28, 1854.

35. FWS to WHS, December 20, 1854; FMS to AHS, December 22, 1854.

36. FMS to AHS, January 6 and 23, February 7, 1855; LMW to WHS, February 2, 1855.

37. FMS to AHS, January 6 and 23, February 7, April 26, July 13, 1855; LMW to WHS, February 2, 1855.

38. FAS to FMS, April 20, 21, 26, May 13, 1855; FMS to AHS, April 26, 1855; FMS to FAS [?], 1855; FMS to FAS [?], 1855.

39. WSJ to FMS, August 7, 1855.

40. FAS to FMS, May 13, 1855; FAS to FMS, May [?] 1855; FAS to FMS, May [?], 1855; FAS to FMS, May [?], 1855.

41. FMS to AHS, October 18, 22, 26, 1855.

42. FMS to AHS, September 15, 1855; SDH to FMS, October 11, 1855; WSJ to FMS, October 23, 27, 28, 1855; WSJ to FWS, October 24, 1855.

43. LMW to WHS, November 17 and 20, 1855; WSJ to FMS, November 19 and 28, 1855; FMS to AHS, December 17, 1855.

44. FMS to AHS, January 2 and 17, February 7, 1856.

45. FMS to AHS, February 17 and 19, March 1, 1856; FMS to LMW, March 7, 1856.

46. FMS to AHS, February 19, 1856; FAW to AHS, April 2, 1856.

47. FMS to LMW, February [?], 1856; FMS to AHS, March 1, 1856; Gary Sackett to FMS, March 17, 1856.

48. FMS to LMW, March 24 and 25, 1856; FMS to AHS, March 24 and 30, 1856; FMS to LMW, March [?], 1856.

49. FWS to AHS, March 24, 1856.

50. FMS to LMW, March 24 and 25, 1856; FMS to AHS, March 24 and 30, 1856; FMS to LMW, March [?], 1856.

51. FMS to LMW, March [?], 1856.

52. FMS to AHS, March 30, 1856.

53. FMS to LMW, April 10, 1856; FMS to AHS, April 19, 1856.

54. GWS to WHS, June 20 and 27, July 5, 17, 30, 1855; FMS to AHS, September 15, 1855; EPS to WHS, April 14, 1856; FMS to CMM, April 17, 1856.

55. FMS to AHS, April 19, 1856; FMS to LMW, April 20 and 23, 1856; WSJ to WHS, May 10, 19, 28, 1856; WSJ to FMS, May 13, 1856; FMS to WHS, June 8, 1856.

56. EPS to WHS, April 14, 1856; FMS to CMM, April 17, 1856; FMS to AHS, April 19, 1856; FMS to LMW, April 20 and 23, 1856.

57. WSJ to FMS, April 26 and 29, 1856; LMW to WHS, April 29, 1856.

58. FMS to AHS, April 30, 1856; FMS to LMW, May 1, 1856; WHS to LMW, May 2, 1856.

59. FMS to LMW, May 4, 1856.

60. Quoted in Walter Stahr, *Seward: Lincoln's Indispensable Man* (New York: Simon & Schuster, 2012), 161; William H. Seward Jr., "Youthful Recollections," delivered March 16, 1903, William Seward Papers, University of Rochester, Department of Rare Books and Special Collections, box 120, file 36, 13.

61. FMS to AHS, May 25, 1856.

62. FMS to LMW, May 30, 1856; Williamjames Hull Hoffer, *The Caning of Charles Sumner: Honor, Idealism, and the Origins of the Civil War* (Baltimore: Johns Hopkins University Press, 2010); "The Caning of Senator Charles Sumner," May 22, 1856, US Senate, https://www.senate.gov/artandhistory/history/minute/The_Caning_of_Senator_Charles_Sumner.htm; "Caning of Charles Sumner," Wikipedia, last updated September 15, 2024, https://en.wikipedia.org/wiki/Caning_of_Charles_Sumner.

63. "Caning of Senator Charles Sumner"; "Caning of Charles Sumner."

64. FMS to LMW, May 30, 1856.

65. FMS to LMW, May 30, 1856.

66. WHS to FMS, June 17, 1856, quoted in Frederick W. Seward, *Seward at Washington*, 2:278; FMS to WHS, June 8, 1856.

67. WHS to FMS, June 17, 1856, quoted in Frederick W. Seward, *Seward at Washington*, 2:278; FMS to WHS, June 8, 12, 14, 18, 1856; Alexander H. Greene to FMS, June 12, 1856.

68. WHS to FMS, June 17, 1856, quoted in Frederick W. Seward, *Seward at Washington*, 2:278; FMS to WHS, June 8, 1856; Thomas C. Miller to FMS, July 19, 1856; WHS to FMS, June 1, 6, 10, 11, 13, 14, 15, 1856, quoted in Frederick W. Seward, *Seward at Washington*, 2:276–79.

15. Sojourners, 1856–1859

1. Alexander H. Greene to FMS, June 12, 1856; FMS to WHS, June 20, 1856.

2. "Know Nothing," Wikipedia, last updated September 27, 2024, https://en.wikipedia.org/wiki/Know_Nothing.

3. FMS to WHS, June 20 and 21, 1856.

4. FMS to WHS, June 21, 1856.

5. FMS to WHS, June 28, July 20 and 31, August 3, 12, 22, 1856.

6. FMS to WHS, July 2, 4, 7, 1856.

7. FMS to WHS, July 17 and 27, 1856; Thomas C. Miller to FMS, July 19, 1856.

8. FMS to WHS, July 24, 27, 31, 1856.

9. FAS to WHS, July [?], 1856; FMS to AHS, August 18 and 21, 1856; FMS to WHS, August 22, 1856.

10. FMS to AHS, August 18, 1856; FWS to WHS, August 19 and 21, 1856.

11. LMW to SDH, August 28, 1856; FMS to AHS, September 25, 1856.

12. FMS to AHS, September 8 and 25, 1856; WHS to GWS, September 14, 1856; FMS to WHS, September 15, 1856; FWS to WHS, October 9 and 14, November 11, 1856; WHS to FWS, October 27, 1856.

13. WSJ to FMS, November 23, 1856.

14. WSJ to FWS, November 30, 1856.

15. FWS to WHS, December 2 and 22, 1856; WSJ to FMS, December 7, 1856; FWS to FMS, December 16, 1856; FMS to AHS, December 16, 1856; WSJ to WHS, December 28, 1856.

16. LMW to WHS, December 4, 12, 17, 1856; CCS to WHS, November 30, 1857.

17. CMM to AHS, December 28, 1856; FMS to AHS, December 29, 1856; FMS to LMW, December 31, 1856.

18. AHS to FMS, January 4, 1857; WSJ to FMS, January 5, 1857.

19. Elisha Kane, *Arctic Explorations* (Philadelphia: Childs & Peterson, 1857); LMW to SDH, January 9, 1857.

20. GWS to WHS, January 17 and 19, 1856; GWS to WHS and GMB, March 21, 1857.

21. FMS to CMM, January 19, 1857; WSJ to FMS, January 25, 1857; FMS to AHS, January 27, February 14, 1857; AHS to FMS, February 4, 1857; FWS to WHS, February 6, 1857.

22. FMS to AHS, February 14, 1857.

23. FAS to LMW, February 15, 1857; FWS to WHS, February 15, 1857; WSJ to FMS, February 21, 1857; FMS to AHS, March 2, 1857.

24. FMS to AHS, March 2 and 9, 1857.

25. FAS to LMW, February 15, 1857; FWS to WHS, February 15, 1857; WSJ to FMS, February 21, 1857; FMS to AHS, March 2, 1857.

26. WSJ to FMS, May 19, 1857; FWS to WHS, May 22, 1857; WSJ to FMS, May 31, 1857.

27. WSJ to FMS, May 6, 1857; FMS to WSJ, May 7, 1857; WHS to WSJ, May 9, 1857.

28. FAS to WSJ, May 18 and 31, June 10, 1857; WSJ to FMS, June 14, 1857; FMS to WSJ, June 24 and 29, July 13, 1857.

29. WHS to FMS, June 18, 1857.

30. FMS to WSJ, June 19 and 24, 1857; FAS to WSJ, June [?], 1857.

31. WHS to FMS, June 21, 1857; FMS to WSJ, June 24, 1857.

32. FMS to WSJ, June 24, 1857.

33. FAS to WSJ, July 12 and 15, 1857; Shannon Murphy, "Tableaux Vivant: History and Practice," Art Museum Teaching, December 6, 2012, https://artmuseumteaching.com/2012/12/06/tableaux-vivant-history-and-practice/.

34. WHS to FAS, July 25, 1857.

35. FMS to LMW, August 20, 1857.

36. WHS to FMS, August 21 and 22, 1857; FMS to AHS, August 30, 1857; FMS to WSJ, September 4 and 9, 1857; WSJ to FMS, September 13, 1857.

37. WSJ to FMS, September 16, 1857; WSJ to FAS, September 20, 1857; FMS to WSJ, September 20 and 23, 1857; FAS to WSJ, September 22, 1857.

38. FMS to AHS, September 23 and 30, 1857; WSJ to WHS, September 29, 1857; "Panic of 1857," Wikipedia, last updated July 18, 2024, https://en.wikipedia.org/wiki/Panic_of_1857.

39. WSJ to FMS, October 4 and 19, 1857; WHS to WSJ, October 9, 1857; FMS to AHS, October 9, 1857; FMS to WSJ, October 31, 1857.

40. FMS to AHS, November 3, 1857.

41. FMS to AHS, November 3, 1857.

42. FMS to AHS, November 12, 1857.

43. FMS to AHS, November 12 and 22, 1857; WSJ to FMS, November 15, 1857; FMS to WSJ, November 19, 1857.

44. FMS to AHS, November 12, 1857; WSJ to FMS, November 15, December 13, 1857; FMS to WSJ, November 19, 1857.

45. WSJ to FMS, November 27, December 13, 1857; FMS to WSJ, November 28, 1857; FMS to WHS, November 29, December 5, 1857.

46. FMS to LMW, December 8, 1857.

47. FMS to LMW, December 8, 1857; WSJ to FMS, January 10, 1857.

48. WSJ to FMS, December 16, 1857; FMS to WSJ, December 18, 1857; FMS to WSJ, [?], 1857.

49. FMS to LMW, December 23, 1857.

50. FMS to AHS, December 27, 1857; LMW to WSJ, December 28, 1857; SDH to FMS, December 31, 1857.

51. FMS to LMW, January 1, 1858; WSJ to FMS, January 1, April 11, May 2, 1858; FMS to WSJ, January 11, March 3 and 18, April 14, 1858; FMS to WHS, January 15, 1858; FMS to AHS, April 1, 1858; AWS to FMS, May 3, 1858.

52. FMS to AHS, January 24, February 13, March 3 and 17, 1858; FMS to WSJ, January 27, June 16, 1858; WSJ to FMS, February 1, March 7 and 21, June 14, 1858; FMS to LMW, February 6, March 20, 21, 24, April 30, 1858; FMS to SDH, February 8, 1858; FAS to LMW, March 8, 1858; FAS to WSJ, March 10 and 14, 1858; FMS to AHS, June 22, 28, 29, 1858; EPS to WHS, May 23, 1858; GWS to WHS, May 29, 1858.

53. FMS to AHS, July 11 and 28, August 3, 17, 29, 1858; FMS to SDH, July 14, 1858; FMS to WSJ, July 25, August 17, 1858; WSJ to FMS, July 26, August 5, 15, 29, September 26, 1858.

54. WSJ to FMS, September 26, 1858; FMS to WSJ, September 28, 1858; FMS to FAS, October 9, 1858.

55. FMS to WSJ, October 21, 1858; WSJ to FMS, November 1, 1858.

56. FMS to LMW, November 29, 1858; FAS to SDH, December 5, 1858; FMS to LMW, January 11, 1859.

57. FMS to LMW, December 5, 8, 19, 24, 1858.

58. FMS to LMW, December 24, 1858; FMS to AHS, December 24, 1858; AHS to CMM, January 20, 1859.

59. FMS to LMW, January 1, 1859; FMS to AHS, January 22, 1859.

60. FMS to LMW, January 3, 7, 14, 23, 28, February 1, 1859; FMS to AHS, January 22, 1859; "Ellen Ternan," Wikipedia, last updated September 8, 2024, https://en.wikipedia.org/wiki/Ellen_Ternan.

61. FMS to CMM, February 2 and 26, 1859.

62. FMS to LMW, February 9, 12, 20, 1859; FMS to AHS, February 16, 1859.

63. FMS to LMW, February 17, 1859.

64. FMS to AHS, March 5, 1859; AHS to FMS, March 6, 1859.

65. FMS to LMW, March 7 and 17, 1859; FMS to AHS, March 16, 1859; LMW to FMS, March 19, 1859.

66. FMS to CMM, March 15 and 19, 1859.
67. FMS to LMW, March 25, 1859; FMS to AHS, March 27, 1859.

16. Launch, 1859

1. *New York Times*, May 9, 1859, 1.
2. *New York Times*, May 9, 1859, 1; WHS to FMS, May 7, 1859.
3. "Home! Sweet Home!," Wikipedia, last updated September 30, 2024, https://en.wikipedia.org/wiki/Home!_Sweet_Home!#.
4. *New York Times*, May 9, 1859, 1; WHS to FMS, May 7, 1859; FWS-FMS May 8, 1859; WHS to FAS, May 9, 1859.
5. *New York Times*, May 9, 1859, 1.
6. *New York Times*, May 9, 1859, 1.
7. *New York Times*, May 9, 1859, 1.
8. *New York Times*, May 9, 1859, 1; Frederick W. Seward, *Seward at Washington*, 2:361.
9. WHS to FMS, May 7, 1859; WHS to FAS, May 9, 1859; *New York Times*, May 9, 1859.
10. WHS to WSJ, May 4, 1859; WHS to FAS, May 9, 1859; WHS to FMS, May 7, 1859.
11. WHS to FWS, April 7, 1859; FAS diary, December 1858–December 1859, 111–12, Seward Papers, Department of Rare Books, Special Collections, and Preservation, Rush Rhees Library, University of Rochester; see also sewardproject.org.
12. FAS diary, 115–16.
13. FAS diary, 117–20, 122.
14. WHS to WSJ, May 4, 1859; WHS to FMS, May 16, 1859; Frederick W. Seward, *Seward at Washington*, 2:360.
15. FAS diary, 122.
16. WHS to FMS, May 12, 1859.
17. WHS to FMS, May 9, 10, 11, 12, 13, 14, 1859.
18. WHS to FAS, May 26, 1859.
19. WHS to FAS, May 26, 1859.
20. WHS to FAS, May 26, 1859.
21. WHS to FAS, July 12, 1859.
22. WHS to FMS, May 27, 1859.
23. WHS to FAS, May 28, 1859.
24. WHS to FAS, June 1, 1859.
25. WHS to FMS, May 26, 27, 28, 29, 1859; WHS to FAS, May 28, 29, 30, 31, 1859.
26. WHS to FAS, June 2, 1859.
27. WHS to FAS, June 4, 5, 6, 7, 1859.
28. WHS to FAS, June 8, 1859.
29. WHS to FAS, June 9, 13, 14, 1859.
30. Henry Austen Layard, *Discoveries among the Ruins of Babylon and Nineveh* (London, 1853; New York: Harper & Brothers, 1856).
31. WHS to FAS, June 13, 14, 20, 21, 23, 1859.

32. WHS to FAS, June 9, 13, 14, 1859.

33. WHS to FAS, June 14, 21, 23, 1859.

34. WHS to FMS, June 26, 27, 1859.

35. WHS to FMS June 29 and 30, 1859; WHS to FAS, June 29, 1859.

36. WHS to FMS, June 30, 1859; WHS to FWS, July 8, 1859.

37. WHS to FMS, July 3, 1859.

38. Harriet Martineau, "Female Education," *Monthly Repository* (1823), quoted in Gaby Weiner, editor's introduction to Harriet Martineau, *Deerbrook* (1839; New York: Dial Press, 1983), ix; *Harriet Martineau's Autobiography, with Memorials by Maria Weston Chapman*, vol. 1 (London: Smith, Elder, 1877), 134; WHS to FMS, July 3, 1859.

39. FMS to WHS, December 12, 1837; FMS to LMW, May 14, 1838.

40. *Harriet Martineau's Autobiography*.

41. WHS to FMS, July 3, 1859.

42. WHS to FMS, July 3, 1859.

43. WHS to FMS, July 3, 1859.; Harriet Martineau to Henry Reeve, November 8, 1861, and Martineau to Henry Bright, May 3, 1863, in Valerie Sanders, ed., *Harriet Martineau: Selected Letters* (New York: Oxford University Press, 1990), 194, 202; Robert Kiefer Webb, *Harriet Martineau: A Radical Victorian* (London: Heineman, 1960); Valerie Kossew Pichanick, *Harriet Martineau: The Woman and Her Work* (Ann Arbor: University of Michigan Press, 1986); Martineau, *Autobiography*.

44. WHS to FMS, July 3, 1859.

45. Harriet Martineau, *Retrospect of Western Travel*, ed. Daniel Feller (1838; Armonk, NY: M. E. Sharpe, 2000), 25.

46. *London Daily News*, January 9, 1866, in Elisabeth Sanders Arbuckle, ed., *Harriet Martineau in the London Daily News: Selected Contributions, 1852–1866* (New York: Garland, 1994), 311.

47. Martineau to Bright, May 3, 1863, and Martineau to Henry Reeve, November 8, 1861.

48. WHS to FMS, July 3, 1859.

49. WHS to FMS, July 4 and 8, 1859.

50. WHS to FAS, July 10 and 11, 1859.

51. WHS to FAS, July 12, 1859.

52. WHS to FAS, July 12, 1859.

53. WHS to FAS, July 20, 1859.

54. Charles Sumner to FMS, August 2, 1859.

55. Sumner to the Duchess of Argyll, March 2, 1860, quoted in David Herbert Donald, *Charles Sumner and the Coming of the Civil War* (New York, 1960; republished in a one-volume paperback edition as part 1 of *Charles Sumner* [New York: Da Capo Press, 1996]), 1:351. According to Donald, Sumner made similar statements to Charles Francis Adams and William W. Story as late as March 1860.

56. Donald, *Charles Sumner*, 1:61, 56.

57. Donald, *Charles Sumner*, chapter 12, "The Vacant Chair," 1:312–47.

58. WHS to FAS, July 20, 1859.

59. WHS to FAS, July 20, 1859.

17. Home Sweet Home, 1859–1860

1. Karen Abbott, "The Daredevil of Niagara Falls," *Smithsonian*, October 18, 2011, https://www.smithsonianmag.com/history/the-daredevil-of-niagara-falls-110492884/; G. Linnaeus Bands, ed., *Blondin: His Life and Performances* (New York: Routledge, Warned, and Routledge, 1862).

2. Abbott, "Daredevil of Niagara Falls"; Bands, *Blondin*.

3. FAS to Sarah Hance, July 17, 1859.

4. FAS to Sarah Hance, July 17, 1859.

5. Frances Worden Chesebro to AHS, July 20, 1859; FMS to AHS, July 28, 1859.

6. FMS to FAS, July 29, 2859; FAS diary, 144–45.

7. WSJ to FMS, August 3 [4], 1859.

8. FAS diary, 151–55.

9. FWS to WSJ, May 27, 1859; WSJ to WHS, July 23, 1859.

10. WHS to FAS, July 21, 22, 23, 31, August 2, 3, 4, 1859; WHS to FMS, July 24, 25, 26, 27, 28, 29, 30, 1859.

11. WHS to FAS, August 11, 12, 13, 14, 15, 1859; WHS to FMS, August 8, 9, 10, 11, 16, 17, 1859.

12. WHS to FAS, August 27, September 6, 8, 9, 10, 15, 16, 17, 18, 19, 20, 1859; WHS to FMS, August 28, 31, September 1, 3, 4, 13, 14, 26, 1859.

13. WHS to FMS, September 30, October 2, 3, 7, 15, 16, 28, 19, 20, 21, 22, 24, November 15, 1859; WHS to FAS, October 8, 9, 10, 11, 12, 13, 14, 24, 1859.

14. WHS to FMS, November 15, 1859.

15. FAS to Sarah Hance, December 1859; FAS diary, 161–70.

16. WHS to FAS, December 12 and 13, 1859; FWS to WSJ, December 21, 1859; FAS to Sarah Hance, December 1859; FAS diary, 161–70.

17. WSJ to FMS, December 27, 1859.

18. FAS diary, 171–73.

19. FAS diary, 178–80.

20. WHS to FAS, December 28, 1859.

21. FAS diary, 178–80; Frederick W. Seward, *Seward at Washington*, 2:437; "Arrival of Senator Seward," *New York Times*, December 29, 1859, 4.

22. Frederick W. Seward, *Seward at Washington*, 2:437; "Arrival of Senator Seward."

23. Frederick W. Seward, *Seward at Washington*, 2:438; "Ovation to Senator Seward," *New York Times*, December 30, 1859, 1.

24. Frederick W. Seward, *Seward at Washington*, 2:440.

25. FAS diary, January 1, 2, 3, 4, 1860.

26. Frederick W. Seward, *Seward at Washington*, 2:441–42.

27. FAS diary, January 5–12, 1860, and p. 171 for accounts; "Prices and Wages by Decade: 1860–1869," University of Missouri Libraries, https://libraryguides.missouri.edu/pricesandwages/1860-1869.

28. FAS diary, January 16 and 17, 1860.

29. FAS diary, January 18, 19, 20, 21, 1860.

30. FAS diary, January 23, 1860.

31. Jane Porter, *The Scottish Chiefs: A Romance* (New York: Derby & Jackson, 1857).

32. FAS diary, January 30, February 1 and 8, 1860.
33. FAS diary, January 29, 1860.
34. WSJ to FMS, February 3, 1860.
35. FMS to WSJ, February 6, 1860.
36. FMS to WSJ, February 6, 1860.
37. WSJ to FMS, February 12, 1860.
38. WSJ to FMS, February 12, 1860.
39. WSJ to FMS, February 12, 1860; FMS to WSJ, February 19, 1860.
40. WSJ to FMS, February 26, 1860.
41. FAS diary, February 12–20, 1860.
42. Frederick W. Seward, *Seward in Washington*, 2:444–45; *New York Daily Tribune*, March 1, 1860, 4.
43. Frederick W. Seward, *Seward in Washington*, 2:444–45; *New York Daily Tribune*, March 1, 1860, 4.
44. FMS to WSJ, February 29, 1860.
45. WSJ to FMS, March 4 and 18, 1860; FMS to WSJ, March 7 and 14, 1860.
46. FAS diary, February 12–March 31, 1860.
47. WSJ to FMS, March 25, 1860; FMS to WSJ, March 29, 1860.
48. "Wendell Phillips in Brooklyn; A Plea for the Dissolution of the Union," *New York Times*, March 21, 1860, 8.
49. FAS diary, April 1–22, 1860; Henry Wadsworth Longfellow, "Maidenhood," in *Ballads and Other Poems*, 3rd ed. (Cambridge, MA: John Owen, 1842), https://etc.usf.edu/lit2go/71/henry-wadsworth-longfellow-selected-works/5020/maidenhood/.
50. WSJ to WHS, April 17 and 19, 1860; WSJ to FMS, April 20, 1860.
51. FAS diary, April 21–22, 1860.
52. FMS to WSJ, April 7 and 18, 1860.
53. FAS diary, April 23–25, 1860.

Conclusion

1. FMS to WHS, April 29, 1860; WHS to FMS, May 5, 1860, quoted in Frederick W. Seward, *Seward at Washington*, 2:449, 451–52.
2. FMS to WHS, April 29, 1860.
3. All three quoted in Frederick W. Seward, *Seward at Washington*, 2:442, 444, 446. Southerners on Seward also quoted in Viola A. Conklin, *American Political History to the Death of Lincoln* (New York: Henry Holt, 1901), 360.
4. FMS to WHS, April 26, May 2, 1860.
5. FMS to WHS, May 6, 1860; GWS to WHS, May 26, 1860.
6. FAS diary, May 16–19, 1860.
7. WHS to FWS, May 18, 1860; WHS to TxW, May 18, 1860. Both letters quoted in Frederick W. Seward, *Seward at Washington*, 2:452–53.
8. Quoted in Frederick W. Seward, *Seward at Washington*, 2:453–54.
9. FAS to Sarah Hance, May 25, 1860.
10. FMS to WHS, May 30, 1860.
11. FMS to WHS, May 30, 1860.
12. FMS to WHS, May 30, June 3, 1860.

13. Charles Sumner, "The Barbarism of Slavery," speech in the US Senate, June 4, 1860, https://publications.cedarville.edu/archives/pamphlets/the_barbarism_of_slavery/, 3; FMS to WHS, June 7, 1860; *New York Times*, June 5, 1860, 1, 5, 8.

14. Sumner, "Barbarism of Slavery," 3; FMS to WHS, June 7, 1860; *New York Times*, June 5, 1860, 1, 5, 8.

15. WHS to FMS, May 30, 1860.

16. WHS to FMS, May 30, June 4, 1860, quoted in Frederick W. Seward, *Seward at Washington*, 2:455–56, 457.

17. WHS to TxW, June 26, 1860, quoted in Frederick W. Seward, *Seward at Washington*, 459.

18. FMS to WHS, June 20, 1860; letters of June 13 and June 19, recipient unclear, quoted in Frederick W. Seward, *Seward at Washington*, 2:458.

19. WHS to TxW, June 26, 1860, quoted in Frederick W. Seward, *Seward at Washington*, 2:459; FAS diary, June 27–28, 1860; WSJ to FMS, June 29, 1860; FMS to WSJ, July 1, 1860; FAS to WSJ, July 3, 1860; WSJ to WHS, July 4, 1860.

20. FAS diary, September 1–8, 1860.

21. Frederick W. Seward, *Seward at Washington*, 2:462; Jon Grinspan, " 'Young Men for War': The Wide Awakes and Lincoln's 1860 Presidential Campaign," *Journal of American History* 9 (2009): 357–78.

22. Frederick W. Seward, *Seward at Washington*, 2:462.

23. FAS diary, September 9–12, 1860; Bayard Taylor, *Views Afoot: or, Europe Seen with Knapsack and Staff* (1846; New York: George P. Putnam, 1852).

24. FAS diary, September 20–28, 1860.

25. FAS diary, September 14–October 2, 1860; Frederick W. Seward, *Seward at Washington*, 2:468–75.

26. FAS diary, September 14–October 2, 1860; Frederick W. Seward, *Seward at Washington*, 2:468–75.

27. WHS to Abraham Lincoln, December 28, 1860; WHS to FMS, December 28 and 31, 1860; WHS to TxW, December 29, 1860; WHS to FWS, December 30, 1860; all quoted in Frederick W. Seward, *Seward at Washington*, 2:487, 489.

28. Conversation with Ray Messenger, June 2015.

Postscript

1. Lawrence Stone, *The Family, Sex and Marriage in England, 1500–1800* (New York: Harper & Row, 1977); John Demos, *Little Commonwealth: A Family Life in Plymouth Colony* (New York: Oxford University Press, 1970); Philip J. Greven, *Four Generations: Population, Land, and Family in Colonial Andover, Massachusetts* (Ithaca, NY: Cornell University Press, 1970); Michael Zuckerman, *Peaceable Kingdoms: New England Towns in the Eighteenth Century* (New York: Alfred A. Knopf, 1970).

2. Natalie Davis, *Society and Culture in Early Modern France* (Palo Alto, CA: Stanford University Press, 1975); John Putnam Demos, *The Unredeemed Captive: A Family Story from Early America* (New York: Knopf, 1994); Rachel Jamison Webster, *Benjamin Banneker and Us: Eleven Generations of an American Family*

(New York: Henry Holt, 2013); David N. Gellman, *Liberty's Chain: Slavery, Abolition, and the Jay Family of New York* (Ithaca, NY: Three Hills, 2022); Keri K. Greenidge, *The Grimkes: The Legacy of Slavery in an American Family* (New York: Liveright, 2023); Chris Dixon, *Perfecting the Family: Antislavery Marriages in Nineteenth-Century America* (Amherst: University of Massachusetts Press, 1997).

3. Megan Marshall, *The Peabody Sisters: Three Women Who Ignited American Romanticism* (New York: Houghton Mifflin, 2005); Phyllis Cole, *Mary Moody Emerson and the Origins of Transcendentalism: A Family History* (New York: Oxford University Press, 1998); Lyndall Gordon, *Lives Like Loaded Guns: Emily Dickinson and Her Family's Feuds* (New York: Viking Penguin, 2010); R. W. B. Lewis, *The Jameses: A Family Narrative* (New York: Farrar, Straus & Giroux, 1991); Milton Rugoff, *The Beechers: An American Family in the Nineteenth Century* (New York: Harper & Row, 1981); Madeline Bedell, *The Alcotts: Biography of a Family* (New York: Clarkson N. Palmer, 1980); Alison Bashford, *The Huxleys: An Intimate History* (Chicago: University of Chicago Press, 2022); Lydia Moland, *Lydia Maria Child: A Radical American Life* (Chicago: University of Chicago Press, 2022); Michael Grossberg, *Governing the Hearth: Law and the Family in Nineteenth-Century America* (Chapel Hill: University of North Carolina Press, 1985); Hendrik Hartog, *Man and Wife in America: A History* (Cambridge, MA: Harvard University Press, 2000); Hendrik Hartog, *Someday All This Will Be Yours: A History of Inheritance and Old Age* (Cambridge, MA: Harvard University Press, 2012).

4. Amy S. Greenberg, *Lady First: The World of First Lady Sarah Polk* (New York: Alfred A. Knopf, 2019); Woody Holton, *Abigail Adams: A Life* (New York: Free Press, 2009); Bruce Chadwick, *James and Dolley Madison: America's First Power Couple* (New York: Prometheus, 2014); Catherine Allgor, *Dolley Madison: The Problem of National Unity* (London: Routledge, 2019); Catherine Allgor, *A Perfect Union: Dolley Madison and the Creation of the American Nation* (New York: Henry Holt, 2006); Jean H. Baker, *Mary Todd Lincoln: A Biography* (New York: W. W. Norton, 1987); Catherine Clinton, *Mrs. Lincoln: A Life* (New York: Harper, 2009); Martha Saxton, *The Widow Washington: The Life of Mary Washington* (New York: Farrar, Straus & Giroux, 2019); Patricia Brady, *Martha Washington: An American Life* (New York: Viking, 2005); Jane Hampton Cook, *American Phoenix: John Quincy and Louisa Adams, the War of 1812, and the Exile That Saved American Independence* (New York: Thomas Nelson, 2013); Louisa Thomas, *Louisa: The Extraordinary Life of Mrs. Adams* (New York: Penguin, 2016); Frank J. Williams and Michael Burkhimer, eds., *The Mary Lincoln Enigma: Historians on America's Most Controversial First Lady* (Carbondale: Southern Illinois University Press, 2012); G. J. Barker-Benfield, *Abigail and John Adams: The Americanization of Sensibility* (Chicago: University of Chicago Press, 2010).

Index

Illustrations are indicated by page numbers in italics. William Henry Seward is abbreviated as WHS and Frances Adeline Miller Seward as FMS in subentries throughout the index.